Experiencing Medieval Art

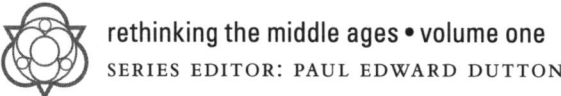

rethinking the middle ages • volume one
SERIES EDITOR: PAUL EDWARD DUTTON

Experiencing Medieval Art
Herbert L. Kessler

UNIVERSITY OF TORONTO PRESS
Toronto Buffalo London

© University of Toronto Press 2019
Toronto Buffalo London
utorontopress.com
Printed in Canada

∞ This book is printed on acid-free paper.

All rights reserved. The use of any part of this publication reproduced, transmitted in any form or by any means, electronic, mechanical, photocopying, recording, or otherwise, or stored in a retrieval system, without prior written consent of the publisher—or in the case of photocopying, a licence from Access Copyright (the Canadian Copyright Licensing Agency) 320–56 Wellesley Street West, Toronto, Ontario, M5S 2S3—is an infringement of the copyright law.

Library and Archives Canada Cataloguing in Publication

Title: Experiencing medieval art / Herbert L. Kessler.
Names: Kessler, Herbert L., 1941–, author.
Description: Series statement: Rethinking the Middle Ages ; volume 1 | Includes bibliographical references and index.
Identifiers: Canadiana 20190132132 | ISBN 9781442600737 (hardcover) | ISBN 9781442600713 (softcover)
Subjects: LCSH: Art, Medieval.
Classification: LCC N5970 .K45 2019 | DDC 709/.02—dc23

We welcome comments and suggestions regarding any aspect of our publications—please feel free to contact us at news@utorontopress.com or visit our internet site at utorontopress.com.

North America
5201 Dufferin Street
North York, Ontario, Canada, M3H 5T8

2250 Military Road
Tonawanda, New York, USA, 14150
ORDERS PHONE: 1–800–565–9523
ORDERS FAX: 1–800–221–9985
ORDERS E-MAIL: utpbooks@utpress.utoronto.ca

UK, Ireland, and continental Europe
NBN International
Estover Road, Plymouth, PL6 7PY, UK
ORDERS PHONE: 44 (0) 1752 202301
ORDERS FAX: 44 (0) 1752 202333
ORDERS E-MAIL: enquiries@nbninternational.com

Every effort has been made to contact copyright holders; in the event of an error or omission, please notify the publisher.

University of Toronto Press acknowledges the financial assistance to its publishing program of the Canada Council for the Arts and the Ontario Arts Council, an agency of the Government of Ontario.

Canada Council for the Arts
Conseil des Arts du Canada

ONTARIO ARTS COUNCIL
CONSEIL DES ARTS DE L'ONTARIO
an Ontario government agency
un organisme du gouvernement de l'Ontario

Funded by the Government of Canada
Financé par le gouvernement du Canada
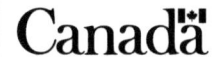

MIX
Paper from responsible sources
FSC® C016245

For

Joey

Mosie

Jeffer

Aurora

Contents

List of Illustrations *ix*
Preface *xiii*

1. Object *1*
2. Matter *31*
3. Making *59*
4. Spirit *91*
5. Book *117*
6. Church *139*
7. Life (and Death) *161*
8. Performance *189*
9. Subject *207*

    Epilogue: Environments of Experience *225*

    Notes *231*
    Photo Credits *317*
    Index *321*

Illustrations

Color Plates (following page 152)

   I Regensburg, Diözesanmuseum, reliquary (fourteenth century)
  II Florence, Museo del Bargello, flabellum (ninth century)
 III León, San Isidoro, Urraca chalice (eleventh century)
  IV Aachen, Dom, ambo (eleventh century)
   V Essen, Domschatz, Theophanu Gospels cover (eleventh century)
  VI Paris, Musée du Louvre, reliquary (thirteenth century)
 VII Chantilly, Musée Condé, MS 65, *Très riches heures*, fol. 158^r (fifteenth century)
VIII Fritzlar, Dom, Pietà (fourteenth century)
  IX London, Westminster Abbey, Cosmatesque floor (thirteenth century)
   X Rosano, Abbazia di Santa Maria, crucifix (twelfth century)
  XI Darmstadt, Hessische Landesbibliothek, Hitda Codex, Cod. 1640, fol. 20^r (eleventh century)
 XII Padua, Scrovegni Chapel (fourteenth century)
XIII Venice, San Marco, atrium (thirteenth century)
 XIV Rome, Santi Quattro Coronati, *aula gotica* (thirteenth century)
  XV Laon, cathédrale de Notre-Dame, rose window (thirteenth century)
 XVI Hereford, cathedral, *mappa mundi* (detail) (c. 1300)

Figures

1 Dublin, National Museum, fidchell board from Ballinderry (tenth century) *2*
2 Den Haag, private collection, pilgrim badge (fourteenth century) *3*
3 Basel, Historisches Museum, reliquary (fourteenth century) *5*
4 Zwiefalten, Katholischer Pfarramt, reliquary (twelfth century, with later elements) *6*
5 Chartres, cathédrale de Notre-Dame, *La belle verrière* (twelfth/thirteenth century) *8*
6 Milan, Sant'Ambrogio, interior (various) *9*
7 Baltimore, Walters Art Museum, mirror (fourteenth century) *10*
8 Paris, École des Beaux-Arts, charter from Saint-Martin-du-Canigou (1195) *11*
9 Hildesheim, Diözesanmuseum, aquamanile (twelfth century) *13*
10 Lisbon, Gulbenkian Collection, MS L.A. 139, Apocalypse, fol. 13^r (thirteenth century) *15*
11 Trier, Stadtbibliothek, MS 1378, *Flores epytaphii sanctorum*, fols. 87^v-88^r (eleventh century) *17*
12 Karlstejn, Castle, chapel of the Virgin Mary, fresco (fourteenth century) *18*
13 London, Victoria and Albert Museum, *arma Christi* booklet (fourteenth century) *19*
14 Budapest, Hungarian National Museum, Coronation Mantle (eleventh century) *21*
15 Rome, Scala Santa, Sancta Sanctorum (ninth/eleventh/thirteenth century) *22*
16 Florence, Biblioteca Laurenziana, MS Tempi 3, *Specchio umano*, fol. 79^r (fourteenth century) *24*
17 Barcelona, Museu nacional d'art de Catalunya, altarpiece from Monastery of Santa Maria de Vallbona de les Monges (fourteenth century) *29*
18 Munich, Residenz, Schatzkammer, Prayer Book, fols. 38^v-39^r (ninth century) *34*
19 Wiesbaden, Nassauische Landesbibliothek (formerly), MS 1, *Scivias*, fol. 51^r (twelfth century) *35*
20 Reichenau (Konstanz), Münster, gilt disk (tenth century) *36*
21 Massa Marittima, Museo di Arte Sacra Medievale, Ambrogio Lorenzetti altarpiece (fourteenth century) *37*

22 Strasbourg, Bibliothèque nationale et universitaire, *Exemplar,* Cod. 2929, fol. 82^r (fourteenth century) *38*
23 Hildesheim, Dom, bronze doors (eleventh century) *41*
24 Moissac, l'abbaye Saint-Pierre, façade (twelfth century) *43*
25 Amiens, cathédrale de Notre-Dame, façade (thirteenth century) *44*
26 Naumburg, Dom, choir screen (thirteenth century) *45*
27 Jaca, Museo Diocesano de Jaca, capital (twelfth century) *46*
28 New York, Metropolitan Museum of Art, shrine Madonna (c. 1300) *49*
29 Salerno, Museo Diocesano, ivory plaque (eleventh century) *50*
30 Lyon, Musée des Beaux-Arts, knob of bishop's crozier (twelfth century) *51*
31 Bayeux, Musée de la Tapisserie de Bayeux, embroidery (eleventh century) *54*
32 Berzé-la-Ville, Chapelle-des-Moines, apse, fresco (twelfth century) *57*
33 Münster, Landesmuseum, stained glass from the Premonstratensian monastery at Arnstein (twelfth century) *63*
34 Jerusalem, Israel Museum, MS 180/57, *Haggadah*, fols. 25^v–26^r (fourteenth century) *65*
35 Paris, BnF, MS fr. 19093, Villard de Honnecourt sketchbook, fol. 22^v (thirteenth century) *66*
36 Aiguamúrcia, Reial Monastir de Santes Creus, cloister (fourteenth century) *69*
37 Ceri, Santa Maria Immacolata, right wall (c. 1100) *71*
38 Utrecht, Universiteitsbibliotheek, MS Bibl. Rhenotraiectinae I Nr 32, Psalter, fol. 82^v (ninth century) *73*
39 León, catedral de Santa Maria, tomb of Rodriguez Alvarez (thirteenth century) *74*
40 Hildesheim, Dombibliothek, MS Saint-Godehard 1, Saint Albans Psalter, fol. 72^v (twelfth century) *76*
41 Escorial, Real biblioteca del Monasterio, MS T.I.1, *Cantigas de Santa Maria*, fol. 177^v (thirteenth century) *80*
42 Jerusalem, church of the Holy Sepulcher, doorways (twelfth century) *81*
43 Écouis, Collégiale Notre-Dame, Mary Magdalene (fourteenth century) *82*
44 Salzburg, Stift Sankt Peter, drawing for a chapel (thirteenth century) *88*

45 Copenhagen, Kongelige Bibliotek, MS Hebrew 11, *Pentateuch*, fol. 104^v (thirteenth century)   *93*
46 Copenhagen, Nationalmuseet, Lisbjerg altar (twelfth century)   *97*
47 Tours, Bibliothèque municipale, MS 193, sacramentary, fol. 71^r (twelfth century)   *99*
48 Brussels, Bibliothèque royale, MS 10074, *Physiologus*, fol. 142^r–143^v (eleventh century)   *102*
49 Aosta, Sant'Orso, mosaic (twelfth century)   *106*
50 Strasbourg, cathédrale de Notre-Dame, south transept (thirteenth century)   *107*
51 Nancy, Musée Lorrain, Hugh of Vaudemont and Aigeline of Burgundy from monastery of Belval (twelfth century)   *115*
52 London, British Library, Additional Manuscript 47682, Holkham Picture Bible, fols. 30^v-31^r (fourteenth century)   *120*
53 Venice, Biblioteca Marciana, MS lat. VIII 22 [2760], *Horologium nocturnum*, fol. 1^r (twelfth century)   *124*
54 Dublin, Trinity College Library, MS A. I. [58], Book of Kells, fols. 291^v-292^r (ninth century)   *128*
55 Cambridge, Trinity College Library, MS 0.7.16, *De spiritu et anima*, fol. 46^v–47^r (thirteenth century)   *133*
56 Paris, Bib. nationale de France, MS fr. 9220, *Vrigiet de solas*, fol. 10^r (thirteenth century)   *134*
57 Lucca, San Martino, labyrinth (twelfth or thirteenth century)   *142*
58 Ferentillo, San Pietro in Valle, fresco (c. 1200)   *147*
59 Barcelona, Museu nacional d'art de Catalunya, fresco from left aisle of Sant Joan de Boí (fourteenth century)   *150*
60 Freckenhorst, Stiftskirche Sankt Bonifatius, baptismal font (twelfth century)   *158*
61 Rodenegg, Castello, fresco (thirteenth century)   *164*
62 Paris, Musée Cluny, erotic pilgrim badge (fourteenth century)   *165*
63 Modena, town square, "La Bonissima" (twelfth century)   *177*
64 Cleveland, Museum of Art, table fountain (fourteenth century)   *182*
65 George Tatge, *Il miracolo e lo specchio* (1995)   *228*

Preface

This book started as a revision of my 2004 *Seeing Medieval Art*, which in turn was an expansion of the article "On the State of Medieval Art History" that I had published some fifteen years before. As the title signals, it has become a completely new work. The shifting field of medieval art history required not only an updating of the eight themes that organized *Seeing Medieval Art* but also a full reconsideration of the topics, most notably the renaming of the "Seeing" chapter to accommodate recent expansion to the entire sensorium; it also led to the addition of a chapter on "Object." In turn, the field's dilation necessitated narrowing the volume's purview. Like its predecessor, *Experiencing Medieval Art* does not cover architectural history and considers questions of style and chronology only in passing; it is more strictly focused on the Latin Middle Ages from Carolingian times until 1400. And, like the antecedent, this volume relies heavily on English-language publications and is limited to books and articles that appeared during the two decades that preceded the start of the project (in this instance, 2017). To a great extent, current scholarly concerns guided the selection of objects and subjects considered and illustrated. The *bibles moralisées* that were a particular interest in the 1990s, for example, are here replaced by the *Cantigas de Santa Maria*, which has grown in importance as Spain has regained its rightful place in medieval studies, and the rich illuminated manuscript is mined for information and theory. Despite the growing attention to interchanges around the entire Mediterranean coast, Islamic art remains beyond the scope of this study except tangentially;

so, too, the "global Middle Ages." An Epilogue touches on such issues of current interest as historiography and display.

Even a glance at the book's illustrations conveys something of medieval art's unusual character. Functional objects—books, reliquaries, altars, doors, tools, liturgical implements—are included alongside the so-called "major arts" of painting and sculpture. Chapter 1 argues that such objects, not just images, were central elements of medieval artistic production and are to be subjected to protocols of examination in their own right. Plundered, exchanged, transported, and arranged in new venues, these included ancient and Islamic reused artifacts (spolia), natural wonders, and the Eucharist itself; assembled as treasures, they were authorized by Scripture and displayed in heterogeneous collections.

Many of the objects are made of materials seldom encountered in the mainstream art of later periods—precious metals and gems, ivory and stained glass, also humble stones, human bones, and even dirt. Chapter 2 explores the ways in which matter mattered. Various materials contributed to meaning through their inherent properties and also were elucidated through biblical allusions, cosmological associations, alchemy, and medicine. Origins played a role, too, as did processes of production and maintenance. Mixed and juxtaposed, matter created a rhetoric of its own.

Chapter 3 examines the place of artisans, patrons, and sponsors in the making of medieval art and the myths of supernatural origins in what was often a complex "web of agency" governing production. It treats the status of craft in medieval society and various techniques of manufacturing and distribution. Chapter 4, in turn, takes up the ways in which the Church accommodated the physical attraction of materials and images to its religious mission and how it redirected pagan legacies to serve Christian spirituality. It also discusses the deployment of such devices as typology, inscriptions, seals, and personation to convey the widely held belief that what humans see with their "carnal" eyes is not necessarily what should enter the "eyes of the mind."

In Judaeo-Christian culture, the written word was God's principal channel of communication with the faithful; hence, parchment books became an essential venue of artistic elaboration. Chapter 5 thus introduces diverse types of books and the forms of decoration developed to adorn, interpret, and facilitate their use. It also analyzes specific components—covers, initials, miniatures, margins, and diptych-like openings—that created presence and structured relationships between words and images.

Chapter 6 turns to sacred environments that religious art helped to create and that many objects served. It studies the ways mural decorations and church furnishings marked functional areas and facilitated movement between them and how art enacted the transition between the Church in which the faithful worshiped and the celestial prototype they sought to enter.

Medieval art also engaged the world outside the sanctuary, sometimes providing an alternative to the sacred realm and in other cases accommodating religious imagery to real-life experience. Chapter 7 considers the importance of classical sources and empirical observation for medieval naturalism, secular art and historical narrative, courts, and the emergence of individual portraiture.

Focused on performance, Chapter 8 treats medieval art's engagement with activities that took place within sanctuaries, domestic environments, and urban settings. Treating art's roles in engendering bodily and psychological responses and attending to movement, it examines the ways pictures and other works of art guided devotion, functioned in the sacred liturgy, engendered play, and served in processions and pilgrimage.

Chapter 9 considers how art was apprehended in a culture with complex attitudes toward the world and sensual experience. Operating within the Augustinian distinction between carnal, spiritual, and intellectual cognition, art relied on various strategies for enacting transitions from physical to mental comprehension even while honoring the claim that only the blessed will confront God "face to face" at the end of time. The chapter studies how, to activate an aesthetics of elevation, medieval art exploited the contrasts between inside and outside, front and back, illusion and object, and mise-en-abîme (the quotation of the object within it to suggest a receding sequence) and cognitive theory.

Reflecting my belief that objects constitute the primary material for art-historical study, *Experiencing Medieval Art* examines selected works in some detail. Even the expanded picture program that the University of Toronto Press generously provided, however, does not permit the inclusion of an illustration of every work referred to in the text. I have chosen the eighty-one objects because they serve the range of conceptual issues discussed in current scholarship and/or because they represent diverse periods, centers, and media. Such well-known works as the Utrecht Psalter, Hildesheim bronze doors, Bayeux embroidery, and San Marco mosaics are still among them because they have remained the focus of interesting scholarship during the past fifteen years. Many less familiar objects are added because they are subjects of interest in recent discussions or represent classes of material that open up new issues.

Many colleagues and friends have contributed to this work in various ways. Philippe Cordez has been an inspiring interlocutor throughout the project. As series editor, Paul E. Dutton read the typescript with care, learning, and intelligence; I have incorporated his comments into the final text. At the University of Toronto Press, Natalie Fingerhut demonstrated a consistent interest in the project and advanced it efficiently and with sensitivity. Michele Bacci, Adam Cohen, Philippe Cordez, Thomas Dale, Vincent Debiais, Francesca Dell'Acqua, Ivan Foletti, Ludovico Geymonat, Fabio Guidetti, Marius Hauknes, Avital Heyman, Allegra Iafrate, Zsombor Jékeley, Jacqueline Jung, Christopher Lakey, Didier Méhu, Rebecca Müller, Joanna Olchawa, Pablo Ordás, Marco Petoletti, Francisco Prado-Vilar, Stefano Riccioni, Marta Serrano Coll, Branislav Slantchev, George Tatge, and Henneke van Asperen provided me with pre-publication copies of forthcoming works or generously helped secure photographs. Now that I am retired, I have not been able to run my ideas past Ph.D. students of my own, but I have been fortunate to present some of the material at the Center of Early Medieval Studies at the Masaryk University in Brno, where I hold the position of Invited Professor, and at Williams College, where I was Croghan Bicentennial Visiting Professor in the autumn of 2018, and have been inspired by the students' lively discussions and pointed challenges.

Chapter 1
Object

PORTABLE OBJECTS constitute a prime category of medieval art.[1] Previously disparaged as "minor" or merely "decorative,"[2] reliquaries, liturgical vessels, game pieces, and personal adornments are the focus of many recent scholarly investigations, transgressing traditional categorizations that privilege monumental painting and sculpture. Some are made of precious materials, others of the basest substances; many are composites.

A delicate enamel locket, probably fashioned in France during the first quarter of the fourteenth century, is an example (see Plate I).[3] Only two inches wide and an inch and a half high, the facsimile insect elicits Christian meaning: just as the worm-like pupa (forming the body), formerly nurtured by the slime of the earth, metamorphoses into a beautiful creature capable of flight, so, too, the resurrected Christ will revivify the faithful and lift them heavenward. Moreover, the pictured Crucifixion and the butterfly's enormous eyes engendered talismanic protection for the person who wore the locket, making visual the amuletic power generated by the relics set in wax in a cross-shaped compartment accessible from the back.

The range of medieval objects is vast and includes many things that served primarily practical functions. A tenth-century wood gaming board found in Ballinderry, Ireland, provided a fictive battlefield for the two-person game of fidchell, something like chess (Figure 1);[4] ten inches square, the surface organized around a circle and corner quarter-circles is punctured with forty-nine holes for pawns (of which one made of

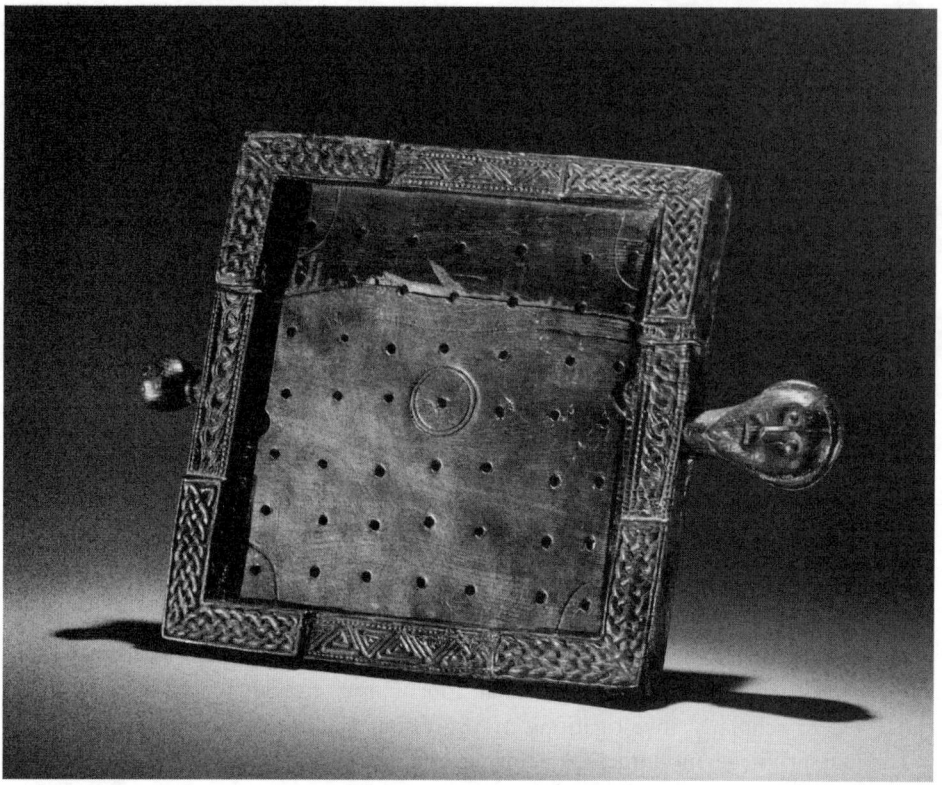

Figure 1. Dublin, National Museum, fidchell board from Ballinderry (tenth century)

horn was excavated with the board) protecting a king against an enemy army. A head and a knob mark the opposing sides, and notched troughs held the "dead men." An inscription describes the purpose of the similarly hands-on, yet elaborate bone, ivory, and painted vellum of a ninth-century fan in Florence: "in summer ... to chase away the relentless flies and to ameliorate the heat" (see Plate II).[5]

Often transported over long distances, plundered, presented as gifts, or traded, objects were collected in heterogeneous assemblies.[6] A Carolingian-period Swedish burial comprehended not only a ladle from Egypt and a Celtic crozier, but also a silver Buddha seated on a lotus-throne from far-off Pakistan, attesting to the global reach of the Middle Ages at a surprisingly early date.[7] Pilgrims seeking salvation left precious things at the holy sites they reached in the hope that they would,

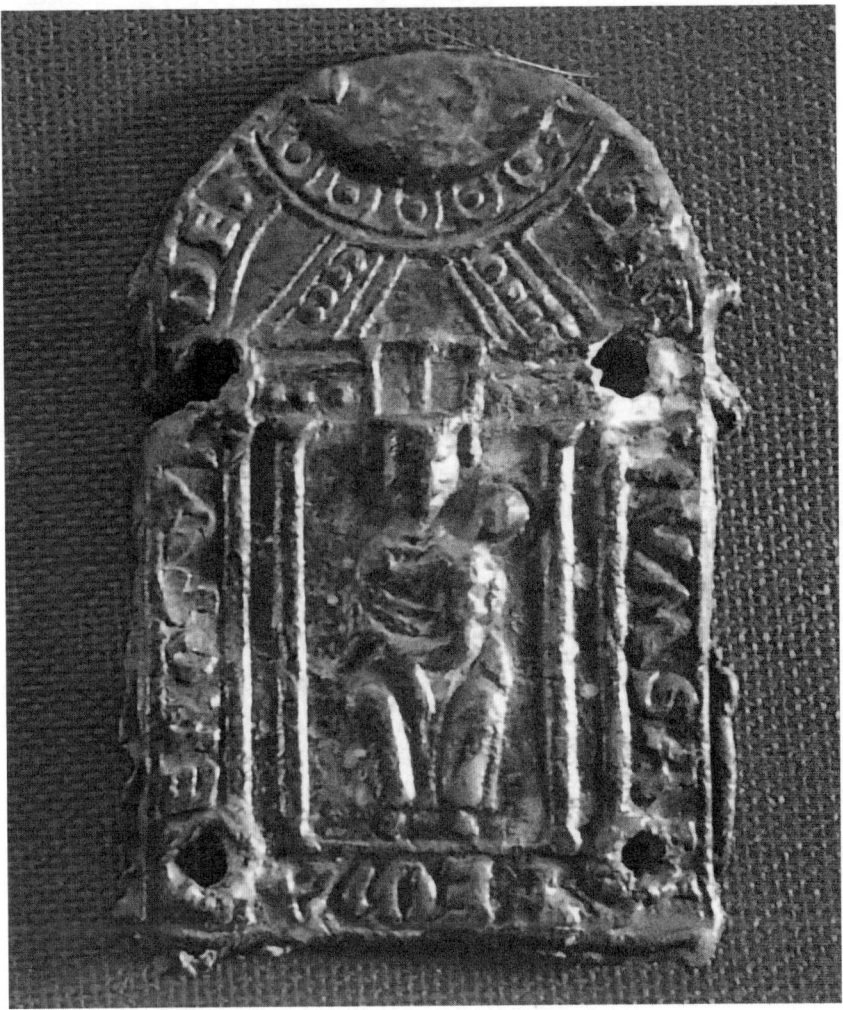

Figure 2. Den Haag, private collection, pilgrim badge (fourteenth century)

in exchange, acquire spiritual benefits, and they brought back souvenirs which they, in turn, offered in gratitude for their safe return home.[8] A fourteenth-century pilgrim's badge, inscribed with "Token of Round Saint Mary" (Figure 2),[9] commemorates a pilgrimage to the Pantheon in Rome that had been transformed into the church of Santa Maria ad Martyres at the start of the seventh century (in part through a miracle-working icon of the Virgin and Child, which is represented at the center of the badge).[10] Sewn onto a devotee's garment originally by means of four eyelets, it documented the wearer's own transitory experience; later punctures attest to its having been removed from the first wearer's clothes and reused. As with so many medieval representations, object and image are perfectly matched; the Pantheon's oculus is mimicked by the token's round top and the columned portico frames the depicted image inside.[11]

Objects took on different meanings when they were displayed in new venues. The incorporation of ancient fragments in works of Christian art had been promoted already by Emperor Constantine and reflected, not economic decline as is often supposed, but a desire to insert Christianity into unfolding history.[12] The eleventh-century maker of the gem-encrusted chalice associated with Doña Urraca (see Plate III) surely chose the Roman bowl and dish that make up its body not only for the antiquity but also because onyx was exalted in Scripture (Ex 28). The shrine commissioned c. 1200 to house the skulls of the Three Magi (Cologne, Dom) uses spolia in an even more precise way: three oversize cameos on the gable (the central one picturing Ptolemy and his wife was removed and is now in Vienna) stand in for the ancient eastern kings who had visited Christ; they are flanked by a Medusa head, reworked to represent Mary; and a sapphire relief of Christ.[13] A Medusa cameo is featured as well on an early fourteenth-century reliquary in Basel (Figure 3), where it forms the face of David on a hybrid object that includes a twelfth-century south Italian gem, a thirteenth-century statuette of the Virgin and Child, and enamel portraits of prophets.[14]

The principle of recycling had been extended as well to earlier medieval works. A throne made during the third quarter of the ninth century for Charlemagne's grandson, Charles the Bald, for example, incorporates ivories in various styles, among them depictions of the Labors of Hercules (themselves in part carved on the planed reverses of seventh-century plaques from Egypt), set within a chair originally adorned with cameos or gems and ivory strips depicting the king within the cosmos.[15] An ambo in Aachen commissioned by the emperor Henry II (see Plate IV) includes Egyptian ivories and rock crystal bottles brought from Egypt across the Mediterranean to Ottonian Germany.[16] The famous wolf in Rome (*lupa romana*), long believed to be a fifth-century BCE Etruscan bronze, which was displayed at the Lateran Palace during the Middle Ages alongside the equestrian statue of Marcus Aurelius, the *spinario*, and other genuine antiquities, seems to be a ninth-century bronze imitation of an ancient figure.[17] And a twelfth-century reliquary in Zwiefalten (Figure 4) is a composite work built around a cross-shaped

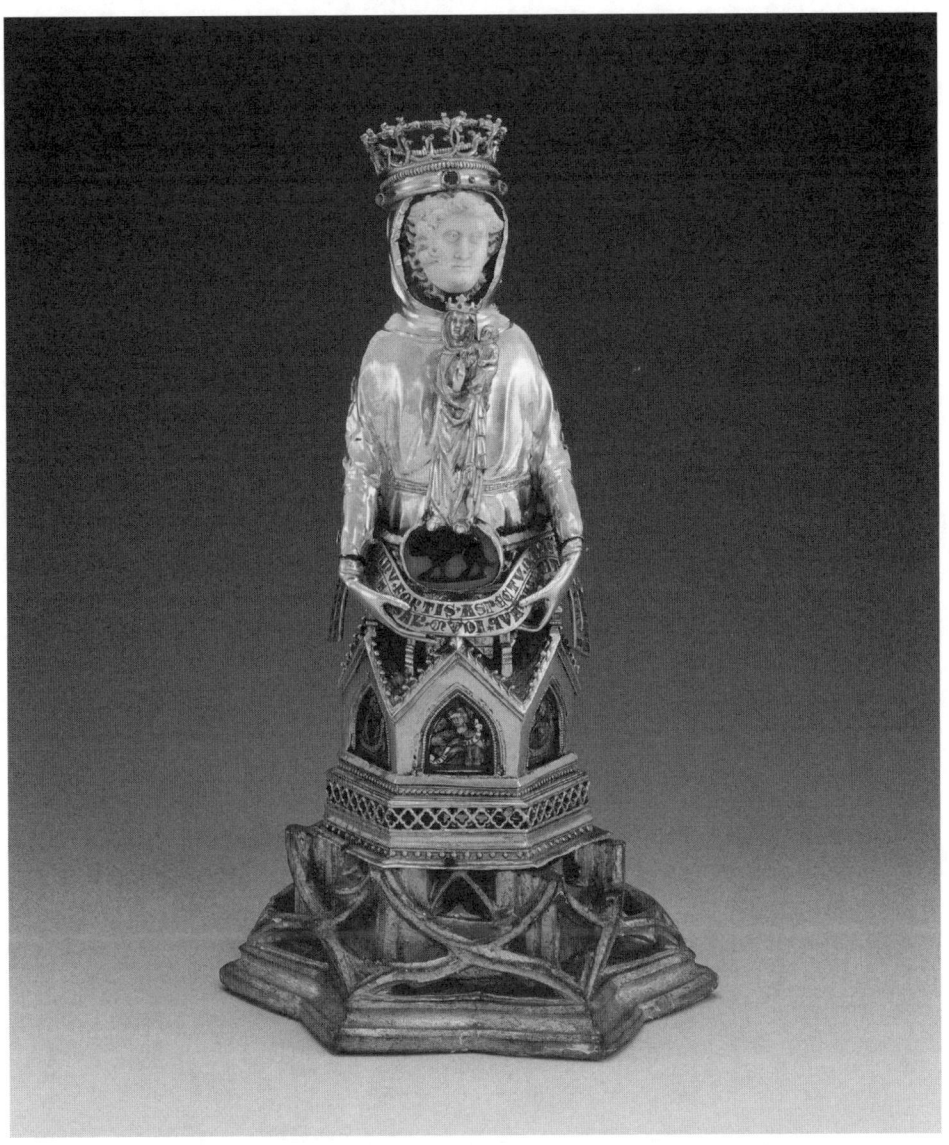

Figure 3. Basel, Historisches Museum, reliquary (fourteenth century)

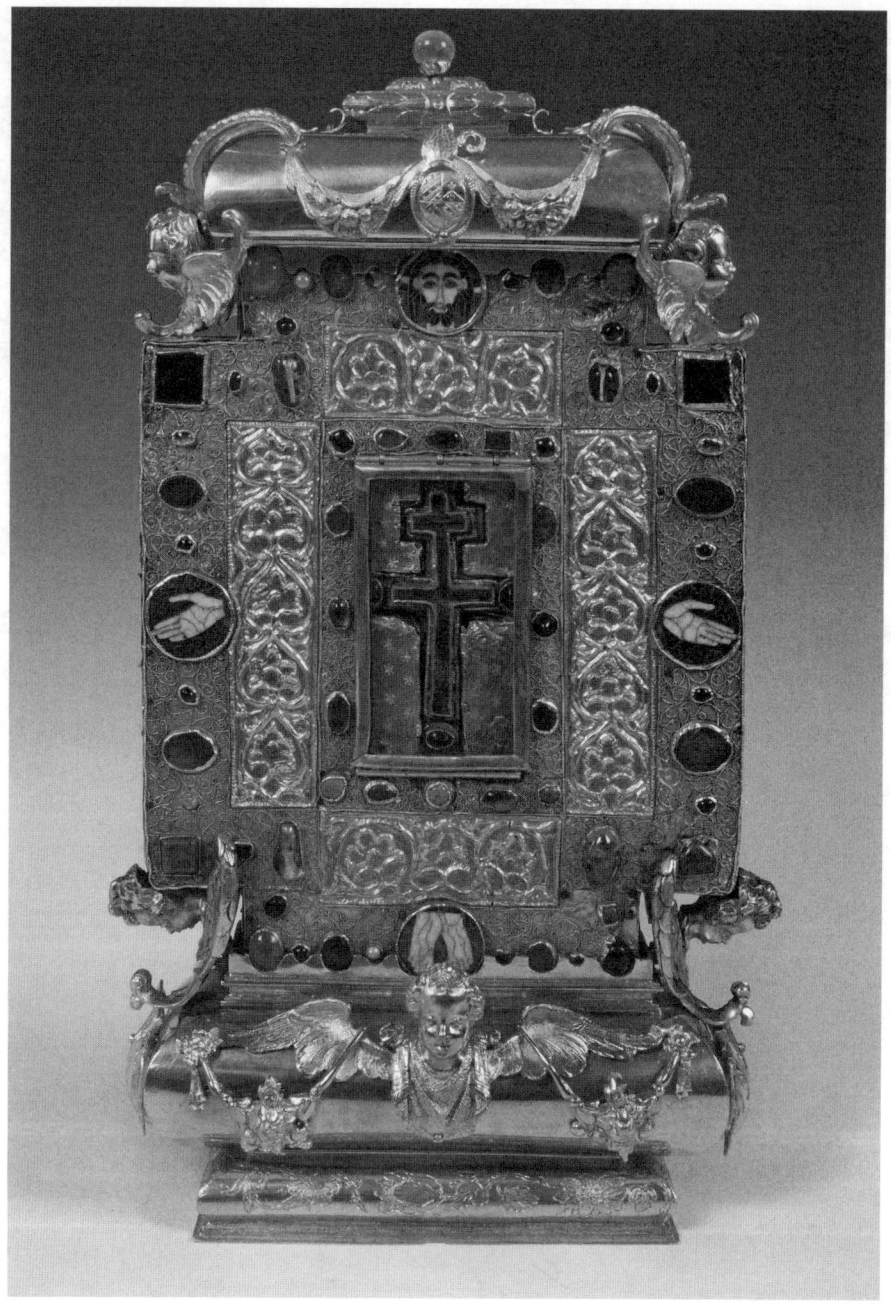

Figure 4. Zwiefalten, Katholischer Pfarramt, reliquary
(twelfth century, with later elements)

box that, the abbey's 1138 chronicle reports, a prior of the Church of the Holy Sepulcher in Jerusalem had acquired during the First Crusade (1096–99) and passed to Berthold von Sperberseck, who commissioned a local goldsmith to provide it with a wide band of filigree, inserted gems, intaglios, polished stones, and enamels that imitate the original box's vine-scroll.[18]

A fragment from a late antique sarcophagus carved with scenes of Jonah was made to serve as the lintel of the ninth-century doorway into the crypt at Santa Prassede in Rome, the Hebrew prophet's submergence in the whale's belly cuing a pilgrim's descent to the saints' graves and the material's reuse itself symbolizing resurrection (depicted in the apse overhead).[19] At the beginning of the fourteenth century, the Dominican friar Giordano of Pisa was buried in a third-century sarcophagus in Santa Caterina d'Alessandria in Pisa where he had preached; the original deceased's face amid Roman putti with extinguished torches on the sarcophagus was recut to resemble Giordano's portrait with tonsure, cape, and mouth open as if delivering a sermon.[20] In the same fashion, a stained-glass window picturing the Virgin and Child, which came to be known as *La belle verrière*, was transferred at Chartres Cathedral (probably from the apse of the Romanesque church) after the fire of 1194 and fitted onto the inside wall of the western wall (counter-façade) of the thirteenth-century building (Figure 5).[21] Only Mary and Christ are preserved from the mid-twelfth-century original; framed later by adoring angels and set off on a red ground, the fragment of a fairly new window is itself a cult object that advertises the cathedral's other relics: the Virgin's chemise and the statue of *Notre-Dame sous terre*.[22]

During the crusades, Islamic spolia displayed with local antiquities in the port cities of Venice, Palermo, Salerno, Amalfi, Naples, Genoa, and Pisa enacted the dynamic, albeit conflictual, relationships of plunder and exchange.[23] For example, the elaborate (probably Andalusian) bronze griffin was installed on the Pisa Duomo (most likely after the Balearic campaign of 1113–15) to symbolize the transition between heaven and earth and to ward off evil.[24] Whole churches are assemblies of spolia. Sant'Ambrogio in Milan (Figure 6), for instance, preserves a Hellenistic serpent on a column paired with a cross near the entrance to the nave and a magnificent fourth-century sarcophagus from the original church that was incorporated into a pulpit constructed c. 1200 from fragments of a twelfth-century ambo and adorned with an eighth-century brass eagle and two saints,[25] a Carolingian altar and apse mosaic (entirely

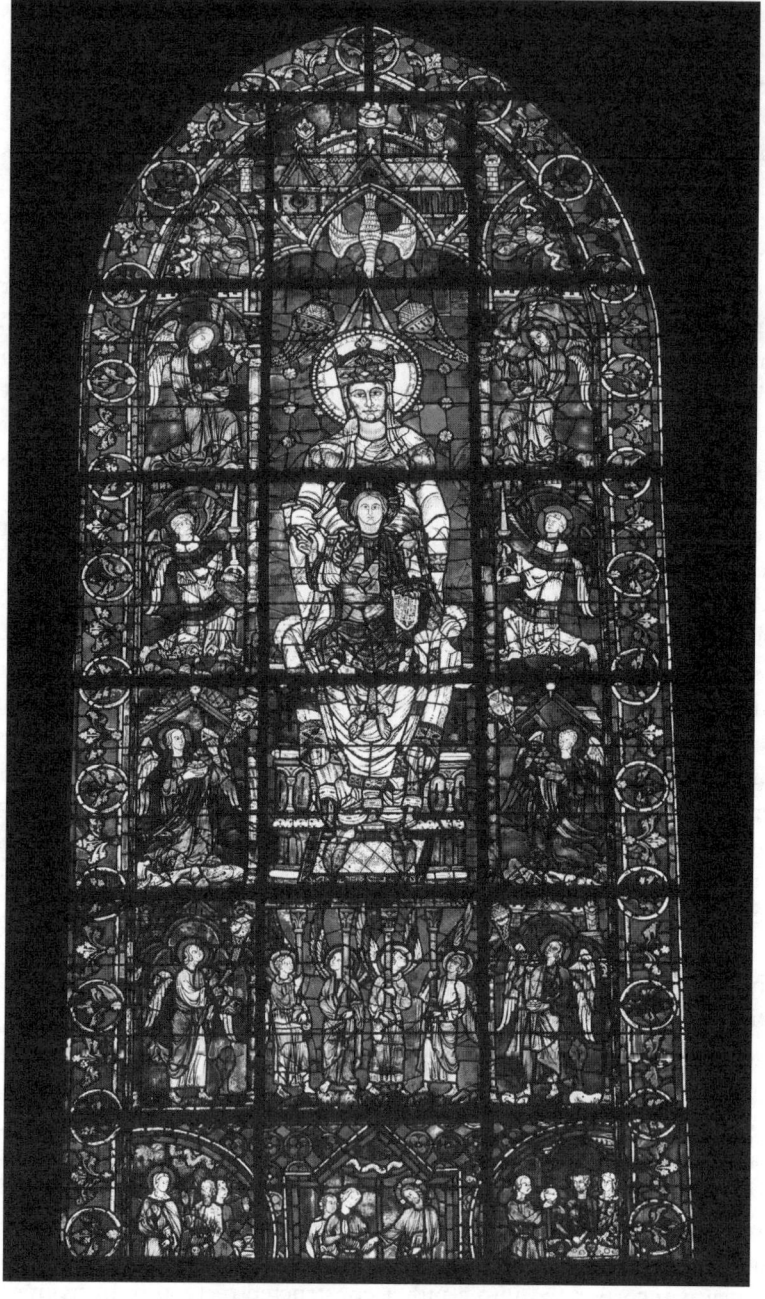

Figure 5. Chartres, cathédrale de Notre-Dame, *La belle verrière* (twelfth/thirteenth century)

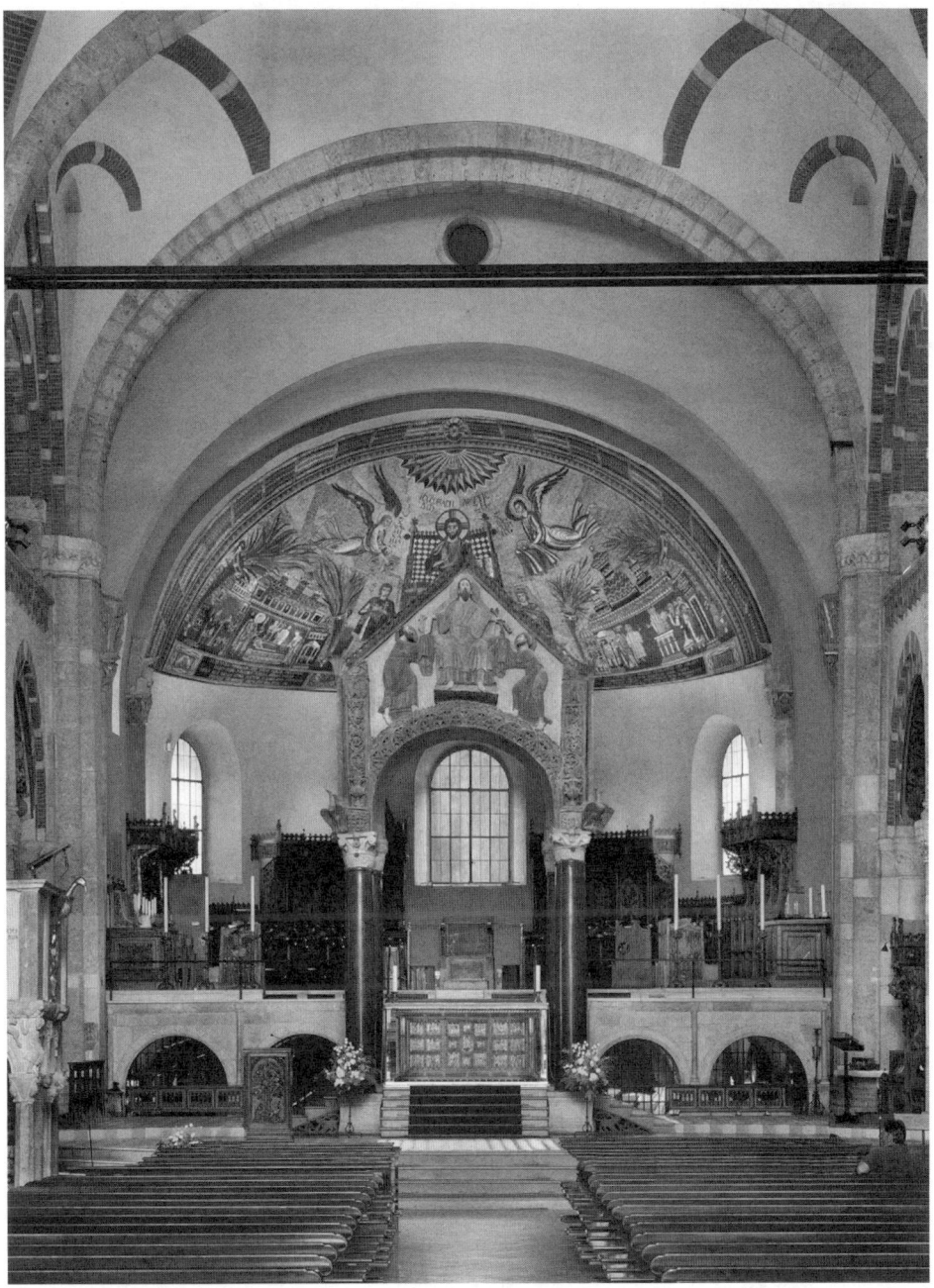

Figure 6. Milan, Sant'Ambrogio, interior (various)

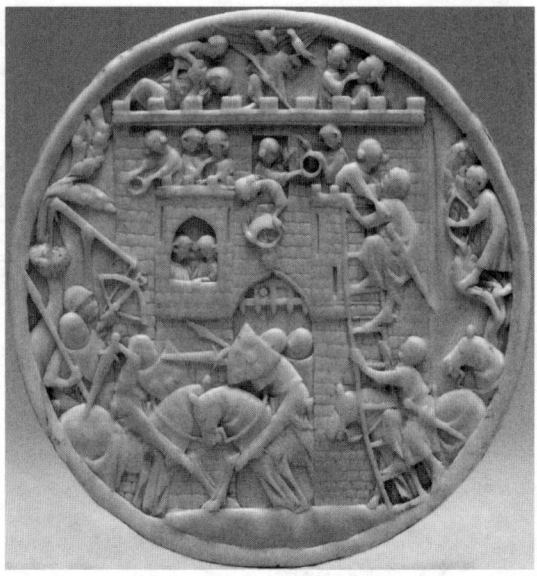

Figure 7. Baltimore, Walters Art Museum, mirror (fourteenth century)

restored), a tenth-century stucco baldachin, and an eleventh-century bishop's throne.[26] Spolia established connections, constructed discontinuities, engaged history, and created meanings.

Many objects were gifts. Charles the Bald presented his throne to San Pietro in Rome, perhaps on the occasion of his coronation as emperor in 875; in the new context, the secular throne came to be identified with Saint Peter, Rome's first bishop.[27] Some, such as the ivory mirror carved with scenes of romance (Figure 7) were private and personal;[28] others were part of more formal traditions of exchange. Rulers, for instance, gave gifts to esteemed visitors at court. According to a medieval legend, the Ayyubid sultan Al-Malik al Kamil presented an early thirteenth-century oliphant (elephant tusk) to Francis when the saint visited Damietta (Egypt) in 1219.[29] Such gift-giving carried with it implications about the relationship of donor and recipient, as when Byzantine emperors sent court silks abroad to co-opt western rulers.[30] The Lateran wolf may have been such a present, its (presumed) secular owner paying homage by adding to the supreme pontiff's collection of bronze sculptures. The "Holy Crown of Hungary" (Budapest, Hungarian Parliament) certainly was—a complex composite of an eleventh-century diadem that the Byzantine emperor Michael VII presented to King Géza and a Latin corona with western

CHAPTER 1: OBJECT 11

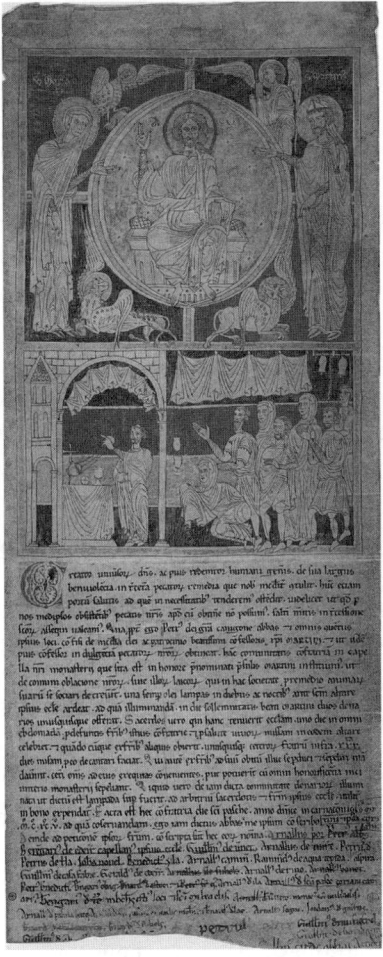

Figure 8. Paris, École des Beaux-Arts, charter from
Saint-Martin-du-Canigou (1195)

enamels attached to it during the second decade of the twelfth century. A political shift westward engendered a legend that it was a gift from the pope to the first king of Hungary.[31]

A charter (cartulary) from the abbey of Saint-Martin-du-Canigou documents corporate gift-giving (Figure 8).[32] It pictures the faithful providing not the objects—the portable cross, chalice, paten, bells, cloths, and lamps—but rather the substance needed to make the latter function, namely, oil. Moreover, the charter itself is an object conveying significance; its scroll form signals that it is a contract, with signatures affixed to the bottom committing confraternity members to continual renewal. The more usual form of book, the codex, was also treated as an object; the cover of the Gospels of Theophanu pictures the queen at the bottom offering the luxury manuscript to the Virgin Mary, represented in the form of Essen's precious Golden Madonna,[33] and to the cathedral itself (see Plate V).[34] Count Fulk may have intended the Psalter that bears the name of his wife Melisende (London, Brit. Lib., MS Egerton 1139) as a token of reconciliation.[35]

The very strangeness of some imported things elicited attention and provoked speculation; embedded in new contexts, they seemed to designate a realm between the earthly and divine. An aquamanile fashioned c. 1130/40 in Hildesheim (Figure 9) imitates Islamic palatine products so well that when it appeared in the art market in 2010 it was identified as a nineteenth-century Ottoman work. Deployed in the eleventh century for priestly handwashing, its exotic quality, allusion to a griffin, and embossed mythological creatures known as *senmurvs* reinforced its geographic intermediacy; it seemed to be an object from the East, where the Holy Land was located.[36] A large piece of exceptionally clear green glass in Reichenau-Mittelzell (Münster, Schatzkammer), most likely once inserted into the center of the monastery's antependium (altar frontal), symbolized Christ or Mary by virtue of its emerald green color and reflective surface, which conjured up Paul's words: "Now we see in an enigmatic mirror, then face to face" (1 Cor 13:12).[37] Medieval objects comprised natural things as well as manufactured ones; the exotic aspect of elephant tusks (transformed as in the case of Saint Francis's oliphant by artistic frames), nautilus shells, narwhal horns, peacock feathers, and coconuts made them seem supernatural.[38] Pilgrims wore the foreign and fascinating scallop shells picked up near the Tomb of Saint James in Santiago de Compostela "back to their own country with great exultation in honor of the apostle and in his memory and as a sign of such a great journey."[39] Taken to be the eggs of griffins, ostrich eggs suspended near altars as signs of the Resurrection attracted the faithful.[40] And, just as the Regensburg butterfly imitated its natural counterpart in size and in the fleeting surface of its iridescent wings,[41] other objects elided the difference between nature and art. Santiago scallop shells were reproduced in metal, perhaps even cast, in a way that makes the object of art almost indistinguishable from the natural thing turned into an object of art.[42]

CHAPTER 1: OBJECT

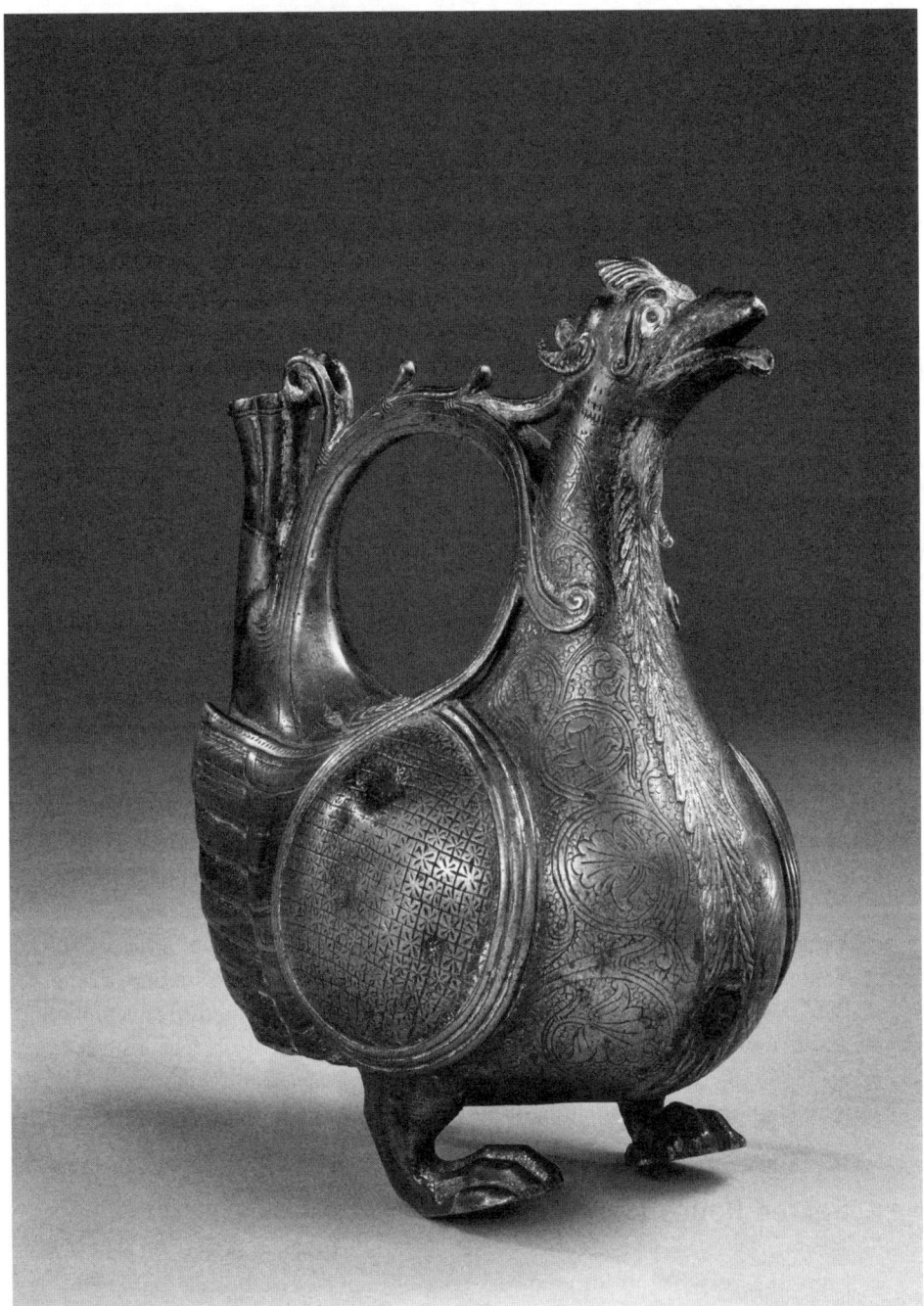

Figure 9. Hildesheim, Diözesanmuseum, aquamanile (twelfth century)

Scriptural Precedents

Christians justified the attachment to physical things by citing objects in Scripture—Noah's ark, Jacob's pillow and ladder, the burning bush in which God appeared to Moses and the Brazen Serpent the prophet set up in the desert, the horn used to consecrate Israelite kings, Solomon's throne, and others. Inscriptions and images affected the associations and uses. A verse on the band of Edward Plantagenet's signet ring in Paris (Musée du Louvre), for instance, connected the wearer with Christ himself and the safe passage He provides: "But Jesus passed among them and went on his way" (Lk 4:30),[43] and the reversed "SIGILLUM SECRETUM," embossed around an intaglio-carved Saint George, conveyed the ring's power to avert evil.

The temple, or tabernacle, and associated objects were particularly potent precedents for Christian liturgical furnishings: the brazen sea, the menorah, Aaron's breastplate and vestments, and in particular the Ark of the Covenant behind the Sancta Sanctorum curtain.[44] Legends arose that certain scriptural objects were actually preserved in medieval churches.[45] Bronze columns in San Giovanni in Laterano, for instance, were revered as Boaz and Jachin from the Jerusalem Temple (1 Kgs 7:21), and the early fourteenth-century *Chronicle of Dalimil* claims that the twelfth-century base of a Baroque candelabrum in a Prague cathedral was "the work of Salomon and nothing can match it. In Jerusalem, it had once stood during Vespasian and Titus's campaign against the Jews."[46] Other objects simply allude to the authorized prototypes; twelve towers adorning the brass chandelier made to hang over the altar in the Stiftskirche Sankt Nikolaus at Groß-Comburg (near Stuttgart) evoke Jerusalem and hence the Heavenly City.[47] A depiction in an Apocalypse manuscript made in England in the 1260s represents Vespasian's troops returning to Rome after destroying the Jerusalem Temple with a curtain as a trophy (Figure 10).[48] The Gospels report that the veil between the Temple's outer courtyard and inner sanctum was rent at the moment of Christ's death and, in accord with medieval legends, the miniature pictures Christ's face (known as the *Veronica*) miraculously impressed on the curtain, making it the most revered spolium of all.

Sacred Relics

From the very beginning, a direct relationship was established between spolia and relics, between Constantine's deployment of fragments of imperial monuments and his gathering of holy remains around his own

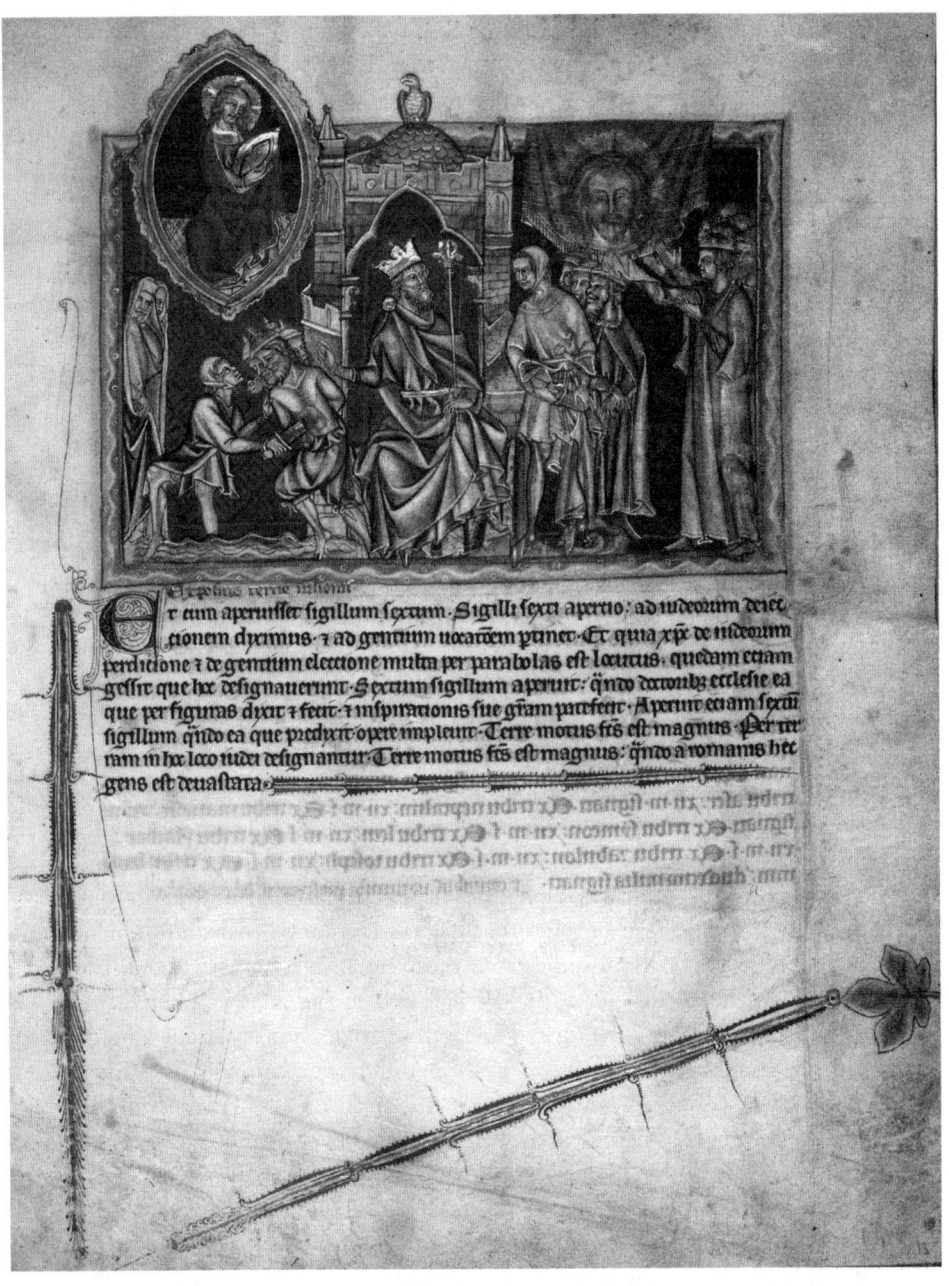

Figure 10. Lisbon, Gulbenkian Collection, MS L.A. 139,
Apocalypse, fol. 13ʳ (thirteenth century)

tomb in the church of the Holy Apostles in Constantinople;[49] the association persisted throughout the Middle Ages. In part, the elision of the difference between corporeal remains and material things was due to the fact that Christ himself was believed to have ascended to heaven without leaving any body parts behind (except his umbilicus, baby teeth, foreskin, and—in the late Middle Ages—also his blood).[50] That meant that in place of body relics, Christians valued material things associated with Jesus's person, especially with his Passion and death—among others, dirt collected in the Holy Land, the lash with which he was flayed, the wreath of thorns used to torment him, his blood and sweat, the nails, sponge, dice, and burial shroud.[51] A lance in Cologne was taken to be Longinus's, the Crown of Thorns was treasured in Paris,[52] and a second-century Roman glass bowl known as the "sacro catino" in Genoa was identified with the cup from which Christ drank at the Last Supper.[53]

Of such things, the cross was the most important. As a sign, it goes back to deep antiquity; as a thing, it acquired particular importance and political valence when Constantine adopted it as his insigne. The emperor's mother Helena allegedly unearthed the actual instrument of Christ's death in Jerusalem;[54] the "True Cross" was fractured into myriad fragments that were distributed throughout the Christian world. Indeed, both the Zwiefalten tablet reliquary and the Regensburg butterfly contain splinters. Crosses could be the simplest of objects, as on the altar pictured in the Saint-Martin-du-Canigou charter and at the center of the eleventh-century frontispiece for Thiofrid of Echternach's tract on relics in Trier (Figure 11).[55] Others were quite elaborate. Between 1358 and 1365, Charles IV built a complex of chapels at Karlstejn outside Prague to house his collection of relics that included, among others, a fragment of the True Cross and a spike from the Crown of Thorns; indeed, the Holy Roman emperor had himself pictured in the antechamber of his private chapel placing the former encased in gold reliquary inside a magnificent container (Figure 12). The Regensburg pendant, enclosed in its own leather cocoon, was deposited in the head of a crucifix carved in eastern Germany,[56] thereby activating a second devotional object through the splinter it houses. Legends grew up around the cross, such as the claim that it had been hewn from the Tree of Life planted at the center of Eden, a reference made by the cross's green color in Thiofrid's frontispiece and in the fragmentary remains of Saint Helena finding the "life-giving cross" on an eleventh-century embroidery in Gerona.[57]

The cross was often replicated, as were the other instruments. A Eucharistic knife in Milan, for instance, is shaped like a spear so that

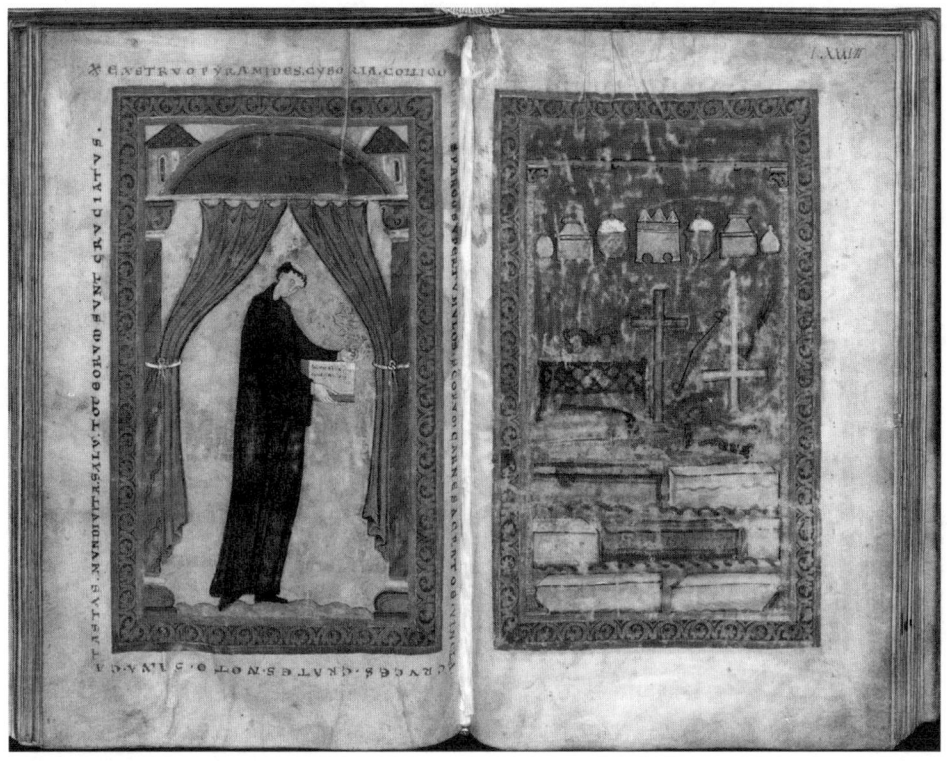

Figure 11. Trier, Stadtbibliothek, MS 1378, *Flores epytaphii sanctorum*, fols. 87ᵛ–88ʳ (eleventh century)

Longinus's stabbing of Christ's chest was re-enacted each time the priest used it to cut a sacramental wafer.[58] In the late Middle Ages, the implements used in the Passion were formed into a virtual complex known as the *arma Christi*. On a fourteenth-century booklet measuring only four by two and a half inches (Figure 13),[59] the implements of the *arma Christi* are pictured separately for contemplation—nails, hammer, tongs, blindfold, Judas's thirty silver coins, cane and whip, cloak and dice, ladder, lance, and sarcophagus. These allowed an easy interchange between object and narrative and also between the instruments used to torture and kill Christ and the healing powers they engendered.[60] In a purposeful inversion of the *arma Christi*, moreover, domestic tools were figured as Passion implements; to convey the idea that a person who violates Church law adds to the Lord's suffering, the "Sunday Christ" at Michael Church in Escley (Herefordshire) surrounds an image of Jesus

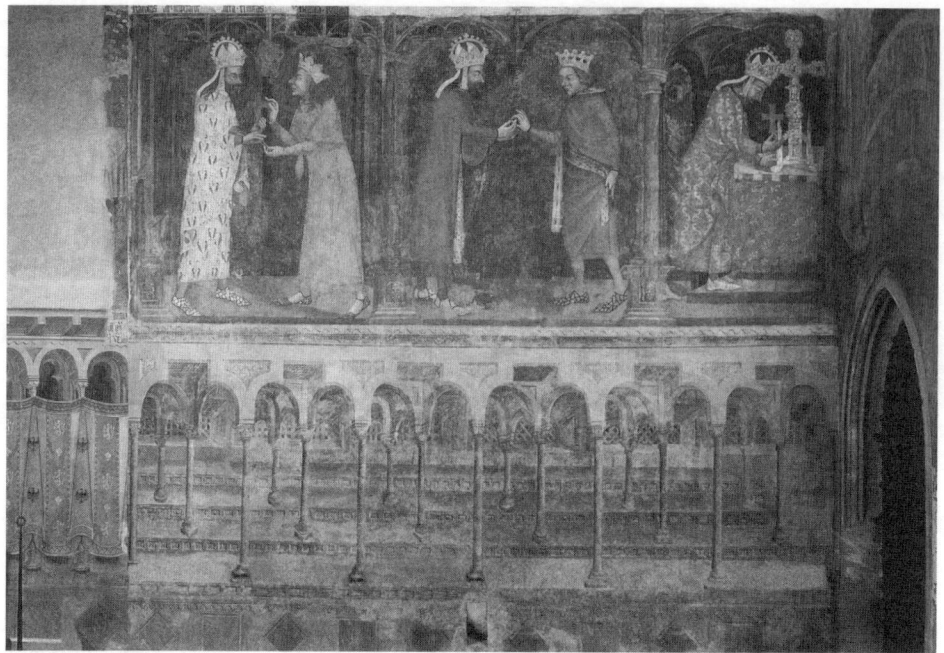

Figure 12. Karlstejn, Castle, chapel of the Virgin Mary, fresco (fourteenth century)

showing his wounds with menacing shears, an adze, saws, hatchets, and other practical objects.[61] Mariotto di Cristofano's painting of the same subject in Florence (San Miniato) bears the warning, "God will damn for eternity anyone who does not respect Sunday and honor Christ."[62]

The idea that divine aura attached to physical objects was extended to Mary, Christ's apostles, and the saints that came after them. The source of his human flesh shared many characteristics with her Son, and, because she, too, was thought to have been assumed bodily into heaven, Mary also was believed to have left few corporal relics. To some extent, contact relics compensated for that lack: clothing, such as her slipper treasured at Soissons, her comb in Valencia, and the belt she dropped to Saint Thomas when she ascended bodily to heaven in the cathedral of Prato (Tuscany);[63] her tears and milk; and her house(s) at Walsingham and Loreto.[64] Images of the Virgin themselves served as reliquaries, like her own person, functioning as intermediaries between the physical world and the divine.[65] The heads of Mary and Christ rendered in

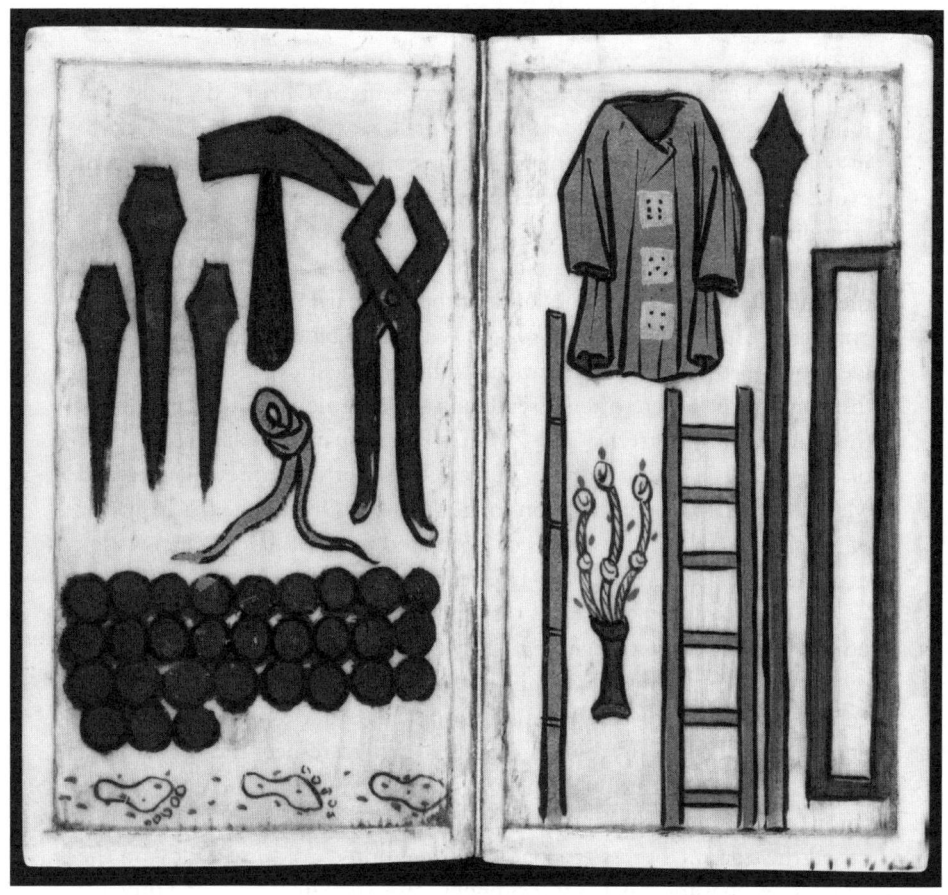

Figure 13. London, Victoria and Albert Museum, *arma Christi* booklet (fourteenth century)

high relief on the panel in Santa Maria Maggiore, Florence, attributed to Coppo di Marcovaldo, sheltered Christ's blood, a fragment of the True Cross, and a piece of the Virgin's veil[66]; these items were discovered during a modern restoration and recall Hugh of Poitiers's report that when the wood statue of the Virgin at Vézelay was opened after a fire in the 1160s almost destroyed it, a "lock of hair of the immaculate Virgin and a part of the same Mary, Mother of God" were found inside.[67] Important for the evolution of three-dimensional sculpture, such figural reliquaries—often called "Thrones of Wisdom"—functioned largely as images, their sacred contents unseen by viewers and probably unknown.

In the Thiofrid miniature, the instrument of Christ's death is surrounded by Peter's cross, Lawrence's grill, a saw, a whip, and other instruments used to martyr the saints; the empty sarcophagi at the bottom evoke the belief that the blessed martyrs have risen, their earthly remains now displayed in vessels pictured at the top, two of simple glass and one at the center, an elaborate gold chest. These vestiges, too, comprised the humblest materials, bones and clothes primarily, but also things the saints had touched or the dirt soaked with their blood. Relics were duly identified with strips of parchments called authentics.[68] Subdivided and distributed, they were often assembled with fragments of the cross, as in the Regensburg butterfly and Zwiefalten reliquary (which has a silver plaque on the back listing relics of John the Baptist, Andrew, James, and Mark adorned with constellations of gold dots).[69] During the third quarter of the thirteenth century, pieces of cloth used to cover Saint Francis's stigmata were enclosed in a flower-like reliquary (see Plate VI).[70]

Art objects were themselves transformed into relics. Abbot Suger reported that he built the choir of Saint-Denis not only to "present the reliquaries of the [three patron] saints, adorned with gold and precious gems," but also to display columns from the earlier building set prominently against the walls dividing each chapel "to respect the very stones, sacred as they are, as though they were relics." Suger also converted the throne of the seventh-century king Dagobert into a secular relic[71] and raised the gemmed cross attributed to the sainted goldsmith Eloy on the altar. The chasuble that King Stephen and Queen Gisela of Hungary donated in 1031 to the Church of the Virgin in Székesfehérvár was refashioned as a coronation mantle, used by King Andrew III in 1290 to honor his sainted predecessor so that he would be "in attire such as St. Stephen wore," and was used continuously in such a way until a century ago (Figure 14).[72] And, in the fourteenth century, a (twelfth-century) paten believed to have been Bernward of Hildesheim's was encased in a monstrance (a vessel used to exhibit the Host) as a relic of the sainted bishop (Cleveland, Cleveland Museum of Art).[73] Proof of a miracle could authorize even mundane objects; at Santo Domingo de la Calzada (near Burgos, Spain), for instance, slave chains bear witness to Saint Dominic's having freed Christian captives from the Saracens.[74]

Images, too, became relics. A seventh-century panel of the enthroned Christ in the Lateran Sancta Sanctorum was considered to be a portrait made by Saint Luke and finished by an angel and, hence,

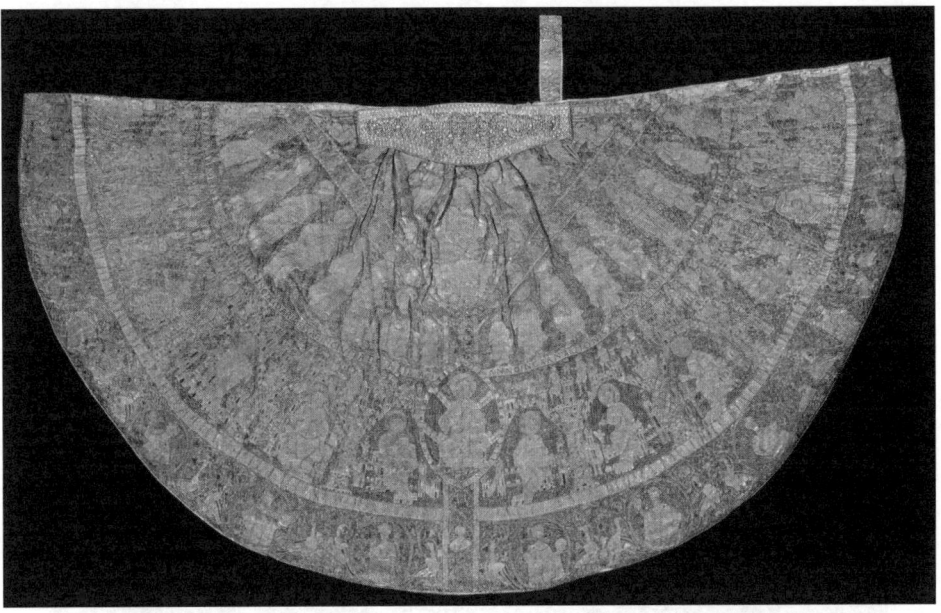

Figure 14. Budapest, Hungarian National Museum, Coronation Mantle (eleventh century)

a semi-*acheiropoieton* (an image made without human hands) (Figure 15); encased in a silver sheath, the "Acheropita" (as it came to be called) was raised on the altar so that its feet rested on other relics, among them significantly a box of stones and soil from the Holy Land kept in a ninth-century wood chest labeled "SANCTA SANCTORUM" and secured by bronze grates around an altar constructed from ancient marble spolia.[75] From the thirteenth century, another miraculously made depiction of Christ came to be venerated as a true image or *vera icona*; derived from the Byzantine *mandylion* (pictured in the Gulbenkian Apocalypse), it was even more fully integrated into the cult of relics by virtue of the fact that it was believed to have been impressed on the cloth that Saint Veronica had allegedly used to wipe the sweat from Jesus's face as he struggled to Golgotha.[76]

As in so many other aspects, the Virgin Mary was matched with her Son. Portraits of her, too, were ascribed to Luke's authorship and considered miraculous; the panel of the Madonna and Child depicted on the pilgrim's badge, for instance, was attributed to the evangelist.[77] Other

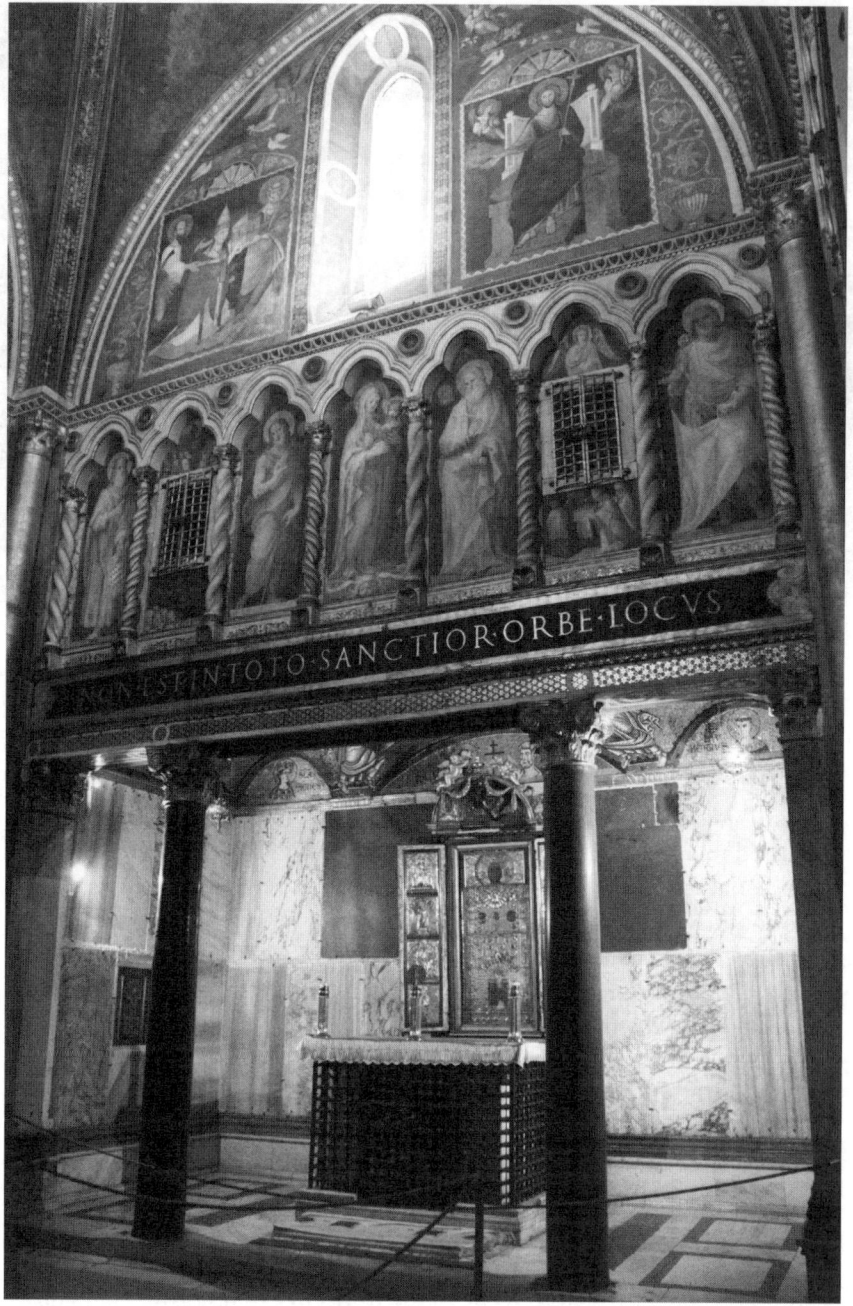

Figure 15. Rome, Scala Santa, Sancta Sanctorum (ninth/eleventh/thirteenth century)

Roman icons claimed the same pedigree,[78] such as the one in Santa Maria Maggiore, known as the *Salus populi romani*. Unlike relics, images could not easily be divided and dispersed, so they were replicated instead and validated by performing miracles. In Florence, for example, a painting of the Virgin and Child in the market that began to be venerated in the late thirteenth century was destroyed and reproduced, and soon became the focus of a cult pictured in Domenico Lenzi's *Specchio umano* (Figure 16).[79] The regal frontal Virgin pictured in the *La belle verrière* at Chartres imitates the ancient variant of Mary icons preserved in the cathedral's crypt, its black coloring distinctive of a family of Madonnas.[80] And in Catalonia, a Marian *Veronica* was mounted in a jeweled reliquary containing Mary's comb (Valencia, catedral); showing only the Virgin's head, albeit without a wisp of hair, it was paraded in Barcelona on the Feast of the Immaculate Conception.[81] Also in Catalonia, the Holy Face of Christ was paired with Mary's to form a diptych.[82] Replicas of the two Lucan icons, framed like precious relics in worked-gold, were depicted in a painting once above the door of the presbytery of the Sainte-Chapelle in Paris, which records Pope Clement VI's presenting the twinned portraits to King Jean le Bon.[83] Following the same pattern, Pope Urban V gave Charles IV three copies of the *Veronica* together with copies of the Madonna icon during the emperor's last visit to Rome in 1368–69.[84]

The assembling of objects from the distant past and far-off places culminated in the amassing of collections and their purposeful display. Over the course of centuries, churches and monasteries accumulated treasuries of relics and related objects; of these, those of Saint-Denis, Conques, Quedlinburg, Essen, Saint-Maurice d'Agaune, and Monza are well documented and partly preserved.[85] In Rome, successive popes constructed, remodeled, and (between 1277 and 1280) rebuilt the San Lorenzo Chapel at the Lateran to accommodate the vast and important collection of body parts and touch relics (now displayed in the Vatican Museum), including Christ's umbilicus and foreskin, a fragment of the True Cross, the Lord's sandals, the Virgin's hair, some of her milk, her veil, bread from the Last Supper, the heads of Saints Peter, Paul, Agnes, and Euphemia, John the Baptist's coat, Matthew's shoulder, and Bartholomew's chin, all inventoried at the entrance of the Sancta Sanctorum. The collection was elevated by rich materials and spolia, including magnificent porphyry columns and slabs looted from ancient Roman monuments, bronze grills and doors taken from a safe made by Pope Innocent III, which he had inserted into the altar, itself constructed from antique marble pieces. Inside the altar, boxes within boxes added to the collection's protection, history, and mystery,

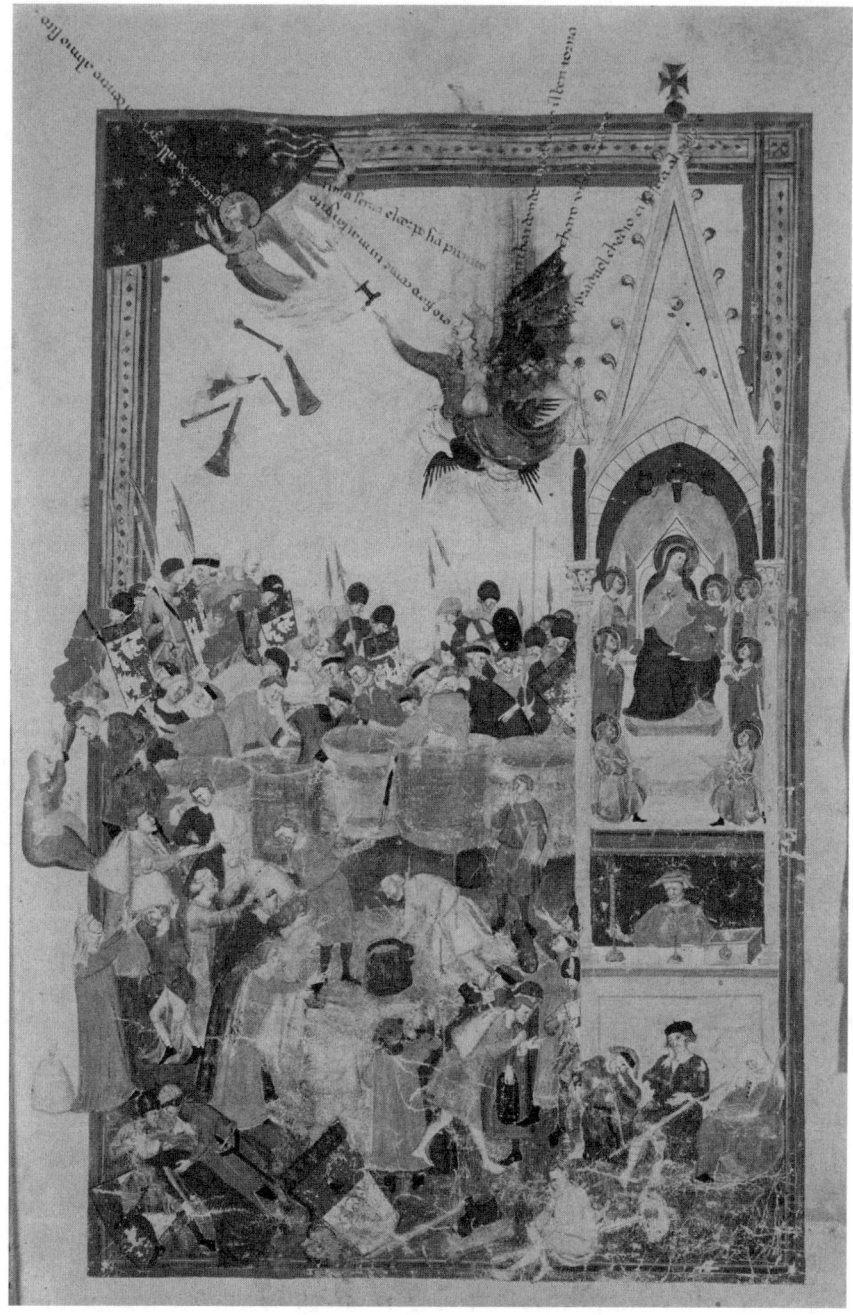

Figure 16. Florence, Biblioteca Laurenziana, MS Tempi 3, *Specchio umano*, fol. 79ʳ (fourteenth century)

including the cypress chest made by Pope Leo III, which contained other reliquary boxes provided by Paschal I, and other containers for relics wrapped in cloths, including one encased in a still earlier gemmed cross.[86]

During the Fourth Crusade, relics looted from Constantinople and elsewhere poured into western Europe. San Marco, the doges' palace in Venice, is adorned outside with sculptural spolia from the Byzantine capital and inside with sacred objects housed in the treasury.[87] In Paris, King Louis IX erected the Sainte-Chapelle to house sacred booty from the Pharos Chapel in the imperial palace of Constantinople that had protected Moses's rod, relics of Christ's Passion, and fragments of Saints John the Baptist, Blasius, Clement, and Simeon.[88] A miniature in the *Très riches heures* (see Plate VII), painted c. 1475 after a late-medieval drawing (Paris, Bibliothèque Mazarine, MS 406, fol. 7), conveys the reliquary-like aspect of King Louis's chapel and the *Grande Chasse* behind the altar that, until the French Revolution, housed the treasure.[89] In turn, the Sainte-Chapelle inspired Pope Nicholas III's new Sancta Sanctorum in Rome and induced the Holy Roman emperor, Charles IV, to emulate (Saint) Louis in his own relic chapel at Karlstejn.

Do ut des?

What motivated the making and collecting of objects? Things given to the Church evoked a process of exchange in which gifts, known as an ex-votos, secured reciprocity, including future redemption.[90] They became part of the age-old practice of offering precious things to the gods in the hope of reaping benefits, known in Latin as *do ut des*. Poems in the First Bible of Charles the Bald (Paris, BnF MS lat. 1), for example, make clear that the monks hoped that the king would respond to the elaborately decorated manuscript they were giving him by renewing the privileges his royal predecessors had conferred on their monastery.[91] Punning on her name Uota, the caption of the early eleventh-century miniature picturing the abbess Uta offering her Gospel Book to the Virgin and Child refers to the act as a "votive," not only for the gift but also for her dedicating her life to God's service in the hope of being granted the "light of eternal life" in heaven (Munich, Bay. Staatsbib., Clm. 13601, fols. 1^v–2^r).[92] In her codex, Abbess Hitda presents the precious tome to Saint Walburga who, portrayed receiving it within the church dedicated to her, simultaneously authorizes the consecrated channel to God and bestows authority on the abbess (Darmstadt,

Hessische Landesbibliothek, MS 1640; see Plate XI).[93] Linked supplications are pictured in a fresco c. 1085 in the lower church in San Clemente in Rome, where, flanking the dedicatory saint, the donors Beno and Maria de Rapiza and their family are portrayed bearing offerings of candles and wax; the inscription makes clear that the gifts, including the painting itself, were for the redemption of the donor's soul.[94] A beautiful inscription on the Rufolo pulpit in the cathedral of Ravello reads, "May this please you, O pious Virgin; and beg your son that he may, because of these gifts, grant them [Rufolo's children] heavenly rewards."[95] Verses on a champlevé plaque (enamel in which the colored glass fills depressions that were formed in the metal base) made during the third quarter of the twelfth century for Henry of Blois, bishop of Winchester, express a similar hope:

> Henry, alive in bronze, gives gifts to God. Henry, whose reputation makes him acceptable to mankind, whose character renders him acceptable to the heavens, a man equal in mind to the Muses and in eloquence higher than Cicero.[96]

It followed that the greater the number of gifts and the more elaborate, the more powerful the saint to whom they were presented would seem to be. An inscription on the great reliquary of Saint Remaclus at Stavelot (destroyed, but known in a drawing in Liège, Archives de l'État) proclaims that Abbot Wibald gave 100 marks for the gold and silver used in its making in the hope of gaining the saint's intercession with God.[97]

Gift-giving recognized gratitude for benefactions already received, as when pilgrims wore tokens from their travels in thanksgiving, or grateful worshippers attached plaster ornaments (*pastiglia*) to the Orsanmichele tabernacle in Florence. Evidence of success inspired others to undertake similar journeys or offer prayers at the shrine. Donating works of art was also a way of inserting one's presence in sacred space. Urraca's chalice and (now lost) paten allowed the queen to be at the altar where, as a woman, she was excluded—likewise Theophanu through her Gospels, and Queen Gisela pictured on the priest's chasuble that was later made into the Coronation Mantle. Around the turn of the tenth century, a widow named Amata provided funds for the *Evangelium longum* of Sankt Gallen in Switzerland (Cod. Sang. 53), not only assuring her presence at the altar but also activating the hope that her gift would provide her a place in heaven's treasury.[98]

Preserving the memory of donors was intended to keep them alive in the prayers of those who came afterward. Theodulf of Orléans made the aim explicit in the titulus of his apse when he called upon those gazing at the mosaic to include "Theodulf's name in your invocations."[99] The inscription beneath the portrait of Saint Clement in Rome also invokes prayer, albeit with an admonition that those who seek him with their devotions must themselves be free of evil. The donor portrayed in a stained-glass window of Le Mans imitates the Virgin Mary commemorated in prayers and hymns, and in so doing, *Ecclesia* (Church).[100] The twelfth-century bronze censer (vessel for burning incense) in Lille is inscribed, "I Reiner, give this sign so that you give your similar prayers when my death has been accomplished, and I ask that the prayers rise [like the smoke of incense] to the face of Christ."[101] The Saint-Martin-du-Canigou charter pictures the sequence of supplications: a gift of oil for lamps, a priest saying Mass, and Saint Martin and the Virgin relaying the invocations to Christ on the donors' behalf. A particularly elaborate example of a benefactor's expectations is evident in the portrait of King Otto IV on the Shrine of the Three Kings in Cologne;[102] inserted behind the three archetypal givers of gifts to the Christ Child, it attests to the king's own tribute to his biblical counterparts—whose skulls are preserved inside—and through them to Mary, the Savior, and God, whose kingdom—pictured at the top—he hopes to enter. A titulus at the bottom of the case Innocent III provided for the Lateran Christ recalls his generosity and positions him in a continuous (and perpetual) process of papal supplications. A final opening of Herrard of Hohenbourg's great compendium *Hortus deliciarum* (Strasbourg, Bibliothèque de la Ville; destroyed in 1870) portrays some sixty members of the community of nuns as a way of staging perpetual veneration for the monastery's founder and book's patron/author by later users of the book.[103]

Eucharist

No object of exchange was more efficacious than God's gift of his own Son to redeem humankind as recapitulated in the Eucharist. Indeed, some theologians considered the sacramental body and blood to be the sole physical presence of Christ,[104] which, like relics, could perform miracles.[105] A fragment of bread from the Last Supper was venerated in Laon,[106] and Hosts were kept in decorated boxes, paraded in Corpus Christi processions, displayed in monstrances and tabernacles, and provided with special sacrament houses.[107] Increasingly, the Eucharist was implicated in gift-giving as an investment for salvation,[108] a notion vividly realized on a mid-thirteenth-century Catalan altar now in Baltimore (Walters Art Museum) where Christ's aureole is adorned with alternating wafers and coins.[109] Not normally thought of as art, sacramental wafers were sometimes treated as images and introduced into other works. A treatise written in the middle of the ninth century by Eldefonsus, "bishop of Spain," illustrates how Hosts might be arranged on altars in forms of the cross or heavenly Christ (*Majestas Domini*) and provides patterns for adorning individual wafers.[110] The objectified Host was elaborated in the altarpiece, c. 1335–45, from the monastery of Santa Maria de Vallbona de les Monges (Urgell) attributed to the Catalan painter Guillem Seguer (Figure 17); the painted and gilt panel centers on a tabernacle containing a wafer (in stucco relief) embossed with a crucifix growing from a life-giving vine.[111] As the flanking narratives also illustrate, the wafer raised over the altar and gazed at by the congregation had the power to exorcise evil and to work miracles.

Eucharistic wine had to be contained in chalices such as the one Doña Urraca gave to Oviedo, and it was thus physically and theologically different from the wafer/body.[112] From an early date, precious materials were recommended to avoid the wine's being corrupted, and a treatise on the Mass produced in England in the early fourteenth century, showing a priest wiping the cup clean after completing the service, illustrates how chalices were treated as special objects (Paris, BnF, MS fr. 13342, fol. 48ᵛ).[113] The Chiarito triptych painted by Pacino di Buonaguida in the middle of the fourteenth century (Los Angeles, J. Paul Getty Museum) pictures Christ himself as the source of the sacramental liquid, drawn from his body by long straws known as fistulae.[114]

Transformed into Christ's body and blood through priestly consecration, the Eucharistic species exemplified a fundamental characteristic of the medieval object more generally: interchangeability. Eldefonsus had already compared the Host to coins as a way of contrasting the earthly king's currency to the celestial Lord's, a trope that twelfth- and thirteenth-century theologians elaborated;[115] and he diagrammed it as both a map of the world and the king who rules it.[116] Held by God in ninth-century depictions of the *Majestas Domini*, it is simultaneously Christ's body, the earth, and the universal Church.[117] The substitution, in turn, fed anti-Semitic propaganda. As the counterexample to Judas's thirty pieces of silver in the *arma Christi*, it evoked the notion of spiritual as against mundane exchange;[118] and it was said that, just as Jews were unable to find the spirit

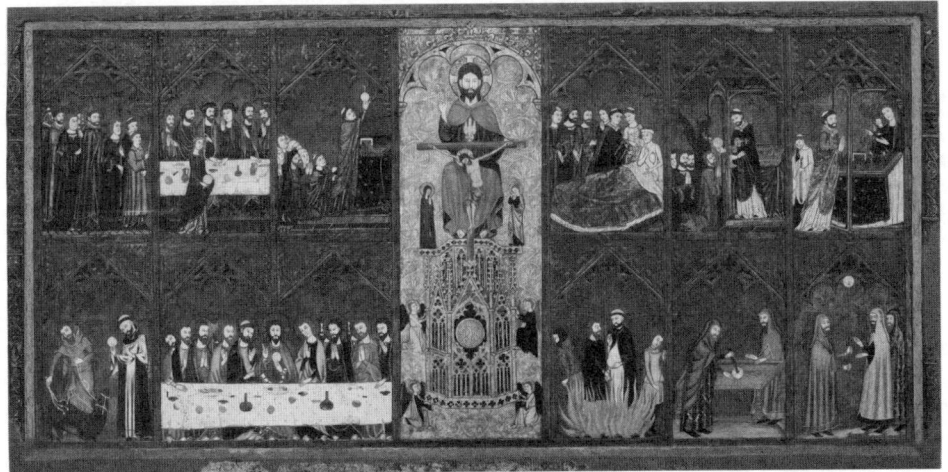

Figure 17. Barcelona, Museu nacional d'art de Catalunya, altarpiece from Monastery of Santa Maria de Vallbona de les Monges (fourteenth century)

in works of art, they could not distinguish a stolen wafer from their money. Legends grew up about Jews desecrating the Host and their conversion when the wafer bled;[119] the story is pictured in lower right of the Vallbona altarpiece where, in a recapitulation of the Crucifixion, a Jew is shown piercing the wafer (which emits blood) and then raising it on a pole.[120]

Chapter 2
Matter

OVERT MATERIALITY is a distinguishing characteristic of much medieval art.[121] The substances used to fashion figures and ornament are apparent in ways that, say, the oil paint on a fifteenth-century Flemish panel or the marble of a neoclassical sculpture are not. Even when wood is painted or parchment covered with pigments and ink, the constitutive substances usually do not vanish from sight through the mimicking of the perception of other things;[122] to the contrary, their very physicality calls attention to a work's essential artifice and interrogates the fact of materiality.[123] The characteristic is obvious on such aggregate works as the Aachen ambo (Plate IV) and Zwiefalten reliquary (Figure 4); not only are the rock crystals and gems patent on one face of the reliquary of Saint Francis (Plate VI), for instance, but the figures and plants on the other are also rendered as imitation jewels of fused glass paste set in gold matrixes. Expressed materiality is fundamental to the typically medieval media of mosaic and enamel, and it is even more evident in stained glass, the most original and important medium of the high Middle Ages. As in *La belle verrière* at Chartres (Figure 5), discrete highly saturated pieces, held in place by stone and metal armatures, declare their physical presence simultaneously as both architecture and images. Even toward the end of the Middle Ages, when verisimilitude led to the effacing of overt materiality, distinctions continued to be deployed; on the Vallbona altarpiece (Figure 17), the gesso Host stands out from the narratives, and, in the Regensburg butterfly (Plate I), the pearls that terminate the antennae assert the facsimile's essential artifice and the object-image's assimilation to God's own artful fashioning of nature. Although the mid-fourteenth-century Pietà in Fritzlar uses paint to convey Mary's smooth white skin, red lips, and cheeks (Plate VIII),[124] the trunk of the lime tree remains discernible in the base and Mary's supportive form; Mary is, in other words, also materially and metaphorically the trunk of the Tree of Jesse on which, in other works, she is often poised (see Figure 33). Moreover, the red paint staining Christ's body assaults the viewer with its own tactility, the scarlet blooms, perhaps originally enhanced by papier mâché drops, evoking flower petals.

Conversely, by sheathing bones and dirt in lustrous materials, the enamel and metal containers made the worth of relics evident by elevating earthly matter and decaying flesh as elements in the heavenly city of Jerusalem.[125] Guibert of Nogent noted that "enclosed ... in a costly shell of gold ... they are visible evidence descending to this age to provide fresh testimony."[126] Thiofrid of Echternach maintained that relics are more precious than gold and gems (Figure 11).[127] A short time later, Rupert of Deutz imagined God himself pointing to golden reliquaries on an altar as the most sublime of all earthly things.[128] Material, color, and ornament served to attract medieval viewers from the chaotic and base world of real life and to construct the spiritual experience. The twelfth-century *De diversis artibus* assures painters that "by setting off the ceiling panels and walls with a variety of kinds of work and diverse pigments, [they] have shown the beholders something of the likeness of the paradise of God."[129] In making his argument, the author, presumably Roger of Helmarshausen, drew on Psalm 25:8: "I love the beauty of thy house, the place where thy glory dwells," one of several scriptural passages deployed to justify the making of art generally.

The relationship between artistic materials and relics became an issue during the Carolingian period, when the *Opus Caroli regis contra synodum* (also known as the *Libri Carolini*, 790s) and the Council of Paris (825) distinguished between the two. Claudius of Turin dismissed both alike as physical matter that cannot participate in the sacred, while Jonas of Orléans and Dungal adopted a moderate middle ground.[130] In these writings, as in later ones, the connection between art and relics inevitably implicated pilgrimage as well; the faithful sought the presence of the saints through their earthly remains, and they also reacted to the visual richness that authenticated the places where the saints were venerated.[131]

Histories

Specific materials had histories that, together with their inherent qualities, imparted meaning to the objects and images constructed of them.[132] Some were associated with the heavens or individual planets, others with particular parts of the world; combined with one another, they created their own rhetoric.

Valued for their cost and luminousness in ancient culture and in Scripture, precious metals and gems were used in Christian art to figure heaven as a place of spiritual reward.[133] Purity was important; just as an eleventh-century description of life in the abbey of Cluny specifies that wheat for the Host had to be chosen grain by grain, so too gold, silver, bronze, and glass used for sacred vessels were valued for untaintedness guaranteed by smelting.[134] Likewise, crystal and amber were worth most if they were without blemish.

Incorruptible, costly, and rare, gold retained the ancient association with power, though its meaning, too, evolved during the course of the Middle Ages.[135] Thus, a tiny prayer book (5.3 × 4.7 inches) made for Charles the Bald, c. 860, deploys the precious material to render the king's crown, to adorn his cape, leggings, and shoes, and to frame the vellum leaves (Figure 18),[136] while embroidery of gold and silver thread transforms the Coronation Mantle into a reflection of heaven (Figure 14).[137] By extension, gold was used to represent the King of Kings in apse mosaics[138] and came to be identified with Church decoration as such, by Bruno of Segni, for example.[139] The precious reflective material distinguishes the personification of *Ecclesia* from other figures in Hildegard of Bingen's *Scivias* (Figure 19),[140] and Pope Innocent III used it to clothe the Lateran Christ panel (Figure 15).[141] An inscription around the *Majestas Domini* on a late tenth-century antependium in Xanten asserts gold's capacity to figure Christ's dual nature: the image renders the form of a man, the gold signifies his divinity.[142] The slightly earlier gilt-copper roundel nearly six and a half feet in diameter of the Savior flanked by angels once set in the east gable of the Münster of Reichenau (Konstanz) of c. 940 implicitly does the same (Figure 20).[143] During the thirteenth and fourteenth centuries, gold was deployed to represent the ineffable Deity in manuscripts and such panel paintings as the altarpiece Ambrogio Lorenzetti painted in 1335–37 for San Piero in Orto in Massa Marittima in south Tuscany (Figure 21).[144]

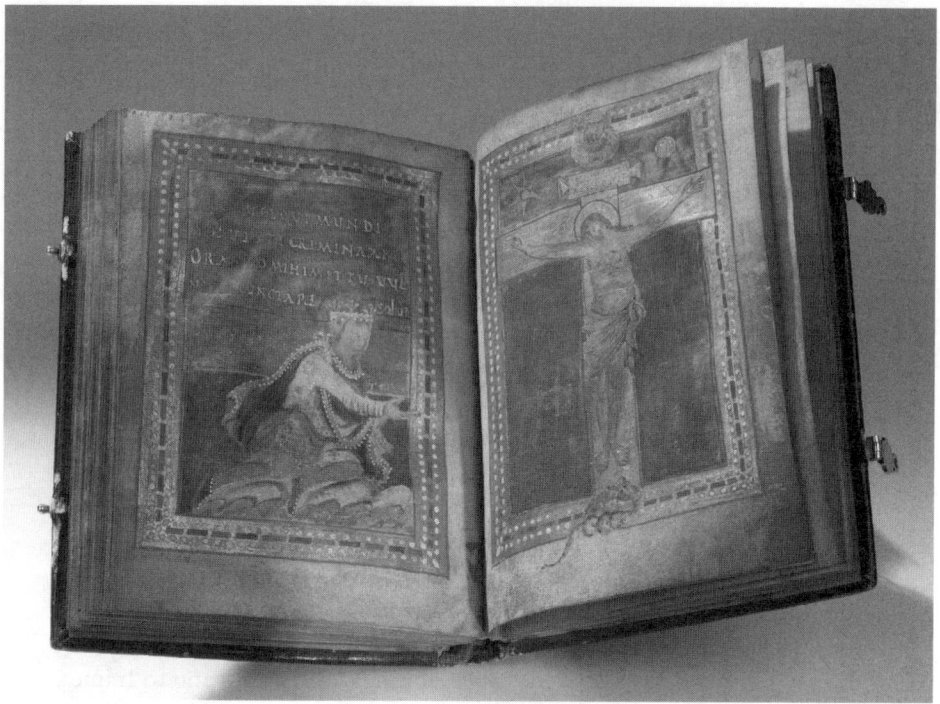

Figure 18. Munich, Residenz, Schatzkammer, Prayer Book, fols. 38ᵛ–39ʳ (ninth century)

Often paired with gold, silver shared many qualities with its more precious counterpart but also differed from it,[145] as Bede, for instance, pointed out in his interpretation of Psalm 11 (12): "For in the Scriptures the splendor of wisdom is often indicated by gold, and the brightness of words by silver." Following the exegesis, the mid-ninth-century Utrecht Psalter illustrated the passage with a picture of the psalmist turning toward Christ while pointing to a silversmith holding tongs at a furnace being stoked by a man working the bellows, the molten metal flowing onto the ground set parallel to the unfurling "words of the Lord" (Universiteitsbibliotheek, MS Bibl. Rhenotraiectinae I Nr 32, fol. 6ᵛ).[146] Silver could also create sound, a quality that fed the notion of eloquence. The metal tarnished and turned black, but when it was polished, silver reflected,[147] a property Ambrogio Lorenzetti exploited when he represented the (unseen and unseeable) Trinity in the framed mirror the personification of Faith holds

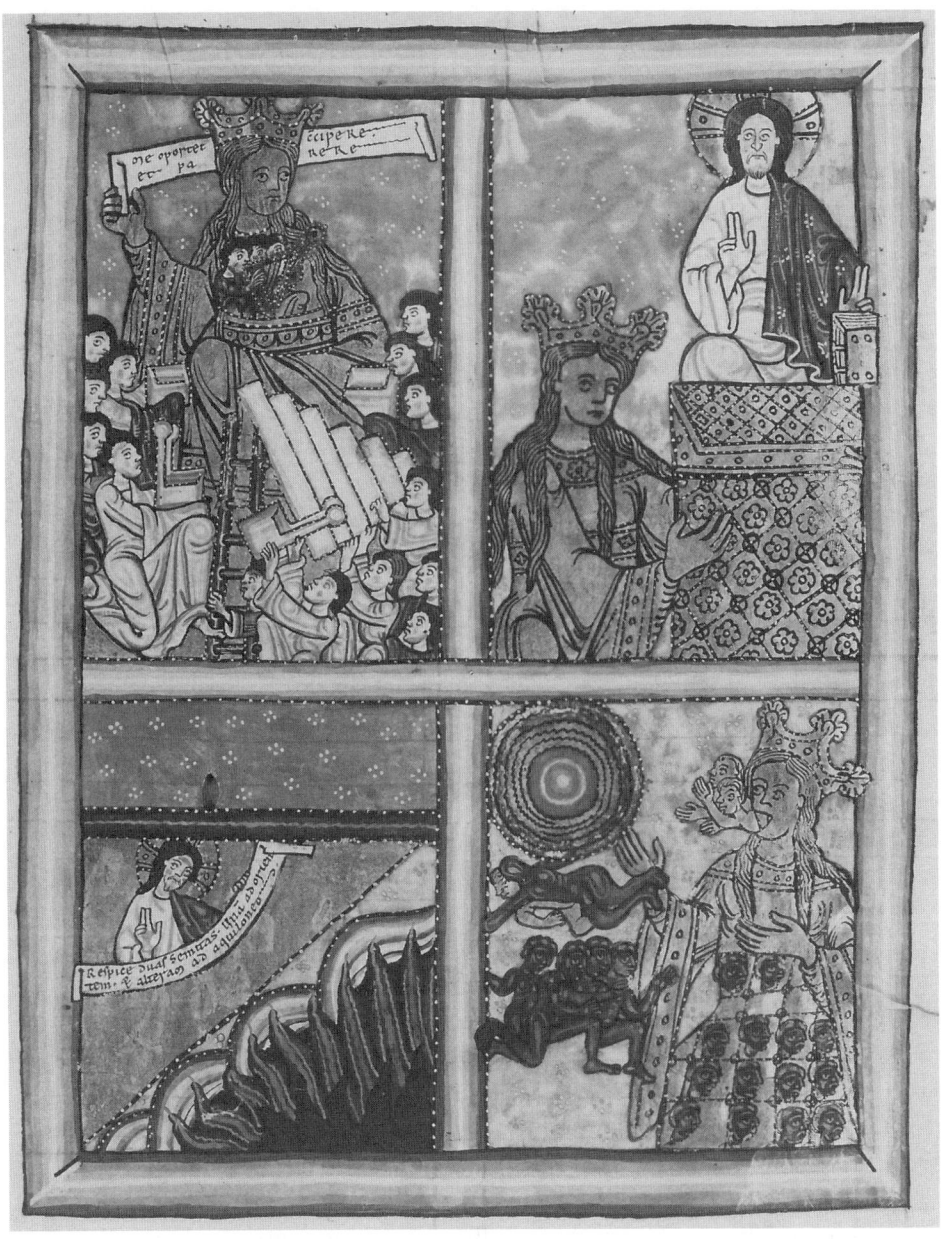

Figure 19. Wiesbaden, Nassauische Landesbibliothek (formerly), MS 1, *Scivias*, fol. 51ʳ (twelfth century)

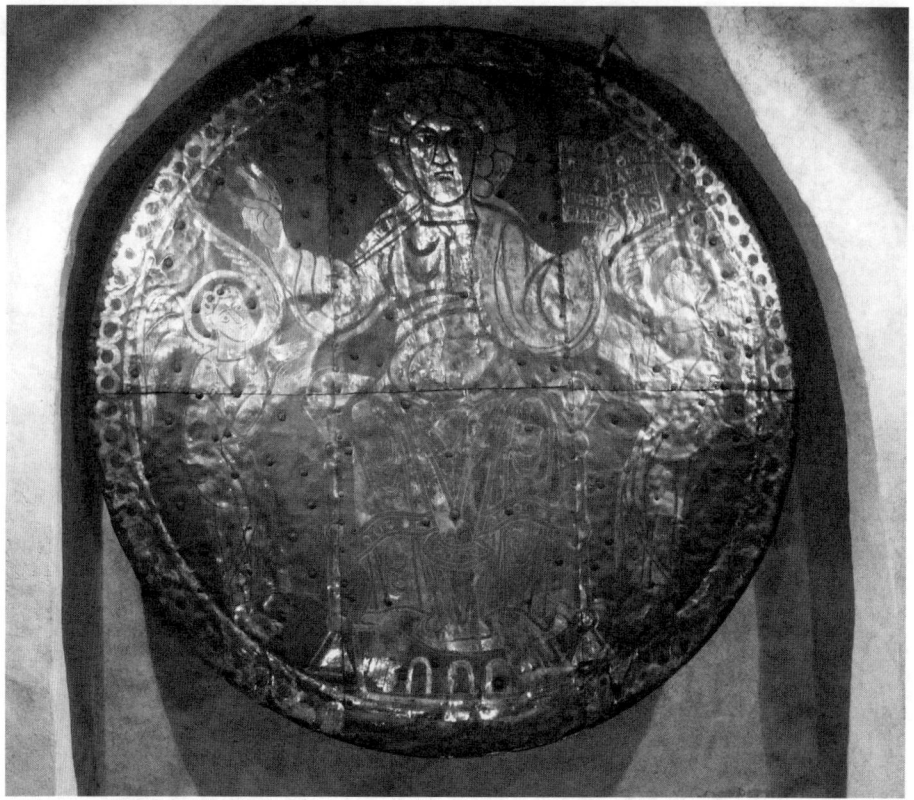

Figure 20. Reichenau (Konstanz), Münster, gilt disk (tenth century)

up to the viewer that was once covered with silver foil inscribed with a Janus-like head and white dove. About the same time, the Salimbeni brothers inserted silvered-glass disks into the wings of angels in a fresco in Urbino,[148] assimilating the intermediary aspect to the angelic virtues. And around 1370, a diagram in a manuscript of Heinrich Suso's *Exemplar* in Strasbourg (Figure 22) used three concentric silver circles to imagine the soul's indwelling with the Trinity at the end of an itinerary of contemplation (speculation). This mirroring allowed a reader-viewer to glimpse her or his own mortal reflection, perceived fleetingly on the page.[149] Silver had negative aspects as well. Judas had sold Christ for thirty silver coins, pictured, for instance, on the London devotional booklet (Figure 13).

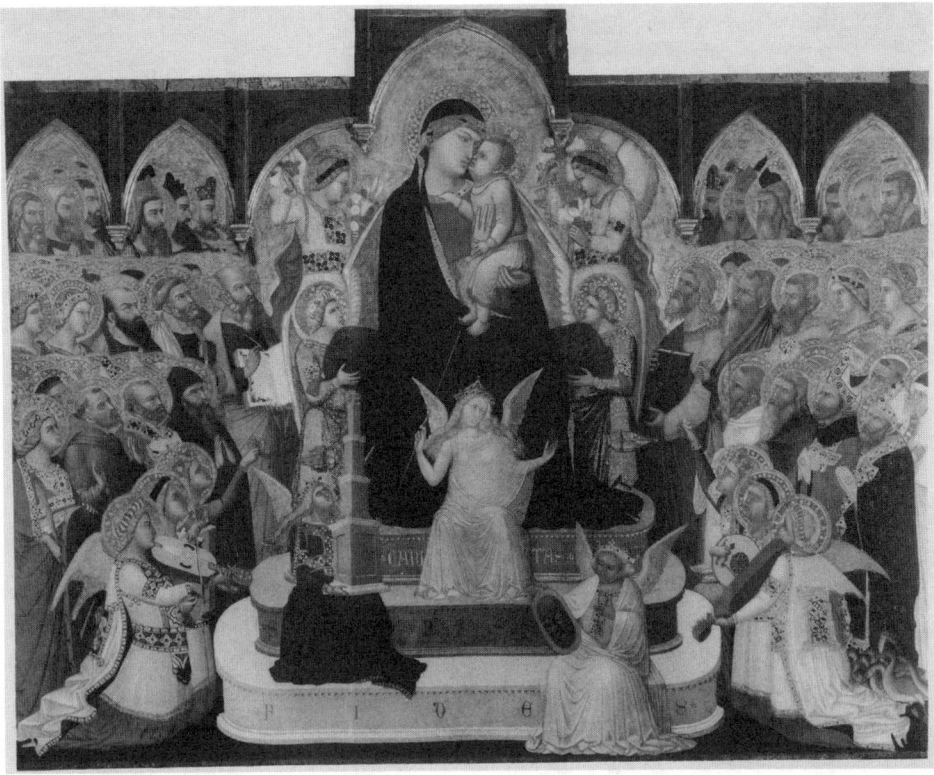

Figure 21. Massa Marittima, Museo di Arte Sacra Medievale, Ambrogio Lorenzetti altarpiece (fourteenth century)

Pure, light-emitting gems also had a biblical pedigree.[150] Ezekiel described Eden as a "garden of God, adorned with gems of every kind: sardin and chrysolite and jade, topaz, cornelian and green jasper, lapis lazuli, purple garnet, green felspar [and] jingling beads of gold" (Ez 28:13), which the Book of Revelation refigured as the celestial city built of "pure gold ... adorned with jewels of every kind" (Rv 21:18–19).[151] Thus, Scripture's beginning and end, both the lost paradise and its promised replacement, are figured in materials prevalent in medieval art. Called "living stones" in 1 Peter 2:4–8, Christ's saints were likened to the gold and gems of which the heavenly city was built; not surprising, the Urraca chalice (Plate III), Aachen pulpit (Plate IV), and Zwiefalten

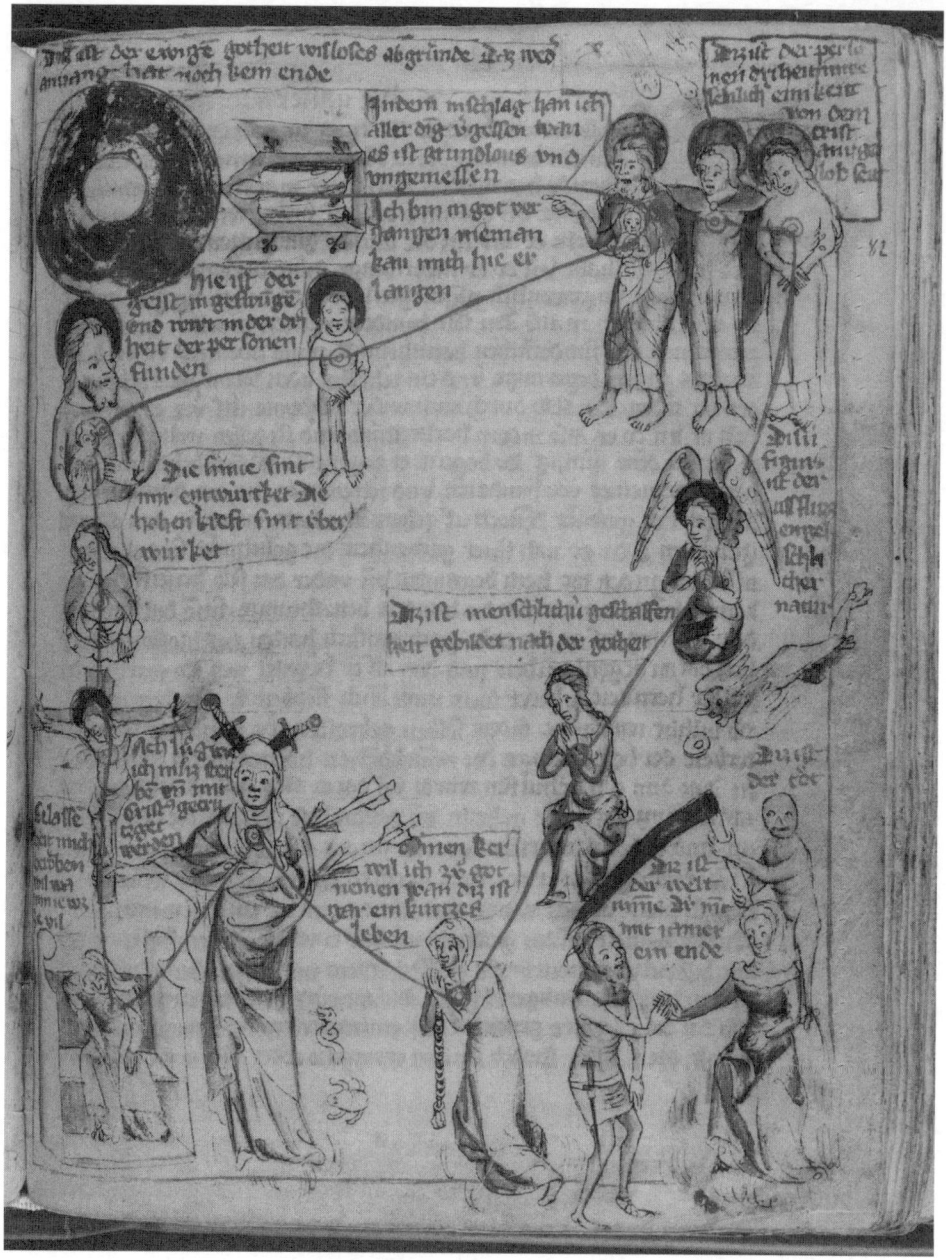

Figure 22. Strasbourg, Bibliothèque nationale et universitaire, *Exemplar*, Cod. 2929, fol. 82ʳ (fourteenth century)

and Francis reliquaries (Figure 4 and Plate VI) are adorned with bands of semi-precious stones.

Aaron's breastplate (*ephod*) was set with twelve gems, each symbolizing a tribe of Israel and identified with the planets believed to govern the power of various material substances (Ex 28:15–29);[152] specific stones therefore took on meaning. Sapphire was considered to be the color of a clear sky and hence a symbol of him who lives there;[153] sculptors of the antechamber to the Camera Santa at Oviedo provided Saint Thomas, alone among the apostles, with a sapphire eye to confirm his ability to see spiritually: "Because you have seen me, you have believed; blessed are those who have not seen and yet have believed" (Jn 20:29).[154] Emerald's green color symbolized the life force, and the gem's purity indexed chastity and eternity;[155] a green bowl occupies the center of the Aachen ambo in much the same way as the slab of green glass set in the center of an antependium in the church of Saints Mary and Mark at Reichenau substituted for Christ (or Mary).[156] Rock crystal was identified with the firmament separating the mundane realm from the region of God and the angels;[157] for Bernard of Clairvaux, it therefore symbolized Mary.[158] On the Francis reliquary, crystal cabochons (polished and shaped gemstones) form a constellation on the front that replicates the wounds on the saint's body pictured on the other side inflicted by the seraph. Citing John's Gospel, "We shall be like him, for we shall see him as he is" (Jn 3:2), Francis's biographer, Bonaventure, argued that crystal embodied Christ's two natures and that, when it is exposed to the sun, it is entirely pervaded by the ray just as the intellectual eye, when it is traversed and filled with divine light, conforms to God.[159] The light-emitting darkness of red garnets symbolized Christ's dual nature, too;[160] and, on Emperor Charles IV's reliquary of the Crown of Thorns (Baltimore, Walters Art Museum), a ruby marks the wound made by the thorn on Christ's forehead.[161]

Cameos, both ancient and newly made, helped to transform "dangerous" stone.[162] On the Urraca chalice, the relief portrait of King Fernando I situates the donor's father among the stars. The ancient medusa used as David's face on the Basel reliquary (Figure 3) simultaneously engages the inherent risk of looking at idols and the transformative aspect of Christian faith,[163] while the intaglio lion of Judah refers to the priestly ephod and the tribe from which Jesse, David's ancestor (and hence Christ's), descended.[164]

Although lapidaries offered methods for distinguishing precious stones from imitations,[165] glass was often deployed to replace gems, not only because it was less expensive but also because it permitted artisans to apply the material symbolism on a large scale.[166] Because of the various metals used in its manufacture—from platinum, to cobalt, to lead—glass was called "metallum"; the transformation from base sand and ash was considered magical.[167] Seemingly made of light itself, windows filled with gem-like glass were used to figure Christ from at least the ninth century,[168] and Abbot Suger, quoting Ezekiel's description of Eden in his account of the Saint-Denis windows, referred to the glass as "sapphiric matter."[169] Sapphire blue dominates *La belle verrière* of Chartres (Figure 5), tying the *mater ecclesiae* to paradise. When Hildegard of Bingen celebrated the consecration of the church of Sankt Rupert, she saw the splendor of the stained glass there as a vision of Jerusalem.[170]

Closely associated with pagan idols, bronze presented special problems to medieval artisans. Ancient works made of the copper and tin alloy were often melted down and reused, but doors made of it were preserved on pagan structures converted into churches, such as the Roman churches of Santa Maria ad Martyres (Pantheon), Santi Cosma e Damiano (Temple of Romulus), and Sant'Adriano (Curia). During the eighth and ninth centuries, popes and emperors vied over the connotations of authority invested in the durable alloy.[171] Charlemagne revived ancient techniques to forge the barriers and doors that secured his chapel at Aachen,[172] an allusion to the Roman precedents he was seeking to revive. At the beginning of the eleventh century, Bernward, bishop of Hildesheim, imitated both Rome and Aachen when he fitted the cathedral with sixteen-foot-high doors pairing creation and the Fall with Christ's birth, death, and resurrection (Figure 23).[173] Later, Abbot Desiderius of Montecassino and other south Italian clerics imported historiated bronze doors from Constantinople for churches in Montecassino, Ravello, Amalfi, and elsewhere.[174] A sequence of bronze doors and grills protected the relics treasured inside the Sancta Sanctorum,[175] tethering them to classical spolia arrayed outside. On Henry of Blois's plaque and in tomb effigies, bronze's permanence fixed the deceased's mortal image whose real body had decayed.[176] A Byzantine bronze door inserted as a spolium into the main portal of San Marco in Venice was imitated and varied during the thirteenth and fourteenth centuries.[177]

Lead, tin, and pewter were used for such modest objects as pilgrims' badges (Figure 2).[178] The *Liber Melorum* written by Herbert of Bosham in 1186 equated lead with Christian humility, and Franciscan poverty was one factor that led to the experimental use of lead white in the transept paintings at Assisi.[179] Like glass, stucco, too, conveyed the

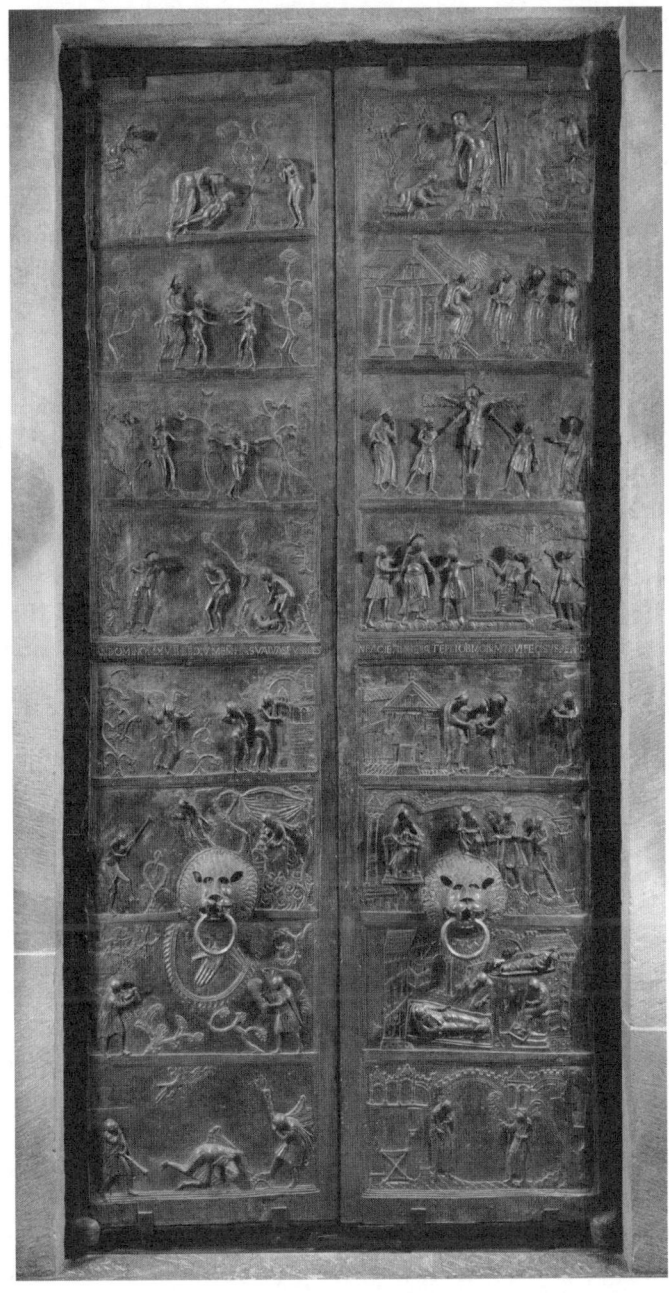

Figure 23. Hildesheim, Dom, bronze doors (eleventh century)

notion of a humble material transformed into something elevated. In Sant'Ambrogio (Figure 6), for example, where it was used for the altar canopy (ciborium), stucco effected the transition between allied materials of stone, fresco, and mosaic and, most important, between images associated with pagan idols and Christian images of God.[180]

Stone, too, had manifold symbolic connotations. In Ephesians 2:19–22, Christ is referred to as a cornerstone, and in 1 Corinthians 10:4, he is compared to the rock from which Moses drew water in the desert.[181] Such passages were evoked to justify the development of altars and monumental stone sculpture;[182] indeed, one of the earliest surviving witnesses, a *Majestas Domini* from Sankt Emmeram in Regensburg, bears the somewhat defensive inscription that makes patent the connection between the material and subject: "Because Christ was called a rock because of his unshakable divinity, it is appropriate to render him in a stone image."[183] At Moissac and other twelfth-century churches, Christ is literally the keystone (Figure 24). Eventually stone sculptures were built into the fabric of medieval sanctuaries to establish physically the connection between Christ, Mary, the saints, the terrestrial church, and the worshippers in that church. Thus, at Amiens Cathedral (Figure 25) and on the screen before the west choir of Naumburg Cathedral (Figure 26),[184] stone figures of Christ seem to support the entire structure.

Idols had long been associated with stone too, but legends of images miraculously formed in it helped to redeem the material. Albertus Magnus described pictures discovered naturally in stone,[185] and an illustration of *Song 29* in Alfonso X's *Cantigas* depicts the story of a stone image of Mary and Christ venerated in Gethsemane (Escorial, Real biblioteca del Monasterio, MS T.I.1, fol. 44^r); most remarkable, it shows Christ actually touching the sculpture with his own fingers.[186] A twelfth-century capital, from the funerary chapel of Don Sanchez Ramirez in Jaca, goes further to assimilate stone's ancient diabolical associations to Christian use (Figure 27): by quoting a pagan Dionysiac nude depicted on an ancient sarcophagus relief, it transforms the dancing man into a Christian image, and by introducing a phoenix on the opposite face, it virtually liquefies the granite and recasts it as a manifestation of resurrection.[187] In the Wenceslaus Chapel of the cathedral of Prague, polished stones covering the walls are assimilated to the column on which Christ is shown tied, the Lord's suffering in this case elevating the base material of which the shrine is constructed into a kind of relic.[188]

Although mostly quarried locally and therefore tethering object to site, in certain cases heavy stone was imported for symbolic reasons. Perhaps

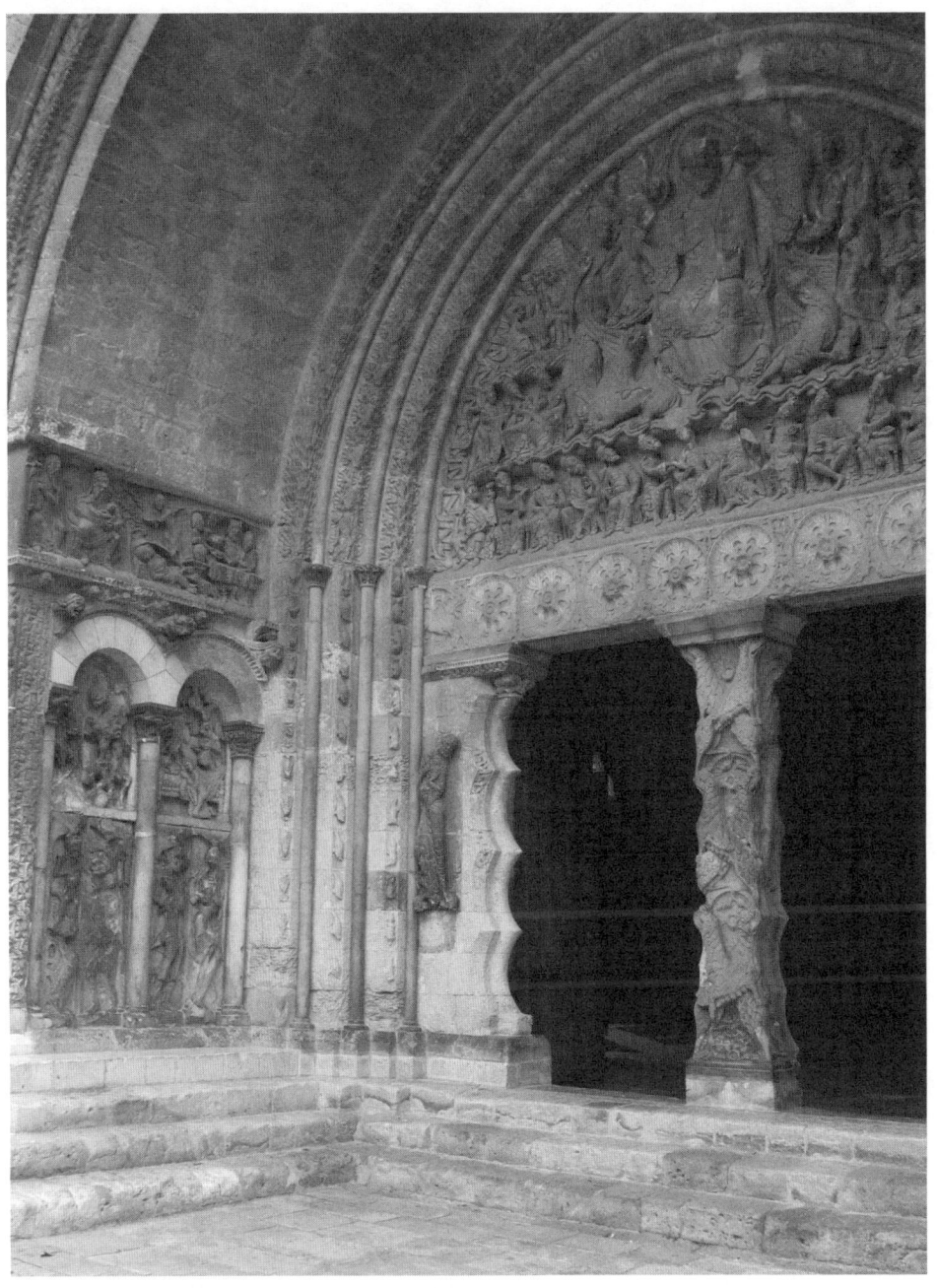

Figure 24. Moissac, l'abbaye Saint-Pierre, façade (twelfth century)

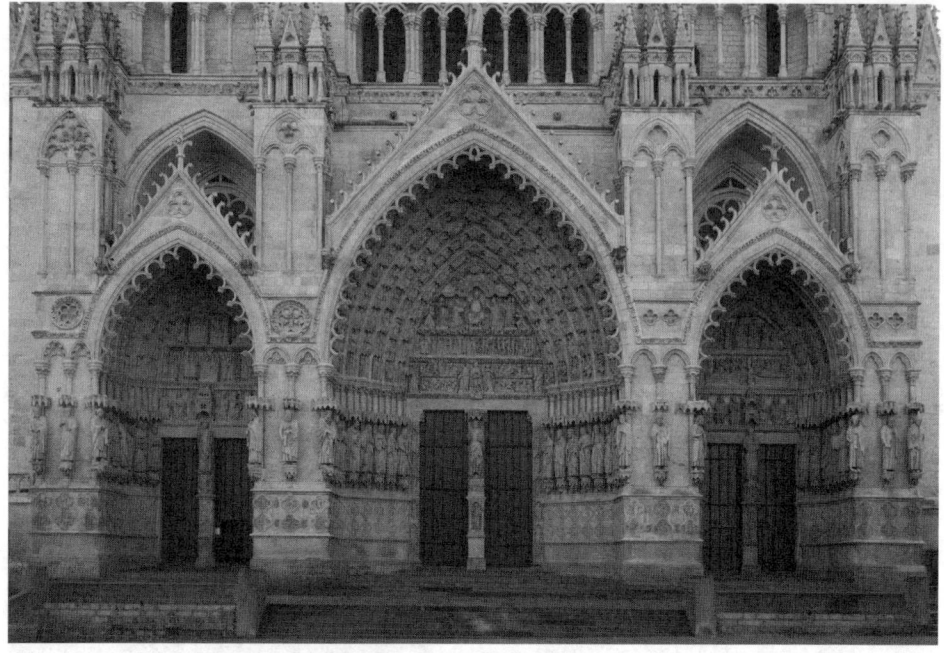

Figure 25. Amiens, cathédrale de Notre-Dame, façade (thirteenth century)

the most valued stone, rich blue lapis lazuli brought from Afghanistan (and hence known as ultramarine), was used from the Carolingian period for frescoes and illuminated manuscripts because of its celestial and Marian connotations.[189] Because of its flame-resistant character, asbestos may have been chosen for a relief picturing the reliquaries that escaped a 1231 fire in San Marco, Venice.[190] Porphyry from Egypt, long associated with Roman imperial power, came to serve the ambitions of popes; the Sancta Sanctorum, for example, features both spolia columns and wall revetments of the purple stuff, as well as disks, cut sausage-like from ancient columns, inserted in the floor to serve as liturgical stage markers. Porphyry columns in Sant'Ambrogio, in turn, "annex" Milan to Rome through the material's historic associations, while the porphyry bathtub reused as Pere III of Aragon's tomb in the royal Catalan monastery of Santes Creus also engages associations with the imperial city (probably via Sicily).[191] The porphyry insets in the pavement King Henry III had laid in front of the altar in Westminster Abbey do the same (see Plate IX); while evoking Rome, they are mixed with marble, alabaster, and other stones from across the Channel and local Purbeck marble to figure London's international ambitions.[192] In contrast with the strict geometry in which it is set, the large onyx disk at the

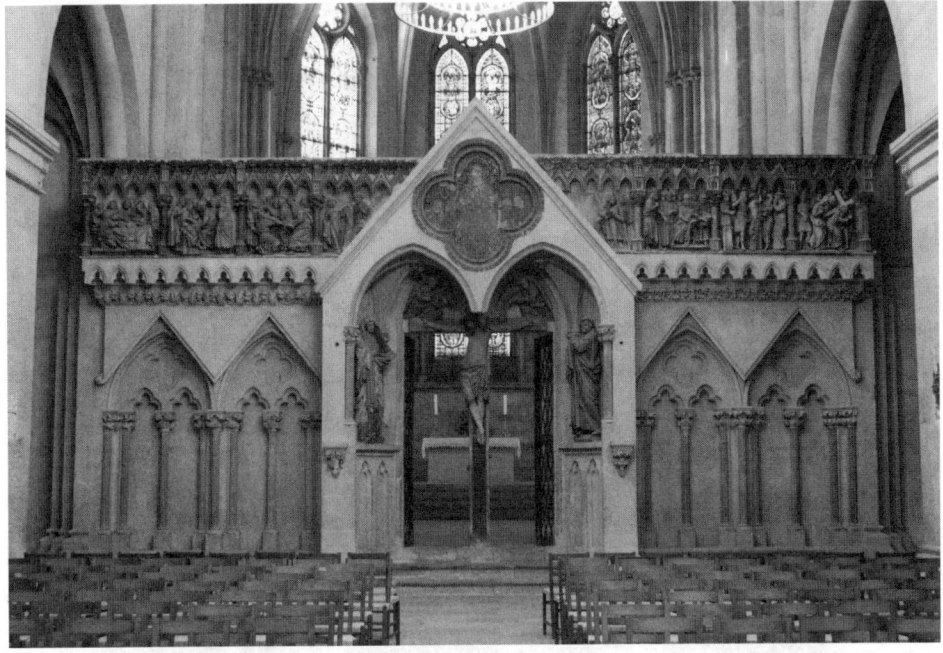

Figure 26. Naumburg, Dom, choir screen (thirteenth century)

center suggests spiritual transformation through its amorphous appearance, in much the same way that the cloud-like forms in the Urraca chalice seem to embody the very essence of the sacramental mutation of wine (that came to be termed transubstantiation).[193] Indeed, the Eucharist provided a metaphor of art's potential to elevate physical matter.[194] No wonder that portable altars, such as the one in Paderborn made by Roger of Helmarshausen (Erzbischöfliches Diözesanmuseum und Domschatzkammer), feature porphyry, veined marble, or alabaster to provide a natural backdrop for the transformation of the Eucharistic species realized on them.[195]

At the other end of the spectrum, stones, even rubble and dirt, were valued if they came from holy sites. The ninth-century pilgrim Bernard the Frank recalled refined "squared marble stones" he had seen in the Valley of Gethsemane,[196] and Matthew Paris reported that Henry III brought a "white stone in which our Lord's footprints appeared" from Mount Olivet.[197] A prized object inside the Sancta Sanctorum altar was the box of pebbles and soil from the Holy Land,[198] and the Karlsteijn Chapel includes a fresco of the Christ rising from a sarcophagus of imitation porphyry, behind which actual relics were immured, among them stones from Christ's tomb and Mary's grave, from the places where

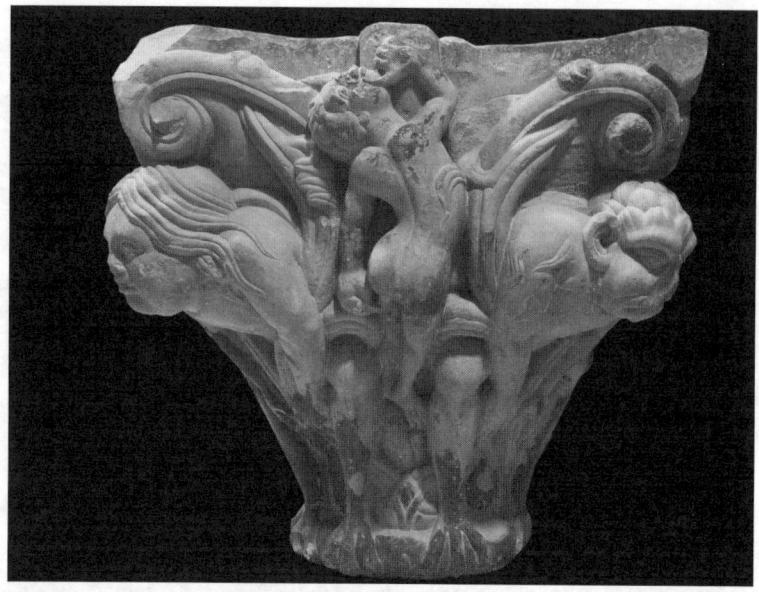

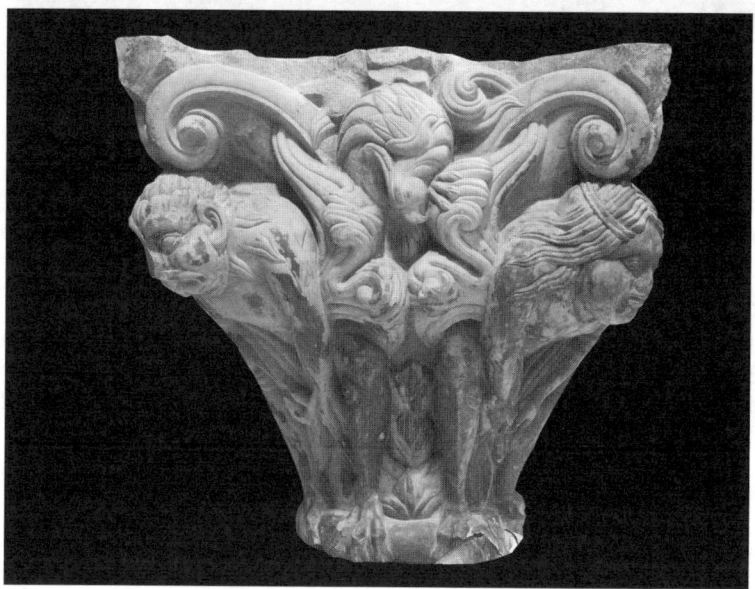

Figure 27. Jaca, Museo Diocesano de Jaca, capital (twelfth century)

Thomas had touched Christ's wounds, and where Christ ascended.[199] In the Book of Genesis, God fashions Adam from clay, a reference Hildegard of Bingen incorporated in her comparison between humans and clay pots filled with inspiration to accomplish God's work.[200]

Water, too, was an essential material. Flowing from the fountain in the center of Eden, it was a metaphor for Christ and the medium of spiritual life through baptism, consecration, exorcism, and purification, as in in the Hildesheim aquamanile (Figure 9).[201] The dedication of the Godescalc Evangeliary (Paris, BnF MS lat. 1203), made to commemorate the baptism of Charlemagne's son at the Lateran, appropriately refers more than once to "sacred waters" and to Christ as a harbor; Jesus is pictured enthroned in a paradisiacal garden, his golden hair rippling over his face and ears and breaking into four rivulets on the recto of a folium that pictures the baptismal font, literally, on the other side.[202] When Peter Damian described a depiction of the *Majestas Domini*, water came to his mind: "For the Fountain of eternal life, who poured out the streams of his wisdom among the other apostles over long periods of time, plunged himself whole, all at once, like a huge torrent, into [Paul]."[203]

Wood was identified with Eden, as well, and also the instrument of Christ's death (allegedly made from the Tree of Life at Eden's center). The Hildesheim doors figure the connection explicitly through the juxtaposition of the Fall and Crucifixion (on a rough-hewn cross),[204] and the green cross at the center of the frontispiece of Thiofrid's tract alludes to the source of life in the primordial garden. Evoking such allusions, wood doors from earliest times and throughout the Middle Ages perpetuated the reference to the Church as a path to eternal life,[205] and ceilings (from the Latin, *caelum*, meaning heaven) made of wood also exploited the material's paradisiacal aspect—as at Sankt Martin at Zillis, in the Cappella Palatina in Palermo, and in Peterborough Cathedral.[206] Wood's most important use was for crucifixes,[207] including one of the first three-dimensional depictions of the dying Christ in San Sepolcro, which carbon-14 dating puts into the first half of the ninth century.[208] A painted crucifix of c. 1100 in Rosano (see Plate X) equates the historical cross from which Christ is shown being lowered (in the upper right narrative) with the blue cross on which he is presented for worship,[209] and a somewhat later wood ensemble in Volterra actually stages the deposition.[210] Wood's association with the tree in the garden of Eden worked both ways, as a medium of corruption or of salvation. The thirteenth-century theologian Peter of Limoges envisioned a wood Madonna that, when seen from the back, was eaten by worms. Moreover, wood was sacred to many pagans and so its use for

Christian cult images or in smelting bronze (requiring the destruction of forests) sent a message of victory over heathen deities.[211]

Cypress wood had a particular connotation because Noah's ark and the Ark of the Covenant were made from it. The early ninth-century cypress box (referred to explicitly as the "*arca cipressina*") containing relics inside the altar of the Lateran Sancta Sanctorum was fashioned from the biblically sanctioned wood,[212] and even though it did not grow in Cantabria, cypress was tellingly used for the agate-covered *arqueta* (probably a book box) in Oviedo.[213] Boxwood was deployed for precious objects like the handle of the Eucharistic knife in Milan;[214] and in the thirteenth century, oak replaced softer woods for sculpture, most likely because of the demands of developed Gothic style.[215] Like the Fritzlar Pietà, a shrine Madonna dating to c. 1300 in New York plays on its material's multiple allusions (Figure 28):[216] wood figures Mary as the tree from which Christ gets his (human) sustenance and also as the Tree of Life on which he redeemed humankind, visible at Christ's feet when the oak figure is opened.[217]

Ivory, the smooth, creamy tusk of an elephant or walrus, retained the political connotations it had acquired in antiquity, attested in literary sources and in such objects as ancient consular diptychs quarried for new works. The vast late eleventh-century ensemble of carved ivory plaques in Salerno, depicting scenes from the Old and New Testaments (Museo Diocesano), may engage classical references to ivory doors and thrones (Figure 29),[218] while the Fatimid-style architecture evokes the material's eastern origins.[219] Imparting the authority of ancient sovereigns to the head of the Church, ivory was also chosen for the knob of a twelfth-century bishop's crozier in Lyon (Figure 30);[220] its whiteness and (presumed) origins from allegedly chaste elephants bestowed symbolism to the images of Christ in Majesty and Virgin and Child.[221] The scene of the Nativity at the very bottom of the central plaque of Theophanu's Gospels cover exploits the incarnational connotation by including the midwife who (according to legend) proved Mary's virginity (Plate V).[222] Even though stone-hard, ivory conveyed fleshiness and invited handling.[223] Chessmen and other game pieces were often made of it, so is the box of the Florence flabellum with carvings from Virgil's *Bucolica*, reinforcing the material's ancient heritage (Plate II).[224] As in so many works, material reinforces subject matter.

Other materials that hovered between organic and inorganic were also tapped because their very ambivalence suggested the amalgam of matter and spirit, especially such "gems" as pearls, mother-of-pearl, coral, and amber.[225] The latter's translucent yellow-orange color, for instance, had since antiquity been likened to the sun, making it especially well-suited for

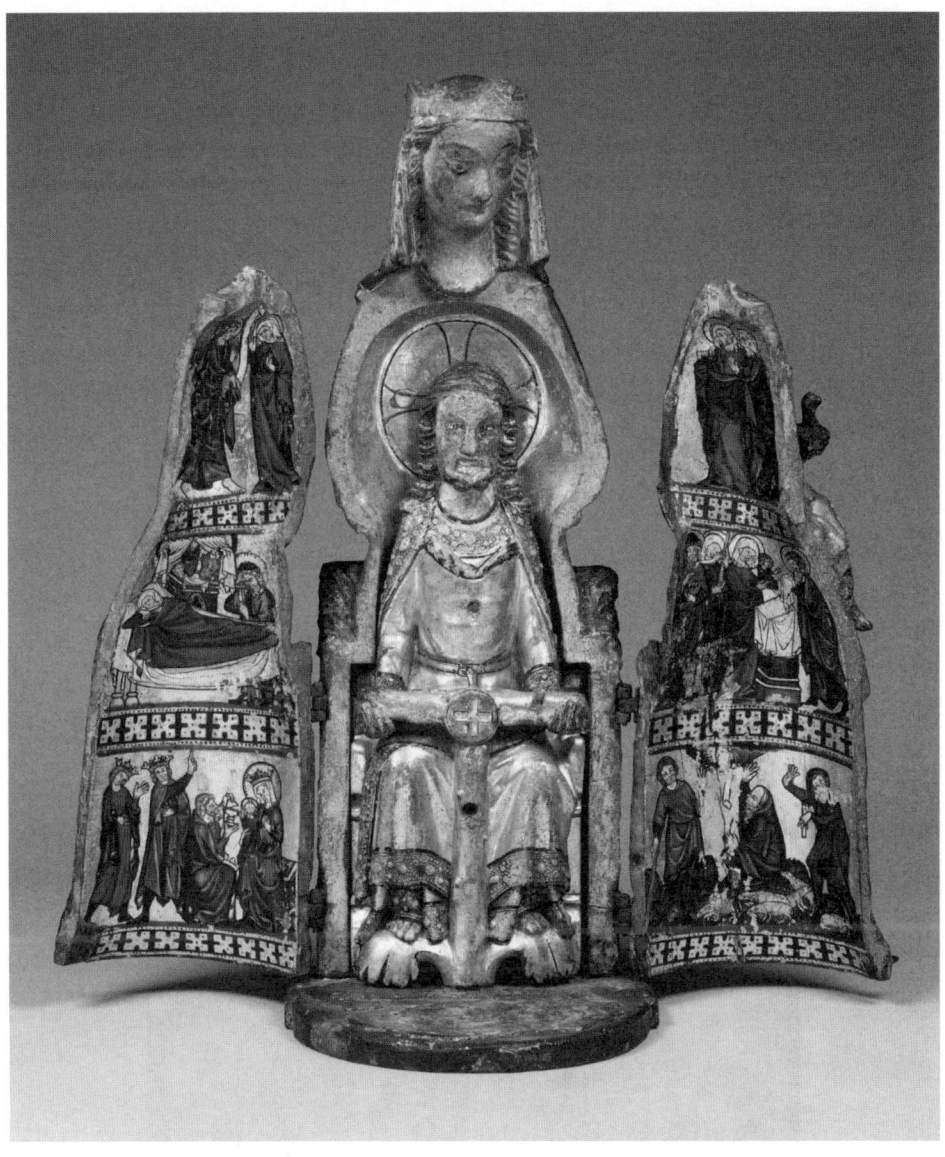

Figure 28. New York, Metropolitan Museum of Art, shrine Madonna (c. 1300)

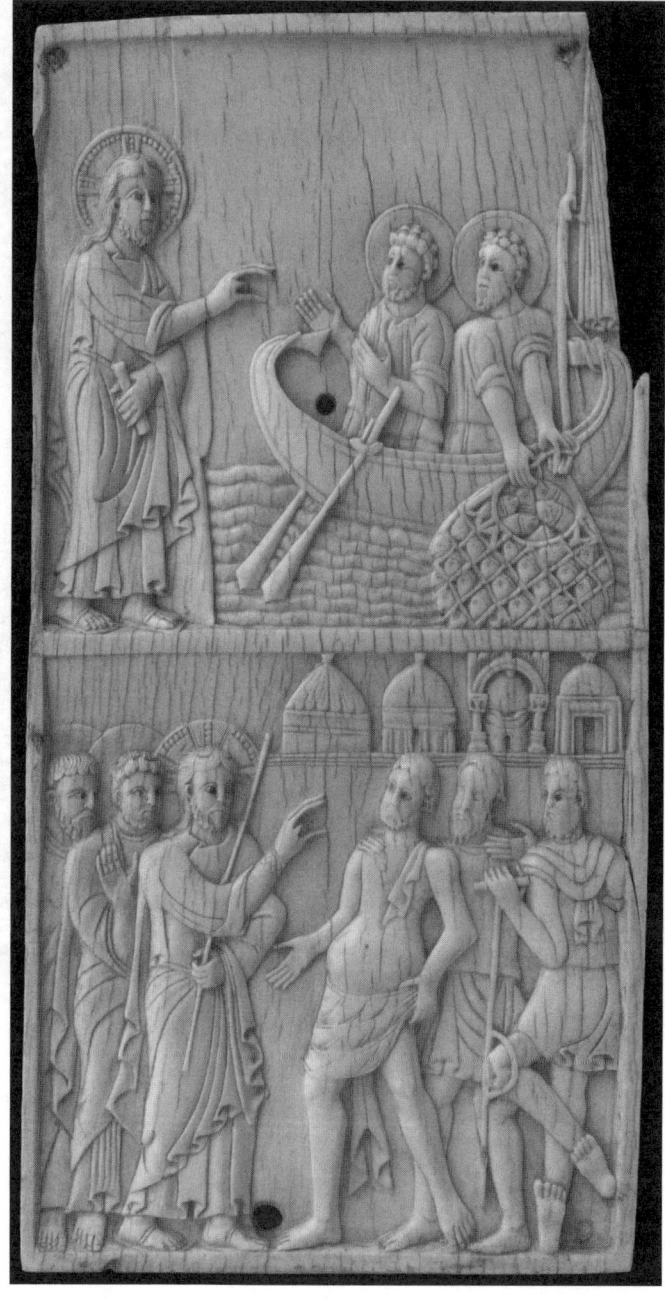

Figure 29. Salerno, Museo Diocesano, ivory plaque (eleventh century)

CHAPTER 2: MATTER

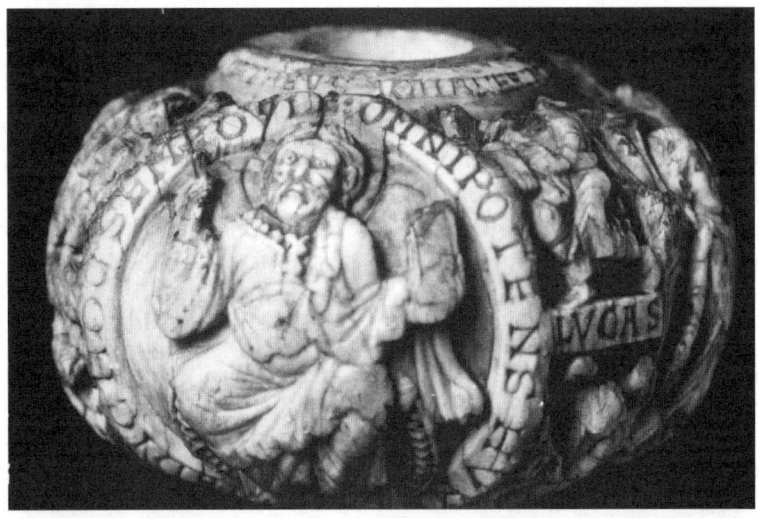

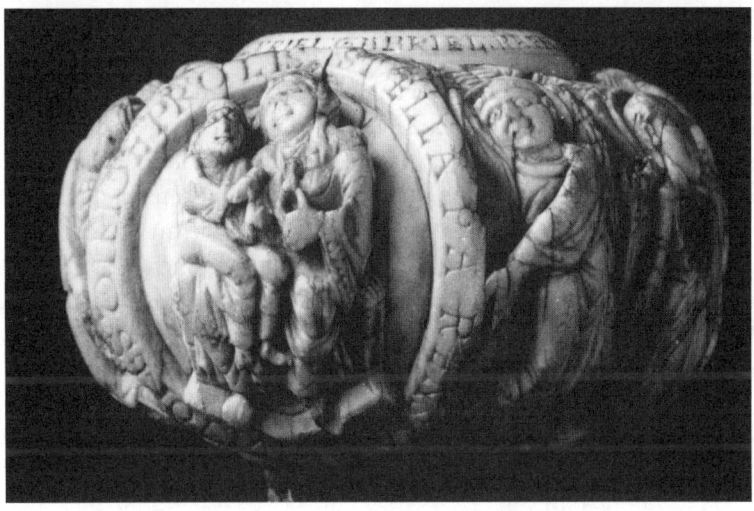

Figure 30. Lyon, Musée des Beaux-Arts, knob of bishop's crozier (twelfth century)

rendering the face of Christ, as on a late fourteenth-century Polish relief in the Metropolitan Museum of Art.[226] Albertus Magnus, among others, attributed medicinal qualities to amber as well, which made it particularly suitable for prayer beads. Wax played an important role in medieval art.[227] Evoking light (through candles) and purity, it was the product of purportedly asexual bees; like Christ's body, it also did not smell. In Canto X of *Purgatory*, Dante invoked wax to describe the imprint of the *ancilla dei* (God's handmaid) that is, the Virgin Mary;[228] in turn, Mechtild of Hackeborn envisioned herself as receiving "the imprint of resemblance [to God] like a seal in wax."[229] Adémar de Chabannes reported that wax figures were deployed against enemies,[230] and a boat full of wax figures saved from a shipwreck was offered to Louis of Toulouse.[231] Since the time of Aristotle, the eye's crystalline humor, which was believed to receive images, was understood to be like wax that could store imaginative force, an important idea for art.[232] As it melted, wax recalled tears, reinforcing the penitential effect of wax votives. Wax residues were also collected as relics.[233]

Made from the skins of animals but rendered ivory-white through preparation processes, parchment (vellum) was the basic material of writing.[234] Its animal origins are everywhere evident; the monumental Hereford map (see Plate XVI), for instance, preserves its bovine source not only in the overall dimensions but also in the placement of rivers at the cow's bladder;[235] and, as on the page in the Gulbenkian Apocalypse, natural scars often were embellished to call attention to the vellum's fleshiness (Figure 10). Ambrogio Lorenzetti incorporated the idea that parchment was a material metaphor of the Word entering flesh by featuring John the Evangelist in his Massa Marittima altarpiece inscribing the letter *I* of "In the beginning was the Word and the Word became flesh" (Jn 1:1) on the open blank codex.[236]

Certain materials were site specific. Derived from the Persian word for raw silk, *gazzatum* (from which the English word gauze derives) was associated with Gaza (Palestine),[237] and, like many substances, the alleged origins of silk tied it to the (sacred) East, in Mary's veil, for instance, and in the loincloth the Virgin fashioned from it to cover Christ's genitals at the Crucifixion.[238] Not only was the fabric luxurious and exotic, but the silkworms that produced it were believed (like bees) to be asexual and hence symbolic of chastity. Relics were often wrapped in silk, and silk was the base fabric of such special fabrics as the Coronation Mantle. Silk also came to be associated with the *Veronica*,[239] as in the Gulbenkian Apocalypse, which pictures the fringed Temple curtain made of shimmering, transparent cloth.

Imported from Fatimid Egypt, crystal spolia took a similar meaning.[240] Alabaster, first deployed for paving and small objects, came in the fourteenth century to be identified with tombs and relief sculptures produced at Nottingham, Tutbury, and Burton upon Trent in England's Midlands.[241] Ivory was imported from more than one place, including from sub-Saharan Africa with such other valued substances as alum used in cloth manufacture.[242] It seems that a single west African tusk, entering Europe through the Mediterranean port city of Amalfi, provided material for the extensive church furnishing in Salerno.[243]

Derived, to a great extent, from associations with gems and other precious materials, color acquired symbolic meaning associated with natural qualities and references in Scripture and lapidaries. Suger, Hildegard of Bingen, and other commentators attest to its significance.[244] Sculpture and ivory were painted in brilliant hues, enhancing both realism and the sense of transformation,[245] and, independent of specific matter, color indexed materiality as such.[246] No wonder that the eleventh-century French rabbi Shlomo Yitzchaki (known as Rashi) argued that it weakened the Israelites' resistance to sin. Colorlessness, in turn, also had its uses, to echo penance during Lent for instance, or to index the elevated state of angels, as in the Sainte-Chapelle miniature (Plate VII).[247]

Material Rhetoric

Matter's transformation released potency.[248] Albertus Magnus and Vincent of Beauvais both regarded the manufacture of glass to be a form of alchemy,[249] so too the making of pigments, such as lead white by applying vinegar or dung to black metal and then firing it.[250] It followed that mixtures could embody meaning: Christ was, himself, a hybrid of man and God, while the Eucharist merged matter with spirit.[251] An alloy of gold and silver, electrum was understood as a material expression of Christ's dual nature and evidence that God can be read in matter. As the twelfth-century Cistercian monk Thomas of Perseigne noted, the mixture of metals evoked Ezekiel's "species electri" (Ez 1:4) and hence the Redeemer's (golden) divinity fused with his (silver) humanity:

> But sometimes God speaks through Angels by things, when nothing is said in words, but future events are announced by an object taken from the elements; as Ezekiel, hearing no words, saw the appearance of "electrum" in the midst of the fire ... For while he presented himself to us as a union of the divine and human natures. He both rendered his human nature more glorious by

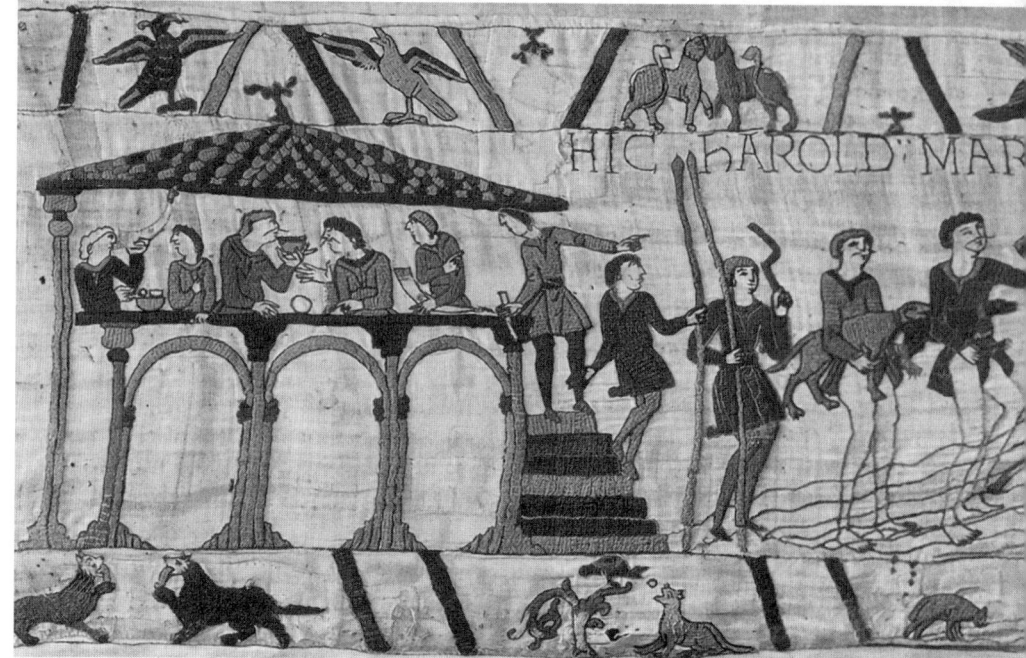

Figure 31. Bayeux, Musée de la Tapisserie de Bayeux, embroidery (eleventh century)

his Godhead and tempered the divine nature to our sight by his manhood. For, since human nature shone forth with so many miracles by the virtue of the Godhead, the silver was improved by the gold; and because God could be recognized through the flesh, and because he endured therein so many adversities, the gold was, as it were, tempered by the silver.

In like fashion, the *Vitiis mystica*, a meditation on Christ's Passion sometimes attributed to Saint Bonaventure, interpreted the amalgamation of metals to make bronze as the merger of Christ's suffering and love on the cross with the eternal life provided by the air of the Resurrection: "Bronze, in truth, because melted together by the red of both charity and passion, red with the blood of the passion and hardened like brass in the Resurrection, because he does not die."[252]

Juxtaposed with one another, substances articulated complex messages. On the simplest level, the contrasting game pieces used on the Ballinderry

CHAPTER 2: MATTER 55

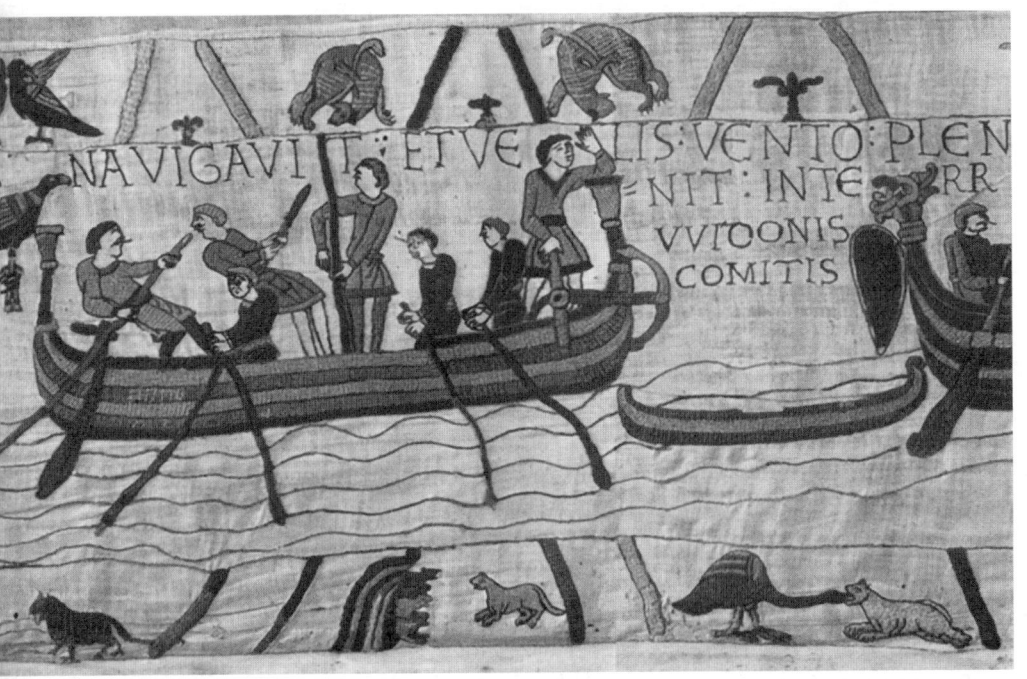

board (Figure 1) represented opposing forces confronting one another on the wood plain. Berthold's chronicle reports that the jewels at the cross's terminal points on the Zwiefalten box (Figure 4) stand for stones from Christ's manger (at the bottom of the cross), Golgotha and the Holy Sepulcher (on the arms), and the Mount of Olives whence Christ ascended (at the top).[253] Ivory was often paired with gold; the twinning of two costly materials represented Christ's dual nature and hence the spiritual elevation of the flesh.[254] The cover of Queen Theophanu's Gospels, for example, fashions scenes of Christ's life in flesh-like ivory and frames them in gold adorned with images that render the ascent from the venerated relic at the bottom, uses saints as lateral ladders, and presents a celestial vision at the top. The stitching of animal yarn onto the vegetal back on the Bayeux embroidery to recount the Norman Conquest reinforces the overall message of harmony the account presents (Figure 31), which is also conveyed by the Aesopian warning about not heeding advice in the fable involving wool and linen pictured in the border.[255]

A Koranic aphorism that likened vellum to the starry sky and ink to the sea is illustrated in the Escorial *Cantigas* by showing a scribe dipping his quill into the ocean beneath an indigo heaven that unfolds onto his writing table (fol. 157ᵛ).[256] The point was to stress the infinity of Mary's virtues, but one result was underscoring the parchment's own intermediacy—a stretch of blank vellum divides heaven from earth.[257] Beginning in the eighth century, purple-stained parchment was associated specifically with Christ's bloodied flesh and gold letters on it with his divinity,[258] as in the prayer book of Charles the Bald. Writing in the mid-thirteenth century, the archbishop of Mainz, Christianus II, saw a similar animating duality in a large gold crucifix set with two rubies or garnets that sparkled in the darkness.[259] Pink, the mixing of red and white as when light transforms the dark world at dawn, was deployed in Carolingian manuscripts and in the tenth-century *Majestas Domini* of the Benedictional of Saint Aethelwold (London, Brit. Lib., Add. MS 49598) to render Christ's advent in the world, where amorphous white clouds symbolizing the divine were mixed with magenta. In the Annunciation miniature in the Hitda Codex of c. 1020 (see Plate XI),[260] the red pigments used to render dark clouds gathering in the upper left translate Gabriel's words into a luminous cloud rippling with gold that spills divinity at Mary's feet, like a curtain pulled back in a theater, or rather, like the (purple) curtain that had separated the outer courtyard from the Temple's inner sanctum (depicted in the background).[261] Mary is the epitome of materialization—the human vessel of divinity; she is also a compassionate mother who mediates between suffering and hope.[262] The analogy with the Passion continued to be amplified throughout the Middle Ages, with the parchment flesh actually rent to connect to Christ's suffering, as in the Fritzlar Pietà.[263]

The incarnational metaphor was also applied to textiles, which were typically constructed by the intermingling of warp and weft.[264] According to legend, Mary was weaving the Temple curtain when the Angel came to her,[265] and in the Epistle to the Hebrews (Heb 10:20), Christ replaced it with his very body. Cassiodorus had already likened Christ to cloth covering God, woven of the thread of compunction and wool of grace, and other theologians developed the analogy. The curtains separating the priest and congregation from the heavenly vision in the Saint-Martin-du-Canigou cartulary refer to the Temple veil (Figure 8), as do the illusionistic cloth dados (parts of walls below waist height) in contemporary churches of north Italy,[266] and in the twelfth-century fresco in the apse of the Cluniac Chapelle-des-Moines at Berzé-la-Ville (Figure 32).[267]

CHAPTER 2: MATTER 57

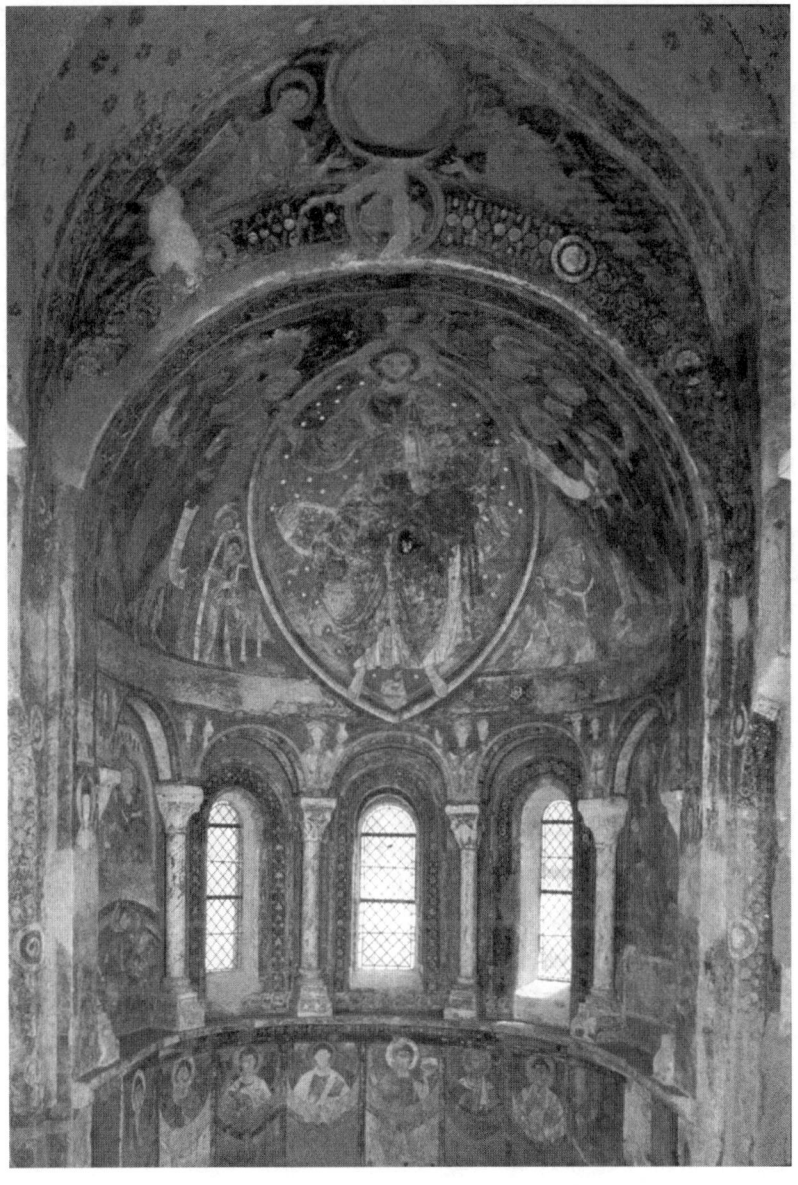

Figure 32. Berzé-la-Ville, Chapelle-des-Moines, apse, fresco (twelfth century)

Christ's shroud also gave importance to textiles; the linen handkerchief with reddish stains in Oviedo was kept as a relic "together with the holy earth where Christ trod."[268]

In Sant'Ambrogio and elsewhere, materials reinforced spiritual vectors, from the marble pulpit, to the golden altar, to the porphyry and stucco baldachin, and, in the apse, the marble bishop's throne beneath the gold mosaic. The Naumburg choir screen contrasts painted three-dimensional sculpture to flat painting to establish levels of reality, leading to the light-emitting stained glass behind; in the chapel that Enrico Scrovegni built, c. 1303–05, adjacent to his palace in Padua (Plate XII),[269] the image of God set in the center at the very top of the apse wall is, alone, a painting on wood,[270] which distinguishes the divine presence from the frescoed narratives and indicates that access to God is available on earth in artificial images alone.[271] More dramatic, still, the silvered "mirror" that (originally) interrupted the illusionism of the painted Massa Marittima panel assaulted the viewer with awareness that the deepest mysteries of Christianity were accessible, not in material images at all, but ultimately only through faith.

The humble flesh of Christ and his saints surpassed even the most lustrous and precious of earthly materials. As Thiofrid of Echternach explained in his tract on relics, the metals and gems used to encase the remains suit human nature because they simultaneously mask the base materials that constituted most remains and attract the higher senses in a way that transforms them into the desire for heavenly reward. At the same time, the saintly objects have greater power because what he called "precious dust" did not engender the monstrous greed that Christ and his saints had themselves disdained.[272]

Chapter 3
Making

MATTER'S MEANING derived not only from inherent qualities, place of origin, and historical allusions, but also from the processes used to convert physical substances into artistic materials and transform them into objects. As an inscription on the bronze door of the cathedral at Trier points out, "The wax gives what should be, the fire takes it away, the bronze gives it back to you."[273] The very fact that wax and oil vanished after they transformed matter into light made the ephemeral materials particularly appropriate votives for the Saint-Martin-du-Canigou confraternity (Figure 8) and for the members of the Orsanmichele brotherhood, who were charged by a 1333 statute to provide the lamp pictured in the *Specchio umano* to burn day and night (Figure 16), which may ironically have fed the fire that destroyed the first image in 1304.[274] Mere transporting of foreign materials could take on meaning,[275] as did the fact that gold was found in nuggets distinguish it from silver, which had to be refined.[276] Craftsmanship added value; Ovid's aphorism that "the workmanship surpasses the material" was much quoted during the period.[277] Like alloys, fused glass and metal in cloisonné enamel (in which soldered wires hold gems and fused glass in place) functioned as a sign of Christ's dual nature. On the Zwiefalten reliquary, the cells that form Christ's face, hands, and feet bridge the fragmentary nature of the body as a whole and the emerald ground studded with blue crosses makes the transition to actual gems that were simultaneously earthly

59

sites and celestial destinations (Figure 4).[278] Objects were also constantly being restored, transposed, erased, and augmented during the Middle Ages to reconfigure their meaning. The ancient spolium used to create the Urraca chalice (Plate III), for example, was reassembled to mark its resanctification by the great Artifex (Creator) himself,[279] and *La belle verrière*'s transposition and reframing re-created it as a relic of the destroyed Romanesque church (Figure 5).

"Artist"

God, who had constructed the world, "formed man from the dust of the ground" (Gn 2:7), and then fashioned Eve from Adam's rib, was, himself, the original artisan. On Queen Theophanu's marriage certificate (Wolfenbüttel, Niedersächsisches Landesarchiv, 6 Urk 11), for instance, a verse declaring that God crafted the first woman "well-built from Adam's rib" ties together the charter's overt artifice and the prospect of progeny it promises.[280] The thirteenth-century mosaics of San Marco in Venice picture Christ, sculptor-like, fashioning Adam from clay and, with his hands, forming the first man's rib into the full figure of Eve (see Plate XIII).[281] In the *Legenda Maior*, Bonaventure compared the marks left on Francis's body by God's hand to an "image of the Crucified" made by a craftsman (Plate VI).[282] Several manuscripts of the *Bible moralisée* imagined the *"artifex mundi"* composing the primordial world by circumscribing the terrestrial orb with an enormous compass,[283] a creative act that the illuminators mimicked when they put their own instruments at the center of the folio and twirled it between their fingers.[284] Inspired by Calcidius's *Commentary on Plato's Timaeus* (Chapter 23 in particular), Hugh of Saint-Victor asserted that there are three works in the world: God, nature, and the artisan imitating nature.[285]

In a culture that distinguished the mechanical arts from the seven "liberal arts" of grammar, rhetoric, dialectics, arithmetic, geometry, music, and astronomy,[286] however, the artisan's conceptual role in relation to advisors and patrons was vexed: how much did an actual maker contribute? But even the distinction between handwork and learning had a complicated history, especially as ancient learning penetrated the West.[287] Roger of Helmarshausen's *De diversis artibus* includes three chapters of recipes intended to instruct artisans in the crafts of making glass, cementing gold, and carving ivory, but it also asserts that manual skill alone does not produce art; to realize talent in the production of images of Christ and the saints, it insists, a craftsperson must exercise a gift of the Holy Spirit. Roger was himself both an artisan and a cleric.[288] Rupert of Deutz and Hugh of Saint-Victor provided positive interpretations of the *artes mechanicae*; the latter, for instance, placed goldsmithing at the top of his list of the mechanical arts and art among the *scientiae mechanicae*.[289] Whereas for Hugh of Saint-Victor and his student Richard of Saint-Victor, manual art was necessary only because the Fall had deformed perfect creation, the maker's role evolved as the created world increasingly came to be accepted as good. In his *De divisione philosophiae* (c. 1150), Domingo Gundisalvo provided a theoretical basis for the elevation of material objects by giving mechanical and liberal arts equal status; Honorius Augustodunensis added the "work of metal, wood, marble, and especially painting, carving, and the manual arts" to the seven liberal arts; and Hildegard of Bingen tied art to the dual nature of paradise, although her (self-)portrait, presumably painted from an autograph design, shows her transcribing a personal vison directly onto waxed tablets.[290] Geoffrey of Vinslauf likewise praised the same combination of artistic skill and intellect in his *Poetria nova* dedicated to Pope Innocent III:

> If a man has to build a house, his hand does not leap into action impulsively. Internally, the line of his heart draws a plan of the work and mentally outlines the successive steps in a particular order; and his heart's hand forms a model of the entire house before the body's hand; and it is an archetype rather than something tangible.[291]

Because the word "artist" (*artista*) was not applied to the manufacture of images and objects until the end of the thirteenth century, that is, until the very moment such persons as Duccio, Giotto, and Arnolfo di Cambio were being valued for individual creativity, the use of the word, with its modern associations of individualism, self-identification, imagination, and innovation, is mostly anachronistic and therefore best reserved only for artisans working during the late Middle Ages.[292] To be sure, many medieval craftspersons signed their productions, but the colophon-like signatures themselves must be analyzed.[293] For example, the role of Hugh, who identified himself as the "painter and illuminator" of the eleventh-century manuscript of Jerome's *Commentary on Isaiah* in Oxford (Bodleian Library, Ms. Bod. 717) has been given various interpretations.[294] Some signatures may even refer not to the person who physically produced a work but rather to the conceiver (*concepteur*) or sponsor. The Guillaume Martin who inscribed his name beneath a sculpted pilaster in Saint-André-le-Bas in Vienne with the date 1152, for example, may well have been the patron, either clerical or lay,[295] and Gislebertus whose name is boldly carved on a sculpted lintel at Autun seems to have been the donor and not, as nineteenth-century writers had it, the sculptor.[296] Indeed, the *me fecit* ("made me") attached to many signatures might simply express pride in fine workmanship not origination,[297] and, by having the object itself speak, as it were, the formula implicated the maker or donor in the act of grace embodied in art.[298] Tuotilo, a monk in the monastery of Sankt Gallen at the turn of the first millennium, is particularly well documented in texts and works of art; a maker of reliefs in both ivory and precious metal, he was later hailed as a painter, architect, and sculptor.[299]

Makers also had themselves portrayed on their products. Eadwine appears in the guise of an evangelist in the copy of the Utrecht Psalter he made (or oversaw) at Canterbury in 1160–70 (Cambridge, Trinity College Library, MS R. 17.1).[300] Gerlach, pictured at the bottom of a stained-glass window from the Premonstratensian monastery at Arnstein, provides a classic example (Figure 33);[301] judging by his habit, he was a lay brother who undertook the work as a votive, his brush completing the inscription beseeching the "illustrious King of Kings [to] have mercy on Gerlachus." The frontispiece of the Holkham Bible sums up the general situation in the early fourteenth century (London, Brit. Lib., Add. MS 47682, fol. 1ᵛ; see Figure 52). Beneath an angel displaying a sort of table of contents, it depicts a layman turning from an easel (on which a portrait of a man and woman is displayed) and toward a Dominican holding a speech scroll exhorting him to "Do the work well and thoroughly, For it will be shown to a rich gentleman." To that the illuminator replies, "If I make it true, and God grants me life, never will you see another such book."[302] Only in the middle of the fourteenth century does something akin to the early modern workshop emerge, in which a master artist supervises artisans, manages the budget over a period of time, and is paid for his talent, not just the work.[303] At the end of the Middle Ages, nature, God, and a bit of personal pride all contributed to the making of art.

Romantic notions of the self-effacing medieval artisan are as misleading as modern conceptions of the autonomous innovator. While historically grounded paradigms of production vary with individual circumstances, they usually reveal a complex inter-working of craft practices, authoritative models, individual talents and experience, and

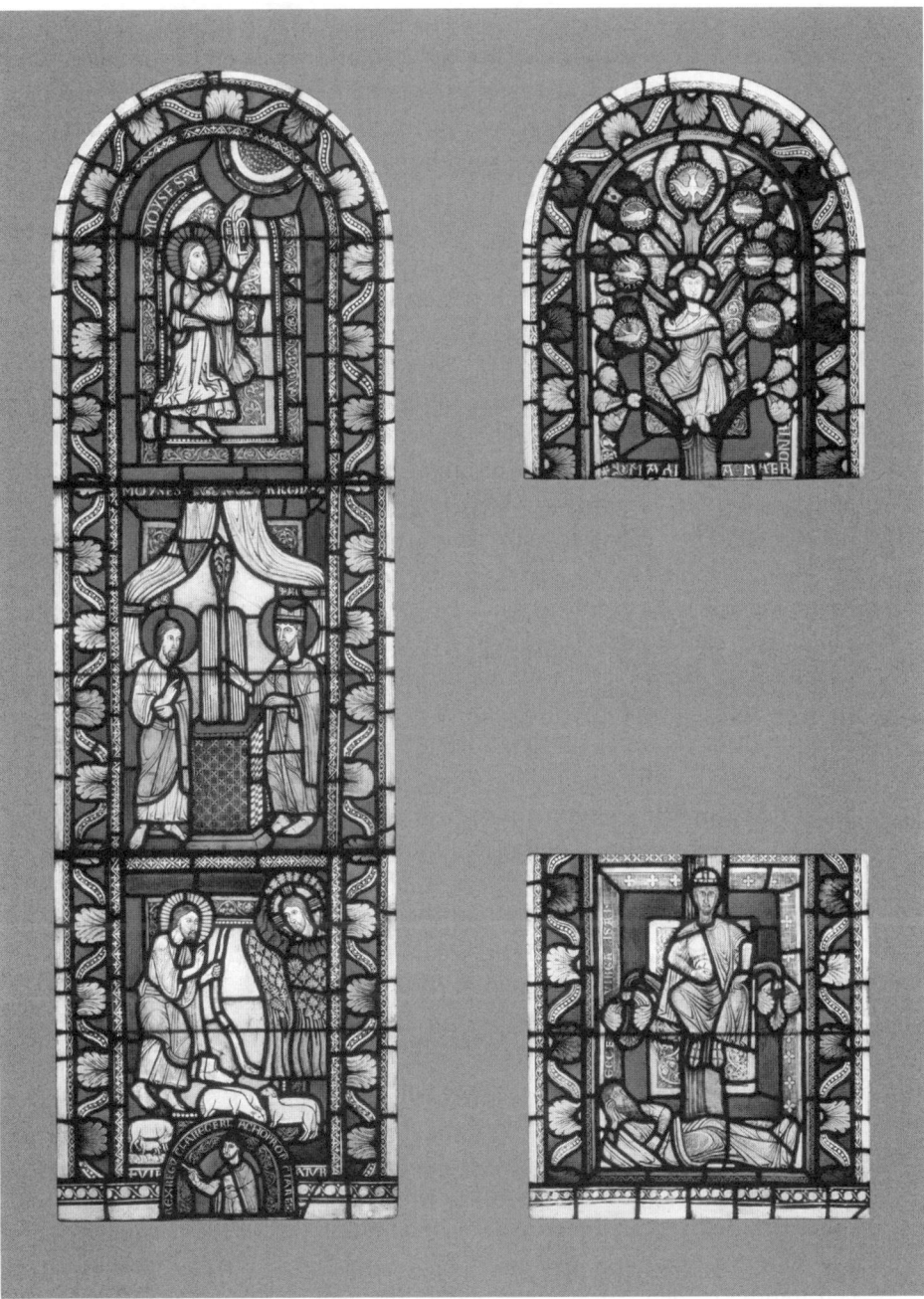

Figure 33. Münster, Landesmuseum, stained glass from the Premonstratensian monastery at Arnstein (twelfth century)

outside supervision.³⁰⁴ In fact, many medieval makers spent only part of their time on what would be called "art"; Tuotilo was a renowned musician, and the illustrious Matthew Paris, a Benedictine at Saint-Alban's (just north of London), may have been a businessman and goldsmith before he took vows, which prepared him for a career as diplomat, metalworker, sculptor, and painter that he followed while a cleric moving between city and monastery.³⁰⁵ In most cases, medieval art is best understood as the product of a web of agency that varied from time to time and place to place but in which the artisan operated within a system by which a donor or other authority provided resources and imposed constraints.³⁰⁶

Artisanal skill required years of training and preparation. In some ways, it was not very different from the techniques used to prepare matzoh illustrated at the turn of the fourteenth century in a Hebrew manuscript used during Passover dinner (Haggadah) (Figure 34),³⁰⁷ beginning with the mixing of ingredients to make dough, the forming and pricking of the circular unleavened breads, and, very much like today's wood-fired pizza-ovens, the using of a paddle to shove the bread into the oven. Blacksmiths, carpenters, and stoneworkers depicted in the mid-thirteenth-century reliefs on the façade of San Marco in Venice, to cite another example, are guided by habit, not written aids or preliminary drawings.³⁰⁸ Such acquired skills and the equipment needed to apply them were independent of content; a goldsmith could fashion a ring as easily as a cross. It is therefore understandable that Jewish manuscripts find close technical parallels in a secular German songbook (Stuttgart, Württembergishe Landesbibliothek, HB XIII 1).³⁰⁹

Medieval specializations did not conform to modern genres and divisions of labor, as the thirteenth-century Parisian magistrate Étienne de Boileau's *Livre des métiers* makes clear.³¹⁰ Carpentry, used for quotidian needs, was, for example, also needed to construct armatures for reliquaries, reliquaries themselves, book covers, painted panels, altarpieces, ceilings, and other objects; the gold and ivory of the Theophanu Gospels (Plate V) are set in oak, which is exposed on the much simpler back cover adorned with five medallions and expresses the object's etymological derivation, "codex" from "caudex" or block of wood.³¹¹ The thirteenth-century architect Villard de Honnecourt was fascinated by wood's tensile properties that enabled the workings of various machines he carefully rendered in his sketchbook: the bent cog of a saw mill, for instance, the taut crossbow, and also the pin and pulley within an eagle-shaped pulpit ornament (Figure 35).³¹² On occasion, wood workers may

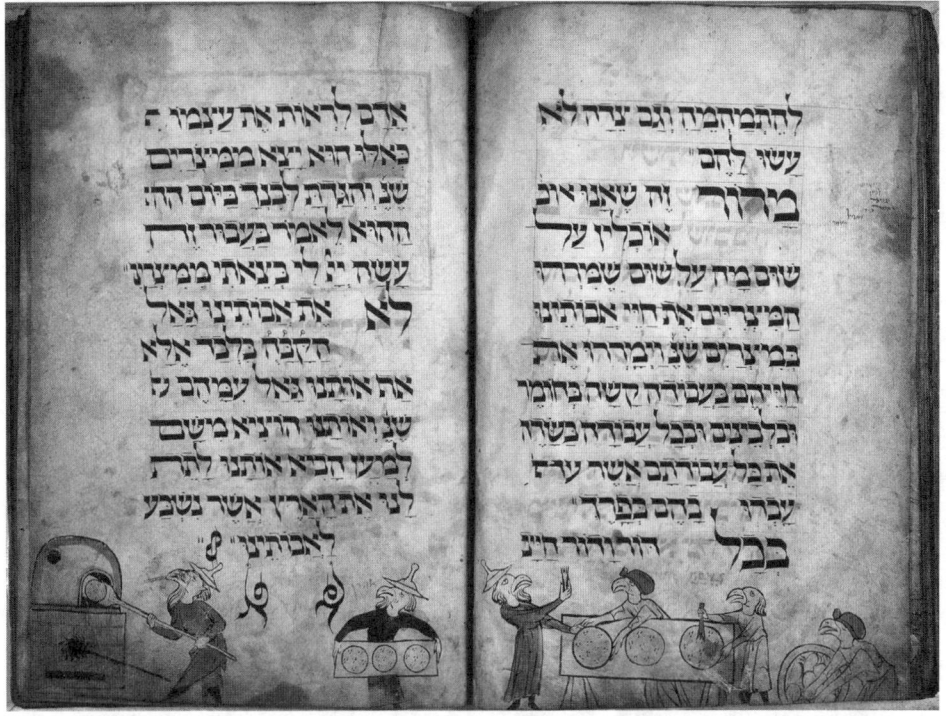

Figure 34. Jerusalem, Israel Museum, MS 180/57, *Haggadah*, fols. 25ᵛ–26ʳ (fourteenth century)

have applied their skills to rarer materials; the rendering of the sail spar tethered to the mast crotch in the scene of Christ Calling Peter and Andrew on the Salerno ivory, the oarlock fixed by a dowel, and the crippled man's crutch in the healing miracle suggest that the ivory carver was familiar with the making of things of humbler materials (Figure 29).[313] Bronze-casters used their techniques to fashion both small objects and large, perhaps with some significant cross-over effect,[314] and stone carvers, too, worked on diverse scales, adapting spolia, imitating ancient remains in columns and capitals they made anew, constructing church furniture of marble, and setting colored stones and mosaics. In the Cappella Palatina in Palermo, for example, masons laid the floors and dados, fashioned the supports, pulpits, barriers, and (some) window mullions, and provided tesserae for the figural decoration.[315]

Many objects required the skills of diverse artisans working together. Surely a unique product, the flabellum of Tournus was the joint effort

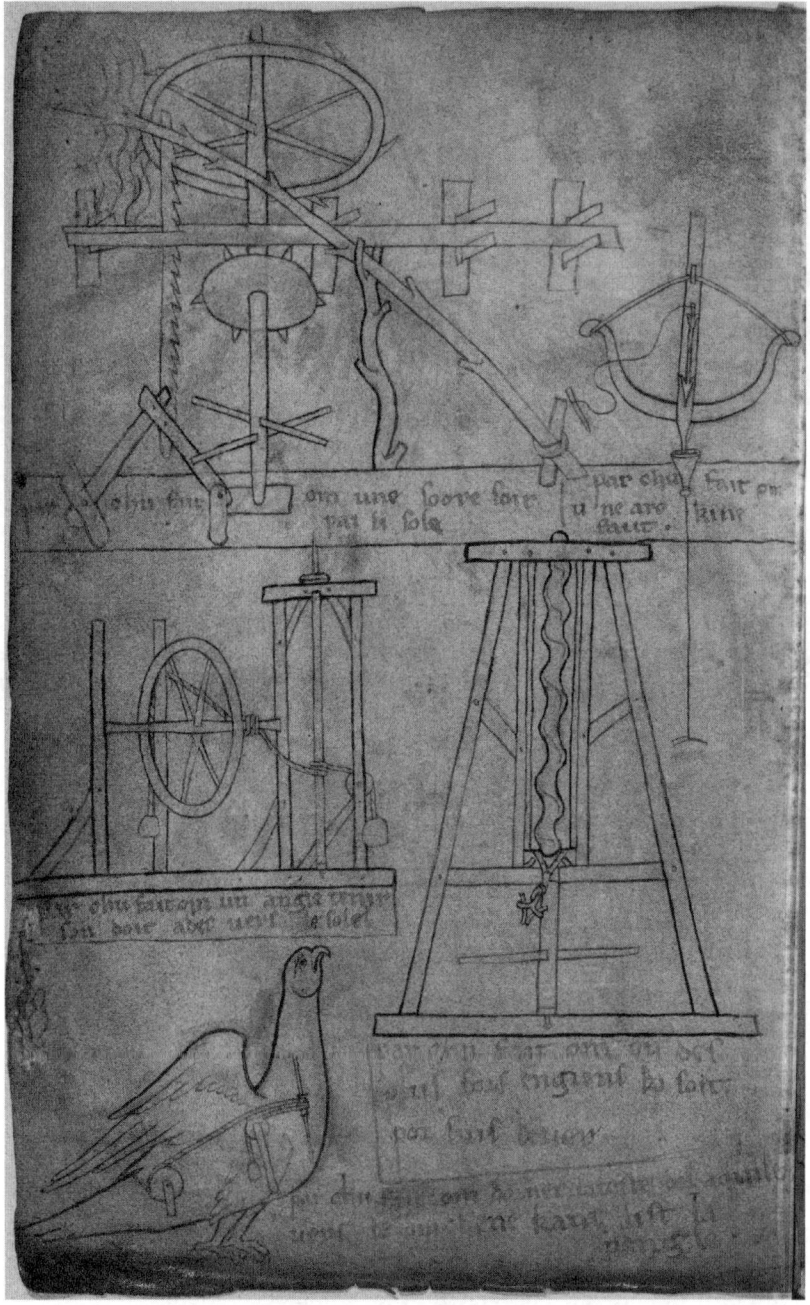

Figure 35. Paris, BnF, MS fr. 19093, Villard de Honnecourt sketchbook, fol. 22ᵛ (thirteenth century)

of an ivory-carver and manuscript illuminator (Plate II). Glass arts required metalworkers to provide matrices to hold and protect the vitreous materials, whether in enamel or stained glass. The Rosano Crucifix engaged not only painters and gilders but also carpenters and tailors (who covered the corpus in cloth attached with glue) in a complicated collaboration that involved the cutting of the torso, arms, and head on separate panels before the painting was begun and the assembly completed (Plate X);[316] similar cooperation was needed to fashion and finish the Fritzlar Pietà (Plate VIII).[317] Ensemble work spurred assimilation; carpenters, for instance, transferred the experiments they introduced to build theater apparatuses to relic displays, as in the *Grande Chasse* of the Sainte-Chapelle in Paris (Plate VII); in turn, wood carving was imitated in stone.[318] In addition to a patron and someone who compiled or composed the contents, manuscript production demanded the skills of those who prepared the materials and laid out the format, and transcribed the words, as well as rubricators and illuminators; depending on the particular circumstances, these might also be one and the same person.[319]

Certain techniques, such as those used to fashion the enamels on the Francis reliquary (Plate VI), required specialized skills that could not be secured everywhere; in this case, the Franciscan brothers at Assisi seem to have outsourced the work to Limoges. Though a monk of Sankt Gallen, Tuotilo traveled some distance on commission; Abbot Suger assembled artisans noted for particular media from across Europe to build and decorate his abbey church and, in so doing, to transform art.[320] When Pope Honorius III needed mosaicists to adorn the apse of San Paolo fuori le Mura in Rome, he had to summon them from Venice;[321] although Rome had had a great tradition of mosaic-making and the composition followed local conventions, the practice was dormant in his day. Palermo's elaborate Islamic ceiling vaulting (*muqarnas*) is the joint product of carpenters imported from North Africa and local painters. Hybridity was not simply the result of practical exigency. When King Henry III, his emissaries, and church authorities brought artisans from France and Rome to work with local masons in Westminster Abbey (see Plate IX), they were expressing political attachments;[322] the painters from Tuscany and England (or France) and glass-makers from Germany assembled at Assisi to adorn the church of San Francesco manifested the Franciscan Order's international ambitions.[323]

By the thirteenth century, regions had become famous for types of production, leading to commercialization. Some kinds of textiles and the carving of alabaster were associated with England, for instance, where materials and skill were available, and, in the late Middle Ages, Silesia seems to have had a monopoly on carved amber.[324] Subject to economic and historical circumstances, regionality of production also underwent changes. Bronze was associated first with Rome, as the bronze caster who fabricated the *lupa Romana* understood and Bernward of Hildesheim acknowledged, but it came later to be identified with Germany, where smelting was developed.[325] In the first phase, silk textiles were manufactured largely in Byzantium; the ground fabric of the Coronation Mantle is Byzantine (Figure 14). Then, production moved to north Africa, Sicily, and Spain, but from the mid-twelfth century, high-grade silk textiles were produced in Lucca, the raw material itself coming through Genoa, with the finished fabric exported through the port to Castile, London, and Asia Minor.[326] Perhaps to replace Constantinople and the Near East after the crusader conquests, Venice emerged in the early thirteenth century as a rival silk producer.[327]

Large, specialized projects required the organization of workshops that might involve a supervisor (*magister operis*) who served as an intermediary between the patron and conceiver, foremen, core workers, and their assistants and apprentices.[328] An English mason, Raynard de Fonoyll, oversaw the completion of the cloister in the Cistercian Reial Monastir de Santes Creus in Catalonia during the 1330s (Figure 36), blending his own training and experience with those of local artisans.[329] Even at Assisi, which is generally taken as the cradle of the Renaissance *artist*, the very nature of medieval production subverts any idea of a unitary creative spirit.

Precedents

Scripture offered precedents for the manufacture of art, if not for "artists" as such; the notion of "artifex" is fluid in the Bible too.[330] God commanded Noah to build an ark, and according to the Book of Exodus, the Lord "filled [Bezalel] with the spirit of God in skill, in understanding, in knowledge, and in all kinds of craftsmanship, to make artistic designs for work with gold, with silver, and with bronze, and with cutting and setting stone, and with cutting wood, to work in all kinds of craftsmanship" (Ex 31:3–5). This passage inspired Durand, the thirteenth-century bishop of Mende, to assert that his handbook on church art, architecture, and accoutrements, known as the *Rationale*, would disclose the celestial model that God had shown Moses on Mount Sinai.[331] The same Scripture

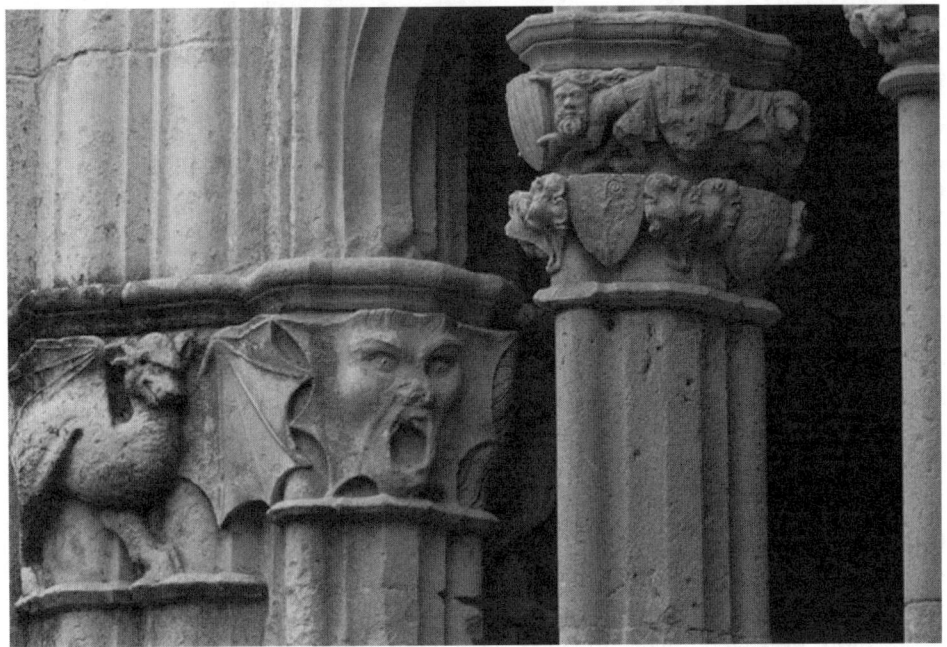

Figure 36. Aiguamúrcia, Reial Monastir de Santes Creus, cloister (fourteenth century)

refers also to "Oholiab ... to whom God has given skill to all the skillful," implying the division of planning and execution realized later, for example, in the dual portraits of Volvinus and Angilbert on the golden altar of Milan (Figure 6).[332] To construct the Jerusalem Temple, Solomon turned to Hiram, "a worker in bronze ... filled with wisdom and understanding and skill for doing any work in bronze" (1 Kgs 7:13–14), but it was the "wise" king of Israel himself who came to be associated with a wide range of objects, especially of exotic manufacture and with refined ornament. Indeed, the imported motifs impressed on the aquamanile (Figure 9), cast in Hildesheim,[333] may have been intended to identify it with the ancient king of Israel.[334]

Moreover, quasi-scriptural legends root art production in the very origins of Christianity. Mary, following Aaron's sister who wove the Temple curtain,[335] was portrayed at the Annunciation with spindle and distaff,[336] and Saint Joseph emerged as a carpenter.[337] Presumably because he was (allegedly) a Greek gentile believed to have authored the Acts of the Apostles with its proselytizing agenda, Luke was regarded as a painter;[338] the Evangeliary of Jan of Oplava of 1368 portrays him in a studio wearing a beret and coloring a drawing of the Crucifixion mounted on an easel (Vienna, ÖNB, Cod. 1182, fol. 91ᵛ).[339] The evangelist was credited with having painted Rome's two original icons, the encaustic Christ Emmanuel in the Lateran, known as the *Acheropita* (Figure 15), and the *Madonna Advocata*, which portrays Mary praying for Christ's intercession with upraised hands which, by the fourteenth century, was also treated as a *vera icona*, a "true image."[340] The enthroned Virgin and Child rendered within the Pantheon on the pilgrim token was also associated with Luke (Figure 2).[341] Nicodemus, the learned Jew to whom Christ himself had cited the Brazen Serpent as a sign of eternal life (Jn 3:12–16) and who had helped lower Christ into the tomb,[342] came to be regarded as the sculptor of a crucifix (*Volto Santo*).[343] Supernatural agency was attributed to others, as when in 1188, Gerald of Wales, who was fascinated by miraculously manufactured images, concluded that because of its subtle intricacy, a manuscript he had seen (that must have resembled the Book of Kells; see Figure 54), was "created more by angelic than human diligence."[344] Reinforcing women's association with textiles, the hemorrhaging woman healed by touching the hem of Christ's garment (Mt 9:20–22, Mk 5:25–34, Lk 8:43–48) became Veronica, one of the holy women who comforted Christ on Golgotha and the "crafter" of the *Veronica* (punning *vera icona*) impressed directly onto the cloth she proffered to relieve his suffering.[345] The earliest rendering in Matthew Paris's *Chronica maiora* of c. 1240 looks like a conventional portrait of Jesus,[346] but the signum of papal Rome appearing on pilgrims' badges and incorporated into the *arma Christi* soon acquired the distinct character of an imprint, as on the London polyptych where the culminating frontal face flanked by the alpha and omega offers a glimpse of the beatific vision the faithful hope to enjoy at the end of time (see Figure 13).

Promoters and Suppliers

The reliance of Noah, Moses, and Solomon on artisans to carry out actual labor authorized the role of patrons, both religious and secular, to provide materials and guide production. As heirs to the Roman emperors and Saint Peter himself, popes were foremost among the commissioners of art.[347] Hadrian I had affirmed and reinforced the legitimacy of images

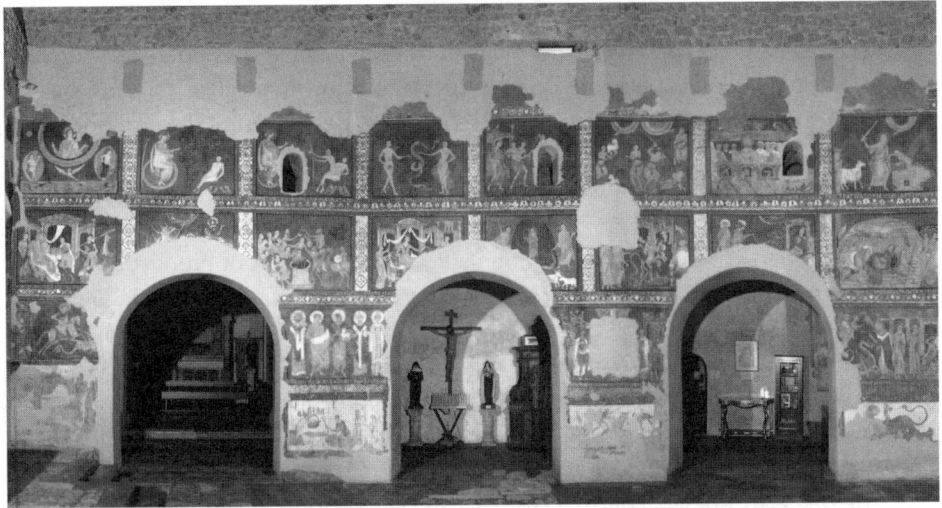

Figure 37. Ceri, Santa Maria Immacolata, right wall (c. 1100)

against Byzantine iconoclasm,[348] and his successors often actively engaged in the promotion, production, and maintenance of art. Gregory VII is associated with the revival of early Christian art known as the Gregorian Reform that was started by his predecessor Leo IX[349] and continued during the reigns of Victor III, Paschal II, and Urban II.[350] As witnessed in the renewal of monumental painting in the lower church of San Clemente in Rome and the production of the so-called *bibbie atlantiche* (giant bibles),[351] retrospective art was deployed as an instrument of papal propaganda. Murals, associated with the San Clemente painters in the church of Santa Maria Immacolata in Ceri just north of Rome, exemplify Gregorian Reform art (Figure 37). In a modest church originally dedicated to an early Christian pope, the decorations include a scene of Saint Sylvester cleaning the Forum of pagan demons under the auspices of the two Roman apostles and, most important, a program of Old Testament scenes from creation through the crossing of the Red Sea that imitates the fourth/fifth-century basilicas of San Pietro and San Paolo fuori le mura. Innocent III, who restored the apse of San Pietro and promoted the *Veronica* cult,[352] was the first of several thirteenth-century popes who were particularly active patrons. Nicholas IV designated the picture roster of early Christian saints and contemporary popes for the embroiderers in England of the *opus anglicanum* cope he intended to present to the bishop of Ascoli in

1288,[353] and he followed a similar procedure when commissioning the apse mosaic in Santa Maria Maggiore signed by the "painter" Jacopo Torriti.[354] Pope Nicholas also became directly involved with the decoration of the upper church of San Francesco at Assisi, virtually eliminating the need for a head master.[355] Even the notorious Boniface VIII was an eager patron of art.[356] When the papacy went into its "Babylonian Exile" in Avignon, the tradition of papal support of art continued albeit within new international dynamics that enabled the development of a new system of production[357] and such hybrid phenomena as Clement VI giving Jean le Bon, a Valois monarch, a diptych of Christ and Mary based on Roman prototypes which was recorded in a painting in the Sainte-Chapelle.[358]

Closer to the ground than the bishop of Rome, cardinals and bishops were also frequent patrons.[359] In the apse mosaic of his private oratory at Germigny-des-Prés, Theodulf, bishop of Orléans and a protagonist of the Carolingian controversy over images, responded to art he had encountered during a trip to Rome.[360] Hincmar, bishop of Reims and an influential Church leader, was a major patron and likely the determining intellectual force behind the creation of such important works as the San Paolo Bible (Rome, Monastery of San Paolo fuori le mura) and the Utrecht Psalter (Figure 38).[361] Bernward of Hildesheim commissioned the bronze doors and a column for his cathedral (Figure 23), smaller works, and such manuscripts as the illuminated Gospel book still in Hildesheim (Dommuseum, MS 18).[362] The archbishop of Tarragona promoted the recuperation of Roman antiquity, inserting an early Christian sarcophagus above the cathedral's right portal dedicated to episcopal use.[363] Lucas, the thirteenth-century bishop of Tuy, sought to impose ecclesiastic control on imagery;[364] in the cathedral of his native city of León, bishops, beginning with Rodriguez Alvarez c. 1250, created a pantheon of (seven) tombs that attests to episcopal munificence (Figure 39).[365] Around the same time, cardinal Stefano Conti, a nephew of Innocent III who was Rome's prefect, had a chapel dedicated to Saint Sylvester at Santi Quattro Coronati adorned with narratives promoting the Donation of Constantine;[366] and he also sponsored the decoration of a vast hall above it, known today as the *aula gotica*, covered with the most advanced art of its time and advancing the culture of knowledge that he and other clerics were promoting (Plate XIV).[367] A century later, cardinal Giacomo Stefaneschi was not only the patron of Giotto's *Navicella* in the atrium of San Pietro but also an advisor to the man who, in later historiography, became the first "artist." The Regensburg butterfly reliquary (see Plate I), discovered in the bishop's residence at Burg Donaustauf, may originally have been the pectoral of Bishop Nikolaus von Ybbs (1283–1340).[368]

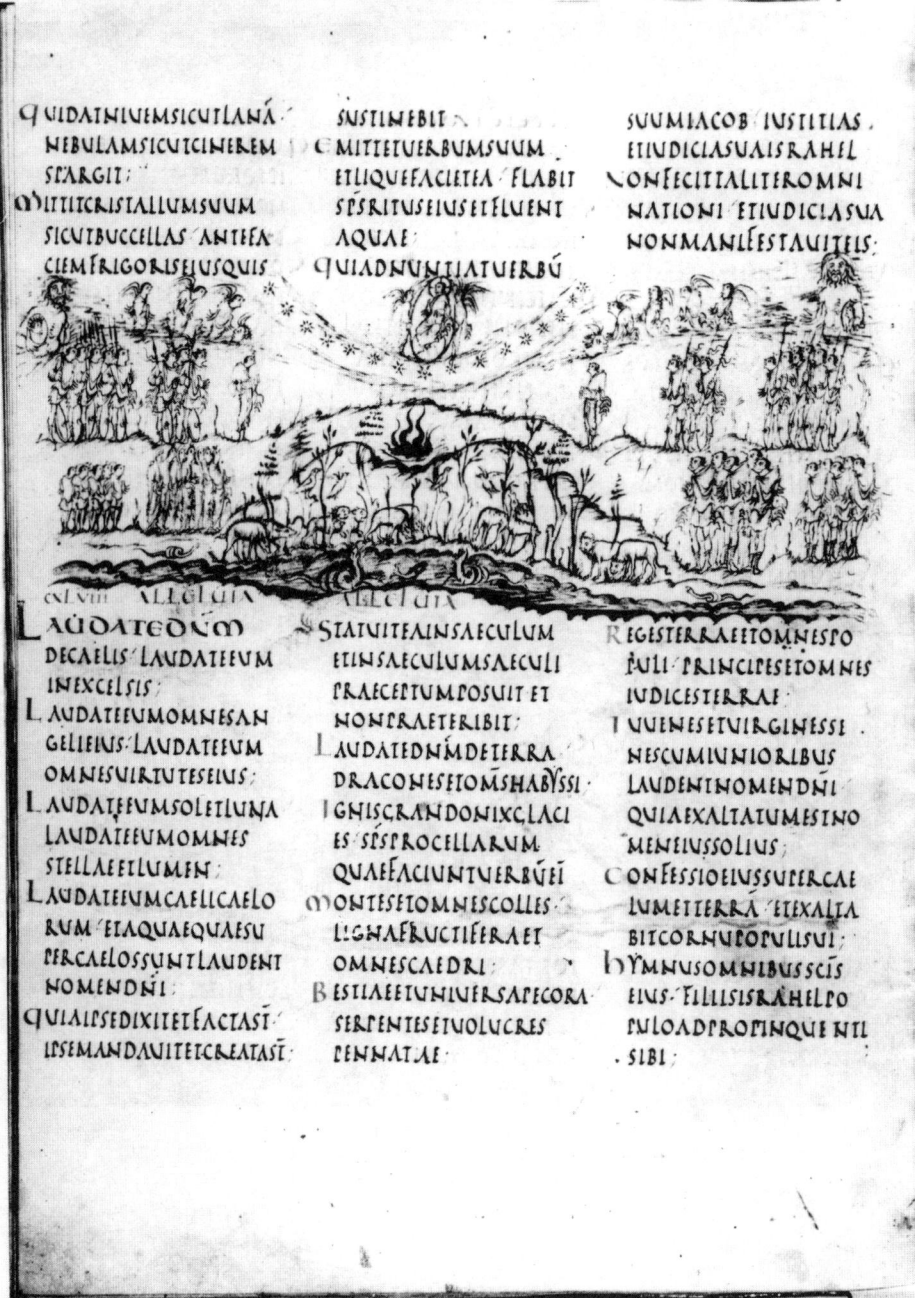

Figure 38. Utrecht, Universiteitsbibliotheek, MS Bibl. Rhenotraiectinae I Nr 32, Psalter, fol. 82ᵛ (ninth century)

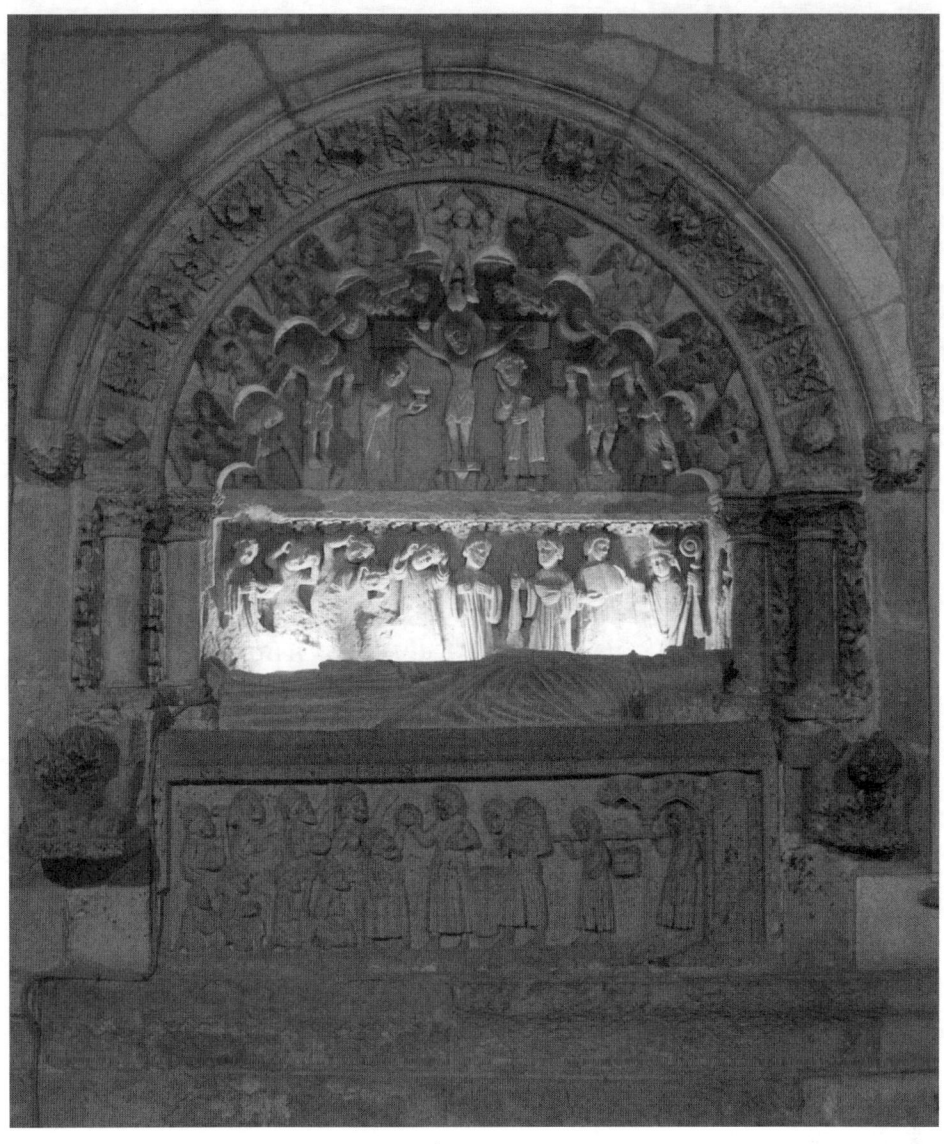

Figure 39. León, catedral de Santa Maria, tomb of Rodriguez Alvarez (thirteenth century)

Abbots and abbesses were particularly active in the production of art, which, in the early Middle Ages especially, was mostly the province of monasteries.[369] Although the *Rule of Saint Benedict* (and, within a wide range, other monastic ordinaries) allowed for work, physical labor was still largely understood as servile and carnal; nonetheless, it was valued and promoted because it demonstrated obedience to God and countered idleness, which was believed to lead to vice.[370] The *Rule* mandated that monks participate in book culture; under Abbot Desiderius, Benedict's own Montecassino was a center of artistic patronage during the eleventh century[371] and Benedictines were particularly active in deploying art for their missionizing of Europe.[372] Cluny in Burgundy established international networks;[373] not surprising, the imagery in the apse of Berzé-la-Ville is distinctly Roman and Early Christian in featuring Christ delivering the New Law to Peter (*traditio legis*), albeit with particular local and contemporary inflection (Figure 32).[374] Farfa provided an artistic nexus for Cluny, Montecassino, and Rome.[375] Inspired by journeys to Rome in 1011 and 1016–17, during the first half of the eleventh century Abbot Oliba of Santa Maria de Ripoll and Saint-Michel-de-Cuxa sponsored the production of art and manuscripts,[376] while Suger of Saint-Denis, who left an account of his consequential involvement in the rebuilding of France's most important church, was the guiding intellect behind the architecture, sculpture, stained glass, and goldsmith's work of the building considered to be the birthplace of Gothic.[377] Suger's Cistercian rival Bernard of Clairvaux railed against artistic excess, although he conceded imagery's usefulness for the lay.[378]

For nuns, Mary's spinning the Temple curtain was the exemplar for art making,[379] but how much cloistered women participated in the planning of works is still being debated. Even though the Gospel lectionary that bears her name was written and painted in the nearby monastery of Saint-Emmeram (Munich, Bay. Staatsbib., Clm 13601), not at Niedermünster where she was abbess, Uta was surely the intellectual force behind its creation;[380] likewise, the precise relationship between Christina of Markyate, an anchoress living near Saint Albans in the 1120s and 30s, and the illuminations in the Saint Albans Psalter remains a vexed question (Figure 40).[381] Scholars also continue to be divided over whether Hildegard of Bingen, the Benedictine abbess of Rupertsberg, turned to a trained miniaturist or designed the intellectually complex illustrations of her idiosyncratic visions in the *Scivias* (Figure 19), but she, like Herrard of Hohenbourg in the *Hortus Deliciarum*,[382] stamped the work's character.

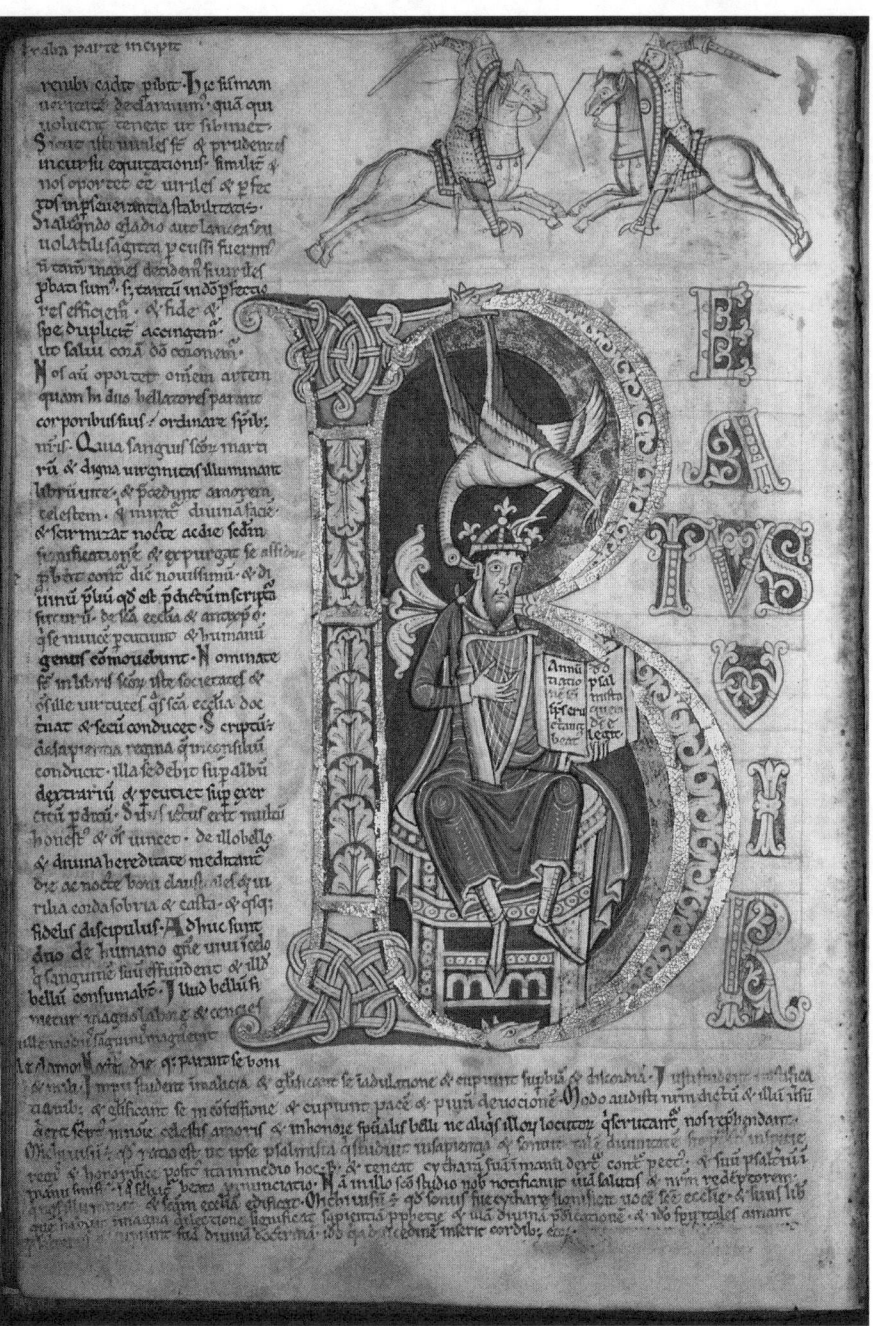

Figure 40. Hildesheim, Dombibliothek, MS Saint-Godehard 1, Saint Albans Psalter, fol. 72ᵛ (twelfth century)

Considerable evidence survives, moreover, that clerics, even bishops, abbots, and abbesses were themselves artisans.[383] The monk Tuotilo produced works, and the tenth-century bishop of Winchester, Æthelwold, not only ordered the Benedictional that bears his name to be adorned with gold, beautiful colors, frames, and various figures (London, Brit. Lib., Add. MS 49598) but is reported also to have been a practicing goldsmith. Bernward's biographer, Thangmar, described the Hildesheim bishop as skilled in art, and Thietmar chronicled his direct involvement.[384]

Clerical connections facilitated the participation of theologians in the production of art. In south Italy, Abbot Ambrosius Autpertus bridged Byzantine and western thought in a way that transformed it, undoubtedly through papal agency.[385] Audradus Modicus, a brother at Saint-Martin in Tours who signed the ornamented frontispiece of the *Liber comitis of Saint-Père of Chartres* (Chartres, Bib. municipal, MS. 24), was the author of both the poems and certain pictures in the First Bible of Charles the Bald (Paris, Bib. nat. MS lat. 1);[386] Hugh of Saint-Victor constructed images for lectures collected in the *Ark of Noah*;[387] and Rupert of Deutz's theology permeates the decorations at Schwarzrheindorf.[388] Suger seems to have relied on Hugh of Saint-Victor (who could have transmitted to him the ideas of the Pseudo-Dionysius) to realize his sophisticated and consequential project at Saint-Denis,[389] and Bishop Anselm played an active role in planning art in Canterbury.[390]

Despite vows of poverty, mendicant orders also sponsored the making of art.[391] Franciscans were particularly active promoters, especially after Assisi became a major pilgrimage site;[392] through their international networks, they became a prime force in the transformation of late medieval imagery.[393] The Order of Saint Clare embraced art, too; the mid-fourteenth-century *Meditations on the Life of Christ* (Paris, BnF, MS Ital. 115) greatly expanded the Gospels with legends and human touches to enhance accessibility, reflecting in the illustrations' style and homey imagery the order's poverty.[394] Dominicans deployed pictures as instruments of pedagogy and piety,[395] like the Franciscans, setting aside the vow of evangelical simplicity. Berthold of Nuremberg was a Dominican, whose refashioning of Hrabanus Maurus's complicated schemata and the addition of Marian *figurae* made the Carolingian text accessible,[396] and a Dominican is portrayed overseeing the illumination of the Holkham Bible, while a monkey gazing in a mirror cautions against vanity and the inherent danger of images.[397]

Lay orders were particularly active. Brother Rufillus, pictured painting the letter *R* in a late twelfth-century Passionale from Weissenau

(Geneva, Bibl Bodmeriana, Cod. 127, fol. 224), was a "white canon"; literate laymen also seem to have made the fourteenth-century Luttrell Psalter (London, Brit. Lib., Add. MS 42130).[398] The importance of such para-clerical groups as confraternities in the commissioning and care of art grew steadily during the thirteenth and fourteenth centuries. In Rome, a confraternity was established to attend the Lateran icon,[399] and, in Florence, a similar lay order was charged in 1291 with maintaining the Orsanmichele Virgin and Child (Figure 16), which itself attracted other miraculous works of art that reinforced its own power, including a crucifix and a stone relief. In 1347, civic authorities commissioned Bernardo Daddi to paint the enormous version, more than ten feet high, set in an elaborate tabernacle sculpted by Andrea di Cione (Orcagna), still visible in Orsanmichele.[400]

The Florence municipality was acting in a venerable tradition of secular patronage. Although members of the clergy were, themselves, mostly aristocrats and royalty fashioned itself as part of the sacred order,[401] courts played a distinct role in the production of art. Charlemagne, for example, gathered artisans to build his palace complex at Aachen,[402] including Einhard (nicknamed Bezalel) who, among other things, later designed a remarkable miniature triumphal arch.[403] One of the earliest witnesses of the revival of manuscript illumination and ivory book carving that Charlemagne sponsored is the "Coronation Gospels" in Vienna (Schatzkammer), written in gold and silver on fine purple-stained vellum, decorated with classical architecture and *faux marbre*, and illustrated with four evangelists in the guise of ancient authors sitting in impressionistic landscapes or before classical *scenae frons* rendered in light and dark.[404] Charles the Bald continued his grandfather's tradition of patronage but relied on monastic scriptoria to produce illuminated manuscripts and other works for his realm, including the personal prayer book in Munich (Figure 18).[405] The emperor Otto III is said to have found the Coronation Gospels together with such objects as the reliquary of Saint Stephen (now in Vienna Cathedral) when he opened Charlemagne's grave in 1000,[406] and many other objects also came to be associated with the first Holy Roman emperor, including an ivory chess set (albeit eleventh-century) in Paris.[407]

Inspired in part by such legends, later rulers continued the tradition of court patronage, among others Frederick Barbarossa, Frederick II, and Charles VI of Anjou.[408] Some looked to Byzantium, others to Constantine or Charlemagne. It is impossible fully to understand the Cappella Palatina in Palermo, for instance, without probing the pan-Mediterranean politics of its patron Roger I.[409] Henry III promoted the cult of Edward the Confessor by refurbishing his sainted royal predecessor's tomb in Westminster (Plate IX). The Capetian court in Paris became an important venue for production of art that included the Psalter of Louis IX (Paris, BnF, MS lat. 10525), the *bibles moralisées*,[410] and the Sainte-Chapelle that King Louis built to house relics he had poached from the great palace of the Byzantine emperors during the Fourth Crusade (Plate VII), including the emblem of sacred kingship par excellence, the Crown of Thorns. Culture thrived in the cosmopolitan court of Alfonso X (the Wise), king of Aragon and León, who promoted translations from Hebrew and Arabic and the study of science, games, and music. Alfonso personally oversaw the compilation of the Galician-Portuguese *Cantigas de Santa Maria*, with its rich blend of religious imagery and material from everyday life (Figure 41). In Venice, doges supervised the creation of San Marco. Years after "Saint" Louis died, his achievement, like Charlemagne's earlier, served as a model: the Holy Roman emperor Charles IV, who participated in rituals in the Sainte-Chapelle and as an old man climbed its stairs to view the relics, was inspired by it to build Karlstejn (Figure 12),[411] and Jean, duc de Berry, actually replicated it at Bourges.[412]

Queens were particularly engaged in art production. During the Carolingian period, they were charged with the chamberlain to oversee gift-giving at court and, hence, were well positioned to function as patrons. Queen Ælfgyfu is pictured with King Cnut presenting the altar cross to the New Minster and Hyde Abbey in the *Liber Vitae* (London, Brit. Lib., Stowe MS 944, fol. 6),[413] and like many royal women, she was involved with the production of textiles and donated luxurious fabrics to the abbey church at Ely. Beginning with the marriage charter and including the Gospels that bear her name (Plate V), Theophanu changed the pattern of Ottonian art. Queen Gisela is featured on the Coronation Mantle (Figure 14). A member of the papal court circle, Matilda of Canosa was a leading force behind Gregorian Reform art in northern Italy;[414] Urraca of León-Castille had a powerful impact on the art of twelfth-century Spain;[415] and Melisende, daughter of King Baldwin II of Jerusalem, wife of Fulk of Anjou, and mother of two future kings of Jerusalem, either commissioned a book of psalms with splendid ivory covers now in the British Library (Egerton MS 1139) or was the recipient of it. She was also responsible for the double portal of the church of the Holy Sepulcher in Jerusalem (Figure 42) and patron of the abbey of Mary in the Valley of Jehoshaphat and the Armenian church of Saint James in Jerusalem.[416] Not only King Louis but also

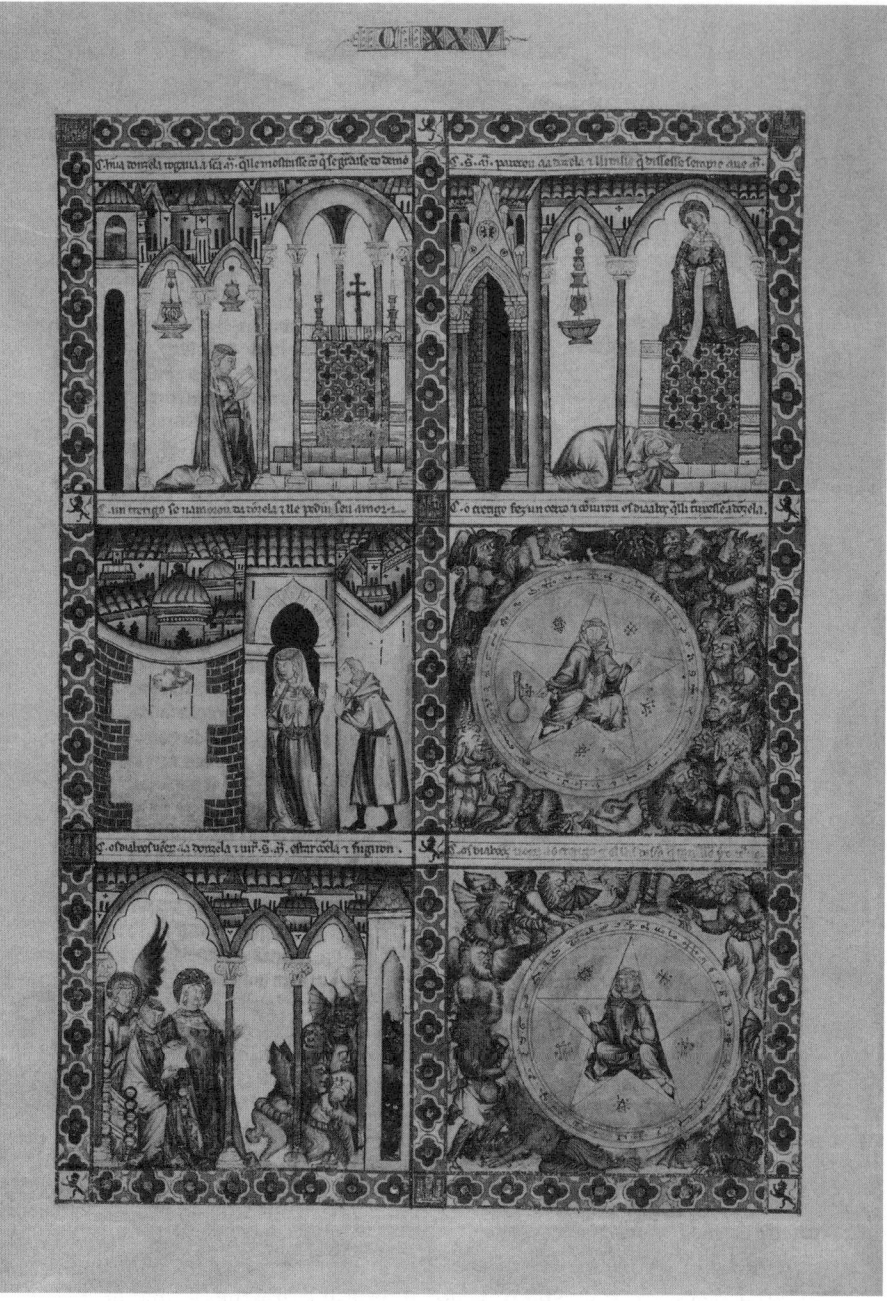

Figure 41. Escorial, Real biblioteca del Monasterio, MS T.I.1, *Cantigas de Santa Maria*, fol. 177ᵛ (thirteenth century)

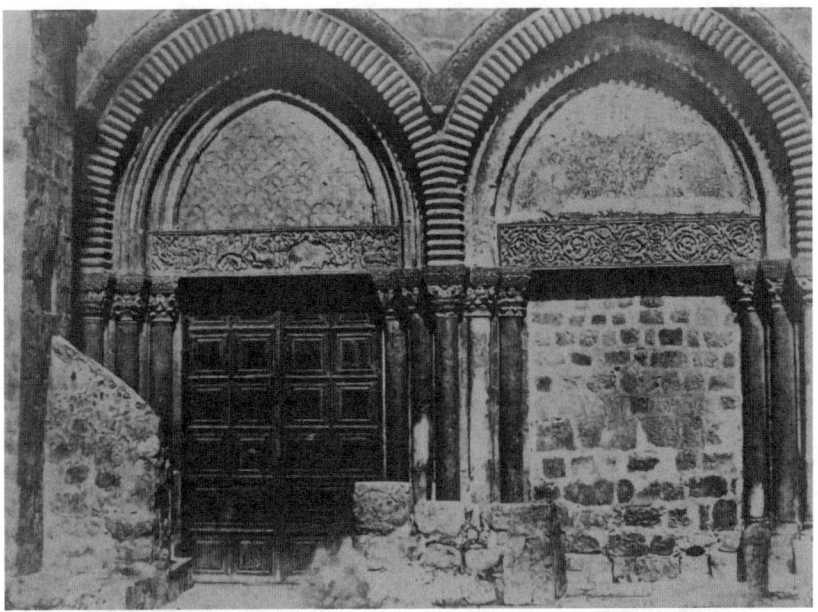

Figure 42. Jerusalem, church of the Holy Sepulcher, doorways (twelfth century)

his mother, Blanche of Castille, is referred to in the subjects chosen for the windows of the Sainte-Chapelle,[417] and the queen is portrayed alongside her son on the frontispiece of the Toledo *bible moralisée* overseeing the production (New York, Pierpont Morgan Library, MS 240, fol. 8^r). Eleanor of Aquitaine specified the iconography of an ivory she commissioned, unlike her king, Henry II, who simply ordered his favorite artisan, William, a monk of Winchester, to make a work that was "proper," "beautiful," and "expensive," and who left to his embroiderer, Mabel, the composition and design of a standard for Westminster Abbey because she "would know best how to see them."[418] When their daughter Eleanor became queen of Castille, moreover, she seems to have channeled French traditions to her new realm.[419] Joan of Navarre may have inspired Enguerrand de Marigny's love of art; after leaving her service in 1302 to serve the chamberlain of her husband, Philip the Fair, Enguerrand built the church of Notre-Dame at Écouis (northwest of Paris) between 1308 and 1313 and decorated it with sculptures that reflected Parisian court tastes (Figure 43).[420]

Dynastic and family connections were strong vectors in court circles.[421] The marriage of Charles the Bald's daughter, Judith, to the

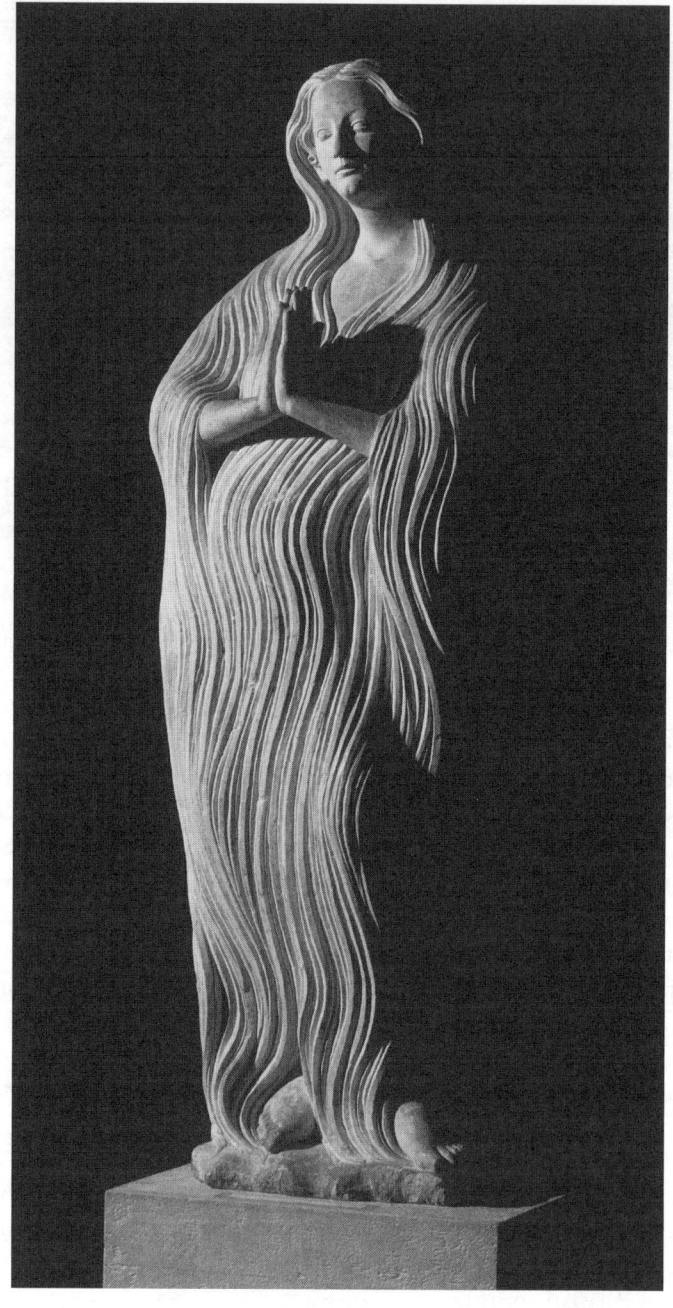

Figure 43. Écouis, Collégiale Notre-Dame, Mary Magdalene (fourteenth century)

king(s) of Wessex may account for the strong influence of Carolingian art in England, and the fact that Theophanu's grandaunt, Mathilde, had installed the Golden Madonna in Essen most likely explains the image-reliquary's inclusion on the cover of the queen's Gospel book.[422] In 1249, Sibylle, the abbess of Montreuil-les-Dames, asked her brother, Jacques Pantaleon (later Pope Urban IV), for a Veronica and he sent her the painting of the Mandylion (*La sainte face*) that is still in Laon.[423] The Toledo *bible moralisée*, mentioned in Alfonso X's will as a bible "in three volumes, illustrated, which King Louis of France [Louis IX] gave to us" (perhaps on the occasion of a wedding intended to unite France with the homeland of his mother, Blanche of Castille),[424] likely provoked the Spanish king's making of the *Cantigas*. Frederick II "authored" the *De arte venandi cum avibus*, the age's most important treatise on natural history, but his son, Conrad, had it illuminated.[425]

How various participants—artisans, clerics, sponsors—interacted with one another varied from case to case. An eleventh-century panel of the Last Judgment in the Vatican documents one mode: an inscription beneath the resurrection of the dead names the makers: "at the sound of the trumpets, the painters Nicholas and John rise from the dust of the earth," and the abbess Constantia, who probably commissioned the panel, and Benedicta, who may have paid for it, are pictured with their offerings outside the walls of paradise.[426] In this instance, the difference between portrait, written name, and the hierarchy of placement may reflect the roles of the persons who conceived the work and the painters. Repentance and judgment are also themes embedded in the choice and placement of words in Guillaume Martin's inscription in Saint-André-le-Bas.[427] On the Toledo *bible moralisée* frontispiece, a cleric is pictured beneath Blanche and Louis with a book in his hand (bearing the words "Let it be left to faith to paint"), instructing a miniaturist at work on a sheet of vellum already subdivided into medallions for the miniatures.

The problem with attributing direct participation to a famous ruler is not that a monarch's role in the work is exaggerated so much as that sponsorship by other court groups might be overlooked. A count, Guido Guerra, apparently commissioned the Rosano Cross to protect a small piece of bone and a reliquary cross (secreted behind the head) that he presumably had brought from the Holy Land, c. 1100.[428] For the façade sculptures of Sankt Theobald at Münster, the patron Johanna von Pfirt seems to have chosen the iconographic sources deployed by an itinerant master and his assistants, including both foreign artisans and local workmen.[429]

In a number of such instances, on the other hand, art functioned to exhort, flatter, and even scold the ruler. A subtext of the overt imagery and poems of the First Bible of Charles the Bald, for instance, actually undercuts the status of Count Vivian (whose name, ironically, is still often attached to the manuscript).[430] And since the identification of the designer and circumstances of production of perhaps the most written-about work of medieval art, the Bayeux embroidery, continue to elude scholars (Figure 31),[431] its partisan or conciliatory message remains the subject of discussion. One recent theory is that Countess Adela of Blois likely commissioned it sometime after William the Conqueror's death to commemorate her father's great accomplishment, but whether the work was manufactured in England, France, or elsewhere continues to be debated, along with the possibility that it was conceived in Normandy but manufactured in Canterbury and displayed there.[432] The role played by lesser nobility is especially complicated in the case of the Pierpont Morgan Library picture Bible, often assigned to Louis IX (MS M 638);[433] here, the *bibles moralisées* offer a guide and a warning: for all the similarity of the manuscripts to one another (Vienna 2554, Vienna 1179, Toledo, and Oxford-Paris-London), their making or the relationship to the commissioners, planners, and the recipients—Louis VIII, Louis IX, and conceivably Marguerite of Provence—was anything but straightforward. Complex motivation is evident in the chapel Enrico Scrovegni built c. 1303–05 adjacent to his palace in Padua (see Plate XII).[434] Prompted by the family's insecurity about how they came by the funds to build and adorn the chapel in the first place, the money-lender is included among the blessed in the Last Judgment, handing over a model to the Virgin Mary and the two other holy Marys.[435]

The role of corporate donors depicted in the lower windows at Chartres has also been variously interpreted. The narratives drawn from Latin and vulgar texts but developed in an original fashion were likely dictated by the clergy or, at the very least, approved by it; clerical donors and members of the nobility were responsible for windows in the transept and high in the choir.[436] In like fashion, the prominence of tradesmen in the lower windows of the apse might suggest that the lay associations who paid for the glass were its "co-authors"[437] or, conversely, that they reflect the chapter's strategy to attach the Church to the artisans and merchants. A principal aim, in either case, was to establish a place for its new class of donors within the history of the Church.

The participation of merchants, manufacturers, and even vassals in the production of art gave rise, especially in the later Middle Ages, to mass production and art markets.⁴³⁸ Trade flourished throughout the period, particularly in the Mediterranean.⁴³⁹ In the thirteenth century, secular workshops for the production of manuscripts were organized in Paris, and a scriptorium near Lake Constance employed Jewish scribes alongside Christian illuminators to produce both Haggadot and graduals in much the same style.⁴⁴⁰ Even as laymen emerged as the principal producers of medieval art, however, their precise status is often unclear, as in the case of the famous Villard de Honnecourt.⁴⁴¹ When commercialization engendered a need to assure quality, guilds arose in the thirteenth century.⁴⁴² Boileau's *Livre des métiers* attests that, by 1270, proto-connoisseurs were able to assess products to insure that they were not "false works."⁴⁴³

Art making ran in some families. Nicola and Giovanni Pisano were father and son,⁴⁴⁴ and the relationship between the Master Honoré and the Papeleu Master, long recognized by means of stylistic affinities, is documented as a relationship between father-in-law and son-in-law; the active participation of spouses is also well attested.⁴⁴⁵ In England, craftsmen sold ready-made alabaster reliefs to the middle class, as well as to local churches, and began exporting their products.⁴⁴⁶

Originality and Standardization

In the eleventh-century *Dialogue on Miracles*, Arnaud of Clermont described a vision of Mary that the abbot Robert de Mozat had had in a dream and then made a statue based on what he had seen,⁴⁴⁷ a literary device that elides the difference between spiritual and material aspects of art. The illustrations in Hildegard of Bingen's *Scivias* betray inspired idiosyncratic imagery; the series begins with an unprecedented image of *Ecclesia*, entirely gold, crowned, enthroned, and bearing Hildegard's words: "I must conceive and give birth." The figure gathers three of the faithful onto her breast while others bring offerings to her in the hope of ascending the ladder to her lap. At the end, the souls of those who enter her womb, still covered in clay-like red skin, are reborn from her mouth and rise toward a celestial disk of gold, silver, and blue floating on a sky dotted with white stars. Like the exegesis that follows each written vision, the pictures draw freely on tradition to render the eccentric imagery comprehensible; imagining the Trinity as three concentric circles, for instance, goes back to late antique art, and *Ecclesia* as a queen has a long history. Nevertheless, the strange combinations are personal; the souls "moving in the air like fishes in water" in the lower right or caught in the net of *Ecclesia*'s womb are unique. Any argument that the makers of earlier medieval art were "artists" in the modern sense would have to be based on a case like Hildegard's—or on Opicino di Canistris, who reconciled practical experience with theology in highly personal expressions of the relationships between science, art, and the Church.[448]

In general, the production of medieval art drew heavily on tradition, often on the copying of available material. The Utrecht Psalter, for example, which had made its way from Reims to Canterbury perhaps as part of Judith of Wessex's dowry already in the ninth century, generated three twelfth-century "copies" in England (Brit. Lib., Harley MS 603; Cambridge, TCL R.171; and Paris, BnF, MS lat. 8846), each with its own distinctive character.[449] Hrabanus Maurus's *In honorem Sanctae Crucis* was replicated in various styles over the course of the Middle Ages.[450] The Book of Revelation and Beatus of Liebana's commentary on it have come down in so many copies that art historians have been able to construct diagrams of derivation (stemmas) of the illustrations of the sort that philologists do for textual transmission.[451] Models, or earlier works, often bore meaning. Just as the Gregorian Reform painters of Ceri had before, the *concepteurs* of Assisi tethered the new Franciscan mother church to the early Christian apostolic basilicas in Rome by incorporating well-known sequences from the Book of Genesis and life of Christ in San Pietro; in the very cradle of artists' identity, the makers of medieval art seem to have privileged venerable models.[452] In turn, the Franciscans circulated forms and models to assure a level of coherency in their dependencies.[453]

Even among "copies," however, each version inevitably introduced modifications and re-interpretations, not only through changes of style, format, and contents, but also with respect to purpose. Thus, for example, the army of the beast (Rv 19) in the Trinity Apocalypse written c. 1260 in Anglo-Norman French translation (Cambridge, Trinity College, Ms. R.16.2, fol. 23ʳ) is clothed in contemporary chain mail and an entirely original narrative life of Saint John replaces the traditional author portrait.[454] The English versions of the Utrecht Psalter differ from one another in size and are concerted re-thinkings,[455] and the production of the *bibles moralisées* involved commonalities but also simultaneity and particular interventions.[456] Crafters participated actively in the process. The post-classical casting techniques of the Capitoline wolf suggest that the person who commissioned the work may have sought to tie himself to the glorious past, even while relying on his metal workers to reinvent the methods by studying ancient remains.[457] Sculptors used clay models that enabled them to gauge visual distortions due to standpoints.[458] And when the mosaicists of the San Marco atrium copied the imagery from a fifth-century Genesis manuscript, most likely acquired during the Fourth Crusade,[459] they fleshed out the damaged ancient codex by turning to sources available in their own medium; the birds and fishes that stand in for the fifth day of creation, for example, derive from Roman mosaics.[460]

Craftspersons also moved about. During the crusades, western painters and sculptors worked in the Holy Land and Constantinople, issuing coins, decorating churches, illuminating manuscripts, and carving sculptures.[461] Their work is western but distinct, and when some of them returned home, they imported eastern motifs and methods. Certain capitals carved in the 1170s to adorn the church of the Annunciation in Nazareth are distinctly French in style and feature Saint Peter,[462] and while the left lintel of the entranceway to the Holy Sepulcher has much in common with French Romanesque sculpture, perhaps through a common derivation from late antique sources,[463] the inhabited scrolls over the right door seem more Italian. In turn, the doorway in Jerusalem is closely related to the double Porta de las Platerías in the cathedral of Santiago, attaching Christ's tomb to the burial place in Spain of his disciple James and tethering the remotest pilgrimage destinations to one another.[464] Villard de Honnecourt's carnet provides evidence that the Picard architect-sculptor moved throughout France and into Italy. Giotto was itinerant, working in Florence, Naples, Rome, Padua, and Milan. Matteo Giovannetti followed the popes from Italy into exile in Avignon where he became the official "papal painter";[465] and Charles IV summoned Tomaso da Modena to Bohemia to help decorate his castle at Karlstejn.[466]

Although such craft ephemera as Villard's were normally discarded, a few working drawings survive and some artistic trials have been discovered beneath finished work.[467] Most models comprise details or single figures, as in the pen and wash copied from the sculptures and mosaics of San Marco, and other works were made perhaps for personal training and recollection, as those assembled in a sketchbook now in Wolfenbüttel (Herzog August Bibliothek, Cod. Guelf. 61.2 Aug. 8°, fols. 75–94) reused in Saxony soon after they were made.[468] A large mid-thirteenth-century drawing (measuring some 16 x 23 inches) for the vaults and walls of a chapel provides unique evidence of what might have been a more common practice in which motifs and texts are assembled within architectural schemata for transfer to monumental surfaces (Figure 44). Constructed first by imposing a geometric schema on the flat surface to designate the architectural matrix, it was then

Figure 44. Salzburg, Stift Sankt Peter, drawing for a chapel (thirteenth century)

filled with figures and inscriptions intended to adorn the cupola and adjacent spaces. A parchment scroll in Vercelli (Archivio e Biblioteca Capitolare) served special circumstances; illustrating episodes from the Book of Acts with accompanying captions, it too was made as a model for decorating a church ceiling. But, as it records, the purpose was to preserve earlier compositions that, apparently, had to be destroyed and replaced.[469] Drawings that laid out an original concept to be followed by subordinate craftsmen in a workshop became increasingly common as the mode of production changed during the fourteenth century with the emergence of master artists.[470]

Captions, too, were circulated in compendia;[471] in rare cases, whole compositions were transmitted through writing.[472] Baudri, the abbot of the Benedictine monastery of Bourgueil and then archbishop of Dol-de-Bretagne, and a leading poet of his age, composed verses intended to be copied "around an altar table" and "around a Crucifix," including a couplet: "It is neither God nor man, which you discern in the present figure, But God and man, which the sacred image represents" that actually survives on sculptures, manuscripts, enamels, panel paintings, and on the fresco at Ceri where it explicates the scene of Moses at the Burning Bush.[473] A caption authored by Fulcoius of Beauvais recurs on the Rosano Cross,[474] and a titulus very close to one composed by Hildebert of Lavardin is inscribed on the Nativity mosaic in the Cappella Palatina in Palermo.[475] The *Pictor in Carmine*, an extensive compilation constructed c. 1200, was intended to offer painters a choice of explanatory captions (tituli or titles), with the explicit intention of curbing their freedom of imagination.[476]

Serial production is also well documented.[477] Badges, such as the one picturing Santa Maria Rotonda and its icon (Figure 2), were impressed from molds, a process deployed also in making coins, wax seals made from signet rings, and Eucharistic wafers. Impressing allowed a crossover of functions. From the early thirteenth century, the face of the Lucca "Volto Santo" was stamped onto the money that pilgrims used along the via Francigena, such as two deposited in Mont-Saint-Michel; in turn, the holy face was impressed onto the coins of Otto IV of Braunschweig.[478] Tokens of the *Veronica* were made for pilgrims at San Pietro by adding a few details to outlines transferred from parchment or leather stencils,[479] thereby enacting both the fleshy aspect of the Holy Face and the claim of being not manufactured by human hand. Stamping was, in itself, rife with meaning because it skirted the issue of human manufacture.[480] Jews favored stencil art to avoid "making" images. Honorius Augustodunensis's little tract, *Sigillum sanctae Mariae*, applied the seal metaphor to Mary's having received divinity in her flesh.[481] And it may be no coincidence that the seven compartments of the Metropolitan Museum's shrine Madonna (Figure 28) seem to conform to Honorius's description of the womb as having seven cells, each one "with the shape of a man stamped on them as if on a coin." The theologian Peter Abelard used the metaphor to articulate Trinitarian arguments, claiming that wax and an image in wax are simultaneously the same and different, just as the Father and Son are, and he and other pre-scholastics extended the analogy also to God's relationship to humankind made, according to Genesis 1:26, "in God's image." Francis embodied the idea in his own person, as pictured on the Paris reliquary, where he receives the "sacred seals" of Christ's wounds as he looks at the vision of the seraph.[482]

Chapter 4
Spirit

EVEN MOST skeptics accepted the argument Pope Gregory I had promulgated c. 600 that art is a useful instrument for teaching the faith to gentiles and illiterate Christians "who read in them what they cannot read in books."[483] The iconoclastic Theodulf of Orléans, for instance, conceded that material images could depict Christ's earthly life but asserted that they offered food for the eyes devoid of all spiritual nourishment.[484] Still, as the dictum's continuous repetition and endless rephrasing attest, art continued to engender anxiety throughout the Middle Ages. Many church authorities harbored concerns that images, particularly those in three dimensions, would engender idolatry. Bernard of Angers reported in the early eleventh-century *Liber miraculorum sancte Fidis* that, when he first saw the statues of the saints Gerard and Faith at Conques "fashioned out of the purest gold and the most precious stones," he reacted as if they were "idols of Jupiter or Mars and Venus or Diana."[485] Aware of the dangerous allure of luxurious substances and intricate craftsmanship, others expressed concern about their essential materiality.[486] Bernard of Clairvaux argued that those who promote art "stimulate the devotion of a carnal people with material ornaments because they cannot do so with spiritual ones,"[487] and Richard of Saint-Victor considered craftsmanship to be an "adulterous" result of the sin that seduced humankind away from the spiritual to the physical.[488]

Bernard's "carnal people" were first and foremost Jews. Despite the Second Commandment's explicit ban on images,[489] Christians pointed to the Israelites' worship of the golden calf while Moses was receiving the commandments (which included the image prohibition) on Mount Sinai, and the brazen serpent the prophet had raised up in the desert, which they came to abuse.

In fact, Jews did not reject art; indeed, from the tenth century until the end of the Middle Ages, Jewish art flourished under diverse styles and modes,[490] constituting a distinctive tradition within the cultural practices of Christian and Muslim neighbors.[491] And, like Christians, Jews expressed a range of opinions about representation. Rashi acknowledged the value of art as an instrument of learning and reinterpreted the story of the brazen serpent in terms of belief and rejection.[492] The thirteenth-century rabbi of Rothenburg, Meir ben Baruch, voiced concern that pictures in books might distract worshippers whose focus should be on God, and Rabbi Joseph Bekhor Shor of Orléans pointed contemptuously to "the heaps of [Christian] statues whose number has no end."[493] At the end of the period, the philosopher Profiat Duran advanced the argument that Solomon's Temple justified book illumination: "just as God wished to adorn the place of his Sanctuary with gold, silver, and precious stones, so is this appropriate for his holy books, especially for the book which is 'his sanctuary' [the Bible]."[494] Jews developed a mode of representation known as micrography,[495] deployed for instance on the opening to Leviticus in the thirteenth-century Bavarian Ebermannstadt Pentateuch containing the Five Books of Moses and various other texts (Figure 45). Seeming literally to realize Profiat Duran's idea, the Temple (in the form of a Gothic sanctuary) is constructed of minuscule lines of Scripture that elide the difference between text and image.[496] Jews did mostly avoid rendering faces, as in the "bird's head" Haggadah (Figure 34), which portrays Pharaoh and his men as humans because there was no risk that the gentile evildoers would be venerated, but obscures Jewish visages behind curious griffin-like masks.[497] Moreover, while the Haggadah does establish a parallel between the preparations for the Seder and the historic Exodus that the ceremonial dinner recalls and re-enacts, it goes no further; like virtually all Jewish art of the Middle Ages, it rejects any attempt to affect a transition from the world to an imagined spiritual realm.[498]

Art's Spiritual Nature

Christians transformed this Jewish restraint into a weapon. Thus, an early eleventh-century cleric in the court of Emperor Henry II accused his coreligionists who understood crucifixes only as material objects of

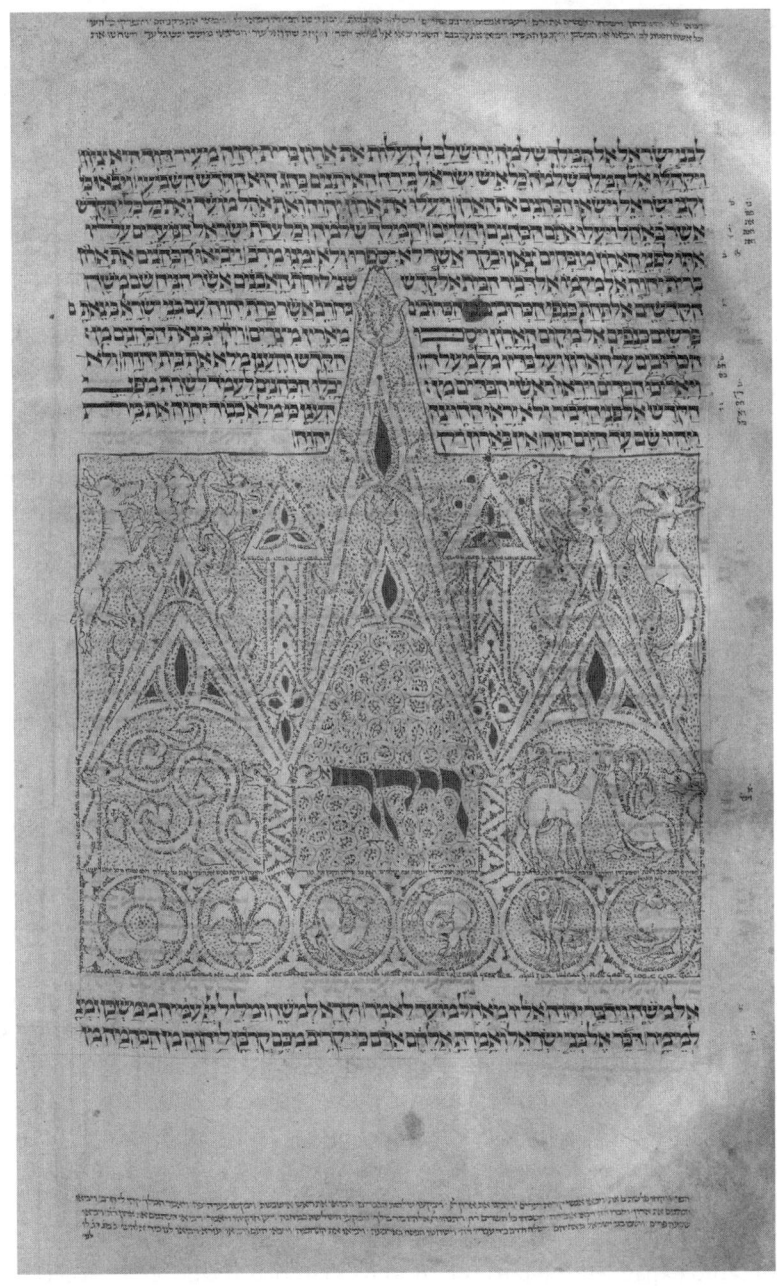

Figure 45. Copenhagen, Kongelige Bibliotek, MS Hebrew 11, *Pentateuch*, fol. 104ᵛ (thirteenth century)

being like Jews, who saw only "with carnal and not spiritual eyes."[499] And, in 1286, the same language was deployed in a Jewish-Christian (*Contra judaeos*) debate: "We do not adore these images that you see in churches, but the holy mother Church sets them out as a kind of mirror, so that seeing them with corporal eyes they see them with the eyes of the mind."[500] Some Christians, too, maintained that art could, at best, serve only mundane subjects. Henry of Ghent denied that corporal images can represent the invisible God, and he was followed by Durand of Saint-Pourçain. who reiterated the basic tenet that images are arbitrary signs that can reproduce only the accidents of appearance and not the substance; hence, veneration of them constitutes idolatry.[501] Like Luke of Tuy and Alexander of Halles before him, Durand objected specifically to attempts to represent theological mysteries as in the Throne of Mercy, the Trinitarian image of God holding the crucified Christ and joined by the dove of the Holy Spirit, at the center of the Metropolitan Museum shrine Madonna (Figure 28) and the Vallbona altarpiece (Figure 17). John Wycliffe and other fourteenth-century reformers continued to rail against Christian idolatry, citing such "abominable" confections as images of the Trinity.[502]

Pope Gregory's argument that Christ's Incarnation made possible the eye's oscillation between matter and spirit in art prevailed nevertheless,[503] and, especially after the attack on images in the Byzantine Empire known as Iconoclasm (726–843), defenses of images' spiritual potential were reinforced. Already in the mid-eighth century, someone in the papal entourage strengthened the original papal dictum by linking it explicitly to Christ's dual nature: "He appeared visible to show us the visible," and embedded the new argument in Gregory's widely circulated *Registrum*, where it passed as a genuine edict of the Church Father.[504] Baudri of Bourgueil built on the eighth-century Gregorian interpolation: "I venerate these things, but it is Jesus himself that I always adore." Alan of Lille maintained that painting made visible what cannot be seen and concluded that "just as you see completely the total person of Christ, that is the head with limbs painted in visible form, so you can understand more easily those parts that are said to be invisible."[505] Honorius Augustodunensis distilled the arguments in support of images in a so-called *triplex ratio*: instruction, affect, and recall,[506] and Jacobus da Voragine expanded the purpose to four: memory, devotion, instruction, and moral example.[507] Circa 1200, when the dicta were paraphrased in the prologue to the *Pictor in Carmine*, an elevating aspect was assumed: "Since the eyes of our contemporaries are apt to be caught by a pleasure that is not only vain, but even profane ... it is an excusable concession that they should enjoy at least that class of pictures that can put forward divine things to the unlearned."[508]

Most theologians advanced and elaborated the authoritative arguments. Bonaventure staged the process, beginning with the clearing away of worldly distractions through focusing on Christ's human life and ending with pure contemplation.[509] Thomas Aquinas claimed among other things that the devout could distinguish the physical object from the "rational creature" represented on it and, therefore, could be led to venerate not the representation but God himself.[510] Referring to Aristotle's *De memoria et reminiscentia*, he argued that veneration of an image of Christ rises, de facto, to reverence of God.[511] At the end of the century, Durand of Mende defended the power of pictures to span the visible and the numinous by pointing out that the Savior's dual nature facilitated the movement from the material realm to the spiritual: "It is not Christ, but through it, I believe in Christ; I do not worship the pictured picture, but I honor the figure."[512] Ugo Panziera da Prato's *Trattato della Perfezione* of c. 1320 brought the incarnational argument full circle when it compared Christ himself to a panel painting that must first be conceived and imagined mentally, then sketched, outlined, and modeled, colored and enfleshed, and finally rendered in relief.[513] And a few years later, the Sienese sculptor Lando di Pietro, who covered a crucifix with parchment to imitate Christ's skin and wounds, left a note inside the head that reads: "It is [Jesus Christ crucified Son of God living and true] that one must adore and not this wood."[514]

It followed that, as Durand had asserted in theory, Christ's own person was used in practice to bridge this world and the next. Thus, "Saint Luke's" Lateran panel in the Sancta Sanctorum came to be positioned between the altar containing the reliquary with stones and soil from the Holy Land and a mosaic of angels bearing him to heaven, figuring Augustine's assertion that Christ had himself never fully ascended (Figure 15).[515] Matthew Paris incorporated the idea in his *Historia Anglorum*, where he depicted Christ disappearing into a cloud to illustrate his discussion of the impression of the Lord's feet that had been brought to England (London, Brit. Lib., Roy. MS 14. C. VII, fol. 146); but he also reminded the reader that the image of Christ's face was preserved in the *Veronica* so that his "memory might be cherished on earth." Interpreting the opening of the sixth seal as the destruction of the Jews, the Gulbenkian Apocalypse figures the epochal event in terms of the introduction of images (Figure 10), curiously picturing Christ's face as a classical bust merging with the Temple curtain, thereby encapsulating Christian art's own twin origin in Judaism and paganism. A play between image and spirit also activates the Rosano Crucifix (Plate X): the God-Made-Man is suspended on a blue cross framed with ornamental bands punctured by gold disks that echo the red-ringed nails attaching the pictured Christ to it.

Words on Images

As Augustine had already noted, the very ornamenting of matter was elevating;[516] following him, Matthew of Vendome asserted that paintings ennoble stone as rhetorical figures decorate poems,[517] and Matthew Paris elaborated the notion when he claimed that the value of a reliquary's metal actually proves that the saint's life depicted on it is true and contributes to the people's faith in the relics inside.[518] The job of inspiriting often fell also to inscriptions, which, as Pope Gregory had already acknowledged, were epistemologically like pictures and in dialogue with them. Indeed, a foundation of Christian theology was the belief that Christ was the "word-made-flesh" who had replaced Jewish Scripture in his very person (Jn 1:14, 1:17).[519] On the Arnstein window (Figure 33), for instance, the dark tablets of Law inscribed by God's finger reinforce the notion conveyed in the images that Jews had petrified the covenant and no longer understood its true meaning. Symbolizing animate Christianity, the flowing scroll in the *Traditio legis* in the Berzé-la-Ville apse manifests the process of God's establishing his Church on earth (Figure 32).[520] Words borrowed from liturgical texts and other writings in the twelfth-century apse of the upper church of San Clemente in Rome function together with the panoply of pictorial motifs to create enigmas that parallel Gilbertus Crispinus's claim that "as letters are figures and signs of words, so are pictures similitudes and annotations of written things."[521] An inscription beneath the Crucifixion on an altar of 1135–40 from Lisbjerg (near Aarhus in Denmark) exhorts the faithful: "Believe and doubt not that my death is life" (Figure 46).[522]

From at least the ninth century, God's names were impressed onto Eucharistic wafers—*XPS, IHS, DS,* or ☧ (the monogram of Jesus's epithets)[523]—to identify the generic body with the specific person.[524] Honorius Augustodunensis explained:

> The image of the Lord with letters is imprinted onto the bread because the image and name of the emperor is inscribed on the

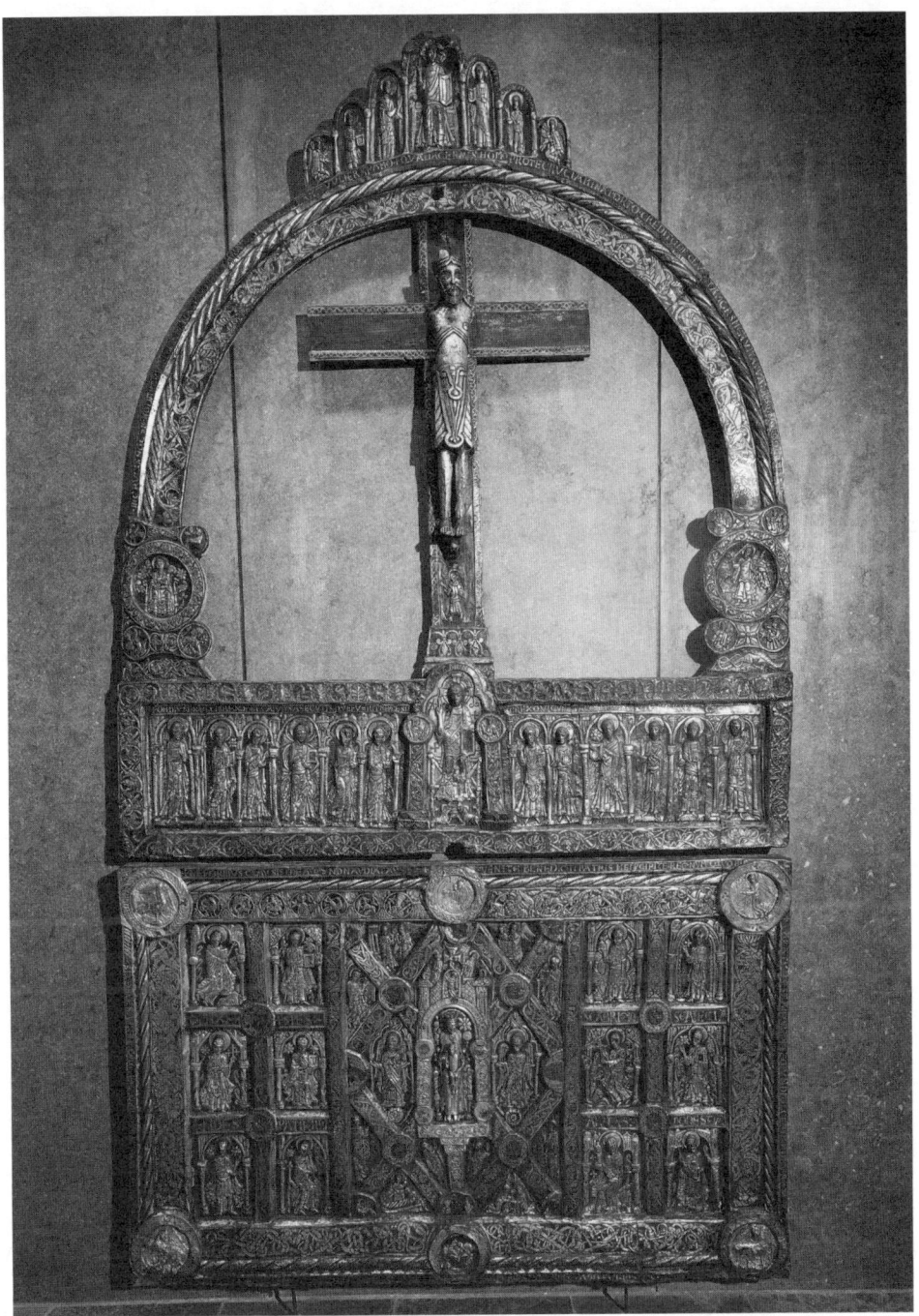

Figure 46. Copenhagen, Nationalmuseet, Lisbjerg altar (twelfth century)

coin and through this bread, God's image is restored in us and our name is written in the book of life.⁵²⁵

Increasingly, images of the Crucifixion and similar motifs were also embossed on Hosts, as on the Vallbona altarpiece.

Like labels on relics, inscriptions also controlled the potential for images to open up more than one meaning that had worried such critics of pictures as Theodulf.⁵²⁶ Even though the learned readers of a late twelfth-century sacramentary in Tours would have had no doubt what the two personifications stand for (Figure 47),⁵²⁷ identifying labels in the upper margins identify *ECCL[ES]IA* and *SYNAGOGA*. The *MOYSES* on the Arnstein window and the *SANCTA MARIA ROTONDO* on the pilgrimage badge (Figure 2) serve the same function. Such other labels as the *PARAω* in the Exodus from Egypt at Ceri (Figure 37) encode meaning through their incorporation of exotic alphabets; the use of the Greek omega there indexes not only the Egyptian king's foreignness but also, at the conclusion of the cycle, the idea that Christ is the alpha and the omega (as on the Saint-Martin-du-Canigou cartulary (Figure 8), thereby linking the Old Testament cycle to the adjacent Last Judgment. Some labels underscored the protagonist's aspects; the OMNIPOTENS, STELLA SOLIS PARENS, and PROLIS on the Lyon ivory (Figure 30),⁵²⁸ for instance, sort out the divine Father, Mary as the Mother of the Sun, and the Son. At the same time, they construct an ascent from the God-Made-Man to the heavenly ruler through the Holy Spirit. *HERETICI* on the Salzburg drawing leaves no doubt as to what the Apocalyptic dragon symbolizes (Figure 44).⁵²⁹ The placement of the inscriptions and their material also created meaning; writing on tombs, for instance, animated the defunct within.⁵³⁰

More extensive labels reinforced or on occasion even cast doubts on images' ability to convey spiritual truths. Legends reported that Saint Helena, for example, had had to rely on the original titulus, *INRI*, to distinguish Christ's cross from the those of the two thieves after a Jew disclosed the three in the burial spot on Golgotha.⁵³¹ A caption beneath the depiction of Abraham Greeting the Angels in the late twelfth-century church of San Pietro in Valle near Ferentillo (Umbria) underscores the belief that even Abraham was unable to understand the (Trinitarian) meaning of the Old Testament epiphany: "He sees three with his mind and intensely praises one."⁵³² The "neither God nor man" caption beneath Moses at the Burning Bush in Ceri confirms the episode's basic argument that before the Incarnation, even prophets

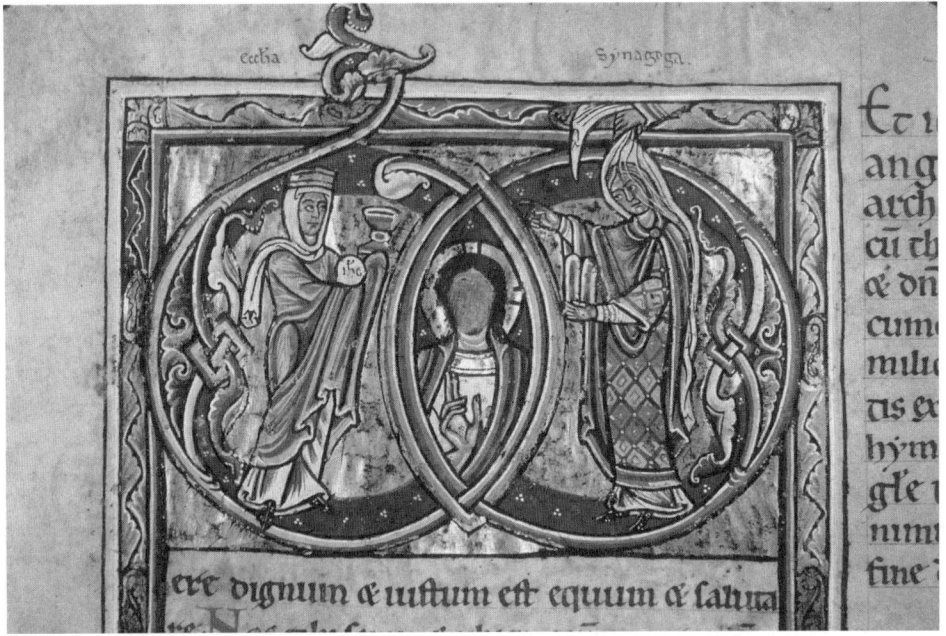

Figure 47. Tours, Bibliothèque municipale, MS 193, sacramentary, fol. 71ʳ (twelfth century)

could not see God. The narrative cycles in the atrium of San Marco are accompanied by extensive written texts that explain and often interpret the pictures (Plate XIII); and biblical personages are included holding passages from their inspired writings.

Typology

Providing a foundation of the very making of art, the acceptance of the Old Testament as a prophecy of Christ was embedded in the Gospels. John, for instance, proclaimed that "the law indeed was given through Moses; grace and truth came through Jesus Christ" (Jn 1:17).[533] In addition to Moses (represented in the Arnstein window receiving the *LEX DEI*), David was particularly important because he was Christ's human ancestor whose poetry, Christians believe, prophesied the Messiah. Thus, following a series of full-page miniatures illustrating Christ's life, the Saint Albans Psalter portrays the Old Testament king being inspired by the dove of the Holy Spirit (Figure 40).[534] The Basel reliquary elaborates the concept by representing the Virgin and Child standing on the Lion of Judah held by David and supported by other Old Testament prophets rendered in enamel around the base (Figure 3); an inscription makes the point: "King David, strong in hand, desirable to look at; Here my descendent and savior of the world that I have prophesied by God." The long cylindrical form supported on architecture itself alludes to the Tower of David in Jerusalem and thereby evokes the celestial city introduced through the relics inside.

Called "typology" from the Greek for seal (*typos*) which becomes legible only when the matrix is impressed in matter, the concept that the words of Hebrew Scripture were incarnated in Christ provided a fundamental paradigm of art's spiritualizing potential. Bede had maintained that the secrets of faith were revealed though meditation on the multiple meanings contained in the Bible; Bruno of Segni recognized that only Christian faith could tease out art's underlying truth;[535] Hugh of Saint-Victor echoed an assault going back to Augustine that Jews read God's words literally without probing their true significance, that is carnally, not spiritually, which Hugh's protégé, Abbot Suger, incorporated into a depiction in the stained-glass windows at Saint-Denis of prophets pouring grain into a mill that Saint Paul grinds into New Testament "flour," "urging us onward from the material to the immaterial."[536] The argument is diagrammed in the Tours Sacramentary, tellingly within intersecting letters; God's hand emerges from heaven to lift the veil from the face of *Synagoga*, who holds the tablets of the Law and wears a highly ornamented aqua, pink, and vermillion dress to emphasize her superficial, sensual appeal. *Synagoga* points to her successor, the simply garbed *Ecclesia*, who presents a chalice and a Host, Christ's blood and body. The realization of the two covenants and a fusion of word and flesh, Christ himself (his facial features obliterated later) emerges at the intersection of the framing letters *V* and *D* of "uere dignum" (the opening of the Preface to the Mass).

Not just the words but also Old Testament objects imbued with divine aura were read as typologies in Christian art, foremost among them the Tabernacle and Jerusalem Temple. *La belle verrière*, for instance, portrays Christ bearing the text of Isaiah 40:4 (recycled through Luke 3:5) to contrast the dark, imageless words with the full Christian realization in vivid, light-filled colors (Figure 5); the glass's thirteenth-century setting reframes the earlier image-relic within the tabernacle of Hebrew

Scripture, supported on four columns.⁵³⁷ The Virgin Mary above the right portal of Amiens is flanked by Moses and Aaron and crowned by the Ark of the Covenant (Figure 25). The curtain that had blocked the view into the Holy of Holies in these sacred structures, torn asunder at Christ's death (depicted in the middle panel of the Arnstein glass; Figure 33), is displayed at the bottom of the Theophanu Gospels cover to reveal Mary and Christ (Plate V); likewise, it is drawn back in the scene of the Annunciation in Padua to emphasize the belief that, unlike the first covenant, the new one is open to all (Plate XII). The interface between the outer precinct and sancta sanctorum underlies the use of fictive hangings decorating the lower registers in many fresco cycles, for example, at Berzé-la-Ville and in the white dado of Ceri; it was an essential metaphor of art as such, asserting the capacity to figure one thing under the image of another.⁵³⁸

Realizing the Old Testament typology, the bowl of a gilded bronze censer in Trier (Domschatz) evokes the earthly Jerusalem presided over by the crowned king Solomon, seated on his lion-throne and holding an orb, and populated by Moses, Isaiah, Jeremiah, Aaron, Melchizedek, Abraham, Isaac, and Abel and covered by a lid with Peter, Paul, James, and John, and the enthroned Christ: "Solomon, while caring for the terrestrial realm, prefigures the true king of peace though all times." And other Old Testament objects, too, participated in typological inspiriting. Among the most important was the brazen serpent that Christ himself had adduced to explain the Crucifixion: "This Son of Man must be lifted up as a serpent was lifted up by Moses in the wilderness, so that everyone who has faith in him may in him possess eternal life" (Jn 3.14).⁵³⁹ In a late-eleventh-century manuscript from Liège containing the *Physiologus* (a late antique treatise on animals), the typology is deployed to illustrate the entry on the plover, a bird believed to have diagnostic power, and in turn, redemptive healing through Christ's death on the cross (Figure 48).⁵⁴⁰ The scene in the lower right labeled "where Moses raised the serpent in the desert" shows the prophet reading a book while pointing to a snake entwined below (damaged) slithering up a tree (to recall the source of sin in the garden of Eden). Two Jews focus on Moses's words, while four beardless (gentile) men begin to turn toward Jesus rising from a hillock with arms outstretched—a hybrid of the crucified and resurrected Savior labeled "This one takes away our sins."⁵⁴¹

Citing the brazen serpent among other typologies, Bede had already in the eighth century applied an art metaphor to juxtaposed scenes from the Old and New Testaments (including the Brazen Serpent) by noting

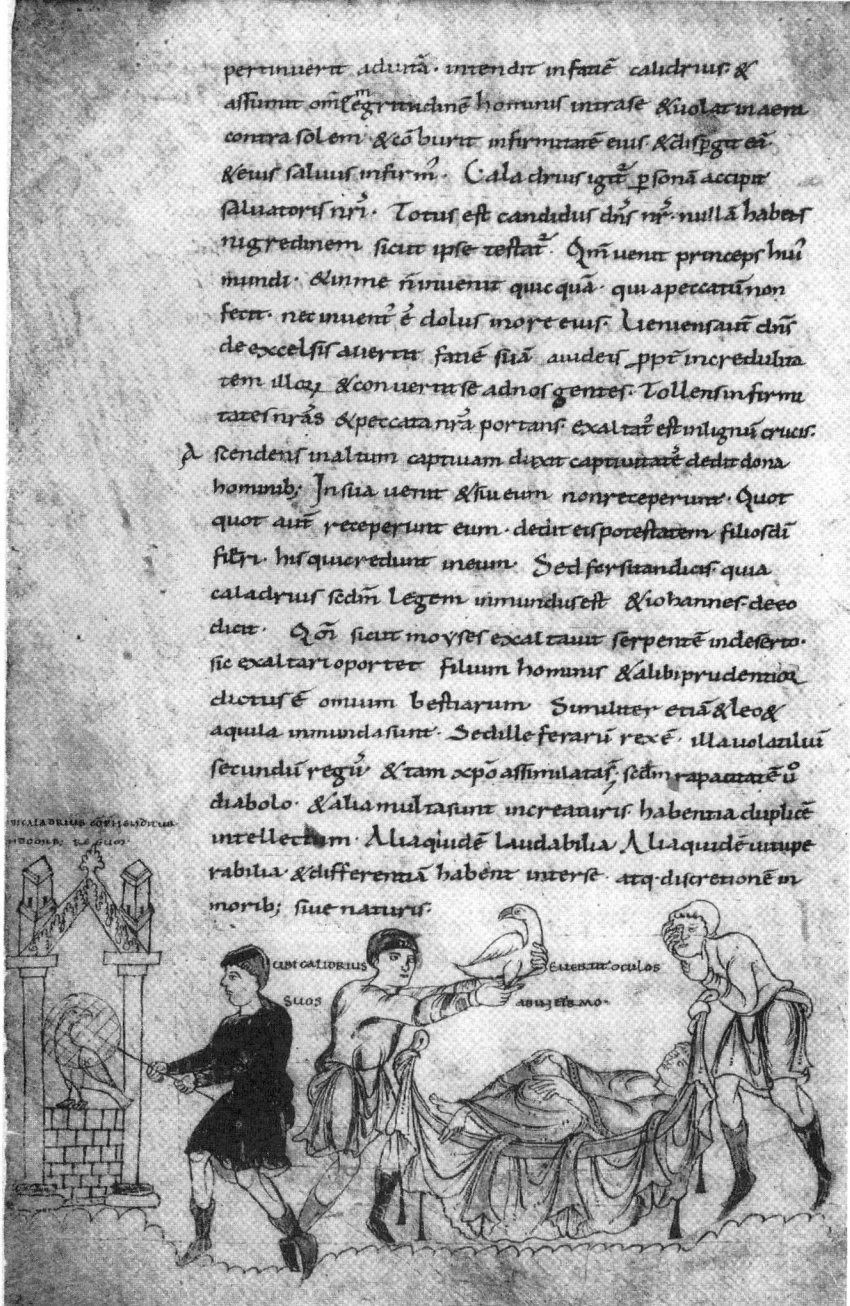

Figure 48. Brussels, Bibliothèque royale, MS 10074, *Physiologus*, fol. 142ʳ–143ᵛ (eleventh century)

CHAPTER 4: SPIRIT

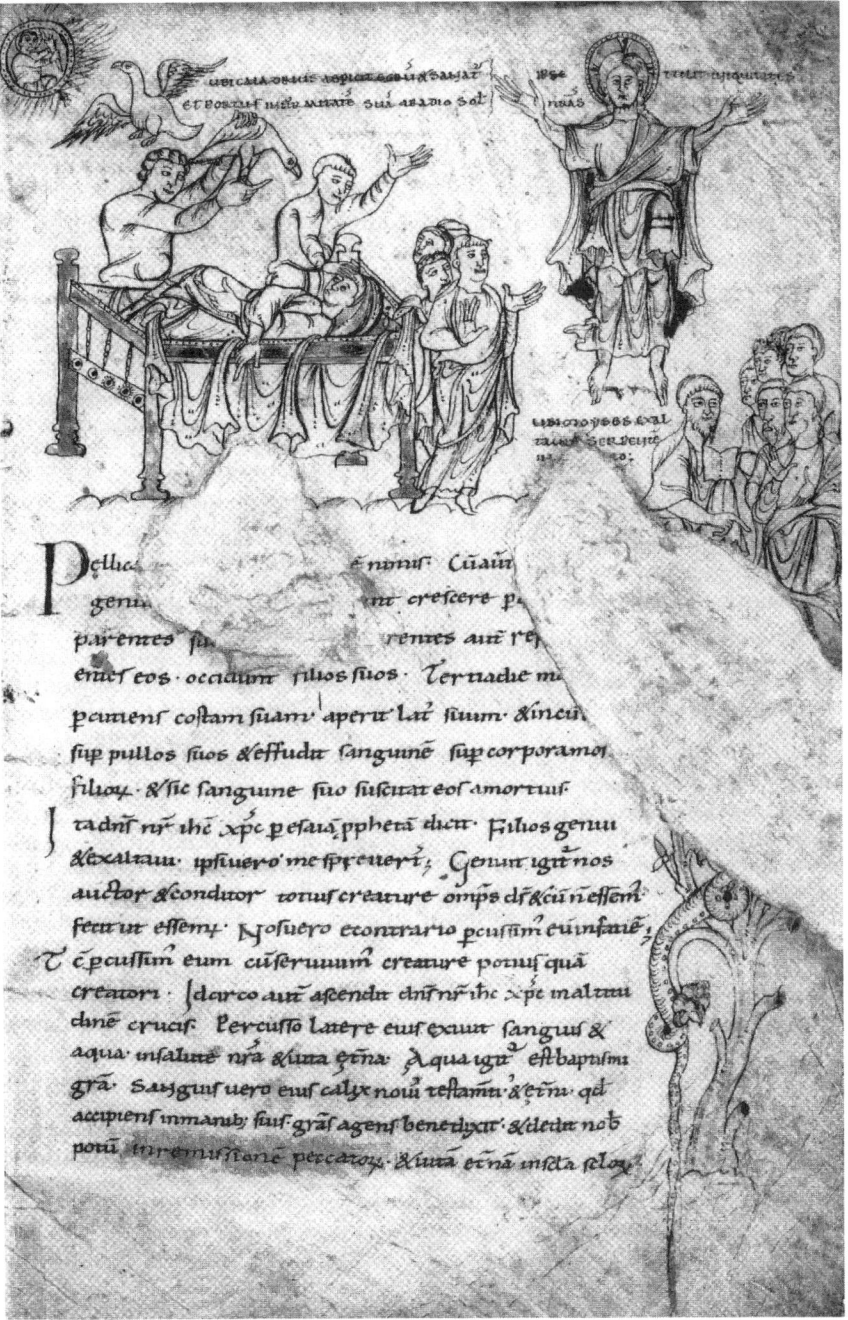

Pelli........ enuit cuaui
genu............... creſcere p.....
parenteſ ſu............ renteſ aũt re.....
enuſ eoſ · occidunt filioſ ſuoſ. Ter uache m.....
patienſ coſtam ſuam aperit lat ſuum & incu.....
ſup pulloſ ſuoſ & effudit ſanguine ſup corpora mo....
filio·. & ſic ſanguine ſuo ſuſcitat eoſ a mortuiſ
J radn̅ſ n̅r ih̅c x̅p̅c p eſaia· ppheta dicit. Filioſ genui
& exaltaui. ipſi uero me ſpreuerũt. Genuit igit̃ noſ
auctor & conditor totiuſ creature om̅pſ dſ & cũ n eſſem̃
fecit ut eſſemuſ. Noſ uero econtrario pcuſſim̃ eũ in faciẽ
&̃ c p cuſſim̃ eum cũ ſeruuum creature potiuſ quã
creatori. Idcirco aut aſcendit d̅n̅ſ n̅r ih̅c x̅p̅c in altitu
dine cruciſ. Percuſſo latere eiuſ exiuit ſanguiſ &
aqua in ſalute n̅r̅a & uita etn̄a. Aqua igr̃ eſt baptiſmi
gr̃a. Sanguiſ uero eiuſ calix noui teſtam̃t̃ & etn̄i. qd
accipienſ in manibuſ ſuiſ gr̃aſ agenſ benedixit & dedit nob
potũ in remiſſione peccator̃. & uita etn̄a in ſcła ſcło·.

that the Greek word for picture is *zoographia* (literally "living writing.")[542] Other exegetes pointed to under-drawing covered by paint or the clay mold destroyed when a bronze figure is made using the lost-wax process to argue that spiritual elevation was inherent in typology. The seal also offered up an argument according to which things are perceived but their matter is not transferred; a perfect analogue to divine entrance into the world,[543] it was cited in discussions of the Incarnation, vision, memory, human soul, and the Eucharist.[544] Christ's image itself functioned in the fashion of a seal matrix, as in the seal-shaped frame of the Tours Sacramentary and the sixth seal of the Lisbon Apocalypse. The connection is implied in Matthew Paris's *Chronica Maiora* (Cambridge, Corpus Christi College, MS 16, fol. 53ᵛ) by the fact that, other than the *Veronica*, the only image pasted in as an object is the emperor's seal, and it is explicit in prayers to the *Veronica* as an "impression" on the cloth.[545] On the Fritzlar Pietà (Plate VIII) and Victoria and Albert booklet (Figure 13), Christ's chest wound has the form of the mandorla-shaped seal, which in turn resembles an eye, lips, and a vulva.[546]

Scriptural concord came to be understood as fundamentally pictorial.[547] After affirming the importance of the historical sequence unfolded in Scripture's literal account, Anselm of Canterbury, for example, maintained at the start of his widely read *Why God Became a Man* that "these appropriatenesses may be set out as pictorial representations of this physical reality ... All these are beautiful notions, and are to be viewed like pictures."[548] Hugh of Saint-Victor rephrased the argument: "In an image the mystical understanding is painted, and through accessible similitudes, of those things that are understood spiritually, a clear demonstration is figured"; and he even reverted to a pictorial simile: "Just as in the same passage of Scripture the [foolish man] will commend the color or the form of the figures, so [the wise man] will praise the sense and the signification."[549] Typological currents ran throughout fictive debates with Jews, such as the one on Mallorca in 1286, that continually reiterated and refreshed image theory.

In much medieval art, Christian understanding is mapped directly onto depictions of Old Testament subjects. The Utrecht Psalter, for instance, imagines the "Lord" of Psalm 148 as *Christ in Majesty* (Figure 38); the Hildesheim doors (Figure 23) and the walls of Ceri present Christ as the agent of creation;[550] and the Coronation Mantle realizes the traditional interpretation of Psalm 90 (91) by picturing Christ trampling the beasts (Figure 14). A terse depiction of the separation of Light and Dark at the start of the Salerno ivories actually activates the movement from word to Christ's human presence by extending one arm of the X in *LUX* (light) to form a cross that drops into the next depiction, which portrays an anthropomorphic Christ as agent. Old Testament types flank the Arnstein Tree of Jesse, itself the embodiment of (re-)creation and restoration. It renders Isaiah's prophecy "And there shall come forth a rod out of the stem of Jesse, and a branch shall grow out of his roots" (11:1) as a genealogical schema with King David at the bottom (Mary's progenitor) and Christ at the top infused by the seven gifts of the Holy Spirit.[551] Moses at the Burning Bush pictures the patriarch able only to look at the desiccated, thistle-bearing side so that the (Christian) viewer alone is led to *understand* the plant not-consumed-by-fire as a type and hence *see* Christ. A depiction of Samson subduing the lion on an early twelfth-century mosaic behind the altar of Sant'Orso in Aosta assumes a typological reading (Judg 14:15); the Jewish hero with flowing tresses subduing the lion is a precursor of Christ's victory over the devil (Figure 49).[552]

Going back to the very earliest Christian art, such juxtapositions of Old Testament figures and events with their Christian "fulfillments" demonstrated the supersession of the one by the other and, in so doing, spiritual elevation. Two wheel windows from c. 1230 over the entrance to the south transept of Strasbourg Cathedral (Figure 50) (adorned outside with the famous flanking sculptures of *Church* and *Synagogue*) set the carnal Jewish sacrifices and their perpetrators Moses, Aaron, and others alongside the New Covenant, centered on Melchizedek, a type of Christian priesthood, all overseen by Christ himself.[553] Bernward's doors at Hildesheim extend the principle to history; the narrative begins at the upper left with the creation of humankind and descends to the Fall and Murder of Abel and then ascends on the right from the Annunciation of Mary to the Return to Paradise. Horizontal parallels reinforce the dynamic—the crucifix opposite the Tree of Life, for instance, and Eve holding Cain back to back with Mary and Jesus.[554] The palatine art in Louis the Pious's palace at Ingelheim had already deployed a similar structure.[555] At Ceri, where the Old Testament cycle most likely faced a New Testament series on the (destroyed) left wall, Joseph Fleeing Potiphar's Wife presents the Hebrew youth as a type of Christian virtue escaping from the temptress—whose pink robe embroidered with gems and patterns, jeweled tiara and earrings, and elaborate palace represent the seductiveness of material ornament itself. The "real" meaning of Joseph pulled from the well is established by fashioning the sacrificed brother after the Crucified Christ. The Savior actually appears to Moses in the flaming bush above the caption declaring the Lord's (and the image's)

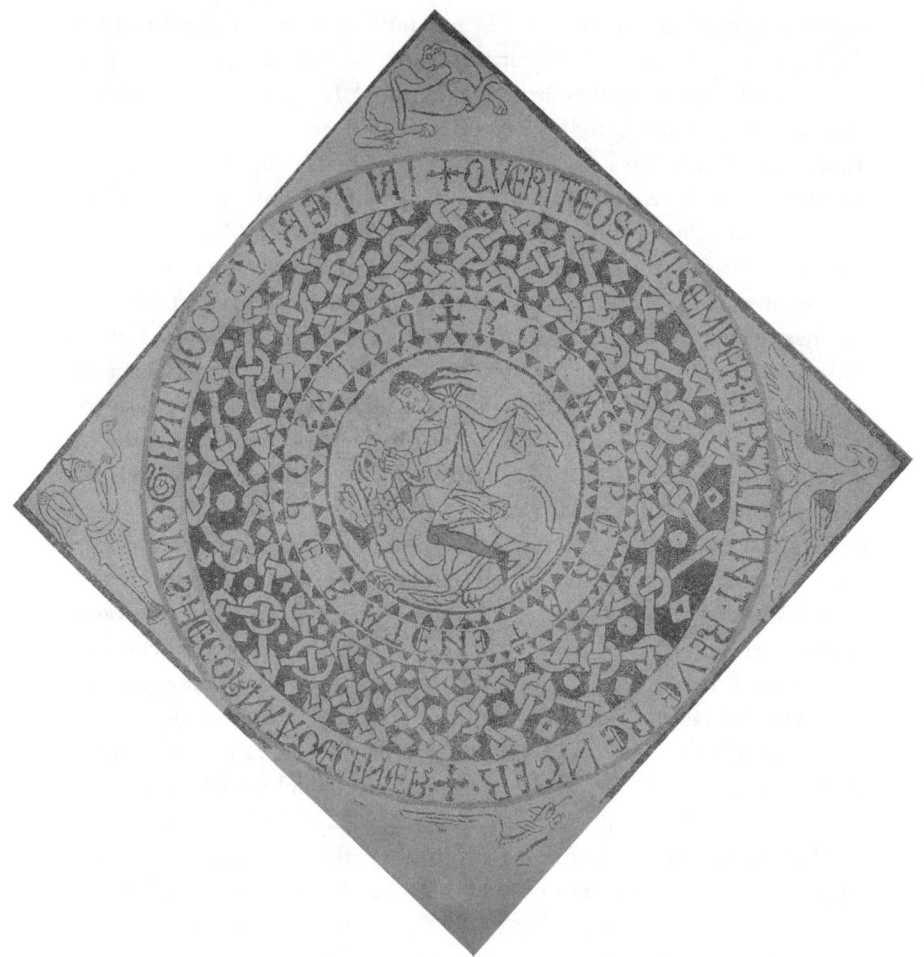

Figure 49. Aosta, Sant'Orso, mosaic (twelfth century)

duality, and the Last Judgment around the corner underscores the reading of Moses and the Israelites crossing the Red Sea as the baptized entering heaven. Similar typological depictions on the Salerno ivories are articulated through format, placement, and even style (see Figure 29).[556]

New Testament subjects tracked spiritual itineraries too. Rendering Christ's earthly life in organic, flesh-like ivory, the cover of Queen Theophanu's Gospels begins with the Nativity and then moves upward through the Crucifixion and Christ's return to heaven, itself evoking Moses's receiving the Ten Commandments on Mount Sinai

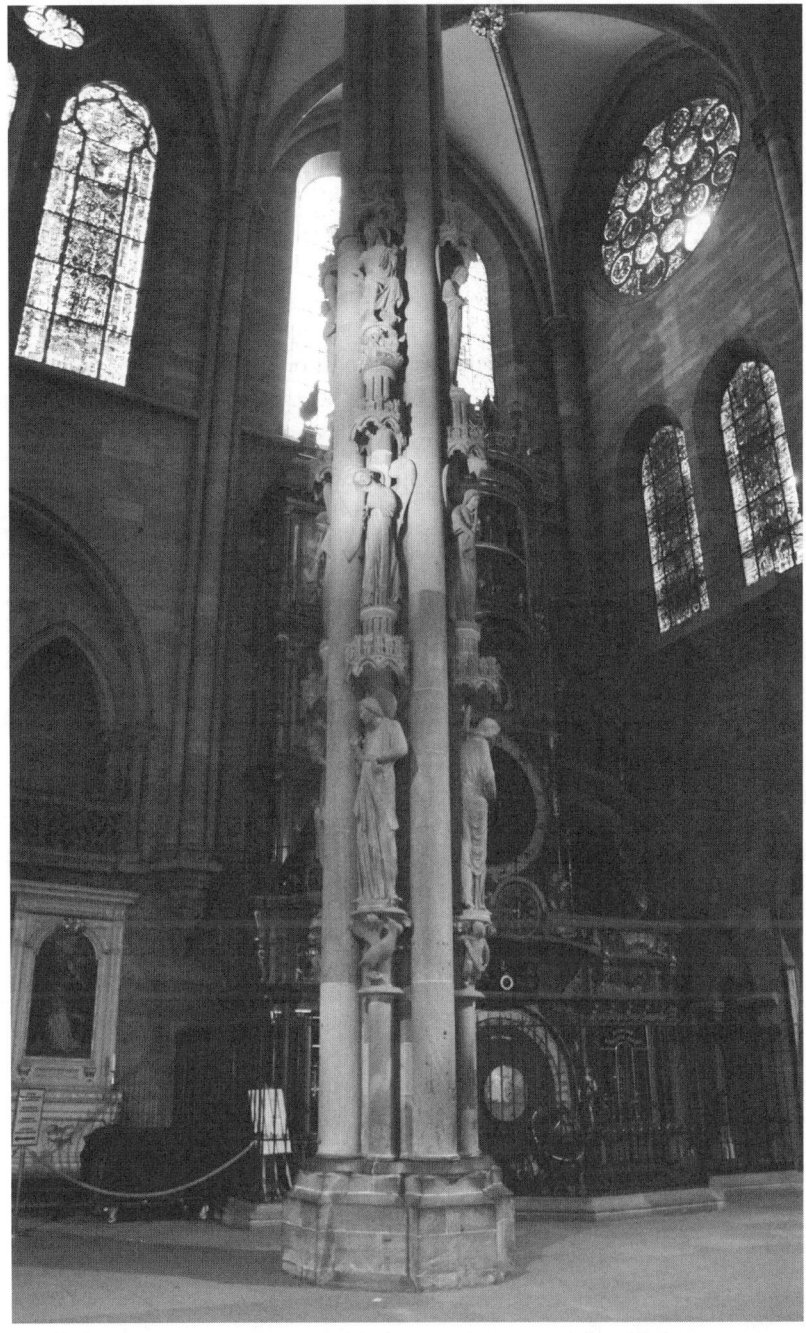

Figure 50. Strasbourg, cathédrale de Notre-Dame, south transept (thirteenth century)

to realize the claim that Jesus fulfilled the old law.[557] The gem-encrusted gold frame repeats the same trajectory in a different register and inserts it into image theory, beginning with the depiction of the queen kneeling before the Golden Madonna and then ascending through the local saints Pinnosa and Walpurg (portrayed within the convent area), Cosmas and Damian, Peter and Paul, and only then rising to the angels bearing Christ.[558] The flanking narratives on the Rosano Cross function in much the same way; beginning with Peter's Denial, an exemplar of penance that establishes the proper viewing tenor, they move upward through Christ's body framed by scenes of his Passion and post-Resurrection miracles, pause at the face, evoke compassion through the lamenting John and the Marys, and (most likely) directed the viewers to gaze with the apostles upon a scene of the Ascension (now missing).[559] On the Zwiefalten reliquary (Figure 4), the Holy Land stones (interpreted in Berthold's report) themselves map a virtual pilgrimage from the Savior's birth on earth, his death, and his return to heaven—echoed in the enamels. The apse of Berzé-la-Ville charts the spiritual journey in much the same way, beginning with saints at the bottom, passing through local saints and apostles, moving through Christ's feet and legs to his increasingly hieratic upper body, and to the head that intersects with the celestial wreath, and directing the gaze to an oculus (perhaps once filled with figured glass) again borne by angels, beings that partook in the divine nature and hence served as intermediaries.[560]

Saints, humans who had imitated their Lord in deed and death, played important roles in this elevating process. The thirteenth-century theologian Radulfus Ardens,[561] for instance, recommended that mortals imitate holy men and women as part of the hierarchical ascent. Saint Martin on the Saint-Martin-du-Canigou charter serves as the bridge between the confraternity of a church containing his relics and (with Mary) the heavenly Redeemer; at Ceri, the crucifixion of Andrew establishes an eye level micro ascent from devils attacking the evil executioner Egeas, the saint's own person (now destroyed but preserved in old photographs) being put to death in the same way Christ had been, and divine light radiating from above. A mid-thirteenth-century German version of Gregory's dictum maintained that "paintings of the saints in the churches" are particularly effective in redirecting vain thoughts toward the divine by virtue of the feelings they stir inwardly.[562] Depicted receiving wounds through looking at the heavenly seraph, Francis's imitation of Christ on the Paris reliquary is exemplary (Plate VI). The ecstatic gaze and praying gesture of the full-length figure of Mary Magdalene at

Écouis channels the viewer's attention (Figure 43). The veil of hair that simultaneously reveals and obscures her body modulates between stone, water, and cloud to convey her aspect as sinner and saint and, in so doing, conjures up redemption through Christ's dual nature.[563] In the Lateran Sancta Sanctorum (Figure 15), hagiographic frescoes are framed as independent panels that elide the traditional distinction between temporal history and an icon that directs attention to heaven, inviting the viewer to excavate the spiritual meaning of each event.[564] Likewise, the calling of Saint Peter which Giotto isolated as the subject of his famous *Navicella* that confronted those exiting San Pietro elevated a New Testament event into an allegory of the Church.[565]

Principles of typology also incorporated real persons and contemporary events in God's plan. Indeed, at the start of the thirteenth century, Thomasin von Zerclaere had already applied the Gregorian precepts to advance the educational value of vernacular literature, arguing in *Der welsche Gast* that mundane tales, too, could teach moral lessons[566]: "Whoever cannot comprehend higher things ought to follow the example [of the romances] ... As the priest looks at writing, so should the untaught man look at the pictures, since he recognizes nothing in the writing."[567] The *Majestas Domini* image was appropriated for the German emperor Otto III to assert that, while he rules on earth, his authority to do so comes from heaven.[568] The pope in the thirteenth-century Salerno *Exultet roll* (Museo Diocesano) is fashioned after Christ of the *Traditio legis*.[569] And the New York picture bible reads the crusades into the story of the Chosen People through the updating of costumes and weapons, while the stained-glass windows of King Louis IX's Sainte-Chapelle are permeated with allusions to Old Testament kingship.[570] In the contemporary stained-glass window donated by the furriers' guild in the ambulatory of Chartres Cathedral, scenes of battle alternate with ecclesiastical ceremonies to demonstrate the consonance of clerical with chivalric missions.

Inspiriting Things

Many works triggered spiritual elevation by manipulating materials, itself a form of typology. God had transformed Moses's staff into a serpent and empowered the prophet to do the same—as pictured both at Ceri and Arnstein, and Aaron's rod had budded, also pictured at Arnstein. The stone figure quoted from classical antiquity on the Jaca capital likewise signals Christianity's rejuvenating power (Figure 27) and, in turn, the ecstatic ascendance from mere matter, mirrored in the phoenix and other hybrids. The bird-beast-sea monster, a dragon originating in Sassanian art as a "senmurv,"[571] that forms the Hildesheim aquamanile activates transmorphic spiritualization (Figure 9); the vines growing upwards on its breast embody the cleansing and salvific power of the water that issues from its mouth. The eyes of the peacock feathers on the stem of the Francis reliquary (the birds of paradise pictured on the base symbolize the ever-changing character of beauty) engage the turquoise insets on the boss and the multi-eyed seraph that transforms the saint's very person. The Regensburg butterfly's translucent wings not only mimic nature but also suggest the intermediacy of Christ's two natures (Plate I), and the clever act of artistic legerdemain also assimilates the humble grub's metamorphosis into a beautiful creature to Christ's death on the cross for humankind. The relics and insect larvae in the capsule at the back share the aspect of dead matter brought back to life, but it is the craftsmanship itself that effects the idea of dematerialization, the transmutation of sand and pigments into luminescent enamel and the gold and pearls made to seem like antennae.

Whether dictated by economy or not, the common practice of transforming basic substances into facsimiles of more elevated ones operated in the way typology did, namely, putting lie to sensual impression and provoking spiritual meditation.[572] Fictive matter had its own rhetoric.[573] The imitation pearls around the page frames of the prayer book of Charles the Bald (Figure 18), for instance, or the markings of the Regensburg butterfly, like other illusionistic devices, assert art's fundamental deceptiveness. From the very beginning of Christian ecclesiastical building, decorations were framed in bands of painted gems that identify churches with the heavenly city of which they were deemed to be images; the tradition was perpetuated in the distinctly "Roman" apse at Berzé-la-Ville, where the main architectural fields are bordered with frescoed cabochons and pearls. Written on parchment painted to look like silk, the marriage charter of Otto II and Theophanu manifested the princess's Byzantine origins,[574] while the imitation cameo on the Urraca chalice (Plate III) inserts the contemporary king into the line of ancient rulers. Giotto introduced painted stucco to enhance the naturalism of leaves in certain frescoes of the Scrovegni Chapel,[575] and he orchestrated *faux marbre* panels and fictive sculptures along the dado to petrify astral and vegetal forms that simultaneously confirm art's power and expose its trickery. The manipulation of artistic effects served the process of spiritual transitus that engages, most notably, the imitation windows on the apse wall; human artifice is inferior to God's immanence through real glass, truth from shadow.[576] A verse on an enamel made for Henry of Blois succinctly sums up the concept: "Art comes before gold and gems, the creator before everything."[577] In the secular realm, too, surface fictions (allegories) clothed greater truths; illusionistic art was among them.[578] In applying the anagogical principle, Petrarch argued that allegorical painting could inspire the viewer to virtue.

Geometry, too, imbued art with spiritual content. In his influential *Isagoge geometriae*, the late eleventh-century French schoolmaster Gerbert of Aurillac (later Pope Sylvester II) maintained that mathematics enabled those who were not able to see with the mind's eye to comprehend the spiritual meaning in worldly things.[579] Ironically, to some extent a natural byproduct of procedures and tools used to fashion objects, mathematics was also understood to underlie God's created world.[580] Thus the compass and straight-edge deployed to form the letter *B* and text blocks in the Saint Albans Psalter convey Platonic concepts of nature's underlying perfect state,[581] and the circle in the Rothschild Canticles (New Haven, Yale University, Beinecke Rare Book and Manuscript Library, MS 404) enacts the author's conception of God as having a "center everywhere and a circumference nowhere."[582] The cosmological orbs in the Hildegard's *Scivias* (Figure 19), the summit of the Salzburg Chapel design (Figure 44), Suso's *Exemplar* (Figure 22), the Aosta and Westminster pavements (Plate IX), and Strasbourg transept windows likewise assimilate art to God's primordial creation.

Divine Light

In Scripture and medieval texts, light was the fundamental figure of the Divinity and the means through which God communicated with the human soul.[583] Christ declared himself the "light of the world" (Jn 8:12),[584] and the epithet on the Lyon ivory identifies Mary as "Mother of the Sun." Depictions of the Annunciation, for example in the Hitda Codex (Plate XI), show God entering as light. The *Annales regni Francorum* reports a miracle in the year 823 in which light transformed an ancient and nearly invisible picture of the Adoration in Como, rendering only the Virgin and Child and the gifts visible, but not the magi themselves;[585] and, indeed, light on the gold mosaics in churches (often inscribed with Latin words meaning shining or flashing: "micat," "rutilat," "resplendens," "perlustrans," or synonyms thereof) made the figures in them at least momentarily ungraspable and, in that way, re-enactments of the Incarnation.[586] At Berzé-la-Ville, the window at the top of the painted decoration symbolizes the invisible God who activates the perception of the created world,[587] and reflective disks once inserted into Christ's mandorla spiritualized the plaster to reinforce the iconography's claim that, when he established the Church by delivering the laws to Peter, he created a tie between heaven and earth.[588] The rising sun shining on the Reichenau disk would have served as a beacon, a light-house summoning the faithful to church (Figure 20).

By combining *lux* (light) and *lumen* (illumination), stained-glass windows fully realized the trope of inspiriting. Pierre de Roissy, chancellor of the Chartres chapter during the first decade of the thirteenth century, described stained-glass windows as "divine writings ... that throw the light of the true sun, that is to say the light of God, into the interior of churches, that is, into the hearts of the faithful by filling them with light."[589] The two round windows in Strasbourg evoke God's eyes. The effect is evident in the merging of the pictured Trinitarian rays with the actual light passing through *La belle verrière*'s halo, and it is manifested in the Arnstein glass's doves, the seven gifts of the Holy Spirit that fall into the world like Jupiter's gold coins that impregnated Danae. Indeed, light passing through glass without damaging it offered proof of the Incarnation and, hence, the efficacy of the earthly Church.[590] Alan of Lille asserted explicitly that glass represents the *sigillum virginitatis*, Mary's unbroken hymen through which the Holy Spirit entered her body, and the mid-twelfth-century Early Middle High German *Arnsteiner Mariengebet*, to which the Arnstein windows are closely related, stated the argument succinctly: "When you bore the child, you were in all ways clean and pure from congress with men. Whoever thinks that impossible, should consider glass, which is similar to you: the light of the sun shines directly through the glass, it is as intact and clean as it was before."[591] The Christmas Mass in the *Très riches heures* underscores similar ecclesial symbolism by merging the descending angels with the grisaille glass (which did not exist in the Sainte-Chapelle) (Plate VII). In contrast to the heavenly creatures, the saints in the windows are colored and the sculptures, *Grande Chasse*, and the altar are covered in reflective gold.

Differentiating God's irradiation of earth from the apparent elevation of physical matter brought about through the changing effects of time of day or shifting reflections from flickering candles and moving lamps, the Sainte-Chapelle miniature distinguishes worldly and divine light,[592] as Hildegard's *Scivias* does too by contrasting the painted flames with gold overlays. Changing sunlight on the pendentives of the San Marco creation cupola makes real the claim in the encircling titulus: "Here the flaming cherubim burn with Christ's love, always radiating the splendor of the eternal Sun." The Chiarito triptych also manipulates light to stratify spirituality:[593] on the right wing, painted rays descend from the Throne of Mercy unto the heads of nuns listening to a sermon; on the base (predella) of the central panel, light represents Eucharistic grace; and actual light reflected from the gilt-stucco relief that forms the main subject of Christ's ascension triggers a dynamic transformation that animates its subject, Christ's return to heaven.

The fundamental darkness of stained glass (called "divine gloom") placed an upper limit on what humans are capable of apprehending, in the same way that the distinctly deep tonality of some renderings of the *Veronica* created a tension that enacted Christ's dual nature,[594] or the way that the Trinity painted on the silvered mirror in Lorenzetti's Massa Marittima altarpiece did when it flashed in and out of perception (Figure 21). Darkness, too, activated a viewer's imagination and memory.[595]

Affect

Gregory's dictum had already recognized art's capacity to activate emotions and redirect them away from the material object toward the Deity, and the eighth-century interpolation introduced the idea of longing by likening images of Christ to portraits that set persons in search of departed lovers: "When you see the picture, you are inflamed in your soul with love of him whose image you wish to see."[596] Augustine himself claimed that Christ had had to disappear even from the apostles' sight after he showed himself following the Resurrection so that his followers could transfer to his divinity the love they felt for his person.[597] And in the middle of the twelfth century, Nicholas Maniacutius applied the idea to the Lateran *Acheropita*, comparing Luke's depiction of Christ to portraits of the deceased kept by mourners, which would comfort both his followers and those who never knew him with his appearance in the flesh and would stir them emotionally. Extending the argument to affection for all material objects, Hugh of Saint-Victor maintained that the engendered passion had to be directed to higher things:

> Now you are wandering in exile because, while you are attracted by the desire for temporal goods, you cannot find the love for

those things that are eternal. Indeed, the important beginning of your salvation can be that you have learned to change your love for the better, since you can be separated from all love of finite things, if a greater beauty be shown you that you would more gladly embrace.[598]

Understood as facilitating the channeling of contemplation from the object before the eyes to its spiritual counterpart, art's affective function grew in importance during the course of the Middle Ages.[599] On the Rosano Crucifix, Mary, John, and the two Marys at the ends of the cross's arms cue the proper kind of response, echoed in the scenes below by Christ's friends lowering the dead Savior's corpse and the weeping Peter embodying contrition. When Jacques Pantéleon sent the *Veronica* to his sister, he expressed the hope that "through contemplation of the image the nuns' pious affections might be more inflamed so that their minds might be made purer."[600] Around the same time, Matthew Paris included a representation of the Holy Face in a Psalter (London, Brit. Lib., Arundel MS 157) "in order for the soul be stirred to devotion."[601] And, although king Alfonso X had banned excessive grieving as evidence of a gentile lack of faith in the Resurrection,[602] compassionate sorrow engages visitors to Rodriguez's tomb (Figure 39) where, triggered by Mary and John's mourning at Christ's Crucifixion above, the lamenting figures evoke feelings that Isidore of Seville had already claimed would admonish the mind to remember the person.[603]

Compassion is the essence also of the virtual pilgrimage on the Victoria and Albert polyptych, which forces each object of Christ's suffering into the devout's consciousness, for instance, the pathetic blood-marked footprints. Suso also incorporated emotions into his diagram of "image" (Figure 22). From the existential abyss represented by the abstraction of the Divinity closed off by a curtain suspended in a triptych,[604] a red thread connects to gold disks on the chests of three men portraying the Trinity; it then divides and passes through a series of figures each with a disk on his or her breast, converging at the bottom on a figure praying the rosary, probably Suso's disciple Elsbeth Stagel, bypassing her alter ego, the elegantly dressed woman in the lower right whose "worldly love ends in grief" when death mows her and her lover down.[605] Although the caption reads, "Behold I must die and be crucified with Christ," the woman directs her prayers not at the Crucified, at least not directly, but toward a second depiction of herself holding a crucifix, fashioned after Mary stricken by grief at the foot of the cross (*mater dolorosa*)—the model of *compassio* (literally "suffering with").[606]

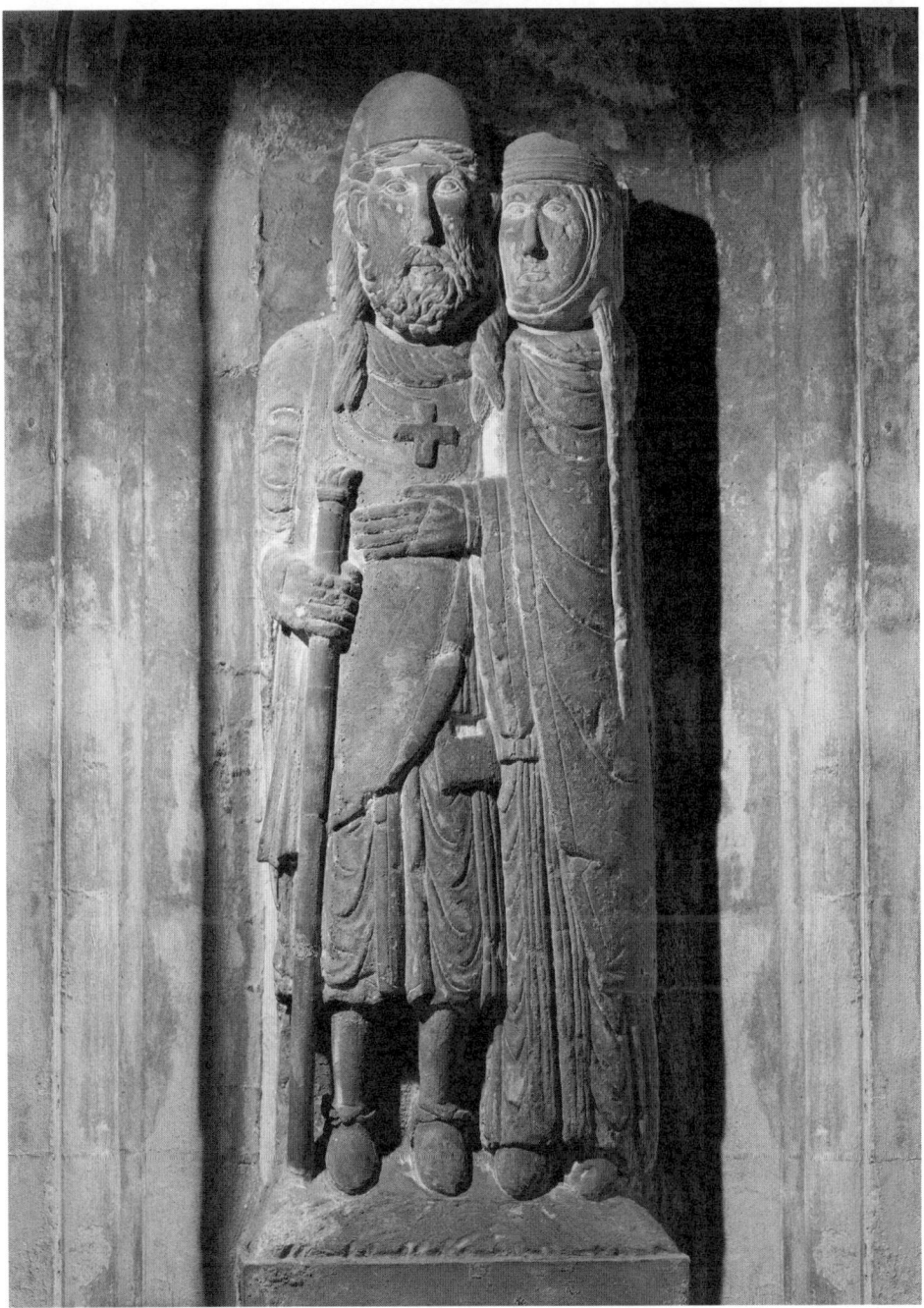

Figure 51. Nancy, Musée Lorrain, Hugh of Vaudemont and Aigeline of Burgundy from monastery of Belval (twelfth century)

Christ's scabrous skin and fountain-like wounds on the Fritzlar Pietà engender a similar kind of intimacy, first in Mary and then in the viewer, at once both repellent and sublime.[607]

Art elicited other emotions as well. Perhaps responding to the pseudo-Gregory image-dictum, love and longing imbue the funeral monument made after Hugh of Vaudemont's death in 1165 in the monastery of Belval (northern France), in its portrayal of the count tenderly embraced by his wife, Aigeline of Burgundy, upon his return from the crusades (Figure 51).[608] The couple is portrayed alive and standing to confirm faith in Christ's power to resurrect the dead, and the woman's affection for the man who had served God inspires others to do the same.[609] Tender compassion also unites Christ with his beloved John (and presumably the viewer) in devotional images excerpted from the Last Supper during the fourteenth century and set up separately for private devotion; in contrast to the violence of the Fritzlar Pietà, John has fallen asleep on Christ's breast and is being comforted by the Lord's gentle embrace.[610] At Lincoln Cathedral, sculpted angels adorning the choir convey paradisiacal bliss with their radiant smiles, representing the joyous return to God affected through the sacramental blessing staged at the altar.[611] The Écouis Magdalene's smile expresses the ultimate happiness of uniting with God. Fear was perhaps the dominant emotion art evoked, as in the lower right of Suso's *Exemplar*, a reminder that death lurks everywhere and that earthly love is a temporal trap. Shocking awareness is a theme of the *vanitas* imagery on the Moissac portal (Figure 24), and it is the theme of Last Judgments that dwell on the tortures awaiting the wayward in hell. The Holkham Picture Bible begins by reminding its viewers that those who believe in Christ portrayed on its pages "will know joy," but it concludes with sinners being boiled in a cauldron, "suffer[ing] pain without relief."[612]

Chapter 5
Book

RELIGIONS OF written revelation, Judaism and Christianity treated books of Scripture as sacred objects.[613] They retained the classical scroll form (*rotulus*) for special uses as liturgical rolls, devotional devices, prompts for interlocutors, amulets,[614] and charters (such as the Theophanu and Otto II marriage document and the Saint-Martin-du-Canigou cartulary; Figure 8).[615] The flowing scrolls in the *Traditio legis* on the Sant'Ambrogio ciborium (Figure 6) and Berzé-la-Ville apse (Figure 32), for example, represent God's contract with his Church on earth, a reference appropriated as well by the banderole (long scroll) with the exhortation "*sempre Ave M[aria]*" that the Virgin unfurls in the *Cantigas* to counter the demonic *characteres* (branding marks) locked within the circle and pentacle (Figure 41). Christians also deployed wax tablets on occasion; Hildegard is portrayed in the *Liber divinorum operum* translating her visions into texts and pictures on smoke-darkened surfaces;[616] conversely, the diptych inscribed by God's finger that Moses receives at the summit of the Arnstein window conveys the notion that the Old Covenant is both petrified and provisionary (Figure 33) and, as on the cover of Theophanu's Gospels (Plate V), replaced with God's own presence.

The codex comprising pages of animal skin stitched together and bound between covers (itself an Early Christian development) was, however, the dominant form of medieval book; it is Christ's principal attribute on the Saint-Martin-du-Canigou cartulary itself, *La belle verrière* (Figure 5), the Reichenau disk (Figure 20), and the Lyon ivory (Figure 30). Jews who treated the *sefer torah* (the scroll containing the Pentateuch) as a divine presence, (eventually) fitting it with a crown and clothing with a breastplate and mantle, did not embellish the sacred scrolls themselves; but, by the tenth century, near eastern Jews had appropriated the codex form for study and commentary,[617] and by the thirteenth century had begun to ornament some texts, including Passover Haggadot and study books (Figures 34 and 45).[618]

Codices varied in size and shape, although even the largest were portable. Hildegard of Bingen's Rupertsberg codex weighed 33 pounds (Figure 19); Charles the Bald's prayer book measures a mere 5 × 4 inches (Figure 18); and, at 3.8 × 2.7 inches, a contemporary devotional book in Montpellier (BU Médecine, H 396) is even tinier.[619] The depiction of the Christmas Eve Mass in the *Très riches heures* features three types of books (Plate VII), each with a history: the sacramentary through which the priest consecrates the Eucharist (see also Figure 47), the enormous antiphonals the choir follows,[620] and the Books of Hours from which pious women pray privately.

Most scriptural manuscripts comprised individual units or small compendia of texts and incorporated supplementary materials that enabled their use; the Copenhagen Pentateuch, for instance, includes liturgical texts and the Targum (rabbinical interpretation of biblical passages) in addition to the Hebrew Bible. In the Pentateuch, as in many manuscripts, frontispieces mark the main divisions. The Book of Psalms, essential in monastic rites and church services, circulated as a separate book,[621] and, like the Utrecht and Saint Albans psalters (Figures 38 and 40), it usually incorporated the canticles and/or such other texts as the calendar.[622] Gospels were almost always bound together to manifest the fundamental unity of the four accounts of Christ's life and included prologues that argued the canonicity of Matthew, Mark, Luke, and John, and canon tables that set concordant passages alongside one another. The Book of Revelation was often a stand-alone Scripture, frequently accompanied by a commentary that interpreted the esoteric visions; the Gulbenkian Apocalypse (Figure 10), for instance, includes Berengaudus's twelfth-century allegorical gloss, which accounts for such details of the illustration of the Breaking of the Sixth Seal as the weeping women of Jerusalem at the far left.

Until the development of the "University Bible" in thirteenth-century Paris, single volumes comprehending the Old and New Testaments were relatively rare and followed various patterns of adornment.[623] Charlemagne's undertaking to issue a revised and standardized Vulgate text generated such remarkable illustrated examples as the First Bible of Charles the Bald (Paris, BnF, MS lat. 1), in which intricate visual cross-references in the eight frontispieces disclose the relationship between Moses, Paul, and John—three men privileged to see God—and between David and his descendent Christ.[624] The Carolingian enterprise culminated in the San Paolo Bible of c. 870 with its (originally) twenty-five full-page miniatures, many rife with typological allusions.[625] The mid-twelfth-century Floreffe Bible (London, Brit. Lib., Add. MS 17737–38) goes further in figuring the reconciliation of diverse biblical accounts as a process of spiritual contemplation;[626] six full-page miniatures (once) brought together Old Testament prophecies, Gospel narratives, portraits, and symbols to engage the viewer in an erudite meditation on the mystery of God's plan as it is revealed in his Word. The so-called *bibbie atlantiche*, produced in the wake of the Gregorian Reform, deploy diverse systems.[627] A two-volume edition in Cividale del Friuli (Museo archeologico nazionale, Bib. cap., I-II) includes two full-page miniatures, one picturing the Fall of Adam and Eve, the other Christ and the Apostles, while the later Pantheon Bible (Vatican, Bib. Apos., Cod. Vat. lat. 12958) introduces narrative pictures throughout and formulates certain Old Testament subjects, Ezekiel, for example, as prophecies of Christ (fol. 152^v). Arguably, some of these Bibles were meant not to be read but rather to preserve Christianity's fundamental Scripture and to serve as monuments of the Church itself.[628] As gifts, they were also vehicles of interchange between patrons, including royals, and the religious foundations they sponsored.

Biblical paraphrases in vernacular tongues circulated from at least the ninth century and engendered expansions of sacred writ in response to new literary and social contexts.[629] A tenth-century Old English paraphrase of Genesis and other texts is embellished with such new material as the Fall of the Rebel Angels (Oxford, Bodleian Library, MS Junius 11),[630] and a twelfth-century Anglo-Saxon paraphrase of the first six books of Hebrew Scripture (London, Brit. Lib., MS Cotton Claudius B.IV) introduced extra-biblical legends that gained authority from the extensive cycle of traditional illustrations and, at the same time, provided a new way to read God's word.[631] The Paris manuscript of the *Meditations on the Life of Christ* greatly expanded the Gospels with legends and human touches to enhance accessibility;[632] it emphasizes Joseph's presence in Christ's life, for instance, elaborates Mary's role, and imagines such moments as when angels provided a banquet for Jesus after the Temptation (fol. 71^v). True picture books emerged during the thirteenth century, such as the one in New York (Pierpont Morgan Library MS M 638), in which texts were added (in three languages) by later users.[633] The early fourteenth-century Holkham Picture Bible (Figure 52) is accompanied by Anglo-Norman captions that provide the

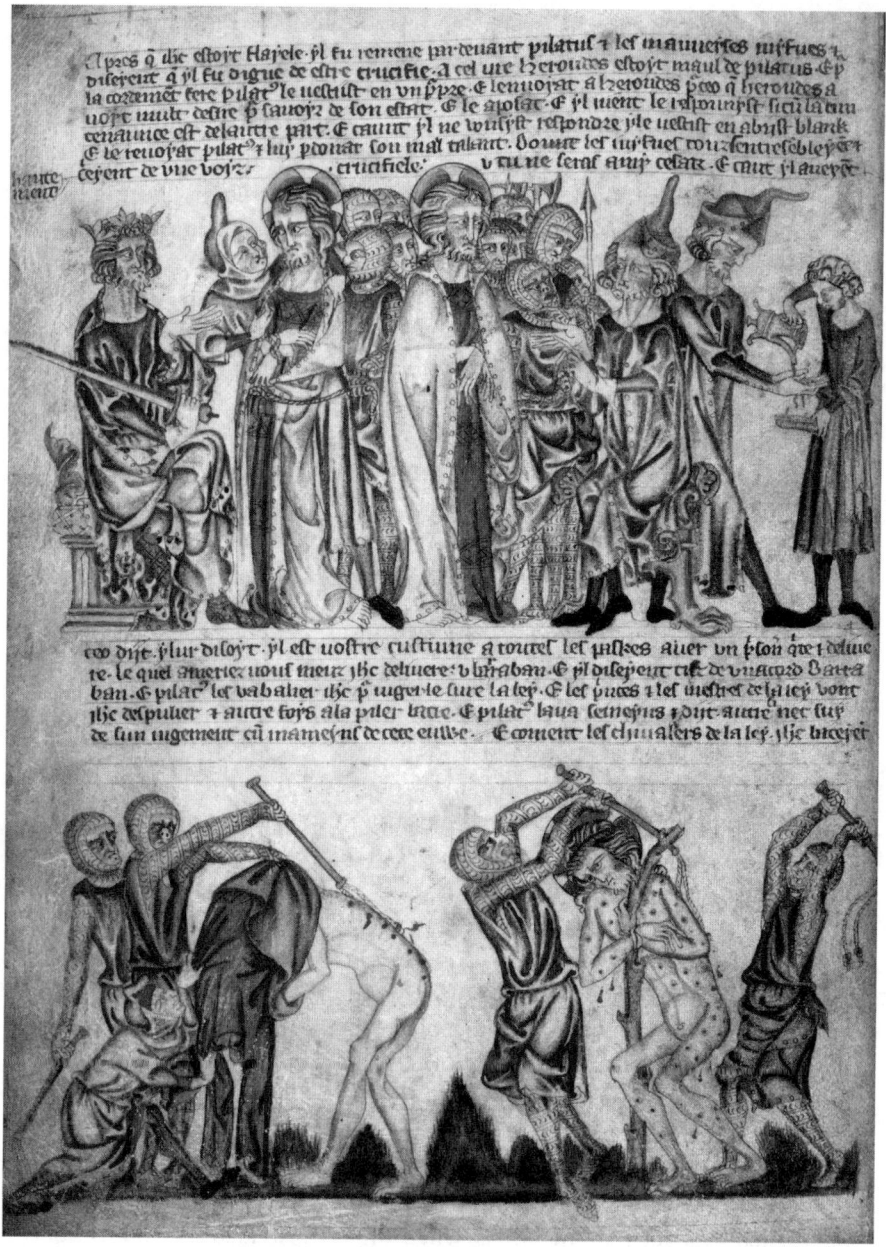

Figure 52. London, British Library, Additional Manuscript 47682, Holkham Picture Bible, fols. 30ᵛ–31ʳ (fourteenth century)

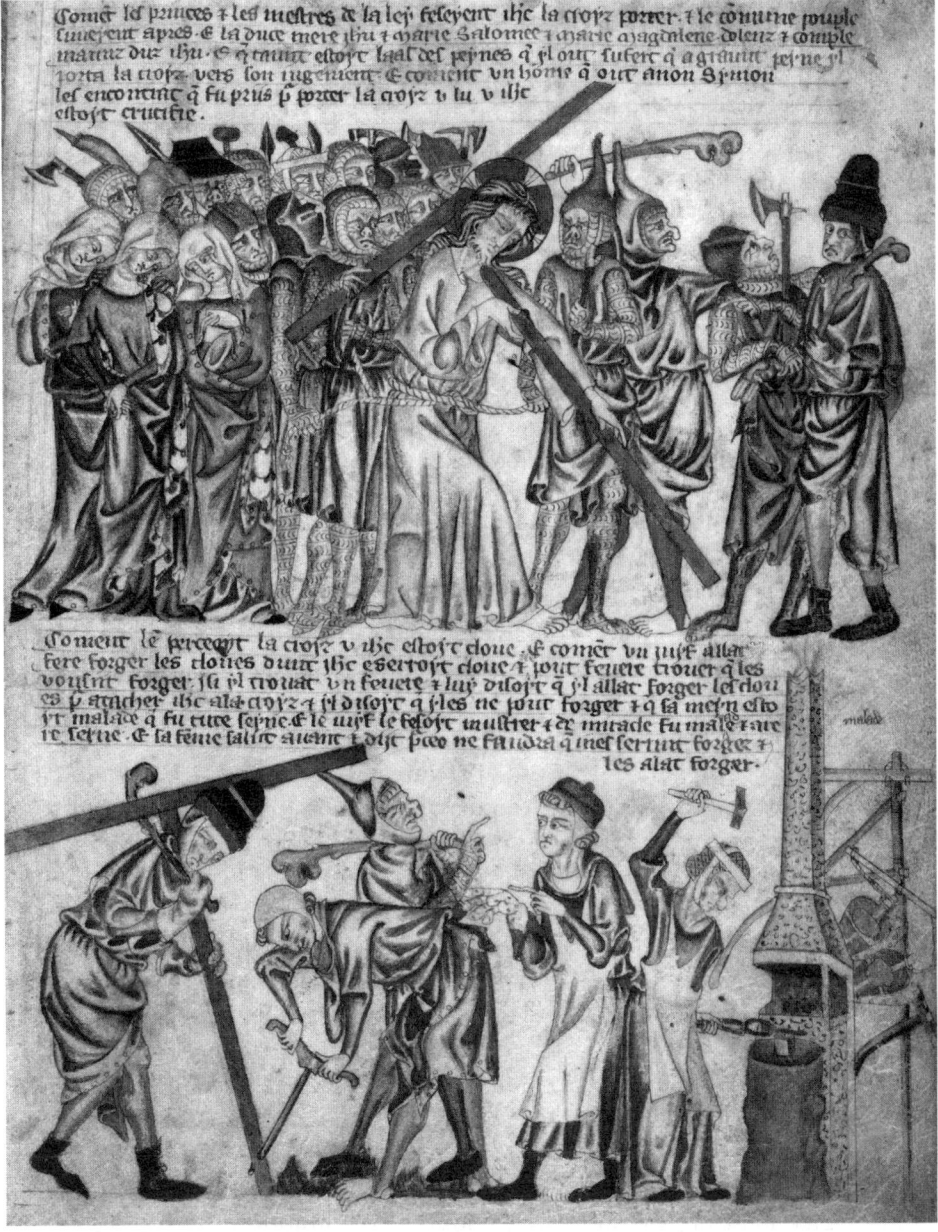

vivid depictions with details from legend and lore to explain the how ("*com[m]ent*"), not just the what, of Scripture. To account for where the nails used in Christ's Crucifixion came from, for instance, it portrays a woman (variously named Hédroit, Malembouchée, and Grumaton in popular paraphrases) working at a forge after her husband had deceived the Roman soldiers into believing that he was not up to the task because his hands were diseased.

Manuscript contents were also diverse. In addition to Scripture and scriptural paraphrases,[634] medieval books comprise *libelli* of saints' lives,[635] compendia of verses suitable for use as picture captions,[636] practical texts such as the financial manual in Florence (Figure 16), works of ancient culture and current-day science, and history. From the tenth century, books of saints' lives were profusely illustrated as means for promoting cults and attracting the interest of lay supporters.[637] The *Vita sancti Martini* illustrated c. 1100 in Tours (Bib. mun. MS 1018, fol. 18ʳ), where Saint Martin had long been venerated, is characteristic; in the manner of Christ and his immediate followers, Martin is shown reviving a slave who had been hanged on the noose shown dangling over his head. The power of the saint's "home" is also often underscored, as in the twelfth-century *Life of Saint Edmund* (New York, Pierpont Morgan Library, MS 736, fol.18ᵛ), which represents how thieves breaking into Edmund's church were paralyzed by the force of his "presence" there.[638]

Texts were bound together to configure new arguments.[639] Vegetius's *Epitoma rei militaris*, a fifth-century treatise on the principles and practices of war, is appended to an illustrated tenth-century Book of Maccabees in Leiden (Universiteitsbibliotheek, Cod. Perizoni, F.17), for example, to underscore the nature of the biblical account as part of a spiritual battle that came to include Christian saints, Church reformers, and the struggling soul.[640] The same themes are tapped in a gathering of folios (quire) containing heterogeneous pictures and texts inserted near the front of the Saint Albans Psalter to present Saint Alexis as Christ's counterpart and, in so doing, to further the local cult (Figure 40). Vitruvius's *De architectura,* added to a mid-twelfth-century copy of Theophilus's *Schedula diversarum atrium,* asserts continuity with ancient technical knowledge.[641]

Like most objects, moreover, books were transformed during their lifetimes.[642] A composite manuscript produced in Sankt Gallen, containing psalms and various other texts written and assembled over centuries, includes a reused page (palimpsest) with Pacificus of Verona's

Horologium nocturnum, a diagram for calculating the liturgical hours by measuring the movements of stars around Polaris (Sankt Gallen, Cod. 18; fol. 43ʳ).[643] The same diagram is included as well in a twelfth-century Anglo-Norman astrological compendium (Figure 53), but in a different context, including, among other things, the Latin *Aratea* and the *Liber Nemroth*, itself a compilation of various sources with diverse histories, and later annotations in English and Italian hands.[644] Texts and the constitution of books containing them remained fluid, especially secular writings, and included illustrations that were likewise sometimes stable but also often variable. Others such as Peter of Eboli's *Liber ad honorem Augusti* (Bern, Burgerbibliothek, Cod. 120.II) were painted over in acts of censorship.[645]

Decorated encyclopedias brought all knowledge together.[646] Isidore of Seville's *De natura rerum* was written because the seventh-century Visigothic king Sisebutus wanted to know the "reasons behind the nature of phenomena and material substances."[647] Isidore's enterprise not only served intellectual and practical purposes, but also invested the natural world with spiritual content, and it became the basis for many later works on natural history, including Hrabanus Maurus's *De natura rerum*, passed down in an eleventh-century volume illustrated with more than 300 traditional and invented miniatures drawn from various sources and organized in a Christian structure beginning with the Trinity and ending with secular themes (Montecassino, Abbazia, Cod. 132).[648] Herrard of Hohenbourg's twelfth-century *Hortus deliciarum* reorganized a remarkable array of pictorial sources based on Scripture, Prudentius, and moralizing literature, as well as new compositions, for use in the instruction of nuns (Strasbourg, Bib. de la Ville, now destroyed).[649] A mid-thirteenth-century English compendium assembled miscellaneous texts to form a preacher's manual (London, Brit. Lib., Harley MS 3244) and introduced diagrams to fix them in the mind,[650] and a codex illustrated by Matthew Paris (Oxford, Bodleian Library, Ashmole 304) collected tracts bearing on prognostication adorned with composite author portraits and pictures.[651] James le Palmer's *Omne bonum* (London, Brit. Lib., MS Royal 6.E.VI), a vast encyclopedia written and illustrated during the third quarter of the fourteenth century, is arranged alphabetically (with cross-references), preceded by a pictorial preface of 106 scenes tracing sacred history from Creation to the Last Judgment, with three devotional miniatures.[652] Another fourteenth-century anthology of Anglo Norman, English, and Latin

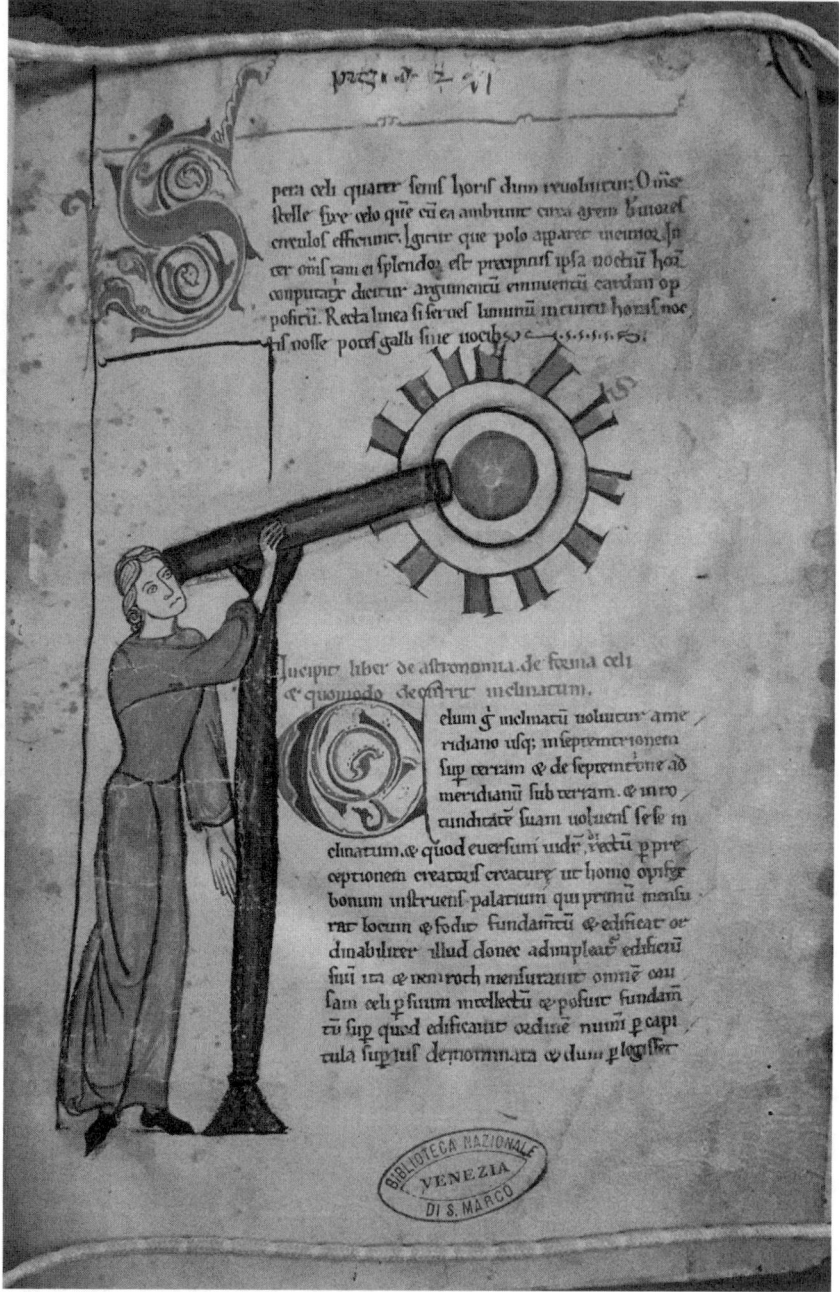

Figure 53. Venice, Biblioteca Marciana, MS lat. VIII 22 [2760], *Horologium nocturnum*, fol. 1ʳ (twelfth century)

religious and scientific texts (Cambridge, University Library, MS Gg 1.1) was compiled and illustrated to instruct laypersons on how best to live in this world and prepare for the next.⁶⁵³

Many manuscripts, both biblical and purpose-written, were used in the liturgy. As the oldest service book, the Psalter was furnished with liturgical markings and such additional texts as litanies of the dead.⁶⁵⁴ Illustrations in sacramentaries, antiphonals, benedictionals, missals, hymnals, and pontificals, meant for clerical eyes,⁶⁵⁵ were sites of special artistic inventiveness. Depictions in the Gellone (Paris, BnF, MS lat. 12048, fol. 143ᵛ) and Drogo sacramentaries (Paris, BnF, MS lat. 9428),⁶⁵⁶ for example, not only tack the texts read during the church celebrations onto their historical bases but also interpret the events in terms of the ceremonies they engendered. Miniatures in a late tenth-century sacramentary from Fulda pictures feasts not based on biblical events and inserts them into the historical sequence, providing a meditation on the liturgy.⁶⁵⁷ Illustrations in the late eleventh-century sacramentary of Warmond of Ivrea (Ivrea, Bib. Capit. Cod. LXXXVI) go further still, making visual the hoped-for harmony between Church and empire.⁶⁵⁸ A depiction of Giacomo Stefaneschi placing the papal tiara on Boniface VIII's head in the *De coronatione* of c. 1299 (Vatican, Bib. Apos. 4933, fol. 7ᵛ) was intended to help legitimize the unusual succession after the retirement of Celestine V, who is shown literally leaving the scene.⁶⁵⁹ Exultet rolls used during Holy Week included illustrations of the blessing of the paschal candle as well as such scriptural events as Christ appearing to Mary Magdalene after the Resurrection.⁶⁶⁰

The development of para-liturgical manuscripts was particularly important for art during the later Middle Ages, reflecting a shift of patronage and use toward the private sphere. Emerging from Psalters, the illustrated prayer book evolved in the context of the pastoral care of nuns and came to acquire singular importance for private devotion during the thirteenth and fourteenth centuries.⁶⁶¹ Like their more formal cousins, these books were themselves compendia and so were their illustrations, comprising scriptural narratives, scenes from the lives of saints, and occasional additions such as portraits of the recipient in prayer. From c. 1300, Jews in Catalonia and northern Europe decorated Haggadot that included rabbinical commentaries, folklore, and details from everyday life to enliven and interpret the biblical narratives and to render the story of Jewish persecution vivid and present, the "bird's head" Haggadah being one of the earliest (Figure 42).⁶⁶²

The Word Incarnate

Identified with the Word and, through Christ's declaration at the end of the Book of Revelation that he is the "alpha and omega," with the alphabet itself,[663] sacred books were understood to be the spirit "in libration." Christian of Stavelot proposed that vellum pages marked with the pen were to be perceived as a recapitulation of the Incarnation,[664] a notion already introduced in the dedication of the Godescalc evangeliary,[665] realized in the prayer book of Charles the Bald (Figure 18), and continued into the late Middle Ages. Hrabanus Maurus developed the trope in his *De laudibus sanctae crucis*, a collection of figured poems composed for Louis the Pious in 814 and frequently copied.[666] The opening picture of Christ, his arms extended as if on the cross, comprises words written on the unpainted vellum that express "his human and divine nature," the one "like a vestment" hiding the other from "human sight,"[667] and the *A*, *M*, and *Ω* inscribed in the halo, the beginning, middle, and end, and the *O* that forms Christ's umbilicus, the middle of the alphabet, is the center of Christ's body.[668] The thirteenth-century Cistercian monk Caesarius of Heisterbach went so far as to equate with Christ the letters written by the lash, rubricated by the nails, and punctuated by thorns. In turn, the prickings used to lay out the lines of text and the stitching for assembling the folios were likened to the Passion and integrated with the prayer texts.[669]

Elaborating the Jewish tradition of deploying contractions that stand in for sacred names and pronouns (*nomina sacra*), initials mimicked the understanding of Christ's own person as the perfect amalgam of human and divine in the Word-Made-Flesh,[670] in particular, the hybrid form of Christ's name known as the chrismon that served simultaneously to evoke Christ's name and to imagine the cross.[671] The concept was applied to the development of initials that served as frames for little scenes. In the Book of Kells, produced in Iona (Scotland) c. 800 (Figure 54),[672] for instance, the *In principio* that opens John's Gospel is as much a picture as a text; the *I* and *N* intersect to form a cross that progresses into the Scripture and the tangles of interlace confined by the letters symbolize the Word subduing the forces of evil.[673] By extension, the book was also equated with Mary in the tenth-century Gospel Book of Bernward of Hildesheim (Hildesheim, Dom-Museum, MS 18, fols. 16ᵛ–17ʳ)[674] and on the cover of the Theophanu Gospels, where the Virgin is understood to be the vessel of the divine's embodiment, simultaneously concealing and re-presenting the body inside. In the fourteenth century, Peter Berchorius described Scripture as the Holy Spirit written on virginal parchment.⁶⁷⁵

Perhaps in reaction to Christian incarnational claims, Jews also began constructing pictures from words in the ninth century, as exemplified by the Leviticus frontispiece in the Copenhagen Pentateuch (Figure 45).⁶⁷⁶ The large ויקרא ("And he spoke") at the center, representing the opening line "and the Lord summoned Moses and spoke from him from the tent of meeting," stands in for God's voice calling out from the Holy of Holies, the Gothic façade, formed entirely of writing.⁶⁷⁷ The minuscule texts engage the reader in a process of puzzling out the divine words and, in so doing, lead him or her into the pictured sacred precinct. Voice, text, image, and book are fully unified.

Books were often deemed to have amuletic power,⁶⁷⁸ and, like relics, they were occasionally enshrined in elaborately adorned boxes,⁶⁷⁹ for example, the early eleventh-century book shrine known as the Soiscél Molaise (Dublin, National Museum).⁶⁸⁰ In turn, they constituted sacred spaces, vested with precious silks and other fabrics, repositories for inventories of church treasures and souvenirs.⁶⁸¹ Covers often figured the corporal aspects; recalling reliquaries in their materials, they frequently featured Christ or an author whose "body" was secreted within. Thus, the covers of the Lindau Gospels in New York and the Uta Codex in Munich both present portraits of Christ in high relief. The Theophanu Gospels cover focuses on the three most important moments of Christ's life—birth, death, and return to heaven—and represents the four evangelists busily transcribing their texts to assert the orthodox belief in the veracity of the four texts within. For practical reasons, the lower cover is flat and simple, comprising four medallions engraved with the evangelist symbols arranged around the Lamb of God with the open apocalyptic book to be revealed at the end of time—a perfect coda.

Continuing ancient custom, medieval codices portrayed the authors at the start of volumes.⁶⁸² The Book of Kells follows a widespread system of Gospel illustration by picturing each evangelist before his Gospel followed by an elaborate initial leading into the text itself, as well as canon tables and various harmony pages. As he often was, John is distinguished from the three co-authors to underscore his special status as the Lord's beloved and most spiritual evangelist;⁶⁸³ he is given Christ's features and cocooned within a frame from which the head, hands, and feet emerge to indicate that he is the disciple who rested on Christ's breast at the

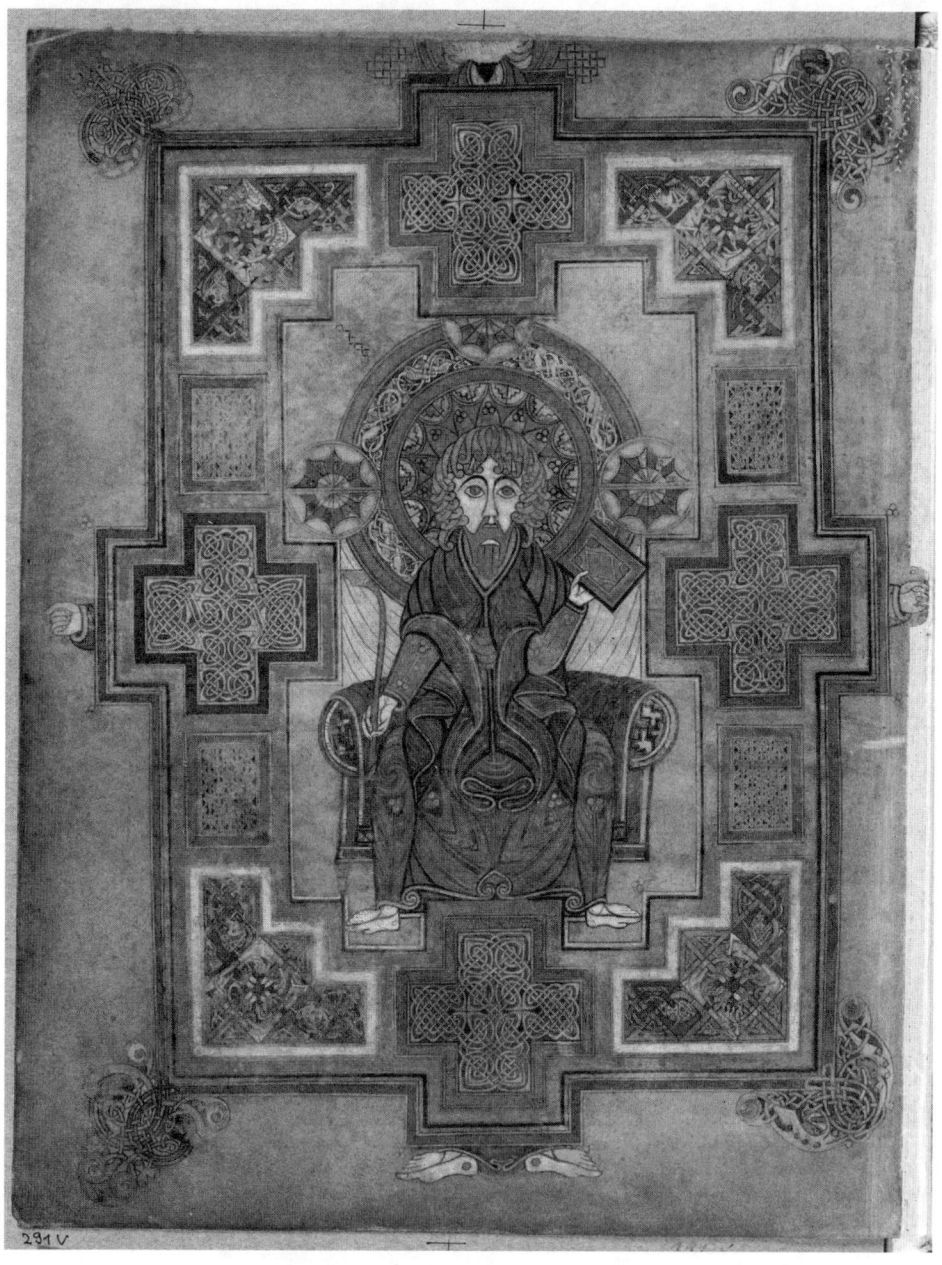

Figure 54. Dublin, Trinity College Library, MS A. I. [58], Book of Kells, fols. 291ᵛ–292ʳ (ninth century)

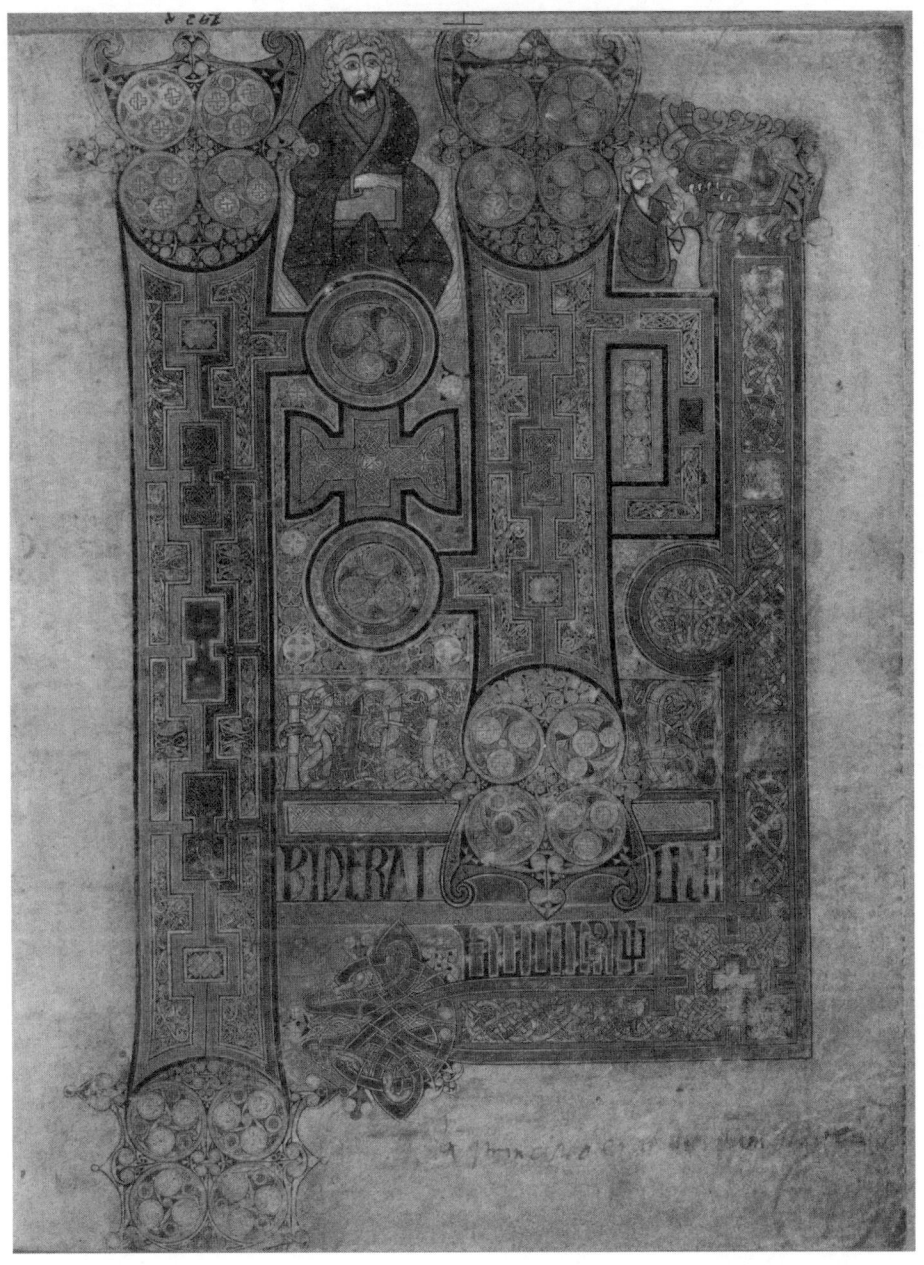

Last Supper, a theme cued also by the figure drinking from the red chalice in the upper right corner of the facing page.[684] Indeed, by covering up Christ, John realizes the words of the Prologue of his Gospel: "No man has seen the Father at any time: the only begotten Son who is in the bosom of the Father, he has declared him" (Jn 1:18).[685] Holding the pen with which he wrote the Gospel that revealed Christ's divinity and a book adorned with a rhombus, the symbol of the world, the Christ-like John is thus shown to be one layer in a sequence of revelations: word, man, *persona* of Christ, image of the unseeable Godhead.[686] In the Bible of Stephen Harding (Dijon, Bib. mun., MS 12–15), on the other hand, a heretic takes the Evangelist's place and the eagle-symbol attacks his mouth, ears, and eyes for proclaiming the Arian belief that "there was a time when he was not" against John's assertion of Christ's co-eternity.[687]

When King David was portrayed dictating to four co-psalmists, the depiction connected him to Christ and the evangelists as set out in the common Bible preface, *Origo psalmorum*. The twelfth-century copies of the Utrecht Psalter picture Christ himself as the anonymous *Beatus vir* of the first verse.[688] The Saint Albans Psalter portrays the Hebrew poet in the guise of Gregory the Great with the dove on his shoulder whispering into his ear, not only as the author of Psalms, in other words, but also as the surrogate of the defender of pictures whose dictum is, in fact, transcribed a couple of folios earlier: "it is one thing to worship a picture; another to learn, through the story of a picture, what is to be worshipped." Translators and editors assumed similar guises. By representing Pope Damasus commissioning Jerome to prepare a good Latin rendering of psalms as the counterpart to David composing the text itself, the ivory cover of the Dagulf Psalter (Paris, Musée du Louvre) not only figured the Church father as David's successor, but also entered the controversy about translation that engaged Charlemagne's court.[689] A short time later, illuminators at Tours portrayed Jerome, the translator of the accepted Latin version of the Bible (known as the Vulgate), as a new Virgil by incorporating elements borrowed from a fourth-century illuminated *Aeneid* (Vatican, Bib. Apos., MS. Vat. lat. 3225),[690] thereby implicating the abbot Alcuin whom Charlemagne had dispatched to a monastery to prepare a standard edition of the biblical text in the succession of authoritative Latinists. In his turn, Stephen Harding was figured as Jerome's spiritual heir, portrayed at the start of his Bible delivering his emended text into the hands of Pope Damasus.[691]

Visual Glosses

Pictures adjacent to relevant texts in many manuscripts rendered the words directly;[692] in so doing, they perpetuated a system that originated in antiquity and survived in early Christian manuscripts and numerous medieval replicas of them.[693] Even poetic texts were illustrated in this literal fashion. The delicate pen and wash sketches in the Utrecht Psalter, for instance, translate the "wild beasts and cattle, creeping things and winged bird" of Psalm 148 into pairs of four-footed animals, serpents, fishes, and birds (Figure 38).[694] Like many "word-illustrations," some were copied from pre-existing pictorial models; in this case, the animals were based on an illustrated *Physiologus*, which, like the personifications holding disks of the sun and moon and, indeed, the rustic capitals of the text itself, add an air of antiquity that fooled modern scholars up to the present into thinking that the Carolingian work was, in fact, a facsimile of an ancient book. By imparting a venerable aspect to the whole work, the Utrecht Psalter's classicism authorized the complicated iconographic inventions that, in fact, responded to and fix Carolingian theological discussions.[695]

Even more important, the organization of the pictures and the process of reading them are often themselves poetic. The Book of Revelation offered a particularly fertile field for contemporary apocalyptic ideas. The early eleventh-century Bamberg manuscript (Staatsbibliothek, Misc. Bibl. 140), for instance, incorporates millennial hopes in its "literal" illustrations,[696] and thirteenth- and fourteenth-century miniatures filtered the same text through crusader ambitions and concern for Church reform.[697] Pictures interacted with the accompanying words as dynamic elements of interpretation. The *Meditations on the Life of Christ* took the reader-viewer on an imagined spiritual pilgrimage, replete with pauses, struggles, and rewards.[698]

Exegetical texts were also illustrated. The eighth-century commentary on the Apocalypse by Beatus of Liebana was almost as popular as the subject of illustration as its canonical source.[699] Although based on the accompanying vernacular paraphrase and probably the result of a scribe-painter collaboration, the pictures in the Ælfric Hexateuch are more commentaries than translations.[700] Distance from holy writ facilitated greater freedom of decoration, as in the illustrations of Haimo of Auxerre's *Commentary on Ezekiel* (Paris, BnF, MS lat. 12302),[701] Honorius Augustodunensis's *Expositio in Cantica Canticorum* (Munich, Bay. Staatsbib., Clm 4450), and many other theological tracts. In fact, some of the most experimental illustrations occur in such exegetical works as the anonymous *Dialogus de laudibus sanctae crucis*, illuminated in Regensburg in the 1170s with its remarkable series of typologies (Munich, Bay. Staatsbib., Clm 14159),[702] and the *Moralia in Job* of c. 1111 in Dijon (Bib. mun., MS 173), which contains both the biblical book and Gregory the Great's commentary on it adorned with historiated initials that lead the reader-viewer into meditation on both.[703] Traditional and innovative iconographies were incorporated into the highly original *bibles moralisées* to create a set of typological commentaries built largely of the pictures themselves.[704] Responding to the Capetian enterprise, Alfonso X drew freely on diverse sources for the poetry and music of his *Cantigas*, including Islamic and Jewish works; one result is that the accompanying illustrations appealed to diverse audiences in the kingdom albeit with a consistent proselytizing goal; in many of the miniatures, the king is shown explicating the pictures to a group comprising noble women and men, not just the "illiterates" often claimed to be the principal audience of art. The illustration of Cantiga 125 (Figure 41), for instance, appropriates the *bible moralisée*'s general format of paired vignettes explicated by terse texts to tell the story of a holy man and a holy woman led astray; the monk conjures up demons but the Virgin Mary wins out, shielding the woman who, in an autoreferential trope, uses a book to chase away the harassing demons in an example of the confrontation of sacred text and magic also found elsewhere in the manuscript.[705]

From the twelfth century, theological speculation was illustrated with diagrams that elucidated complex concepts that eluded verbal explication, figuring the book page as a kind of mirror that attests to the real things beyond it and hence as an intermediary between the intelligible and higher human understanding.[706] An early thirteenth-century copy of the pseudo-Augustinian *De spiritu et anima* in Cambridge depicts the way the brain was understood to process impulses from sight, sound, smell, taste, and touch (Figure 55), facing a tree that diagrams how the soul comprehends sense, spirit, intellect, mind, reason, and memory.[707] Paired with a tree of virtues in the late-thirteenth-century diagrammatic collection known as *Vrigiet de solas* (*Orchard of Solace*), the "mirror of life and death" is constructed as a polished gold circle against a framed diapered background on which interpretive texts are displayed (Figure 56).[708] The designer subsumed the etymological derivation of *codex*, *liber*, and *folio* from tree trunks, bark, and leaves[709] by picturing a tree at the page's center, its crown supporting a personification of earthly life and its roots descending into the dirt of the seven deadly sins,

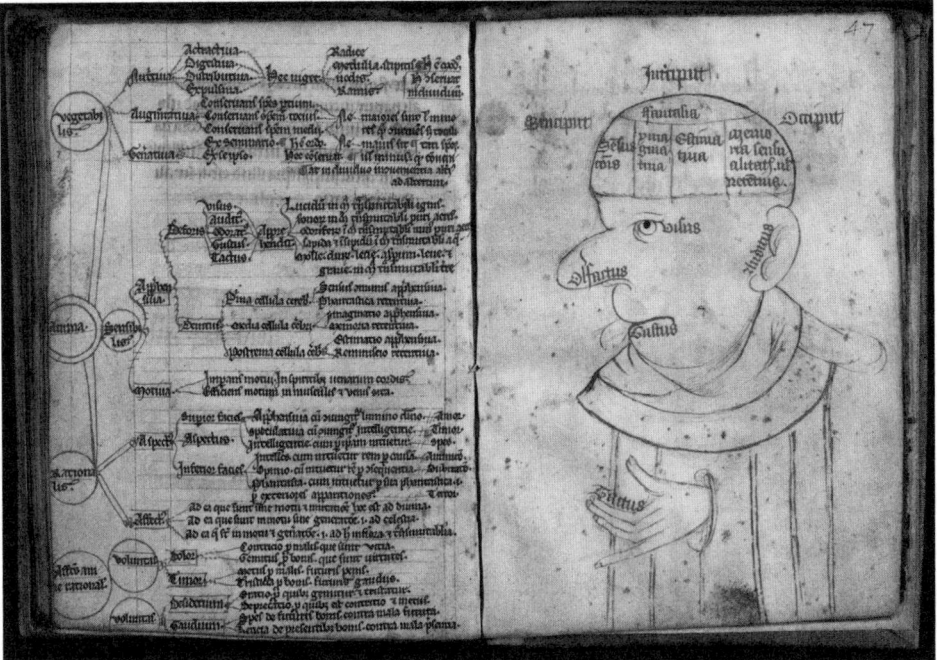

Figure 55. Cambridge, Trinity College Library, MS 0.7.16, *De spiritu et anima*, fol. 46ᵛ–47ʳ (thirteenth century)

centered on Pride. Suso treated the page surface, not as a mirror, but as a map for spiritual pilgrimage, using the corners to create antitheses—the lower right representing death and temptation and the upper left eternal redemption, the lower left Christ's sacrifice on the cross and the upper right the mysterious Trinity (Figure 22).[710]

Many manuscripts deployed the facing pages of the open codex to organize messages,[711] most often simply oscillating between picture and text but sometimes making a pictorial argument through the juxtaposition of miniatures. The opening of John's Gospel in the Book of Kells moves from the author to his (smaller) doppelgänger enthroned on the opening letters of the text facing him; in his Munich prayer book (Figure 18), Charles the Bald confronts his sovereign Lord across the book's gutter, setting up a resonance between the gold ornament on the king's earthly vestment and Christ's red wounds, and transforming the reciprocity itself into a prayer for the viewer, in the first case

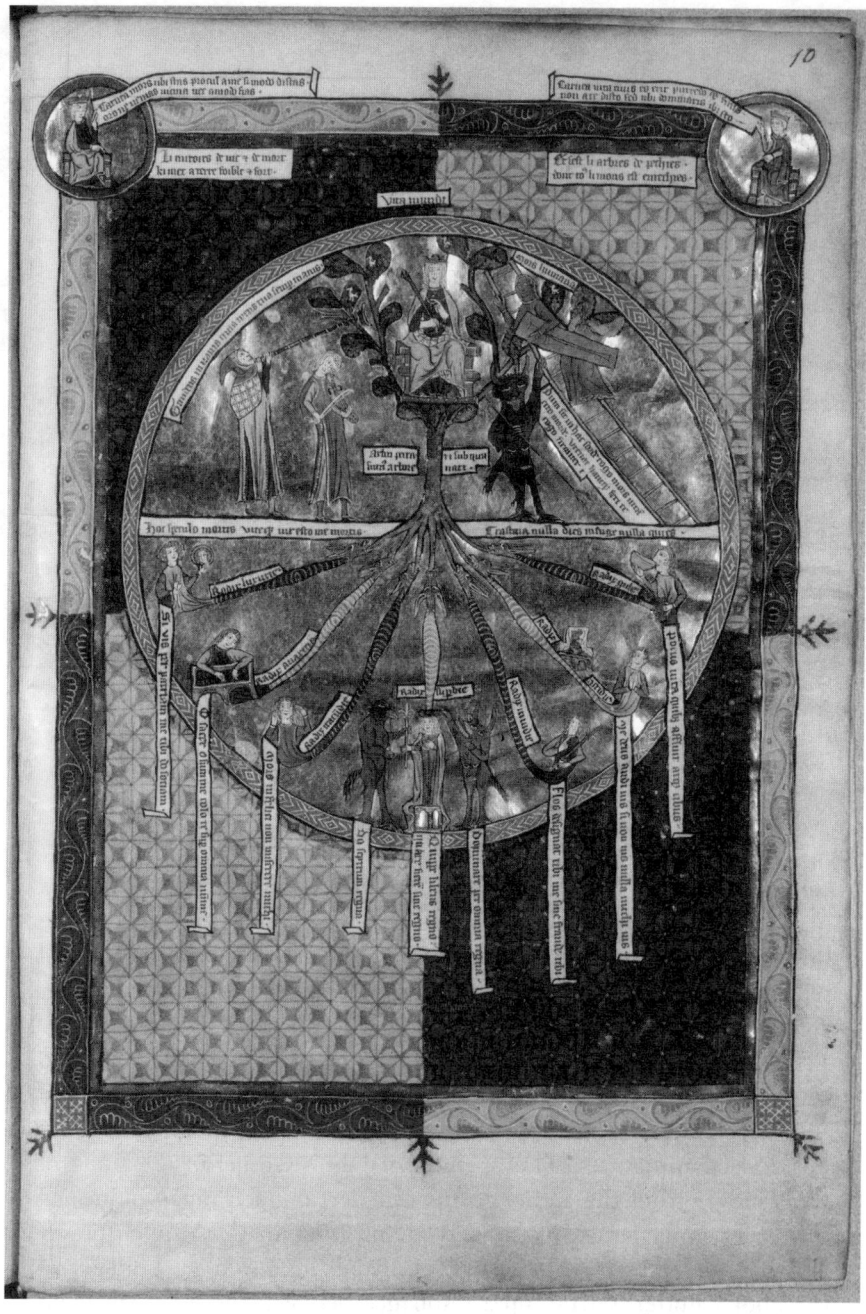

Figure 56. Paris, Bib. nationale de France, MS fr. 9220, *Vrigiet de solas*, fol. 10ʳ (thirteenth century)

the Carolingian monarch himself.[712] Picturing Christian exegesis, the earthly and heavenly Churches are made to confront one another in a composite volume made c. 1000 in Reichenau containing the Song of Songs, the Book of Daniel, and other Old Testament prophecies (Bamberg, Staatsbibliothek, MS Msc. Bib. 22);[713] Thiofrid opened his treatise by presenting a flowering plant on the left-hand page, introducing the life-giving power of the relics on the facing leaf, centered on the green cross (Figure 11). The Psalter of Louis the IX (Paris, BnF, MS lat. 10525) is organized as a succession of such "diptychs."[714] And, in the Rothschild Canticles, an extraordinary pairing opens a sequence of miniatures based on the Song of Songs, which itself provides continuous commentaries on the text passages written on the facing pages; beneath a depiction of Christ embracing the "sponsa" (bride) and then leading her into paradise, a woman is shown seated with a lance in her hand looking across the gutter at the naked Christ, who points out his wound simultaneously to the pictured woman and to the manuscript's reader-viewer.[715]

Margins and frames were active features of manuscript decoration, not only enclosing images but also supplementing texts.[716] They created semantic fields in which different levels of reality intermingled, sometimes benign and at other times arenas of struggle. In the Book of Kells, a fire-spitting demon demarcates the sacred precinct within, for instance, and creatures adorning the edges of the pictured platform protect the Copenhagen temple portal and the book itself. The Brussels bestiary uses the margins to illustrate the text and carefully arranges the pictorial elements to express its meaning (Figure 48); the plover and its counterpart Christ penetrate the titulus at the top of folio 143, and the serpent reaches the text's very bottom. Likewise, Gabriel's wing and right foot transgress the outer border of the Hitda Codex's Annunciation to convey the movement from the world of flesh to the divine impregnation (Plate XI). In the Gulbenkian Apocalypse, Christ hovers outside the pictorial space enclosed by the frame, while the Roman eagle and Temple curtain mark its limits. God's voice enters from beyond the upper confine of the *Specchio umano* and the tabernacle's cross extends beyond it (Figure 16), while at the left two women begging for grain cross from outside into the commercial precinct. In a manuscript of 1270–75, marginal miniatures alongside Wolfram von Eschenbach's *Willeham*, a vernacular text previously known only in oral tradition, imagine the written words explicated by the author marked by a large red *W* (Munich, Staatsbibliothek, Cod. Germ. 193, III, fol.1^r).[717] And in Frederick II's *De arte venandi cum avibus* in the Vatican (MS Pal. Lat. 1071), commissioned by the emperor's son Manfred, ample outer margins and narrower gutters come alive with the creatures inventoried in the words.

Initials served to organize books visually; even modest ones, as in the Utrecht Psalter, created a hierarchy among the textual passages. So-called kinetic initials developed in Ireland and England, and represented brilliantly in the Book of Kells, effected the transition between decorative elements and text. Contemporaneously, initials transformed the letters themselves into pictures to introduce texts and sometimes comment on them.[718] For instance, the late eighth-century Gellone Sacramentary figured the *T* of the *Te Igitur*, the cross on which Christ's body is suspended, and mapped the intersecting circles that Calcidius had deployed to diagram the intersection of fixed and moveable stars to generate the third substance,[719] the cross where the *V* and *D* intersect, perpetuated 400 years later in the Tours Sacramentary (Figure 47).[720] The French theologian John Beleth explained how the two entwined letters represent Christ's dual economy: "The *D*, enclosed on all sides, signifies the divine nature which has neither beginning or end; the *V* stands for Christ's human nature, which originated in the Virgin."[721] Also taking root in the ninth century, initials were deployed as frames for figures and little scenes. Following a venerable tradition of using Psalter initials as sites of spiritual combat,[722] the *B* of Psalm 1 in the Saint Albans manuscript is formed of a serpent biting its tail and includes David the author as the intermediary between the earthly realm and the heavenly, figured by the initial's shape.[723] Mary and Joseph praying before the infant Jesus in the *Très riches heures* establishes the text's function in the Feast of the Nativity while also cuing the proper act of adoration for the reader and the pilgrims shown approaching in the margins.

Interpretive Probes

Illustrations functioned in books just as supplementary textual materials did to interpret the contents and uncover spiritual significance.[724] They activated accompanying texts, provided meditations, helped navigate the contexts, or worked against them.[725] In the Godescalc Lectionary, the Fountain of Life inscribed with the capitulum of the Christmas vigil on the verso of the Christ page makes the transition from figures to text when the reader turns the pages; the emblem of the unity of the Gospels and symbol of the Incarnation bridges the portraits to the first scriptural extract (pericope) on the facing page.[726] A diagram of the Jerusalem Temple inserted in the twelfth century at the head of the ninth-century Valenciennes Apocalypse (Bib. municipale, MS 99) anticipates the depiction of the heavenly city at the end and thus prompts the reading of the Book of Revelation as this world ceding to the next,[727] while the insertion of a Veronica at the very end of the Lambeth Palace Apocalypse pictures the reward promised at the Last Judgment when the blessed "face to face, with confidence might see the judge coming upon [them], our Lord Jesus Christ" (London, Lambeth Palace Library, MS 209, fol. 53ᵛ).[728]

Writing and reading sacred texts were understood as a spiritual battle through which superficial meaning yielded to profound understanding. The claim is represented by the jousting knights in the Saint Albans Psalter and in many of the initials that activate a kind of combat for the soul (*psychomachia*) through depictions of Christ's struggles, the fashioning of intertwined letters, and the disentangling of meaning.[729] The hybrids and violent struggles that fill the initials of the Dijon *Moralia in Job* ensnare readers of the text in conflict,[730] following a long tradition of inspiriting the sacred words on a page and engaging the reader in a process of unraveling their true significance.[731] In the *Speculum Virginum*, schemata and figures are deployed to explain the dialogue between "Peregrinus" (Conrad of Hirsau) and his student Theodora (and hence all readers of the widely read text);[732] and a diagram copied from a mural painting at Saint-Victor that Hugh had used to lecture his students was made available to readers in the *Mystic Ark*.[733] Adam the Premonstratensian's *De tripartito tabernaculo* is organized around a diagram of Moses's tabernacle so that the monks of his abbey could construct a harmony between "what they read in the book and saw in the picture." A late-thirteenth-century treatise for instruction of Dominican novices deploys illustrations to teach the ways the Christian soul can aspire spiritually, incorporating an original variant of the diagram from *De sex alis cherubim* (London, Brit. Lib., Arundel MS 83, fol. 5v), a popular scheme in which each feather of the cherubim leads to the next, progressing toward God.[734]

At the heart of the struggle in which decoration played an important role was discovering the fundamental unity of Scripture's message. In the *Moralia in Job*, for example, bookended miniatures anchor the central theme; Job at the beginning is figured as an example of the restored good man, and a knight at the end stands for Christ's soldier (*miles Christi*) who has triumphed in spiritual battle.[735] Word and image in the

First Bible of Charles the Bald had a similar agenda; in its complex imagery and even in its positioning at the close as a replacement for the Apocalypse picture originally intended for the place, the portrait of the young king receiving the enormous codex completes the expression of hope that Charles will read Scripture and make it part of his very person.[736] The idea is triggered by a vignette of Saint John eating a book in the vision on folio 415^v of Moses, Paul, and John shown to be *personae* of a single spirit.[737] The trope of eating underlies the juxtaposition in the Tours Sacramentary of the Eucharist (proffered by *Ecclesia*) and Christ, the large Host embossed with the *christogram* providing a paradigm for the circular initial letters and, in turn, for the consecratory texts they adorn. The steps for preparing azymes (matzot), pictured in the Jerusalem Haggadah, have the same reach of relating the accompanying text to the activity it describes and, in turn, the (para-)liturgy it serves. In other words, the art in these books engaged the very processes of interpreting and understanding that enabled readers to assimilate Scripture in their own persons.[738]

Chapter 6
Church

SACRED ART, today displayed largely in museums and libraries, was originally encountered during the Middle Ages mostly in churches and other consecrated spaces, often in complex interactive ensembles with in-situ sculpture, painting, stained glass, and other monumental decorations.[739] A few medieval spiritual purists, to be sure, had denied the need for fitted-out structures, but at the Synod of Arras in 1025, Gerard, bishop of Arras and Cambrai, insisted that Christianity required a "holy church which is God's house" to insulate sacred devotions from the profane world and, thereby, elevate them.[740] Such houses included parish churches, many of them modest in scale and ornament,[741] as well was grand cathedrals and royal chapels furnished with dazzling decorations and crafted objects. Such stand-alone substitutes as portable altars and the London diptych (Figure 13) themselves conveyed sanctity, but they mostly served the special circumstances of missions, pilgrimages, and battles. King Louis IX carried a portable altar aboard ship on crusade to the Holy Land.[742] Understanding the contexts enhances the appreciation of objects constituting the *ornamenta ecclesiae*,[743] although the original location and function of even some elaborate works have still not been determined.[744]

The church was simultaneously a replacement for the Jerusalem Temple and a precursor of the heavenly city.[745] The famous relief on the Arch of Titus was taken as evidence that the Ark of the Covenant and other spolia had actually been brought to Rome in 70 CE, a claim the Gulbenkian

Apocalypse miniature builds on by picturing Titus returning from the conquest of Jerusalem with the Temple curtain (here embellished with Christ's face) and delivering it to the emperor Vespasian (Figure 10), and, following the crusader capture of Jerusalem in 1099, the ninth-century cypress chest in the popes' private chapel was labelled "Sancta Sanctorum" (see Figure 15).[746]

The Temple typology was incorporated in reliquaries, including the agate box in Oviedo and the reliquary chest beneath the altar of Sant'Ambrogio (Figure 6); when *La belle verrière* at Chartres (Figure 5) was moved (most likely from the apse), it was reframed within an Ark of the Covenant. The ancient metaphor of Mary, the vessel of the incarnate God and, in turn, of the Church that Christ had instituted through her, engaged a sequence of references that authorized Chartres as a successor of the Holy Land.[747]

The Temple typology had been subjected to exegesis and meditation that, by the High Middle Ages, was extended to virtually every church element.[748] Curtains, grills, and solid barriers controlled movement and perception,[749] in many churches segregating an inner sanctum accessible only to priests, and the creation of hierarchies of experience and itineraries for diverse groups extended to such subsidiary structures as baptisteries, chapels, cloisters, refectories, and chapter houses.[750] Suger's anagogical windows, for example, were intended for priests, and, by the thirteenth century, even cathedral cloisters were reserved for the clergy.[751] At the same time, the richly decorated spaces were believed to restore something of the sacred spectacle that humankind had been privileged to see before it was expelled from Eden and, in so doing, to provide a glimpse of the new Jerusalem that only saints now enjoy in heaven.[752]

Church art also engaged Christianity's pagan legacy; in his *Sententiae*, Bruno of Segni claimed that Constantine had introduced church decoration as part of the process of weaning from heathen traditions. References to antiquity are perpetuated through the incorporation of spolia, quotations, and evocations of triumphal arches;[753] the classical Greek quadriga and other sculptures that marauding crusaders had purloined from Constantinople were assembled on the façade of San Marco to assert Venice's claim to ancient origins.[754]

Entering the Sacred Precinct

At the boundaries of human spaces of habitation and commerce, church exteriors often signaled the transition to a cleansed and ceremonially consecrated interior.[755] The soaring medieval structures set on hilltops distinguished mundane existence from spiritual aspiration. In their Gothic manifestations resembling reliquaries, they advertised precious contents from afar, and, dematerialized in reflected light, the heavy metal roofs seemed even to defy gravity.[756] Lenzi's *Specchio umano* may dramatize the distinction between earthly and spiritual (Figure 16), but the contrast it constructs between the marketplace's chaos and tension and the calm created around the tabernacle captures the principle.[757]

Exteriors not only distinguished profane from sacred but also channeled the transition from the one to the other.[758] When the sun activated the adoring angels on the gleaming gilt copper disk in Reichenau's east gable (Figure 20), for instance, it softened the aspect of the fearsome Christ proffering the scriptural welcome: "Come to me, all you that are weary and I will give you rest" (Mt 11:28).[759] Words above the left-hand portal of San Marco announce, "Let all those who have confessed, who are not weighed down by their crime, and who will have pardon, enter free from care,"[760] and the lintel of Santa Pudenziana in Rome advertised the fact that "This place is famous for the saints' relics. Were there space on this stone, we could list the names of many of them. Through their merits, may we reach the summit of the heavens."[761] The dedicatory saints, whose relics are preserved inside, were also featured on façades, usually among myriad other holy men and women that constitute the stones of Jerusalem; thus, Mary is the highlight at the south portal of Amiens and Saint Firmin at the north (Figure 25),[762] and the dense population of other saints conjures up the Heavenly City.[763]

Following Augustine, churches also took on body symbolism, with the sanctuary as head, the nave as torso, the barrier as waist, and the entranceway as feet;[764] in this construct, the terrestrial church's "face" was nothing more than Christ's soles,[765] as pictured in the Ascension on the Theophanu Gospels (Plate V), which shows Mary and the Apostles gazing from below as Christ raises one foot onto a cloud, or on the façade at Vézelay which depicts his head breaking through the arch's upper boundary (archivolt).[766] Church exteriors warned that entering this body was not easy. Greeting pilgrims making their way to Rome or Jerusalem along the road from France and Spain (via Francigena) with the idea that only faith in the resurrected Lord can redeem them, a labyrinth at San Martino in Lucca (originally picturing the Greek hero defeating the minotaur) warns, "This labyrinth was constructed by Dedalus of Crete. No one who enters can exit, except Theseus who did so with the help of Ariadne's thread" (Figure 57).[767] The ingenious structure represents the Church and the thread, faith needed to achieve salvation.[768] Sculptures introduced during the second quarter of the twelfth century on the

Figure 57. Lucca, San Martino, labyrinth (twelfth or thirteenth century)

north transept of Saint-Étienne in Beauvais fashion the circular window as a wheel of fortune to remind those entering the sacred precinct of the world's vagaries, with grotesques at the base of the slit window above staring down demons who might try to get in.[769] Porches extended into the urban fabric were supported on triumphant animals (*telemones*) and sometimes emblazoned with inscriptions that advertised their force; part of the urban scenography, such spaces mediated between Church and civil authorities.[770]

Generally of stone, façade decorations realized the identification of the Church founded on the rock (Peter) with the building itself, and they visualized the metaphors in Scripture of Christ as the keystone of the Lord's holy temple built on a foundation laid by the prophets and apostles and as the door.[771] Christ's entry into Jerusalem tethers the church of the Holy Sepulcher to the historical event that took place at that spot (Figure 42), and it also engages the faithful who pass under it in imitation of their Savior's passion, which had redeemed human sin.[772] The point is underscored by the entrance into the chapel beneath Golgotha at the right (where Adam's remains were venerated and where the crusader kings of the Holy Land were buried), adorned with vine scrolls inhabited by men battling beasts.[773] Like Islamic ceramics (*bacini*) inserted into façades of Italian and Sardinian churches,[774] the peopled scroll was not mere ornament but warded off imminent threats through the incorporation of motifs evoking Christianity's defeat of its enemies. In Rome, San Pietro was adorned with a Last Judgment, with the Apostle himself replacing the traditional intercessor at Christ's left,[775] and following the eponymous church in Rome, the early twelfth-century entry of Saint-Pierre at Moissac (Figure 24) also presents the sovereign Lord who will judge humankind at the end of time, here being adored in heaven by the twenty-four elders (Rv 4–5) and with commentaries on the Last Judgment in the wings.[776] Eliciting a Roman triumphal arch in its shape, the portal is supported on a trumeau (pillar) decorated with sexually activated lion guardians, that forms, with the lintel, a *T*-shaped cross (Tau-cross), simultaneously protecting against evil and preparing those about to enter the church for the world inside.[777] Six serpentine columns with an array of images of combat against snakes drawn from antique sarcophagi greeted pilgrims at their destination in Santiago de Compostela.[778]

Church façades reinforced the fundamental requirement that Christians lead a Christian life. At Moissac, a shocking depiction, at the left of the portal, of a cadaverous Lust being devoured by demons converts sensual attraction into revulsion,[779] and the parable of the rich man and Lazarus (Lk 16:19–31) glosses the Last Judgment with the message that those who live worldly lives will not enter heaven by recalling Christ's warning about admittance: "It is easier for a camel to go through the eye of a needle than for a rich man to enter the kingdom of God" (Lk 18:25). A century later at Amiens, the themes were reconfigured. Christ *is* the door (of John's Gospel [Jn 10:1–9]) perched above King Solomon, the founder of Jerusalem Temple; flanked by the ten virgins, the exemplars of preparedness and frivolity in Matthew 25:1–13,[780] each in her own church, he greets those who enter. The themes are taken up in the tympanum (the triangular space between the arch and lintel): beneath a trumpet-sounding angel, the Savior displays his wounds and Mary and John the Evangelist pray for humankind's salvation, while in the register below, demons push sinners into a hell mouth at the right and, at the left, Peter ushers the blessed into heaven, led by the then recently canonized Saint Francis. The fourteenth-century mosaic over the south transept of the cathedral of Saint Vitus in Prague likewise assimilates the church entrances to heaven and hell through a Last Judgment that includes the local patron saints as intermediaries.[781]

Some of the same imagery was also introduced within porticoes, liminal spaces preceding some churches that often functioned as burial chambers and, in so doing, reinforced the transition from the mundane to the sacred. Frescoes within the porticoes of San Clemente, San Pietro, and San Lorenzo fuori le mura in Rome appropriately traced the stories of the dedicatory saints' martyrdoms, burials, and translations. In Santiago de Compostela, the main atrium portals feature the Last Judgment,[782] actually encompassing the faithful in a dramatization of the penultimate moments at the end of days. Last Judgment imagery also covers two walls in the chamber at Karlstejn leading into the Catherine Chapel (Figure 12), the rock-covered walls evoking the Holy Sepulcher and, at the same time, the Heavenly Jerusalem.[783] "Roland from Braca" (Portugal) is buried below the labyrinth in Lucca; and in San Marco in Venice, the doges are interred in the elaborate atrium adorned with mosaics (Plate XIII).[784] Preparing the faithful for the itinerary they would follow, porticoes were also preludes to naves:[785] the Vézelay tympanum offered pilgrims a kind of map of the church's interior itinerary.[786]

Doors participated in the schemes, and texts on them underscored their roles as passageways between the profane and the sacred. At Saint-Pierre-de-l'Isle, the doorway is inscribed: "This is God's house and the doorway to Heaven,"[787] and lion-headed pulls at Aachen and Hildesheim are meant to ward off evil (apotropaic) (Figure 23).[788] In the former, visitors' vanishing reflections on the mottled bronze surfaces, it has been proposed, enacted the transformation from one condition to another;[789] in the latter, the presentation of the Christian order would have sent a resounding message to hostile pagans in the East.[790] The Hildesheim reliefs feature Eve, through whose sin Eden was lost, juxtaposed to Mary, whose many epithets included "heaven's gate."[791] The depiction of the Expulsion features a closed-off gateway, and the concluding episode of Christ's cautioning Mary Magdelene not to touch him (*Noli me tangere* [Jn. 20:17]) portrays him inviting the woman—standing for all penitent Christians—into the door of heaven, that is, through the door of the church and the Church. The Virgin Mary was featured on the right portal of Amiens, a classic type of the Church itself. A mosaic of Mary and Christ with angels in a flowering meadow over San Marco's Porta da Mar (since the early sixteenth century, blocked off by Cappella Zen) effected the same typology, with the inscription asserting that the

Virgin is the New Eve who gave birth to the Redeemer of the progenitors' sin, cuing the mosaics of the Creation and Fall in the dome behind and, in turn, the hope of the dead buried in the atrium.[792] Secondary portals constructed a hierarchy of subjects.[793]

Arenas of Spiritual Combat

Entering the church did not automatically result in spiritual respite; as Sicard of Cremona noted, the nave remained a place of patient forbearing and even struggle on the route to the heavenly country.[794] Floors were filled with images of encounters between hybrid animals, mythological beasts, competing athletes, and other depictions of battle between good and evil drawn from ancient Roman traditions of representing creatures on pavements and from medieval bestiaries.[795] A mid-twelfth-century labyrinth on the floor near the entrance of the San Savino in Piacenza bore an inscription exhorting those who entered to crush worldly sins,[796] and at Otranto, the story of Adam and Eve, Cain and Abel, Noah, and Babel, as well as pictures of the labors of the months, activate recollection of life's tribulations.[797] The pavement in the cathedral of Cremona represents a satyr fighting a centaur, dueling personifications of Cruelty and Godlessness, and Faith plunging a lance into the mouth of a defeated Discord,[798] and behind the altar in the cathedral of Aosta, Samson shown subduing a lion symbolizes Christian victory over forces of evil that still threaten at the edges—another lion, a merman struggling with a snake, an eagle with two bodies, and a dragon (Figure 49).[799]

A similar vocabulary populates many column capitals; evolved from ancient Corinthian forms, the vegetal ornament expresses the vitality of the supports and alludes to the tree of life in paradise.[800] In contrast to the systematic arrangement of façade sculptures, nave carvings are normally devoid of any predetermined order, realizing in their very chaos one of the consequences of sin and the need to persist in the struggles they depict.[801] At Vézelay, the Fall of Adam and Eve and other scenes of temptation and conflict are integrated into the nave supports,[802] among them an Israelite, arriving with a sacrifice for the golden calf, being confronted by Moses brandishing the tablets of the law and a club to exorcise the devil of idolatry.[803] Indeed, monstrous evil abounds in medieval art,[804] another consequence of the Fall and the disorder that followed that requires humankind to engage in a continuous spiritual battle.[805]

As in Theophilus's *De diversis artibus*;[806] ceilings were traditionally reserved for cosmological themes, thereby reinforcing the spatial hierarchy. At Beverly Minster, for example, the eleventh-century archbishop Ealdred "covered the whole church on top ... with the work of a painter which they call a *caelum* [heaven]"; and, in his general defense of images, Honorius Augustodunensis cited "paintings on ceiling panels of exemplary deeds of virtuous men"—the saints whose lives earned them a place in heaven. Beginning appropriately by showing God penetrating the vaulted room where Mary (*Ecclesia*) assembled in Jerusalem at Pentecost, lost frescoes on the ceiling of San Eusebio at Vercelli emphasized the role of the Roman saints Peter and Paul in converting the Jews and pagans.[807] The ceiling at Sankt Martin at Zillis, painted with Christ's life and that of the dedicatory saint, provides a celestial vision bordered by the terrestrial world, and the choice of the Tree of Jesse for the extravagant painted ceiling of Sankt Michael at Hildesheim may engage both the wood medium and the imagery of God's entry into the world through *Maria-Ecclesia*.[808] Developing an old Roman tradition, a frieze running just beneath the ceiling in San Pietro in Valle (Ferentillo) deploys a three-dimensional meander to effect the transition between earth and heaven, populated by fish symbolizing the subterrestrial realm and birds and griffins the heavenly (Figure 58).[809] In the Cappella Palatina in Palermo, too, the ceiling functions as part of the mapping of the earthly and heavenly realms; the courtly images of animals, musicians, and dancers on the Fatimid-style work inscribed in Arabic evoke paradise, a region distant in time and place from the world lost by Adam and Eve pictured on the walls below.[810] The same idea inspired the vault of Saint-Savin-sur-Gartempe in northwest France, where the creation of the universe begins a narrative cycle of some sixty scenes that ends with Moses Receiving the Laws on Sinai and Building the Tabernacle.[811] The vault of the Scrovegni Chapel is painted lapis blue and studded with gold stars (Plate XII), and the fourteenth-century wood ceiling of Peterborough Cathedral provides an overall paradisiacal effect and a response to elements below, becoming more animated above the altar.[812] Entering the Sainte-Chapelle (Plate VII), the theologian John of Jandun declared in 1323, was "like entering one of the chambers of Paradise."[813]

Following Gregory the Great's often-repeated justification of art as the "bible of the illiterate," narratives disposed on lateral walls generally served several pedagogical purposes at once. Their sequential flow

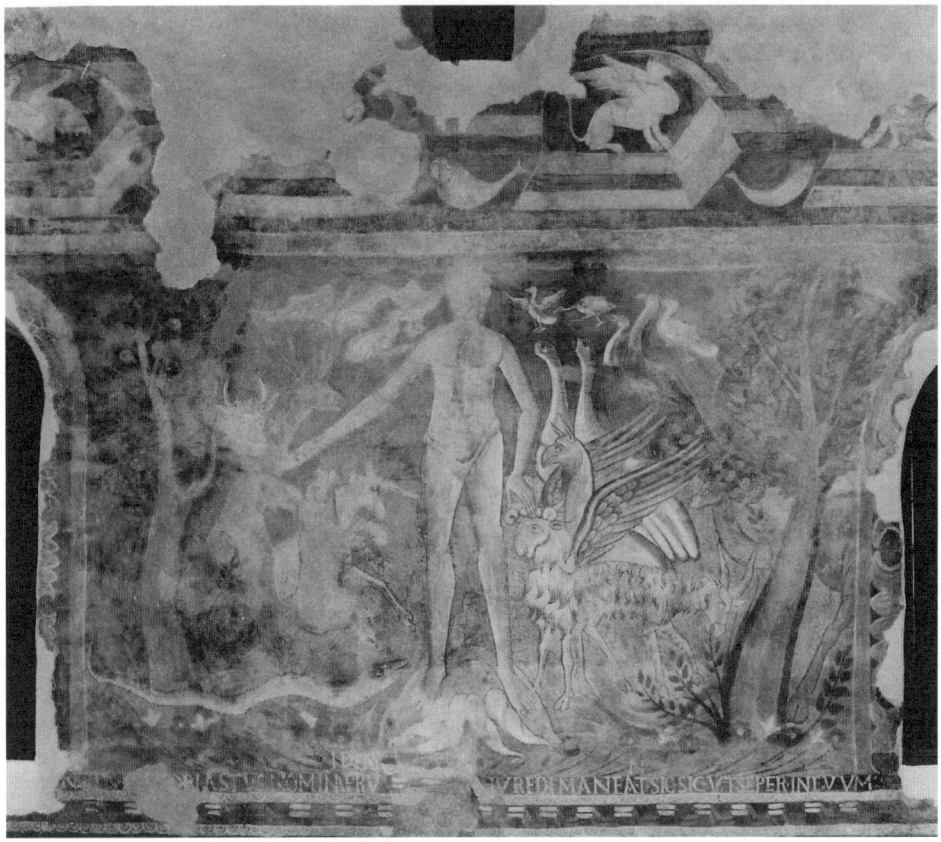

Figure 58. Ferentillo, San Pietro in Valle, fresco (c. 1200)

asserted God's working in historical time; juxtapositions, oppositions, and thematic repetitions revealed the divine plan; and spatial positioning plotted their spiritual movement.[814] Santa Maria Immacolata at Ceri (Figure 37), for instance, traces the story of Genesis and Exodus, from the Creation of the World through the Israelites leaving Egypt for the Promised Land. The reading of the scenes is complicated by their disposition; the parallel sequences are subdivided into meaningful clusters, e.g., the Temptation of Adam and Eve directly above Potiphar's Wife Attempting to Seduce Joseph, and Noah's Family in the Ark and the Crossing of the Red Sea near the saved pictured in the adjacent Last Judgment. In San Pietro in Valle, too, the narrative imagery is inflected by location; the Naming of the Animals inserted at the midpoint of the standard Old Testament system creates an axis opposite the centralized scene on the facing wall of Christ adored by angels, toward which Adam gazes.[815]

New Testament cycles were generally more straightforward; their basic purpose, after all, was to affirm the reality of Christ's Incarnation, death, and resurrection. They often emphasized subjects bearing on the establishment of the Church after Christ returned to the "right side of his Father," and hence to the continuity between sacred history and the present time and place.[816] The scenes from Revelation on the drawing in Salzburg pertain to the Church (Figure 44); at the top of the dome, the invisible Hand of God encircled by four angels stands for Heaven, and the other imagery connects the actual space with the Heavenly Jerusalem (featuring the Lamb at the center of a circular city originally in the drawing's upper right corner),[817] which will replace the world at the end of time, evoked by the apocalyptic horsemen, seas, and winds in the lunettes. In basilical churches, judgment at the end of days was often introduced on the counter-façade,[818] the darkest place in the church, at Ceri, for instance, and at the abbey of San Pietro al Monte in Civate, where the great lunette over the vestibule pictures Christ's ultimate victory over death and the forces of evil, reminding the exiting faithful of the burden they still must bear if they were to enter the celestial paradise.[819] Those leaving the Becket Chapel in Anagni were confronted not only with the Last Judgment but also with the five wise virgins above the exit, the perfect portal imagery to remind those leaving of the need for constant vigilance.[820] Twelfth-century frescoes in Saint-Julien at Tours, though copied from a late antique Pentateuch, were disposed to alert the faithful that, like the Israelites in the desert, they had yet to reach the Promised Land.[821] While the Last Judgment over the principal door of the Scrovegni Chapel includes Enrico's ex-voto, personifications above the secondary portal leading into his palace reminded the patron of the need to continue to battle vice if he wished to pass through the "narrow gate" of eternal life.[822]

Many churches included cycles of pictures that comprehended the life of the dedicatory saint in sacred history and, hence, provided a historical context and authentication for the relics they preserved and the power to ward off evil.[823] The pictured miracle at the Mass of Saint Clement is positioned close to the altar in the lower church of San Clemente in Rome;[824] in the crypt of Aquileia Cathedral, the choice between good and evil is presented beneath depictions of saints, in the form of personifications of the vices, battles between crusaders and infidels, and representations of pilgrimage;[825] and the Ceri dado includes a depiction of Pope Sylvester freeing the Roman forum of the menacing dragon-like chimaera near the door (leading from Rome).[826] Assisi integrates the life of Saint Francis into the narrative;[827] the Scrovegni Chapel goes farther by expanding the Gospels narrative to assimilate Mary more fully into the scriptural account and, thereby, establishing the Virgin—to whom the building is dedicated—as her Son's near equal and the compassionate intermediary between humankind and God. The thirteenth-century paintings in the Lateran Sancta Sanctorum elevate the saints' earthly lives into icons of heavenly ascent (Figure 15), in a sense dilating the schema of the *Acheropita* on the altar below.[828]

Opening onto naves but clearly subordinate, aisles as well were often used to accommodate hagiographical cycles. In the Premonstratensian abbey church at Türje in Hungary, Saint Ladislaus's victory over the Cumans provides a vivid account that leads the faithful from the doorway toward the altar.[829] Frescoes painted c. 1100 in the Pyrenees church of Sant Joan de Boí, by contrast, segregate nave and aisle (Figure 59);[830] while Saint Martin and the martyrdom of Saint Stephen adorn the main walls, animals drawn from the bestiary filling the intrados of the arches separate the lateral space where a pictured dancer playing the harp, a juggler, and an acrobat evoke the lively celebration of God's house and, at the same time, caution that church art must not (as Bernard of Clairvaux admonished) simply draw attention to itself as entertainers do, but rather redirect the onlookers' gazes to heaven.[831]

The vast expanses of stained glass that fill Gothic buildings continued traditions of narrative, allegorical, and moral subjects found in earlier churches, the translucent material itself elevating stone figures encountered nearer the ground into celestial portals and binding the macrostructure to reliquaries.[832] In Saint-Remi at Reims, for instance, a relief of Moses and Aaron with the brazen serpent in the choir provides the material and intellectual counterpart for the Crucifixion at the center of the glazed apse above;[833] at Chartres, thirty episodes devoted to the story of the Prodigal Son engage the congregation in a journey of sin and repentance, phrased appropriately in the material's own transformation from darkness to light.[834] Like other narrative media, windows provided material for contemplation when services were not being performed.[835]

Mimicking the mountain on which Moses had received the tablets and Christ had preached God's word to the faithful, pulpits converted naves into theaters where preachers coached congregants on their spiritual struggles.[836] The Aachen ambo, for instance, figures the platform as

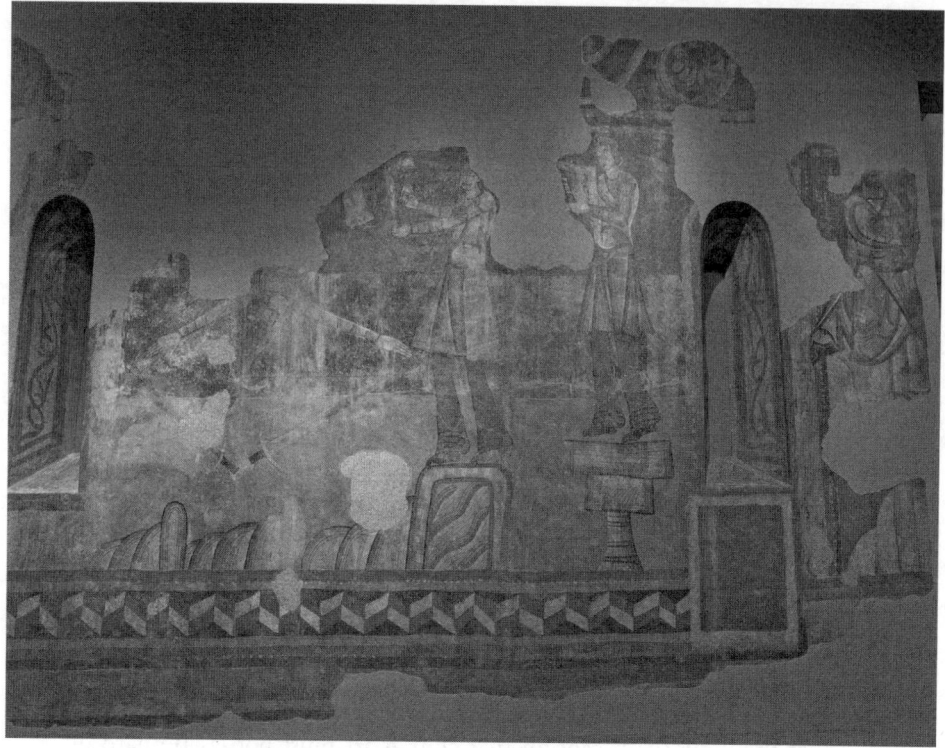

Figure 59. Barcelona, Museu nacional d'art de Catalunya, fresco from left aisle of Sant Joan de Boí (fourteenth century)

a book with the four evangelists in the corners of the cross (Plate IV), providing a fitting foundation for the priest's living voice.[837] In south Italy, pulpits divided the clergy from the congregation, their very structures effecting transitions from the lower spaces representing Christ's *sepulchrum*,[838] the bema's stairs offering an anagogical ladder, and the bookrest—often adorned with an eagle and open book—introducing John's "logos" that soars to heaven.[839] The concept is also realized in Sant'Ambrogio in Milan, where the pulpit, adorned with a (spoliate) eagle, serves simultaneously as a canopy for the sarcophagus in the nave and as a bridge to the main altar.[840]

In some churches, pulpits also provided pedestals for the display of relics; in others, special tabernacles served the purpose.[841] At San Pietro in Rome, Pope Celestine III constructed a ciborium for the altar of the *Veronica* surmounted by a stone safe enclosed in a bronze grate,[842] and similar tabernacles were built for the icon and relics in Santa Maria Maggiore and other Roman churches.[843] The *Specchio umano* miniature offers a likeness of such shrines, with the icon raised on a pedestal and an altar-like marble table below,[844] and the *Très riches heures* records the most elaborate of all, the *Grande Chasse*, commissioned by Louis IX for the relics pilfered from Constantinople (Plate VII).[845] Albeit smaller, such similar tabernacles as the one represented at the center of the Vallbona altarpiece (Figure 17) also came to be used to protect the Eucharist and precious vessels used during the Mass.[846] Rife with symbolism, the form was also appropriated for special tombs (Figure 39).

Transepts joined congregations and clergy. In the Dom of Freiburg-im-Breisgau, the northern arm was a place to mete out justice, with the stained-glass window appropriately featuring the works of mercy (Mt 25) and related themes of judgment.[847] At Strasbourg, the south arm served the same purpose (Figure 50); there, a sixteen-foot column supporting the roof vaults is adorned with trumpeting angels and Christ in judgment, picking up the theme of the judicious king Solomon on the portal.[848] In Assisi, Francis's special devotion to Michael, remembered on his feast day, is commemorated by frescoes over the altar in the left transept.[849]

In every way liminal and often the oldest parts of churches, crypts derived from ancient traditions were carpeted with mosaics teeming with pagan motifs.[850] They engaged the reference in the Book of Revelation to "the souls of those who had been slaughtered for God's word" beneath the altar.[851] The scriptural verse is itself pictured at Anagni, south of Rome, where the crypt is actually a separate church once enterable directly from the outside,[852] and where a passageway (with a sarcophagus) leads to the Becket Chapel (originally a temple of Mithras, which still preserves the ancient altar for blood sacrifices adorned with a bull).[853] At Berzé-la-Ville (Figure 32), which has neither a crypt nor transept, the martyrdoms of saints Blaise and Vincent flank the triple window behind the altar and nine other saints venerated at Cluny are portrayed below it,[854] effecting a spiritual pilgrimage from relics and altar, through the death and life of the honored saints, to God in heaven.

Communion with God

Church interiors were subdivided.[855] The lay confraternity pictured on the Saint-Martin-du-Canigou cartulary looks into but does not enter the priest's precinct (Figure 8), for example, and various types of barriers divided congregations from the clerical spaces. In San Clemente, a sixth-century *schola cantorum* was refitted in the twelfth century to provide an enclosed space for the clergy within the nave, furnished with a candlestick and pulpits for the reading of the Gospels and Epistles.[856] A rare separate choir survives at Palencia and a few other cathedrals. At Saint-Martin de Vicq, altars abut a dividing wall painted with the life of Christ.[857] In the double church dedicated to Saints Mary and Clement at Schwarzrheindorf, the effect is quite dramatic, with the dark lower rooms adorned with Ezekiel's prophecies pierced by an octagonal oculus through which Christ is visible in heaven.[858] Membranes comparable to the curtain that isolated the Holy of Holies from the outer courtyard of the Jewish Temple also closed off the Orsanmichele tabernacle and many other precincts;[859] a sixteenth-century inscription declares that the chamber with the altar of the supreme pontiff's Sancta Sanctorum (originally hidden by curtains) is the "holiest place in the world." In the Sainte-Chapelle, the king was privileged to occupy a private booth,[860] while the rest of the court and the common people were separated by a bench-like barrier in front of the altar; a bracket surviving in San Francesco at Assisi attests to the existence of a beam for displaying images of the sort pictured in the church's fresco of the verification of Saint Francis's relics.[861]

For aesthetic and ecclesiological reasons, most of these fixed barriers that provided interfaces between the public and clergy have been destroyed. In Italian churches, a *tramezzo* screened the sanctuary from the lay; in the basilica of San Antonio in Padua, the saint's sarcophagus set on the west of the screen provided a meaningful bridge between the two spaces.[862] The mid-thirteenth-century screen before the west choir in Naumburg Cathedral functions as a site of transition and passage in a particularly charged fashion (Figure 26);[863] reliefs along the top trace the story of Christ's Passion, but the Crucifixion itself is arranged at the doorway to the sanctuary to realize the Pauline typology of Christ's flesh as the Temple curtain rent at the moment of the Savior's death. The barriers introduced the new sacrifice and the officiants of it, inviting visual penetration to the altar and service beyond.[864] Elevated through material and imagery by the frescoed bust above of the Judging Christ flanked by angels in heaven, Christ hovers between life and death to engage that transitional moment and to proclaim that devoting oneself to the Church, as the founders portrayed beyond had two centuries earlier, promotes redemption.

In many churches, the decoration of apsidal and triumphal arches linked the historical narratives on nave walls to the liturgical spaces below; in the Capella Palatina at Palermo and the Scrovegni Chapel,

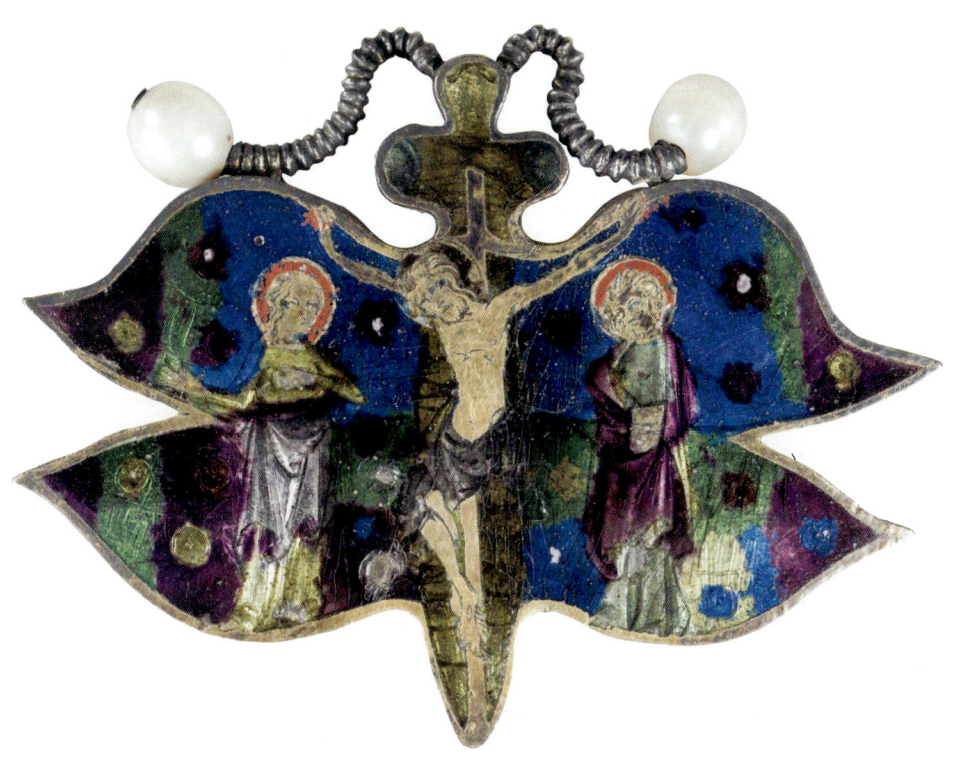

Plate I. Regensburg, Diözesanmuseum, reliquary (fourteenth century)

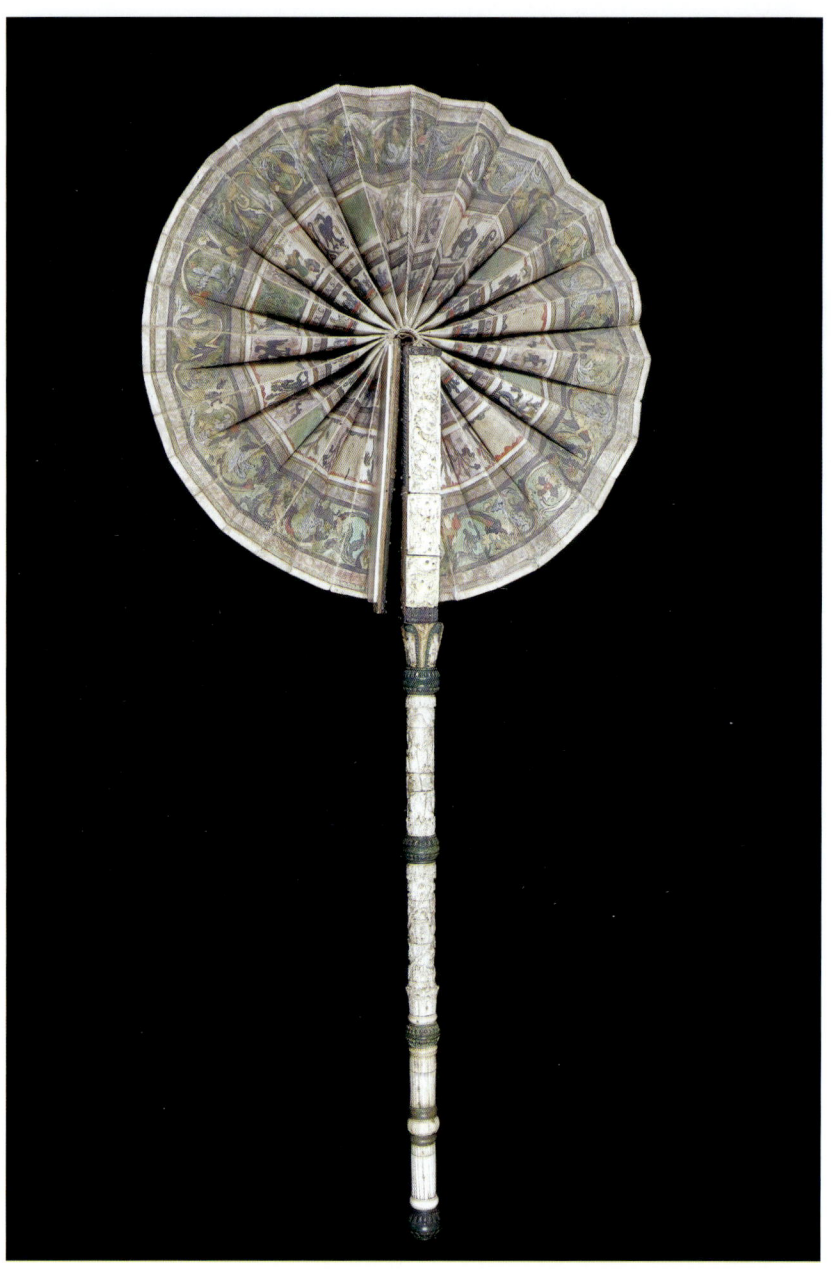

Plate II. Florence, Museo del Bargello, flabellum (ninth century)

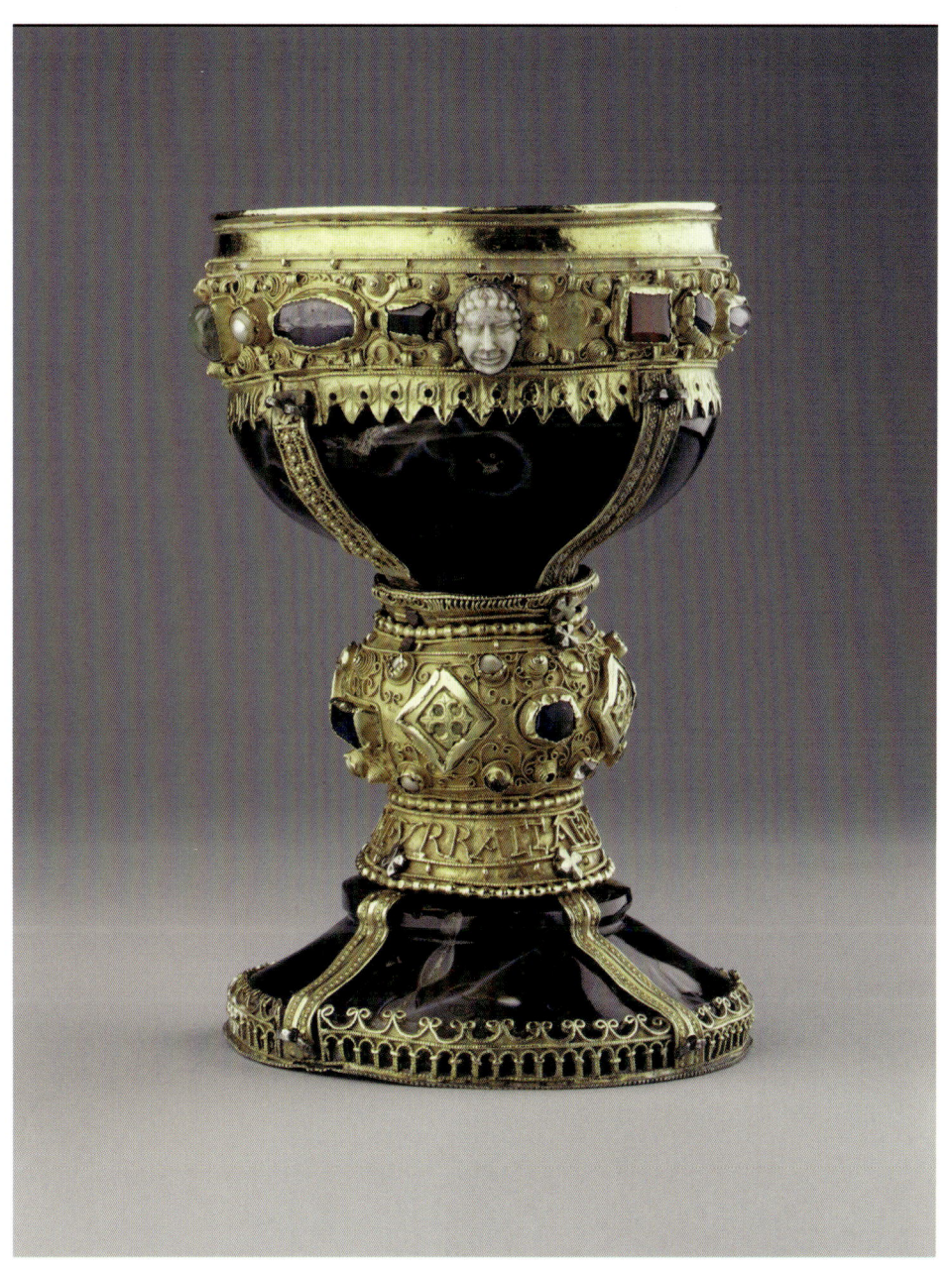

Plate III. León, San Isidoro, Urraca chalice (eleventh century)

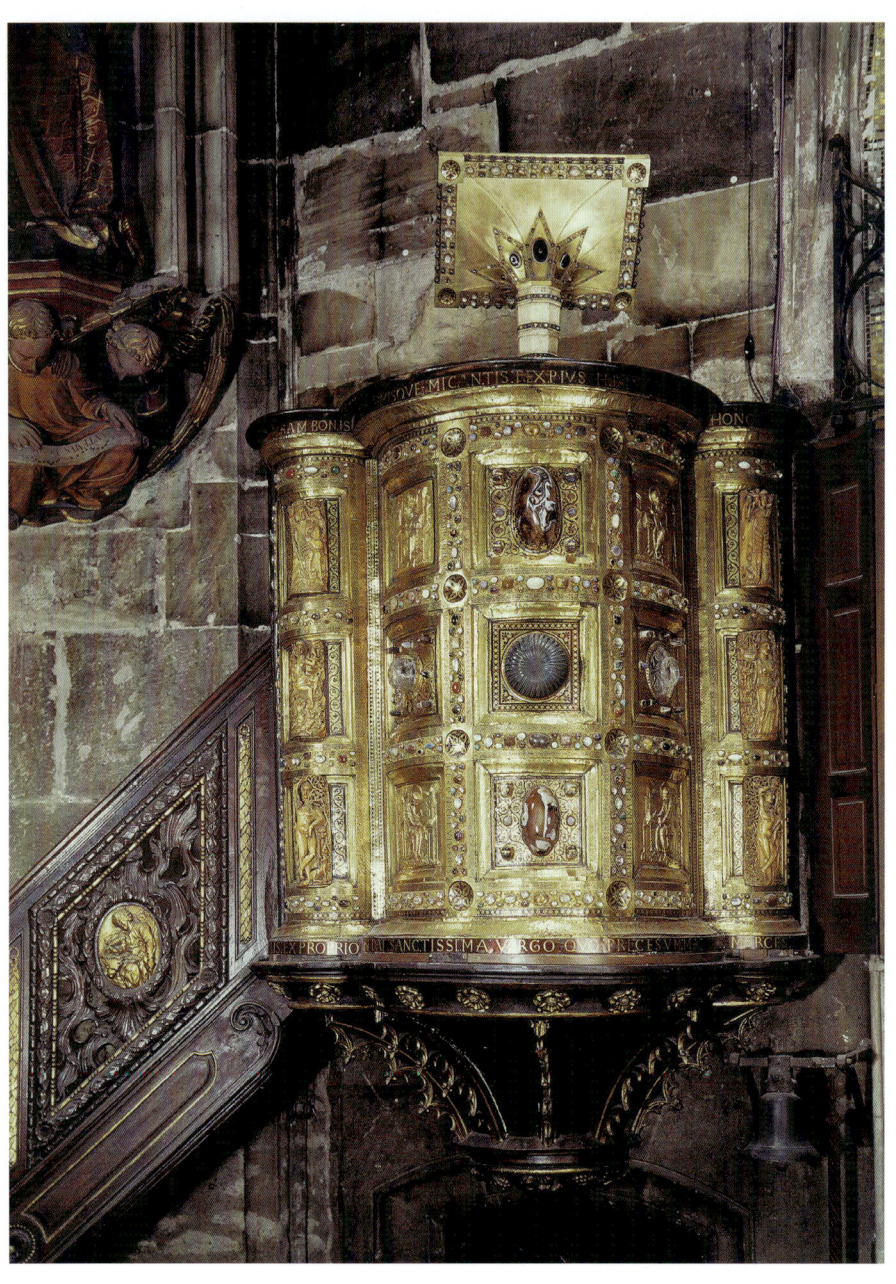

Plate IV. Aachen, Dom, ambo (eleventh century)

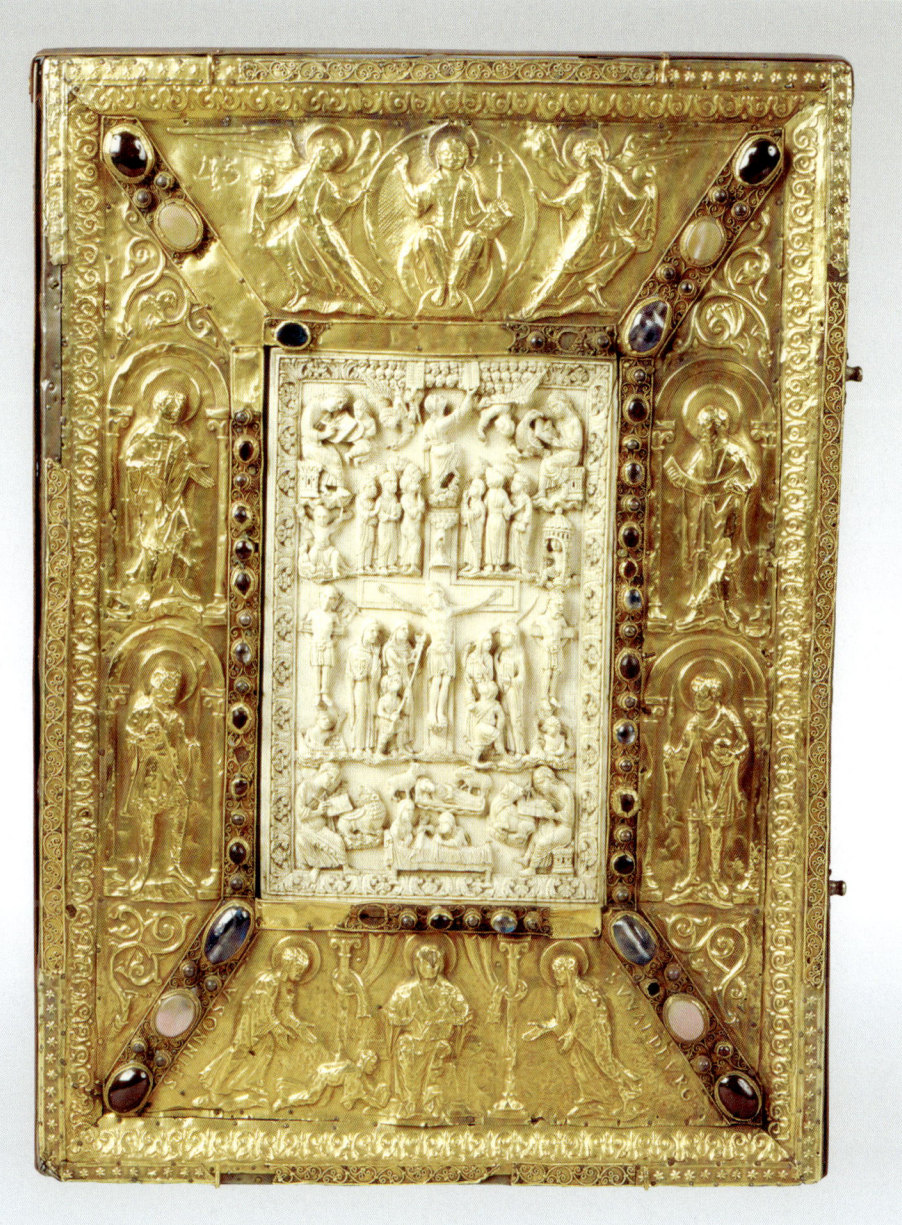

Plate V. Essen, Domschatz, Theophanu Gospels cover (eleventh century)

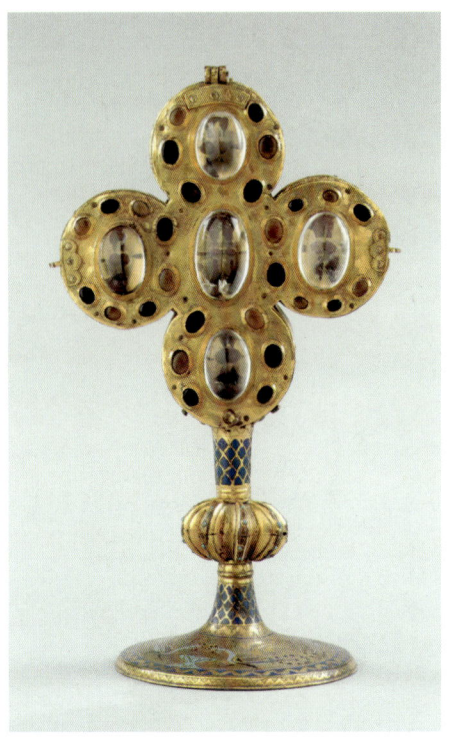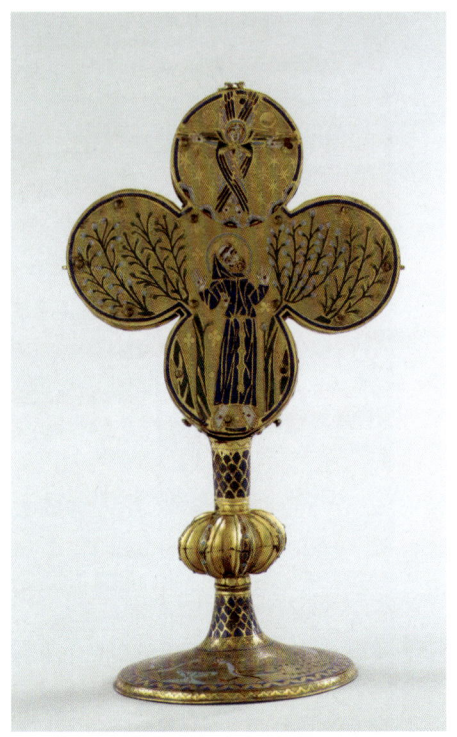

Plate VI. Paris, Musée du Louvre, reliquary (thirteenth century)

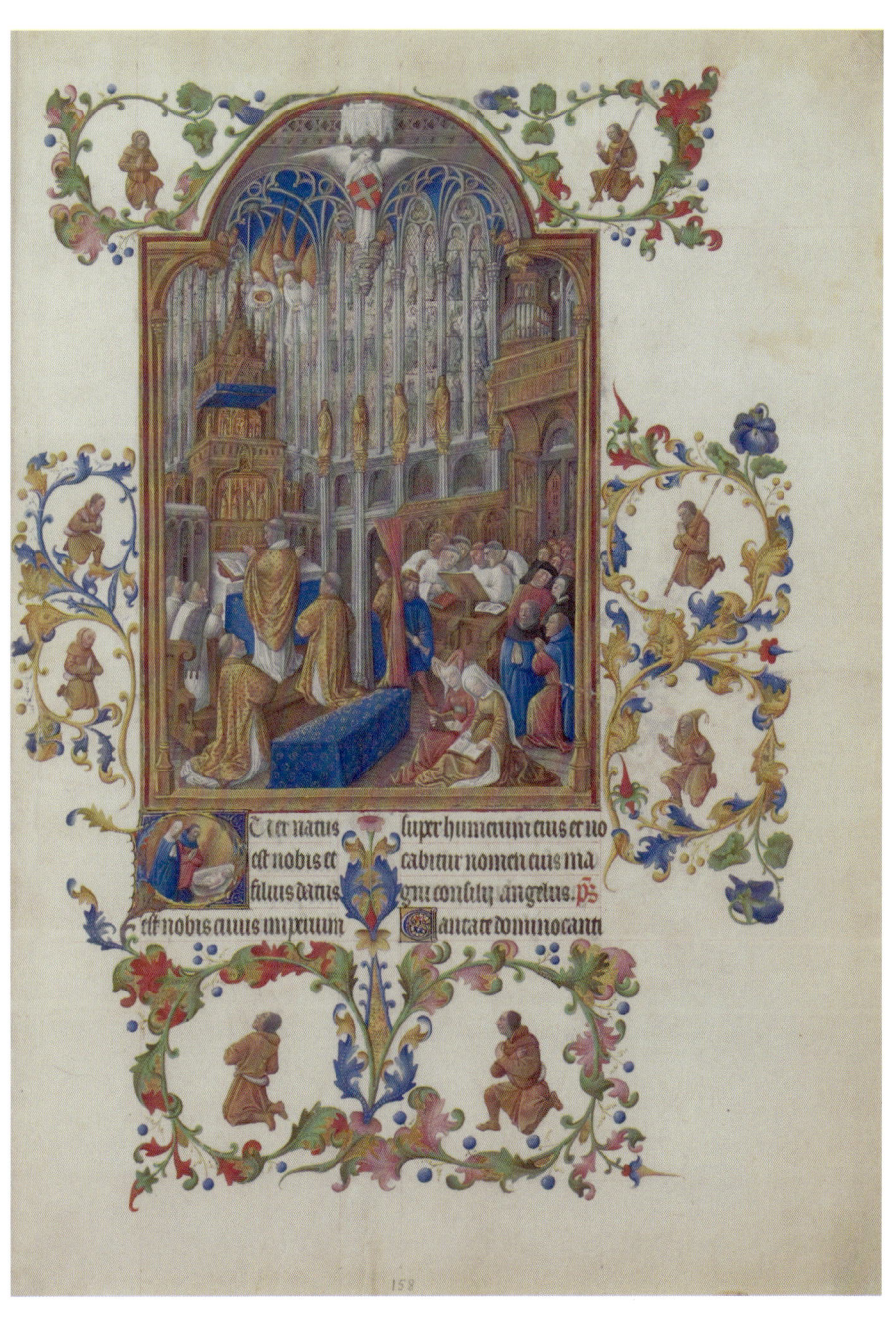

Plate VII. Chantilly, Musée Condé, MS 65, *Très riches heures*, fol. 158ʳ
(fifteenth century)

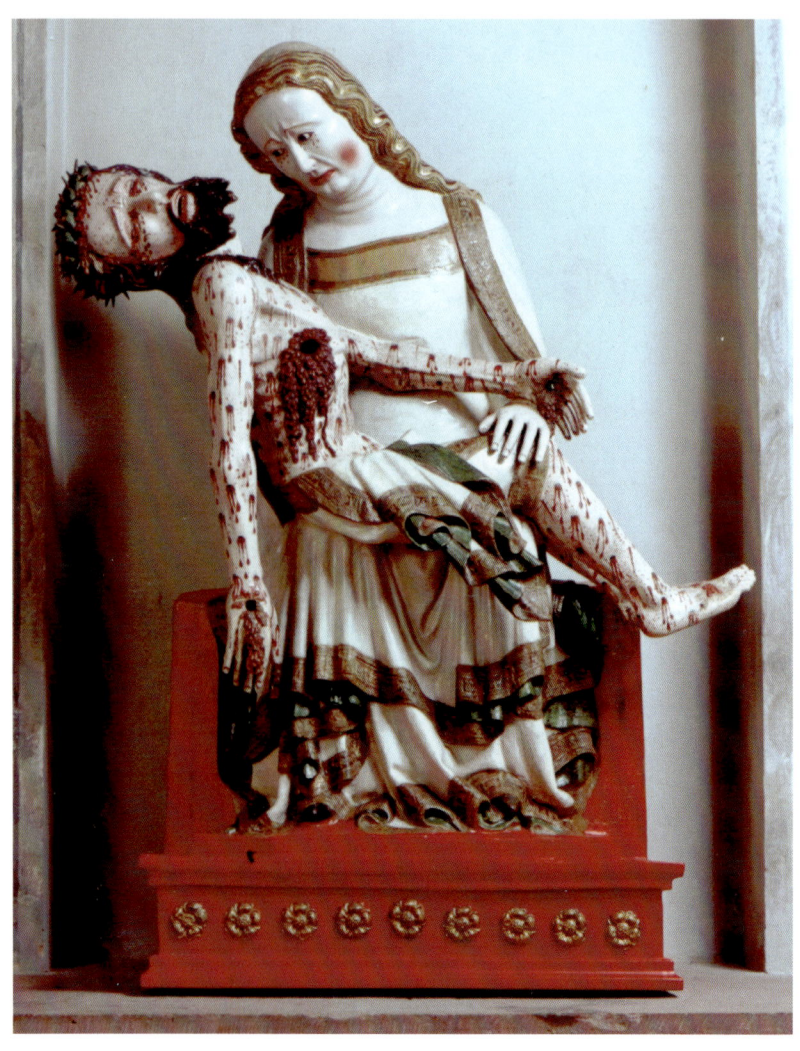

Plate VIII. Fritzlar, Dom, Pietà (fourteenth century)

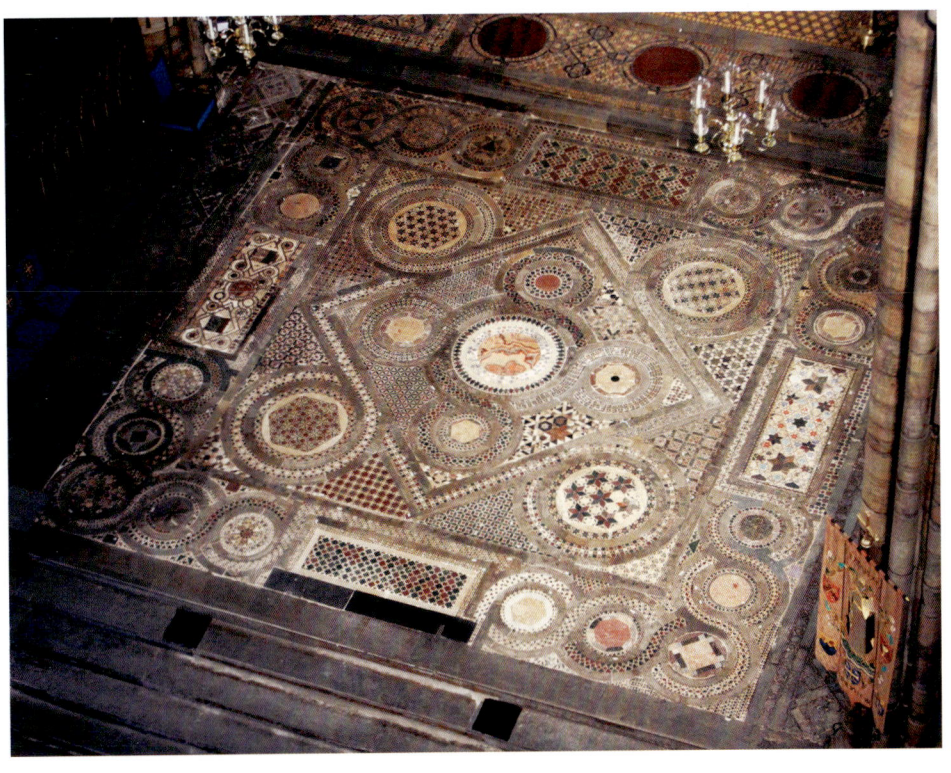

Plate IX. London, Westminster Abbey, Cosmatesque floor (thirteenth century)

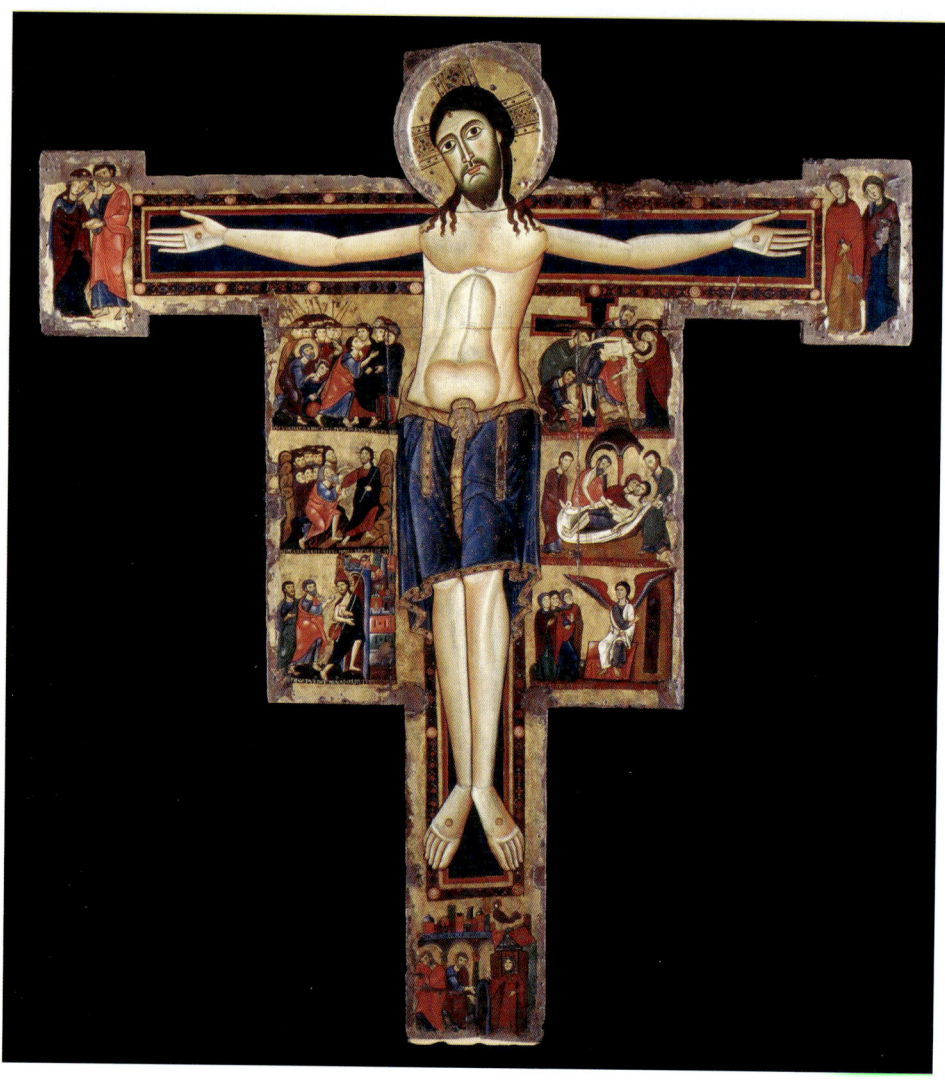

Plate X. Rosano, Abbazia di Santa Maria, crucifix (twelfth century)

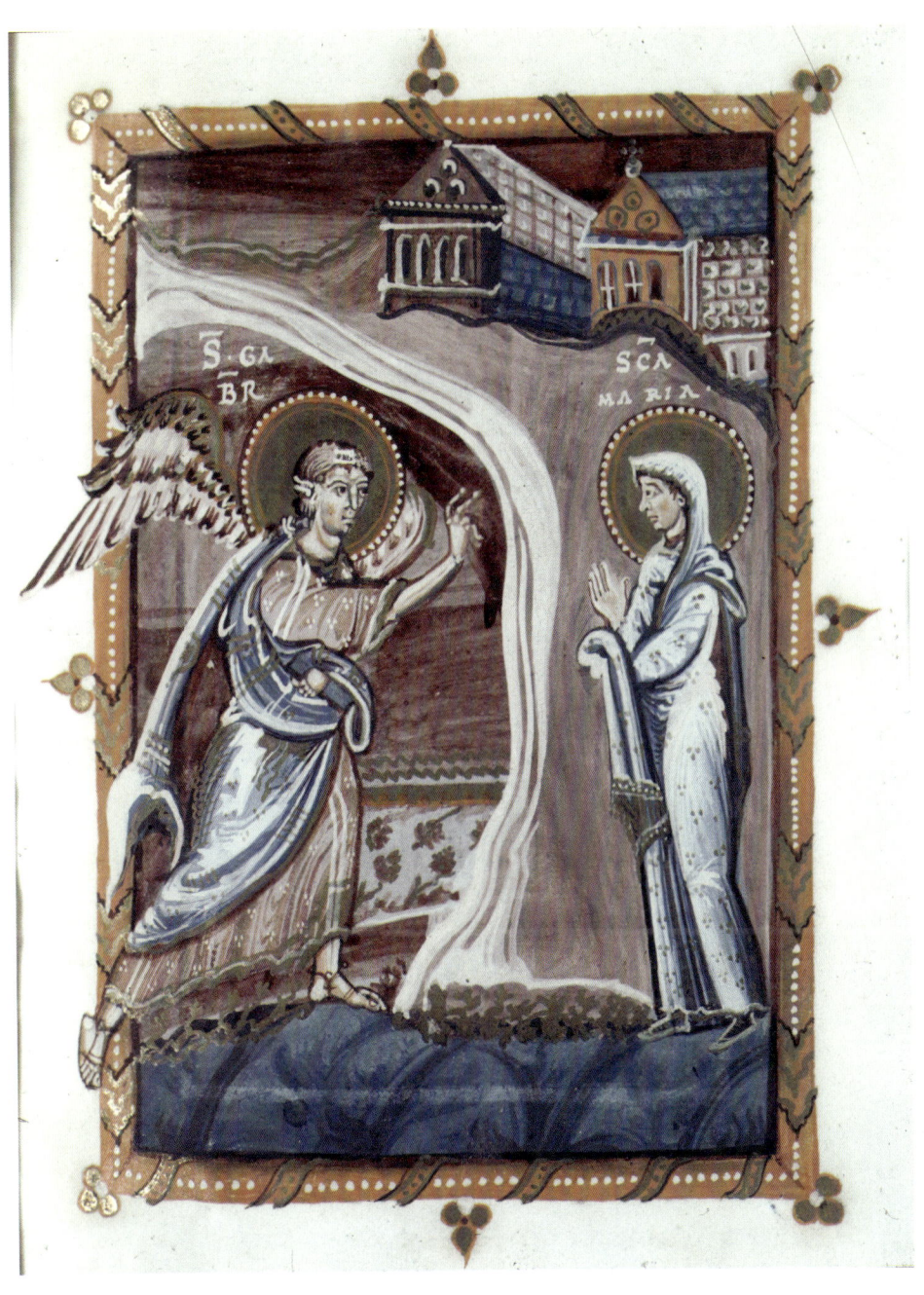

Plate XI. Darmstadt, Hessische Landesbibliothek, Hitda Codex, Cod. 1640, fol. 20ʳ (eleventh century)

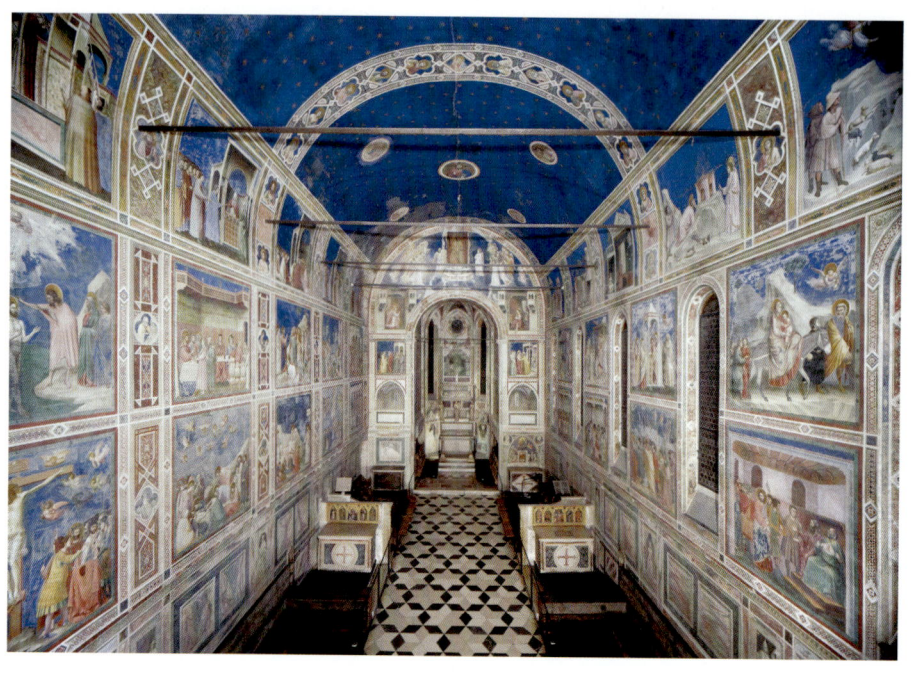

Plate XII. Padua, Scrovegni Chapel (fourteenth century)

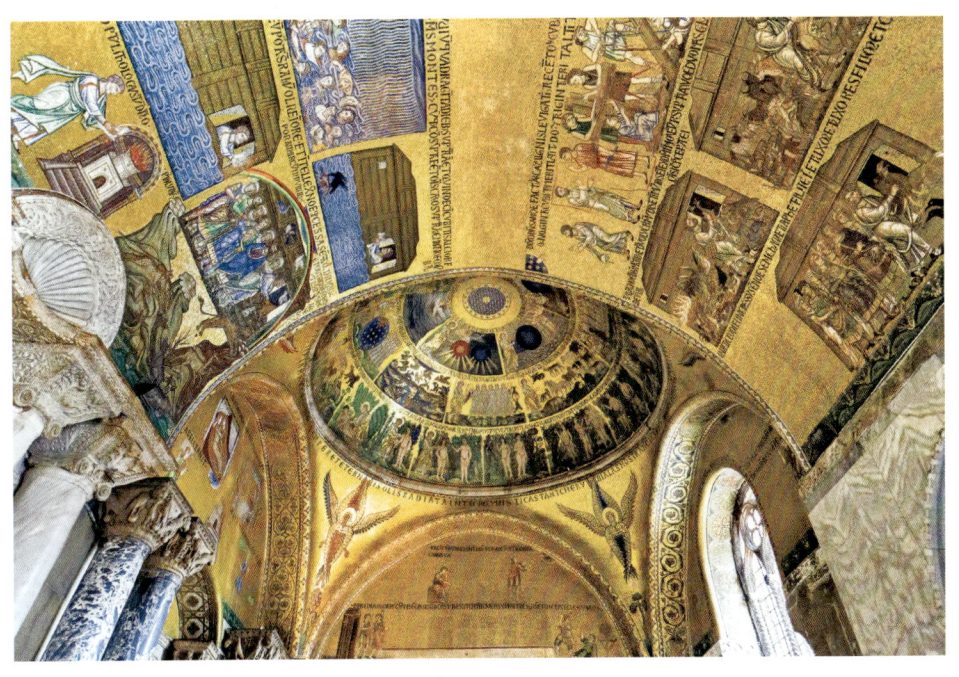

Plate XIII. Venice, San Marco, atrium (thirteenth century)

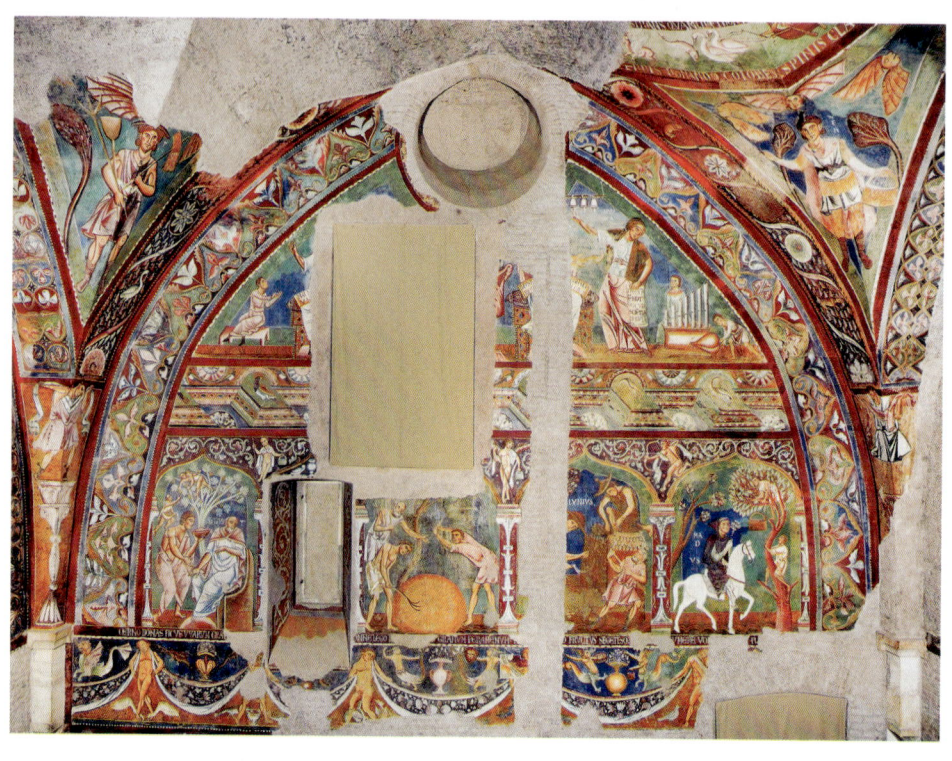

Plate XIV. Rome, Santi Quattro Coronati, *aula gotica* (thirteenth century)

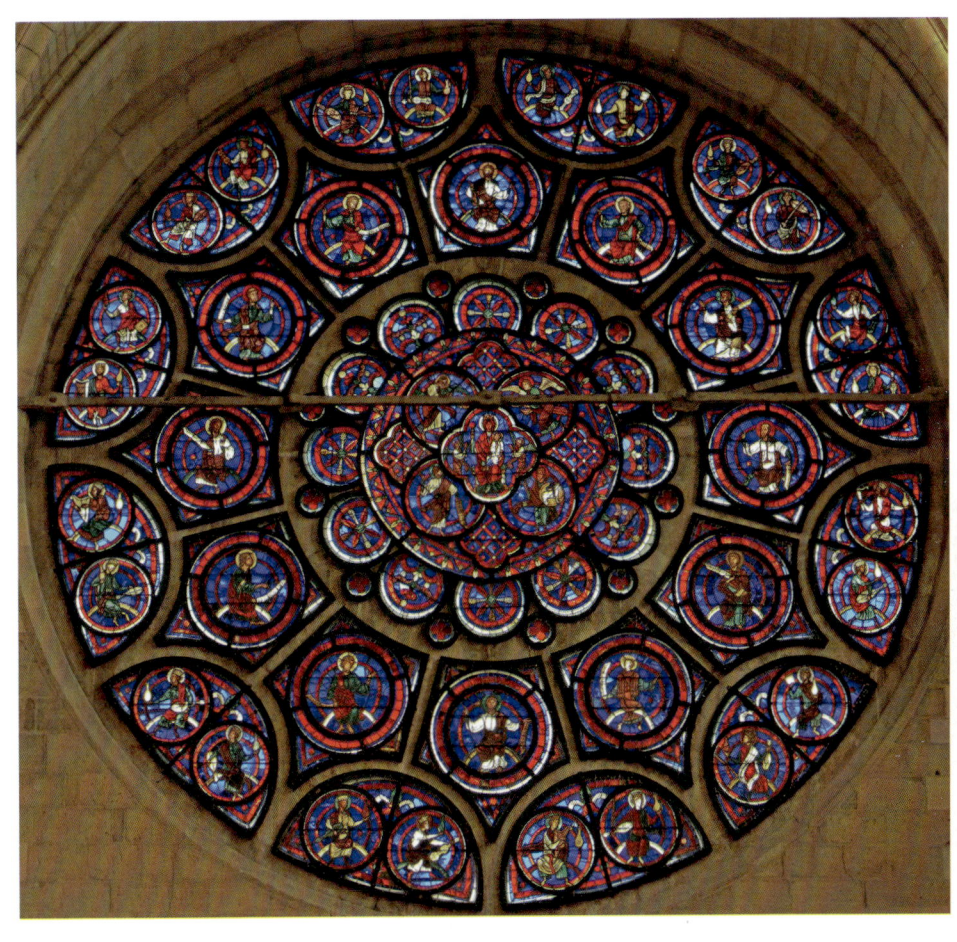

Plate XV. Laon, cathédrale de Notre-Dame, rose window (thirteenth century)

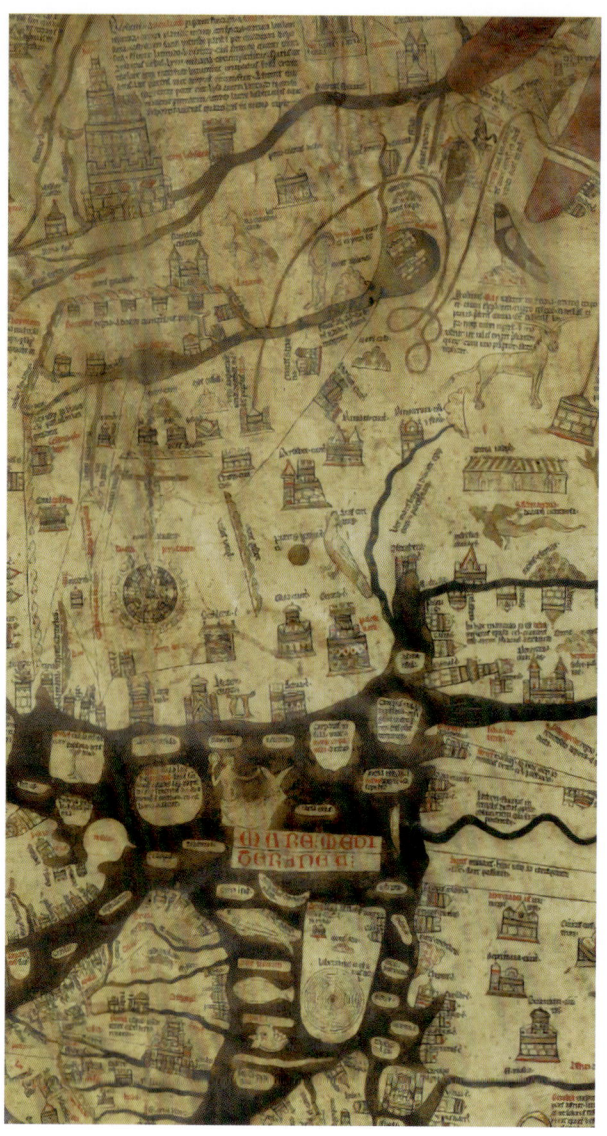

Plate XVI. Hereford, cathedral, *mappa mundi* (detail) (c. 1300)

the conjoining is realized by the Annunciation to the Virgin, at Berzé-la-Ville and elsewhere, by the Lamb of God.[865] In some churches, balconies were constructed also for the display of relics: in the Camera Santa at Oviedo, for example, and at Norwich Cathedral, where a platform was raised north of the altar to present a large crystal container of Christ's blood beneath a canopy of painted vine scrolls, forming a cavernous Easter sepulcher below.[866]

The sanctuary lay beyond.[867] Lighted by the rising sun, it was generally a particularly luminous space, the locus of the church's principal relics and the stage of the liturgical mysteries. In Rome, shimmering gold mosaics rendered the notion that Christ embodied the eastern light.[868] According to Bonizo, the eleventh-century bishop of Sutri, the Trinity dwells there with the angels.[869] At Lincoln Cathedral, paradisiacal ecstasy is evoked by the smiling sculpted angels that adorn the choir, representing the joyous return to God affected through the sacramental blessing staged at the altar.[870] Materials were deployed to reinforce the sense of sacrality. At Westminster Abbey, the Cosmatesque floor (Plate IX) maps the cosmos onto the material world, and, as Suger attests, precious metals and gems clustered near the altar in Saint-Denis and reinforced by the style and imagery of stained-glass windows were intended to affect a mental transition to its celestial archetype:

> Conjoin[ing] the material with the immaterial, the corporeal with the spiritual, the human with the Divine, and sacramentally reform[ing] the purer ones to their original condition. By these and similar visible blessings, you invisibly restore and miraculously transform the present [state] into the Heavenly Kingdom.[871]

The Arnstein glass exemplifies the concept (Figure 33), where the light-infused doves of the seven gifts enter a bud of the Tree of Jesse rising, through David, out of the sleeping ancestor.

The apse was where, it was believed, angels bore the offerings to heaven. At Saint-Savin, the Eucharistic typologies of Noah in the vineyard and Noah enjoying the grapes are represented above the altar; the *Très riches heures* illustrates the idea literally by picturing angels descending on the altar. The effect is well preserved at Notre-Dame in Laon, where three lancets behind the altar "support" a rose window centered on a quatrefoil featuring the Virgin and Child flanked by angels (Plate XV), by the Prophet Isaiah with his prophecy "behold a virgin shall conceive" (Is 7:14), and by John the Baptist bearing a disk with a

Lamb ("behold the Lamb of God" [Jn 1:29]). The small inner quatrefoil generates a cross, and then a sequence of deep blue segments (in the fashion of celestial charts) presents the twelve apostles and twenty-four elders of the Apocalypse.[872] Mary clothed in blue holds the Child in one arm and a brilliant red rose in the other, the "rose without thorns," like the material an emblem of her purity and a metonym of the blossom-like window itself.[873]

A church within the church, the sanctuary contained the altar where the priest consecrated the Eucharist.[874] The "tomb" on which Christ's body and blood are laid was simultaneously the manger where the Magi presented their gifts, a repository of relics, and the Virgin Mary.[875] The altar embodied both material presence and spiritual aspiration, where, Bruno of Segni maintained, the invisible God became present to the human senses. During the Carolingian period, ivory seems to have been reserved almost exclusively for this most sacred of places—covers of liturgical books, chalices, and flabella such as the one preserved in Florence (Plate II). On the Saint-Martin-du-Canigou charter, the altar is covered by simple white cloth, but, in fact, the Christ in Majesty above may be intended to represent the painted antependium of the sort that was common in Catalonia and eventually evolved into elaborate altarpieces of the Valbona type.[876] Altars were often decorated with lavish textiles, as in the Arnstein glass where the Old Testament type is visible through the parted curtains, and at Karlstejn. Altars themselves were often made of marble and adorned with crosses and other symbols of regeneration; for example, on the twelfth-century altar at Saint-Guilhem-le-Désert, a crucifixion is paired with the *Majestas Domini* framed in vines to visualize the sacrifice and elevation that takes place there.[877]

Altars usually contained relics of saints honored in the church, a practice that was officially adopted at the Lateran Council of 1215 and that reinforced their sepulchral aspect. The marble coffin made of spolia in the Sancta Sanctorum, for example, housed various types of relics. The ninth-century altar of Sant'Ambrogio in Milan is adorned with narrative reliefs of the life of Christ facing the nave and the story of Saint Ambrose (whose body is interred in the crypt directly below) facing the choir,[878] configuring the titular saint as an alter-Christus and empowering his burial church.[879] The reliefs picture the fifth-century saint working a miracle while standing at an altar and an angel lifting his soul to heaven from his body lying on an altar-like bed; he is also featured as an active church administrator, like the patron Angilbert, a bishop in pursuit of heretics. In Saint-Remi at Reims, themes related to altars are figured on the floor, including the sacrifice of Isaac and Jacob's ladder at Bethel (before the steps).[880]

The Lisbjerg altar merges several of the themes (Figure 46).[881] Covered with gold and (originally) set with colored gems and crystal (and hence a replica of the Heavenly Kingdom described in Revelation 21), the solid base alludes to Christ's human nature and to a sarcophagus with figures that refers to the earthly city where he had died. The Virgin and Child occupy the gate of the "City of Jerusalem"; Mary's death and assumption are pictured in the irregular fields around her, and her virtues are personified by twelve women on either side. From the *mensa* (or table) formerly housing a bone relic on which the Eucharist was prepared, an arch rises from a band of apostles flanking Christ trampling the beasts, and an inscription beckons the faithful to compare mortal time to everlasting peace: "I urge you to enter into [eternal] rest while you still have time." And between two Old Testament types—the sacrifice of Isaac and Abraham—the crucifix rises, the archetype of the Eucharist that reaches toward the heavenly kingdom, separated by ornament and an inscription that evokes Adam and Eve's sin and Christian healing: "In the sign of the cross, cure is given by the tree." Christ is portrayed again at the very top of the triumphal arch, enthroned and flanked by Mary and John, the medical saints Cosmas and Damian, and angels. For all the multiplicity of images and inscriptions, the Lisbjerg altar is united by the visual sequences of epigrams and repetitious forms and, most of all, by the gleam of the precious metals suggesting the presence on it of the "light of the world."

Because it provided the historical basis of the sacraments while engaging the process of the transformation of *historia* (narrative) into *icona* (image) recapitulated in the liturgy itself, the cross or Crucifixion was the most common theme pictured near the altar. As with the one on the Saint-Martin-du-Canigou cartulary, some crosses were portable and simple, while others, such as that on the Lisbjerg altar, were figured and elevated.[882] Fittings on the back indicate that the Rosano Crucifix (Plate X), like other Italian painted crosses, was suspended over the altar and helped make the transition from Eucharist to Archetype, as pictured in several panels of the Vallbona antependium, where the central monstrance-like tabernacle with the embossed wafer borne by angels to heaven provided a backdrop. The reliquary of the corporal in the Duomo of Orvieto, made in 1337–38 by Ugolino di Vieri, is even more dramatic, displaying the cloth stained with the blood of the Host that demonstrated the truth of Transubstantiation during a Mass at Bolsena.[883]

The open arch of the Lisbjerg altar also recalls baldachins (canopies) that, beginning in the fourth century, were erected over altars to shelter the precious tables and to recall the presence of the honored body.[884] The cloth hanging from the arch above the priest in the Saint-Martin-du-Canigou charter evokes one too; and the scene of Christ's Deposition on the Rosano cross pictures a ciborium to link the narrative of Christ's death to the place where it was being re-enacted. Baldachins are pictured as well above Mary in *La belle verrière* and the miracle scenes at the upper right of the Vallbona altarpiece.[885] The stucco and porphyry ciborium in Sant'Ambrogio is characteristic of the developed type, and the *Majestas Domini* on the early thirteenth-century baldachin of Tost (Vic, Museu Episcopal) conveys the underlying idea that such canopies represent the interface between heaven and earth.[886] The white marble Gothic image of the Heavenly Jerusalem adorned with gold mosaics atop severe dark columns in San Paolo fuori le mura in Rome follows early Christian practice,[887] while the more or less contemporary wood canopy in Hoppertad (Norway) is adorned with fine fret work, surmounted by a bust of Christ and inside two painted angels swinging censers over the altar.

Thrones for the archbishop or bishop, often flanked by benches for lesser clergy, filled the crowns of apses and situated the seated officiants as images of the saints and Christ they represented. In Sant'Ambrogio, for instance, an enormous marble chair framed by the baldachin connects the living incumbent to Christ portrayed in the *Traditio legis* relief enthroned in heaven; Bruno of Segni ended his discussion of Church ornament (*De ornatu*) with a vision of Saint Benedict seated on an ivory throne; and, following a tradition established in sixth-century Ravenna and Grado, the Salerno ivories may once have constituted an elaborate bishop's chair (see Figure 29).[888] Thrones made manifest the pope's secular power and rivalry with rulers, beginning with Solomon, and, through the wise king of the Israelites,[889] they evoked the notion of the Throne of Wisdom (*sedes sapientiae*) and hence Church and Mary. Taken to be Saint Peter's seat and hence a relic of the first bishop of Rome, Charles the Bald's ivory and gold throne authorized the pope as the wise ruler who occupied the heavenly throne on earth.[890]

Candelabra suspended from church ceilings reinforced the cosmic symbolism. The inscription on the wheel chandelier in Sankt Nicholas at Groß-Comburg asserts that the fixture's circular shape and towers signify the Church constructed of the prophets and apostles and uncovers symbolism in the light (faith) and the chain (hope).[891] The usually implicit comparison to the Heavenly Jerusalem is expressed explicitly in the inscription on the famous Barbarossa chandelier at Aachen.[892] In Rome and south Italy, candlesticks fashioned after ancient triumphal columns promoted themes of Christ's victorious resurrection.[893]

Derived ultimately from Roman nymphaea (sacred grottoes),[894] semicircular apses provided a dramatic termination of the nave and redirected the spiritual vector upward, sometimes recapitulating the imagery encountered on the portal and elevating it.[895] Transforming Christ's death and humiliation introduced in frescoes of the Entry into Jerusalem and Last Supper on the west wall of Berzé-la-Ville, the apse represents his eternal reign in heaven with Peter and Paul and local saints, windows framed by Edenic flora and articulated by the wise virgins (who, in the biblical parable, had entered paradise), and capped by the angels flanking an oculus. Conch decoration often figured the sacred conversion through allusions to water that betray continuity with the four rivers of paradise, which flow from the Tree of Life, as in the apse of the upper church of San Clemente in Rome.[896] Symbolizing the Church that brings renewed life, similar streams divide the earthly realm in Santa Maria Maggiore's apse from the celestial vision above.[897] Suger had the idea in mind in his account of the Saint-Denis choir, when he invoked Ezekiel's description of Eden as "a garden adorned with gems" existing "neither entirely in the slime of the earth nor entirely in the purity of Heaven," which reinforced his yearning to be "transported from this inferior to that higher world." Mary, the vessel of Christ's Incarnation and heavenly intercessor, was featured wearing the robe and crown relics in *La belle verrière* originally above the altar that housed them,[898] and she is also featured in stained glass once above Duccio's *Maestà*, moving from her earthly to her heavenly realm by means of medial progression (Siena, Museo del Duomo).[899]

Other Spiritual Spaces

As churches were subdivided to accommodate the developing liturgy, imagery was deployed to mark off diverse functions and to effect the transition between various spaces. Of numerous domains created to serve specific liturgical functions, none was more important than the baptistery. Sometimes a separate building or subdivision of the church, the place of initiation around the font often bore rich decoration. The twelfth-century stone baptismal font in the Stiftskirche Sankt Bonifatius at Freckenhorst, for example, engages several elements (Figure 60).[900]

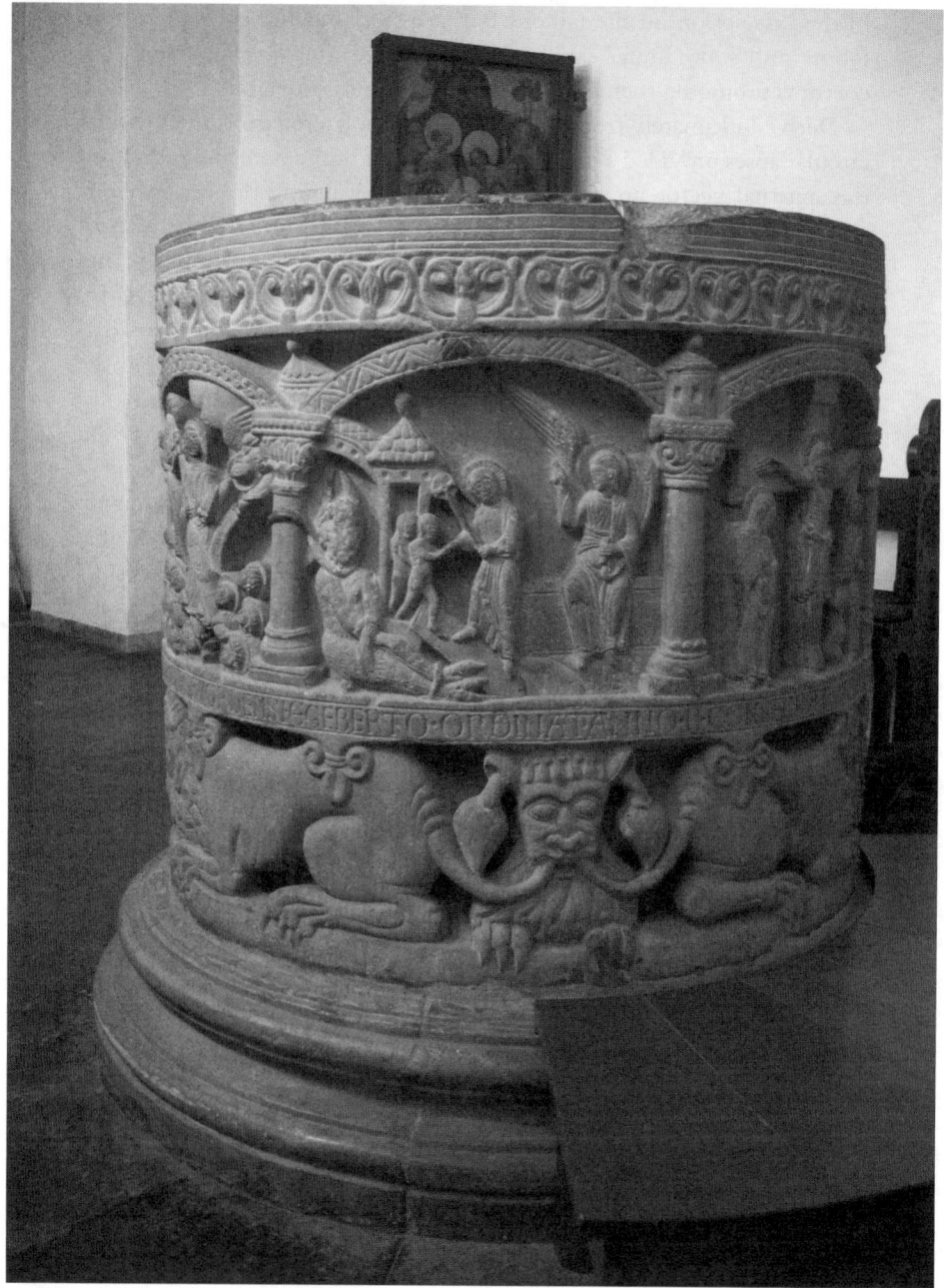

Figure 60. Freckenhorst, Stiftskirche Sankt Bonifatius, baptismal font (twelfth century)

Carved from a single block of stone from nearby Münster, its basin rests on the scene of Daniel in the Lions' Den, a subject of exorcism recapitulated in the depiction of Christ pulling Adam and Eve from hell, one of seven events from Christ's life pictured beneath the arches of the main register.

Separate oratories, chapels, and chapter houses, many containing relics and furnished with altars, provided rooms for private devotion and pilgrim visits and became venues for artistic innovation.[901] Side chapels, for instance, seem to have prompted the development of the altarpiece.[902] Eleventh-century paintings of Christ charging Peter provided an appropriate backdrop for monastic administration conducted in the chapter house at Vendôme;[903] there, in the manner noted by the contemporary theologian Hildebert de Lavardin, Christ is shown at Emmaus raising the Eucharist in the mode of the liturgical rite of breaking the sacramental bread (*fractio panis*). The chapter house in Santa Maria Novella in Florence, decorated in the 1360s by Andrea Bonaiuto, promotes the Dominican Order's place in the history of salvation and the Church and features a magnificent fresco with a portrait of the Florence Duomo as the point of entry of the path toward heaven.[904] The scenes from the Book of Revelation suggest that the Salzburg drawing may have been intended for a burial chapel.

In monastic cloisters, sculptures served various purposes.[905] At San Paolo fuori le mura, the Cosmatesque courtyard completed in 1230 included admonitory vignettes such as Adam and Eve (in another garden) eating from the forbidden tree and a fox in monastic garb distracted from his reading by a tempting goat.[906] At Saint-Michel-de-Cuxa, early twelfth-century capitals filled with monstrous and overtly lascivious figures conjured up evil thoughts, precisely in an effort to convert them into pious aspirations.[907] Images of the veiled Sancta Sanctorum on the piers of the thirteenth-century cloister in the Cistercian monastery at Santa Maria la Real de Las Huelgas (Burgos), invited nuns (especially those in the adjacent infirmary) to meditate on the Virgin and the heavenly Jerusalem they aspired to enter.[908] At Santes Creus (see Figure 36), a capital on the southwest pier depicting Adam and Eve sinning, being called by God, and being expelled into the world leads in a straight diagonal to the Last Judgment and the Virgin Mary at the entrance to the church—the door through paradise is regainable if one is not distracted by the randomly placed drolleries in between.[909]

Other buildings served different ecclesiastic functions. Pope Leo III built reception and dining halls at the Lateran decorated with mosaics that promoted the agenda of establishing papal ties to the Franks,[910] and nearly half a millennium later, the remarkable array of painting in the *aula gotica* of Santi Quattro Coronati (probably a courtroom and banquet hall) emphasized Christian orthodoxy (Plate XIV).[911] Some monastic refectories were adorned with such appropriate subjects as the Last Supper or the Miracle of Loaves and Fishes;[912] others underscored the danger of allowing carnal food to distract from spiritual nourishment.[913] The abbot's quarters at the monastery of Tre Fontane in Rome were decorated with contentious frescoes built around the theme of *contemptus mundi* (disdain for physical existence).[914]

Powerful rulers erected private chapels that were the near equal of churches. When he established a permanent residence at Aachen, Charlemagne fitted it with a *capella palatina*, which his successors embellished and emulated. Edward the Confessor began to rebuild Westminster Abbey as the royal burial church, finished by Henry III. Roger II's Cappella Palatina in Palermo is one of the most elaborate churches preserved from the Middle Ages. In Rome, a succession of popes built and steadily augmented the chapel of San Lorenzo at the Lateran palace, emulating both the Pharos Chapel of the Byzantine emperors in Constantinople and King Louis IX's Sainte-Chapelle in Paris.[915] In turn, Charles IV continued the sequence when he built Karlstejn, as did Jean, duc de Berry, at Bourges. Lesser figures emulated royalty. Enrico Scrovegni constructed the chapel adjacent to his palace in Padua and had the most eminent painter of his age decorate it. And eventually, the Florentine guilds elaborated the tabernacle of Orsanmichele as a separate oratory and fitted it with stained-glass windows that confirmed the market panel's miraculous powers.

Chapter 7
Life (and Death)

THE REAL world was often deemed a distraction from the eternal life that much medieval art was fashioned to serve. The *Hortus deliciarum*, for instance, devoted a page to the wheel of fortune, which also includes two men working puppet soldiers labeled *vanitas vanitatum,* to remind even its cloistered readers that everything in this life, including artifacts and the pleasures they afford, are destined to perish. As one of the men looks intently at battling rod puppets (*simulacra*) in front of him, the other begins to turn away toward Solomon, the author of the verses quoted on the facing page that declare that human endeavors are useless (Eccl 1:2). Likewise, Lenzi's *Speccio umano* sets up a contrast between devotion to a miraculous image and the panic and chaos caused by the catastrophic famine of 1329 (Figure 16). The miniature conveys the devastating event's actuality through details of the setting arranged in a receding space; people interacting with one another and with things—including large barrels of grain—and by enhancing the pathos with such poignant vignettes as a pregnant woman swooning from hunger in the lower left and a mother pleading with a menacing member of the civic militia. In contrast, the icon of Mary and Christ within the Gothic tabernacle at the right provides an island of peace, attended by a member of the confraternity that provided alms for the cripple, blind man, and pregnant woman below.[916] In fact, the miniature blurs the distinction between sacred and profane. It illustrates an account book of monthly grain prices, and it pictures God governing the forces of nature and the confraternity caring for the miraculous image with resources generated in the market.

Secular life, in short, was inextricably mixed with religion. Prelates controlled the Liberal Arts curriculum.[917] Astronomy served to calculate the liturgical hours and calendrical matters (as illustrated in Pacificus of Verona's nocturnal clock; Figure 53); herbals were illuminated in monasteries; and monarchs promoted the study of theology and collected relics (Figure 12). The Aachen pulpit (commissioned by an emperor) was adorned with treasured pagan spolia and secular game pieces, displayed as if on a game board (Plate IV).[918] The Coronation Mantle, originally a secular silk (Figure 14), was transformed by embroidery into a chasuble and given to the church by Queen Gisela and King Stephen I of Hungary; the latter, in turn, was later canonized as a saint and ultimately his cape became a part of the imperial regalia. Rulership descended from the biblical David; Louis's Sainte-Chapelle treasured the "rod of Moses," putting the French king in line with the kings of Israel.[919] King Louis was also canonized, like Stephen of Hungary and myriad other rulers including Clovis, Charlemagne, Ladislav, and Elisabeth of Hungary.[920] Divinely sanctioned kingship was dramatized in the painted chamber at Westminster by an angel and prophet on the ceiling overlooking the state bed that abutted a mural of the bishops crowning Saint Edward the Confessor.[921] Crusader knights and their sponsors believed that they were pursuing God's mission when they recaptured the Holy Land. Integrating adventure with a moral lesson, the *Chanson de Roland* was represented in the Charlemagne window at Chartres and Montebourg Psalter,[922] above a portal of the Modena Cathedral, on nave pavements,[923] and in the apse of the duomo of Aquileia,[924] as well as in Bremen's town square.[925]

Created by God, the natural world was ambivalent, embodying both splendor and divine principles.[926] The early fourteenth-century anthology of Anglo Norman, English, and Latin texts in Cambridge was compiled and illustrated to instruct lay persons on how best to live here while preparing for the future; the scientific diagram of the brain confronts a schema of the nature of the soul (Figure 55).[927] Franciscans promoted the study of optics;[928] one brother, Peter of Limoges, wrote a treatise entitled *The Moral Treatise of the Eye* that cited Aristotelean theories of vision (made available through Ibn al-Haytham, known in the west as Alhacen) as exempla for teaching lay persons the proper way to live a Christian life.[929]

Many works of art assert a reciprocity between secular and sacred. Baudri de Bourgeuil's eleventh-century description of the decoration of countess Adela's chamber emphasizes the continuity between ancient origins and Christian culture; it inventories scenes of Creation, Eden, the Flood, and other Old Testament subjects together with episodes from Greek mythology, Roman history, and the Norman conquest of England. The autograph text, moreover, is included in a composite manuscript that contains religious tituli (Vatican, Bib. apos., Cod. Reg. lat. 1351).[930] The contrast of geometric and organic ornament on the Hildesheim aquamanile may be understood as a migration of Islamic court culture to Christian church use (Figure 9), implying superiority while, at the same time, applying the apotropaic principle of "like cures like."[931] Decorating a multifunctional space that most likely served curial gatherings, tribunals, and perhaps banquets, the frescoes in the *aula gotica* include only two scriptural types (Plate XIV), Cain Killing Abel and King Solomon, subjects from Hebrew Scripture appropriate to the space's judicial functions. The overarching theme of the learned imagery is humankind's temporal condition within the dynamics of salvation conveyed through a panoply of virtues and vices, labors and sins, ancient gods and rulers, prophets and Christian holy men, including the near-contemporary saints Francis and Dominic. Under a vast lapis lazuli ceiling encircled by a zodiac and other constellations, quotations from Roman sculpture including swag-bearing putti and a lion attacking a deer enhance the fresco's ancient aura and anchor the painting in the bygone classical world, strengthening the notion of historical unfolding within a typological discourse.[932]

Secular art was often in dialogue with religious themes. Whether the Bayeux embroidery itself (Figure 31) originally was displayed in a Norman keep, a church setting, a mausoleum, or an abbot's residence, Baudri de Bourgeuil's prose description (*ekphrasis*) imagines a similar tapestry adorning a secular hall with a *mappa mundi* pavement, histories on the walls, and an astrological ceiling.[933] As the earliest surviving example of purely profane art within a secular building, the paintings in Rodenegg castle (near Brixen; Figure 61), apparently dating to the 1220s,[934] draw on conventions long used in religious narratives to structure and interpret the chivalric tale of Iwein; the scene of Lady Laudine grieving over Ascalon's body, for instance, was patterned after a Lamentation of Christ. And shocking lead badges depicting sexual organs, such as one on which two erect male members are represented walking on a flowery field with a crowned vulva on their shoulders and

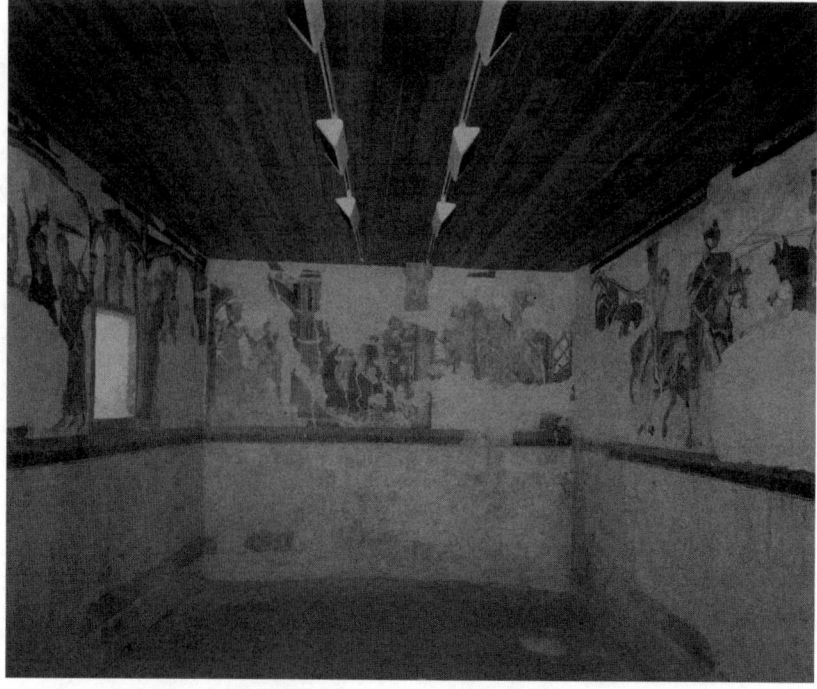

Figure 61. Rodenegg, Castello, fresco (thirteenth century)

a third ready to penetrate it (Figure 62), are to be understood as snarky inversions of the ubiquitous religious tokens found with them (such as the one featuring the Madonna and Child; Figure 2),[935] and thus as parodies of the solemn pilgrimages the others commemorate. The burlesque badges also caricature Christ's bleeding chest wound that, increasingly, was emphasized on such contemporary depictions as the Fritzlar Pietà (Plate VIII).[936] On one level, the aisle paintings in Sant Joan de Boí enhance spiritual celebrations (Figure 59), but the joyful pageant of jugglers also mocks martyrdom (specifically Stephen's stoning) and the dancing harpist provides a secular counterpoint for David's sacred music.[937] The map of the world produced in Hereford c. 1300 comprehends the complex dialogue between nature and religion perfectly (Plate XVI);[938] unlike the celestial map of the Salzburg drawing, which was constructed to accommodate the faithful's aspiration to glimpse heaven (Figure 44),[939]

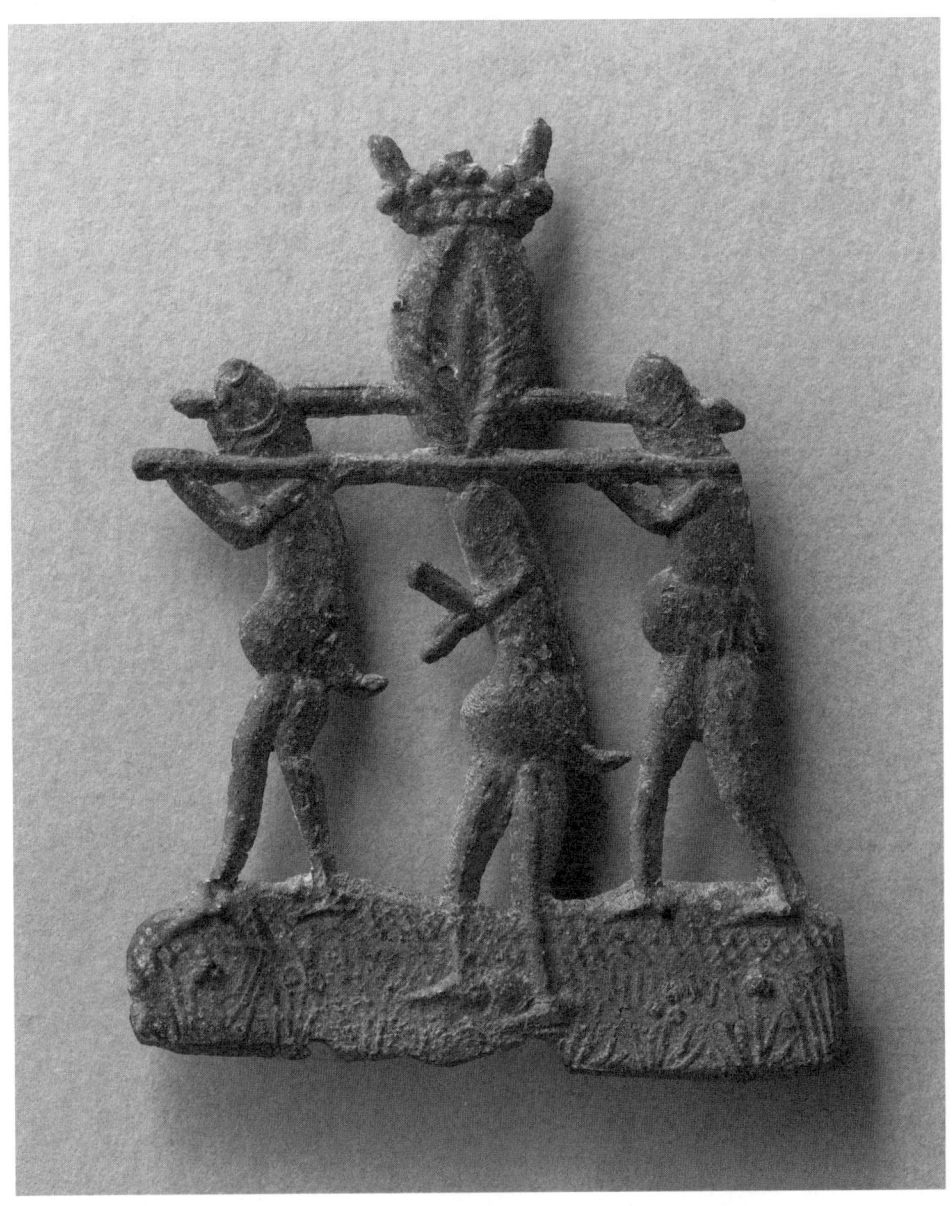

Figure 62. Paris, Musée Cluny, erotic pilgrim badge (fourteenth century)

it represents God's view of a world centered on Jerusalem, where humans had put his Son to death; and it identifies sites mentioned in Scripture (including paradise, where Adam and Eve violated his commandments), situating them in places known from classical literature (such as the labyrinth of Crete). Accompanying texts cite the Bible, Alexander legends, Orosius's *Historiae adversus paganos*, and the bestiary; and pictures include a portrait of the emperor Augustus (who had ordered the census that caused the Virgin Mary to journey to Bethlehem), myriad creatures, and narratives of the Exodus and Last Judgment. Likewise, Cimabue's remarkable *Ytalia* in Assisi, the imagined destination of Saint John's Gospel, envisions Rome as a harmonious agglomeration of a long history, with (appropriately) San Giovanni in Laterano closest to the Evangelist, the three-staged Castel Sant'Angelo with Nero's pyramid near the entrance, the medieval Torre delle Milizie, the Pantheon, and San Pietro and the Palazzo Senatorio on the Capitoline Hill as counterparts of one another, one adorned with a mosaic of the judging Christ and the other emblazoned with alternating coats of arms of the reigning pope's Orsini family and the ancient acronym for the Senate and People of Rome, SPQR.[940] The same artisans who produced ivories for aristocratic amusement in fourteenth-century Paris carved similar precious objects for intense religious devotion (see Figure 7). An ivory box in Paris (Musée du Louvre) deploys the microarchitecture that on contemporary religious works represented the Ark of the Covenant for cherished tokens of human love.[941] Secular and religious, in other words, are often dynamically balanced and productively integrated with each other.

Classical Heritage

Pagan antiquity provided a vast and varied reservoir of secular art that the Middle Ages quarried, revised, augmented, and transformed.[942] Especially in Italy, Spain, and parts of France rich in Roman remains, classical forms were often perpetuated or recycled. At the Lateran, the second-century bronze equestrian statue of Marcus Aurelius became Constantine; in Oviedo, imperial imagery from a consular diptych, including circus scenes, was copied onto the doors of the Asturian palace.[943] The ancient heritage and fascination with Rome were continuously revived elsewhere, too; even if they assimilate local pagan traditions as well, the Hildesheim bronze monuments betray Bishop Bernward's travels and fascination with the imperial city (Figure 23). And, working near his hometown in northeast France during the twelfth century, Nicholas of Verdun surely studied the classical treatment of clothed figures and elegant contrapoised limbs (contrapposto) of the personifications adorning the fourth-century Nicomachi-Symmachi diptych he had mounted in the shrine of Saint Berchaire.[944]

Cosmological knowledge amassed by Aratus in the third century BCE and passed down in Latin translation was incorporated in manuscripts illustrated in Carolingian monasteries and, in turn, conveyed to later centuries;[945] the figural representations of constellations transmitted something of the mythological iconography and even the classical style of the late antique models.[946] Likewise, the *corpus agrimensores Romanorum* transferred not only ancient surveying techniques to later centuries but also vestiges of landscape painting. The Westminster Abbey Cosmatesque floor mapped Roman cosmology and references onto contemporary politics (Plate IX),[947] and ancient knowledge of plant species and their particular characteristics was preserved in the ninth-century *Pseudo-Apuleius* in Kassel (Landesbibliothek und Murhadsche Bibliothek, 2° ms phys. et hist. nat. 10) and myriad other manuscripts,[948] including an illuminated herbal in Copenhagen (Kongelige Bibliotek, MS Thott 190 2°) based ultimately on the Greek *Dioscurides*.[949]

Some of the ancient sources were themselves Christian—the *Physiologus*, for instance, which applied to fauna the kind of moralizing reading that Christians mapped onto Hebrew Scripture to tease out signs of the Incarnation in nature,[950] as was Prudentius's popular *Psychomachia*,[951] transmitted in manuscripts and incorporated in church decorations and the *aula gotica* frescoes. Labors of the months were transmitted in calendar pictures, of which the ninth-century copy of the Calendar of 354 is perhaps most famous,[952] but they were elaborated in contemporary language, as in the *aula gotica*'s threshers and grape-harvesters. Transmission was often complex; some ancient material passed directly, other detoured through the Byzantine and Muslim worlds. Much was original but some was already converted, for example, the late Carolingian *De arithmetica* in Lund (University Library, Medeltidshandskrift 1), which seems to have been based on Boethius's mathematical diagrams transmitted through a Hiberno-Saxon intermediary already imbued with cross-symbolism.[953]

The Carolingians had collected classical literary texts, among others at least two illustrated late antique Virgil manuscripts[954] as well as illustrated manuscripts of Terence's comedies.[955] Centuries before it was deployed for the Hereford *mappa mundi*, Orosius's *Historiae adversus paganos* had been incorporated into the decorations of Ingelheim and was illustrated in the antique manner in an early twelfth-century manuscript now in the Vatican (BAV, Ms. Vat. lat. 3340).[956] Depictions of history and romance were also rooted in antiquity.[957] A late tenth-century fragment of the *History of Apollonius of Tyre* (Budapest, Országos Széchényi Konyvtár, Cod. Lat. 4) is illustrated in the manner of ancient books written in narrow columns interrupted by myriad narrative pictures;[958] a thirteenth-century manuscript of Godfrey of Viterbo's *Pantheon* illustrates the Life of Alexander the Great in the same manner.[959]

Perhaps most important for art were practical manuals that conveyed ancient science in diagrams.[960] While some favored pure geometrical shapes and others introduced ladders, trees, and more intricate diagrammatic forms,[961] they enabled the embedding of universal principles in renderings of nature and the correlating of conceptual connections with theological concepts.[962] The brain map in the Cambridge compendium, for instance, imposes order to make a theory of cognition easily readable, and a miniature in Honorius Augustodunensis's *Clauis physicae* (Paris, BnF, MS lat. 6734) presents a Platonic understanding of the relationship between primal causes and the world of matter as passed down through Eriugena's *Periphyseon*.[963] Much art deployed diagrams to chart clear, ordered pathways between things and ideas; the *Vrigiet de solas*, for instance, creates a productive dialogue between several diagrammatic forms (Figure 56).[964] Like the texts included in the compendium that served the Dominican preacher's rhetorical practices involving enumeration and antithesis, a miniature before Peraldus's *Summa de virtutibus et virtiis* (London, Brit. Lib., Harley MS 3244, fols. 27ᵛ–28ʳ) gathers miscellaneous passages from Scripture, diagrams, and images to construct a memorable chain of correspondences based on spiritual combat.[965] Fully painted and most earthly, a knight engages the viewer directly, his sword, helmet, and other pieces of armor symbolizing virtues and his shield the *scutum fidei* of Ephesians 6:14–19. An angel descending from heaven bestows on him seven beatitudes, and the seven gifts of the Holy Spirit form a phalanx before him as he sets out to conquer the cardinal vices, each one generating secondary and tertiary vices rendered as demons neatly set in a grid. Even seemingly simple appropriations were intellectually ambitious. The intersecting circles drawn from Calcidius's commentary on Plato's *Timeaus* map geometry onto Christ's dual natures in the Tours Sacramentary initial (Figure 47),[966] moving from word to image and Law to Eucharist in a manner that mimics transubstantiation.

Revamping

Medieval art transformed inherited subjects and systems to serve new needs. The highly classical Leiden *Aratea* (Universiteitsbibliotheek, VLQ 7) produced under Louis the Pious, for instance, modifies the source pictures, refiguring Castor and Pollux as Christian soldiers and incorporating a diagram that corresponds to the heavens at Aachen just before Easter 816.[967] The archetype of a computus handbook illustrated for Bishop Ebo of Metz in a refined classical style in 809 (Madrid, Bib. nac., MS 3307) introduced a chapter from Bede to counteract the pagan constellation pictures and extend their iconography to make exegetical arguments;[968] the Pythagorean diagram of the harmonic intervals of the planets, for example, was "corrected" to demonstrate Christian renewal.[969] A ninth-century collection of astrological texts, preserved in copies in Munich (Bay. Staatsbib., Clm 210) and Vienna (Nationalbibliothek, MS 387), includes among its traditional diagrams and pictures a schema of the winds derived from a *Majestas Domini*,[970] and Aesculapius portrayed at the front of the Kassel herbal (Landesbibliothek und Murhadische Bibibliothek, 2 ° MS phys et hist. nat. 10, fol. 14^v), enthroned within a mandorla while transmitting his prescriptions to doctors, surely owes more to contemporary depictions of the *Traditio legis* than to any classical author portrait.[971] An illustrated composite manuscript produced in or near Canterbury in the first quarter of the eleventh century (London, Brit. Lib., Cotton MS Vitellius C III) contains various ancient pharmacological texts translated into Old English and updated for use in northern Europe,[972] and the astrological compendium in Venice containing the Pacificus diagram also includes the Carolingian revision of the *Aratus latinus* that had rearranged the ancient constellations to enhance the text's usefulness.[973]

Classical art was quarried for new creations. Not only were the creatures illustrating Psalm 148 in the Utrecht Psalter taken from an illustrated *Physiologus* (Figure 38), for example, but the zodiac accompanying the words of Psalm 64 was also copied from an *Aratea*.[974] The scenes from Virgil adorning the ivory case of the flabellum of Tournus establish a bucolic aura for the breeze-generating liturgical fan (Plate II). The mosaicists in the atrium of San Marco supplemented the (by the thirteenth century, defective) fifth-century Greek Genesis manuscript that served as their basic model with suitable motifs copied from ancient models (Plate XIII);[975] and, to gloss the scribe's irrepressible activity, the illuminator of the *Cantigas* interpolated cranes from a bestiary to emphasize the pictured scribe's ability, like the birds', to stay awake day and night.[976]

Borrowings generated new meanings. Not only did motifs copied from the Vatican Virgil into the First Bible of Charles the Bald authorize Jerome's Vulgate translation as a worthy Latin text, but they also transformed the account of Saint Paul's travels to Damascus into a new *Aeneid*.[977] The animal lore incorporated on the right lintel of the church of the Holy Sepulcher in Jerusalem asserts Christianity's triumph over the evil Saracens (Figure 42).[978] *Abyssus* in the first Day of Creation pictured among the mosaics of the cathedral of Monreale illustrates the opening words of Genesis and also distinguishes the world of non-believers from the faithful who understand the Trinity-Creator above,[979] and in a similar way, the same personification's inclusion on the undersides of south Italian lectern-pulpits introduces the notion of profane evil defeated by God's word.[980] A satyr inspired by a Roman Bacchus was reborn on the Jaca capital as a Christian soul delirious for God (Figure 27).[981] The same principle underlies Adam's fashioning in San Pietro in Valle after a Roman sarcophagus (still in the church), which not only characterizes humankind before the Fall as perfect physically and spiritually (Figure 58)[982] but also contrasts the pagan deity's lustful embrace of a demonic faun on the ancient relief to the first man's gift of judgment over the assembly of naturalistically rendered birds and beasts (among which geese, a hog, a camel, and a ram are easily recognized).

Geometry was particularly important because it was believed to disclose the principles underlying creation.[983] No basic shape was more important than the circle;[984] a vision of the eternal God (Christ) who made the world occupies the center of the circular map of paradise on the eleventh-century tapestry in the Gerona cathedral, anchored by the four rivers of paradise and framed by the labors of the month, medallions of year, day and night, and the seasons.[985] A mid-ninth-century tract on the Eucharist maintained that the Host was appropriately round because God has no beginning and no end and, like the center point, is motionless; it also likened the wafer to the coins of earthly monarchs, picturing a circle subdivided by a cross and inscribed with Christ's epithets.[986] A circular *spolium* replaces God on the Aachen ambo (Plate IV), and the basic shape forms the universe in Pacificus's *Horologium*. Hildegard of Bingen and Heinrich Suso both introduce it to figure the celestial realm (Figures 19 and 22), and the *aula gotica* ceiling is structured as a diagram based on a circle.[987] An inscription on a chandelier in Groß-Comburg extends the symbolism to the "immortal Church."[988]

The universal shape mediated between this world and the next, as the oculus also does at the top of the Berzé-la-Ville apse and the Salzburg Chapel, and it effects a transition from the present to the future (Figures 32 and 44). Occupying the space between the mundane and sacred, circles were also used as consecration signs;[989] inscribed with christograms, circles above the entrances of Romanesque churches in Spain and southern France negotiated between Christ's two natures (one not representable and the other visual). Likewise, *mappae mundi* were circular and locate Jerusalem at the world's middle point,[990] and the Aosta pavement amplifies the circle's unending character by encircling it with the ancient palindrome *sator arepo tenet opera rotas* (the precise meaning of which is still not known), written so that the alternating vowels and consonants form a chain that rhymes with Solomon's knots (Figure 49).

Books, on the other hand, were rectangular, and their bindings and protective boxes often took advantage of the basic shape to present ecclesiological concepts to the reader. The Soiscél Molaise, for example, extends the arms of the cross beyond a central circle to subdivide the rectangular field into four spaces for the Evangelist symbols in a pattern like the carpet pages inside contemporary manuscripts.[991] The rhombus (*tetragonus mundi*) serves the same function on the book John proffers on the Book of Kells frontispiece (Figure 54) and on the base of the Lisbjerg altar (Figure 46); as on many depictions of the *Majestas Domini*, it distinguishes the earthly domain from the celestial.[992]

The triangle was particularly pregnant with meaning because other polygons could be reconstituted from it and because it was the basis for measuring distances essential for surveying, astronomy, and other practical uses including the carving of sculpture.[993] Thus, the margins of a twelfth-century manuscript of Gerbert of Aurillac's *Isagoge geometriae* diagram the forms of the triangle (University of Pennsylvania, Rare Books Collection, MS LJS 194, fol. 12^v), and Ambrogio Lorenzetti organized the Massa Marittima altarpiece (Figure 21) around the shape rife with Trinitarian implications.[994]

More complex geometry elaborated conceptual connections.[995] The John portrait in the Book of Kells is a series of variations on circles, squares, rectangles, and crosses, while the geometry used to organize the Saint Albans Psalter expresses the sacred music that the poems also engage (Figure 40).[996] The eleventh-century Uta Codex creatively deployed schemata to reveal the harmony of diverse representations,[997] and a (mostly lost) inscription on the Westminster Abbey pavement identified Rome at its center, likened the quincunx to the "eternal pattern of the world" and the "measure" of the outermost circle of the universe, evoking the end of time when the primordial world, represented by the cloudy onyx disc at the center, would be restored.[998]

Geometric schemata were also orchestrated. The Freckenhorst baptismal font (Figure 60), for instance, sets lines of text, images, and ornament in opposing circular directions.[999] Cued by portraits of Hippocrates and Galen discussing the origin of the world and Moses's narrative account,[1000] frescoes in the crypt at Anagni deploy the zodiac, a diagram of the microcosm, and a syzygy (drawn from diagrams found in manuscripts of Boethius, Bede, and other natural philosophers) to assert the fundamental agreement between the elements, seasons, humors, and ages of humankind, and to set up a contrast between knowledge derived from human reasoning and the divine. Number and geometry control the iconographic elements of rose windows, such as the one above the altar in Laon (Plate XV), disclosing the harmony between biology (embodied in the flower Mary proffers), the cosmos, and theology. Mapped onto female reproductive anatomy (transmitted from classical sources recycled through Muslim intermediaries), the diagrammatic rendering in the late thirteenth-century treatise in Oxford (Bodleian, MS Ashmole, 399) evokes the cross and, in turn, the *arma Christi*.[1001] The seraph that Francis saw in his vision was based on a schema that constructed what Bonaventura called a mental itinerary to God (Plate VI).[1002]

Contempt and Contention

Inscriptions on the "trattoria" scene at Ceri picturing a man basting the barbecued pig against a white background (Figure 37) point to a source in Terence's *Andria*;[1003] the painter ingeniously deployed the illustrated classic in much the same way Hrotsvit of Gandersheim had, who modeled her own plays on the gentile theater as a way to create new and improved Christian dramas. Likewise, topped by Christ in the Heavenly Jerusalem looking down at the moment of the Last Judgment, the Hereford *mappa mundi*'s detailed rendering treats the world as God's ornament (just as *cosmetics* adorn a body), what the ninth-century monk of Saint-Riquier, Micon, had described as "an image of the world destined to perish."[1004] Indeed, Adam and Eve are expelled from the circle of Eden directly below God, and the path the Israelites take through the Sinai traverses a world full of traps set by the devil. At the very moment Moses receives the Ten Commandments, the Israelites worship the Golden Calf and, as they approach Jerusalem, the Jews rescued from Egyptian bondage pass Lot's wife, a previous disobedient sinner turned into a statue of salt.[1005]

Full of tempting distractions, the world is a dangerous place. The lures included food, which can overwhelm spiritual nourishment,[1006] a theme at Moissac (Figure 24), where the avaricious rich man and his wife are shown banqueting while the emaciated Lazarus is being eaten by dogs. The *Specchio umano* implies a more complex relationship in which spiritual devotion feeds carnal needs, the candles sold to illuminate the miraculous image providing funds to relieve the impoverished (Figure 16). As at Ceri, references to food (and other earthly seductions) are pictured on the dados that ring altars at Aquileia and Summaga,[1007] and something of the same idea is introduced by the depiction of a woman offering a pig's head and feet to Saint Blasius at Berzé-la-Ville, which not only represents carnality but, engaging local customs, also sets up a contrast between flesh and spirit intended to direct contemplation heavenward. In the Saint-Denis Moses window, the Israelites are pictured banqueting while Moses is on Sinai, evidence of alleged Jewish preoccupation with material things. Monks, of course, fasted, but controlling consumption and other carnal temptations was a constant struggle for them. Guillaume le Clerc's *Bestiaire divin*, written in 1210–11, makes the conflict explicit by drawing on lore that the antelope's two horns are the Old and New Testaments that are to be studied assiduously and reconciled lest Christians become ensnared in worldly pleasures that render them incapable of fending off the devil. A manuscript of the *Bestiaire* illustrated in England c. 1270 (Paris, BnF, MS fr. 14969, fol. 5^r) pictures the choice by portraying a Dominican holding a cross and pointing out the heavenly Christ to a rapt congregation while a devil embraces a cleric consumed by "rich foods, fine drinks delicate and choice, beautiful women, beautiful clothes, palfreys ambling and fat, gold and silver and money."[1008]

No sensual temptation was of greater concern to medieval Christianity than sex, shockingly introduced at Sant Joan de Boí by a man masturbating, but also pictured by lewd subjects in many other medieval churches. At Moissac, a depiction of *Luxuria* being attacked in the breasts and genitals by reptiles contrasts with chaste conception represented by the Annunciation and Visitation across the entranceway;[1009] in the cloister of Saint-Michel-de-Cuxa, sirens and other seducers are presented in a scheme intended to test and hence prove the monks' (spiritual) love of God;[1010] and in the Egerton Genesis, the Sodomites are pictured in activities deemed so offensive to a later viewer that he or she erased their genitals (as someone did also in Sant Joan de Boí).[1011]

Magic and necromancy were worldly risks to which Christian art also responded. The Franciscan empiricist Roger Bacon associated talismans with infidels from the East and contrasted them to sacred relics.[1012] The seducer in the *Cantigas* miniature is portrayed summoning demons to do his wooing by deploying Solomon's seal (Figure 41), the pentagram understood to refer to Christ's five wounds within a magical circle framed with *characteres* of necromancy, including ring-signs and keys derived from antiquity through Arabic and Hebrew sources that Alfonso the Wise had had translated.[1013] A written refrain, however, makes the truth clear: "The benevolence of the Holy Virgin Mary is much greater than the devil's power or man's perversity."[1014] In the Scrovegni Chapel (Plate XII), Giotto personified *Faith,* brandishing a scroll inscribed with the Creed in one hand and a processional cross in the other, destroying a pagan idol standing atop a tattered magic handbook (grimoire) on which a pentacle and other occult signs are visible.[1015]

Christians succumbed to superstition, nonetheless, and assimilated it to their faith. A mid-thirteenth-century amulet in Canterbury (Cathedral Library, MS Add. 23) is adorned with some forty signs, including *chrismons* and other apotropaic versions of the cross, meant to be worn for protection.[1016] Subduing magic is the theme also of the Aosta pavement; medieval magical texts included the *sator arepo tenet* palindrome because it was believed to disclose the *Pater noster* (Our father) and the cross.[1017] Midwives used amulets to facilitate the birth process and to protect the newborn from sudden death; an actual-size image of Christ's bloody wound, such as the one isolated at the bottom of a fourteenth-century Genoese amulet in Princeton (University Library Ms. 138.44),[1018] recalls lips and bleeding vaginal labia.[1019] A painting of young women plucking penises from a tree encloses a communal fountain in Massa Marittima, amplifying the theme of fecundity,[1020] and the obscene lead badges, although on one level clearly parodic, also engaged the magical power of Christ's wound and Mary's vagina.[1021]

Religious imagery was, itself, part of the transformation of sensual attraction into spiritual elevation. Hugh of Fouilloy still expressed an ambivalence toward mural paintings of Christ's deeds that he deemed "pleasing" but empty of character, and for Bernard Silvestris, pictures "are not good but seem so." The author of the *Pictor in carmine* acknowledged the problem when he recommended that profane imagery be replaced by "the panorama of the Old and New Testaments." In many monuments, secular subjects were introduced as a kind of bait-and-switch, seducing the eye and then engaging the mind in a process of elevation.

Art and Nature

The representations in the *Specchio umano* of peasants gathering crops and selling them in Florence's grain and legume market reveal the increasingly positive understanding of the real world that emerged during the twelfth century and led ultimately to the integration of observed natural detail into art during the thirteenth. Alongside renewed contact with Byzantium during the crusades and ambitions to revive the grandeur of antiquity, naturalism had been used for specific purposes throughout the period. Real observation already imbued the statue of Hugh of Vaudemont, who is shown wearing a pilgrim's cap, pectoral cross, and kit and holding a rod (Figure 51), and it extends well beyond the identifiable paraphernalia to the portraits of the husband and wife and the sentiment the woman expresses. Reference to medical knowledge, possibly imported by Constantine Africanus, who brought Islamic medicine to south Italy in the eleventh century, may be detected in the rendering of the "dropsical" man's swollen belly on the Salerno ivory and the lame man's upturned feet (Figure 29); it makes Christ's miracle vivid and directly understandable. Villard de Honnecourt betrayed an even greater interest in the world. To be sure, the lion he famously claimed to have drawn "from life" was, in fact, constructed from two compass-drawn circles in a ratio of 2:1 that mapped Platonic idealism onto his empiricism,[1022] and he copied other material from ancient or Byzantine sources.[1023] But his water-driven saw, crossbow, primitive clock, and windlass, as well as numerous buildings and figures, were surely added from direct observation (Figure 35).[1024]

Villard was not alone among thirteenth-century image-makers who straddled convention and new observation. The elephant represented by his contemporary Matthew Paris (Cambridge, Corpus Christi College, MS. 16, fol. 4) was surely pictured from the animal that King Louis IX sent to Henry III, even if it is explained in the accompanying text by passages from Scripture, Bernard Silvestris, Virgil, Horace, and the bestiary.[1025] And, although refreshed with new observations, the scientific naturalism associated with Frederick II's court also had a strong classical foundation constructed, in part, by Michael Scot, the emperor's court astrologer and the translator of ibn Rashd (Averroës) and Aristotle, as manuscripts of the *Varia medica* in Florence (Bib. Med. Laur., MS Plut. 73.16) and Vienna (Öst. Nationalbib., Cod. 93) witness.[1026] The emperor's *De arte venandi cum avibus* also engaged Aristotle, while the illustrations in Manfred's copy of it are rife with naturalistic details.[1027] The *aula gotica* betrays the same heterogeneity, refreshing the old tradition of labors of the months (still represented schematically on the Amiens façade, Figure 25) with observed details. More realistic still are the labors portrayed in relief around the main portal of San Marco in Venice carved a century later, which detail local trades overseen by the port city's guilds, including fishing, boat construction, carpentry, shoe-making, hair-cutting, barrel-making, and other activities.[1028] "La Bonissima," the personification of "just measure" that, from the early thirteenth century, stood atop a ciborium in the main square near the cathedral of Modena, is clothed in simple town dress and perhaps originally held scales in her hand and had standard measures at her feet that assured uniformity in actual commercial transactions (Figure 63).[1029] The famous "Catalan Atlas" (Paris, BnF, Espagnol 30), produced in Mallorca by Jewish cartographers in 1375, is a similar hybrid of real and imagined.[1030] Commissioned by Pedro IV of Aragon as a gift to his cousin King Charles V of France, it is full of geographic and nautical information and is populated with exotic animals, ruler figures (including the three Magi), and architecture that merge the exotic and the familiar. Thus, Sumatra is personified by a two-tail siren and "Musse Melly, lord of the blacks of Geneua" is portrayed as a conventional European monarch enthroned, crowned, and holding a fleur-de-lis scepter, but with dark skin.

Naturalistic elements introduced into narratives served to connect sacred history to contemporary life.[1031] At San Marco, the real carpenters and masons of the type introduced on the facade are paralleled in the men building Noah's ark and the Tower of Babel in the portico mosaics. More significant, the biblical tower that symbolized humankind's futile aspirations is portrayed in the guise of the basilica's own bell-tower (campanile), visible through the adjacent portal;[1032] drawing the moral lesson is hard to avoid: earthly activities can serve either good or evil. Likewise, the elision of past and present in the thirteenth-century Morgan Library picture book made a political point, through the incorporation of crusader armor and contemporary war machines envisioning the attempt to capture the Holy Land as an extension of the Book of Kings.[1033] In a similar spirit, marginal pictures in the "birds head" Haggadah represent Pharaoh and his soldiers in hot pursuit of the Israelites, led by Moses and provided with unleavened bread (proleptically, as in Ex 13:6–7; fols. 24^v–25^r). When the page is turned, the fulfillment is depicted—"You shall tell your

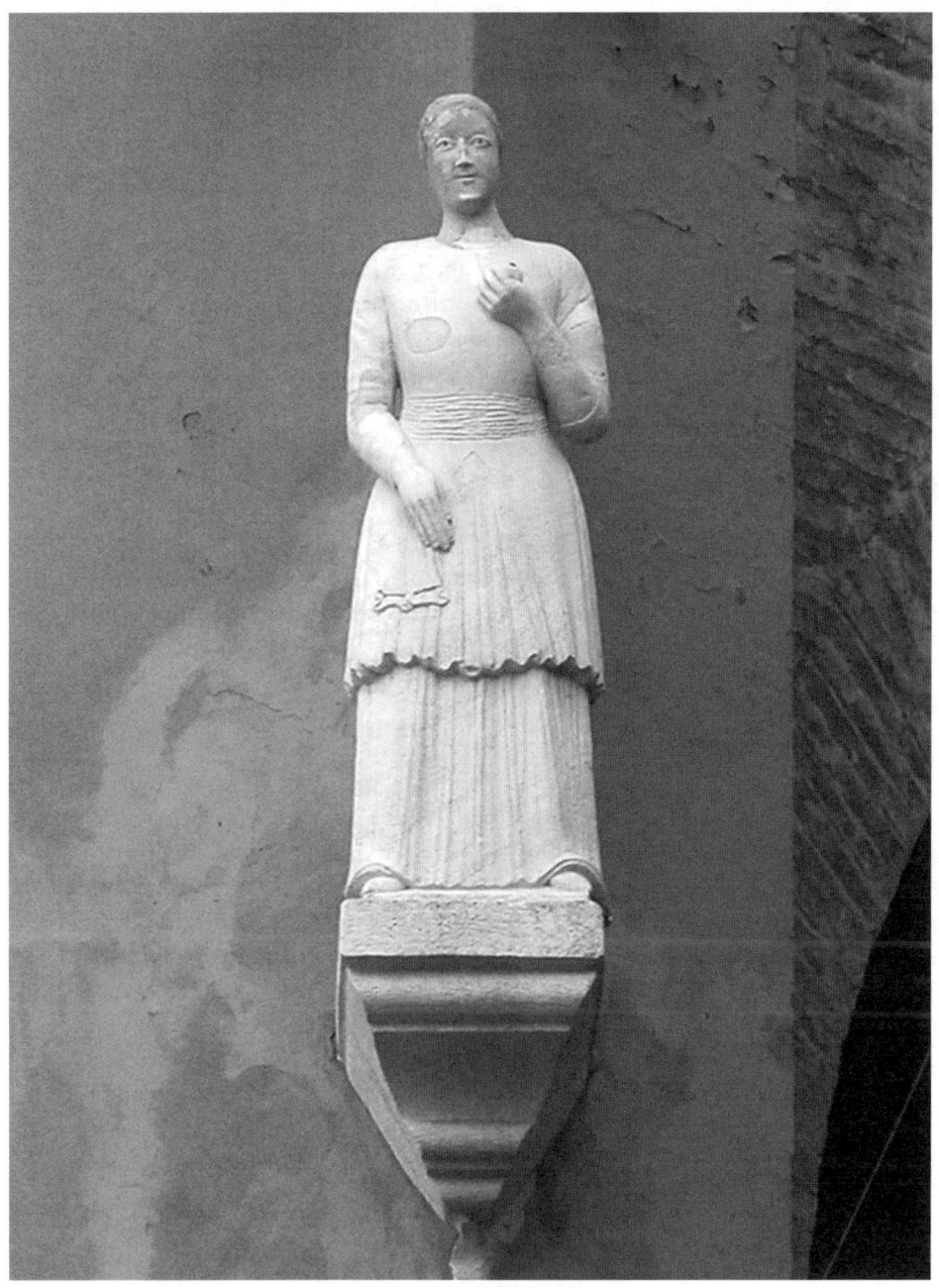

Figure 63. Modena, town square, "La Bonissima" (twelfth century)

child on that day, 'It is because what the Lord did for me when I came out of Egypt'"—by contemporary women wearing headscarves (*tichels*) and men in conical "Jews caps" (Figure 34). The up-turned loaves and the man ostentatiously holding the piercing fork aloft delivers a contemporary message as well. Jews were accused of using the blood of Christian boys to make matzot, the infamous "blood libel";[1034] the depiction would thus have assured the Haggadah's users that they are not to be seen as profaners of sacramental Hosts (as they are pictured on the Vallbona altarpiece; Figure 17) or worse, murderers, but used the knife-like tool only to keep unleavened bread from rising. Host desecration may underlie a detail of the Hereford *mappa mundi*, as well, which pictures the simian "golden calf" on an altar defecating tiny wafer-like disks marked with crosses,[1035] perhaps alluding to King Edward I's 1290 expulsion of the Jews from England. A different kind of political message was also embedded in the early fourteenth-century frescoes in Türje that depict the eleventh-century king Ladislaus as a knight; it sends a message to the contemporary Angevin ruler Charles I that, if he wanted to be a worthy successor to the nation's saint, he would have to undertake a new crusade against the pagan enemies.[1036]

Lifelike

Steadily, naturalism aligned art with Christianity's growing attention to bodies and emotions.[1037] On the Naumburg choir screen (Figure 26), for example, Christ is fully human and Mary and John react to him as mortals, cuing the response of viewers below. And within the choir, the portraits of the church's founders are made vivid by polychrome and facial specificity—the wrinkles around Ekkehard's eyes and double chin, for instance—that provide the historical figures with a sense of presence. The Franciscans and other mendicant orders fostered art that rendered biblical stories and even theology directly apprehensible through deployment of familiar details that engaged audience sentiments. Less than a decade after Francis was canonized, Giunta Pisano painted a crucifix for the saint's successor Elias of Cortona on which the kneeling brother was portrayed beneath Christ's bleeding feet and an inscription appealed: "Merciful Jesus Christ have mercy on the praying Elias," thus transforming compassion into an instrument of elevation.[1038] It is not by chance that Francis is portrayed on many of the most naturalistic works of the late Middle Ages, including the apse of Santa Maria Maggiore and Ambrogio Lorenzetti's Massa Marittima altarpiece. The Franciscan *Meditations on the Life of Christ* rethought sacred history in human terms by imagining the holy family's daily activities, which go unaccounted for in Scripture; the feast the angels provide Christ after the Temptation, for instance, is set out on a tablecloth which, as the accompanying text makes clear, cues compassion for Jesus's humiliating need for "food of the flesh."[1039] In the early fourteenth century, the Franciscan theologian Ugo Panziero argued that the image of Christ "outlined and shadowed" seemed fully incarnate in the mind of the faithful.[1040] An object/image's realism nonetheless still posed the danger that it would appeal to sensual needs rather than subvert and transcend them and hence risked idolatry or, even worse, sensual satisfaction that would short-circuit anagogical ascent. Indeed, a Yorkshire chronicle reports that Abbot Hugh of Meaux fashioned the crucified Christ on the altar after a naked man and that it attracted the devotion of women especially.[1041]

By rendering images accessible and realistic while simultaneously imposing geometrical distancing, perspective reconciled the empirical with divine principles. Experiments relating vision to representation had been undertaken during the twelfth and thirteenth centuries, primarily in artisanal practice. The sculptor of the tympanum relief of Saint George defeating a dragon (c. 1135) above the porch door of San Giorgio in Ferrara was able to adjust the appearance to accord with a viewer's apprehension from below,[1042] and constructed through the use of chalk snap-strings, the perspectival frieze occupied by fishes and birds beneath the rafters at San Pietro in Valle sitting atop the illusionistic frame of the historical narratives negotiates the here and now with heaven beyond (Figure 58).[1043] Villard de Honnecourt knew how to deploy sightlines and triangles to calculate the height of towers that could not be measured directly, apparently from the surveying manual known as *Quadrans vetus*,[1044] and the *aula gotica* introduces a perspectival frieze in a program that emphasizes knowledge of earthly matters. The Passion scenes in Naumburg Cathedral occupy "space boxes" that distinguish them as histories distinct from the presences of Christ on the cross;[1045] on the other side, the founders exchange glances with one another to encompass the living viewers in the dramatic scenario staged by the historical simulacra.[1046]

A radical transformation of vision theory contributed to the conversion of the early probings into a new form of art. Competing hypotheses about sight known as extramission (according to which rays leave the eye, mingle with light in the air, touch things, and return to the eye) and intromission (according to which reflected light enters the pupil as species) coexisted already in antiquity and were passed on through Galen and Aristotle's optics (translated c. 1200 into Latin by al-Hacen as *De aspectibus*). Peter of Limoges, for instance, likened painting to the eye's crystalline humor on which God's emanation is unified with rays from the eyes,[1047] a mirror that, even while engaging the real world, provides an image of that which cannot be seen.[1048] Intromission gradually gained acceptance during the second half of the thirteenth century in writings by Robert Grosseteste, Roger Bacon, John Pecham, and other (chiefly Franciscan) students of optics because its mathematics could be reconciled with the physiological mechanism of sight and the psychology of cognition.[1049] Indeed, precisely at the moment when the artistic experiments were reaching an early culmination in the Sancta Sanctorum commissioned by Nicholas III (where the pope is shown presenting a model of his new chapel that is an actual portrait of his structure as a believable three-dimensional projection; Figure 15), Pope Gregory X, perceiving empirical learning's utility for abstract theology, assembled Bacon, Pecham, and another leading optics scientist, Vitelo, at the papal court in Viterbo.[1050]

The primal integration of art with life was manifested at Saint Francis's mother church in Assisi, where Cimabue collected discrete portraits of buildings into a believable three-dimensional assembly in his depiction of *Ytalia*,[1051] and where, a short time later, Giotto depicted the saint's life on the lowest level of the nave as a series of tableaux framed by a classical *scaenae frons* that makes the events that took place in the town and nearby seem real and present.[1052] A generation later, Giotto himself furthered the experimental art in the Scrovegni Chapel, and his successors created illusionistic paintings and sculptures that steadily approximated natural vision. For instance, Ambrogio Lorenzetti deployed optical devices to conduct viewers step-by-step from the altar table to God's (fictive) presence; at the same time, he made patent the artifice he deployed by providing each of the cardinal virtues seated on the steps with tools used in practical manuals to survey the unmeasurable, a mirror, tower, and rod.[1053] The heavenly court constructed by means of art, these instruments caution the viewer, is only imperfectly imagined and ultimately unreachable.

Everyday Life

Driven by earthly needs, ambitions, desires, and fears, royalty, nobles, and other persons with sufficient resources wore regalia. Charles the Bald, for example, sported a gold crown, a cape adorned with pearls and gold, and red leggings (Figure 18), and Charles IV wore rich and varied mantles and a double crown (Figure 12). They took delight in jewelry and other precious objects, and engaged in such pastimes as fidchell (Figure 1). The Hildesheim aquamanile could have embellished a banquet table as easily as an altar, and the spectacular fourteenth-century ornament in Cleveland, worked with all the splendor of the most elaborate reliquary, seems to have served pleasure alone, its shimmering surfaces, turning wheels, tingling bells, and scented water amusing only the senses (Figure 64).[1054]

Probably part of a trousseau, the Walters Art Museum mirror inverts the language of heroic depictions of classical culture and Scripture to tease the owner about romantic love.[1055] Centered on the attack on the castle of love, an allegory of courting, the battle in the foreground is a joust, but the siege engine at the left catapults flowers not pellets, and the soldier climbing the ladder is embraced by a lady, not repelled by a combatant. The fourteenth-century artistic elaboration derives ultimately from troubadour performance, written down in the Romance literature of the twelfth and thirteenth centuries. The erotic references would surely have been recognized in the profusion of lances, openings, and penetration, common also in illustrations of the *Roman de la rose* (a text that itself incorporates numerous references to visual art) that frequently gloss the allegorical poetry as a commentary on sacred and erotic love, barely disguised in contemporary theater. Its deployment on a mirror, moreover, may reflect on the *speculum sine macula* (unblemished mirror), the Virgin Mary unsullied by sex. Late-thirteenth-century paintings in the Communal Palace at San Gimignano depict hawking, hunting, and jousting, as well as a love tryst that culminates in a depiction of the couple bathing together; the good life that a properly governed commune affords, it shows, is an alternative to salvation provided by the Church.[1056]

Royal courts had long promoted an interest in antiquity and science. Charlemagne, for instance, had imported works from Italy to his permanent residence at Aachen and, in turn, sent objects back to the capital of the empire they emulated. Similarly, Pope Hadrian's epitaph in San Pietro in Rome was prepared in the north, and so, perhaps, was the *lupa Romana*, displayed with genuine antiquities outside the

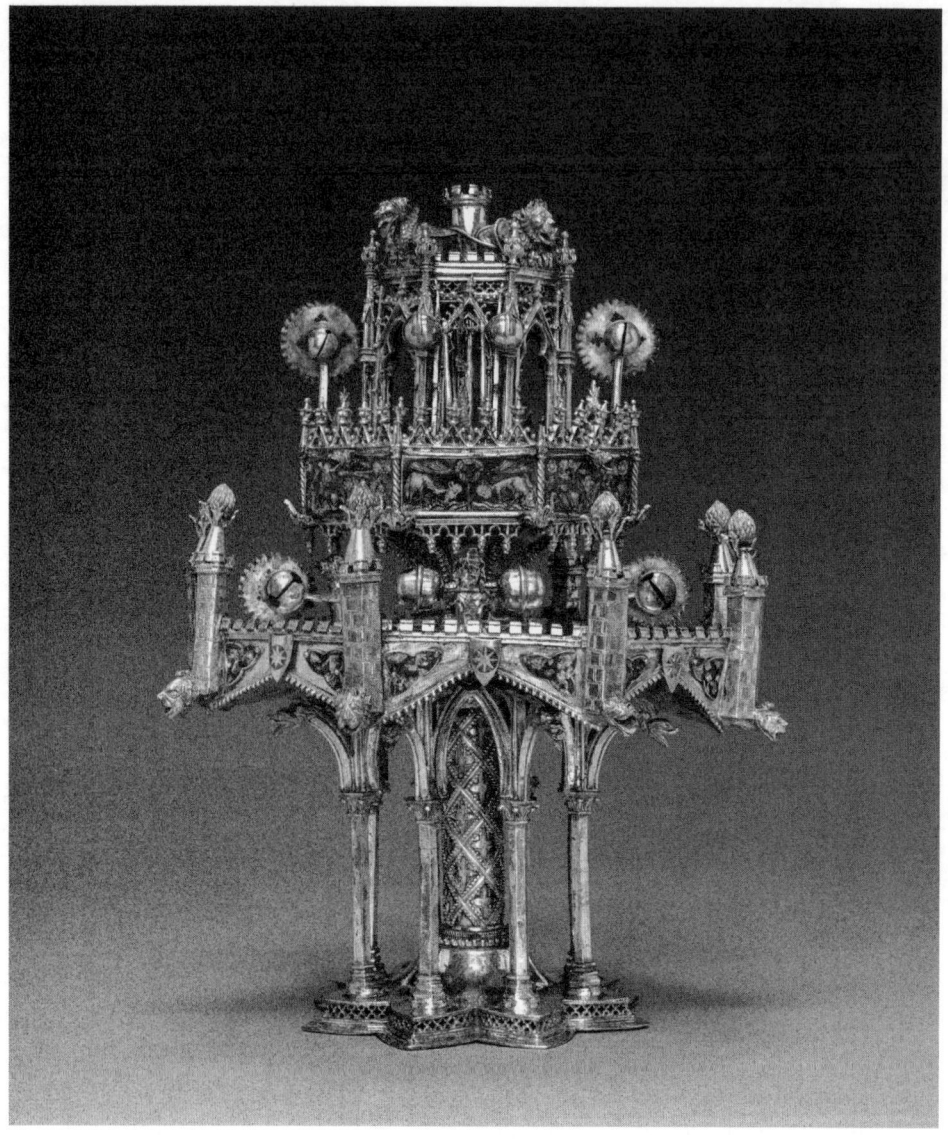

Figure 64. Cleveland, Museum of Art, table fountain (fourteenth century)

Lateran palace of the Christian *pontifex maximus*. Ottonian ties with Byzantium led to a resurgence of luxury art, including the marriage charter of Otto II and Theophanu, which used imperial forms, purple-stained vellum inscribed with gold letters, and medallions of facing birds and animals interrupted by portraits of Christ, Mary, and saints as seals of the contract.[1057] Other courts were also centers of learning and art. In Palermo, Roger II assembled craftsmen and intellectuals from Byzantium, north Africa, and Norman areas; Stefano Conti's *aula gotica* is an encyclopedia of contemporary knowledge; and Alfonso X had compilations of Arabic astronomy (and astrology) translated into Galician-Portuguese, from which his artists incorporated elements into the *Cantigas*.

Assimilating folklore and oral traditions, such medieval secular texts as German love-songs performed by minstrels (*Minnesänger*)[1058] were written down and illustrated with pictures that are, themselves, interpretive retellings. Breton inscriptions elucidate the Arthurian tale pictured in relief on the twelfth-century Porta della Pescheria of the cathedral in Modena.[1059] The paintings in Rodenegg are elucidated with Bavarian tituli and recount the legend of Iwein known from Chrétien de Troyes's and Hartmann von Aue's redaction, and also transmitted orally throughout the period. Richard of Fournival's mid-thirteenth-century *Bestiaire d'amour* asserts at the beginning that text and pictures are of equal effect, and, indeed, both are materializations of the oral tradition that the author is portrayed writing down.[1060] An early fourteenth-century tapestry in Wienhausen (monastery) tracks the Tristan story in three registers, each with its own theme and pictorial rhetoric, and interlards the narrative with words and rows of coats of arms.[1061] Like almost all prominent clergymen, Pope Clement VI was an aristocrat, so it is not surprising that he had his private chambers at the Palais des Papes in Avignon adorned with lyrical frescoes incorporating realistic details to represent an imagined earthly paradise.[1062] The discovery of meaning in the outward signs of secular imagery functioned much as typology did; for Cennino Cennini and others, art's very essence was in the discovery of things not seen.[1063]

Courts sponsored the depicting of actual historical events as well. Though carefully constructed within artistic conventions and literary genres, including the classical triumphal columns, the Bible, and epic poetry, the Bayeux embroidery derives veracity from the incorporation of details from real life and the matter-of-fact Latin tituli.[1064]

Accompanying the caption near the beginning of the pictured epic, "Here Harold sailed the sea, and with the wind full in its sails, he came to the land of Count Guy," a man is shown summoning Harold and his men from a banquet, who then descend the steps of the manor house at Bosham and, with trousers rolled up, wade to the craft carrying oars, dogs, and a hawk. To cross the Channel, the Viking-type ship is driven by man power as well as wind, and, as the French coast comes into sight, a sailor at the prow makes ready to cast anchor. In contrast to the essentially non-temporal structure of typology that governed much religious art, the event is presented in a linear fashion, but illustrations from Aesop's fables in the lower margin—a fox tricking the crane to drop a piece of cheese, a dog unwilling to leave her den after her litter is grown, and a crane removing a bone from a wolf's mouth—provide an ironic, perhaps even subversive commentary on the military encounter.[1065]

Other wars also provoked the production of histories. Crusader illuminators produced copies of William of Tyre's *Histoire d'Outremer*,[1066] and Matthew Paris continued the tradition of historical art in his densely illustrated *Chronicles*, which picture gems and seals, maps and itineraries, genealogies, relics and elephants, and numerous events, both ancient and contemporary.[1067] Although he was a Benedictine monk of Saint Albans and his *Chronica majora* is a monastic history, Matthew's work was encouraged by Henry III and is full of secular material. As the author himself informs the reader, the illustrations were directed so that "what the ear hears the eyes may see." The historical attitude transformed hagiography in Matthew Paris's *Passions of Alban and Amphibalus* (Dublin, Trinity College Library, MS 177), designed to move its courtly audience. Peter of Eboli's *Liber ad honorem Augusti* was intended to convey accuracy but is full of artistic political tropes,[1068] and the fourteenth-century Hungarian chronicle (Budapest, Orzságos Széchényi Konyvtár, Clmae 404) merged myth and fact to advance the monarchy.[1069] Inscribed on vellum suspended for viewing or painted on walls and other surfaces, maps symbolized power as much as they served actual practice; a *mappa mundi* was included in Henry III's painted chamber at Westminster, for instance, perhaps as a reminder of the ephemeral nature of worldly power. A royal present, the "Catalan Atlas" nonetheless tracked navigational routes for the extensive fourteenth-century mercantile exchanges.

Such public monuments as the Bonissima provided a source of civic cohesion that unified persons of various classes. Perhaps imitating the

Lateran wolf, duke Henry the Lion had a bronze lion erected outside his Dankwarderode Castle in Braunschweig, and the Fontana Maggiore adorned with labors of the months dominates the center of Perugia.[1070] In Rome, the senate was reinstituted in the fourteenth century and a senatorial palace built on the Capitoline, fitted with such civic accoutrements as standardized measures for wine and oil fashioned from reworked ancient columns and decorated in the classical manner;[1071] in Florence, the commune and wool guild sponsored the renewal of Orsanmichele. Enormous statues of Roland in Hanseatic League cities represent communal identity.[1072]

Portraiture

Fashioning recognizable faces reflects the interest in history.[1073] Although Villani reported that Giotto used a mirror to make a self-portrait, during the early Middle Ages commonality was generally more important than individual features,[1074] and authority was encoded through symbolic references.[1075] In the (largely reconstructed) apse mosaic in Sant'Ambrogio in Milan, for example, Saint Martin of Tours has the same features as Saint Ambrose (who appears miraculously at Martin's funeral) and—through him—Saint Peter; the point is to establish an ecclesiastic lineage between the men and, in turn, their churches.[1076] The portrait of Maestro Mateo in Santiago de Compostela accommodates an assertion of artistic pride to that of humble labor for God.[1077] Even today, the precise identity of the female hermit portrayed at Écouis is debated and her general resemblance to Veronica standing nearby noted (Figure 43); only an inscription or attribute would resolve whether she is Mary Magdalene or Mary of Egypt. Theodulf of Orléans had deployed this kind of ambiguity to attack images (*Opus karoli*, 4.16); medieval portraitists used it to express the community of the blessed. Articulated in language transcribed from Roman art, Arnolfo di Cambio's portrait of Charles I of Anjou on Rome's Capitoline Hill is a convincing likeness; the knit brows, high cheekbones, and creases around the mouth add vitality and presence to the ancient conventions.[1078] Likewise, the regalia and the emperor's long straight nose and shrunken cheeks leave no doubt that it is Charles IV who receives the relics at Karlstejn, even though the portrait also indexes the emperor's namesake and illustrious predecessor, Charlemagne.[1079]

The declaration of personal likeness "*imago noster*" (our image) on generic types of seals was an attempt to subsume individual persons within groups through inscribed names and titles, although some impressions literally prolonged the body by including imprints of fingers or teeth.[1080] Seals were closely related to another form of personal representation, namely the coat of arms;[1081] in the Morgan Library Picture Book, for instance, the helmets that obscure the fighters' faces are emblazoned with shields that substitute for their individual features. Ekkehard's shield secures his identity among the historic founders of Naumburg, and coats of arms prominently displayed on the platform and summit of his tomb in the north transept of León cathedral incorporate Cardinal Rodriguez Alvarez into his familiar group and, through it, to his earthly benefactions to the Church (Figure 39). Dynastic lineage is petrified on the central pillar of the Santes Creus cloister by the coats of arms of James II and Blanche of Anjou and Naples (Figure 36).[1082]

Real life was nowhere more evident in medieval art than in representations of the dead: visible proof of the unseeable deceased's absence. Directly below the scene of the banquet at Moissac, the rich man is shown dying; as his wife grieves beside his bed, devils fight for his soul,[1083] and, to the left, he is pictured again suffering the torments of hell to make the essential Christian point about a sinful life: its rewards are eternal damnation. Although made in God's image, humankind had sinned and acquired accidental features after being expelled from Eden;[1084] in the aspiration to regain paradise, physical existence ceded to theology at a person's death. Individual persons commemorated on early tombs were assimilated to conventions used on such reliquaries as Henry of Blois's, beginning with the 1080s slab effigy of Rudolph of Swabia (Merseburg, cathedral).[1085] A twelfth-century gravestone in Sankt Callixtus, Riesenbeck, shows the dead Reinhildes watching an angel carry her miniscule soul heavenward, and an inscription proclaims, "At once she ascended, taking her place on the starry thrones, having become a blessed coheir of Christ."[1086] For all the conventionality of the eyes and facial structure, Hugh of Vaudemont would have been recognizable in his memorial at Belval. The Rodriguez Alvarez tomb demonstrates the relationship between being and spiritual aspiration perfectly.[1087] The eulogy in stone was designed to affirm the deceased's authority and inspire his successors by demonstrating the relationship between the bishop's life on earth and the fate of his soul. A relief at the bottom pictures the bishop's charitable deeds; at eye level, an effigy atop his remains preserves his appearance in the flesh; and a relief behind of Alvarez's successor and priests solemnly accepting the bishop's death and desperate laymen who tear their hair and clothes in grief provides a mirror for visitors to the grave. Christ's own saving death on the cross is portrayed above, mourned by John the Evangelist and Mary (who catches the blood), and at the apex, two angels bear Rodriguez's naked soul upward on an eagle.[1088] Enrico Scrovegni is recognizable in two portraits in his chapel, once among the blessed in the Last Judgment fresco and, at the opposite end, in a sculpture praying for eternity in the presbytery. At the close of the century, Arnolfo di Cambio applied the conventions even more dramatically in his tomb monument for Guillaume De Bray in Orvieto (San Domenico),[1089] the cardinal's dead body exposed to the living by two acolytes who draw back curtains.

Chapter 8
Performance

TO A GREAT EXTENT, medieval art operated as phenomenal reality. Frequently put into motion or apprehended in changing environments, it was contingent on performative contexts and was constantly refashioned by them.[1090] Art participated in the physical and emotional spectacles enacted in church liturgy, court ceremonies, and processions, and served instruction, preaching, and devotional exercises. Liturgy was itself a drama acted out with props and sets beneath arches descended ultimately from Roman theater architecture and on pulpits derived from ancient stages.[1091] Every time a priest washed his hands from an aquamanile such as that in Hildesheim (Figure 9) or one of the faithful crossed herself with holy water, the action joined him or her to the sacred; deacons reciting Scripture from books assumed God's voice.[1092] As ambient conditions changed, even stationary art performed; colors metamorphosed and the appearance of the figures mutated. On the façade of Amiens (Figure 25), for instance, God the Father is obscured by shadows at the apex of the tympanum. In Giovanni del Biondo's altarpiece from the sacristy of Santa Maria Novella (Florence, Galleria dell'Accademia),[1093] he and his heavenly cohort are shaded beneath a canopied frame so that only the *painted* rays emanating from Christ are visible in the picture space, in that way assimilating the triptych itself to the sacred event it imagines. When congregants inside the Scrovegni Chapel kneeled and recited the "Ave Maria," they became like Gabriel on the apsidal arch conveying God's word to Mary as depicted on either side (Plate XII).[1094]

Active Objects

Some works of art were moved casually. Doors on objects and buildings confirmed the fluidity of experience—opening and closing, protruding, receding, blurring, and revealing.[1095] Collected as souvenirs at various sites, pilgrim badges attached to clothes bore witness to the completion of arduous journeys (Figure 2).[1096] The Regensburg butterfly enacted a succession of movements (Plate I): first hidden from view in a bag suspended from the bishop's neck, the creature was released from its leather and horn cocoon to reveal its contents, then displayed again as a necklace on a moving body, its opalescent enamels changed from earthly green and dark red to celestial blue in a fluctuation that enhanced the crucifix's amuletic character and animated its symbolic spiritual flight upward.[1097] The act of dressing in appropriate garb during ordinations invested the clergy with God's grace;[1098] whoever donned the Coronation Mantle not only inserted his person into the hierarchy of saints (Figure 14) but also became the persona of Christ's judgment and victory over evil pictured in the trampling of the beasts and *Majestas Domini* of the two main fields on the garment's spine. Whether on the altar to purify a priest's hands before he touched the Eucharist or on a banquet table for washing fingers in a society that ate without forks, aquamanili were gripped, tipped, and their contents emptied, as pictured in the Holkham Picture Bible, an action with both ethical and moral implications (Figure 52).[1099]

Books exploited the process of opening and page-turning to construct sequences of experiences.[1100] Successive miniatures in the *De modo orandi corporaliter sancti Dominici*, for instance, stage exercises linked to one another in the text.[1101] And while reading generally proceeded from beginning to end, ornament created systems of organization that generated contrapuntal actions as well. Verses in the First Bible of Charles the Bald exhort the king to read and reread the book, and the proleptic presentation portrait at the close refers back to the beginning and to the contract between ruler and brethren sealed by the gift volume.[1102] The Holy Face that terminates the Lambeth Palace Apocalypse is the reward offered to readers who engage in the dialogic process of reading and viewing the preceding texts and illustrations—distilled in the allegory on the facing recto of Penance warding off the vices threatening to distract her.[1103] The round mirror that organizes the *Vrigiet de solas* page (Figure 56) invites the viewer's visual participation, while the words inscribed on skewed banderoles spin (in her or his imagination) the wheel of fortune depicting *Worldliness* enthroned at the top and *Pride* at the bottom;[1104] the horizontal band makes the point of the action explicit: "in flight, there is no rest."

The reading process was applied to other objects as well. Thumbing through the Victoria and Albert ivory booklet (Figure 13), a traveler correlated her or his real journey with a virtual pilgrimage through time and place, beginning with Pilate washing his hands and finishing at Christ's face awaiting the blessed at the end of time; in the interim, he or she walks mentally in the Savior's bloody footprints, which are pictured at the bottom of one leaf, and prays on each of the *arma Christi*. Prayer rolls bearing the *arma Christi* did the same,[1105] and James le Palmer's *Omne bonum* promises that "whoever recites in the presence of the arms of Christ the Pater Noster and the Ave Maria, and as often as he does so, shall be pardoned of 20,000 years of punishment in purgatory."[1106] The New York shrine Madonna embodies the idea, too (Figure 28); like the painted tree of the *Vrigiet de solas*, the effigy of the Mother and Child is a "caudex," enclosing leaves (growing from a plant at the center) representing the Word becoming flesh and thus integrating the life cycle from tree to wood sculpture with the notion of Mary as heaven's gateway.[1107] Movements often effected a shift of time and status, as when the Assisi reliquary was turned from bits of bloodstained cloth magnified by the five rock crystals on one side to the image of their source on the other (Plate VI), the change from fragment to whole enacting a move from present to historic past.

Some objects were animated mechanically.[1108] A legacy of ancient, Byzantine, and Islamic culture, automata are well documented in medieval texts and include a few survivors,[1109] such as the Cleveland table fountain (Figure 64);[1110] mechanical devices were used to activate sacred objects. Villard de Honnecourt sketched a kind of "dippy bird" that could drink wine from a bowl,[1111] and, on the same page where he depicted a crossbow and water-driven saw (Figure 35), he pictured a mechanism for animating an angel to point toward the sun, and an eagle with pulleys and weights inside that, when mounted on a lectern, would turn the evangelist symbol's head toward the reader of the Gospel lesson.[1112] Fitted with hidden gears, the thirteenth-century *Virgen de los Reyes* in Seville could be made to respond to worshippers,[1113] and a statue of Saint James holding a sword in Santa Maria la Real de Las Huelgas is said to have knighted crusaders going off to the Holy Land.

Conversely, desecrations performed on images were understood to degrade the person depicted. Extending ancient traditions of *damnatio memoriae*, full-length effigies of noblemen who failed to pay their taxes or were guilty of more serious crimes (*pitture infamanti*) were suspended upside down on city walls or civic palaces.[1114]

Works were also activated through movements that were simultaneously random and controlled. Although the Ballinderry fidchell board would have been carried from place to place within a residence or on a journey (Figure 1), strict rules governed the moving of pieces itself.[1115] Likewise, crosses were paraded to the altar before Mass began and placed beside the chalice and paten, and the priest swung a censer to consecrate them, releasing fragrant smoke that drifted heavenward, as pictured, for instance, on the Saint-Martin-du-Canigou cartulary (Figure 8).[1116] The flabellum of Tournus depended on an interplay of orchestrated motions (Plate II). Folded into its coffin-like ivory box adorned with scenes from the *Bucolica*, it was brought to (Christian) life when a deacon opened the pleated vellum like a dazzling peacock-tail and waved it (as the inscription explains) to "refresh the air" and "to drive away flies" from the Eucharist; then, moved through the church for all to see, it was mounted beside the cross on the altar as a standard of a priest's faith and clean heart.[1117] Depicting his transformation from infant (with his mother) into the celestial God, the Lyon ivory knob enacted Christ's two natures (Figure 30), and when the officiant carried it through the church at the beginning and end of the liturgical celebration, his gestures and movements channeled the almighty's benediction and guided those who, literally, follow the Incarnate Lord.[1118] In like fashion, reliquaries fashioned as arms (so-called speaking reliquaries) functioned as priestly prostheses; at Essen, the reliquary of Saint Blaise was taken from the altar and used to transmit sacred authority when the priest pronounced the final benediction.[1119] Figures of the baby Jesus and of the dead Savior were subjected to caressing and the rites of clothing and unclothing, which dramatized Christ's two natures.[1120]

Art authorized the Mass. Raising the Host against the pictorial backgrounds of apses or altarpieces helped congregations visualize the mystery in the white wafer, which itself was blank or embossed with *nomina sacra* or ghost-like images,[1121] as pictured in the Vallbona retable (Figure 17), which shows Christ raising the Host in the Last Supper and features an enormous wafer borne by angels at the center. Responding to the *sursum corda* that enjoined the faithful to abandon earthly things and lift their souls to God in heaven, canopies, apses, and framing arches figured the imagined unity of the earthly and heavenly liturgies

(Figure 6).[1122] Thus, the Saint-Martin-du-Canigou cartulary portrays Christ enthroned on an altar-like throne above the depicted celebration flanked by Mary and Saint Martin, and the Lisbjerg altar sets up a similar parallel (Figure 46), with the *Civitas Hierusalem* on the base and the heavenly counterpart above.[1123] Realizing the concept by portraying *Ecclesia* bearing the chalice and Host intertwined with the unveiled *Synagoga*, the Tours Sacramentary reveals Christ within the letters of the liturgy's opening, *Vere dignum* (Figure 47). In Santissima Annunciata in Florence, the raising of the Host inserted the "body of Christ" visually between Gabriel and Mary depicted on the miraculous Annunciation painting, establishing a relationship between the historical event and its sacramental celebration.[1124] Ambrogio Lorenzetti was careful to show two angels lifting the cushion on which Mary and Christ sit to indicate that the sacred celebration is not anchored to the earth (Figure 21). Implicit in the relationship of art to the Mass was a conflict or at least a competition with the Eucharist, deemed to be the only true image of Christ.[1125] Already in the ninth century, sacramental wafers were arranged on the altar to form figures or stamped with inscriptions alluding to the *Majestas Domini*,[1126] but the Fourth Lateran Council, convened by Innocent III, who generally endorsed Church art, contrasted the "real presence" to the empty outward appearance of paintings and sculpture.[1127]

Church objects were set in motion especially in Holy Week celebrations, mimicking Christ's own peripatetic final days. Just before the paschal candle was lighted, Exultet rolls were unfurled over the ambo on Holy Saturday to dramatize God's descent to earth and his resurrection as rendered in the pictures displayed on them; the congregation viewed the illustrations while the priest singing the hymns read the words and notes transcribed in the opposite direction.[1128] Sculptures of the Crucified Christ were "buried" in wood Easter sepulchers, wall niches, or altars and "resurrected" at Easter.[1129] The early thirteenth-century *Vision of Edmund, Monk of Eynsham* (near Oxford) reports that "before Lent, the sexton of the church had let down this cross to the ground and left it till Good Friday between the altar and the wall";[1130] in Durham, a crucifix was moved from a shrine Madonna to the main altar;[1131] and in Poitiers, a container of consecrated Host (pyx) was placed in the tomb during the liturgy.[1132] A hook on the back of the Rosano Crucifix (Plate X) indicates that it, too, was an art-actor that could be removed from its regular station for the annual transfer to the altar, recapitulating Christ's entombment beneath a baldachin as in the Lamentation pictured in it at the right; the cross token from the site of Christ's death in Jerusalem secreted behind the head amplified the drama. Some crucifixes were fitted with moveable arms to accommodate the Holy Week tradition,[1133] which also facilitated direct physical contact with the image-objects.[1134] Accessible from the presbytery by a narrow staircase, the so-called crypt of the Siena Duomo, featuring a fresco of the deposition flanked by depictions of the Crucifixion and Lamentation, may have served the Easter ceremony.[1135] Figures of the resurrected Christ were fashioned and hoisted into church vaults on Ascension Day, doves were lowered on Pentecost, and angels on the Feast of the Assumption lifted images of Mary.[1136]

Outside churches, performances sanctified whole communities.[1137] Some processions were occasional, as when Pope Leo IV dedicated the new walls protecting the neighborhood around Rome's San Pietro in 846.[1138] Others followed the Church calendar. Sculptures of Christ astride a donkey were led through towns on Palm Sunday, engaging the populace in the religious drama.[1139] Already in the eleventh century, William of Volpiano devised an elaborate dramatization of Christ's entry into Jerusalem for a small north Italian town in which a representation of Christ was carried in procession to his monastery of Fruttuaria and was greeted there with hymns and acclamations, thereby merging the sacred past with the present and identifying the monastery with the Holy City.[1140] In Paris, the ceremonies of the Sainte-Chapelle were extended into the city's public spaces.[1141] From 1350, relics stored at Karlstejn (Figure 12) were transported to Prague and shown publicly on a wood platform in the Market Square, among them the magnificent reliquary of the True Cross, the Holy Lance, John the Baptist's tooth, and bust reliquaries of local saints;[1142] in addition to these processions, Charles IV also instituted special rituals for coronations.[1143]

In Rome, a regular "stational" liturgy symbolically wove the city's many churches together under a single bishop, that is, the pope. Preceded by a subdeacon carrying a cross, the papal entourage journeyed from the Lateran Palace on feast days and staged various acts at different churches.[1144] During the Pentecost station at the Pantheon, for instance, roses were released to enact the descent of the Holy Spirit onto the Virgin Mary and apostles (perhaps represented on the pilgrim's badge as rows of balls). And, as still today, rose petals were released onto the worshippers in Santa Maria Maggiore to re-enact the miraculous snowfall in 358 (depicted in the mosaic introduced onto the façade at the end of the thirteenth century).[1145] Symbolizing Mary in the two churches dedicated to her, roses also stood for the congregation of the faithful that constitute the *Ecclesia* she personifies.[1146] The most dramatic of the Roman processions took place on the evening of the Feast of the Assumption of the Virgin, 14–15 August, when the Lateran *Acheropita* (Figure 15), was paraded along a ceremonial route to Santa Maria Maggiore to meet the Madonna;[1147] enclosed in its silver box, it passed through the Arch of Titus with its first-century relief of Roman soldiers returning with the Ark of the Covenant and spoils from the Jerusalem Temple (see also Figure 10), paused at Santa Maria Nova where the pope opened little doors to wash the icon's feet, and spent the night in the Roman Curia (Sant'Adriano) before proceeding out of the Forum.[1148] When he instituted an annual procession of the *Veronica* from the Vatican to the hospital of Santo Spirito on the feast of the Marriage at Cana (a Eucharistic celebration also symbolizing the marriage of the divine and human in Christ), Innocent III had this Assumption Day procession in mind.[1149]

Art served particular rituals too. A brass lunette over the doorway to the crypt of San Pietro reflects the ecclesiastical liturgy celebrated in the memorial basilica on Saint Agnes's day, when the wool-bands (*pallia*) about to be bestowed on new archbishops were consecrated by being kept overnight near the bones of the first bishop of Rome.[1150] Reliquaries were paraded on saints' feast days, and some were opened to display their precious contents: at Tournai, for instance, the relics of the first bishop, Saint Eleutherius,[1151] and at Cologne, where the shrine of the three kings was transported on the Feast of the Epiphany and the three skulls inside exposed by removing its front lid.[1152] Used to establish authority at papal coronations, the "throne of saint Peter" was removed from the transept on the feast of *Cathedra Petri*, wreathed with candles, and displayed on the altar.[1153] On the feast of the Annunciation, the panel picturing God conversing with the angels in the Scrovegni Chapel, it seems, was folded back to allow light from a window behind (and possibly a dove) to enter the room, symbolizing the Holy Spirit's descent onto Mary (portrayed below) and sanctifying the entire assembly.[1154]

Some of the faithful believed that even stationary images could become animate. Bernard of Angers reported that the golden effigy of Saint Gerald on the altar at Aurillac "seemed to see with its attentive, observant gaze the great many peasants seeing it and gently to grant with its reflecting eyes the prayers of those before it."[1155] The *Sermo de vita et morte gloriosae Virginis Maurae* (attributed to the ninth century but most likely composed later) tells of Saint Maura praying regularly in the church at Troyes before separate representations of the Virgin and Child, Crucified Christ, and *Majestas Domini* until, one day, the depicted infant cried, the man groaned, and the God thundered.[1156] Caesarius of Heisterbach reported several instances in which devotional images granted expiation and prevented sin,[1157] and the rapidly evolving hagiography of Saint Francis incorporated a painted crucifix that spoke to him, while as a young man he was praying in the church of San Damiano, and effected a conversion of purpose. Francis's *vitae* also refashioned the legend of the stigmata to incorporate the form of the crucifix as pictured on the Paris reliquary.[1158] Interactions between art and people often sparked miracles.

Light contributed to the effect.[1159] Shimmering in the flickering candles on the altar, the vitreous insets at Berzé-la-Ville dematerialized the surrounds of Christ's starry mandorla (Figure 32),[1160] ceding to actual light let into the church through the oculus between two angels. Dancing candlelight would have brought the resurrected firebird and soul to life on the Jaca capital (Figure 27). Christ was pictured on an axis in Arnstein and Chartres so that the sun rising in the east would function as the spirit entering through him into the church (Figure 33).

People in Motion

Most medieval works were animated not by being moved or moving, but as persons circulated within their orbits.[1161] The underlying typological structure of the Salerno ivories (see Figure 29), for instance, was activated when a viewer passed the first panel and set the *X* of the embossed *LUX* in motion as a cross that falls into the created world pictured in the second panel, affirming the belief that Christ was present from the beginning of time.[1162] Enclosed between menacing grotesques, the Jaca capital begins with an image of the soul desiring God derived from a classical inebriated satyr, proceeds to a lion battling evil, and culminates in the phoenix reborn from ashes in a succession that re-enacts the deceased Don Sanchez Ramirez's aspiration for salvation.[1163] And plotted seeing is what makes the early fourteenth-century *Lady World* at Worms Cathedral effective; the smiling, elegantly dressed anti-Mary who greets those entering the sacred precinct evokes horror when her rotting flesh eaten by reptiles and worms becomes visible from the back as they pass by.[1164]

Art provided backdrops for activities, both informal and staged. Every time the pope departed or returned from his palace at the Lateran, for instance, the assembly of ancient Roman spolia in the piazza outside affirmed his temporal authority.[1165] The first thing visitors saw when they arrived at Ceri from Rome was the picture of Pope

Sylvester that guided them into the sacred space with a reminder of the Church's power to exorcise evil (Figure 37), and, when they exited, they tracked the Israelites crossing into the Promised Land after Moses laid low the demonic Pharaoh. On the San Leonardo-al-Frigido lintel (New York, Metropolitan Museum of Art, The Cloisters), the apostles that follow Christ's entry into Jerusalem are shown singing, just as the twelfth-century congregants would as they entered the Tuscan church at the start of Holy Week.[1166] *La belle verrière* (Figure 5) and the sculptures on the three portals of the Chartres Cathedral façade elevated the bishop's entry into the cathedral accompanied by singing, and the music-making shepherds on the Mary portal engaged the liturgy of the purification of the Virgin.[1167] The atrium of San Marco in Venice was the stage for the ritual that proceeded from the Porta da Mar on the south and followed the Genesis narrative (Plate XIII);[1168] other doors into the atrium space generated different meanings: the Porta Sant'Alippio opens onto a series that emphasizes Israel's history in Egypt, the land Saint Mark converted to Christianity, and, interrupting the flow of the Genesis story, Abraham Greeting the Angels displayed above a portal into the basilica welcomed the faithful and introduced the benefaction offered them on the altar within. Joseph and Moses cycles displayed in the atrium's north wing, in turn, provided biblical antecedents for the doge's governance and set an approving tone for the mercantile activities that took place there.[1169] And the Crossing of the Red Sea and Desert Miracles at the very end fashioned the series for pilgrims to Palestine as a gateway to the Promised Land.

Settings engaged particular liturgies, too, that can be reconstructed only in relatively few cases. Christ's entry into Jerusalem at the center of episodes from the last days on the lintel above the western door of the church of the Holy Sepulcher resonated with Palm Sunday celebrations that took place on the spot and, in turn, with the historic event they commemorated and reanimated (Figure 42).[1170] At Berzé-la-Ville, the paintings bridged local customs to the official liturgies; the depiction of the woman presenting the head and feet of a pig incorporated popular practices into the official ritual. The insertion of important relics in the cloister at Moissac and the liturgical response appear to have determined the disposition of sculptures,[1171] while at Saint-Denis, an inscription in the scene of Benedict's assumption in the stained glass clearly refers to the last responsory of the service on the saint's feast, leaving no doubt that the depicted *transitus* envisions the words spoken in the chapel during feast day. Scenes of the finding of the True Cross, the miracle in Beirut, and the legend of Saint Alexander on the thirteenth-century Berardenga antependium in Siena (Pinacoteca nazionale) offered pictorial counterparts to the lections read during the 14 September feast.[1172] Penitents passed the *Ecclesia* and *Synagoga* and entered the right transept of Strasbourg Cathedral on Maundy Thursday, positioning themselves below Christ the judge atop the angel column (Figure 50).[1173] After the Lateran *Acheropita* reached its destination in Santa Maria Maggiore, the depiction in the apse of Christ retrieving Mary's soul and crowning her (in the form of the two icons brought together) provided an appropriate backdrop for the Assumption day meeting.[1174]

The exceptionally rich illustrations in a manuscript from the time of Louis IX containing the coronation ordo (Paris, BnF MS lat. 1246) served to interpret the "sacre royal" and to convey, through their aesthetic formalism and color, the balance between ritual and ceremony inherent in the liturgy.[1175] Meditating on Christ's crown and humankind's sin, coronation liturgies in the Sainte-Chapelle promoted connections between the monarch and the history of salvation pictured in the light-filled glass (see Plate VII).[1176]

Churches were consecrated as sacred precincts in rituals that involved inscribing signs on the floor, bringing relics into the space, and sprinkling the walls with holy water to exorcise demons and make space for the inhabiting spirit.[1177] In turn, anniversaries of consecrations, which provided occasions to re-enact mythic beginnings and thereby telescope sacred time, were celebrated through art. A fresco at the entrance to the lower church of San Clemente, for example, features the ninth-century translation of Clement's body from the Vatican with the papal entourage preceded by a stational cross and banners, thereby authorizing the relics inside and tying the foundational moment to annual processions.[1178] At the summit of the north portal of Amiens, the remains of the local saint, Firmin, are shown being carried in the reliquary shrine that, until the French Revolution, occupied the apse as they were on the day the church was consecrated and repeated on the saint's feast day of 13 January.[1179] The Baptism of Christ on the Freckenhorst font reminded those entering the nave of their own initiations (Figure 60), and the faithful's viewing of the bands of narratives and inscriptions encircling the drum recapitulated the movements of the original consecration.[1180] By extension, the acts of charity pictured on the Rodriguez tomb in León (Figure 39) offered a paradigm for the commemorative lamentation repeated on the anniversary of the bishop's death and the annual renewal of alms of food, drink, and clothes (mentioned in the epitaph).[1181]

Art engaged paraliturgical rites. In the cloister of Gerona Cathedral, a depiction of Abraham washing the angels' feet provided a biblical paradigm for the monastic ceremony of cleansing the feet of the poor that took place on the stone bench below, and a capital showing a monk shaving another for the clerical tonsuring.[1182] Rubrications in the Song of Songs of the early eleventh-century Saint-Vaast Bible (Arras, Bib. mun., MS 559) indicate that the dialogue between the bride and bridegroom of Hebrew Scripture pictured in the miniature served monks in the refectory.[1183] In Pisa, the confraternity of *flagilanti* conducted rituals in the Campo Santo interwoven with the figures in the pictured triumph of death.[1184]

Particularly in the complicated environments of large churches that changed with the time of day, liturgical circumstances, and status of person, interactions between pious people and art were multilayered. Accessibility was often controlled; screens closing off the Holy of Holies where the priest effected the miraculous transformation of the Host and wine often represented Christ's historical presence in images (Figure 26). Although the direct impact of the Lateran Council on the development of church retables may be exaggerated,[1185] changes in liturgy resulted in the development of altarpieces, as when Charles the Bald's antependium was refashioned at Saint-Denis. The connection between image and ceremony was complex: the altarpiece engaged the liturgy, but it also constructed its own concept, presenting one message to the laity and another to the clergy, for example on the Vallbona altarpiece, which features the Virgin and Child on the verso. Continuous reconfiguration of secondary liturgical spaces resulted in other transformations, even on occasion the removal, transfer, and modification of stained-glass windows.[1186]

Guiding Devotion

Art generated motion.[1187] Renowned images attracted the faithful from afar; just as the Shroud of Turin brings pilgrims to Genoa today,[1188] the *Veronica* was a major lure to Rome in the Middle Ages, especially after Pope Innocent granted indulgences for pilgrimage to it.[1189] Pope Boniface VIII instituted regular jubilee years in which veneration of the *Veronica* in San Pietro became a prime goal and earned pilgrims remission for sins;[1190] Giotto painted a fresco commemorating the promulgation of the Jubilee indulgence in a papal benedictional loggia at the Lateran, the backdrop's accurate rendering of portraits and historical detail making the pope (who was actually away in Avignon) present and potent when pilgrims flocked to the city.[1191] Pilgrims came to expect art at their destinations,[1192] not only in Rome, but also at the grave of Saint James at Santiago de Compostela, the Holy Land sites, and the tomb of Thomas Becket, celebrated by Geoffrey Chaucer in the *Canterbury Tales*.[1193] Figures in the border of the *Très riches heures* record the fact that the Sainte-Chapelle, too, was a pilgrimage goal, the relic of Christ's Crown of Thorns in Paris serving to authorize Louis IX's sanctioned reign.

Art at pilgrimage destinations was believed to work physical and spiritual changes. Bernard of Angers described peasants venerating the Conques relic-sculpture and the healings and punishments affected during processions in the town. The depiction of all kinds of ailments on the tympanum at Vézelay advertises the effectiveness of pilgrimage to Sainte-Madeleine.[1194] Saints' tombs were designed during the twelfth and thirteenth centuries to enable pilgrims suffering from diseases and defects to crouch beneath, walk around, and touch the sacred resting place;[1195] a seventeenth-century watercolor copy of a fourteenth-century fresco records the practice at the tomb of Saint Margaret of Cortona, as does Andrea Bonaiuto's fresco of pilgrims to Peter Martyr's grave in the Santa Maria Novella chapter house in Florence.[1196] Transferred to portable objects, a saint's aura could be brought home; following ancient custom, an early thirteenth-century ampulla from Canterbury picturing Thomas Becket is inscribed, "Thomas is the best doctor of sick people [who are spiritually good]."[1197]

In turn, art regulated movement. The Westminster Cosmatesque pavement appropriated Roman use of porphyry disks to mark liturgical positions to plot coronation ceremonies (Plate IX). At Ceri, the martyrdom of Saint Andrew interrupted the passage from door to apse to invite the faithful to pause for prayer; frontal and on eye level, the vignette represents the legend that even while being crucified, the apostle preached and made converts introduced in the caption, "Hanging, he lived for two days and taught the people."[1198] The dialogue of Old and New Testament images not only tethers the church to its divine prototype but also asserts that worshiping Christ in this world leads to the redemption of Adam's sin. Each position in the *aula gotica* brought new images into view, creating a tension between physical enclosure and aspiration even more sophisticated than the somatic experience generated by the related murals at Anagni.[1199]

The back-and-forth between pictured subjects and actions within church spaces engaged the cause-and-effect relationship between sin, guilt, punishment, and redemption.[1200] Art followed patterns more like chess moves than straight vectors, or engendered a labyrinth's false steps and recoveries, as at Lucca (Figure 57), which require the thread of faith to navigate. Aligned with Daedalus's labyrinth on the Hereford *mappa mundi* (Plate XVI),[1201] the Israelites' journey offers a paradigm of such artistic itineraries. God's chosen people traverse the waters divided for them and pass mythical creatures before they reach Mount Sinai where, while Moses receives God's law, a renegade group of Israelites succumbs to worshiping the idol labeled "Mahum" (Mohammed), simultaneously "othering" Christianity's two perceived religious enemies.[1202] Continuing to the Promised Land, the exiles' path loops around itself twice, doubles back, forks into two paths, converges again, and rounds Sodom and Gomorrah, where, descending, it continues past Lot's naked, disobedient wife. Temptation lurks everywhere. Thus, a devout Christian at Cremona traversing the figures on the floor would, herself, have enacted the pictured *psychomachia*, authorized by Christ's trampling the beasts. More dramatically, trammeling the demons and lion on the Aosta pavement, a visitor would re-enact Samson's vanquishing the lion and hence the triumph over evil and, reading the inscription in the circular frame, spin her or his body in an elevating ecstasy (Figure 49). A labyrinth of Saint-Étienne in Auxerre provided the matrix for a similar sacred circular dance (or "ball") in which, at Easter time, the bishop and clerics chanting *Victimae paschali laudes* re-enacted Christ's descent into Hades on Holy Saturday to defeat the devil and his return (like Theseus using a ball of string) to restore order in the world.[1203] Writing c. 1170, John Beleth disapproved of a similar paschal dance on the labyrinth of Reims Cathedral.[1204] In the late Middle Ages, rituals of flagellants and other mystics assumed the form of a dance,[1205] and, during carnival, the Church used dance to instrumentalize sin.

Private devotion, too, could be quite energetic,[1206] engaging art to effect an anagogical *transitus*.[1207] Peter Lombard argued that praying before depictions of the human Christ distinguished true from false worship,[1208] and Matthew Paris acknowledged that the *Veronica* activated prayers uttered before the image. The fact that almost every small Italian painting was worked on the back implies that the panels now displayed in cases or on museum walls were originally held in worshipers' hands and opened and closed during meditation.[1209] A treatise attributed to Peter the Chanter distinguishes seven gestures of prayer, each justified by the Bible or a Church father and designed to express the humility and emotional response of a devout lay person. Similarly, the handbook, written by a Dominican brother between 1280 and 1288, describes, documents, and illustrates nine prayer positions, of which the third is like that of Charles the Bald, lurching toward a crucifix on his knees with the right arm raised and the left hand opened (Figure 18).[1210] Angela of Foligno engaged in such an intense dialogue with a painted crucifix that its appearance was impressed on her person, and Elsbeth Stagel at the bottom of Suso's *Exemplar* page meditates on her paradigm, the Virgin of Sorrows, using the newly popular rosary to regulate her devotions (Figure 22). The concept is integrated into the several forms of veneration figured in the miniature, initial, and margins of the *Très riches heures* Sainte-Chapelle page; and, cued by the statue of Enrico Scrovegni kneeling in prayer in the presbytery and by inscriptions in the frescoes, it configures the Scrovegni Chapel as a perpetual "Ave Maria" for the patron's redemption.[1211]

While considered a worthy first step, experiencing art impeded sacred imagining. In the upper register of the *Cantigas* miniature (Figure 41), the Virgin appears and speaks only when the woman bows down and averts her eyes,[1212] and the *La sainte abbaye* manuscript in London (Brit. Lib. Yates Thompson, MS 11, fol. 29ʳ) tracks the proper process—through confession, prayer before an image of the Coronation of the Virgin, imageless meditation in a prostrate position, and finally a mental vision of the Trinity.[1213] Walter Hilton noted that "those who wish to pray spiritually usually close the exterior eye or avert it from the object of the image."[1214] Induced to decipher the lines of text that constitute the imagery, the reader of the micrography of the Leviticus frontispiece in the Copenhagen Pentateuch (Figure 45), by contrast, moved from image to word in a manner antithetical to contemporary Christian practice.

Speaking

People reinforced meaning when they spoke in front of works of art.[1215] Hugh of Saint-Victor used a diagram to teach the fine points of theology,[1216] and, according to Jacques de Vitry, the Dominican preacher Johannes Tauler delivered a sermon to nuns in Cologne that was inspired by a painting in the refectory based on Hildegard of Bingen's *Scivias* (see Figure 19).[1217] King Alfonso is portrayed in the *Cantigas* pointing out the pictured stories to his pious subjects and, in so doing, incorporating the explanatory voice of the texts he transcribed or composed. The antiphon that Sicardus introduced at the start of his discussion of *Ecclesia* cued the reading of the gem-like glass as both holy Scripture and the walls of

Jerusalem, and the recitation of the responsorial *Stirps Jesse* would have conveyed the significance of the Tree of Jesse, and the *clara chorus* that of *La belle verrière*. The *Mariengebet* seems to have been written to be recited before the contemporary Arnstein windows, rendering Latin liturgical tropes in the vernacular to explain the erudite Marian imagery and provide an account of the subjects' relationship to the vitreous medium itself:

> Moses, a holy man, saw a burning bush,
> But the bush was not consumed
> It burned without damaging it ...
> The bush retained its beauty,
> As your body did its chastity.[1218]

On-site interlocuters sometimes provided interpretive services.[1219] A roll preserved in the cathedral of Canterbury (Cathedral Archives and Library, MS C 246), for instance, would have helped resident guides explain the complicated imagery of the stained-glass windows to visitors.[1220] Adam of Eynsham recounted how Hugh of Lincoln, "wishing to apply this lesson specifically to John Lackland" (a son of Henry II and Eleanor of Acquitaine who would soon be crowned king), pointed to the wicked kings at Lincoln Cathedral "who cannot govern themselves and so become the slaves of demons" and commented that church portals were good places for Last Judgments because they remind "those who enter that they must implore God's pardon for sins," praying being the best way to enter heaven.[1221] John then turned the tables in his response, drawing attention to the kings entering heaven and promising to follow their lead so that one day he "might share their company for all eternity."[1222] (At Lincoln, the Last Judgment portal led into the angel choir where Saint Hugh was later buried.[1223])

Public orations also made images come alive. The façade of León Cathedral was a backdrop for sermons preached in the cathedral parvis and the *scaenae frons* for such rites of transition as baptism and marriage in which the priest greeted the participants at the church threshold.[1224] Preaching engaged with pictures in a mutually reinforcing didactic strategy. A sermon by a Vézelay monk named Julian, for instance, directed the audience to "look" at the kings adoring Christ as a way to understand that the dirty and humble Holy Family was indeed divine and exhorted the congregation to "follow the path and faith of the magi."[1225] A vernacular sermon delivered at Amiens in the middle of the thirteenth century offers insight into how a clerical interlocutor would have made the complex theological constructs of the cathedral façade accessible to the largely illiterate faithful;[1226] direct references are few, but the overall meaning is elucidated. A homily preached on the feast of Saint Francis in 1265 assured the faithful that the homage paid to a painted portrait is equivalent to veneration of the saint himself; for the Franciscan Peter of Limoges, the crucifix deployed by a priest was the Gregorian "book of the lay." Preachers also reminded the faithful to redirect their attention to the celestial archetype rather than the material image before them; to that end, sermons sometimes deployed diagrams.[1227] Opicino de Canistris, moreover, warned that the vivid exempla deployed to animate sermons held the danger of idolatry unless they were subjected to an elevating imagination,[1228] and for the Franciscan preacher Giordano of Pisa, the physical crucifix was only the beginning of spiritual ascent.[1229]

Within an overall order that conveyed ecclesiological authority, spoken words reinforced the stratification of audiences affected by the images' complex rhetoric of style and inscription. Parallelling the way in which polychromy made the statues resemble living persons, the vernacular language of sermons would have appealed directly to rustic viewers in the same way such familiar motifs as an attendant testing the temperature of water for an infant being baptized and even the use of humor to render Scripture immediately intelligible did.[1230] The Passion narrative on the Naumburg choir screen contains palpable examples that were useful for instructing uncultured people.[1231] At the other extreme, sermons also incorporated philosophy and even technology to drive home pastoral messages. Peter of Limoges's preacher's manual is rife with references to modern optics, and Giordano of Pisa cited the recently invented eyeglasses and studies of vision to contrast corporal and spiritual vision.

Another means for rendering Scripture accessible, liturgical drama had a symbiotic association with artistic renderings.[1232] Originating in Holy Week rituals, the enactment of the dialogue between the three Marys at Christ's tomb and the angel, beginning *Quem quaeritis* (Whom do you seek?), is documented in the mid-tenth century. The *Sponsus*, which ends with Christ's expelling the five foolish virgins from "the threshold of this court," resonated with depictions of Matthew's parable on such church façades as that of Amiens and interior decorations as that in Berzé-la-Ville and at Anagni.[1233] The eleventh-century chapterhouse paintings at Vendôme provided an appropriate backdrop for the liturgical drama *Peregrinus*, enacted there on Holy Thursday;[1234] and the depiction of two women in the adoration of the magi at Lambach are the midwives who, in a dialogue with the Magi in the Christmas Eve play *Officium stellae*, exalt Mary and Christ. The woman wearing a white apron at the forge and her husband displaying his hands in the Holkham Picture Bible's rendering of Christ's Passion appear in the plays of Autun, Semur, Arras, and Auvergne.[1235]

Whether text engendered image and then drama, or drama based on text generated picture, varies from instance to instance. Illustrations in manuscripts of liturgical drama may have provided intermediaries, as attested by the fourteenth-century example in Besançon (Bib. mun., MS 579), which productively blends images and texts.[1236] By the fourteenth century, images themselves, like other church accoutrements, served as props.[1237]

Art used in secular ceremonies followed similar patterns. With its Latin inscriptions and "footnoted" narratives, the Bayeux embroidery (Figure 31) may have been a portable history set up in various baronial keeps or halls and elucidated by interlocutors speaking different languages who could bend the narrative to appropriate audiences. A fragment of Wolfram von Eschenbach's *Willehalm* in Munich (Bayerische Staatsbibliothek, Cgm 193, III) uses formulae found also in the contemporary *Cantigas* to suggest the epic's essentially performative aspect; Wolfram is the pivotal figure in the sequence of "acts" and is indexed to the accompanying text to establish continuity between the gesturing figures and lines of poetry. At Rodenegg (Figure 61), where subjects were known through recitations of chivalric poetry, the frescoes provided a setting for social events hosted by an aspiring ministerial family; at San Gimignano, paintings may also have contributed to dinner-time entertaining.[1238] The attack on the castle of love pictured on the Walters Art Museum mirror was an allegory of courting actually enacted during festivals (Figure 7).

Playing

Literates were captivated by puns and word games; in addition to saints' lives and other texts, a tenth-century compendium from southwest England contains almost 100 riddles (Exeter Cathedral Library, MS 3501).[1239] When Gerlachus understood the rod (*virga*) of Moses and Aaron as signs of Mary's virginity (*virgo*) on the Arnstein window, he was acting like the Latin exegetes and etymologists who delighted in such play.[1240] Gerlachus extended the punning to art itself when he pictured himself resting his brush between *regu[m]* and *clare* (meaning brightly, clearly) on the glass, constructing an alternative reading with the adjacent *vir* as *virgu[it]um*, meaning brush. Like Moses's transformed staff, Aaron's rod that blossomed, and the "*virga isai*," art, it shows, was another instrument of God's power to animate dead matter. Plants engaged Calcidius's use of *silva* (forest) to refer to primordial matter,[1241] and the word *desidera* on David's banner on the Basel reliquary puns desire with both stars (*de sidera*) and the lustful king's Medusa face (Figure 3).[1242] Image-makers made visual puns (many rooted in Latin), too; the gold ornament on Charles the Bald's regalia in the prayer book, for instance, rhymes with Christ's red chest wounds to reinforce the opposition of the world's vanity and redemption through Christ's death.[1243] The fashioning of the pilgrim badge vulva as a wound (*vulnus*) dramatized a similar play (Figure 62),[1244] alluding to the prevailing tradition exemplified by the Fritzlar Pietà's assimilating of the gash in Christ's chest to lips (Plate VIII).[1245]

Serious playfulness energizes the acrobats, jugglers, and wrestlers on the Bayeux embroidery, at Sant Joan de Boí (Figure 59), in Villard's sketchbook, and in other works,[1246] as well as such inversions as Phyllis riding Aristotle (paired with Adam and Eve expelled from Eden) in the León cloister.[1247] For Bernard of Clairvaux, such parodic figures represent earthly distractions from the sacred life, which "is not a game for children of the theater where lust is excited by the effeminate and indecent contortions of actors it is a joyful game, decent, grave, and admirable, delighting the gaze of heavenly onlookers."[1248] The monkey shown picking his bottom while looking at his face in a mirror at the start of the Holkham Picture Bible was included to poke fun at the illuminator's boast below about the mimetic imagery.[1249] Secular art also sometimes parodied sacred imagery;[1250] for instance, Charles V of France owned a wood figurine of a fox in Franciscan garb holding up pearls representing the Eucharistic Host.[1251] Fun is an aspect of drolleries both formal and provisory,[1252] and the user's reflection in the Walters ivory mirror inserted her into the joyous frolicking depicted on the back, inverting the vanity trope in a complicated game of cat's-cradle crossings.

The search for salvation also acquired a ludic character. The dynamic structure of the Ballinderry fidchell board is mapped onto the pages in the Book of Kells (Figure 54) and other books, for instance, and ornament was disposed in churches in hopscotch arrangements sometimes actually cued by dice and chess pictured on church pavements.[1253] Doll-like sacred figures generated intimacy,[1254] and mathematical games (*ludi matematici*) structured habits of seeing.[1255]

Chapter 9
Subject

WRITING AT his monastery on Mont Saint-Michel in 867, Bernard the Frank concluded a detailed account of his travels to the far end of the world by recalling stones he had seen at Gethsemane on which "one could catch the sight of all the things a person might possibly wish to see as if on a mirror."[1256] Even simple worked matter of the sort inserted into the Urraca chalice (Plate III), Aachen pulpit (Plate IV), Sancta Sanctorum walls (Figure 15), or Westminster floor (Plate IX), Bernard implied, elicits memory that conjures knowledge worth having. At heart, his is an Augustinian theory of cognition,[1257] according to which things and the way they are perceived are inextricably intermingled with one another. Object implicates subject.[1258] As diagrammed in the Cambridge *De spiritu et anima* (Figure 55), the mind takes in impressions that arrive at its "common sense" from fingers, nose, tongue, ears, and eyes, are controlled by the cognitive faculty ([*vis*] *imaginativa* directly above the eye) and judgment ([*vis*] *estimativa*), and are stored in the memory (*memoria sensualitatis ut retentitiva*), all monitored by the inner sense of imagination believed to retain a spark of divine wisdom (*phantasia* at the crown).[1259] Bruno of Segni had applied the understanding to complex images, maintaining that, without "the gleam of apostolic teaching, no ornament is truly beautiful or instructive," and Peter of Celle noted that, on earth, "spiritual seeing is constructed by means of our recollection of images of corporeal things."[1260] Bonaventure declared that "there is nothing in the soul that was not perceived by the senses," concluding that "the soul does not make new things but, in painting and sculpture, expresses outwardly new compositions it made interiorly."[1261] Roger Bacon underscored the essential identity of objects and the perception of them.[1262]

Herman, the twelfth-century abbot of Scheda, bore witness to how the process was deemed actually to work. He reported that, while still a Jew, he could see only a "monstrous idol" in juxtaposed depictions of the Crucifixion and heavenly Lord he encountered in Mainz Cathedral because he lacked the "mental eyes" "to detect the light of truth" in the material images he had perceived with his corporal eyes.[1263] A late twelfth-century depiction of the Mass of Saint Gregory from Weingarten (Chicago, Art Institute) underscores the inadequacy of "fleshly eyes,"[1264] and in 1276, Inghetto Contardo rebutted a Jew's putative challenge in language remarkably like Bernard the Frank's four centuries earlier.[1265] Giordano of Pisa elaborated the claim that physical perception was the beginning of a series of actions that had to be processed mentally: "You must gaze so that you have within you some likeness ... [so that] the form and image is born within you and enters you."[1266]

In short, a culture that read Hebrew Scripture as prophecy of Jesus, accepted the Eucharistic species as Christ's body and blood, and put faith in the power of things to ward off invisible evil forces believed that *subjects* transformed inert things into *objects* by filtering sensual perception through learning and memory.[1267] Thus, Pacificus exhorts the *curiosus* (both the pictured monk and the reader of the text) to follow the line of the tube that bridges the corporeal world to the heavens and to find the nails of Christ's Crucifixion in the diagram of the stars, that is, to allow seeing things with physical eyes to trigger the memory of salvific objects (Figure 53).[1268] Both outer and inner eyes must work together in an instructive process analogous to apprehending religious truth in the visible sacraments.[1269]

The manipulation of matter could energize such binocular seeing, as in the use of contemporary visual language on the Naumburg choir screen lintel to cajole viewers into a state of repentance and atonement (Figure 26),[1270] or the assimilating of Mary Magdalene's hair to water in the statue at Écouis to dematerialize the stone's physical qualities and hence the saint's bodily presence (Figure 43).[1271] But according to the theory of cognition in which memory guided experience, art was, by definition, different for a literate Christian from what it was for a semi-illiterate or unschooled person, a layperson or nun, a Jew, Muslim, heretic, or even Byzantine, woman or man, child or sick person, a rich Lord or a peasant.[1272] Only imagination, forged through faith, could convert things and signs perceived by the senses into worthy objects and images. As Bruno of Segni, among others, asserted:

> Heretics, pagans, philosophers, and Jews seem to wear the very same ornaments as those worn by the Spouse of Christ. But their ornaments differ in this: however much they may look like gold, they are not gold, for no other wisdom is golden except that which the teaching of the Gospel and the Apostle authenticates.[1273]

The defecating monkey on the Hereford *mappa mundi* encapsulates the same dead-end seeing (Plate XVI), deploying the classic metaphor for imitative art (found also at the start of the Holkham Picture Bible; see Figure 52) for "Jews" unable to elevate an idol spiritually. Ambrogio Lorenzetti also realized the claim in the Massa Marittima altarpiece when he positioned the three cardinal virtues on steps leading to Mary and Christ (Figure 21) to mark the distance to the divine that can never be fully bridged, and furnished Faith with a mirror to assert that the deepest mystery is apprehensible only through belief.[1274]

Seeing

Resting on the assumption that what is perceived by the senses is at best partial, art is in its essence a fiction. Nonetheless, it could be a useful instrument for mediating between corrupting corporeal experience— deemed to be defecation, ejaculation, and fornication—and intellectual perception.[1275] Sight was considered the principal instrument of such mental conversion;[1276] thus, Gerard of Arras defended Christian art by claiming that the "mind of the inner man is to be aroused through that visible image [of the cross], on which the passion and death of Christ [which he] assumed for us is inscribed as if on the membrane of the heart. ... Likewise, the images of saints are permitted ... not that they should be adored by humankind, but so that through them minds are excited interiorly to contemplation of the working of divine grace, and also through their deeds we are influenced in our own behavior."[1277] And Gertrude of Hefta acknowledged that material images are appetizers before the "hidden manna" of true visions;[1278] they attract the devout through images of the Son while asserting that God is glimpsed through, and not in, those images.

Precisely *how* art might transform corporal seeing into a credible perception of the divine was therefore the central issue.[1279] Faith was essential. Indeed, beginning (perhaps) with Gregory's response to Serenus of Marseilles and continuing throughout the Middle Ages, Jews came to epitomize exterior-seeing because they denied the Incarnation.[1280] Saint Helena, for example, discerned cogency within chaos in the dirt on Golgotha by distinguishing Christ's cross;[1281] and in the Brussels bestiary (Figure 48), the brazen serpent that healed only those who demonstrated trust in God by gazing at it separates Christians from Jews. In turn, images themselves provided training for what has been termed "sacramental vision."[1282]

Even the faithful had to be content in this world to experience God in his human aspects and through images; the belief that true beatific vision awaits the blessed when they will be united with their bodies at the Last Judgment underlies much medieval art.[1283] An inscription framing the image of *Year* hovering above the earth and sea while holding sun and moon aloft within concentric circles occupied by the seasons, elements, and months on the cloth shrine cover in the church of Saint Kunibert in Cologne, for instance, expresses confidence that "The entire people gazes at that which is produced by art."[1284] The play here is between God's making of the world using geometric principles and humankind's artful imitation of it, and hence an affirmation of the relationship between what one sees in images and the world beyond. Art's fictionality is exposed in San Pietro in Valle, where God's face (and that of Saint Peter) was painted on separate panels inserted into the plaster to distinguish it from the narratives of scriptural history,[1285] and at the summit of the Scrovegni Chapel, where the celestial image of Christ is also distinguished materially from the frescoes (Plate XII). The Victoria and Albert polyptych (Figure 13) also enacts the concept on which the sequence of images of instruments of the Passion concludes with a representation of the vision promised to the faithful at the end of time.

Considered to have been corrupted by the original sin (itself precipitated by sensual desire), human sight no longer enabled direct perception of God of the sort that Adam and Eve had initially enjoyed in Eden.[1286] The narratives on the Hildesheim doors spell out the argument, beginning with an angel watching over the creation of Eve as Adam looks on and allowing the spectator below to gaze on God's face (Figure 23).[1287] Clouded by the Fall, expulsion, and Abel's murder, vision requires regeneration through Christ's Incarnation and sacrifice; thus, the narrative ends with proof that the disciples could see Christ after the Resurrection, and with the Savior's beckoning Mary Magdalene to a new (Christian) paradise (Jn 20:14–18). The penitent saint assumes the prayerful pose of the first angel and is led by the resurrected Christ toward a new garden occupied by eagles, birds fabled for their ability to soar high enough to see his divinity in heaven.[1288] The Salerno ivories track the divine plan, too, mapped also in botanical details from Genesis and ending with Christ's farewell to the (two) Marys after the Resurrection.[1289] And San Pietro in Valle meditates on the difference between the prelapsarian perception that the first man had shared with the angels and humankind's carnal seeing after the Fall, which it has in common with irrational beasts (Figure 58);[1290] the animals all gaze at the man and await his judgment, but standing, Christ-like, on the hillock from which the four rivers flow, the man looks across the nave to Christ being adored by angels in Heaven inscribed "SANCTUS, SANCTUS, SANCTUS" (Is 6:3). Mimicking Adam, human viewers below, in turn, see God only in images that reflect the primordial vision, echoing the "Holy, Holy, Holy, the whole earth is full of his glory" recited during the liturgy.[1291] The peacock feathers that decorate the stem of the Saint Francis reliquary evoke the same idea (see Plate VI); alluding to the birds of paradise pictured around the base and the garden in which Francis receives the stigmata, the iridescent "eyes" acknowledge the ambivalence of human sight.

Pictures were considered particularly effective in rendering the words of Scripture memorable because, through sight, they engendered emotions.[1292] Richard of Saint-Victor maintained that the beauty of images was not just "lust for the eyes" but could, by exciting desire, engage the imagination.[1293] Through intelligent contemplation, in other words, art had the capacity to meditate between the sensible and the intellectual. Imagination, in turn, rested on Trinitarian speculation,[1294] which is evoked through meditation on the ornamental forms in eighth- and ninth-century Hiberno-Saxon art, by the ubiquitous juxtapositions of the crucified Christ and *Majestas Domini*, and in such popular iconographies as the Tree of Jesse and Throne of Mercy (which, understandably, became special targets of iconographic reformers).

Sight's access to higher truths was, nonetheless, limited; many works of art engaged words and other devices to activate higher theological speculation.[1295] As Gregory I had already acknowledged in his dictum and others asserted over and over again, especially in the context of debates with Jews, inscriptions were epistemologically like pictures and in dialogue with them. Interacting with representations, tituli frequently cast doubt on images' ability to convey essential truth. The "It is neither God nor Man ..." couplet beneath Moses at the Burning Bush at Ceri (Figure 37) engages the question of what the prophet saw on Sinai and, in turn, what faithful Christians discern in the typological rendering of the event. And, directly below Adam gazing at God in Ferentillo, the Trinitarian caption beneath the scene of Abraham greeting the three angels cues skepticism about relying on corporeal sight to disclose divine mysteries. For all its appeal to the senses, the *Meditations on the Life of Christ* asserted that true contemplation is blind.[1296]

Moreover, seeing was itself regulated. From an early time, cloths were suspended before sacred depictions, re-enacting art's capacity simultaneously to reveal and hide divinity and identifying images with the curtain before the inner sanctum of the Jewish tabernacle.[1297] The Virgin Hodegetria in Santa Maria ad Martyres pictured on the pilgrim's badge is known to have been hidden behind a curtain hanging on rings from two columns (Figure 2);[1298] veils obscuring the Golden Madonna of Essen pictured at the base of the Theophanu cover were parted for the queen's devotions and tied around the column shafts. The confraternity at the Orsanmichele garnered income, not only by furnishing candles for devotees of the Madonna and Child panel but also by opening and closing the curtains, a drama that enhanced the impact of seeing the miraculous image (Figure 16).[1299] A silk cloth over Christ's face protected viewers of the Lateran *Acheropita* because, according to Gervase of Tilbury, the true image of Christ "caused such violent trembling in people who gazed at it too intently that there was a risk of death."[1300] Later in the thirteenth century, Juliana of Cornillon, the instigator of the Feast of Corpus Christi, is reported to have unfolded a Veronica so that she could look Christ in the eyes.[1301] Shutters on altarpieces permitted the main subjects to remain invisible except when revealed during special feasts,[1302] and, as panel painting passed from church to domestic setting during the thirteenth century, triptychs transferred and transformed the (touched) mundane world into a visible image of the sacred.[1303]

Corporeal sight could mimic the Incarnation through which the divine entered the world, but, as Peter of Limoges argued, it was also the portal of sin.[1304] Sight readily led to *in-vidia* (non-seeing), that is, the twisted desire that perceives bad things.[1305] Thus, the Medusa head and inscriptions on the Basel David reliquary assert that even the longing for relics needed to be redirected from the material body to the heavenly (Figure 3); David, after all, had himself become a monster because of urges aroused when he watched Bathsheba bathing.[1306] Following optical theories in Francesco da Barberino's *Documenti d'Amore*, Giotto painted a personification of circumspection over the door into the palace in the Scrovegni Chapel to remind those exiting the sacred space to remain on guard against vice, which was believed to distort vision.[1307]

Seeing had to be concerted, lest surface things obscure the deeper, spiritual meanings.[1308] Eyes were, after all, the instruments of original sin and, in medieval medical tracts, the agents of contagion.[1309] Curiosity and, worse, prurience, were among seeing's dangers.[1310] Thus, pictures of Christ, God's own image, were particularly effective in exorcising evil ones.[1311] Scrutinizing such small objects as the Regensburg butterfly (Plate I) or intricate ornament of the sort in the Book of Kells (Figure 54) and Copenhagen Pentateuch (Figure 45) engendered an amuletic effect.[1312] For Saint Francis, among others, emotions elicited by images and directed toward God catalyzed the unification of flesh with soul, but when reflected back to the viewer, they could, on the contrary, expose disunity. The Franciscan *Vrigiet de solas* ensnared the reader-viewer into looking and then chastised her for her vanity (Figure 56).[1313] The Paris reliquary alternates up-close scrutiny of tiny cloth fragments magnified with lenses and looking from afar at Francis gazing at the seraph.

Hugh of Saint-Victor and Richard of Saint-Victor compared images to mirrors that reflect God but that, like the soul, must be burnished of the blotches of sin.[1314] Mirrors were affixed to some pilgrim badges, and according to Giovanni Dominici, children would benefit from images of Jesus or Mary in which to mirror themselves.[1315] Engaging the Latin pun on *speculum* (mirror) and *specula* (watchtower), seeing from a distance underlay the juxtaposition of Faith's mirror in Lorenzetti's Massa Marittima altarpiece with Hope's tower. Rendered in perspective, the latter—like Pacificus's telescope—directs the viewer toward the envisioned Heavenly Jerusalem; the former provides a glimpse of the Trinitarian truth that is beyond direct seeing. The idea of a macro-microcosmic relationship that so intrigued theologians[1316] is manifested as well in the *aula gotica*, Hereford *mappa mundi* (Plate XVI), and many other works that employ binocular seeing to foreground the human role in activating sight and to contrast it with God's perfect and all-encompassing vision.[1317] The Christ of the Rosano Crucifix (Plate X), for instance, is present to the viewer but at the same time inserted into historic time by the framing narratives; tellingly, the painted cross pictures Christ as the first pilgrim, equipped with kit and staff on the way to Emmaus. The Metropolitan Museum Virgin Mary contains sacred history and the entire Trinity (Figure 28), and, prepared by the mourning Mary, the compassionate viewer of the Fritzlar Pietà can visually enter Christ's wound in a kind of rebirth and (if indeed the Host was stored there) partake ocularly of his body (Plate VIII).[1318]

Seeing also had a history,[1319] in fact, two—one objective, the other subjective—which became productively intertwined at various periods and intersected in diverse ways with art production.[1320] Particularly during periods of intense artistic exchange, politics governed aesthetics.[1321] Peter of Limoges, for example, drew on Augustine when he maintained that there are three types of vision—carnal, rational, and contemplative—and that, just as the first requires physical light, the latter needs God.[1322] For him, painting corresponds to carnal vision and the mirror to reason that processes it; both are needed to effect contemplation. Given these histories, the question arises: Do modern persons see as people did in the Middle Ages?[1323] To the extent that medieval writings about vision can be relied on, the answer is no: controlled by memory, sight had to be learned and guided.[1324] The Trinity College brain imagines memory as a controlling element of cognition, while the later version of the diagram in the Cambridge University Library pictures impulses from two eyes crossing before they enter the common sense and the imagination.

Simulating the processes of seeing in pictures,[1325] Giotto successfully elided the difference between object and subject;[1326] in the Scrovegni Chapel, for instance, he had the viewer look up from a standpoint into the chambers where the Annunciation takes place and, even more dramatically, deceived them into believing that the space extends beyond the wall that separates the public space from the presbytery. Giotto's followers, including Taddeo Gaddi and Ambrogio Lorenzetti, perfected the devices—in the Massa Marittima altarpiece, the latter guides the viewer into the painting on rising steps that symbolize the cardinal virtues needed to approach God.[1327] During the 1330s, Opicinus de Canistris applied optics to merge the system of real navigational maps (known as portolan charts) to imagine the world as God sees it, to figure the relationship of earth to heaven, and to disclose the spiritual truths in empirical depiction.[1328] In the chapel at Karlstejn (Figure 12), Charles is portrayed preparing his cross reliquary within an antechamber that mimics the vaulted Sancta Sanctorum he is about to enter, and a receding bank of four steps below creates the illusion of the outer courtyard of Solomon's temple where lesser people had to remain.[1329]

Such painterly tricks only confirmed corporeal sight's unreliability. Indeed, the theorists based many of their conclusions on optical illusions, such as the apparent distortion of a stick seen in water, and Peter of Limoges made it a theme of his moralizing tract when he argued that only perpendicular rays form a distinct impression on the eye's crystalline humor, and oblique viewing therefore was sinful.[1330] Thus, while much Trecento painting orchestrates an orderly ascent toward God, some works also assert the belief that the senses can never reach the ineffable presence.[1331]

Mise-en-abîme

A widely used and varied mechanism for demonstrating the chasm between objects seen with fleshly eyes through art and the true vision that the faithful seek was the generating of a chain of references between things in this world and an imagined (paradisiacal) prototype, through duplicating an object on a reduced scale within the work itself—"mise-en-abîme."[1332] The miniature orb adorned with a cross atop the horse in the lower right of the Hereford Map, for instance, mimics the *mappa mundi* and, in so doing, provides the viewer with the kind of perspective God himself enjoys when looking at the entire cosmos.[1333] Giotto deployed mise-en-abîme systematically in his Stefaneschi altarpiece (Vatican, Pinacoteca; first decade of the fourteenth century) when he included a portrait of the cardinal-donor in the foreground offering a precisely rendered miniature of the polyptych in which he appears again holding a miniature of the ex-voto entirely of gold.[1334] The viewer of the altarpiece (in the first instance, Giacomo Gaetani Stefaneschi) thus occupied a place between the pictured patron being ushered into the congregation of saints and angels organized in a perspective space, then into an overt image of the celestial realm, and ultimately into a distilled dematerialized world at the very edge of perception's abyss.

Giotto's perfect application of mise-en-abîme had numerous antecedents, including Bernard the Frank's polished Gethsemane stones. The burning bush in Ceri is a classic example; shaped like a church apse enclosing the figure of Christ (as at Berzé-la-Ville; Figure 32), it asserts that the Old Testament appearance of God (theophany) yields ultimately to the Word-Made-Flesh, as the accompanying titulus asserts.[1335] Boxes-within-boxes dilate the cross's significance on the Zwiefalten altar (Figure 4), transforming the cross fragment mounted against a star-studded gold field into a tree, framed by golden vines, and into Christ's body through delicate enamels of the Savior's face, hands, and feet, set among gems on an outer cross-shaped field. Theophanu's Gospel cover relies on a similar succession to move the owner from the shrine in Essen with its reliquary and saints, through the historical Christ and his return to heaven itself. So does the tiny Regensburg butterfly, not only through the fragile creature's encompassing the entire Crucifixion but also through the relics the enamel encloses, the case in which it was protected, and the crucifix in which the ensemble was inserted. Opened to disclose something physically smaller but spiritually greater inside, shrine Madonnas operated in the same way; as Candide, a sister at Maubuisson recorded: "When it was thus opened, it was not a Virgin, but a world—and more than a world, a paradise, purgatory, and hell were there with all the mysteries of the Old and New Testament, from the creation of the universe through the Last Judgment, and all represented in figures no larger than a finger, arranged on shelves in separate groups, all very well done and the most delightful thing in this world."[1336] Whenever Andrew III or a later monarch wrapped himself in the Coronation Mantle (Figure 14), he became the representative of Christ through images of the sovereign God shown enthroned in his heavenly court on the back and the victorious ruler by way of his predecessor the sainted king Stephen, whose cape it had been.

Diagrams, so frequently employed in medieval works, facilitated the effect of mise-en-abîme, as in the concentric circles that formulate the relationship of World-Year-Man[1337] or Opicinus de Canistris's interplay of maps and anthropomorphic forms.[1338] The *Vrigiet de solas*, for example, opens with a Tree of Jesse and, a few pages later, collapses the arboreal metaphor in the "mirror of life and death," here the "tree of sin under which we are born" at the center in which human life is shown about to yield to dirt-colored human death (Figure 56).[1339] Microarchitecture generated similar relationships between real objects and an imagined celestial abode. The buildings represented on the Hildesheim doors, for instance, connect the entrance into the church to sacred history, while a miniature Jerusalem on a capital in the cloister at Las Huelgas encouraged meditation on invisible places.[1340] As at Lucca, where the labyrinth refigures Christian pilgrimage and salvation (Figure 57), Daedelus's structure on Crete is a mise-en-abîme of the Hereford *mappa mundi*, that is, for the perilous itineraries through the world depicted on the circular map.[1341] Framed by a succession of arches that mimic the windows themselves and that move from lustrous words against black, life-evoking green vines, and red devoid of imagery, Gerlach is portrayed completing the votive inscription that beseeches the King of Kings to have mercy on him (Figure 33), the first link in a visual and linguistic chain that, in the *Arnsteiner Mariengebet*, is understood as an entreaty to the Virgin Mary to intercede so that humans might glimpse "God's inextinguishable light" through the medium itself:

> You are the intact glass, through which came
> the light, which rid the world of darkness....
> The rod [of the Tree of Jesse] points to you, holy maiden,
> and the flower means your beloved son.

The Eucharistic wafer operated as a mise-en-abîme par excellence. Understood to embody Christ and also to concentrate the entire universe in a palpable object, it is pictured in between the Savior's fingers in some *Majestas Domini* pictures;[1342] milled and stamped like a coin, imprinted with the crucifix and vine scrolls, and set within a micro-tabernacle on the Vallbona altarpiece (Figure 17), the image of God's beneficence recalls the recompense for the faithful who bring offerings to his altar. As a "sign of the fear of the Lord,"[1343] the Host is also referred to in coin-like disks representing the gifts of the Holy Spirit in the Arnstein window (Figure 33), which applies the device of recurring series specifically to the making of art.

Beyond Looking

As the Cambridge diagram documents, knowledge, feeling, and belief were understood to enter the mind through all the senses, and although sight was considered foremost and, for art, the principal one, sound, touch, smell, and taste were also important aspects of the experience of many works.[1344]

Hearing was, in fact, deemed almost as potent as seeing. According to Bernard of Clairvaux, Mary conceived through her ear,[1345] and the *Cantigas* imagines King Alfonso singing Mary's praises as the "flesh which can be seen and heard" (fol. 157ᵛ).[1346] Repeated over and over again in the "Ave Maria," Gabriel's salutation is not only featured in the Scrovegni Chapel but also actually embodied by it.[1347] Church bells summoned people to regular worship and also frightened demons away,[1348] as the Pisa griffin did when wind caused it to roar.[1349] In turn, trumpet blasts were understood to herald the Last Judgment, as in the depictions of the Second Coming in Strasbourg (Figure 50) and the *Specchio umano*.[1350] The gleaming Reichenau roundel (Figure 20) beckoned the faithful with both a vision of God's divinity and a verbal summons. Reading aloud, a central element of the liturgy, created communal listening.[1351] Inscriptions were massed around altars where spoken words effect objects;[1352] although sometimes associated with Judaism, words thus represented the Incarnation and so provided a second transmaterial bridge.[1353]

Liturgical objects made sacrality audible during church services: flabella, for instance, which were sometimes fitted with bells. Statutes of Guillaume de Seignelay, bishop of Paris 1219–24, ordered that "when the body of Christ is elevated, at the elevation or slightly beforehand, the bell should be rung ... so that the minds of the faithful are roused to prayer." Portable bells were likened to preachers' voices,[1354] and oliphants treasured in many churches were sounded,[1355] as the silver mount on Francis's ivory horn attests: "With this bell, Saint Francis summoned the people for his sermon," while the paired wood batons did the opposite: "striking these sticks he imposed silence." Clay pots inserted into the vaults of churches served acoustic purposes, following Vitruvius's discussion of ancient theaters.[1356] In the scene of the coronation of the Virgin in Sankt Severin in Cologne, an acoustical jar is inserted at the end of an angel's trumpet, linking the congregation's chant with divine music and sound with sight;[1357] it is perhaps no mere coincidence that a ceramic horn in the San Silvestro Chapel of Santi Quattro Coronati provided an acoustical channel to the *aula gotica* above, proclaiming the priesthood's power and interconnecting the sacred and mundane worlds to each other.[1358]

Although heaven was sometimes conceived of as a place of silence,[1359] it was more often imagined as filled with joyous music. Processions were accompanied *cum hymnis et canticis spiritalibus*; music stood in for the Holy Spirit and conveyed a dynamic harmony that united the community.[1360] It established a resonance between Church and the harmony of the spheres that governed the universe, and the persons occupying it whose comings and goings figured by echoes.[1361] Repetitive arches of the south transept portal of Aulnay Cathedral evoke the cosmic music circling around an empty tympanum, symbolizing God's unknowable nature.[1362] With arithmetic, geometry, and astrology, music was a manifestation of the quadrivium (four mathematical sciences), as depicted in the *aula gotica* where *Musica*, ringing bells and conducting organ-playing boys alongside *Num[erus]*, proffers the Augustinian definition, passed on in Guido Aretinus's theoretical *Micrologus*, that "music is the movement of pitches and the science of modulating well (rhythm)"[1363]—the celestial geometry moving the soul from the corporeal to the incorporeal figured at the room's summit.[1364] Sung at Chartres, the *Clara chorus* knitted together architectural metaphors, images, relics, and the very validity of human sensory experience,[1365] and the *Arnsteiner Mariengebet* refers to singing the Virgin's praise in imitation of the heavenly chorus. It is no surprise that, responding to the new Franciscan emphasis on sensuality, an organist is shown on the façade of the cathedral of León accompanying the blessed marching to heaven.[1366] In the Rothschild Canticles, musicians are integral to the apophatic images, adding to the interplay of senses deployed to figure the Trinity and subverting humans' attempts to comprehend fully the mystery corporeally.[1367]

Like the other senses, sound was also implicated in sin;[1368] the devil, after all, tempted Eve by whispering in her ear. An early twelfth-century Psalter from Reims (Cambridge, Saint John's College, MS B 18, fol. 1ʳ) is preceded by a miniature that opposes profane and sacred music; David composing the psalms with his holy musicians is contrasted to a bear-like man playing a tambourine accompanied by dancers and, as at Sant Joan de Boí, acrobats turning somersaults.[1369] The *Vrigiet de solas* pictures the seductive power of mundane music; the *Beatus Vir* page in the thirteenth-century Luttrell Psalter (London, Brit. Lib., Add. MS 42130, fol. 13r) makes the same contrast, albeit more discreetly, by picturing a man with a bagpipe in the margin across from David playing the harp. Rashi may have had Christian sound effects in mind when he imagined the golden calf the Israelites worshiped at the foot of Mount Sinai as a kind of satanic automaton animated by sound effects.[1370] Sound could also frighten the faithful; at Santes Creus, the bat and a screeching bat-monster assault the ears as much as the eyes (Figure 36).

Many works of art appealed to touch, not only such personal ornaments as rings and liturgical objects carried from place to place but also images that, like moving pieces on the Ballinderry game board (Figure 1), engaged the mind by coordinating sight with touch. The grooved labyrinth at Lucca invites pilgrims to retrace with their fingers the steps they had taken to trek the via Francigena,[1371] setting up a *psychomachia* between sight and feel to thematize Theseus's victory of good over evil through effort.[1372] Initials in the Saint Albans Psalter engage touch to effect a connection between Christ's physical mistreatment on earth and the struggle needed to transcribe and comprehend his sacred message.[1373] Likewise, Elsbeth Stagel's fingering the rosary in Suso's scheme of meditation mimics the interplay of sight and sound in her prayers before the Crucifixion and, in turn, the reader-viewer's progressive spiritualization when they follow the red thread with both eyes and fingers (Figure 22).[1374] A play of sight and touch also entered Trinitarian speculations in the Rothschild Canticles.

Through the theory of extramission, touch was in fact assimilated to sight.[1375] Sicard of Cremona tapped into the theory when he wrote that "in some books, the majesty of the Father and the cross of the crucifix are portrayed so that it is almost as if we see as present the one we are calling to, and the passion that is depicted imprints itself on the eyes of the heart."[1376] Strong but distributed throughout the body, feeling also verified corporeality; it was introduced in two of Christ's post-Resurrection appearances: the doubting Thomas and *noli me tangere,* which, for that reason, were pictured together on a single plaque of the Salerno ivories.[1377] Christ on the trumeau of the Naumburg screen was brought into proximity with those approaching the west choir so that he could be felt as well as seen.[1378] John's falling onto Christ's breast at the Last Supper and Mary cradling Christ's dead body after the Crucifixion are moments involving touch that became an important subject in fourteenth-century art. In the one, the Evangelist closes his eyes as he contemplates union with Christ realized by the Lord's hands;[1379] in the other, the grisly attention to Christ's suffering was part of a trend to deploy art as an instrument of spiritual exercises in which the torments of judgment become present in the viewer's body, through desire, pain, tears, and joy.[1380] As in the detailed sequence of flagellation, scourging, and clubbing of Christ in the Holkham Picture Bible (Figure 52) and in the stretched arms, broken legs, scabrous flesh, and gushing wounds of the Fritzlar Pietà, touch shocked.

Some objects were accompanied by tituli enjoining the faithful to kiss them,[1381] or were fashioned to accommodate expressions of passion.[1382] The eleventh-century *Life of Saint Dominic of Sora* tells of the miraculous cure of a child at the saint's tomb, though only after the father promised a donation of wax or oil; the boy kissed and embraced the saint's image (and the father repeatedly invoked the saint's name). Rupert of Deutz went even further when he recorded a vision in which, when he kissed a crucifix, Jesus opened his mouth so that the monk could kiss him deeply.[1383] And Innocent III decreed that when a priest kissed the altar, he was recapitulating the celestial embrace of Christ (the *sponsus*) and Maria-Ecclesia (the *sponsa*).[1384] If ivory is chaste because of its frigidity, as ancient texts indicated, it also yielded to human passion when handled and caressed.[1385] Touching, in turn, left its mark as a sign of devotion. The *Acheropita*'s feet offer evidence of the annual ceremony when the pope opened the little doors and washed them, and the abrading of Christ's face in the Tours Sacramentary initial is undoubtedly evidence of devotion (Figure 47). Likewise, the silver used on the ivory polyptych and Suso manuscript had to be rubbed to retain its luster; renewing the (divine) radiance was an ex-voto activity that refreshed a devotee's personal identification with Christ's suffering.[1386] Indeed, Suso maintained that a soul must be polished of any blemish.[1387]

The haptic sense could, obviously, also be evil. Directly beneath the obscene Sodomite in the Egerton Genesis, a soldier guarding the city is pictured provocatively fondling the pommel of a sword resting between his legs while another in fool's costume batters an alms seeker.[1388] In the aisle of Sant Joan de Boí (Figure 59), the juggler's dangerous twirling swords reinforce the sensual cacophony introduced by the music-making reveler inverting the anagogic power of the psalms. A caveat on the bottom of the Oviedo box alerts those who wish to touch it that they had better not, except the priest who might carry it in process: "May God, with divine thunder, destroy anyone who removes this gift."[1389]

An important element of Church ceremonies, smell too played a role. To reinforce the contrast with the outside world, churches were perfumed by incense, flowers, and beeswax that evoked the saints' presence and, in turn, thoughts of paradise, particularly during rites of baptism and burial.[1390] Thiofrid of Echternach evoked smell when he noted that perfume proved that relics did not putrefy and that the "precious materials [used to encase them] suit human nature because they simultaneously mask the nauseating matter that constituted most relics and attract the higher senses in a way that transforms them into the desire for heavenly reward" (Figure 11). The caption accompanying the translation of Saint Clement's relics in San Clemente in Rome underscores the belief that "Pope Nicholas ... buried him with divine hymns and aromas"; the pictured censing engages the perfume of lovers in the Song of Songs and, in so doing, the union of humankind with God.[1391] The depiction of Saint Michael bearing a censer in *La belle verrière* (Figure 5) is related to the saint's feast when the main altar was censed and the "aromatic smoke rises in the sight of God."[1392] The *Très riches heures* renders censer-bearing angels descending onto the altar (Plate VII). The reused crystal flacons inserted on crucifixes and reliquaries elicited perfume. Rose petals drifting down at the Santa Maria Rotonda and Santa Maria Maggiore injected fragrance into feast-day celebrations. Meant also to be touched and kissed, rosaries (especially those made of amber) elicited smell through association with the "rose without thorns," that is, beautiful form and fragrance devoid of pain that Mary proffers at the center of the Laon window (Plate XV) and that the petal-shaped wounds allude to on the Fritzlar Pietà. Scented water, together with the fascination of the mechanism and tinkling bells on the Cleveland device (Figure 64), on the other hand, were probably only for pleasure, like the gardens with music-making lovers depicted in the enamels.[1393]

Taste seduced Adam and Eve. Mundane food's temptation is pictured at Ceri adjacent to the altar, where a man is shown beneath sausages and prosciutti, basting a pig on a spit as two women enter with jugs of wine, the allure of carnal nourishment distracting those about to receive spiritual food. In turn, the mundane feast engages the iconic image of five saints, which includes John the Baptist proffering the *agnus dei* on a charger.[1394] The rich man's banquet at the entrance to Moissac is set in opposition to the liturgical offerings inside (Figure 24),[1395] which provide a foretaste of the paradisiacal banquet at the end of time.[1396] A Eucharistic reference is embedded in the *Vision of Saint Edmund,* which reports that feeling blood dropping from a crucifix behind an altar, the saint "put one drop to my lips and swallowed it";[1397] likewise, Mechthild of Magdeburg imagined communion with Christ by eating a Host embossed with the Lamb.[1398] The Eucharist, in turn, became increasingly spiritualized, manifesting its power visually in what has been dubbed "ocular communion," as pictured, for instance, toward the upper left of the Vallbona altarpiece.[1399]

Sacred texts were themselves ruminated. The First Bible of Charles the Bald, for instance, likened Scripture to bread and drink and exhorted the king to become one with it,[1400] and, in the twelfth century, Peter the Venerable directed monks to imitate Saint Benedict, whose "mouth is unceasingly ruminating on the divine words,"[1401] a notion of meditation realized, appropriately, in the Tree of Life, abundant with figures that fill the apse mosaic of the upper church of San Clemente.[1402] In such decorated manuscripts as the Book of Kells, the deep-looking at the ornamented word—itself full of devouring creatures—was understood as a form of ingestion whereby the message became part of the believer's very person.[1403]

Art engaged many senses at once, though not always all five. In the *Vision of Saint Edmund,* for instance, a voice directs the monk to the altar, where he sees the crucifix and anoints his nostrils before tasting the blood. The inscription on the Bargello flabellum not only refers to the fan's cooling capacity and use in chasing away black flies with their painful bites (Plate II),[1404] but also notes its usefulness against the smell threatened by "disgusting" spoiling Hosts. Pilgrims sang, gestured, and fell onto their knees,[1405] and the twelfth-century life of Saint Alpais mobilized censers, musical instruments, and candlesticks.[1406] The scene of Moses at the burning bush in Ceri details seeing (and not-seeing) and also engages hearing God's voice and removing the sandals made of skin that had touched the ground. The naming of the animals in San Pietro in Valle orchestrates the sound of Adam's voice and hand imposing names, chirping birds and baying animals, fragrant flowers, and luscious fruit to transform the vision of the earthly paradise into an allegory of Church. And, below the vision of God and his saints in heaven, the Saint-Martin-du-Canigou cartulary (Figure 8) conspicuously pictures lamps, bells, a censer, and the Eucharistic species about to be ingested. The Passion week liturgy in Italy involved lighting the Paschal candle and inhaling the pleasant scent of the beeswax candle, unravelling the Exultet roll, and chanting the hymns.[1407] Ambrogio Lorenzetti's altarpiece provides a setting for the Mass that offers entry into the celestial realm through sight (the mirror, tower, and steps rendered in perspective), touch (Charity's bow and flaming heart), music made by angels fingering and bowing instruments, and the smell of incense, lilies, and roses borne by angels. The miniature in the *Très riches heures* captures something of the saturated environment: it pictures the Sainte-Chapelle alive with singing and organ music, with people entering through a door adorned with figures; worshippers kneeling in humility within a space filled with ornament, effigies, and narrative; members of the faithful reading books or praying privately in the royal box; clergy in brilliant vestments celebrating the Mass at the altar fitted with the elaborate *Grande Chasse*; and, in the margins, approaching pilgrims praying by crossing their hands on their chests and clasping them together.

Art's Temptation

Although Hugh of Saint-Victor maintained that corporal attraction was a useful preparation for the greater beauty that awaits the faithful,[1408] the Middle Ages generated no autonomous aesthetics.[1409] Instead, medieval art embraced the early Christian notion of *varietas*, according to which images, objects and materials, words, and ornament are organized into a kind of poetry that appeals to the subject, often through various senses, and that cross one another in a simulation of the Incarnation itself.[1410] The fourteenth-century *Compendium de musica* summed up the aesthetic when it explained how music "does not follow the order of reason nor the order of nature ... but delights the ear through mixtures of sounds as the eye [does] by mixtures of colors and the palate by mixtures of flavors" and is structured so that "everything corresponds to each other in a firm order."[1411] The Aachen pulpit is a potent witness to *varietas* (Plate IV), with its late antique imperial ivories, Fatimid crystal chess pieces, multicolored gems, and agate and glass bowls ordered by inscriptions and strict geometry to serve the delivery of God's word; the Basel David is too.

As it had in the Garden of Eden, sensual delight could seduce.[1412] The long passage from Honorius Augustodunensis opposite the miniature of the puppet joust labelled "the game of monsters signifies the vanity of vanities" in the *Hortus deliciarum* makes the point that, just as Perseus had to use a mirror to defend himself from the Medusa's libidinous beauty, art's sensual attraction requires a shield to guard against the threat of diverting the faithful from the path to the invisible God.[1413]

Only the new Adam and new Eve can conduct the faithful's minds back to paradisiacal beauty.[1414] Thus, Adam at San Pietro in Valle presents an idealistic figure (in contrast to the animals) that the faithful could delight in and, indirectly at least, glimpse the perfection across the nave,[1415] and Christ on the central trumeau of Amiens exhibits proportion and classical harmony as he beckons the faithful to church and begins a *transitus* effected through the hierarchical composition (Figure 25).[1416] In the late eleventh-century *Salve regina*, which became increasingly popular during the twelfth and thirteenth centuries, the faithful beckon the Virgin to turn her merciful gaze at the "banished children of Eve" and show them the *fruit* of her womb, Christ.[1417] The Queen of Heaven occupies the center of the cosmic kaleidoscope of color and images at Laon, holding her Son in one hand and a mise-en-abîme rose composed of a disk encompassed by circles that is the perfect synecdoche of the light-infused glass in a church dedicated to her and the glimmer of divine beauty it provides the faithful.[1418] As Peter of Limoges exclaimed, "how great the glorious Virgin's beauty is and how delightful it is to see her with one's eyes."[1419] Embodying the fragile, divine beauty that is always just behind the reach of human senses, Mary who conceived the Child played a central role in making the Divinity apprehensible through art.

Epilogue
Environments of Experience

BECAUSE THE experience of medieval art was contingent on conditions of viewing and temporal unfolding processed through memory and faith, *presenting* it poses special problems. Photography, which since the nineteenth century has been the principal instrument of study, is troublesome because of the camera's built-in perspectival bias and scholars' tendency to deploy it in ways that assimilate medieval objects to post-medieval easel paintings and sculptures.[1420] More important, traditional photography imposes an aesthetic on works that originally had depended on experienced contexts to distinguish the things of this world from an imagined fixity promised the blessed at the end of time.[1421] As Peter of Limoges explained, "After the resurrection we will see with full directness, but before that only at an oblique angle to that directness,"[1422] which the Saint-Martin-du-Canigou charter (Figure 8) conveyed, for instance, by contrasting the temporal event with the timeless vision above it. Hildegard's *Scivias* renders the contingencies of medieval seeing even more emphatic (Figure 19); it presents Christ and the cosmos frontally and shows *Ecclesia*, alone, directing her eyes toward the eternal signs; the Church is intermediary, enterable on oblique stairs by a humanity pictured in profile. No wonder that Luke of Tuy condemned Manichaean heretics (who presumably denied Christ's dual nature) for rendering "the image of the most holy mother of God one-eyed and misshapen."[1423] Computers can restore aspects of the medieval experience, such as by sequencing images and text in a manuscript as the "pages" are "turned" or by creating a virtual reality of movement and shifting conditions in a cathedral.[1424] The *Cenobium* project at the Kunsthistorisches Institut in Florence is an ambitious attempt to compensate for some of conventional photography's failings, and the abbey at Fontevraud has applied available technological resources to re-create the experience of medieval art, including music and pageantry, and also narrators and theater. At the very least, users of traditional photographs need to try to re-enact the distinctive standpoints and contexts that, for medieval viewers, were essential to the comprehension of art,[1425] and historians should acknowledge how different medieval conditions of experiencing art are from those that prevail today.[1426]

Recognition of medieval art's contextual imperatives has long been dealt with, in part, by expanding the environments of display, as at the Musée Cluny in Paris, the Cloisters in New York, and other venues that reconstitute aspects of original settings.[1427] The recent re-installation of the treasury of Saint-Maurice d'Agaune takes full advantage of the monastery's exceptional collection of reliquaries and other liturgical objects and rich documentation, within a dignified modern setting.[1428] The Knight's Hall in the Walters Art Museum in Baltimore is, in my opinion, less successful because its attempt to provide a secular environment by assembling armor, furniture, and secular and religious objects in a castle setting and inviting visitors to sit at the central table and play checkers ignores the incongruous application of modern notions of domestic privacy to the Middle Ages and ends up subordinating objects to display. *Chroma* at Amiens also is only a mixed success; while the *lumière* (light) serves the useful function of reconstructing the appearance of the façade's polychromy, the *son* (sound) degrades the spectacle into a tourist show. Processions staged in Rome and elsewhere are more historically evocative, even if they do not involve precious objects from the Middle Ages. This medievalist will never forget the Good Friday staging of Christ's Passion in Gubbio with its hissing rattles, hymns, and candle-lit penitents walking along the walls, the Easter morning launch of a combustible dove into the Duomo culminating the *scoppio del carro* in Florence, or the priests swinging an enormous censer during Sunday Mass at Santiago de Compostela, suffocating the entire transept in fragrant clouds of smoke.

Temporary exhibitions that confront museum visitors with "modern" aspects of medieval art have also been provocative. The 2009 Rothko/

Giotto in Berlin's Gemäldegalerie (and the essays in the accompanying catalogue) not only probed such medieval verities as color and touch but also asked the question of what it means to be an artist.[1429] And by juxtaposing medieval objects with modern counterparts, the modest 2011 exhibition at Hunter College in New York, *Objects of Devotion and Desire: Medieval Relics to Contemporary Art*, made evident some of the complications of experiencing medieval art today.[1430] More ambitious undertakings such as the Jeffrey Koons installation in Frankfurt, however, obscured rather than elucidated the treasures of medieval objects in the Städel Museum; and while *Heavenly Bodies* seems to have gotten many visitors through the doors of the Cloisters and the Metropolitan Museum of Art's downtown medieval galleries,[1431] the superficial bling and the facile resemblances to adjacent religious objects did more to satisfy a chic clientele's materialism than elucidate the genuine medieval conflicts about clothing novelties that are revealed in thirteenth- and fourteenth-century sumptuary laws.[1432]

Contemporary artists who have struggled with issues of site-specific objects, materiality, veiling, multisensory activation, and performing have generally succeeded better than museum curators in conveying essential aspects of medieval art. Among many other works, Andres Serrano's 1987 *Piss Christ*, one of the photographic series entitled Immersions, is fully medieval in its powerful exploitation of (disgusting) matter, medial ambiguity, and elevating light to render the mystery of Christ's Incarnation; not surprisingly, the artist was fully aware of the medieval justification of sacred images that Lando di Pietro had used half a millennium before:[1433] "what the nuns told us when I was going to religious instruction was that we worship not the crucifix but Christ."[1434] Chris Ofili, too, seems to have understood the medieval notion of art as "dung clinging to carnal eyes" in his Holy Virgin Mary of 1996 (Private Collection),[1435] the obscene votive "badges" conjuring up the *pastiglia* medieval devotees applied to miraculous images (for example, the Orsanmichele Madonna [see Figure 16]). Each in her or his own way, Banksy, Joseph Beuys, Judy Chicago, Sam Gilliam, Damien Hirst, Allan Kaprow, Barnett Newman, Robert Smithson, and numerous other contemporary artists perpetuate medieval forms with intelligence and force and, in turn, refigure the old objects themselves.[1436] In his 1995 photograph *Il miracolo e lo specchio*,[1437] George Tatge (Figure 65), for example, incorporates ex-voto plastic roses in front of a painting of Mary's miraculous appearance before a local woman to create a

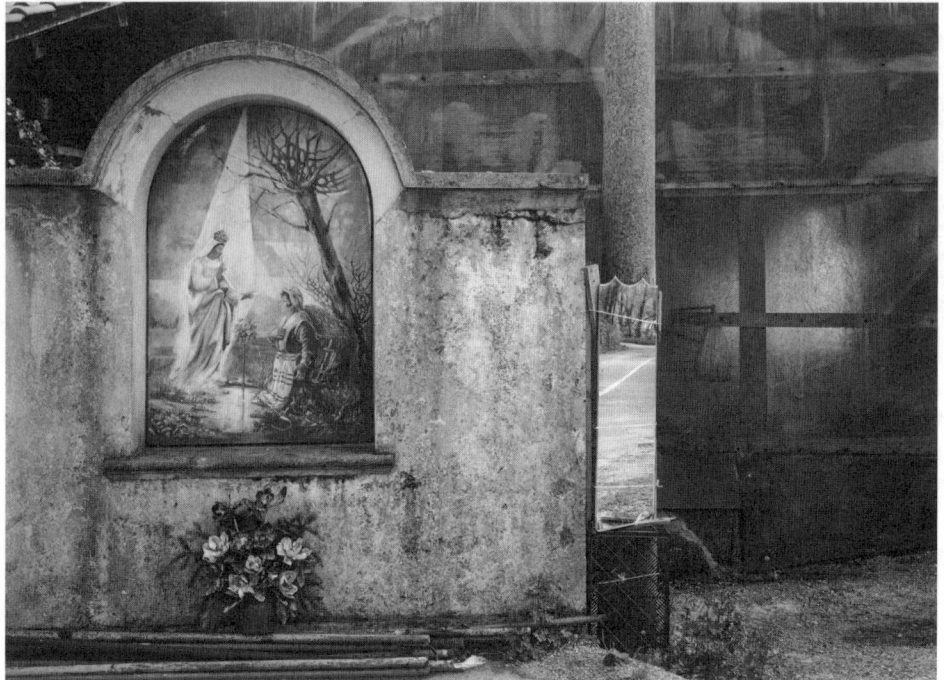

Figure 65. George Tatge, *Il miracolo e lo specchio* (1995)

medieval-like mise-en-abîme between the viewer of the photograph, the human-made spolia in the foreground, and the painted symbolic rosebush. He also sets up a comparison between the divine emanation that illuminates the pictured Virgin and the "real" light captured on the emulsion; passing through a curtain, that light creates a silhouetted cross and also the image itself, re enacting the powerful and persistent incarnational metaphor from Hebrews 10:20. As in Ambrogio Lorenzetti's Massa Marittima altarpiece (Figure 21), moreover, the angled mirror (featured in the titulus/title) breaks the photograph's insistent illusionism to provide a glimpse of an Edenic landscape that lies beyond this world's material clutter. *Il miracolo e lo specchio*'s profoundly medieval aspects might be serendipitous, what Erwin Panofsky dismissed as pseudomorphism, but they also may be more than coincidental. Tatge works in Italy and France, and, while employed by Fratelli Alinari in Florence, he made photographs of medieval objects such as the one of the flabellum of Tournus used in this book (Plate II). Modern art often meditates on medieval.

Recent focus on historiography has increased awareness of the myriad ways in which post-medieval engagement has conditioned the reception and study of medieval art. The Renaissance paradigm of a radical decline, initiated by Constantine's conversion to Christianity, and its reversal by "artists" who, during the thirteenth century, gradually returned art to nature through principles recovered from ancient art and texts remain tenacious. The prevailing narrative promulgated by Lorenzo Ghiberti and canonized by Giorgio Vasari of a Dark Age steadily illuminated through contact with the Greek east continues to prevail, distilled in the infelicitous neologism "Byzantinizing," still used even by sophisticated medievalists.[1438] The examination of counter-reformation medievalism, extraordinary continuities outside Italy, Romantic revivals, and Fascist period recuperations has not dislodged the Vasarian paradigm, in large part because the History of Art institutionalizes it in departmental structures and teaching.[1439]

Fortunately, new publications are steadily undermining disciplinary walls, not only by considering such oddities as the composite twelfth- and fifteenth-century *Marmo Osiriano* (Viterbo, Museo Civico),[1440] but also by taking seriously the continuities in medieval cults, forms, and ideas during the fifteenth century and beyond. Renaissance medievalisms are acknowledged;[1441] one new book with "late medieval" in the title considers sixteenth-century works;[1442] another is called *Gothic Renaissance*;[1443] and yet others focus on fifteenth- and sixteenth-century relic cults and pilgrimages[1444] and medievalisms in Golden Age Spanish art.[1445] Accepting and embracing such continuities is the only way to reckon with the fact that Alberti's own *Ludi mathematici*, considered essential for understanding perspective, essentially plagiarized the medieval *Quadrans vetus*, or to grasp the fact that Sister Candide of Maubuisson wrote her vivid account of the shrine Madonna at a moment when her compatriots Nicholas Poussin and Georges de La Tour were already passing from the scene. Moreover, medieval monuments were, themselves, continuously updated; the recent restorations at Santiago de Compostela, for instance, revealed that Maestro Mateo's great portico sculptures were covered over with rich new polychromy in the early sixteenth century, benefitting from the wealth pouring in from the New World, and that the portrait of Mateo's evangelist namesake was once refigured as a pilgrim.[1446] This is not to say that there was no Renaissance; it is to question whether there was a Middle Ages with a distinct medieval art.

How else to comprehend Benedetto da Maiano's 1490 monument in the Florence Duomo (no less), accompanied by Angelo Poliziano's inscribed panegyric of Giotto "through whom painting, dead, returned to life," which portrays the originary "artist" not emerging *ex nihilo* by tracing a perfect O, as the Vasarian myth would have it, but rather adding one more cube to an existing mosaic of Christ's black, flat, acheiropoietic, and distinctly medieval face?[1447]

Notes

1. Caroline Walker Bynum, *Christian Materiality: An Essay on Religion in Late Medieval Europe* (Brooklyn: Zone Books, 2011); *The Challenge of the Object: Die Herausforderung des Objekts* (Proceedings of the 33rd Congrès international d'histoire d'art), ed. G. Ulrich Groß et al. (Nuremberg: Verlag des Germanischen Nationalmuseums, 2013); Philippe Cordez, "Die kunsthistoriche Objektwissenschaft und ihre Forschungsperspektiven," *Kunstchronik: Monatsschrift für Kunstwissenschaft, Museumswesen und Denkmalpflege*, 67 (2014), 364–73; *Schatz Gedächtnis Wunder. Die Objekte der Kirchen im Mittelalter* (Regensburg: Schnell & Steiner, 2015) (French version *Trésor, mémoire, merveilles: Les objets des églises au Moyen Âge* [Paris, École des Hautes Études en Sciences Sociales, 2016]; English trans. *Church Objects in the Middle Ages: Treasure, Memory, Wonder* [London: Harvey Miller, forthcoming]); John Sutton and Nicholas Keen, "Cognitive History and Material Culture," in *The Routledge Handbook of Material Culture in Early Modern Europe*, ed. Catherine Richardson et al. (New York: Routledge, 2017), 46–58.
2. *From Minor to Major: The Minor Arts in Medieval Art History*, ed. Colum Hourihane (Princeton: Department of Art and Archaeology, 2012).
3. Danielle Gaborit-Chopin, "Reliquaire en forme de papillon," in *L'Art au temps des rois maudits: Philippe le Bel et ses fils, 1285–1328* (cat. of an exhib., Paris) (Paris: Galeries du Grand Palais, 1998), 233–34; Friedrich Fuchs, "Das Schmetterlingsreliquiar," in *Christus: Das Bild des unsichtbaren Gottes* (Regensburg: Schnell & Steiner, 2004), 49–51; Silke Tammen, "Bild und Heil am Körper: Reliquiarhänger," *Kanon Kunstgeschichte* 1 (2013), 299–322; Cordez, "Objektwissenschaft," 366–70; *Ludwig der Bayer: Wir sind Kaiser!* (cat. of an exhib., Regensburg), ed. Peter Wolf et al. (Regensburg: Schnell & Schneider, 2014), 318–19; Philippe Cordez, "Object Studies in Art History," in *Object Fantasies: Experience and Creation* (Berlin: De Gruyter, 2018), 24–27.
4. Dominique Barbet-Massin, *L'enluminure et le sacré: Irlande et Grande-Bretagne VIIe–VIIIe siècles* (Paris: Presses de l'université Paris-Sorbonne, 2013), 331–415; Jan Niehues, "Brettspiele des mittelalterlichen Irland und Wales," in *Sport und Spiel bei den Germanen: Nordeuropa von der römischen Kaiserzeit bis zum Mittelalter*, ed. Matthias Teichert (Berlin: De Gruyter, 2013), 217–43.
5. Renate Kroos and Karl-August Wirth, "Flabellum (und Scheibenkreuz)," in *Reallexikon zur deutschen Kunstgeschichte* 9 (2003), 428–507; Marie-Pasquine Subes,

"Art et Liturgie—Le Flabellum et l'ostension de la patène dans le cérémonial de la messe," *Bibliothèque de l'École des Chartes* 162, no. 1 (2004), 97–118; Daniel Joyner, "The Flabellum of Tournus," in *The Virgilian Tradition: The First Fifteen Hundred Years*, ed. Jan Ziolkowski and Michael Putnam (New Haven: Yale University Press, 2008), 436–38; *Karolingische und Ottonische Kunst*, ed. Dieter Blume, Bruno Reudenbach, and Klaus Gereon Beuckers (Munich: Prestel Verlag, 2009), 454–55; Isabelle Cartron, *Les pérégrinations de Saint-Philibert: Genèse d'un réseau dans la société carolingienne* (Rennes: Presses universitaires de Rennes, 2009), 81–89; "Le *flabellum* liturgique carolingien de Saint-Philibert: du don d'un souffle à la geste des moines," *Revue belge de philologie et d'histoire* 88, no. 2 (2010), 153–176; Herbert L. Kessler, "Images Borne on a Breeze: the Function of the Flabellum of Tournus as Meaning," in *Charlemagne et les objets: Des thésaurisations carolingiennes aux constructions mémorielles*, ed. Philippe Cordez (New York: Peter Lang, 2012), 57–85.

6 Such treasuries recapitulated and transformed burial hoards, the most famous being the Sutton Hoo ship and the recently discovered Straffordshire hoard; Michelle P. Brown, *Art of the Islands: Celtic, Pictish, Anglo-Saxon and Viking Visual Culture, c. 450–1050* (Oxford: Bodleian Library, 2016); Robert Sharp, *The Hoard and Its History: Staffordshire's Secrets Revealed* (Studley: Brewin Books, 2016); *Anglo-Saxon Kingdoms: Art, Word, War* (cat. of an exhib., London), ed. Claire Breay and Joanna Story (London: British Library, 2018), 82–92.

7 Eric Ramirez-Weaver, "Islamic Silver for Carolingian Reforms and the Buddha-Image of Helgö: Rethinking Carolingian Connections with the East, 790–820," in *China and Beyond in the Mediaeval Period: Cultural Crossings and Inter-Regional Connections*, ed. Dorothy C. Wong and Gustav Heldt (New Delhi: Manohar Publishers, 2015); Lawrence Nees, "Notes on Collecting in the First Millennium of the Common Era: Perspectives from West of China," in *Collecting China: The World, China, and a History of Collecting*, ed. Vimalin Rujivacharakul (Newark: University of Delaware Press, 2011), 184–93.

8 *Voyager au Moyen Âge* (cat. of an exhib., Paris) (Paris: Réunion des musées nationaux, 2014) ([Italian trans. *Il medioevo in Viaggio* [Florence: Giusti, 2015]; Catalan and English trans. *Viatjar a l'edat Mitjana/Travel in the Middle Ages* [Vic: Museu Episcopal, 2015]).

9 Holger Grönwald, "Am Einzelfund ins Detail: Das mittelalterliche Bild des Pantheon und seiner Ikone im Spiegel von Pilgerzeichen," in *Wallfahrer aus dem Osten: Mittelalterliche Pilgerzeichen zwischen Ostsee, Donau und Seine*, ed. Hartmut Kühne, Lothar Lambacher, and Jan Hrdina (Frankfurt: Peter Lang, 2013), 275–320; Robert Maniura, "Two Marian Image Shrines in Fifteenth-Century Tuscany, the 'Iconography of Architecture' and the Limits of 'Holy Competition,'" in *Architecture and Pilgrimage, 1000–1500: Southern Europe and Beyond*, ed. Paul Davies, Deborah Howard, and Wendy Pullan (Farnham: Ashgate, 2013), 213–29; Hanneke van Asperen, "'And They Were Always in the Temple': The Pilgrims' Experience in S. Maria Rotonda," in *Monuments & Memory: Christian Cult Buildings and Constructions of the Past; Essays in Honour of Sible de Blaauw*, ed. M. Verhoeven, L. Bosman, and H. van Asperen (Turnhout: Brepols, 2016), 85–93.

10 Philippe Buc, "Conversion of Objects," *Viator* 28 (1997), 99–143; Gerhard Wolf, "Icons and Sites: Cult Images of the Virgin in Medieval Rome," in *Images of the Mother of God: Perceptions of the Theotokos in Byzantium*, ed. Maria Vassilaki (Aldershot: Ashgate, 2005), 23–49; Beate Fricke, *Fallen Idols and Risen Saints: Sainte Foy of Conques and the Revival of Monumental Sculpture in Medieval Art* (rev. trans. of *Ecce fides: Die Statue von Conques, Götzendienst und Bildkultur im Westen* [Munich: Wilhelm Fink Verlag, 2007]).

11 Drop-shaped rock crystal ampulae containing water from Sainte Larme in Vendôme transferred the sacred power of Christ's tears venerated in the church and expressed it

in both form and material; Hans Henrik Lohfert Jørgensen, "Sensorium. A Model for Medieval Perception," in *The Saturated Sensorium: Principles of Perception and Mediation in the Middle Ages*, ed. Hans Henrik Lohfert Jørgensen and Laura Katrine Skinnebach (Aarhus: Aarhus University Press, 2015), 24–70.

12 Dale Kinney, "The Concept of Spolia," in *A Companion to Medieval Art: Romanesque and Gothic in Northern Europe*, ed. Conrad Rudolph (Malden, MA: Blackwell Publishing, 2006), 233–52; "Ancient Gems in the Middle Ages: Riches and Ready-mades," in *Reuse Value: Spolia and Appropriation in Art and Architecture from Constantine to Sherrie Levine*, ed. Richard Brilliant and Dale Kinney (Farnham: Ashgate, 2011), 97–120; *Persistenz und Rezeption: Weiterverwendung, Wiederverwendung und Neuinterpretation antiker Werke im Mittelalter*, ed. Dietrich Boschung and Susanne Wittekind (Wiesbaden: Reichert Verlag, 2008), 237–84; Maria Fabricius Hansen, *The Spolia Churches of Rome: Recycling Antiquity in the Middle Ages*, trans. Barbara J. Haveland (Aarhus: University of Aarhus Press, 2015).

13 Werner Telesko, "Das theologische Programm des Kölner Dreikönigenschreins," *Jahrbuch des Kölnischen Geschichtsverein* 68, no. 1 (1997), 25–47; Hiltrud Westermann-Angerhausen, "Spolia as Relics, Relics as Spoils? The Meaning and Functions of Spolia in Western Medieval Reliquaries," in *Saints and Sacred Matter: The Cult of Relics in Byzantium and Beyond*, ed. Cynthia Hahn and Holger Klein (Washington, DC: Dumbarton Oaks Research Library and Collections, 2015), 173–92; Philippe Cordez, "El arrepentimiento de un mago? Los camafeos de la estatuilla del rey David en la catedral de Basilea (hacia 1310–1320)," *Codex Aqvilarensis* 33 (2017), 127–36. Nicholas of Verdun, the goldsmith who oversaw the making of the shrine, seems to have incorporated one of the most glorious of all spolia, the late fourth-century ivory diptych of the Nicomachi and Symmachi ivory diptych, into a reliquary for Saint Berchaire, framing it between columns and bordering it with angels, enamels, precious stones, and pearls; Samuel Vitali, "*Sicut explorator et spoliorum cupidus*: Zur Methode und Funktion der Antikenrezeption bei Nicolaus von Verdun," *Wiener Jahrbuch für Kunstgeschichte* 52 (2002), 9–46; Philippe George, "Entre pays mosan et Champagne: Le trésor des reliques de Montier-en-Der," *Cahiers archéologiques* 53 (2011), 63–88; Laurence Terrier Aliferis, *L'imitation de l'Antiquité dans l'art médiéval (1180–1230)* (Turnhout: Brepols, 2016), 51–74.

14 The crown and wood socle are post-medieval. Dorothee Engenberger, "Goldene König David-Figur," in *Der Basler Münsterschatz*, ed. Brigitte Meles (Basel: Merian, 2001), 37–42; Beth Fischer, "Facing Medusa: A Thirteenth-Century Reliquary of King David," in *Gender, Otherness, and Culture in Medieval and Early Modern Art*, ed. Carlee A. Bradbury and Michelle Moseley-Christian (New York: Palgrave Macmillan, 2017), 15–41; Cordez, "Arrepentimiento."

15 Jean-Pierre Caillet, *L'art carolingien* (Paris: Flammarion, 2005), 158–61; Stefan Trinks, "Eingehüllt in Gold und Bein—Die 'techné' des Chryselephantin als 'Mitstreit' im Mittelalter," *Zeitschrift für Kunstgeschichte* 79, no. 4 (2016), 481–507; Benjamin Anderson, *Cosmos and Community in Early Medieval Art* (New Haven and London: Yale University Press, 2017), 34–42.

16 Avinoam Shalem, "Islamic Rock Crystal Vessels: Scent or Ampullae," in *Rezeption in der islamischen Kunst*, ed. Barbara Finster, Christa Fragner, and Herta Hafenrichter (Stuttgart: Steiner, 1999), 289–99; Gia Toussaint, "Blut oder Blendwerk? Orientalische Kristallflakons in mittelalterlichen Kirchenschätzen," in ... *das Heilige sichtbar machen: Domschätze in Vergangenheit, Gegenwart und Zukunft* (Regensburg: Schnell & Steiner, 2010), 107–20. The Christ relief on the Three Magi shrine is Carolingian; Genevra Kornbluth, "The Heavenly Jerusalem and the Lord of Lords: A Sapphire Christ at the Court of Charlemagne and the Shrine of the Magi," *Cahiers archéologiques* 49 (2001), 47–68.

17 Anna Maria Carruba, *La Lupa Capitolina* (Rome: De Luca Editore d'Arte, 2006); *Die römische Wölfin: Ein antikes Monument stürzt von seinem Sockel* (English trans. *The Lupa romana: An Antique Monument Falls from Her Pedestal*), ed. Maria R. Alföldi, Edilberto Formigli, and Johannes Fried (Stuttgart: Franz Steiner Verlag, 2011); Nadja Horsch, *Ad astra gradus: Scala Santa und Sancta Sanctorum in Rom unter Sixtus V (1585–1590)* (Munich: Hirmer Verlag, 2014), 32–65; Ittai Weinryb, *The Bronze Object in the Middle Ages* (Cambridge: Cambridge University Press, 2016), 79–80. A close parallel is found in the Amiens Psalter of c. 800; Heather Pulliam, "Exaltation and Humiliation: The Decorated Initials of the Corbie Psalter (Amiens, Bibliothèque municipale, MS 18)," *Gesta* 49, no. 2 (2010), 97–115.

18 Bruno Reudenbach, "Visualizing Holy Bodies: Observations on Body-Part Reliquaries," in *Romanesque: Art and Thought in the Twelfth Century*, ed. Colum Hourihane (Princeton: Department of Art and Archaeology, 2008), 95–106; "Holy Places and Their Relics," in *Visual Constructs of Jerusalem*, ed. Bianca Kühnel et al. (Turnhout: Brepols, 2014), 197–206; Holger A. Klein, *Byzanz, der Westen und das "wahre" Kreuz: die Geschichte einer Reliquie und ihrer künstlerischen Fassung in Byzanz und im Abendland* (Wiesbaden: Reichert Verlag, 2004), 198–206; Sara Ritchey, *Holy Matter: Changing Perceptions of the Material World in Late Medieval Christianity* (Ithaca: Cornell University Press, 2014), 203; Jan Klípa et al., "Reliquary Panel from Zwiefalten," in *Open the Gates of Paradise: The Benedictines in the Heart of Europe 800–1300* (cat. of an exhib., Prague) (Prague: National Gallery, 2015), 326–27.

19 Marizio Caperna, *La basilica di Santa Prassede: Il significato della vicenda architettonica* (Rome: Monaci Benedettini Vallombrosani, 1999); Herbert L. Kessler and Johanna Zacharias, *Rome 1300: On the Path of the Pilgrim* (New Haven: Yale University Press, 2000), 111–12.

20 Joanna Cannon, *Religious Poverty, Visual Riches: Art in the Dominican Churches of Central Italy in the Thirteenth and Fourteenth Centuries* (New Haven and London: Yale University Press, 2013), 103–05.

21 Brigitte Kurmann-Schwarz and Peter Kurmann, *Chartres: Die Kathedrale* (Munich: Schnell und Steiner, 2001), 235–36 et passim; Margot E. Fassler, *The Virgin of Chartres: Making History through Liturgy and the Arts* (New Haven and London: Yale University Press, 2010); Christine Hediger and Brigitte Kurmann-Schwarz, "Reliquie und Skulptur im Glasfenster: Intermediale Auratisierung am Beispiel von Notre-Dame de la Belle Verrière," in *Aura und Auratisierung: Mediologische Perspektiven im Anschluss an Walter Benjamin*, ed. Ulrich Beil et al. (Zurich: Chronos Verlag, 2014), 135–60.

22 Claudine Lautier, "The Sacred Topography of Chartres Cathedral," in *The Four Modes of Seeing: Approaches to Medieval Imagery in Honor of Madeline Harrison Caviness*, ed. Evelyn Staudinger Lane et al. (Aldershot: Ashgate, 2009), 174–96.

23 Rebecca Müller, *"Sic hostes Ianua frangit": Spolien und Trophäen im mittelalterlichen Genua* (Weimar: VDG, 2002); Jill Caskey, *Art and Patronage in the Medieval Mediterranean: Merchant Culture in the Region of Amalfi* (Cambridge: Cambridge University Press, 2004); Karen Rose Mathews, *Conflict, Commerce, and an Aesthetic of Appropriation in the Italian Maritime Cities, 1100–1150* (Leiden: Brill, 2018).

24 Anna Contadini, "Translocation and Transformation: Some Middle Eastern Objects in Europe," in *The Power of Things and the Flow of Cultural Transformation: Art and Culture between Europe and Asia*, ed. Lieselotte Saurma-Jeltsch and Anja Eisenbeiss (Berlin: Deutscher Kunst-Verlag, 2010), 42–65; Weinryb, *Bronze Object*, 140–43; Mathews, *Conflict*, 128–29.

25 Anat Tcherikover, "The Pulpit of Sant'Ambrogio at Milan," *Gesta* 38, no. 1 (1999), 35–66; Ivan Foletti and Irene Quadri, "Un dialogo inevitabile: l'ambone palinsesto di Sant'Ambrogio a Milano," in *Survivals, revivals, rinascenze: Studi in onore di Serena Romano* (Rome: Viella, 2017), 305–21.

26 Ivan Foletti, *Oggetti, reliquie, migranti: La basilica Ambrosiana e il culto dei suoi santi (386–972)* (Rome: Viella, 2018).
27 Kessler and Zacharias, *Rome 1300*, 208; Jean-Pierre Caillet, "Gli avori: circolazione, contatti, testimonianze," in *Carlo Magno e le Alpi* (Acts of an International Conference, October 2006) (Spoleto: CISAM, 2007), 399–412; Anderson, *Cosmos*, 36–42.
28 Martina Bagnoli and Kathryn Gerry, *The Medieval World: The Walters Art Museum* (London: Giles, 2011), 154–55.
29 *L'arte di Francesco: Capolavori d'arte italiana e terre d'Asia dal XIII al XV secolo* (cat. of an exhib., Florence), ed. Angelo Tartuferi and Francesco D'Arelli (Florence: Giunti, 2015), 166–69; Mariam Rosser-Owen, "The Oliphant: A Call for a Shift of Perspective," in *Romanesque and the Mediterranean*, ed. Rosa Maria Bacile and John McNeill (Leeds: British Archaeological Association, 2015), 15–58.
30 Warren T. Woodfin, "Presents Given and Presence Subverted: The Cunegunda *Chormantel* in Bamberg and the Ideology of Byzantine Textiles," *Gesta* 47, no. 1 (2008), 33–50.
31 Cecily J. Hilsdale, "The Social Life of a Byzantine Gift: The Royal Crown of Hungary Re-Invented," *Art History* 31 (2008), 603–31.
32 Herbert L. Kessler, "Object as Subject in Medieval Art," *The Haskins Society Journal* 23 (2011), 201–24; Éric Palazzo, "Missarium sollemnia: Eucharistic Rituals in the Middle Ages," in *The Oxford Handbook of Medieval Christianity*, ed. John Arnold (Oxford: Oxford University Press, 2014), 238–53; *L'invention chrétienne des cinq sens dans la liturgie et l'art au Moyen Âge* (Paris: Les Éditions du Cerf, 2014), 301–59.
33 Anna Pawlik, *Das Bildwerk als Reliquiar? Funktionen früher Großplastik im 9. bis 11. Jahrhundert* (Petersberg: Michael Imhof Verlag, 2013), 205–12.
34 *Goldene Pracht: Mittelalterliche Schatzkunst in Westfalen* (cat. of an exhib., Münster) (Munich: Hirmer Verlag, 2012), 144–47; Géza Jászai, "Christus als neuer Mose? Zur Ikonologie des Einbandes vom Evangeliar der Äbtissin Theophanu im Essener Domschatz," *Das Münster: Zeitschrift für christliche Kunst und Kunstwissenschaft* 66, no. 1 (2013), 40–49; "Was heißt 'Christliche Ikonologie'? Ein Beispiel," *Das Münster: Zeitschrift für christliche Kunst und Kunstwissenschaft* 69, no. 2 (2016), 118–120; David Ganz, *Buch-Gewänder: Prachteinbände im Mittelalter* (Berlin: Dietrich Reimer Verlag, 2015), 192–223.
35 Janet Backhouse, "The Case of Queen Melisende's Psalter: An Historical Investigation," in *Tributes to Jonathan J.G. Alexander: Making and Meaning in the Middle Ages and Renaissance*, ed. Susan L'Engle and Gerald B. Guest (London: Harvey Miller, 2006), 457–70; Jaroslav Folda, *Crusader Art in the Holy Land, From the Third Crusade to the Fall of Acre, 1187–1291* (Cambridge: Cambridge University Press, 2005) and "Melisende of Jerusalem: Queen and Patron of Art and Architecture in the Crusader Kingdom," in *Reassessing the Roles of Women as "Makers" of Medieval Art and Architecture*, ed. Therese Martin (Leiden: Brill, 2012), 429–77.
36 *Drachenlandung: Ein Hildesheimer Drachen-Aquamanile des 12. Jahrhunderts*, ed. Claudia Höhl et al. (Regensburg: Schnell & Steiner, 2017).
37 Ingeborg Krueger, "Zu einigen großen Smaragden aus Glas," *Journal of Glass Studies* 53 (2011), 103–27.
38 Avinoam Shalem, *Islamic Objects in Historical Context* (Leiden: Brill, 2004); Pierre-Alain Mariaux, "Trésor et collection: Le sort des 'curiosités naturelles' dans les trésors d'église autour de 1200," in *Le trésor au Moyen Âge: Questions et perspectives de recherche*, ed. Lucas Burkhart et al. (Neuchâtel: Institut d'Histoire de l'art et Muséologie, 2005), 27–53; Sebastian Bock, *Ova struthionis: Die Straußeneiobjekte in den Schatz-, Silber- und Kunstkammern Europas* (Freiburg im Breisgau/Heidelberg: Bock, 2005); Nile Green, "Ostrich Eggs and Peacock Feathers as Cultural Exchange between Christianity and Islam," *Al-Masaq* 18, no. 1 (2006), 27–66; Cordez, *Schatz*, 127–40.

39 As the twelfth-century *Liber Sancti Jacobi* affirms; Wendy Pullan, "Tracking the Habitual: Observations on the Pilgrim Shell," in *Architecture and Pilgrimage*, 59–85.
40 Green, "Ostrich Eggs"; Bock, *Ova struthionis*; Mariaux, "Trésor," 35–36.
41 Cordez, "Objektwissenschaft," 366–70.
42 Marc Sureda I Jubany, "La salvezza dell'anima," in *Viaggio*, 134–42.
43 Benedetta Chiesi, "Anello d'oro con sigillo, detto del 'Principe Nero,'" in *Viaggio*, 195.
44 Jeffrey Hamburger, "Body vs. Book: The Trope of Visibility in Images of Christian-Jewish Polemic," in *Ästhetik des Unsichtbaren: Bildtheorie und Bildgebrauch in der Vormoderne*, ed. David Ganz and Thomas Lentes (Berlin: Reimer Verlag, 2004), 110–45; "The Medieval Work of Art: Wherein the 'Work'? Wherein the 'Art'?," in *The Mind's Eye: Art and Theological Argument in the Middle Ages*, ed. Jeffrey Hamburger and Anne-Marie Bouché (Princeton: Department of Art and Archaeology, 2006), 374–412; Dominique Iogna-Prat, *La maison dieu: Une histoire monumentale de l'Église au Moyen Âge* (Paris: Seuil, 2006), 575–605; Éric Palazzo, *L'espace rituel et le sacré dans le christianisme: La liturgie de l'autel portatif dans l'Antiquité et au Moyen Âge* (Turnhout: Brepols, 2008); Ivo Rauch, "Die Bundeslade und die Wahren Israeliten: Anmerkungen zum mariologischen und politische Programm der Hochchorfenster der Kathedrale von Chartres," in *Glas, Malerei, Forschung: Internationale Studien zu Ehren von Rüdiger Becksmann*, ed. Hartmut Scholz et al. (Berlin: Deutsche Verlag für Kunstwissenschaft, 2004), 61–71; Lawrence Nees, "Theodulf's Mosaic at Germigny, the Sancta Sanctorum, and Jerusalem," in *Discovery and Distinction in the Early Middle Ages: Studies in Honor of John J. Contreni*, ed. Cullen J. Chandler and Steven A. Stofferahn (Kalamazoo: Medieval Institute Publications, 2013), 167–86; *Judaism and Christian Art: Aesthetic Anxieties from the Catacombs to Colonialism*, ed. Herbert L. Kessler and David Nirenberg (Philadelphia: University of Pennsylvania Press, 2011); Cynthia Hahn, *Strange Beauty: Issues in the Making and Meaning of Reliquaries, 400–circa 1204* (University Park: Pennsylvania State University Press, 2012), 240–42; Gerardo Boto Varela, "Velum lapideo: Lapides veligerae dans des cloîtres romans castillans; Révéler l'invisibilité de Dieu," in *Voiler/Devoiler: Le rideau dans la culture chrétienne de l'Antiquite et du Moyen Âge* ed. Éric Palazzo and Vincent Debiais (Paris: forthcoming).
45 Allegra Iafrate, "*Opus Salomonis*: Sorting Out Solomon's Scattered Treasure," *Medieval Encounters* 22, no. 4 (2016), 326–78.
46 *Open the Gates*, 139.
47 Hiltrud Westermann-Angerhausen, "Incense in the Space between Heaven and Earth: The Inscriptions and Images on the Gozbert Censer in the Cathedral Treasury of Trier," *Acta ad archaeologiam et artium historiam pertinentia* 23, no. 10 (2011), 227–41; Rolf Dieter Blumer and Inès Frontzek, "Recherchiert und kartiert: Der Comburger Hertwig-Leuchter," *Denkmalpflege in Baden-Württemberg: Nachrichtenblatt der Landesdenkmalpflege* 41 (2012), 194–99; Vincent Debiais, "Mostrar, significar, desvelar: El acto de representar según las inscripciones medievales," *Codex Aqvilarensis* 29 (2014), 169–86; *La croisée des signes: L'écriture et les images médiévales (800–1200)* (Paris: Éditions du Cerf, 2017), 139–41.
48 Herbert L. Kessler, "The Icon in the Narrative," in *Spiritual Seeing: Picturing God's Invisibility in Medieval Art* (Philadelphia: University of Pennsylvania Press, 2000), 1–28; *Apocalipsis Gulbenkian* (Museu Fundação Calouste Gulbenkian, Lisbon), ed. Emílio Rui Vilar et al. (Barcelona: M. Moleiro, 2002); Barry Windeatt, "'Vera Icon'? The Variable Veronica of Medieval England," in *The European Fortune of the Roman Veronica in the Middle Ages*, ed. Amanda Murphy et al. (Brno: Center for Early Medieval Studies, 2017), 58–71.
49 Jas Elsner, "From the Culture of *Spolia* to the Cult of Relics: The Arch of Constantine and the Genesis of Late Antique Forms," *Papers of the British School at Rome* 68 (2000), 149–84.

50 Caroline Walker Bynum, *Wonderful Blood: Theology and Practice in Late Medieval Northern Germany and Beyond* (Philadelphia: University of Pennsylvania Press, 2007); *Materiality*, 138–39; Cordez, *Schatz*, 90–96.

51 Mitchell B. Merback, *Pilgrimage and Pogrom: Violence, Memory, and Visual Culture at the Host-Miracle Shrines of Germany and Austria* (Chicago: University of Chicago Press, 2012).

52 On the politics of Passion relics: Merback, *Pilgrimage*, 187–214.

53 Krueger, "Smaragden"; Rebecca Müller, "Il 'sacro catino': Percezione e memoria nella Genova medievale," in *Intorno al Sacro Volto: Genova, Bisanzio e il Mediterraneo (secoli XI–XIV)*, ed. Anna Rosa Calderoni Masetti et al. (Venice: Marsilio Editori, 2007), 91–104.

54 Barbara Baert, *A Heritage of Holy Wood: The Legend of the True Cross in Text and Image* (Leiden: Brill, 2004); Éamonn Ó Carragáin, *Ritual and the Rood: Liturgical Images and the Old English Poems of the Dream of the Rood Tradition* (London and Toronto: The British Library and University of Toronto Press, 2005); Richard Viladesau, *The Beauty of the Cross: The Passion of Christ in Theology and the Arts from the Catacombs to the Eve of the Renaissance* (Oxford: Oxford University Press, 2006).

55 Hahn, *Strange Beauty*, 205.

56 *Ludwig der Bayer*, 318–19.

57 In the Gotha manuscript of Thiofrid's tract (Forschungs- und Landesbibliothek Gotha, MS Memb. 170, fol. 99^r), the cross is gold and Peter's (inverted) cross is green; Hahn, *Strange Beauty*, 25. For the Gerona embroidery, Manuel Castiñeiras González, *El Tapiz de la Creación* (Eng. trans., *The Creation Tapestry*) (Gerona: Cathedral, 2011), 76–78.

58 Francesca Tasso, "Il medioevo nella Milano ottocentesca: Qualche nota sulla costituzione delle raccolte civiche di arte suntuaria," *Rassegna di Studi e Notizie* 34, no. 31 (2007–08), 163–83.

59 Marius Rimmele, "Geordnete Unordnung: Zur Bedeutungsstiftung in Zusammenstellung der Arma Christi," in *Das Bild im Plural*, ed. David Ganz and Felix Thürlemann (Berlin: Dietrich Reimer Verlag, 2010), 219–42; Lisa H. Cooper and Andrea Denny-Brown, "Introduction," in *The Arma Christi in Medieval and Early Modern Material Culture*, ed. Lisa H. Cooper and Andrea Denny-Brown (Farnham: Ashgate, 2014), 1–19.

60 Cynthia Hahn, *The Thing of Mine I Have Loved the Best: Meaningful Jewels* (London: Paul Holberton, 2018), 174.

61 Philippe Cordez, "Werkzeuge und Instrumente in Kunstgeschichte und Technikanthropologie," in *Werkzeuge und Instrumente*, ed. Philippe Cordez and Matthias Krüger (Berlin: Walter de Gruyter, 2012), 1–19; Ann W. Astell, "Retooling the Instruments of Christ's Passion: Memorial *Technai*, St. Thomas the Twin, and British Library, Additional MS 22029," in *Arma Christi*, 171–202.

62 Cordez, "Werkzeuge," 9–11.

63 *Legati da una cintola: L'Assunta di Bernardo Daddi e l'identià di una città* (cat. of an exhib., Prato), ed. Andrea De Marchi and Cristina Gnoni Mavarelli (Florence: Libri Mandragora, 2017).

64 Madeline H. Caviness, *Visualizing Women in the Middle Ages: Sight, Spectacle, and Scopic Economy* (Philadelphia: University of Pennsylvania Press, 2001); Rachel Fulton, *From Judgment to Passion: Devotion to Christ & the Virgin Mary, 800–1200* (New York: Columbia University Press, 2002), 201.

65 Pawlik, *Bildwerk*, et passim.

66 "*Immagine antica*": *The Madonna and Child of Santa Maria Maggiore*, ed. Marco Ciatti and Cecilia Frosinini (Florence: Edifir, 2003).

67 Aliya Bhatia, "Virgin and Child: The Status of Reliquaries without Relics," *Saeculum Journal* 9, no. 2 (2014), 16–21.

68 Bruno Galland, *Les authetiques de reliques du* Sancta Sanctorum (Vatican: Biblioteca Apostolica Vaticana, 2004); Julia M.H. Smith, "Les reliques et leurs étiquettes," in *L'abbaye de Saint-Maurice d'Agaune 515–2015*, ed. Bernard Andenmatten and Laurent Ripart (Gollion: Infolio éditions, 2015), 2:220–57.
69 Borne by cherubim in a seventeenth-century mount, it is, itself, presented as a precious object worthy of contemplation.
70 Roland Recht, *Le croire et le voir: L'art des cathédrales (XIIe–XVe siècles)* (Paris: Gallimard, 1999), 124–26 (English trans. Mary Whittal, *Believing and Seeing: The Art of the Gothic Cathedrals* [Chicago: University of Chicago Press, 2008]), 90–93; Rosalind Brooke, *The Image of St Francis: Responses to Sainthood in the Thirteenth Century* (Cambridge: Cambridge University Press, 2006), 168; Élisabeth Antoine-König, "New Dating of the Limoges Reliquaries of the Stigmatization of St. Francis," in *Matter of Faith: An Interdisciplinary Study of Relics and Relic Veneration in the Medieval Period*, ed. James Robinson and Lloyd de Beer (London: British Museum, 2014), 84–91; Michel Pastoureau, "The Place of Animals in Medieval History," in *Art and Nature in the Middle Ages*, ed. Nicole R. Myers (Dallas: Dallas Museum of Art, 2016), 27–37 and 63.
71 *Les temps mérovingiens: Trois siècles d'art et culture (451–751)* (cat. of an exhib., Paris) (Paris: Musée du Louvre, 2016), 60–61.
72 Ernõ Marosi, "The Székesfehérvár Chasuble of King Saint Stephen and Queen Gisela," in *The Coronation Mantle of the Hungarian Kings* (Budapest: Hungarian National Museum, 2005), 109–39.
73 *Treasures of Heaven: Saints, Relics, and Devotion in Medieval Europe* (cat. of an exhib., Cleveland, Baltimore, and London), ed. Martina Bagnoli et al. (New Haven: Yale University Press, 2011), 87; Martina Bagnoli, "The Stuff of Heaven: Materials and Craftsmanship in Medieval Reliquaries," in *Treasures of Heaven*, 136–47.
74 At Conques, the chains given as ex votos are displayed within the church pictured on the tympanum; Marcello Angheben, *D'un jugement à l'autre: La représentation du jugement immédiate dans les jugements derniers français: 1100–1250* (Turnhout, Brepols, 2013), 236.
75 Marius Hauknes, "Emblematic Narratives in the Sancta Sanctorum," *Studies in Iconography* 34 (2013), 1–46.
76 Jeffrey Hamburger, "Vision and the Veronica," in *The Visual and the Visionary* (New York: Reaktion Books, 1998), 316–82; Gerhard Wolf, "'Or fu sì fatta la sembianza vostra?' Sguardi alla 'vera icona' e alle sue copie artistiche," in *Il volto di Cristo* (cat. of an exhib., Rome), ed. Giovanni Morello and Gerhard Wolf (Milan: Electa, 2000), 103–14, and *"Alexifarmaka*: Aspetti del culto della teoria delle immagini a Roma tra Bizanzio e Terra Santa nell'Alto Medioevo," in *Roma fra Oriente e Occidente* (Spoleto: CISAM, 2002), vol. 2, 755–96; Tiziana Di Blasio, *Veronica il mistero del Volto: Itinerari iconografici, memoria e rappresentazione* (Rome: Città Nuova, 2000); Christiane Kruse, *Wozu Menschen malen: Historische Begründungen eines Bildmediums* (Munich: Wilhelm Fink Verlag, 2003), 269–306; Rémi Gounelle, "Les origines littéraires de la légende de Véronique et de la Sainte Face: La Cura Sanitatis Tiberii et la Vindicta Salvatoris," in *Sacre impronte e oggetti "non fatti da mano d'uomo" nelle religioni* (acts of an international congress, Turin, 2010), ed. Adele Monaci Castagno (Alessandria: Edizioni dell'Orso, 2011), 231–51; Jean-Marie Sansterre, "Variation d'une légende et genèse d'un culte entre la Jérusalem des origines, Rome et l'Occident: quelques jalons de l'histoire de Véronique et de la Veronica jusqu'à la fin du XIIIe siècle," in *Passages: Déplacements des hommes, circulation des textes et identités dans l'Occident médiéval* (acts of an international congress, Bordeaux, 2007), ed. Joëlle Ducos and Patrick Henriet (Toulouse: Editions Méridiennes, 2013), 217–31; Herbert L. Kessler, "The Literary Warp and Artistic Weft of Veronica's Cloth," in *European Fortune*, 11–29.
77 Probably painted for the conversion of the Pantheon into a church in 609; Giorgio Leone, *Icone di Roma e del Lazio*, vol. 1 (Rome: L'Erma Di Bretschneider, 2013), 59–60.

78 Annemarie Weyl Carr, "Thoughts on Mary East and West" in *Images of the Mother of God*, 277–92; Michele Bacci, "The Legacy of the Hodegetria: Holy Icons and Legends between East and West" in *Images of the Mother of God*, 321–36; *Tavole miracolose: Le icone medioevali di Roma e del Lazio del Fondo Edifici di Culto* (cat. of an exhib., Rome), ed. Giorgio Leone (Rome: "L'Erma" di Bretschneider, 2012).

79 Véronique Rouchon Mouilleron, "Miracle et charité: Autour d'une image du *Livre du Biadaiolo* (Florence, Bibliothéque Laurentienne, MS Tempi 3)," *Revue Mabillon*, n.s. 19 (2008), 157–89; *Florence at the Dawn of the Renaissance: Painting and Illumination*, ed. Christine Sciacca (Los Angeles: Getty Publications, 2012), 52–53; Megan Holmes, *The Miraculous Image in Renaissance Florence* (New Haven and London: Yale University Press, 2014), 70–71, 146–51; Sergio Tognetti, "Florentine Economy Between the 13th and 14th Centuries," in *Textiles and Wealth in 14th Century Florence: Wool, Silk, Painting*, ed. Cecilie Holberg (Florence: Giunti, 2017), 30–41.

80 Sophie Cassagnes-Brouquet, *Vierges noires* (Rodez: Éditions du Rouergue, 2000).

81 Marc Sureda Y Jubany, "From Holy Images to Liturgical Devices: Models, Objects and Rituals around the Veronicae of Christ and Mary in the Crown of Aragon (1300–1550)," in *European Fortune*, 194–217.

82 Herbert L. Kessler, "Paradigms of Movement in Medieval Art: Establishing Connections and Effecting Transitions," *Codex Aqvilarensis* 29 (2013), 45.

83 The painting is preserved in a drawing by the antiquarian François-Roger de Gagnieres (Paris, BnF, Est. Oa 11, fol. 85); "Man of Sorrows/Mater Dolorosa," in *Prayers and Portraits: Unfolding the Netherlandish Diptych* (cat. of an exhib., Washington), ed. John Hand et al. (Washington, DC: National Gallery of Art, 2006), 50–61; *Byzantium: Faith and Power (1261–1557)*, ed. Helen C. Evans (New Haven: Yale University Press, 2004), 565–67; Kessler, "Paradigms"; Sarah K. Kozlowski, "Toward a History of the Trecento Diptych: Format, Materiality, and Mobility in a Corpus of Diptychs from Angevin Naples," *Zeitschrift für Kunstgeschichte* 81, no. 1 (2018), 3–29.

84 *The Mother and the Son: Gothic Paintings of the Madonna and Veronica Images from St. Vitus Cathedral in Prague* (cat. of an exhib., Prague), ed. Ivana Kyzouravá (Prague: Správa Prazského Hradu, 2014), 25–36.

85 Buc, "Conversion"; *Les dominicaines d'Unterlinden* (cat. of an exhib., Colmar) (Colmar: Musée d'Unterlinden, 2000); *Le trésor de la Sainte-Chapelle* (cat. of an exhib.) (Paris: Musée du Louvre, 2001); *Le trésor de Conques* (cat. of an exhib.) (Paris: Musée du Louvre, 2001); *L'abbaye de Saint-Maurice d'Agaune*; Fricke, *Fallen Idols*, 213–64 (*Ecce fides*, 249–310); Bernadette Burchard and Holger Kempkens, "Mittelalterliche Kirchen- und Heiltumsschätze in Westfalen," in *Goldene Pracht*, 68–77.

86 Ingo Herklotz, "Die Fresken von Sancta Sanctorum nach der Restaurierung: Überlegungen zum Ursrpung der Trecentomalerei," in *Pratum Romanum: Richard Krautheimer zum 100. Geburtstag*, ed. Renate Colella et al. (Wiesbaden: Reichert Verlag, 1997), 180; Mario Cempanari, *Sancta Sanctorum Lateranense: Il Santuario della Scala Santa delle origini ai nostril giorni* (Rome: Città Nuova, 2003); Erik Thunø, *Image and Relic: Mediating the Sacred in Early Medieval Rome* (Rome: "L'Erma" di Bretschneider, 2002); Serena Romano, *Il duecento e la cultura gotica, 1198–1287 ca.* (*Corpus della pittura medieval a Roma 312–1431: Corpus e atlante*, vol. 5) (Milan: Jaca Book, 2012), 321–38; Hauknes, "Emblematic Narratives," 2–21.

87 Karin Krause, "Feuerprobe, Portraits in Stein. Mittelalterliche Propaganda für Venedigs Reliquien aus *Constantinopel* und die Frage nach ihrem Erfolg," in *Lateinisch-griechisch-arabische Begegnunngungen: Kulturelle Diversität im Mittelmeerraum des Spätmittelaters*, ed. Margit Mersch and Ulrike Rizerfeld (Berlin: Akademie Verlag, 2009), 111–62; Holger A. Klein, "Refashioning Byzantium in Venice, ca. 1200–1400," in *San Marco, Byzantium, and the Myths of Venice*, ed. Henry Maguire and Robert S. Nelson (Washington, DC: Dumbarton Oaks, 2010), 193–225.

88 *Trésor de la Sainte-Chapelle*; Johannes Tripps, "Der Kirchenraum als Handlungsort für Bildwerke: 'Handelnde' Altarfiguren und hyperwandelbare Schnitzretabel," in *Kunst und Liturgie im Mittelalter*, ed. Nicolas Bock et al. (Munich: Hirmer Verlag, 2000), 235–47; Alexei Lidov, "A Byzantine Jerusalem: The Imperial Pharos Chapel as the Holy Sepulchre," in *Jerusalem as Narrative Space: Erzählraum Jerusalem*, ed. Anette Hoffmann and Gerhard Wolf (Leiden: Brill, 2012), 63–103.

89 Meredith Cohen, "An Indulgence for the Visitor: The Public at the Sainte-Chapelle of Paris," *Speculum* 83 (2008), 840–83; Barbara Schellewald, "Konstantinopel-Paris: Ein Schatz im neuen Gewand," in *Heilige sichtbar*, 161–80. On the reconstruction of Louis's Grande Chasse and its use in the Middle Ages, see Jannic Durand, "La Grande Chasse aux reliques," in *Trésor de la Sainte-Chapelle*, 107–112; on the windows, see Alyce A. Jordan, *Visualizing Kingship in the Windows of Sainte-Chapelle* (Turnhout: Brepols Publishers, 2002).

90 Esther Cohen and Mayke B. de Jong, *Medieval Transformations: Texts, Power, and Gifts in Context* (Leiden and Boston: Brill, 2001); *Negotiating the Gift*, ed. Gadi Algazi et al. (Göttingen: Vandenhoeck & Ruprecht, 2003); *Sauver son âme et se perpétuer: Transmission du patrimoine et mémoire au haut Moyen Âge*, ed. François Bougard et al. (Rome: École Française de Rome, 2005); *The Languages of Gift in the Early Middle Ages*, ed. Wendy Davies and Paul Fouracre (Cambridge: Cambridge University Press, 2010); Cecily J. Hilsdale, "Gift," *Studies in Iconography* 33 (2012), 171–82; Ittai Weinryb, "Introduction: Ex-Voto as Material Culture," in *Ex Voto: Votive Giving Across Cultures*, ed. Ittai Weinryb (New York: Bard Graduate Center, 2016), 1–22; Michele Bacci, "Italian Ex-Votos and 'Pro-Anima' Images in the Late Middle Ages," in *Ex Voto*, 76–105; Lucy K. Pick, *Her Father's Daughter: Gender, Power, and Religion in the Early Spanish Kingdom* (Ithaca: Cornell University Press, 2017), 169–226; *Agents of Faith: Votive Objects in Time and Place* (cat. of an exhib., New York), ed. Ittai Weinryb (New York: Bard Graduate Center, 2018).

91 Paul Edward Dutton and Herbert L. Kessler, *The Poetry and Paintings of the First Bible of Charles the Bald* (Ann Arbor: University of Michigan Press, 1997), 89–101.

92 Adam S. Cohen, *The Uta Codex: Art, Philosophy, and Reform in Eleventh-Century Germany* (University Park: Pennsylvania State University Press, 2000), 39–51, 191–96.

93 *Krone und Schleier: Kunst aus mittelalterlichen Frauenklöstern* (cat. of an exhib., Essen and Bonn), ed. Jeffrey F. Hamburger, Robert Suckale, et al. (Munich: Hirmer Verlag, 2005), 167–69 (English trans. *Crown & Veil: Female Monasticism from the Fifth to the Fifteenth Centuries*, ed. Jeffrey F. Hamburger and Susan Marti [New York: Columbia University Press, 2005]).

94 Patrizia Carmassi, "Die hochmittelalterlichen Fresken der Unterkirche von San Clemente in Rom als programmatische Selbstdarstellung des Reformpapsttums," *Quellen und Forschungen aus italienisichen Archiven und Bibliotheken* 81 (2001), 1–66; Cristiana Filippini, "La chiesa e il suo santo: gli affreschi dell'undicesimo secolo nella chiesa di S. Clemente a Roma," in *Art, Cérémonial et Liturgie au Moyen Âge* (acts of a colloquium, Lausanne-Fribourg), ed. Nicolas Bock et al. (Rome: Viella, 2002), 107–24.

95 Nino Zchomelidse, *Art, Ritual, Civic Identity in Medieval Southern Italy* (University Park: Pennsylvania State University Press, 2014), 145–48.

96 Marian Campbell, "An Enamelled Plaque Showing Bishop Henry of Blois," *Journal of the British Archaeological Association* 154 (2001), 191–93; James Robinson, *Masterpieces of Medieval Art* (London: British Museum Press, 2008).

97 Susanne Wittekind, "Liturgiereflexion in den Kunststiftungen Abt Wibalds von Strabo," in *Art, Cérémonial*, 503–24; Barbara Baert, "'A Brilliant Resurrection': Enamel Shrines for Relics in Limoges and Cologne, 1100–1230," in *Treasures of Heaven*, 148–61.

98 David Ganz, "An Artist-Monk in Pieces: Towards an Archeology of Tuotilo," in *Tuotilo: Archäologie eines frühmittelalterlichen Künstlers*, ed. David Ganz und Cornel Dora (Basel: Schwabe Verlag, 2017), 21–51.

99 Ann Freeman +++and Paul Meyvaert, "The Meaning of Theodulf's Apse Mosaic at Germigny-des-Prés," *Gesta* 40, no. 2 (2001), 125–39.
100 Marcello Angheben, "Résonances sacramentelles, dévotionnelles et sensorielles des images: La Vierge à l'enfant et la crucifixion sur les vitraux de la cathédrale du Mans," in *L'Église, lieu de performances: In locis competentibus*, ed. Stefanie Daussy and Nicolas Reveryon (Paris: Éditions Picard, 2016), 159–79.
101 Heidi Gearhart, "Word and Prayer in the Fiery Furnace: The Three Hebrews on the Censer of Reiner in Lille and a Case for Artistic Labor," *Studies in Iconography* 34 (2013), 103–32.
102 Lisa Victoria Ciresi, "A Liturgical Study of the Shrine of the Three Kings in Cologne," in *Objects, Images, and the Word: Art in the Service of the Liturgy*, ed. Colum Hourihane (Princeton: Department of Art and Archaeology, 2003), 202–30.
103 Danielle B. Joyner, *Painting the* Hortus Deliciarum: *Medieval Women, Wisdom, and Time* (University Park: Pennsylvania State University Press, 2016), 16–21.
104 Cordez, *Schatz*, 94–95.
105 Bynum, *Materiality*, 139–45.
106 Cordez, *Schatz*, 94.
107 Achim Timmermann, *Real Presence: Sacrament Houses and the Body of Christ, c. 1270–1600* (Turnhout: Brepols, 2009).
108 Michele Bacci, *Investimenti per l'aldilà: Arte e raccomandazione dell'anima nel Medioevo* (Rome and Bari: Laterza & Figli, 2003); Philippe Cordez, "Les usages du trésor des grâces: L'économie idéelle et matérielle des indulgences au Moyen Âge," in *Trésor au Moyen Âge*, 55–88; Thomas Golsenne, "Offrandes alimentaires," in *L'Église, lieu de performances*, 181–96.
109 Kessler, "Object as Subject," 221–28; Bagnoli and Gerry, *Medieval World*, 85–86.
110 Max Wahren, "Zur Geschichte der Hostienbäckerei" in *Panis angelorum—Das Brot der Engel: Kulturgeschichte der Hostie*, ed. Oliver Seifert (Ostfildern: Thorbecke Verlag, 2004), 11–22; Aden Kumler, "The Multiplication of the Species: Eucharistic Morphology in the Middle Ages," *RES: Anthropology and Aesthetics* 59–60, no. 1 (2011), 179–191, and "Manufacturing the Sacred in the Middle Ages: The Eucharist and Other Medieval Works of Art," *English Language Notes* 53, no. 2 (2015), 9–44; Tobias Frese, *Aktual- und Realpräsenz: Das eucharistische Christusbild von Spätantike bis ins Mittelalter* (Berlin: Gebr. Mann, 2013); Roger Reynolds, "Christ's Money: Eucharistic Azyme Hosts in the Ninth Century According to Bishop Eldefonsus of Spain; Observations on the Origin, Meaning, and Context of a Mysterious Revelation," *Peregrinations: Medieval Art and Architecture* 4 (2013), 1–69; "Vetera analecta," *Peregrinations: Medieval Art and Architecture* 4 (2013), 154–172.
111 Marisa Melero Moneo, "Eucaristía y polémica antisemita en el retablo y frontal de Vallbona de les Monges," *Locus amoenus* 6 (2002–03), 21–40; Cèsar Favà Monllau, "Noves consideracions entorn al joc de retaule, i frontal de Vallbona de les Monges," *Butlletí del Museu Nacional d'Art* 10 (2009), 57–85; Rafael Cornudella et al., *Gothic Art in the MNAC Collections* (Barcelona: Museu nacional d'art de catalunya, 2011), 34–37. Also, Klaus Krüger, "Medium and Imagination: Aesthetic Aspects of Trecento Panel Painting," in *Italian Panel Painting of the Duecento and Trecento*, ed. Victor M. Schmidt (Washington, DC: National Gallery of Art, 2002), 57–82; Barbara Baert, "Nourished by Inwardness: The Beato Chiarito Tabernacle (c. 1340)," *Annali dell'Università di Ferrara, Sezione Storia* 2 (2007), 28–40, and in *Speaking to the Eye Sight and Insight through Text and Image (1150–1650)*, ed. Thérèse de Hemptinne et al. (Turnhout: Brepols, 2013), 213–40; Christopher R. Lakey, "The Curious Case of the *Chiarito Tabernacle*: A New Interpretation," *Getty Research Journal* 4 (2012), 13–30; Francesco Saracino, "*Felix umbilicus*: Un tema per Filippo Lippi e Pacino di Bonaguida," *Iconographica* 16 (2017), 115–25.

112 Bynum, *Blood*, 85–111.
113 Aden Kumler, *Translating Truth: Ambitious Images and Religious Knowledge in Late Medieval France and England* (New Haven and London: Yale University Press, 2011), 119–45 et passim.
114 On the disputed identity of the straws, Baert, "Nourished"; Lakey, "*Chiarito Tabernacle*"; Saracino, "*Felix umbilicus*."
115 Kumler, "Multiplication," 187–91.
116 Reynolds, "Christ's Money"; Herbert L. Kessler, "Medietas/Mediator and the Geometry of Incarnation," in *Image and Incarnation: The Early Modern Doctrine of the Pictorial Image*, ed. Walter Melion and Lee Palmer Wandel (Leiden: Brill, 2015), 17–75; "Dynamic Signs and Spiritual Designs" in *Sign and Design: Script as Image in Cross-Cultural Perspective (300–1600 CE)*, ed. Brigitte Bedos-Rezak and Jeffrey Hamburger (Washington, DC: Dumbarton Oaks, 2016), 107–30.
117 François Bougard, "L'hostie, le monde, le signe de Dieu," in *Orbis disciplinae hommages en l'honneur de Patrick Gautier Dalché*, ed. N. Bouloux et al. (Turnhout: Brepols, 2017), 31–62.
118 Martha Rust, "The *Arma Christi* and the Ethics of Reckoning," in *Arma Christi*, 143–69.
119 Miri Rubin, *Gentile Tales: The Narrative Assault on Late Medieval Jews* (London and New Haven: Yale University Press, 1999); Merback, *Pilgrimage*, passim; Sara Lipton, *Dark Mirror: The Medieval Origins of Anti-Jewish Iconography* (New York: Henry Holt, 2014).
120 The transposition from Host to depicted crucifix, based on the *Passio imaginis*, is made on the fourteenth-century Berardenga altar frontal in Siena (Pinacoteca nazionale) and retable of San Salvador de Felanitx (Mallorca); Michele Bacci, "The Berardenga Antependium and the Passio Ymaginis Office," *Journal of the Warburg and Courtauld Institutes* 61 (1998), 1–16; Carlos Espí Forcén, *Recrucificando a Cristo: Los judíos de la Passio Imaginis en la isla de Mallorca* (Palma de Mallorca: Lleondard Muntaner, 2009).
121 William Diebold, "Medium as Message in Carolingian Writing about Art," *Word & Image* 22 (2006), 197–198; Bynum, *Materiality*, 37–123; Aden Kumler and Christopher R. Lakey, "*Res et significatio*: The Material Sense of Things in the Middle Ages," *Gesta* 51 (2012), 1–17; Ittai Weinryb, "Living Matter: Materiality, Maker and Ornament in the Middle Ages," *Gesta* 52, no. 2 (2013), 113–132.
122 Kruse, *Wozu Menschen malen*, 15–23 et passim.
123 Bynum, *Materiality*, 66–82.
124 Uta Rheinhold, "Das Fritzlarer Vesperbild, ein Meisterwerk mittelalterlicher Schnitz- und Fasskunst," *Denkmale und Kulturgeschichte* 2 (2000), 33–38; Bynum, *Materiality*, 177 and caption of Plate 15; Assaf Pinkus, "Transformations in Wood: Between Sculpture and Painting in Late Medieval Devotional Objects," *Viator* 48, no. 3 (2017), 263–91.
125 Cynthia Hahn, "Seeing and Believing: The Construction of Sanctity in Early Medieval Saints' Shrines," *Speculum* 72, no. 4 (1997), 1079–1106; Evan Gatti, "Reviving the Relic: An Investigation of the Form and Function of the Reliquary of St. Servatius, Quedlinburg," *Athanor* 18 (2000), 7–15; Bynum, *Materiality*, 70–79; Dagnoli, "Stuff of Heaven," 137.
126 Cynthia Hahn, *Portrayed on the Heart: Narrative Effect in Pictorial Lives of Saints from the Tenth through the Thirteenth Century* (Berkeley and Los Angeles: University of California Press, 2001).
127 Michele Ferrari, "Gold und Asche: Reliquie und Reliquiare als Medien in Thiofrid von Echternachs 'Flores epytaphii sanctorum,'" in *Reliquiare im Mittelalter*, ed. Bruno Reudenbach and Gia Toussaint (Berlin: Akademie Verlag, 2005), 61–74; Hahn, *Strange Beauty*, 23–26; Robyn Malo, *Relics and Writing in Late Medieval England* (Toronto: University of Toronto Press, 2013).
128 François Bœspflug, "La vision-en-rêve de la Trinité de Rupert de Deutz (v. 1100): Liturgie, spiritualité et histoire de l'art," *Revue des sciences religieuses* 71, no. 2 (1997), 205–29.

129 Daniel Alexandre-Bidon, "Une foi en deux ou trois dimensions? Image et objets du faire coire à l'usage des laïcs," *Annales* (1998), 1155–90.
130 Thomas F.X. Noble, *Images, Iconoclasm, and the Carolingians* (Philadelphia: University of Pennsylvania Press, 2009), 288–313 et passim.
131 Hahn, "Seeing and Believing"; Georgia Frank, "The Pilgrim's Gaze in the Age before Icons," in *Visuality Before and Beyond the Renaissance: Seeing as Others Saw*, ed. Robert Nelson (Cambridge: Cambridge University Press, 2000), 98–115.
132 Henk van Os, *The Way to Heaven: Relic Veneration in the Middle Ages* (The Hague: Koninklijke Bibliotheek, 2000); Kumler and Lakey, "Res et significatio."
133 Dominic Janes, *God and Gold in Late Antiquity* (Cambridge: Cambridge University Press, 1998); Trinks, "Eingehüllt."
134 Francesca Dell'Acqua, "Il fuoco, le vetrate delle origini e la mistica medievale," in *Il fuoco nell'alto Medioevo*, ed. Enrico Menestò (LX Settimana di Studio, Spoleto) (Spoleto: CISAM, 2013), 557–91.
135 Barbara Schellewald, "Gold, Licht und das Potenzial des Mosaiks," *Zeitschrift für Kunstgeschichte* 79, no. 4 (2016), 461–80.
136 Celia Chazelle, *The Crucified God in the Carolingian Era: Theology and Art of Christ's Passion* (Cambridge: Cambridge University Press, 2001), 155–57; Herbert L. Kessler, "Sanctifying Serpent: Crucifixion as Cure," in *Studies on Medieval Empathies*, ed. Rudolph Bell and Karl F. Morrison (Turnhout: Brepols, 2013), 161–81; David Ganz, "Gelenkstellen von Bild und Schrift: Diptychen, Doppelseiten und Bucheinbände," in *Klappeffekte: Faltbare Bildträger in der Vormoderne*, ed. Marius Rimmele and David Ganz (Berlin: Reimer Verlag, 2016), 55–108.
137 Márta Járó, "The Gold Threads of the Hungarian Coronation Mantle," in *Coronation Mantle*, 67–89.
138 Erik Thunø, *The Apse Mosaic in Early Medieval Rome: Time, Network and Repetition* (New York: Cambridge University Press, 2015), 47–51.
139 Herbert L. Kessler, "A Gregorian Reform Theory of Art?," in *Roma e la riforma Gregoriana: Tradizioni e innovazioni artische (XI–XII secolo)* (acts of a conference, Lausanne 2005), ed. Serena Romano and Julie Enckell (Rome: Viella, 2007), 25–48.
140 *Hildegard von Bingen: Prophetin durch die Zeiten*, ed. Edeltraud Forster (Freiburg im Breisgau: Herder, 1997); Madeline Caviness, "Gender Symbolism and Text Image Relationships: Hildegard of Bingen's *Scivias*," in *Translation Theory and Practice in the Middle Ages*, ed. Jeanette Beer (Kalamazoo: Medieval Institute Publications, 1997), 71–111; *Hildegard of Bingen: The Context of her Thought and Art*, ed. Charles Burnett and Peter Dronke (London: The Warburg Institute, 1998); Lieselotte Saurma-Jeltsch, *Die Miniaturen im "Liber Scivias" der Hildegard von Bingen: die Wucht der Vision und die Ordnung der Bilder* (Wiesbaden: Reichert Verlag, 1998); Keiko Suzuki, *Bildgewordene Visionen oder Visionserzählungen: Vergleichende Studie über die Visionsdarstellungen in der Rupertsberger "Scivias"-Handschrift und im Luccheser "Liber divinorum operum"-Codex der Hildegard von Bingen* (Bern: Peter Lang, 1998); Richard Emmerson, "The Representation of the Antichrist in Hildegard of Bingen's Scivias: Image, Word, Commentary and Visionary Experience," *Gesta* 41, no. 1 (2002), 95–110; Bernard McGinn, "Theologians as Trinitarian Iconographers," in *Mind's Eye*, 186–207; Jill Caskey, "Whodunnit? Patronage, the Canon, and the Problematic of Agency in Romanesque and Gothic Art," in *Companion to Medieval Art*, 193–212; Brigitte Kurmann-Schwarz, "Gender and Medieval Art," in *Companion to Medieval Art*, 128–50; Wendelin Knoch, "Visionäre Farbigkeit: Anmerkungen zum *Liber Scivias* der Äbtissin Hildegard von Bingen (1098–1179)," in *Farbe im Mittelalter: Materialität—Medialität—Semantik*, ed. Ingrid Bennewitz and Andrea Schindler (Berlin: Akademie Verlag, 2011), vol. 2, 791–802; Nathaniel M. Campbell, "*Imago expandit splendorem suum*: Hildegard of Bingen's Visio-Theological Designs in the Rupertsberg *Scivias* Manuscript," *Eikón/Imago* 4, no. 2 (2013), 1–68; Joyner,

Hortus deliciarum, 131–35; David Ganz, "The Cross on the Book: Diagram, Ornament, Materiality," in *Graphic Devices and the Early Decorated Book*, ed. Michelle P. Brown et al. (Woodbridge: Boydell & Brewer, 2017), 243–64.

141 *Volto di Cristo*, 39–63; Nino Zchomelidse, "The Aura of the Numinous and Its Reproduction: Medieval Paintings of the Savior in Rome and Latium," *Memoirs of the American Academy in Rome* 55 (2010), 221–62.

142 Herbert L. Kessler, "Image and Object: Christ's Dual Nature and the Crisis of Early Medieval Art," in *The Long Morning of Medieval Europe*, ed. Michael McCormick and Jennifer Davies (Farnham: Ashgate, 2008), 291–319.

143 Ulrich Kuder, "Die Konstanzer Christus Scheibe," *Schriften des Vereins für Geschichte des Bodensees und seiner Umgebung* 115 (1997), 1–50; Rolf Dieter-Blumer and Katrin Hubert-Kühne, "Restaurierung der Konrad-Scheibe vom Konstanzer Münster," *Denkmalpflege in Baden-Württemberg* 1 (2009), 37–39.

144 *Ambrogio Lorenzetti* (cat. of an exhib., Siena, 2018), ed. Alessandro Bagnoli et al. (Cisinello Balsamo: Silvana Editoriale, 2018), 232–60. For the sources of gold in the late Middles Ages, see Anne Dunlop, "On the Origins of European Painting Materials, Real and Imagined," in *The Matter of Art: Materials, Practices, Cultural Logistics, c. 1250–1750*, ed. Pamela Smith et al. (Manchester: Manchester University Press, 2015), 68–96; Sarah M. Guérin, "Gold, Ivory, and Copper: Materials and Arts of Trans-Saharan Trade," in *Caravans of Gold, Fragments in Time: Art, Culture, and Exchange Across Medieval Saharan Africa*, ed. Kathleen Bickford Berzock (Evanston: Northwestern University, 2019), 174–201.

145 *Die Macht des Silbers: Karolingische Schätze im Norden* (cat. of an exhib., Frankfurt and Hildesheim), ed. Egon Wamers and Michael Brandt (Regensburg: Schnell & Steiner, 2005); Jürgen Bärsch, "Gold und Silber im Dienst der Liturgie: Sinn und Funktion von Werken der Goldschmiedekunst im Gottesdienst," in *Goldene Pracht*, 58–77.

146 In the twelfth-century copy of the Utrecht Psalter (Paris, BnF, MS 8846), the flowing metal is actual silver; Herbert L. Kessler, "The Eloquence of Silver," in *L'allégorie dans l'art du Moyen Âge: Formes et fonctions; Héritages, créations, mutations*, ed. Christian Heck (Turnhout: Brepols, 2011), 49–64.

147 Herbert L. Kessler, "Speculum," *Speculum* 86, no. 1 (2011), 1–41.

148 Mauro Minardi, *Lorenzo e Jacopo Salimbeni: Vicende e protagonisti della pittura tardogotica nelle Marche e in Umbria* (Florence: Olshki, 2008), Plate LXXXV.

149 Jeffrey F. Hamburger, "The Use of Images in the Pastoral Care of Nuns: The Case of Henry Suso and the Dominicans" and "Medieval Self-fashioning: Authorship, Authority, and Autobiography in Suso's *Exemplar*," in Hamburger, *Visual and the Visionary*, 197–231 and 233–78; also "Speculations on Speculation: Vision and Perception in the Theory and Practice of Mystical Devotion," in *Deutsche Mystik im abendländischen Zusammenhang: Neu erschlossene Texte, neue methodologische Ansätze, neue theoretische Konzepte*, ed. Walter Haug and Wolfram Schneider-Lastin (Tübingen, 2000), 353–408; McGinn, "Theologians," 199–202; Thomas Lentes, "Der mediale Status des Bildes: Bildlichkeit bei Heinrich Seuse—statt einer Einleitung" in *Ästhetik des Unsichtbaren: Bildtheorie und Bildgebrauch in der Vormoderne* (Berlin: Reimer Verlag, 2004), 13–73; David Ganz, *Medien der Offenbarung: Visiondarstellungen im Mittelalter* (Berlin: Reimer Verlag, 2008), 313–27.

150 Hahn, *Thing of Mine*, 232–33 et passim.

151 *Gemme dalla corte imperiale alla corte celeste*, ed. Graziella Buccellati and Anna Marchi (Milan: Universitá degli studi, 2002); Fricke, *Fallen Idols*, 241–48 (*Ecce fides*, 295–300); Bagnoli, "Stuff of Heaven," 137–43; Hahn, *Thing of Mine*.

152 Felipe Pereda, "Through a Glass Darkly: Paths to Salvation in Spanish Painting at the Outset of Inquisition," in *Judaism and Christian Art*, 115–42; David Nirenberg, "Discourse of Judaizing and Judaism in Medieval Spain," *La corónica: A Journal of*

the *Medieval Hispanic Languages, Literatures, and Cultures* 41, no. 4 (2012), 207–33; Nicolas Weill-Parrot, *Les "images astrologiques" au Moyen Âge et à la Renaissance: Spéculations intellectuelles et pratiques magiques (XIIe–XVe siècles)* (Paris: Champion, 2002), and "Astrology, Astral Influences and Occult Properties in the Thirteenth and Fourteenth Centuries," *Traditio* 65 (2010), 201–30; Cynthia Hahn, "Portable Altars (and the *Rationale*): Liturgical Objects and Personal Devotion," in *Image and Altar 800–1300* (Papers from an International Conference in Copenhagen, 24 October–27 October 2007), ed. Poul Grinder-Hansen (Copenhagen: National Museum, 2014), 45–64.
153 Kornbluth, "Heavenly Jerusalem," 53–55.
154 César García de Castro Valdés, "La reforma románica de la cámara santa de la catedral de San Salvador de Oviedo," in *Monumentos singulares del románico español* (Aguilar de Campoo: Fundación Santa María la Real-Centro de Estudios del Románico, 2012), 43–89.
155 Krüger, "Smaragden.".
156 Krüger, "Smaragden." On the use of green and other colors, Stefano Riccioni, "The Word in the Image: an Epiconographic Analysis of Mosaics of the Reform in Rome," in *Acta ad Archaeologiam et Artium Historiam Pertinentia*, 24 (n.s. 10), ed. Kristin B. Aavitsland and Turid Karlsen Seim (Rome: Sciencze e Lettere, 2011), 85–137.
157 Stefania Gerevini, "Christus crystallus: Rock Crystal, Theology and Materiality in the Medieval West," in *Matter of Faith*, 92–99, and "'Sicut crystallus quando est obiecta soli': Rock Crystal, Transparency and the Franciscan Order," *Mitteilungen des Kunsthistorischen Institutes in Florenz* 56, no. 3 (2014), 254–83; Doron Bauer, "Geological Imagination in Romanesque Sculpture," *Materialidades: Perspectivas en cultura material* 3 (2015), 104–27; Patrick R. Crowley, "Crystalline Aesthetics and the Classical Concept of the Medium," *West 86th Street* 23 (2016), 220–51.
158 Francisco Prado-Vilar, *The Portal of Glory: Architecture, Matter, and Vision*, ed. Francisco Prado-Vilar (Coruña: Fundación Barrié/Andrew W. Mellon Foundation, Barrié Press, 2019), 43.
159 Gerevini, "Sicut," 272–73.
160 Francesca Dell'Acqua, "The Carbunculus (Red Garnet) and the Double Nature of Christ in the Early Medieval West," *Kunsthistorisk tidskrift/Journal of Art History* 86 (2017), 158–172.
161 *Prague: The Crown of Bohemia 1347–1437* (cat. of an exhib., New York), ed. Barbara Drake Boehm and Jirí Fajt (New York: Metropolitan Museum of Art, 2005), 140–41.
162 Erika Zwierlein-Diehl, "Antike Gemmen im Mittelalter: Wiederverwendung, Umdeutung, Nachahmung" in *Persistenz und Rezeption*, 237–84.
163 Fischer, "Facing Medusa," 19–20; Cordez, "Arrepentimiento," 129.
164 Cordez, "Arrepentimiento," 136.
165 Bissera Pentcheva, *The Sensual Icon: Space, Ritual, and the Senses in Byzantium* (University Park: University of Pennsylvania Press, 2010).
166 Spike Bucklow, "The Virtues of Imitation: Gems, Cameos, and Glass Imitations," in *The Westminster Retable: History, Technique, Conservation*, ed. Paul Binski and Ann Massing (London: Harvey Miller, 2009), 143–49.
167 Heidi Gearhart, *Theophilus and the Theory and Practice of Medieval Art* (University Park: The Pennsylvania State University Press, 2017), 59.
168 Jacob Wamberg, *Landscape as World Picture: Tracing Cultural Evolution in Images from the Palaeolithic Period to the Middle Ages* (Aarhus: Aarhus University Press, 2009), vol. 1, 304–16; Francesca Dell'Acqua, "The Christ from San Vincenzo al Volturno (9th century): Another Instance of 'Christ's Dazzling Face,'" in *Panneaux de Vitrail Isolés/die Einzelscheibe/The Single Stained-glass Panel* (XXIV International Colloquium of the Corpus Vitrearum) (Zurich: Peter Lang, 2010), 11–27, and "Il volto di Cristo e il dilemma dell'artista: un esempio di IX secolo," in *"Conosco un ottimo storico dell'arte ..."*

Per Enrico Castelnuovo: Scritti di allievi e amici pisani, ed. Monica M. Donato and Massimo Ferretti (Pisa: Edizioni della Normale, 2012), 21–27.

169 Christine Hediger and Brigitte Kurmann-Schwarz, "[...] et faciunt inde tabulas saphiri pretiosas ac satis utiles in fenestris: Die Farbe Blau in der 'Schedula' und in der Glasmalerei von 1100–1250," in *Zwischen Kunsthandwerk und Kunst: Die "Schedula diversarum atrium,"* ed. Andreas Speer et al. (Berlin: De Gruyter, 2014), 256–73.

170 Madeline H. Caviness, "Artist: To See, Hear, and Know, All at Once," in *Voice of the Living Light: Hildegard of Bingen and her World*, ed. Barbara Newman (Berkeley: University of California Press, 1998), 110–24; Jeffrey F. Hamburger, "Seeing and Believing: The Suspicion of Sight and the Authentication of Vision in Late Medieval Art and Devotion," in *Imagination und Wirklichkeit: Zum Verhältnis von mentalen und realen Bildern in der Kunst der frühen Neuzeit*, ed. Klaus Krüger and Alessandro Nova (Mainz: Philipp von Zabern, 2000), 47–69.

171 Weinryb, *Bronze Object*, 17–23.

172 Weinryb, *Bronze Object*, 39–44; Horst Bredekamp, *Der schwimmende Souverän Karl der Große und die Bildpolitik des Körpers* (Berlin: Verlag Klaus Wagenbach, 2014).

173 Michael Brandt, *Bernwards Säule: Schätze aus dem Dom zu Hildesheim* (Regensburg: Schnell & Steiner, 2009) and *Bernwards Tür: Schätze aus dem Dom zu Hildesheim* (Regensburg: Schnell & Steiner, 2010); *1000 Jahre St. Michael in Hildesheim: Kirche-Kloster-Stifter*, ed. Gerhard Lutz and Angela Weyer (Göttingen: Michael Imhof Verlag, 2012); Ittai Weinryb, *Bronze Object*, 30–33, and "Hildesheim Avant-Garde: Bronze, Columns, and Colonialism," *Speculum* 93 (2018), 728–82; Isabelle Marchesin, *L'arbre & la Colonne: La porte de bronze d'Hildesheim* (Paris: Picard, 2017).

174 Valentino Pace, "Da Amalfi a Benevento: porte di bronzo figurate dell'Italia meridionale medieval," *Rassegna del centro di cultura e storia Amalfitana*, n.s. 13 (2003), 41–69; Weinryb, *Bronze Object*, 82–83, 173–77.

175 Hauknes, "Emblematic Narratives," 7.

176 Campbell, "Enamelled Plaque"; Thomas E.A. Dale, "The Individual, the Resurrected Body, and Romanesque Portraiture: The Tomb of Rudolf von Schwaben in Merseburg," *Speculum* 77 (2002), 707–43.

177 Julian Gardner, "Magister Bertuccius Aurifex and the Bronze Doors of San Marco: A Programme for the Year of Jubilee," *Revue de l'Art* 134 (2001 [2004]), 9–26.

178 Jennifer Lee, "Material and Meaning in Lead Pilgrims' Signs," *Peregrinations* 2 (2009), 152–69.

179 Holly Flora, *Cimabue and the Franciscans (Renovatio atrium)* (Turnhout: Brepols, 2018), 30–48.

180 *Le Stuc: Visage oublié de l'art medieval* (cat. of an exhib., Poitiers) (Paris: Somogy, 2004); Monika E. Müller, *Omnia in mensura et numero et pondere disposita: Die Wandmalereien und Stuckarbeiten von San Pietro al Monte di Civate* (Regensburg: Schnell & Steiner, 2009), 69–98; Foletti, *Oggetti*, 181–221.

181 Peter Low, "'You Who Once Were Far Off': Enlivening Scripture in the Main Narthex Portal at Ste-Madeleine de Vézelay," *Art Bulletin* 85 (2003), 469–89; Thunø, *Apse Mosaic*, 142–45, 159–64 et passim; Henry Maguire, "The Aniketos Icon and the Display of Relics in the Decorations of San Marco," in *San Marco, Byzantium*, 91–111.

182 Palazzo, *L'espace rituel*.

183 Jean Wirth, *L'image à l'èpoque romane* (Paris: Éditions du Cerf, 1999), 202–03; Marcello Angheben, "Christus Victor, Sacerdos et Judex: The Multiple Roles of Christ on Mosan Shrines," in *Sacred Scripture/Sacred Space: The Interlacing of Real Places and Conceptual Spaces in Medieval Art and Architecture*, ed. Tobias Frese, Wilfried Keil, and Kristina Krüger (Berlin: DeGruyter, 2019), 85–108.

184 *Der Naumburger Meister: Bildhauer und Architekt im Europa der Kathedralen; Forschungen und Beiträge zum internationalen wissenschaftlichen Kolloquium in Naumburg vom 05. bis 08.*

Oktober 2011, ed. Hartmut Krohm et al. (Petersberg: Michael Imhof, 2012); Jacqueline Jung, "Beyond the Barrier: The Unifying Role of the Choir Screen in Gothic Churches," *Art Bulletin* 82, no. 4 (2000), 622–57, and *The Gothic Screen: Space, Sculpture, and Community in the Cathedrals of France and Germany, ca. 1200–1400* (Cambridge: Cambridge University Press, 2013), 36–43 et passim; Assaf Pinkus, *Sculpting Simulacra in Medieval Germany, 1250–1380* (Farnham: Ashgate, 2014), 29–70.

185 Bauer, "Geological Imagination"; Finbarr Barry Flood, "'God's Wonder': Marble as Medium and the Natural Image in Mosques and Modernism," *West 86th* 23 (2016), 168–219; Philippe Cordez, "Albertus Magnus und die Steine von Venedig: Ein Beitrag zur 'Bildwissenschaft' des 13. Jahrhunderts," in *Steinformen: Materialität, Qualität, Imitation*, ed. Isabella Augart, Maurice Sass, and Iris Wenderholm (Berlin: De Gruyter, 2019), 191–205.

186 Rocío Sánchez Ameijeiras, "Imaxes e teoria da imaxe nas *Cantigas de Santa Maria*," in *Las cantigas de Santa María*, ed. Elvira Fidalgo (Salamanca: Ediciós Xereis de Galicia, 2002), 247–330; *Los rostros de las palabras: Imágenes y teoria literaria en el Occidente medieval* (Madrid: Ediciones Akal, 2014), 171–75; Francisco Prado-Vilar, "The Parchment of the Sky: Poiesis of a Gothic Universe," in *Las Cantigas de Santa María: Códice Rico, Ms. T-I-1 Real Biblioteca del Monasterio de San Lorenzo de El Escorial*, ed. Laura Fernández Fernández and Juan Carlos Ruiz Souza (Madrid: Colección Scriptorium, 2011), 477–520; Kirstin Kennedy, "Seeing is Believing: The Miniatures in the Cantigas de Santa Maria and Medieval Devotional Practices," *Portuguese Studies* 31, no. 2 (2015), 169–82.

187 Francisco Prado-Vilar, "The *Superstes*: Resurrection, the Survival of Antiquity, and the Poetics of the Body Romanesque Sculpture," in *Transformatio et Continuatio—Forms of Change and Constancy of Antiquity in the Iberian Peninsula 500–1500*, ed. Horst Bredekamp and Stefan Trinks (Berlin and New York: De Gruyter, 2017), 137–88.

188 Jan Royt, *The Prague of Charles IV* (Prague: Karolinum Press, 2016), 94–95; Flood, "God's Wonder," 207–08.

189 Maria Carolina Gaetani, Ulderico Santamaria, and Claudio Seccaroni, "The Use of Egyptian Blue and Lapis Lazuli in the Middle Ages: The Wall Paintings of the San Saba Church in Rome," *Studies in Conservation* 49 (2004), 13–22; Pia Roger, "Étude des couleurs et de la pratique picturale," in *L'évangéliaire de Charlemagne* (Paris: Éditions Faton, 2007), 46–64; Spike Bucklow, *The Riddle of the Image: The Secret Science of Medieval Art* (London: Reaktion Books, 2014), 55–72.

190 Krause, "Feuerprobe"; Klein, "Refashioning," 178–79.

191 Paul Binski, "Cosmati and *romanitas* in England: An Overview," in *Westminster Abbey: the Cosmati Pavements*, ed. Linda Grant and Richard Mortimer (Aldershot: Ashgate, 2002), 116–34; Ruth Siddall, "Westminster Abbey: The Stones of the Sanctuary Pavement," *Urban Geology in London* 22 (2014), 1–5.

192 Bucklow, *Riddle*, 161–66.

193 Bauer, "Geological Imagination," 120.

194 Kumler, "Multiplication," 191. An alabaster jug in Quedlinburg (Domschatz) was associated (from the sixteenth century at least) with the transformation of wine at the Marriage at Cana, while the white in the deep-red sardonyx of an ancient cup used for Abbot Suger's chalice (Washington, National Gallery of Art) appears to embody the very essence of the sacramental mystery.

195 Hamburger, "Seeing and Believing," 53.

196 Michael McCormick, *Origins of the European Economy: Communications and Commerce AD 300–900* (Cambridge: Cambridge University Press, 2001), 134–38; Paul E. Dutton, *Carolingian Civilization: A Reader*, 2nd ed. (Peterborough: Broadview Press, 2004), 472–79, and "The Identification of Persons in Frankish Europe," *Early Medieval Europe* 26 (2018), 135–73 and 166–70; Josef Ackermann, *Das "Itinerarium Bernardi Monachi" Edition-Übersetzung-Kommentar* (Hannover: Hahnsche Buchhandlung, 2010), 8, 127, 135.

197 Kessler, "Object as Subject," 211.
198 Herbert L. Kessler, "Arca arcarum: Nested Boxes and the Dynamics of Sacred Experience," *Codex Aqvilarensis* 30 (2014), 97–100.
199 Kessler, "Arca arcarum," 91.
200 Bénédicte Palazzo-Bertholon, "La spatialisation des pots acoustiques dans l'espace liturgique et la matérialisation du son," in *Les cinq sens au Moyen Âge*, ed. Éric Palazzo (Paris: Éditions du Cerf, 2016), 407–28.
201 Herbert L. Kessler, "Christ's Fluid Face," in *Theologisches Wissen und die Kunst: Festschrift für Martin Büchsel*, ed. Rebecca Müller, Anselm Rau, and Johanna Scheel (Berlin: Gebr. Mann, 2015), 221–34; Kumler, "Manufacturing," 28–30.
202 Bruno Reudenbach, *Das Godescalc-Evangeliar: Ein Buch für die Reformpolitik Karls des Grossen* (Frankfurt: Fischer Verlag, 1998); Lafitte, *L'évangéliaire*; Peter Orth, "Das Widmungsgedicht," in *Das Godescalc-Evangelistar: Eine Prachthandschrift für Karl den Großen*, ed. Fabrizio Crivello et al. (Munich: Faksimile Verlag, 2011), 38–48; Jeffrey F. Hamburger, *Script as Image* (Paris: Peeters, 2014), 20–24; Kathryn M. Rudy, *Postcards on Parchment: The Social Lives of Medieval Books* (New Haven and London: Yale University Press, 2015), 198–201.
203 Peter Damian, Letter 159, in *Die Briefe des Petrus Damiani*, ed. K. Reindel (Munich: Die Briefe der deutschen Kaiserzeit, Munich 1993), vol. 4, MGH..
204 Marchesin, *L'arbre*, 191 et passim.
205 Gaetano Curzi, *Arredi lignei medievali: L'Abruzzo e l'Italia centro meridionale; Secoli XII–XIII* (Cinisello Balsamo: Silvana Editoriale, 2007).
206 Marc Antoni Nay, *Die Bilderdecke von Zillis: Grundlagen und Versuch einer Rekonstruction* (Chur: Verlag Desertina, 2015); Jeremy Johns, "Le pitture del soffitto della Cappella Palatina," in *La Cappella Palatina a Palermo*, ed. Beat Brenk (Modena: Franco Cosimo Panini, 2010), 387–407; *Conservation and Discovery: Peterborough Cathedral Nave Ceiling and Related Structures*, ed. Jackie Hall and Susan M. Wright (London: Museum of London Archaeology, 2015).
207 Baert, *Heritage*; Gerhard Lutz, "The Drop of Blood: Image and Piety in the Twelfth and Thirteenth Centuries," *Preternature: Critical and Historical Studies on the Preternatural* 4 (2015), 37–51; Robin M. Jensen, *The Cross: History, Art, and Controversy* (Cambridge, MA: Harvard University Press, 2017), 29–32, 124–36 et passim; Ritchey, *Holy Matter*, 18–24; Paul Binski, "The Rhetorical Occasions of Gothic Sculpture," *Collegium medievale* 30 (2018), 7–32.
208 Anna Maria Maetzke, "Il Volto Santo di Sansepolcro," in *Il Volto Santo in Europa: Culto e immagini del Crocifisso nel Medioevo* (Atti del Convegno internazionale di Engelberg [13–16 settembre 2000]), ed. Michele Camillo Ferrari and Andreas Meyer (Lucca: Istituto Storico Lucchese, 2005).
209 *La croce dipinta dell'abbazia di Rosano: Visibile e invisibile; Studio e restauro per la comprensione*, ed. Marco Ciatti et al. (Florence: Edifir, 2007); *La pittura su tavola del secolo XII: Riconsiderazioni e nuove acquisizioni a seguito del restauro della Croce di Rosano*, ed. Cecilia Frosinini et al. (Florence: Edifir, 2012).
210 Mariagiulia Burresi, "Il gruppo della Deposizione nella cattedrale di Volterra," in *Medioevo a Volterra: Arte nell'antica Diocesi fino al Duecento*, ed. Mariagiulia Burresi and Antonino Caleca (Ospedaletto: Pacini editore, 2002), 171–81; Antonino Caleca, "Gruppi di Deposizione medievali in Italia centrale," in *Il teatro delle statue: Gruppi lignei di Deposizione e Annunciazione tra XII e XIII secolo*, ed. Francesca Flores D'Arcais (Milan: Vita e Pensiero, 2005), 125–29.
211 Weinryb, "Avant-Garde," 774–76.
212 Hauknes, "Emblematic Narratives," 31–34.
213 César García de Castro Valdés, "La Arqueta de las Ágatas de la Cámara Santa de la Catedral de Oviedo," *Anales de Historia del Arte* 24 (2014), 173–226.

NOTES TO PAGES 48–52   249

214 Tasso, "Medioevo nella Milano."
215 Emmanuelle Mercier, "Évolution du travail du sculpteur sur bois aux XIIIe et XIVe siècles: l'exemple de la sculpture mosan," *Rivista d'arte*, ser. 5, 5 (2015), 1–16.
216 Marius Rimmele, "Die Schreinmadonna: Bild, Körper, Matrix," in *Bild und Körper im Mittelalter*, ed. Kristin Marek et al. (Munich: Fink Verlag, 2006), 41–59; Bynum, *Materiality*, 86–89; Pinkus, *Simulacra*, 148–78; Elina Gertsman, "Performing Birth, Enacting Death: Unstable Bodies in Late Medieval Devotion" in *Visualizing*, 83–104, and *Worlds Within: Opening the Medieval Shrine Madonna* (University Park: Pennsylvania State University Press, 2015); Sarah Elliott Novacich, "Transparent Mary: Visible Interiors and the Maternal Body in the Middle Ages," *JEGP, Journal of English and Germanic Philology* 116, no. 4 (2017), 464–90; Jack Hartnell, *Medieval Bodies: Life, Death and Art in the Middle Ages* (London: Welcome Collection, 2018), 230–31.
217 As in the case of other shrine Madonnas, Mary likely once proffered an apple in her (broken) left hand, symbolizing her role as the new Eve.
218 Francesca Dell'Acqua, "The Hidden Sides of the Salerno Ivories: Hypotheses about the Original Object, Program, and Cultural Milieu," in *The Salerno Ivories: Objects, Histories, Contexts*, ed. Francesca Dell'Acqua et al. (Berlin: Gebr. Mann, 2016), 211–39; Trinks, "Eingehüllt," 482–89; Eve Borsook, "A Solomonic Throne for the Cathedral of Salerno?" *Convivium* 5, no. 1 (2018), 35–39.
219 Sarah M. Guérin, "The Tusk: Origins of the Raw Material for the Salerno Ivories," in *Salerno Ivories*, 21–29, and "Gold, Ivory, and Copper," 192–95. Fatimid ornament on ivory oliphants made in eleventh- and twelfth-century southern Italy apparently served the same purpose; Shalem, *Islamic Objects*; Rosser-Owen, "Oliphant."
220 Debiais, *Croisée*, 298–300.
221 Trinks, "Eingehüllt," 481.
222 Jászai, "Christus," 41.
223 Lucinia Speciale, "Ludus scachorum: I gioco dei re; Forma e iconografia delgi scacchi tra l'Italia meridional e l'Europa," in *L'enigma degli avori medievali da Amalfi a Salerno*, vol. 1, ed. Ferdinando Bologna (Pozzuoli: Paparo edizioni, 2008), 203–30; Philippe Cordez, "O jogo de xadrez: imagem, poder e Igreja (fin X^e–début XIIe siècles)," *Revista de História* 165 (2011), 93–120, and "Images ludiques et politique féodale: Les matériels d'échecs dans les églises du XIe siècle," in *Tempus ludendi: Chiesa e ludicità nella società tardo-medioevale (sec. XII–XV)* (*Ludica: Annali di storia e civiltà del gioco* 13–14, [2007/2008]), 115–36.
224 As on the handle, bone often was substituted for the more precious material.
225 Beate Fricke, "Matter and Meaning of Mother-of-Pearl: The Origins of Allegory in the Spheres of Things," *Gesta* 51, no. 1 (2012), 35–53; Hahn, *Thing of Mine*, 23–32.
226 Rachel King, "Rethinking 'the Oldest Surviving Amber in the West,'" *Burlington Magazine* 155, no. 1328 (2013), 756–62; Hollie Drinkwater, "Material in Context: The Amber Head of Christ of the Wallace Collection Pax," *Journal of the British Archaeological Association* 169 (2016), 95–121.
227 Hugo van der Velden, *The Donor's Image: Gerard Loyet and the Votive Portraits of Charles the Bold* (Turnhout: Brepols, 2000), 247–59; Brigitte Bedos-Rezak, "Medieval Identity: A Sign and a Concept," *The American Historical Review* 105, no. 5 (2000), 1488–1533, and *When Ego was Imago: Signs of Identity in the Middle Ages* (Leiden: Brill, 2011), 142–50 et passim; Fabio Bisogni, "La scultura in cera nel Medioevo," *Iconographica* 1 (2002), 1–15; Sarah Blick, "Pilgrimage to Tomb and Shrine of St Thomas, Canterbury Cathedral," in *Push Me, Pull You: Art and Devotional Interaction in Late Medieval and Renaissance Art*, ed. Sarah Blick and Laura Gelfand (Leiden: Brill, 2011), 21–58; Zchomelidse, *Art, Ritual*, 42–43.
228 Christopher R. Lakey, *Sculptural Seeing: Relief, Optics, and the Rise of Perspective in Medieval Italy* (New Haven and London: Yale University Press, 2018), 144.
229 Hamburger, *Visual and the Visionary*, 350–62.
230 Fricke, *Fallen Idols*, 52 (*Ecce fides*, 66).

231 Michele Bacci, "On the Holy Topography of Sailors: An Introduction," and Vinni Lucherini, "Strategie di visibilità dell'architettura sacra nella Napoli angioina: la percezione da mare e la testimonianza di Petrarca," in *The Holy Portolano/Le Portulan sacré: The Sacred Geography of Navigation*, ed. Michele Bacci and Martin Rohde (Berlin: De Gruyter, 2014), 7–16 and 197–220.

232 *De anima*, 424a, 15–25; Stuart Clark, *Vanities of the Eye: Vision in Modern European Culture* (Oxford: Oxford University Press, 2007), 14–15.

233 Francisco Prado-Vilar, *Tears from Flanders: Memory, Prophecy, and the Consolation of Painting* (Turnhout: Brepols, 2019).

234 Prado-Vilar, "Parchment."

235 Rudy, *Postcards*, 41–43.

236 Kessler, "Speculum," 24–27.

237 Gerhard Wolf, *Schleier und Spiegel: Traditionen des Christusbildes und die Bildkonzepte der Renaissance* (Munich: Wilhelm Fink Verlag, 2002), 210–11; see also the Manopello Christ, Heinrich Pfeiffer, *Il volto santo di Manoppello* (Pescara: CARSA, 2000). On transparent *Veronicas*: Raffaella Zardoni, Emanuela Bossi, and Amanda Murphy, "The Iconography of the Roman Veronica: From the Repertoires of Karl Pearson to the Veronica Route," in *European Fortune*, 286–301.

238 Kessler, "Literary Warp and Artitic Weft," 22; Flora, *Cimabue*, 174–83.

239 Herbert L. Kessler, "Configuring the Invisible by Copying the Holy Face," in *The Holy Face and the Paradox of Representation*, ed. Herbert L. Kessler and Gerhard Wolf (Bologna: Nuova alfa, 1998), 129–151 (reprinted in *Spiritual Seeing*, 64–87).

240 Elisa Pallotini, "The Epigraphic Presence on the Borghorst Cross (c. 1050)," in *Sacred Scripture/Sacred Space*, 63–84.

241 Fergus Cannan, "'If Marble will not serve': Medieval English Alabaster Sculpture, from Quarry to Object of Devotion," in *Object of Devotion: Medieval English Alabaster Sculpture from the Victoria and Albert Museum*, ed. Paul Williamson (Alexandria, VA: Arts Services International, 2010), 22–37; Eamon Duffy, "The Reformation and the Alabaster Men," in *Tributes to Nigel Morgan: Contexts of Medieval Art: Images, Objects and Ideas*, ed. Julian M. Luxford and M.A. Michael (London and Turnhout: Harvey Millar, 2010), 54–65 (reprinted in Eamon Duffy, *Royal Books & Holy Bones: Essays in Medieval Christianity* [London: Bloomsbury Continuum, 2018], 289–300).

242 Sarah M. Guérin, *Gothic Ivories: Calouste Gulbenkian Collection* (London: Scala Arts and Heritage Publishers, 2015), 37–42.

243 Guérin, "The Tusk."

244 Andreas Petzold, "'Of the Significance of Colours': The Iconography of Colour in Romanesque and Early Gothic Book Illumination," in *Image and Belief: Studies in Celebration of the Eightieth Anniversary of the Index of Christian Art*, ed. Colum Hourihane (Princeton: Index of Christian Art, 1999), 125–34; Françoise Gasparri, "La pensée et l'oeuvre de l'abbé Suger à la lumière de ses écrits," in *L'abbé Suger, la manifeste gothique de Saint-Denis et la pensée victorine*, ed. Dominique Poirel (Turnhout: Brepols, 2001), 59–82.

245 *La couleur et la pierre: Polychromie des portails gothiques* (acts of a colloquium, Amiens) (Paris: Picard, 2002); Pinkus, "Transformations."

246 Kumler and Lakey, "*Res et significatio*," 8–10.

247 Madeline Caviness, "Stained Glass Windows in Gothic Chapels, and the Feasts of the Saints," in *Kunst und Liturgie*, 135–48; Marius Rimmele, "Transparenzen, variable Konstellationen, gefaltete Welten: Systematisierende Überlegungen zur medienspezifischen Gestaltung von dreiteiligen Klappbildern," in *Klappeffekte*, 13–54.

248 Bynum, *Materiality*, 53–61.

249 Bucklow, "Virtues," 146.

250 Bucklow, *Riddle*, 11–41; Flora, *Cimabue*, 43–48.

251 Caroline Walker Bynum, *Metamorphosis and Identity* (New York: Zone Books, 2005), 118–27.
252 Weinryb, *Bronze Object*, 33–35.
253 Kumler and Lakey, *"Res et significatio"*; Kozlowski, "Trecento Diptych." The aggregate stone on a crusader portable altar in Agrigento (Museo nazionale) recalls collections of pebbles that pilgrims gathered at the actual sites where Christ had lived and died, providing a meaningful material foundation for the Eucharistic sacrifice; Bianca Kühnel, "L'arte crociata tra Oriente e Occidente," in *Le crociate: L'oriente e l'occidente da Urbano II a San Luigi 1096–1270*, ed. Monique Rey-Delqué (Milan: Electa, 1997), 341–53; Palazzo, *L'espace*, 166.
254 Trinks, "Eingehüllt," 501.
255 R. Howard Bloch, *A Needle in the Right Hand of God: The Norman Conquest of 1066 and the Making and Meaning of the Bayeux Tapestry* (New York: Random House, 2006), 75–81.
256 Sánchez Ameirjeiras, *Rostros*, 171–75; Prado-Vilar, "Parchment"; Elina Gertsman, "Phantoms of Emptiness: The Space of the Imaginary in Late Medieval Art," *Art History* 41, no. 5 (2018), 800–37.
257 The same Islamic trope entered Judaism; *Skies of Parchment/Seas of Ink: Jewish Illuminated Manuscripts*, ed. Marc Michael Epstein (Princeton: Princeton University Press, 2015).
258 Debiais, *Croisée*, 174–75.
259 Dell'Acqua, "Carbunculus," 167.
260 Christoph Winterer, *Das Evangeliar der Äbtissin Hitda—Eine ottonische Prachthandschrift aus Köln: Miniaturen, Bilder und Zierseiten aus der Handschrift 1640 der Universitäts- und Landesbibliothek Darmstadt* (Darmstadt: WBG, 2011); Klaus Gereon Beuckers, *Äbtissin Hitda und der Hitda-Codex (Universitäts- und Landesbibliothek Darmstadt, Hs. 1640): Forschungen zu einem Hauptwerk der ottonischen Kölner Buchmalerei* (Darmstadt: WBG, 2013).
261 Also, the St. Gereon Gospels (Paris, BnF, MS Lat. 817, fol. 12ʳ); Kumler and Lakey, *"Res et significatio,"* 7. A frontispiece to Luke's Gospel in an eleventh-century Rhenish Gospelbook exploits cosmic symbolism by applying thin washes of blue and green tempera onto parchment that remains visible (Darmstadt, Landesmuseum, Cod. AE 679, fol.126ᵛ); *Gold und Purpur: Der Bilderschmuck der früh- und hochmittelalterlichen Handschriften aus der Sammlung Hüpsch im Hessischen Landesmuseum* Darmstadt (Darmstadt: Hessisches Landesmuseum, 2001), 25–37; Herbert L. Kessler, "'Hoc visibile imaginatum figurat illud invisibile verum': Imagining God in Pictures of Christ," in *Seeing the Invisible in Late Antiquity and the Early Middle Ages: Papers from "Verbal and Pictorial Representations of the Invisible 400 to 1000"* (Utrecht, 11–13 December 2003), ed. Giselle de Nie et al. (Turnhout: Brepols, 2005), 293–328; Antonio Iacobini, "'Hoc elementum ceteris omnibus imperat': L'acqua nell'universo dell'alto medioevo," in *L'acqua nei secoli altomedievali* (LV Settimane di Studio, Spoleto) (Spoleto: CISAM, 2008), 985–1027; Bynum, *Materiality*, 53–61; Joshua O'Driscoll, "Visual Vortex: an Epigraphic Image from an Ottonian Gospel Book," *Word & Image* 27, no. 3 (2011), 309–21.
262 Fulton, *From Judgment to Passion*, 194–203 et passim.
263 Silke Tammen, "Blick und Wunde—Blick und Form: zur Deutungsproblematik der Seitenwunde Christi in der spätmittelalterlichen Buchmalerei," in *Bild und Körper*, 85–114.
264 *Weaving, Veiling, and Dressing: Textiles and their Metaphors in the Late Middle Ages*, ed. Kathryn M. Rudy and Barbara Baert (Turnhout: Brepols, 2007).
265 Jeffrey Hamburger, *Nuns as Artists: The Visual Culture of a Medieval Convent* (Berkeley and Los Angeles: University of California Press, 1997), 179–80; Elizabeth Coatsworth, "Cloth-Making and the Virgin Mary in Anglo-Saxon Literature and Art," in *Medieval Art: Recent Perspectives; A Memorial Tribute to C.R. Dodwell*, ed. Gale R. Owen-Crocker and Timothy Graham (Manchester: Manchester University Press, 1998), 8–25; Maureen C. Miller, *Clothing the Clergy: Virtue and Power in Medieval Europe, c. 800–1200* (Ithaca and London: Cornell University Press, 2014), 149–51.

266 Thomas E.A. Dale, *Relics, Prayer, and Politics in Medieval Venetia: Romanesque Painting in the Crypt of Aquileia Cathedral* (Princeton: Princeton University Press, 1997); Holmes, *Miraculous Image*, 218–39.

267 Daniel Russo, "Espace peint, espace symbolique, construction ecclésiologique: Les peintures de Berzé-la-Ville (Chapelle-des-Moines)," *Revue Mabillon*, n.s. II, 72 (2000), 57–87; Éric Palazzo, "Les peintures murales et les pratiques liturgiques dans l'église médiévale," in *Peintures murales médiévales, XIIe–XVIe siècles*, ed. Daniel Russo (Dijon: Université de Dijon, 2005), 57–62; Elizabeth Lapina, "The Mural Paintings of Berzé-la-Ville in the Context of the First Crusade and the *Reconquista*," *Journal of Medieval History* 31, no. 4 (2005), 309–26.

268 Andrea Nicolotti, *Sindone: Storia e leggende di una reliquia controversa* (Turin: Einaudi, 2015), 33–41; for the complicated history of the shroud and related images, Andrea Nicolotti, *From the Mandylion of Edessa to the Shroud of Turin: The Metamorphosis of a Legend* (Leiden: Brill, 2014).

269 Claudio Belinati, *Nuovi studi sulla Cappella di Giotto all'Arena di Padova (25 marzo 1303–2002)* (Padua: Poligrafico, 2003); Laura Jacobus, *Giotto and the Arena Chapel: Art, Architecture and Experience* (Turnhout and New York: Brepols/Harvey Miller, 2008).

270 Chiara Frugoni, *L'affare migliore di Enrico: Giotto e la Cappella Scrovegni* (Turin: Einaudi, 2008), 145–46, 186–87; Andrea De Marchi, "Dieu le Père en majesté," in *Giotto e compagni*, ed. Dominique Thiébaut (Paris: Musée du Louvre, 2013), 102–04; Alessandro Tomei, "Dio Padre in trono," in *Giotto, l'Italia*, ed. Serena Romano and Pietro Petraroia (Milan: Electra, 2017), 76–83.

271 Herbert L. Kessler, "Real Absence: Early Medieval Art and the Metamorphosis of Vision," in *Morfologie sociali e culturali in Europa fra tarda antichità e alto medioevo* (XLV Settimana internazionale di studi, Spoleto) (Spoleto: CISAM, 1998), 1157–1211 (repr. *Spiritual Seeing*, 104–48); "The Icon in the Narrative," in *Spiritual Seeing*, 1–28.

272 Ferrari, "Gold und Asche"; Hahn, *Strange Beauty*, 26; Malo, *Relics and Writing*, 14–17 et passim.

273 Weinryb, *Bronze Object*, 44–51.

274 Paul Davies, "The Lighting of Pilgrimage Shrines in Renaissance Italy," in *The Miraculous Image in the Late Middle Ages and Renaissance*, ed. Erik Thunø and Gerhard Wolf (Rome: "L'Erma" di Bretschneider, 2004), 62–71; Rouchon Mouilleron, "Miracle et charité"; Holmes, *Miraculous Image*; Tanja Klemm, "Corpus animatum—imago animate: Shared Image Practices in the Florentine Church SS. Annunziata in the Renaissance," in *Feelings of Being Alive*, ed. Jörg Fingerhut and Sabine Marienberg (Berlin: De Gruyter, 2012), 259–91; Sergio Tognetti, "Florentine Economy between the 13th and 14th Centuries," in *Textiles and Wealth*, 30–41.

275 Paul Binski, "Reflections on the 'Wonderful Height and Size' of Gothic Great Churches and the Medieval Sublime," in *Magnificence and the Sublime in Medieval Aesthetics: Art, Architecture, Literature, Music*, ed. C. Stephen Jaeger (New York: Palgrave Macmillan, 2010), 129–56.

276 Bagnoli, "Stuff of Heaven," 138.

277 T.A. Heslop, "Art, Nature, and St Hugh's Choir at Lincoln," in *England and the Continent in the Middle Ages: Studies in Memory of Andrew Martindale*, ed. John Mitchell (Stamford: Shaun Tyas, 2000), 60–74; Martin Büchsel, "Materialpracht und die Kunst für Litterati: Suger gegen Bernhard von Clairvaux," in *Materialpracht und Mysterifizierung mittelalterlicher Kunst "Kultbild": Revision eines Begriffs*, ed. Martin Büchsel and Rebecca Müller (Berlin: Gebr. Mann Verlag, 2010), 155–81; Allegra Iafrate, "'Artifex specialis': per una lettura critica della figura di Matthew Paris attraverso le fonti," *Opera, Nomina, Historiae: Giornale di cultura artistica* 2/3 (2010), 1–42.

278 In like fashion, the rock-crystal overlays on painted vellum on the diptych of Andrew III of Hungary can be seen as a kind of imitation enamel; Béla Zsolt Szakás, "From

the Harbour of Venice to the Kingdom of Hungary: Art and Trade in the 11th–13th Centuries," *Hortus atrium medievalium* 22, no. 22 (2016), 294–302.

279 Kumler, "Manufacturing," 22.

280 Eliza Garrison, "Mimetic Bodies: Repetition, Replication, and Simulation in the Marriage Charter of Empress Theophanu," *Word & Image* 33, no. 2 (2017), 212–32.

281 Following ancient depictions of the Prometheus legend; Herbert L. Kessler, "Memory and Models: The Interplay of Patterns and Practice in the Mosaics of San Marco in Venice," in *Medioevo: Immagine e memoria*, ed. Carlo Arturo Quintavale (Parma: Elekta, 2009), 463–75, and "Thirteenth-Century Venetian Revisions of the Cotton Genesis Cycle," in *Das Atrium von San Marco in Venedig: Die Genese der Genesismosaiken und ihre mittelalterliche Wirklichkeit/The Atrium of San Marco in Venice: The Genesis of the Genesis Mosaics and their Medieval Reality*, ed. Martin Büchsel, Herbert L. Kessler, and Rebecca Müller (Berlin: Gebr. Mann, 2015), 75–94.

282 Hans Belting, "Franziskus: Der Körper als Bild," in *Bild und Körper*, 21–36; Bynum, *Materiality*, 113–16.

283 Katherine H. Tachau, "God's Compass and 'Vana Curiositas': Scientific Study in the Old French 'Bible Moralise,'" *Art Bulletin* 80, no. 1 (1998), 7–33; Conrad Rudolph, "In the Beginning: Theories and Images of Creation in Northem Europe in the Twelfth Century," *Art History* 22, no. 1 (1999), 3–55; Sarah Lipton, *Images of Intolerance: the Representation of Jews and Judaism in the Bible moralisée* (Berkeley and London: University of California Press, 1999); John Lowden, *The Making of the Bibles Moralisées* (University Park: Pennsylvania University Press, 2000), and "Under the Influence of the Bibles moralisées," in *Under the Influence: The Concept of Influence and the Study of Illuminated Manuscripts*, ed. John Lowden and Alixe Bovey (Turnhout: Brepols, 2007), 169–85; François Boespflug, "Le Créateur au compass: *Deus geometra* dans l'art d'Occident (IXe–XIXe siècle)," *Micrologus* 19 (2011), 113–30; Jean Wirth, *Villard de Honnecourt, architecte du XIIIe siècle* (Geneva: Droz, 2015), 59–60; Alessio Monciatti, "Figure sorprendenti: Disegni fuori contesto e particolari nascosti fra utilità e divertimento, per la pittura dei secoli XIII e XIV in Italia," in *L'art medieval en joc*, ed. Rosa Alcoy (Barcelona: Universitat de Barcelona, 2016), 175–95; Antonia Martinez Ruipérez, "The Moral Compass and Mortal Slumber: Divine and Human Reason in the *Bibles moralisées*," *Journal of the Warburg and Courtauld Institutes* 81 (2018), 1–33.

284 A similar image is included at the start of the creation cycle in the fourteenth-century Holkham Bible (London, British Library, Add. MS 47682, fol. 2^r); Michelle Brown, *The Holkham Bible Picture Book: A Facsimile* (London: The British Library, 2007), 31–32.

285 Wirth, *Villard*, 57–60; Román de la Calle, "Del *Deus pictor* a la acción creadora del artista, *instar Dei*," *Aisthesis* 38 (2005), 21–41.

286 Hamburger, *Nuns*, 177–211; Alain Erlande-Brandenburg, *De pierre, d'or, et de feu: La creation artistique au Moyen-Âge, IVe au XIIIe siècle* (Paris: Fayard, 1999), and *Le sacre de l'artiste: La création au Moyen Âge, XIVe–XVe siècle* (Paris: Fayard, 2000); Pierre-Alain Mariaux, "Quelques hypotheses à propos de l'artiste roman," *Médiévales: Langues, Textes, Histoire* 44, no. 1 (2003), 199–214; Enrico Castelnuovo, *Artifex Bonus: Il mondo dell'artista medievale* (Rome: Laterza, 2004); Caskey, "Whodunnit?"; Carles Mancho, "Un métier très contemporain: Les artistes du haut Moyen Âge," *Cahiers de Saint-Michel de Cuxa* 43 (2012), 9–14; Mary Carruthers, *The Experience of Beauty in the Middle Ages* (Oxford: Oxford University Press, 2013), 204–05; Aden Kumler, "The Patron-Function," in *Patronage: Power & Agency in Medieval Art*, ed. Colum Hourihane (Princeton: Index of Christian Art, 2013), 297–319; Gearhart, *Theophilus*; Robert Maxwell, "The 'Literate' Lay Donor: Textuality and the Romanesque Patron," in *Romanesque Patrons and Processes*, ed. Jordi Camps et al. (London and New York: Routledge, 2018), 259–77.

287 Laura Cleaver, "The Liberal Arts in Sculpture and Metalwork in Twelfth Century France and Ideals of Education," *Immediations* 1 (2007), 56–75; *Education in Twelfth-Century Art and Architecture: Images of Learning in Europe, c.1100–1220* (Woodbridge: Boydell Press, 2012); Laura Cochrane, "Secular Learning and Sacred Purpose in a Carolingian Copy of Boethius's *De institutione arithmetica* (Bamberg, Staatsbibliothek, Msc. Class. 5)," *Peregrinations: Journal of Medieval Art and Architecture* 5 (2015), 1–35.

288 Andrea Speer and Hiltrud Westermann-Angerhausen, "Ein Handbuch mittelalterlicher Kunst? Zu einer relecture der Schedula diversarum atrium," in *Schatzkunst am Aufgang der Romanik*, ed. Christoph Stiegermann and Hiltrud Westermann-Angerhausen (Munich: Hirmer Verlag, 2006), 249–58.

289 Jacqueline Leclerq-Marx, "Signatures iconiques et graphiques d'orfèvres dans le haut Moyen Âge: Une première approche," *Gazette des Beaux-Arts* 137, no. 1 (2001), 1–16, and "La 'signature' au Moyen Âge: Mise en perspective historique," in *Entre la letra y el pincel: el artista medieval; Leyenda, identidad y estatus*, ed. Manuel Castiñeiras González (Ohrid: Circolo Rojo, 2017), 63–76.

290 Caviness, "Artist"; Knoch, "Visionäre Farbigkeit"; Ganz, *Medien der Offenbarung*, 248–54; Kathrin Müller, "Gott ist (k)eine Sphäre: Visualisierungen des Göttlichen in geometrisch-abstrakten Diagrammen des Mittelalters," in *Handbuch der Bildtheologie: Zwischen Zeichen und Präsenz*, ed. Reinhard Hoeps (Paderborn: Ferdinand Schöningh, 2014), 3: 311–55.

291 *Poetria nova*, rev. ed. (Turnhout: Brepols, 2008), 135; Mary Carruthers, *The Craft of Thought: Meditation, Rhetoric, and the Making of Images, 400–1200* (Cambridge: Cambridge University Press, 1998); Paul Binski, "Medieval Invention and its Potencies," *British Art Studies* 6 (2017); *Maestro Mateo en el Museo del Prado* (cat. of an exhib., Madrid), ed. Ramón Yzquierdo Peiró (Madrid: Museo del Prado, 2016); Manuel Castiñeiras González, "Autores homónimos: el doble retrato de 'Mateo' en el Pórtico de la Gloria," in *Letra y el pincel*, 37–52; Prado-Vilar, *Portal*, 84.

292 Beat Brenk, "Originalità e innovazione nell'arte medievale," in *Arti e storia*, vol. 3, 69; Sherry C.M. Lindquist, "Artistic Identity in the Late Middle Ages: Forward," *Gesta* 41 (2002), 1–2; Lawrence Nees, "Godescalc's Career and the Problems of 'Influence,'" in *Under the Influence*, 21–43.

293 Leclerq-Marx, "Signatures iconiques" and "Signature"; Albert Dietl, *Die Sprache der Signatur: Die mittelalterlichen Kunstinschriften Italiens* (Berlin and Munich: Deutscher Kunstverlag, 2009); Horst Bredekamp, *Theorie des Bildakts* (Berlin: Suhrkamp, 2010) (English trans. *Image Acts: A Systematic Approach to Visual Agency* [Berlin/Boston: De Gruyter, 2018]), 45–61; Pierre-Alain Mariaux, "Women in the Making: Early Medieval Signatures and Artists' Portraits (9th–12th century)," in *Reassessing the Roles of Women*, 393–427; Ganz, "Artist-Monk," 21–51; Stefano Riccioni, Giovanni Maria Fara, Nico Stringa, "La 'firma' nell'arte autorialità: Autocoscienza, identità e memoria degli artisti, Introduzione," *Venezia arti* 26 (2017), 7–14.

294 Enrico Castelnuovo, "Introduzione," in *Artifex Bonus*, xvi.

295 Nurith Kenaan-Kedar and Gil Fishhof, "Patrons and Artists of the Sculptural Program of the Church of Saint-André-le-Bas: Meanings and Identities," *Studies in Iconography* 39 (2018), 87–134.

296 Linda Seidel, *Legends in Limestone: Lazarus, Gislebertus, and the Cathedral of Autun* (Chicago: University of Chicago Press, 1999); Bredekamp, *Theorie*, 70–71 (*Image Acts*, 45–46); Kenaan-Kedar and Fishhof, "Patrons," 111.

297 Kumler, "Patron-Function," 317–19.

298 Bredekamp, *Theorie*, 59–89 (*Image Acts*, 37–54); Iafrate discusses a particularly complex Arabic signature on an aquamanile made in Andalusia c. 1000, in "*Opus Salomonis*," 354–60.

299 Gearhart, *Theophilus*; Ganz, "Artist-Monk."

300 For an analysis of Eadwine's transformation of his Utrecht Psalter model, Sánchez Ameijeiras, *Rostros*, 199–207.
301 Daniel Parello, "Fünf Felder eines typologischen Zyklus aus Arnstein," in *Die Glasgemäldesammlung des Freiherrn vom Stein*, ed. Uwe Gast et al. (Münster: Kulturstiftung der Länder u. LWL-Landesmuseum für Kunst und Kulturgeschichte Münster, 2007), 22–39, 92–93; Francesca Dell'Acqua, "Gerlachus: L'arte della vetrata," in *Artifex bonus*, 56–63; Jeffrey Hamburger, "The Hand of God and the Hand of the Scribe: Craft and Collaboration at Arnstein," in *Die Bibliothek des Mittelalters als dynamischer Prozess*, ed. Michael Embach (Wiesbaden: Reichert, 2012), 53–80.
302 Brown, *Holkham Picture Bible*, 30–31.
303 Étienne Anheim, "Un atelier italien à la cour d'Avignon: Matteo Giovannetti, peintre du pape Clément VI (1342–1352)," *Annales Histoire, Sciences Sociales* 73, no. 3 (2018), 703–35.
304 Ganz, "Artist-Monk," 21–23.
305 Iafrate, "Artifex specialis," 31–37.
306 Kenaan-Kedar and Fishhof, "Patrons," 123.
307 *Skies of Parchment/Seas of Ink* and *Signs/Skies*, 97–104, 123–27; Adam S. Cohen, *Signs and Wonders: 100 Haggada Masterpieces* (New Milford: The Toby Press, 2018), 2–7.
308 Mark Rosen, "The Republic at Work: S. Marco's Reliefs of the Venetian Trades," *Art Bulletin* 90, no. 1 (2008), 54–75. A maker's skills often extended well beyond a single artistic activity; Ittai Weinryb, "Material and Making: Artisanal Epistemology at St Gall" in *Tuotilo*, 265–85; Iafrate, "Artifex specialis."
309 Sarit Shalev-Eyni, "Receiving of the Law: Visual Language and Communal Identity in Medieval Ashkenaz," *Gesta* 55, no. 2 (2016), 239–55.
310 Guérin, *Gothic Ivories*, 42–43.
311 Jászai "Christus," 47; Ganz, *Buch-Gewänder*, 192–223.
312 *The Portfolio of Villard de Honnecourt: A New Critical Edition and Color Facsimile with a glossary by Stacey L. Hahn* (Farnham: Ashgate, 2009); Wilhelm Schlink, "War Villard de Honnecourt Analphabet?" in *Pierre, lumière, couleur: Études d'histoire de l'art du Moyen Âge en l'honneur d'Anne Prache*, ed. Fabienne Joubert and Dany Sandron (Paris: PUF, 1999), 213–21; Wirth, *Villard*.
313 Herbert L. Kessler, "'Veteris testamenti typos evangelicae veritati profecisse monstravimus': *Realia* and *Spiritualia* on the Salerno Ivories," in *Salerno Ivories*, 125–31.
314 Weinryb, "Avant-Garde," 736–38.
315 Patrizio Pensabene, "Marmi architettonici della Cappella Palatina tra reimpiego e recupero dell'antico," in *Cappella Palatina*, 1:137–72.
316 Ciro Castelli, Mauro Parri, and Andrea Santacesaria, "Appunti sulla tecnica di costruzione della Croce di Sarzana," in *Pinxit Guillielmus: Il restauro della croce di Sarzana* (Florence: Edifir, 2001), 55–58, and "Il support ligneo della Croce di Rosano: Tecnica e confronti" in *Croce dipinta*, 105–10.
317 Rheinhold, "Vesperbild."
318 Paul Binski, *Gothic Wonder: Art, Artifice and the Decorated Style 1290–1350* (New Haven and London: Yale University Press, 2014), 133–34.
319 Such collective operations are pictured in a mid-twelfth-century manuscript produced in Michaelsberg Abbey c. 1150 (Bamberg, Staatsbibliothek, Msc. Patr. 5, fol. 1ᵛ). A Benedictine monk holds a pot in one hand and a brush in the other, painting a sculpture and, in eight rondels on the frame, the steps needed to prepare the illustrated book are shown: scraping and stretching the animal skin, preparing quills, transcribing the text, and drawing on a wax tablet; Christopher Clarkson, "Some Representations of the Book and Book-Making from the Earliest Codex Forms to Jost Amman," in *The Bible as Book: The Manuscript Tradition*, ed. J.L. Sharpe III and K. van Kampen (New Castle: Oak Knoll Press, 2002), 197–203; Rudy, *Postcards*, 41–43. Also:

Barbara Newman, "Contemplating the Trinity: Text, Image, and the Origins of the Rothschild Canticles," *Gesta* 52, no. 2 (2013), 133–59.
320 Alain Erlande-Brandenburg, *La révolution gothique* (Paris: Picard, 2012).
321 Romano, *Duecento*, 77–87; Julian Gardner, *The Roman Crucible: The Artistic Patronage of the Papacy 1198–1304* (Munich: Hirmer Verlag, 2013), 219–24.
322 Binski, "Cosmati."
323 Frank Martin, *Die Glasmalereien von San Francesco in Assisi: Entstehung und Entwicklung einer Gattung in Italien* (Regensburg: Schnell & Steiner, 1997); Serena Romano, *La basilica di San Francesco ad Assisi: Pittori, botteghe, strategie narrative* (Rome: Viella, 2001); Donal Cooper and Janet Robson, *The Making of Assisi: The Pope, the Franciscans and the Painting of the Basilica* (New Haven and London: Yale University Press, 2013).
324 King, "Rethinking."
325 Weinryb, "Avant-Garde," 775–80.
326 David Jacoby, "The Movement of Silk and Silk Textiles: Italy and the Mediterranean in the 12th–14th Centuries," in *Textiles and Wealth*, 18–29.
327 Jacoby, "Movement," 26–27.
328 Francis Ames-Lewis, *Tuscan Marble Carving 1250–1350* (Aldershot: Ashgate, 1997); James R. Farr, *Artisans in Europe, 1300–1914* (Cambridge: Cambridge University Press, 2000); Assaf Pinkus, *Workshops and Patrons of St. Theobald in Thann* (Münster: Waxmann, 2006), 28–31 et passim.
329 Markus Hörsch, "Zur bildlichen Ausstattung von Zisterzienserkreuzgängen des 13. und 14. Jahrhunderts," in *Der Mittelalterliche Kreuzgang: Achitektur, Funktion und Programm*, ed. Peter Klein (Regensburg: Schnell & Steiner, 2004), 241–68; Josep Baluja Barreiro and Jesús M. Oliver Salas, *Els capitells del claustre de Santes Creus* (Valls: Cossetánia Ediciones, 2008); Binksi, *Gothic Wonder*, 266–72.
330 Éric Palazzo, *Peindre c'est prier: Anthropologie de la prière chrétienne* (Paris: Éditions du Cerf, 2016), 134–36.
331 Enrico Castelnuovo, "Dedalo e Beseleel," in *Medioevo: Il tempo degli antichi*, ed. Arturo Carlo Quintavalle (Milan: Electa, 2006), 65–68; Gearhart, *Theophilus*, 84–86.
332 Ivan Foletti, "La firma artistica, i miti vasariani e *Wolvinius magister phaber*," *Venezia Arti* 26 (2017), 35–48; *Oggetti*, 145–46; Ganz, "Artist-Monk," 42–43.
333 Michael Brandt, "Made in Hildesheim? Überlegungen zur Niedersächsischen Bronzekunst des 12. Jahrhunderts," in *Drachenlandung*, 45–71.
334 A bronze vessel in the Louvre engraved "opus Solomonis"; Iafrate, "Opus Salomanis." Solomon's knot also became an inspiration for intricate ornament; Allegra Iafrate, *The Long Life of Magical Objects. A Study of the Solomonic Tradition* (University Park, PA: The Pennsylvania State University, 2019), 80–108.
335 Kristin Böse, "Spürbar und unvergänglich: Zur Visualität, Ikonologie und Medialität von Textilien und textile Reliquiaren im mittelalterlichen Reliquienkult," *Marburger Jahrbuch für Kunstwissenschaft* 33 (2006), 7–27; Fiona Griffiths, "'Like the Sister of Aaron': Medieval Religious Women and Liturgical Textiles," in *Vita regularis: Ordungen und Deutungen religiosen Lebens in Mittelalter*, ed. Gert Melville and Anne Müller (Zurich, 2011); Miller, *Clothing*.
336 For example, on a painted chest in Halberstadt (Domschatz); Roland Möller, "Zur Maltechnike des bemalten romanischen Schrankes aus der Liebfrauenkirche zu Halberstadt im Vergleich mit zeitgenössischen Quellenschriften," in *Das Aschaffenburger Tafelbild: Studien zur Tafelmalerei des 13. Jahrhunderts*, ed. Erwin Emmerling and Cornelia Ringer (Munich: Lipp, 1997), 135–51; Johannes Tripps, "Der Schrank aus dem Marienstift zu Halberstadt: Überlegungen zur Form und Funktion" (2011), http://archiv.ub.uni-heidelberg.de/artdok/volltexte/2012/1694/; Gertsman, *Worlds Within*, 23–24.

337 Joseph T. Lienhard, "St. Joseph in Early Christianity: Devotion and Theology," in *Joseph of Nazareth: Through the Centuries*, ed. Joseph F. Chorpenning (Philadelphia: St. Joseph's University, 2011), 15–46.

338 Michele Bacci, *Il pennello dell'Evangelista: Storia delle immagini sacre attribuite a san Luca* (Pisa: Gisem, 1998); Kruse, *Wozu Menschen malen*, 225–68; Anna Eörsi, "The Incarnation of the Word and the Form: Some Thoughts about St Luke the Painter, and about Some Painters of St Luke," *Acta Historiae Artium* 44, no. 1–4 (2003), 47–57.

339 *Magister Theodoricus Court Painter to Emperor Charles IV: The Pictorial Decoration of the Shrines at Karlštein Castle*, ed. Jiří Fajt (Prague: National Gallery, 1998); Eörsi, "Incarnation"; Kruse, *Wozu Menschen malen*, 234–36; Michele Bacci, "San Luca come Petrarca: visioni dell'artista-letterato nell'Evangeliario di Giovanni da Opava (1368)," in *Letra y Pincel*, 53–61; Marco Petoletti, "'Ut patenter omnibus innotescat': Il trattato di Nicola Maniacutia (Sec. XII) sull'immagine archeroptia del Laterano," in *Auctor et Auctoritas in Latinis Medii Aevi Litteris/Author and Authorship in Medieval Latin Literature*, ed. Edouardo d'Angelo and Jan Ziolkowski (Florence: SISMEL, 2014), 847–64; Herbert L. Kessler, "*Fenestra obliqua*: Art and Peter of Limoges's Modes of Seeing," in *Optics, Ethics, and Art in the Thirteenth and Fourteenth Centuries: Looking into Peter of Limoges's Moral Treatise on the Eye*, ed. Herbert L. Kessler and Richard G. Newhauser (Toronto: Pontifical Institute for Mediaeval Studies, 2018), 139–58.

340 Michele Bacci, "*Kathreptis*, o la Veronica della Vergine," *Iconographica* 3 (2004), 11–37; Kessler, "Paradigms"; Marc Sureda I Jubany, "From Holy Images to Liturgical Devises: Models, Objects and Rituals around the Veronicae of Christ and Mary in the Crown of Aragon (1300–1500)," in *European Fortune*, 194–217.

341 Bacci, *Pennello*, 235–36, 278–79 et passim; Leone, *Icone di Roma*, 1:59–60.

342 Michele Camillo Ferrari, "Il *Volto Santo* di Lucca," in *Il volto di Cristo*, 253–75; Celia Chazelle, "An Exemplum of Humility: The Crucifixion Image in the Drogo Sacramentary," in *Reading Medieval Images: The Art Historian and the Object*, ed. Elizabeth Sears and Thelma Thomas (Ann Arbor: University of Michigan Press, 2002), 27–35; Michele Bacci, "Nicodemo e il Volto Santo," in *Volto Santo*, 15–37.

343 Ferrari, *Volto Santo*; Maetzke, "Il volto santo di Sansepolcro," 193–207.

344 Mildred Budny, "Deciphering the Art of Interlace," in *From Ireland Coming*, ed. Colum Hourihane (Princeton: Department of Art and Archeology, 2001), 183–210; Adam S. Cohen, "Magnificence in Miniature: The Case of Early Medieval Manuscripts," in *Magnificence and the Sublime*, 79–101; Tina Bawden, "Describing Spaces: Topologies of Interlace in the St Gall Gospels," in *Sacred Scripture/Sacred Space*, 11–36.

345 *Volto di Cristo*, 194–95; Wolf, *Schleier und Spiegel*, 141–42; Alexa Sand, *Vision, Devotion, and Self Representation in Late Medieval Art* (New York: Cambridge University Press, 2014), 77–79.

346 *Volto di Cristo*, 169–71; Kessler, "Literary Warp and Artistic Weft"; Nigel Morgan, "'Veronica' Images and the Office of the Holy Face in Thirteenth-Century England," in *European Fortune*, 84–99.

347 Generally: *Corpus della pittura medievale* and *La committenza artistica dei papi a Roma nel Medioevo*, ed. Mario d'Onofio (Rome: Viella, 2016).

348 Noble, *Images*, 216–18 et passim. Paschal I also promulgated new arguments to support images and was an important patron of mosaics and church objects; Alia Englen, "La difesa delle immagini intrapresa dalla chiesa di Roma nel IX secolo," in *Caelius I: Santa Maria in Domnica, San Tommaso in Formis e il Clivus Scauri* (Rome: "L'Erma" di Bretschneider, 2003), 257–84; Erik Thunø, *Image and Relic: Mediating the Sacred in Early Medieval Rome* (Rome: "L'Erma" di Bretschneider, 2002); *Apse Mosaic*, 52–55; Francesca Dell'Acqua, "Iconophilia in Italy, c. 680–880: A European Project and Its Method,"

IKON 11 (2018), 31–46; *Iconophilia: Religion, Politics, and Sacred Images in Italy c. 680–880* (Birmingham: Byzantine and Ottoman Studies, forthcoming).

349 Robert Suckale, *Das mittelalterliche Bild als Zeitzeuge* (Berlin: Lukas Verlag, 2002), 12–122; *Roma e la Riforma gregoriana*; Stefano Riccioni, "Le Arti a Roma al tempo di Leone IX," in *La reliquia del sangue di Cristo: Mantova, l'Italia e L'Europa al tempo di Leone IX*, ed. Glauco Maria Cantarella and Arturo Calzona (Verona: Scripta edizioni, 2012), 341–58; Lucinia Speciale, "*Un art dirigé*: vent'anni dopo," in *Reliquia del sangue*, 409–20.

350 Serena Romano, *Riforma e tradizione* (*Corpus della pittura medievale a Roma*, vol. 4) (Milan: Jaca Book, 2006).

351 Cristiana Filippini, "Functions of Pictorial Narratives and Liturgical Spaces: The Eleventh-Century Frescoes of the Titular Saint in the Basilica of San Clemente in Rome," in *Shaping Sacred Space and Institutional Identity in Romanesque Mural Painting: Essays in Honour of Otto Demus*, ed. Thomas E.A. Dale and John Mitchell (London: Pindar, 2004), 122–38; Romano, *Riforma*, 129–50; *Le bibbie atlantiche: Il libro delle Scritture tra monumentalità e rappresentazione* (cat. of an exhib., Montecassino and Florence), ed. Marlena Maniaci and Giulia Orofino (Rome: Ministero per i Beni Culturali, 2000); Giulia Orofino, "La decorazione delle Bibbie atlantiche tra Lazio e Toscana nella prima metà del XII secolo," in *Roma e la Riforma gregoriana*, 357–79; Lila Yawn, "The Italian Giant Bibles" in *Practice of the Bible in the Middle Ages: Production, Reception, and Performance in Western Christianity*, ed. Susan Boynton and Diane J. Reilly (New York: Columbia University Press, 2011), 126–56; Maria Alessandra Bilotta, "La réforme grégorienne et ses programmes iconographiques: Le cas des peintures murales de l'ancien palais des papes du Latran à Rome et leur rapport avec l'illustration des bibles atlantiques," in *Les Bibles Atlantiques: Le manuscrit biblique à l'époque de la réforme ecclésiastique du XIe siècle* (Acts of a conference, Geneva 2010), ed. Nadia Togni (Florence: SISMEL, 2016), 103–27.

352 Christoph Egger, "Papst Innocenz III. und die Veronica: Geschichte, Theologie, Liturgie und Seelsorge," in *The Holy Face and the Paradox*, 181–203; Ann Van Dijk, "The Veronica, the *Vultus Christi* and the Veneration of Icons in Medieval Rome," in *Old Saint Peter's, Rome*, ed. Rosamond McKitterick et al. (Cambridge: Cambridge University Press, 2013), 229–56; Thunø, *Apse Mosaic*, 35–36; Rebecca Rist, "Innocent III and the Roman Veronica: Papal PR or Eucharistic Icon?," in *European Fortune*, 114–25.

353 *English Medieval Embroidery*, 144–46; Julian Gardner, "Papal Exactions, Royal Gifts and Fashionable Cardinals: The Curial Clientele for Opus Anglicanum c. 1300–70," in *The Age of Opus Anglicanum: A Symposium*, ed. Michael A. Michael (Turnout: Brepols, 2016), 22–35.

354 Alessandro Tomei, "Dal documento al monumento: Le lettere di Niccolò IV per Santa Maria Maggiore," *Studi medievali e moderni* 1 (1997), 73–92; Valentino Pace, "Per Jacopo Torriti, frate, architetto, e 'pictor,'" in Valentino Pace, *Arte a Roma nel Medioevo: Committenza, ideologia e cultura figurative in monumenti and libri* (Naples: Liguori Editore, 2000), 399–414; Gardner, *Roman Crucible*, 260–67; Thunø, *Apse Mosaic*, 37–38; Serena Romano, *Apogeo e fine del Medioevo 1288–1431* (Corpus della pittura medievale a Roma 312–1431, vol. 6) (Milan: Jaca Book, 2018), 116–27.

355 Serena Romano, *La O di Giotto* (Milan: Electa, 2008), 67.

356 *Bonifacio VIII e il suo tempo: Anno 1300 il primo giubileo*, ed. Marina Righetti Tosti-Croce (Milan: Electa, 2000); Romano, *Apogeo*, 208–12.

357 Étienne Anheim, "La 'Chambre du cerf': Image, savoir et nature à Avignon au milieu du XIVe siècle," in *I saperi nelle corti*, ed. Mattia Cavagna (Florence, Sismel-Edizioni del Galluzzo, 2008), 57–124, and "Atelier italien"; Cathleen A. Fleck, The *Clement Bible at the Medieval Courts of Naples and Avignon: A Story of Papal Power, Royal Prestige, and Patronage* (Farnham: Ashgate, 2010); Claudia Bolgia, "Images in the City: Presence, Absence and Legitimacy in Rome in the First Half of the 14th Century," in *Images and Words in Exile:*

Avignon and Italy during the First Half of the 14th Century, ed. Elisa Brilli et al. (Florence: SISMEL, 2015), 381–401.
358 *Prayers and Portraits*, 50–55; Kessler, "Paradigms."
359 Éric Palazzo, *L'évêque et son image: L'illustration du Pontifical au Moyen Âge* (Turnhout: Brepols, 1999), 55–71; Pierre-Alain Mariaux, "The Bishop as Artist? The Eucharist and Image Theory around the Millennium," in *The Bishop: Power and Piety at the First Millennium*, ed. Sean J. Gilsdorf (Münster: LIT-Verlag, 2004), 155–67; *L'évêque, l'image, et la mort: Identité et mémoire au Moyen Âge*, ed. Nicolas Bock et al. (Rome: Viella, 2014).
360 Freeman and Meyvaert, "Theodulf's Apse Mosaic"; Herbert L. Kessler, "The Place of Rome between Judea and Francia in Early Medieval Art," in *Roma fra Oriente e Occidente* (XLIX Settimana internazionale di studi [Spoleto, 2002]) (Spoleto: CISAM, 2003) 2: 695–718; Jean-Pierre Caillet, *L'art carolingien* (Paris: Flammarion, 2005), 28–31; Gillian V. Mackie, "Theodulf of Orléans and the Ark of the Covenant: a New Allegorical Interpretation at Germigny-des-Prés," *Racar* 32, no. 1/2 (2007), 45–58; Ivan Foletti, "Germigny-des-Prés, il Santo Sepolcro e la Gerusalemme celeste," *Convivium* 1 (2014), 32–49.
361 Lawrence Nees, "Problems of Form and Function in Early Medieval Illustrated Bibles from Northwest Europe," in *Imaging the Early Medieval Bible*, ed. John Williams (University Park: The Pennsylvania University Press, 1999), 9–59; Celia Chazelle, "Archbishops Ebo and Hincmar of Reims and the Utrecht Psalter," *Speculum* 72, no. 4 (1997), 1055–77, and *Crucified God*, 241–54.
362 Mariëlle Hageman, "Between the Imperial and the Sacred: Gesture of Coronation in Carolingian and Ottonian Images," in *New Approaches to Medieval Communication*, ed. Marco Mostert (Turnhout: Brepols, 1997), 127–63; Adam Cohen and Anne Derbes, "Bernward and Eve at Hildesheim," *Gesta* 40 (2001), 19–38; Harvey Stahl, "Eve's Reach: A Note on Dramatic Elements in the Hildesheim Doors," in *Reading Medieval Images*, 162–75; Jennifer P. Kingsley, *The Bernward Gospels: Art, Memory, and the Episcopate in Medieval Germany* (University Park: University of Pennsylvania State Press, 2014); Weinryb, *Bronze Object*, 30–33, and "Avant-Garde"; Michael Brandt, "Mentem et oculos pascere," *Niederdeutsche Beiträge zur Kunstgeschichte*, n.s. 2 (2017), 9–26; Marchesin, *L'arbre*; Kristina Krüger, "St Michael's at Hildesheim: Scripture Networks and the Perception of Saced Space," in *Sacred Scripture/Sacred Space*, 109–36.
363 Marta Serrano and Gerardo Boto Varela, "Memoria per corporis sensum combibit anima: Relato histórico en la catedral de Tarragona; presencia y secuencia de escenarios de memorias arzobispales," *Codex Aqvilarensis* 34 (2018), 115–42.
364 *De altera vita*, ed. E. Falque Rey, CCCM 74A (Turnhout: Brepols, 2009); Patrick Henriet, "Sanctissima patria, point et thèmes communs aux trois oeuvres de Lucas de Tuy," *Cahiers de Linguistique Hispanique Médiévale* 24 (2001), 249–78; Jean-Marie Sansterre and Patrick Henriet, "De l'inanimis image à l'omagem mui bella: Méfiance à l'égard des images et essor de leur culte dans l'espagne médiévale (VIIe–XIIIe siècle)," *Edad Media* 10 (2009), 37–92.
365 Rocío Sánchez Ameijeiras, "*Monumenta* and *Memoria*: The 13th Century Episcopal Pantheon of León Cathedral," in *Memory and the Medieval Tomb*, ed. Elizabeth Valdez de Álamo and Carol Pendergast (Farnham: Ashgate, 2000), 269–300, and *Rostros*, 108; Alicia Miguélez Cavero, "Embodied Emotions: Action, Reaction and Interaction in León Cathedral," in *L'Église, lieux de performances*, 283–300. Also: Anísio Miguel de Sousa Saraiva, Carla Varela Fenandes, and Maria do Rosário Barbosa Morujão, "Mémoire au-delà de la mort: Les évêques portugais et leurs monuments funéraires au Moyen Âge," in *L'évêque*, 141–89.
366 Wolfgang Christian Schneider, "Bild und Text in der Silversterkapelle des päpstlichen Herrschaftsbaus von SS. Quattro Coronati in Rom," in *Sacred Scripture/Sacred Space*, 287–322.

367 Andreina Draghi, *Gli affreschi dell'aula gotica nel monastero del Santi Coronati: Una storia ritrovata* (Milan: Skira, 2006); Romano, *Duecento*, 136–76; Marius Hauknes, "The Painting of Knowledge in Thirteenth-Century Rome *Gesta* 55, no. 1 (2016), 19–47; Dieter Blume, "Die Aula Gotica von Santi Quattro Coronati-Kosmos, Antike und Tugenden im Selbstverständnis der Kurie," in *Die Päpste und Rom zwischen Spätantike und Mittelalter*, ed. Norbert Zimmermann et al. (Regensburg: Schnell & Steiner, 2017), 213–33. Stefano Conti seems to have summoned painters from his ancestral town of Anagni; *Un universo di simboli: Gli affreschi della cripta nella cattedrale di Anagni*, ed. Gioacchino Giammaria (Rome: Viella, 2001); Lorenzo Cappelletti, *Gli affreschi della cripta anagnina: Iconologia* (Rome: Editrice della Pontificia Università Gregoriana, 2002).

368 *Ludwig der Bayer*, 318–19.

369 Gearhart, *Theophilus*, 83–88.

370 Hamburger, *Nuns*, 95.

371 *Desiderio di Montecassino e l'arte della Riforma Gregoriana*, ed. Faustino Avagliano (Montecassino: Pubblicazioni Cassinesi, 1997); *Il monaco, il libro, la biblioteca*, ed. Oronzo Pecere (Cassino: Università degli Studi Cassino, 2003); *Roma e la Riforma gregoriana*; *Rome Re-imagined*, ed. Louis Hamilton and Stefano Riccioni, *Medieval Encounters* 17 (2011).

372 Valentino Pace, "Committenza Benedittina a Roma: Il caso di San Paolo fuori le mura nel XIII secolo," in *Arte a Roma*, 125–36.

373 Daniel Russo, "La réforme de l'église et le moment figuratif dans l'art religieux (XIe-XIIe siècles)," *Bulletin du Centre d'Etudes Médiévales d'Auxerre* 2 (2008), 1–11.

374 Jean-Claude Bonne, "'Concordia discors temporum': Le temps dans les peintures murales de Berzé-la-Ville," in *Metamorphosen der Zeit*, ed. Éric Alliez et al. (Munich 1999), 145–175; Russo, "Espace peint"; Lapina, "Mural Paintings"; Juliette Rollier-Hanselmann, "La traditio legis de Berzé-la-Ville entre tradition et innovation," *Hortus Artium Medievalium* 17 (2011), 275–87; Armin F. Bergmeier, "The *Traditio Legis* in Late Antiquity and Its Afterlives in the Middle Ages," *Gesta* 56, no. 1 (2017), 27–52.

375 Julie Enckell Julliard, *Au seuil du salut: Les décor peints de l'avant-nef de Farfa en Sabine* (Rome: Viella, 2008).

376 *Oliba Episcopus: Millenari d'Oliba, bisbe de Vic* (cat. of an exhib., Vic), ed. Marc Sureda i Jubany (Vic: Museu episcopal, 2018).

377 Martin Büchsel, *Die Geburt der Gotik: Abt Sugers Konzept für die Abteikirche Saint-Denis* (Freiburg im Breisgau: Rombach Verlag, 1997); Kessler, *Spiritual Seeing*, 190–204; *Abt Suger von Saint-Denis: Ausgewählte Schriften: Ordinatio, De consecratione, De Administratione*, ed. Andreas Speer and Günter Binding (Darmstadt: Wissenschaftliche Buchgesellschaft, 2000); *L'abbé Suger, le manifeste gothique de Saint-Denis et la pensée victorine: Actes du Colloque organisé à la Fondation Singer-Polignac* (Paris) (Turnhout: Brepols, 2001); Conrad Rudolph, "Inventing the Gothic Portal: Suger, Hugh of Saint Victor, and the Construction of a New Public Art at Saint-Denis," *Art History* 33, no. 4 (2010), 568–95, "Inventing the Exegetical Stained-Glass Window: Suger, Hugh, and a New Elite Art," *Art Bulletin* 93, no. 4 (2011), 399–422, and *The Mystic Ark: Hugh of Saint Victor, Art, and Thought in the Twelfth Century* (New York: Cambridge University Press, 2014), 365–74.

378 Carruthers, *Craft of Thought*, 84–87; *The Experience of Beauty*, 147–40; Diane J. Reilly, *The Cistercian Reform and the Art of the Book in Twelfth-Century France* (Amsterdam: Amsterdam University Press, 2018).

379 Hamburger, *Nuns*, 186–87.

380 Cohen, *Uta Codex*, 183–90.

381 Kristine Haney, *The St. Albans Psalter: An Anglo-Norman Song of Faith* (New York: Peter Lang Publishing, 2002); Katherine Gerry, "The Alexis Quire and the Cult of Saints at St Albans," *Historical Research* 82 (2009), 593–612, and "The Psalmist and

the Saint: David, Alexis, and the Construction of Meaning in a Twelfth-Century Composite Manuscript," in *St. Albans and the Markyate Psalter: Seeing and Reading in Twelfth-century England*, ed. Kristen Collins and Matthew Fisher (Kalamazoo: Medieval Institute Publications, 2017), 116–32.
382 Joyner, *Hortus deliciarum*, 17–26 et passim.
383 Ganz, "Artist-Monk."
384 Dieter von der Nahmer, "Sünde: Zur Chronik Thietmars von Merseburg und zu einigen Werken Bernwards von Hildesheim," *Studi Medievali*, ser. 3, 54 (2013), 541–628.
385 Dell'Acqua, *Iconophilia*.
386 Dutton and Kessler, *Poetry and Paintings*.
387 Carruthers, *Craft of Thought*, 243–46 et passim; Rudolph, *Mystic Ark*.
388 Peter Kern, "Das Bildprogramm der Doppelkirche von Schwarzrheindorf, die Lehre vom vierfachen Schriftsinn und die 'memoria' des Stifters Arnold von Wied," *Deutsche Vierteljahrsschrift* 77 (2003), 353–79.
389 Rudolph, "Exegetical Stained-Glass Window."
390 T.A. Heslop, "St Anselm, Church Reform, and the Politics of Art," *Anglo-Norman Studies* 33 (2011), 103–36.
391 Dominique Donadieu-Rigaut, *Penser en images les orders religieux (XIIe–XVe)* (Paris: Éditions Arguments, 2005); Victor M. Schmidt, *Painted Piety: Panel Paintings for Personal Devotion in Tuscany 1250–1400* (Florence: Centro D, 2005), 218–29; Anne Dunlop, "Introduction: The Augustinians, the Mendicant Orders, and Early Renaissance Art," in *Art and the Augustinian Order in Early Renaissance Italy*, ed. Louise Bourdua and Anne Dunlop (Farnham: Ashgate, 2007), 1–15.
392 Louise Bourdua, *The Franciscans and Art Patronage in Late Medieval Italy* (Cambridge: Cambridge University Press, 2004); Rosalind B. Brooke, *The Image of St Francis: Responses to Sainthood in the Thirteenth Century* (Cambridge: Cambridge University Press, 2006); *Beyond the Text and the Construction of Religion: Franciscan Art*, ed. Xavier Schubert and Oleg Bychlov (Saint Bonaventure, NY: Franciscan Institute, 2012); Roberto Rusconi, "Francesco, i frati e le immagini," in *Le immagini del francescanesimo* (Spoleto: Centro italiano di Studi sull'alto Medioevo, 2009), 5–29; *L'arte di Francesco: Capolavori d'arte italiana e terre d'Asia dal XIII al XV secolo* (Florence: Giunti, 2015).
393 Cooper and Robson, *Assisi*, 17–33; Gardner, *Giotto*, 115; Donal Cooper, "Gothic Art & the Friars in Late Medieval Croatia 1213–1480," in *Croatia: Aspects of Art, Architecture and Cultural Heritage*, ed. Jadranka Beresford-Peirce (London: Frances Lincoln, 2009), 76–97.
394 Holly Flora, *The Devout Belief of the Imagination: The Paris Meditationes vitae Christi and Female Franciscan Spirituality in Trecento Italy* (Turnhout: Brepols, 2009) and *Cimabue*.
395 Cannon, *Religious Poverty*; Donal Cooper, "Preaching Amidst Pictures: Visual Contexts for Sermons in Late Medieval Tuscany," in *Optics, Ethics*, 31–45.
396 Jeffrey Hamburger, "*Haec Figura demonstrat*: Diagrams in an Early Thirteenth Century Copy of Lothar de Segni's *De missarum mysteriis*," *Wiener Jahrbuch für Kunstgeschichte* 58 (2009), 7–78, revised and translated as *Hrabanus redivivus*: Berthold of Nuremberg's Marian Supplement to *In honorem sanctae crucis*," in *Diagramm und Text Diagrammatische Strukturen und die Dynamisierung von Wissen und Erfahrung*, ed. Eckart Conrad Lutz et al. (Wiesbaden: Reichert Verlag, 2014), 175–204.
397 Brown, *Holkham Picture Bible*, 16–17, 30–31.
398 Michael Camille, *Mirror in Parchment: The Luttrell Psalter and the Making of Medieval England* (London: Reaktion Books, 1998).
399 Kirstin Noreen, "Sacred Memory and Confraternal Space: The Insignia of the Confraternity of the Santissimo Salvatore (Rome)," in *Roma Felix—Formation and Reflections of Medieval Rome*, ed. Éamonn Ó Carragáin and Carol Neuman de Vegvar (Aldershot: Ashgate, 2007), 159–87.

400 *La Madonna di Bernardo Daddi negli "horti" di San Michele*, ed. Licia Bertani and Muriel Vervat (Florence: Sillabe, 2000); Holmes, *Miraculous Image*, 69–74; Thomas Golsenne, "Les images qui marchent: performance et anthropologie des objets figuratifs," in *Les images dans l'occident medieval*, ed. Jérôme Baschet and Pierre-Olivier Dittmar (Turnout: Brepols, 2015), 179–92.

401 Jacques Le Goff et al., *Le sacre royal à l'époque de Saint Louis* (Paris: Gallimard, 2001).

402 *799, Kunst und Kultur der Karolingerzeit: Karl der Große und Papst Leo III. in Paderborn*, ed. Christoph Stiegemann and Matthias Wemhoff (cat. of an exhib., Paderborn) (Mainz: Philipp von Zabern, 1999); *Trésors carolingiens: Livres manuscrits de Charlemagne à Charles le Chauve*, ed. Marie-Pierre Lafitte and Charlotte Denoël (cat. of an exhib., Paris) (Paris: Bibliothèque nationale de France, 2007); Rainer Kahsnitz, "Die Elfenbeinskulpturen der Adagruppe: Hundert Jahre nach Adolph Goldschmidt," *Zeitschrift des Deutschen Vereins für Kunstwissenschaft* 64 (2010), 9–170; *Karl der Grosse/Charlemagne: Orte der Macht*, ed. Frank Pohle (cat. of an exhib., Aachen) (Dresden: Sandstein Verlag, 2014).

403 *Charlemagne's Courtier: The Complete Einhard*, ed. Paul E. Dutton (Peterborough: Broadview Press, 1998).

404 Fabrizio Crivello, "Die Handschrift und ihr Schmuck," in *Das Krönungsevangeliar des Heiligen Römischen Reiches*, Wien, Kunsthistorisches Museum, Weltliche Schatzkammer, Inv.-Nr. XIII 18 (Gütersloh and Munich: Faksimile Verlag, 2013), 23–85.

405 Dutton and Kessler, *Poetry and Paintings*.

406 Hermann Fillitz, "Die Geschichte der Handschrift," in *Krönungsevangeliar*, 13–22.

407 Nathania Girardin, "Charles le Chauve et les objets 'de Charlemagne,'" in *Charlemagne et les objects*, 115–34; Philippe Cordez, "Vers un catalogue raisonné des 'objets légendaires' de Charlemagne: Le cas de Conques (XIe-XIIe siecles)," in *Charlemagne et les objets*, 135–67.

408 Max Kerner, "Mythos Karl: Wie die Nachwelt Karl den Großen sieht," in *Orte der Macht*, 400–07; Viola Belghaus, "*Intravimus ergo ad Karolum*—Grab, Reliquien und Reliquiare Karls des Großen," in *Charlemagne et les objets*, 169–208.

409 William Tronzo, *The Cultures of His Kingdom: Roger II and the Cappella Palatina in Palermo* (Princeton: Princeton University Press, 1997); *Petrarch's Two Gardens: Landscape and the Image of Movement* (New York: Italica Press, 2014), 24–67; Beat Brenk, "L'importanza e la funzione della Cappella Palatina di Palermo nella storia dell'arte," in *Cappella Palatina* 1:27–78.

410 Le Goff et al., *Sacre royal*.

411 *Magister Theodoric*, 126.

412 *La Sainte-Chapelle de Bourges: Une fondation disparue de Jean de France, duc de Berry* (cat. of an exhibition, Bourges), ed. Béatrice de Chancel-Bardelot and Clémence Raynaud (Paris: Somogy, 2004); Clémence Raynaud, "*Ad instar capelle regie parisiensis*: la Saint-Chapelle de Bourges, le grand dessein du duc de Berry," *Bulletin monumental* 162, no. 4 (2004), 289–302.

413 Elizabeth Parker, "The Gift of the Cross in the New Minster *Liber Vitae*," in *Reading Medieval Images*, 176–86.

414 *Matilde e il tesoro dei Canossa, tra castelli, monasteri e città* (cat. of an exhib, Reggio Emilia), ed. Arturo Calzona (Cinisello Balsamo: Silvana Editoriale, 2008); Dorothy Glass, *The Sculpture of Reform in North Italy, ca. 1095–1130: History and Patronage of Romanesque Facades* (Farnham: Ashgate, 2010), 26–33; Arturo Quintavalle, "Matilda and the Cities of the Gregorian Reform," in *Romanesque Patrons and Processes*, 15–29.

415 Therese Martin, "The Art of a Reigning Queen as Dynastic Propaganda in Twelfth-Century Spain," *Speculum* 80, no. 4 (2005), 1134–71, and *Queen as King: Politics and*

Architectural Propaganda in Twelfth-Century Spain (Leiden: Brill, 2006), 1–30, 95–135, 146–53, 177–200; Pick, *Her Father's Daughter* 199–204.

416 Jaroslav Folda, "Melisende of Jerusalem: Queen and Patron of Art and Architecture in the Crusader Kingdom," in *Reassessing the Roles of Women*, 465–67; Helen A. Gaudette, "The Spending Power of a Crusader Queen: Melisende of Jerusalem," in *Women and Wealth in Late Medieval Europe*, ed. Theresa Earenfight (New York: Palgrave, 2010), 135–48; Margaret Tranovich, *Melisende of Jerusalem: The World of a Forgotten Crusader Queen* (London: East & West, 2011), 115–38; Avital Heyman, "Un reto para el 'taller de Melisenda': la decoración de Santa María en el Valle de Josafat y el proyecto monumental de la Jerusalén cruzada," in *Entre la letra y el pincel*, 263–78, and "The Deēsis of the Valley of Jehoshaphat: Melisende and the Monumental Sacred Deēsis Topography of Crusader Jerusalem," *Israel Museum Studies* (forthcoming); Armen Kazaryan, "The Armenian Cathedral of Saints James in Jerusalem: Melisende and the Question of Exchange between East and West," in *Romanesque Patrons and Processes*, 83–92.

417 Alyce A. Jordan, "Stained Glass and the Liturgy: Performing Sacral Kingship in Capetian France," in *Objects, Images*, 274–97.

418 Guérin, *Gothic Ivories*, 50–51.

419 Elizabeth Valdez del Álamo, "Leonor Plantagenet: Reina y Mecenas," in *Alfonso VIII y Leonor de Inglaterra: Confluencias artísticas en el entorno de 1200*, ed. Marta Poza Yagüe and Diana Olivares (Madrid: Ediciones Complutense, 2017), 249–68.

420 Sabine Berger, "Chute et Réhabilitation (1315–1475): La mémoire d'Enguerran de Marigny, de l'église des Chartreux de Vauvert à la collégiale de Notre Dame à Écouis," *Art sacré* 32 (2017), 171–79; Binski, "Rhetorical Occasions."

421 Jitske Jasperse, "Matilda, Leonor and Joanna: the Plantagenet Sisters and the Display of Dynastic Connections through Material Culture," *Journal of Medieval History* 43 (2017), 523–47.

422 Eva Schlotheuber, "*Misere mei deus:* Stifter und Stifterinnen in Westfalen," in *Goldene Pracht*, 50–57.

423 Annemarie Weyl Carr, "Images. Expressions of Faith and Power," in *Byzantium: Faith and Power*, 174–75; Jean-Marie Sansterre, "Deux témoignages sur la Sainte Face de Laon au XIIIe siècle," *Revue belge de philologie et d'histoire* 86 (2008), 273–85.

424 Lowden, *Bibles Moralisées*, 1:132–34.

425 Julian Gardner, "Torriti's Birds," in *Medioevo: i modelli* (acts of a congress, Parma), ed. Arturo Carlo Quintavalle (Milan: Electa, 2002), 605–14.

426 Suckale, *Mittelalterliche Bild*; Romano, *Riforma*, 45–55.

427 Kenaan-Kedar and Fishhof, "Patrons," 102–08.

428 Maria Rosaria Marchionibus, "La croce-reliquia trovata all'interno della Croce di Rosano," in *Croce dipinta*, 89–97.

429 Pinkus, *Workshops*.

430 Dutton and Kessler, *Poetry and Paintings*, 71–87.

431 Elizabeth Carson Pastan and Steven D. White, *The Bayeux Tapestry and its Contexts: A Reassessment* (Woodbridge: Boydell Press, 2014); Xavier Barral I Altet, *En souvenir du roi Guillaume: La broderie de Bayeux* (Paris: Éditions du Cerf, 2016).

432 Barral I Altet, *Souvenir*, 369.

433 *The Book of Kings: Art, War, and the Morgan Library's Medieval Picture Bible* (cat. of an exhib., Baltimore), ed. William Noel and Daniel Weiss (London: Third Millennium, 2002); Alison Stones, "Questions of Style and Provenance in the Morgan Picture Bible," in *Between the Picture and the Word*, ed. Colum Hourihane (Princeton: Princeton University Press, 2005), 112–21; Richard Abels, "Cultural Representations of Warfare in the High Middle Ages," *Journal of Medieval Military History* 6 (2008), 1–31; Judith

Oliver, "Between Flanders and Paris: Originality and Quotation in the Montebourg Psalter," *Getty Research Journal* 10 (2018), 17–36.

434 Claudio Belinati, *Nuovi studi sulla Cappella di Giotto all'Arena di Padova (25 marzo 1303–2002)* (Padua: Poligrafo, 2003); Laura Jacobus, *Giotto and the Arena Chapel: Art, Architecture and Experience* (Turnhout and New York: Brepols/Harvey Miller, 2008).

435 Belinati, *Nuovi studi*, 25–31; Anne Derbes and Mark Sandona, *The Usurer's Heart: Giotto, Enrico Scrovegni, and the Arena Chapel in Padua* (University Park: The Pennsylvania State University Press, 2008). The apsidal zone was embellished after 1339. Giotto seems to have collaborated with the patron's confessor, Altegrado Cattaneo di Lendinara, a canon of the Padua cathedral, presumably portrayed bearing the Chapel's model on his shoulder.

436 Kurmann-Schwarz and Kurmann, *Chartres*, 139–73.

437 Wolfgang Kemp, *The Narratives of Gothic Stained Glass* (Cambridge: Cambridge University Press, 1997), 163–77.

438 Achim Timmermann, "The Workshop Practice of Medieval Painters," in *Making Medieval Art*, ed. Phillip Lindley (Donington: Shaun Tyas, 2003), 42–53; Caskey, *Art and Patronage*, 56–60; *Mendicant Cultures in the Medieval and Early Modern World: Word, Deed, and Image*, ed. Sally J. Cornelison, Nirit Ben-Aryeh Debby, and Peter Howard (Turnhout: Brepols, 2016).

439 McCormick, *Origins*, 614–38 et passim.

440 Sarit Shalev-Eyni, *Jews Among Christians: Hebrew Book Illumination from Lake Constance* (Turnhout: Brepols, 2010), 105–44.

441 Schlink, "Analphabet?"

442 Gervase Rosser, "Crafts, Guilds and the Negotiation of Work in the Medieval Town," *Past and Present*, 154 (1997), 3–31; *Craftsmen and Guilds in the Medieval and Early Modern Periods*, ed. Eva Jullien and Michel Pauly (Stuttgart: Franz Steiner, 2016).

443 Elizabeth Sears, "Craft Ethics and the Critical Eye in Medieval Paris," *Gesta* 45, no. 2 (2006), 221–38.

444 Max Seidel, *Nicola and Giovanni Pisano: Father and Son*, trans. (Chicago: University of Chicago Press, 2012).

445 Richard H. Rouse and Mary A. Rouse, *Manuscripts and their Makers: Commercial Book Producers in Medieval Paris, 1200–1500* (Turnhout: Harvey Miller, 2000).

446 Cannan, "Albaster Sculpture," 28–29.

447 Marie José Mondzain, "The Holy Shroud/How Invisible Hands Weave the Undecidable," in *Iconoclash: Beyond the Image Wars in Science, Religion, and Art* (cat. of an exhib., Cambridge, MA), ed. Bruno Latour and Peter Weibel (Cambridge, MA: MIT Press, 2002), 324–35.

448 Victoria M. Morse, "Seeing and Believing: The Problem of Idolatry in the Thought of Opicino de Canistris," in *Orthodoxie, Christianisme, Histoire*, ed. Susanna Elm et al. (Rome: École Française, 2000), 163–76; Karl Whittington, *Body-Worlds: Opicinus de Canistris and the Medieval Cartographic Imagination* (Toronto: Pontifical Institute of Medieval Studies, 2014).

449 *Anglo-Saxon Kingdoms*, 344–51.

450 Arturo Carlo Quintavalle, "Medioevo: i modelli, un problema storico," in *Medioevo: i modelli*, 11–52; *In honorem sanctae crucis*, ed. Michel Perrin (*Corpus Christianorum, continuatio medievalis*, vols. 100–100A) (Turnhout: Brepols, 1997); Hamburger, *Hrabanus redivivus*.

451 Ganz, *Medien der Offenbarung*, 189–246; Nigel Morgan, "The Iconography," in *The Trinity Apocalypse* (Trinity College Cambridge, MS R.16.2), ed. David McKitterick et al. (Toronto: University of Toronto Press, 2005), 45–75; Peter K. Klein, "The Valenciennes Apocalypse and the Pictorical (*sic*) Tradition," in *Apocalypsis Carolingio de Valenciennes (Ms. 99)* (Valenciennes: Orbis Mediaevalis, 2012), 175–89; "The Role of Prototypes

and Models in the Transmission of Medieval Picture Cycles: The Case of the Beatus Manuscripts," in *The Use of Models in Medieval Book Painting*, ed. Monika E. Müller (Newcastle on Tyne: Cambridge Scholars Publishing, 2014), 1–28.

452 Alessandro Tomei, *Pietro Cavallini* (Milan: Silvana Editoriale, 2000); Romano, *San Francesco ad Assisi*, 207–20 ; Bruno Zanardi, *Giotto e Pietro Cavallini: la questione di Assisi e il cantiere medievale di pittura a fresco* (Milan: Skira, 2002). On the employment of three-dimensional models, see Bisogni, "La scultura in cera."

453 Louise Bourdua, "The Religious Orders and Their Fresco Cycles in the Later Middle Ages," in *Immagini del francescanesimo*, 195–215.

454 John Williams, *The Illustrated Beatus: A Corpus of the Illustrations of the Commentary on the Apocalypse* (London: Harvey Miller, 1994–2003); Klein, "Prototypes and Models"; Richard K. Emmerson, "Framing the Apocalypse: The Performance of John's Life in the Trinity Apocalypse," in *Visualizing Medieval Performance: Perspectives, Histories, Contexts*, ed. Elina Gertsman (Aldershot: Ashgate, 2008), 33–56.

455 Sánchez, *Rostros*, 181–213.

456 Lowden, *Bibles Moralisées*, 2:204–09.

457 Carruba, *Lupa*, 16–32.

458 Jacqueline Jung, "Moving Viewers, Moving Pictures: The Portal as Montage on the Strasbourg South Transept," in *Mouvement, Bewegung: Über die dynamischen Potenziale der Kunst*, ed. Andreas Beyer and Guillaume Cassegrain (Berlin: Deutscher Kunstverlag, 2015), 23–43; Lakey, *Sculptural Seeing*, 96.

459 Penny Howell Jolly, *Made in God's Image? Eve and Adam in the Genesis Mosaics at San Marco, Venice* (Berkeley and Los Angeles: University of California Press, 1997); Karin Krause, "Venedigs Sitz im Paradies. Zur Schöpfungskuppel in der Vorhalle von San Marco," *Mittelungen des Kunsthistorischen Institutes in Florenz* 48, no. 1–2 (2004), 9–54; Annette Reed, "Blessing the Serpent and Treading on Its Head: Marian Typology in the S. Marco Creation Cupola," *Gesta* 46, no. 1 (2007), 41–58; Herbert L. Kessler, "Memory and Models"; "The Cotton Genesis and Creation in San Marco, Venice," *Cahiers archéologiques* 53 (2009–2010), 17–32, and "Introduction" and "Thirteenth-Century Venetian Revisions," in *Atrium*, 9–18, 75–94; Martin Büchsel, "Theologie und Bildgenese. Modelle der Transformation antiker und frühchristlicher Vorlagen," in *Atrium*, 95–130.

460 Herbert L. Kessler, "The Cotton Genesis *in situ*: An Early Christian Manuscript Cycle on the Walls of a Thirteenth-Century Venetian Church," in *Antique Memory*, ed. Ivan Foletti (Rome: Viella, 2015), 11–28.

461 *Le Crociate: L'oriente e l'occidente da Urbano II a San Luigi 1096–1270* (cat. of an exhib., Toulouse and Rome), ed. Monique Rey Delqué (Milan: Electa, 1997); Jaroslav Folda, *Crusader Art in the Holy Land, From the Third Crusade to the Fall of Acre 1187–1291* (New York: Cambridge University Press, 2005).

462 Neil Stratford, "Le chapiteau de la tentation du Christ à Plaimpied revisité," *Bulletin Monumental*, 173–74 (2015), 307–31; *Jerusalem 1000–1400: Every People under Heaven*, ed. Barbara Drake Boehm and Melanie Holcomb (cat. of an exhib., New York) (New York: Metropolitan Museum of Art, 2016), 187–93.

463 Nurith Kenaan-Kadar, "The Two Lintels of the Church of the Holy Sepulchre in Jerusalem," in *Knights of the Holy Land*, 176–85; Melanie Holcomb and Barbara Drake Boehm, "Experiencing Sacred Art in Jerusalem," in *Jerusalem*, 113–28; Avital Heyman, "Fulcher's Bestiary at the Door of the Holy Sepulchre," *Ad limina* 6 (2015), 99–147.

464 Manuel Castiñeiras González, "Compostela, Bari and Jerusalem: in Search of the Footsteps of a Figurative Culture on the Roads of Pilgrimage," *Ad Limina* 1 (2010), 15–51, and "Puertas y metas de la peregrinación. Roma, Jerusalén y Santiago hasta el siglo XIII," in *Peregrino, ruta y meta en las peregrinaciones mayores* (VIII Congresso Internacional de Estudios Jacobeos, Santiago de Compostela, 2010), ed. Paolo Caucci von Sauken

and Rosa Vásquez Santos (Santiago de Compostela: Xunta de Galicia, 2012), 327–77; Heyman, "Bestiary," 107–11.
465 Anheim, "Atelier italien."
466 Robert Maniura, *Pilgrimage to Images: The Origins of the Cult of Our Lady of Częstochowa* (Woodbridge: Boydell & Brewer, 2004).
467 Quintavalle, "Medioevo: i modelli"; Monciatti, "Figure," 178–84; *Les modèles dans l'art du Moyen Âge (XIIe–XVe siecles): Models in the Art of the Middle Ages (12th–15th Centuries)*, ed. Laurence Terrier Aliferis and Laurence and Denise Borlée (Turnhout: Brepols, 2018); Anne Leturque, "The Scope of Competence of the Painter and Patron in Mural Painting in the Romanesque Period," in *Romanesque Patrons and Processes*, 313–25.
468 Annemarie Weyl Carr, "The 'Model Book' of Wolfenbüttel," in *The Glory of Byzantium*, ed. Helen C. Evans and William D. Wixom (New York: Metropolitan Museum of Art, 1997), 482–484; Harald Wolter von dem Knesebeck, "Das Wolfenbütteler Musterbuch in seinem sächsischen Umfeld," in *Manuscripts in Transition: Recycling Manuscripts, Texts, and Images*, ed. Brigitte Dekeyzer and Jan van der Stock (Dudley, MA: Peeters, 2005), 99–108; Eberhard König, "Une nouvelle lecture du livre de modèles de Wolffenbüttel," *Les Cahiers de Saint-Michel de Cuxa* 37 (2006), 21–32; Maria Andaloro, "Gli Atlanti della memoria. La memoria delle immagini e le immagini della memoria," in *Medioevo: immagine e memoria*, 564–577; Ludovico Geymonat, "Drawing, Memory and Imagination in the Wolfenbüttel Musterbuch," *Medieval Encounters* 18 (2012), 518–82.
469 Enrica Pagella, "Vedere, copiare, interpretare: Artisti e circolazione di modelli nell'ambito ecclesiastico," in *Arti e storia*, 1, 477–511; Sofia Uggè, "Rotolo in pergamena con scene degli *Atti degli Apostoli*," in *Et verbum caro factum est ... La Bibbia oggi e la sua trasmissione nei secoli*, ed. Sofia Uggè e Gianmario Ferraris (cat. of an exhib., Vecelli) (Vercelli: Museo del Tesoro del Duomo, 2005), number 81.
470 Anheim, "Atelier italien."
471 Arwed Arnulf, *Versus ad Picturas: Studien zur Titulusdichtung als Quellengattung der Kunstgeschichte von der Antike bis zum Hochmittelalter* (Munich and Berlin: Deutscher Kunstverlag, 1997); Nicolas Bock, *De Titulis: Zur Vorgeschichte des modernen Bildtitels* (Berlin and Munich: Deutscher Kunstverlag, 2018).
472 Herbert L. Kessler, "The Codex Barbarus Scaligeri, the *Christian Topography*, and the Question of Jewish Models of Early Christian Art," in *Between Judaism and Christianity: Pictorials Playing on Mutual Grounds: Essays in Honour of Prof. Elisabeth (Elisheva) Revel-Neher* (Leiden: Brill, 2008), 139–54.
473 Nino Zchomelidse, "Das Bild im Busch: Zur Theorie und Ikonographie der alttestamentlichen Gottesvision im Mittelalter," in *Die Sichtbarkeit des Unsichtbaren: Zur Korrelation von Text und Bild im Wirkungskreis der Bibel*, ed. Bernd Janowski and Nino Zchomelidse (Stuttgart: Laupp & Göbel, 2003), 165–89; "Liminal Phenomena: Framing Medieval Cult Images with Relics and Words," *Viator* 47 (2016), 243–96; Herbert L. Kessler, *Neither God Nor Man: Words, Images, and the Medieval Anxiety about Art* (Freiburg i Br.: Rombach Verlag, 2007).
474 Arnulf, *Versus*, 273–85; Tommaso Gramigni and Stefano Zamponi, "Le iscrizioni della Croce di Rosano," in *Croce dipinta*, 71–88.
475 Tronzo, *Cultures*, 56; Herbert L. Kessler, "Inscriptions on Painted Crosses and the Spaces of Personal and Communal Meditation," in *Inscriptions in Liturgical Spaces*, 161–84.
476 Arnulf, *Versus*, 293–95; *Pictor in Carmine: Ein typologisches Handbuch aus der Zeit um 1200*, ed. Karl-August Wirth (Berlin: Gebr. Mann, 2006).
477 *Bibbie atlantiche*.
478 Lucia Travaini, *Monete, mercanti e matematica: Le monete medievali nei trattati di aritmetica e nei libri di mercatura* (Rome: Jouvence, 2003); Alessio Montagano, "Quattrini 'del signore'

e 'della Vergine Maria': L'immagine sacra nella moneta in Toscana dal Medioevo al Rinascimento," in *Moneta e divozione: Le offerte alla Sacra Cintola, gli Angiò e le immagnini sacre nelle monete tra Medioevo e Rinascimento a Prato* (Calenzano: La Marina, 2013), 23–30, 40; Aden Kumler, "*Signatus ... vultus tui*: (Re)impressing the Holy Face Before and After the European Cult of the Veronica," in *European Fortune*, 102–13.

479 Hanneke van Asperen, "'Où il y a une Veronique attachiée dedens,' Images of the Veronica in Religious Manuscripts with Special Attention for the Dukes of Burgundy and their Family," in *European Fortune*, 233–49.

480 Fourteenth-century irons in Vic (Museu Episcopal) and Toulouse (Musée Paul-Dupuy) include the Crucifixion (as on the Vallbona altarpiece) and Lamb of God; Lluisa Amenós, "Hostiers i Neulers medieval del Museu Episcopal de Vic," *Quaderns del Museu Episcopal de Vic* 1 (2005), 91–113; Kumler, "Multiplication," 184–87; "Manufacturing," 15–19.

481 Fulton, *Judgment to Passion*, 254–65; Bedos-Rezak, *Ego*, 142–50.

482 Suzannah Biernoff, *Sight and Embodiment in the Middle Ages* (London: Palgrave McMillan, 2002), 139–40. Silvia Pedone, "Vedere Bisanzio da nessun luogo: I limiti di una visione 'estetica' condizionata," in *ΦΑΝΤΑΖΟΝΤΕΣ: Visioni dell'arte bizantina*, ed. Valentina Cantone and Silvia Pizzone (Padua: Cleup, 2013), 1–31.

483 Creighton Gilbert, *The Saints' Three Reasons for Paintings in Churches* (Ithaca: Clandestine Press, 2001); Jérôme Baschet, *La civilisation féodale: De l'an mil à la colonisation de l'Amérique* (Paris: Flammarion, 2004), 460–502; Lawrence Duggan, "Reflections on 'Was Art Really the "Book of the Illiterate"?,'" in *Reading Images and Texts: Medieval Images and Texts as Forms of Communication*, ed. Mariëlle Hageman and Marco Mostert (Turnhout: Brepols, 2005), 63–119; *Mind's Eye*; Celia Chazelle, "Art and Reverence in Bede's Churches at Wearmouth and Jarrow," in *Intellektualisierung und Mystifizierung mittelalterlicher Kunst: "Kultbild"—Revision eines Begriffs*, ed. Martin Büchsel and Rebecca Müller (Berlin: Gebr. Mann, 2010), 79–98; Alejandro García Avilés, "*Transitus*: actitudes hacia la sacralidad de las imágenes en el Occidente medieval," in *Imágenes medievales de culto: Tallas de la colección El Conventet* (Murcia: Museo arqueológico, 2010), 22–25; Herbert L. Kessler, "*Aliter enim videtur pictura, aliter videntur litterae*': Reading Medieval Pictures," in *Scrivere e leggere* (Settimana di studio LIX, 2011) (Spoleto: CISAM, 2012), 701–29; "Gregory the Great and Image Theory in Northern Europe during the Twelfth and Thirteenth Centuries," in *Companion to Medieval Art*, 151–72.

484 Noble, *Images*, 220–24; García Avilés, "*Transitus*," 26.

485 Fricke, *Fallen Idols*, 160–61 (*Ecce fides*, 186–87).

486 Conrad Rudolph, "La resistenza sull'arte nel Occidente," in *Arti e storia*, 3:49–84.

487 Tobias Frese, *Die Bildkritik des Bernhard von Clairvaux: Die Apologia im monastischen Diskurs* (Bamberg: Arthis, 2006); Büchsel, "Materialpracht," 166–70.

488 Kemp, *Narratives*, 167.

489 Fricke, *Fallen Idols*, 97–105 (*Ecce fides*, 133–44); Weinryb, *Bronze Object*, 115–21; David Nirenberg, *Aesthetic Theology and Its Enemies: Judaism in Christian Painting, Poetry, and Politics* (Lebanon, NH: University Press of New England, 2015).

490 Marc Michael Epstein, "Mapping the Territory: 'Arb'ah kanfot ha'arez—the Four Corners of the Medieval Jewish World," in *Skies of Parchment*, 47–87.

491 Bezalel Narkiss, *The Golden Haggadah* (London: British Library, 1997); Katrin Kogman-Appel, "Hebrew Manuscript Painting in Late Medieval Spain: Signs of a Culture in Transition," *Art Bulletin* 84, no. 2 (2002), 246–272.

492 Kalman P. Bland, *The Artless Jew: Medieval and Modern Affirmations and Denials of the Visual* (Princeton: Princeton University Press, 2000), 116–29 et passim.

493 Shalev-Eyni, *Jews Among Christians*, 67; Bland, *The Artless Jew*, 124–28.

494 Vivian B. Mann, *Jewish Texts on the Visual Arts* (Cambridge: Cambridge University Press, 2000).

495 Katrin Kogman-Appel, *Jewish Book Art Between Islam and Christianity: The Decoration of Hebrew Bibles in Medieval Spain* (Leiden: Brill, 2004); "Jewish Art and Cultural Exchange: Theoretical Perspectives," *Medieval Encounters* 17 (2011), 1–26, and "The Role of Hebrew Letters in Making the Divine Visible," in *Sign and Design*, 153–71; Epstein and Frojmovic, *Skies of Parchment*; Shalev-Eyni, *Jews Among Christians*, 130–40.

496 Eva Frojmovic, "Jewish Mudejarismo and the Invention of Tradition," in *Late Medieval Jewish Identities: Iberia and Beyond*, ed. Carmen Caballero-Navas and Esperanza Alfonso (New York: Palgrave Macmillan, 2010), 233–58; Sarit Shalev-Eyni, "Tradition in Transition: Mudejar Art and the Emergence of the Illuminated Sephardic Bible in Christian Toledo," *Medieval Encounters* 23 (2017), 531–59.

497 Cohen, *Signs and Wonders*, 2–3.

498 Epstein, *Skies of Parchment*, 97–104, 123–27; Shalev-Eyni, *Jews Among Christians*, 29–66.

499 Lipton, *Dark Mirror*, 35–45; Nirenberg, *Aesthetic Theology*, 29.

500 Kessler, *Neither God nor Man*, 29; Felipe Pereda Espejo, *Las imágenes de la discordia: Polita y poética de la imagen Sagrada en la España del 400* (Madrid: Marcial Pons, 2007), 79–80 (English trans. *Images of Discord: Poetics and Politics of the Sacred Image in 15th century Spain* [Turnhout: Brepols, 2018], 39–40); García Avilés, *"Transitus."*

501 Jean Wirth, "La critique scolastique de la théorie thomiste de l'image," in *Crises de l'image religieuse: De Nicée à Vatican II*, ed. Olivier Christin and Dario Gamboni (Paris: Éditions de la Maison des Sciences de l'homme, 1999), 93–109; Jérome Baschet, *Corps et âmes: Une histoire de la personne au Moyen Âge* (Paris: Flammarian, 2016), 85–89.

502 Kathleen Kamerick, *Popular Piety and Art in the Late Middle Ages: Image Worship and Idolatry in England 1350–1550* (New York: Palgrave, 2002), 23; Stephen Perkinson, "'As They Learn It by Sight of Images': Alabasters and Religious Devotion in Late Medieval England," in *Object of Devotion*, 38–53; Malo, *Relics and Writing*, 164–80; Duffy, "Alabaster Men," 55 (*Royal Books*, 290).

503 Palazzo, *L'invention*, 72–73.

504 Alberto Ricciardi, "Gli *inganni della tradizione*: Una silloge del *Registrum* di Gregorio Magno nei rapporti fra Carolingi e papato e nel dibattito sulle immagini sacre," *Studi Medievali*, ser. 3, 56 (2015), 79–126; Dell'Acqua, *"Iconophilia in Italy,"*, 34–35.

505 Kruse, *Wozu Menschen malen*, 324–25; Kessler, "Object as Subject," 214.

506 Gilbert, *Saints' Three Reasons*, 13–16; Frank Büttner, *Giotto und die Ursprünge der neuzeitlichen Bildauffassung: Die Malerei und die Wissenschaft vom Sehen in Italien um 1300* (Darmstadt: WBG, 2013), 28–37.

507 Cannon, *Religious Poverty*, 51–52.

508 *Pictor in Carmine*, 109.

509 Lynn Ransom, "The Eyes Have It: The Question of Redemptive Vision in the *Verger de Soulas* (Paris, Bibliothèque Nationale de France, MS fr. 9220)," in *Beyond the Text*, 177–95.

510 *Summa theologica*, 3a, quast. 25, art. 4, 4:2149. Jean Wirth, "Peinture et perception visuelle au XIIIe siècle," in *La visione e lo sguardo nel Medioevo*, ed. Jean-Claude Schmitt (Florence: SISMEL, 1998), 2:113–128.

511 Thomas Lentes, "Inneres Auge, äußerer Blick und heilige Schau: Ein Diskussionsbeitrag zur visuellen Praxis in der Frömmigkeit und Moraldidaxe des späten Mittelalters," in *Frömmigkeit im Mittelalter: Politisch-soziale Kontexte, visuelle Praxis, körperliche Ausdrucksformen*, ed. Klaus Schreiner (Munich: Wilhelm Fink, 2002), 179–220.

512 Kirstin Faupel-Drevs, *Vom rechten Gebrauch der Bilder im liturgischen Raum: Mittelalterliche Funktionsbestimmungen bildender Kunst in* Rationale divinorum officiorum *des Durandus von Mende (1230/1–1296)* (Leiden: Brill, 2000), 249–55 et passim.

513 Lars R. Jones, "*Visio Divina*? Donor Figures and Representations of Imagistic Devotion: The Copy of the 'Virgin of Bagnolo' in the Museo dell'Opera del Duomo, Florence," in *Italian Panel Painting*, 31–55; Lakey, *Sculptural Seeing*, 164.

514 Pamela Smith, *The Body of the Artisan: Art and Experience in the Scientific Revolution* (Chicago: University of Chicago Press, 2004), 9–11; Donal Cooper, "Projecting Presence: The Monumental Cross in the Italian Church Interior," in *Presence: The Inherence of the Prototype within the Image and Other Objects*, ed. Robert Maniura and Rupert Shepherd (London: Routledge, 2006), 47–69; Cannon, *Religious Poverty*, 172.

515 Hauknes, "Emblematic Narratives," 4–6.

516 Didier Méhu, "Augustin, le sens et les sens: Réflexions sur le processus de spiritualisation du charnel dans l'Église médiévale," *Revue historique* 317, no. 2 (2015), 271–302.

517 Sánchez, *Rostros*, 34.

518 Iafrate, "Artifex specialis," 33–36.

519 Hans Belting, *Das echte Bild: Bildfragen als Glaubensfragen* (München: Verlag C.H. Beck, 2005), 86–89.

520 Debiais, *Croisée*, 72–80.

521 Stefano Riccioni, *Il mosaico absidale di S. Clemente a Roma: Exemplum della Chiesa riformata* (Spoleto: CISAM, 2006).

522 Klaus Krüger, "'Hoc est corpus meum': Bild und Liturgie im gemalten Altaraufsatz des 13. Jahrhunderts," *Westfalen* 80 (2002), 221–44 (reprinted in Klaus Krüger, *Zur Eigensinnlichkeit der Bilder: Acht Beiträge*, ed. Matthias Weiß et al. [Munich: Wilhelm Fink, 2017], 24–52), and Kristen B. Aavitsland, "Visual Splendour and Verbal Argument in Romanesque Golden Altars," *Acta ad archaeologiam et artium historiam pertinentia* 24 (2011), 205–25, and "Civitas Hierusalem: Representing Presence in Scandinavian Golden Altars," in *Image and Altar*, 179–93.

523 Herbert L. Kessler, "Christ's Name as Image and Object," *Heilige Namen*, ed. Michele C. Ferrari (Erlangen: FAU Studien aus der Philosophischen Fakultät, forthcoming).

524 These appear on a Host press in the Museu Episcopal in Vic (Catalonia), dating perhaps from the twelfth century, incised with six circles rimmed with coin-like dots; Kumler, "Multiplication," 184–87.

525 Kumler, "Multiplication," 188.

526 Noble, *Images*, 158–206 et passim; Alejandro García Avilés, "*Transitus*," 25, and "Este rey tenno que enos idolos cree: Imagenes milagrosas en Las *Cantigas de Santa Maria*," in *Cantigas*, 523–59.

527 Stephan Waldhoff, "Synagoga im Sakramentar: Zur *revelatio synagogae* in der Handschrift 193 der Bibliothèque municipale in Tours," *Frühmittelalterliche Studien* 43 (2009), 215–70; Cécile Voyer, "L'allégorie de la Synagogue: Une représentation ambivalente du judaïsme," in *L'allégorie dans l'art*, 2:95–109.

528 Debiais, *Croisée*, 299.

529 Ludovico Geymonat, "Apocalypse Drawing," in *Pen and Parchment: Drawing in the Middle Ages*, ed. Melanie Holcomb (New York: Metropolitan Museum of Art, 2009), 130–33; "Un disegno preparatorio del XIII secolo per un ciclo pittorico sull'Apocalisse," *Ikon: Journal of Iconographic Studies* 6 (2013), 55–64.

530 Vincent Debiais, "Le chant des formes: L'écriture épigraphique entre matérialité du trace et transcendance des contenus," *Revista de poética medieval* 27 (2013), 101–29.

531 Baert, *Heritage*, 27.

532 Giulia Tamanti, "Il restauro degli affreschi di San Pietro in Valle: aspetti tecnici e novità," in *Gli affreschi di San Pietro in Valle a Ferentillo: Le storie dell'antico e del nuovo testamento*, ed. Giulia Tamanti (Naples: Elekta, 2003), 11–40.

533 Frans van Liere, "Biblical Exegesis Through the Twelfth Century," in *The Practice of the Bible*, 57–78.

534 Christian Heck, *L'échelle celeste dans l'art du Moyen Âge: Une image de la quête du ciel* (Paris: Flammarion, 1997); Felix Heinzer, "'Wondrous Machine': Rollen und Funktionen des Psalters in der mittelalterlichen Kultur," in *Der Albani-Psalter: Stand und Perspektiven der Forschung/The St. Albans Psalter: Current Research and Perspectives*, ed. Jochen Bepler and Christian-Heitzmann (Hildesheim: Olms, 2013), 15–31.

535 Herbert L. Kessler, "Gregorian Reform," 26–29, and "'To Curb the License of Painters': The Functions of Some Captions in the Construction and Understanding of Pictured Narratives," in *Figure et récit/Figura e racconto: Narrazione letteraria e narrazione figurativa in Italia dall'Antichita al primo Rinascimento*, ed. Marco Praloran and Serena Romano (Florence: SISMEL-Edizioni del Galluzzo, 2009), 25–52.

536 Büchsel, "Materialpracht," 174; Kurt Ambrose, *The Nave Sculpture of Vézelay: The Art of Monastic Viewing* (Toronto: Pontifical Institute of Mediaeval Studies, 2006), 93–94, and "The 'Mystic Mill' Capital at Vézelay," in *Wind and Water: Fluid Technologies from Antiquity to the Renaissance*, ed. Steven A. Walton (Tempe: Center for Medieval and Renaissance Studies, 2006), 235–58.

537 Herbert L. Kessler, "'Thou Shalt Paint the Likeness of Christ Himself': The Mosaic Prohibition as Provocation for Christian Images," in *The Real and Ideal Jerusalem in Jewish, Christian and Islamic Art: Studies in Honor of Bezalel Narkiss on the Occasion of his Seventieth Birthday (Jewish Art*, 23, 1997/98), ed. Bianca Kühnel (Jerusalem: Center for Jewish Art, 1998), 124–39; Hediger and Kurmann-Schwarz, "Reliquie und Skulptur."

538 Dale, *Relics, Prayer*. Tempera paintings participated in the same layering of meanings; the colors and inscriptions of the Rosano Crucifix, for instance, are applied not to the wood frame itself but to a fabric glued onto it.

539 Stefan Trinks, *Antike und Avantgarde: Skuptur am Jakobsweg im 11. Jahrhundert; Jaca-León-Santiago* (Berlin: Akademie Verlag, 2012), 44–54; Suger included the subject in his exegetic windows.

540 Ron Baxter, *Bestiaries and Their Users in the Middle Ages* (London: Sutton Publishing, 1998); Debra Higgs Strickland, "The Jews, Leviticus, and the Unclean in Medieval English Bestiaries," in *Beyond the Yellow Badge: Anti-Judaism and Antisemitism in Medieval and Early Modern Visual Culture*, ed. Mitchell B. Merback (Leiden: Brill, 2008), 203–32; Herbert L. Kessler, "Christ the Magic Dragon," in *Making Thoughts, Making Pictures, Making Memories: a Special Issue in Honor of Mary J. Carruthers*, ed. Anne D. Hedeman and Clark Maines (*Gesta* 48, no. 2 [2009]), 119–34; Cynthia White, "*Potiones ad sanandum*: Text as Remedy in a Medieval Latin Bestiary," in *Bodily and Spiritual Hygiene in Medieval and Early Modern Literature*, ed. Albrecht Classen (Berlin: De Gruyter, 2017), 221–75.

541 Celia Chazelle, "An *Exemplum* of Humility: The Crucifixion Image in the Drogo Sacramentary," in *Reading Medieval Images*, 27–33; Kessler, "Sanctifying Serpent." On the underlying anti-Jewish polemics in bestiaries, see Strickland, "Jews."

542 Kessler, *Spiritual Seeing*, 195.

543 Michael Camille, "Before the Gaze: The Internal Senses and Late-Medieval Practices of Seeing," in *Visuality Before and Beyond the Renaissance*, 197–223; Katharine Park, "Impressed Images: Reproducing Wonders," in *Picturing Science, Producing Art*, ed. Caroline A. Jones and Peter Galison (London: Routledge, 1998), 254–71; Suzanne Conklin Akbari, *Seeing through the Veil: Optical Theory and Medieval Allegory* (Toronto: University of Toronto Press, 2004).

544 Akbari, *Veil*, 29; David Summers, *Vision, Reflection, and Desire in Western Painting* (Chapel Hill: University of North Carolina Press, 2007), 46–47; Lakey, *Sculptural Seeing*, 132–55.

545 Hamburger, *Visual and the Visionary*, 355–58; Eamon Duffy, *Marking the Hours: English People and Their Prayers 1240–1570* (New Haven and London: Yale University Press, 2006), 23–52; Rudy, *Postcards*, 7–14; Zchomelidse, "Liminal Phenomena," 268–71.

546 Tammen, "Blick und Wunde," 88–92.

547 Christoph Winterer, *Das Fuldaer Sakramentar in Göttingen* (Petersberg: Michael Imhof Verlag, 2009), 409.
548 Heslop, "Anselm," 124.
549 Functioning like a picture, ekphrasis could displace vision; Vincent Debiais, "La vue des autres: l'ekphrasis au risque de la littérature médiolatine," *Cahiers de la civilisation médiévale* 55, no. 220 (2012), 393–404.
550 *Coronation Mantle*, 222–23.
551 Parello, "Fünf Felder"; Ivo Rauch, "Die Bundeslade und die wahren Israeliten: Anmerkungen zum mariologischen und politischen Programm der Hochchorfenster der Kathedrale von Chartres," in *Glas, Malerei, Forschung*, 61–71; Rudolph, "Exegetical Stained-Glass Window," 411; Marie-Pierre Gelin, "*Stirps Jesse in Capite Ecclesiae*: Iconographic and Liturgical Readings of the Tree of Jesse in Stained-Glass Windows," in *The Tree: Symbol, Allegory, and Mnemonic Device in Medieval Art and Thought*, ed. Pippa Salonius and Andrea Worm (Turnhout: Brepols, 2014), 13–33.
552 Xavier Barral I Altet, *Le décor du pavement au Moyen Âge: Les mosaïques de France et d'Italie* (Rome: École française de Rome, 2010), 303–05.
553 On the religious context: Nina Rowe, *The Jew, the Cathedral, and the Medieval City: Synagoga and Ecclesia in the Thirteenth Century* (New York: Cambridge University Press, 2011), 191–237.
554 von der Nahmer, "Sünde"; Marchesin, *Arbre*, 97–99.
555 As Ernold Nigellus recalled; Dutton, *Carolingian Civilization*, 252–54.
556 Kessler, "*Realia* and *Spiritualia*," 125–31.
557 Jászai, "Christus als neuer Mose?" and "'Christliche Ikonologie'"; Ganz, *Buch-Gewänder*, 193–206. Also, William Diebold, "'Except I shall see ... I will not believe' (John 20:25): Typology, Theology, and Historiography in an Ottonian Diptych," in *Objects, Images*, 257–73.
558 Karen Blough, "The Princess-Abbesses of Essen and the Golden Virgin," in *De re metallica: The Uses of Metal in the Middle Ages*, ed. Robert O. Bork et al. (Aldershot: Ashgate, 2005), 147–61; Barbara Newman, "Die visionären Texte und visuellen Welten religiösen Frauen," in *Krone und Schleier*, 104–17 (*Crown & Veil*, 151–71); Bredekamp, *Bildakts*, 238–39 (*Image Acts*, 199–200); Ganz, *Buch-Gewänder*, 193–206.
559 As does the painted cross of Guillielmo in Sarzana; *Pinxit Guillielmus*.
560 Katrin Müller, "Fragwürdige Bilder: Die Genesismosaiken in Monreale," in *Atrium*, 124–39.
561 Wirth, *Villard*, 49–50.
562 Jeffrey Hamburger, "The 'Various Writings of Humanity': Johannes Tauler on Hildegard of Bingen's *Liber Scivias*" in *Visual Culture and the German Middle Ages*, ed. Kathryn Starkey and Horst Wenzel (New York: Palgrave MacMillan, 2005), 161–205, and "Introduction," *Mind's Eye*, 3–10.
563 As in the final scene on the Hildesheim doors; Marchesin, *Arbre*, 205–17. On the Magdalene's hair, Katherine Ludwig Jansen, *The Making of the Magdalen: Preaching and Popular Devotion in the Later Middle Ages* (Princeton: Princeton University Press, 2000), 130–34. Also, Bauer, "Geological Imagination," 105–10.
564 Hauknes, "Emblematic Narratives," 8–39.
565 Hauknes, "Emblematic Narratives," 24–26; Romano, *Apogeo*, 246–63.
566 Michael Curschmann, "*Der aventiure bilde nemen*: The Intellectual and Social Environment of the Iwein Murals at Rodenegg Castle," in *Wort-Bild-Text: Studien zur Medialität des Literarischen in Hochmittelalter und früher Neuzeit* (Baden-Baden: Koerner, 2007), 447–55.
567 James A. Rushing Jr., "Images at the Interface: Orality, Literacy and the Pictorialization of the Roland Material," in *Visual Culture*, 115–34.

568 Ulrich Kuder, "Die Ottonen in der ottonischen Buchmalerei: Identifikation und Ikonographie," in *Herrschaftsrepräsentation in ottonischen Sachsen*, ed. Gerd Althoff and Ernst Schubert (Sigmaringen: Thorbecke, 1998), 137–234.
569 Zchomelidse, *Art, Ritual*, 75.
570 C. Griffith Mann, "Picturing the Bible in the Thirteenth Century," in *Book of Kings*, 38–59; Alyce A. Jordan, "Stained Glass and the Liturgy: Performing Sacral Kingship in Capetian France," in *Objects, Images*, 274–97.
571 Stefano Riccioni, "Dal ketos al sēnmurv? Mutazioni iconografiche e transizioni simboliche del kētos dall'Antichità al Medioevo (secolo XIII)," *Hortus Artium Mediaevalium* 22 (2016), 130–44; Sara Kuehn, "On the Transcultural and Transreligious Dimension of the So-called 'Sēnmurw,'" in *Drachenlandung*, 103–26. The creature dominates the seascape of the fifth day of creation in San Marco, and a variant expels Jonah on Italian pulpits (symbolizing salvation and delivery); Zchomelidse, *Art, Ritual*, 12.
572 Carruthers, *Beauty*, 190.
573 Bucklow, "Virtues" and *Riddle*, 185–88 et passim; Büttner, *Giotto*, 35–37; Binski, "Rhetorical Occasions," 27–28.
574 Anthony Cutler and William North, "Word Over Image: On the Making, Uses, and Destiny of the Marriage Charter of Otto II and Theophanu," in *Interactions: Artistic Interchange between the Eastern and Western Worlds in the Medieval Period*, ed. Colum Hourihane (Princeton: Princeton University Press, 2007), 167–87; Garrison, "Mimetic Bodies," 213–21.
575 Romano, *La O*, 144–65 et passim; Laura Jacobus, *Giotto and the Arena Chapel* (Turnhout: Brepols, 2008); Derbes and Sandona, *Usurer's Heart*, 150–52.
576 John Osborne, "Dado Imagery in the Lower Church of San Clemente, Rome, and Santa Maria Immacolata at Ceri," in *Shaping Sacred Space*, 35–50; Jill Bain, "Signifying Absence: Experiencing Monochrome Imagery in Medieval Painting," in *A Wider Trecento: Studies in 13th and 14th Century European Art Presented to Julian Gardner*, ed. Louise Bourdua and Robert Gibbs (Leiden: Brill, 2012), 5–20; Philippe Cordez, "Les marbres de Giotto: Astrologie et naturalisme à la Chapelle Scrovegni," *Mitteilungen des Kunsthistorischen Institutes in Florenz* 55, no.1 (2013), 8–25.
577 Campbell, "Enamelled Plaque"; Robinson, *Masterpieces*; Bucklow, "Virtues," 147.
578 Anne Dunlop, "Allegory, Painting and Petrarch," *Word & Image* 24 (2008), 77–91.
579 Megan C. McNamee, "Picturing as Practice: Placing a Square above a Square in the Central Middle Ages," in *Canonical Texts and Scholarly Practices*, ed. Anthony Grafton and Glenn W. Most (Cambridge: Cambridge University Press, 2016), 200–23; Christopher R. Lakey, "'To See Clearly': The Place of Relief in Medieval Visual Culture," in *Optics, Ethics*, 119–38.
580 Robert Bork, *The Geometry of Creation: Architectural Drawing and the Dynamics of Gothic Design* (Farnham: Ashgate, 2011).
581 Isabelle Marchesin, "Proportions et géométrie signifiante," in *Images dans l'occident*, 213–26.
582 Newman, "Trinity," 141–45.
583 Hans Belting, *Bild-Anthropologie: Entwürfe für eine Bildwissenschaft* (Paderborn: Wilhelm Fink, 2011), 189–211 (English trans. *An Anthropology of Images: Picture, Medium, Body*, trans. Thomas Dunlop [Princeton, NJ: Princeton University Press, 2011], 125–43).
584 Valentino Pace, "Cristo-Luce a Santa Prassede," in *Per assiduum stadium scientiae adipisci margaritam: Festgabe für Ursula Nilgen zum 65. Geburtstag*, ed. Annelies Amberger (St. Ottilien: EOS, 1997), 185–200 (repr. Pace, *Arte e Roma*, 105–23).
585 Jean-Marie Sansterre, "Attitudes occidentales à l'égard des miracles d'images dans le haut Moyen Âge," *Annales HSS* 53, no. 6 (1998), 1219–41.
586 Erik Thunø, "Inscription and Divine Presence: Golden Letters in the Early Medieval Apse Mosaic," *Word & Image* 27, no. 3 (2011), 279–91.

587 Kessler and Zacharias, *Rome 1300*, 119.
588 In St. Georg Oberzell at Reichenau, gilt metal inserts fallen from frescoes in the nave and the apse exterior have been recovered: Dörthe Jacobs, *Sankt Georg in Reichenau-Oberzell: Der Bau und seine Ausstattung; Bestand, Veränderungen, Restaurierungsgeschichte* (Stuttgart: Konrad-Theiss-Verlag 1999), 1:203–208, 2:509–523 et passim; Matthias Exner, "L'avant-nef occidentale de l'église Saint-Georges à Oberzell (Reichenau): État, bilan et interprétation," in *Les Avant-nefs et espaces d'accueil dans l'église entre le IVe et le XIIe siècle*, ed. Christian Sapin (Paris: CTHS, 2002), 127–49.
589 Elizabeth Pastan, "The Torture of Saint George Medallion from Chartres Cathedral in Princeton," *Record of the Art Museum of Princeton University* 56, no. 1/2 (1997), 11–34.
590 Andrew Breeze, "The Blessed Virgin and the Sunbeam through Glass," *Celtica* 23 (1999), 19–29; Pentcheva, *Sensual Icon*, 147–48; Brigitte Kurmann-Schwarz, "'Fenestre vitree [...] significant Sacram Scripturam': zur Medialität mittelalterlicher Glasmalerei des 12. und 13. Jahrhunderts," in *Glasmalerei im Kontext: Bildprogramme und Raumfunktion* (Akten des XXII. Internationalen Colloquiums des Corpus Vitrearum, Nürnberg, 29. August–1. September 2004), ed. Rüdiger Becksmann (Nuremberg: Germanisches Nationalmuseum, 2005), 61–73.
591 Parello, "Fünf Felder"; Hamburger, "Hand of God"; Herbert L. Kessler, "'Consider the Glass, It Can Teach You,'" in *Dictionary of Stained Glass*, ed. Brigitte Kurmann-Schwarz and Elizabeth Pastan (Leiden: Brill, 2019), 143–56.
592 Gabriella Federici Vescovini, "Vision et réalité dans la perspective au XIVe siècle," *Micrologus* 5 (1997), 161–80; Ruth Siddall, "Westminster Abbey: the stones of the Sanctuary Pavement," *Urban Geology in London* 22 (2014), http://www.ucl.ac.uk/~ucfbrxs/Homepage/walks/LOUGS-Westminster.pdf.
593 Lakey, "*Chiarito Tabernacle*"; Baert, "Nourished"; Saracino, "*Felix umbilicus*," 115–25.
594 Hamburger, *Visual and the Visionary*, 317–82; Joseph Leo Koerner, "The Icon as Iconoclash," in *Iconoclash*, 164–213.
595 Krüger, "Medium and Imagination."
596 Kessler, "Object as Subject," 214–15; Ricciardi, "*Inganni*."
597 Robert Deshman, "Another Look at the Disappearing Christ: Corporeal and Spiritual Vision in Early Medieval Images," *Art Bulletin* 79 (1997), 518–546 (repr. in *Eye and Mind: Collected Essays in Anglo-Saxon and Early Medieval Art by Robert Deshman*, ed. Adam S. Cohen [Kalamazoo: Western Michigan University, 2010], 242–76).
598 Kessler, "Object as Subject," 215.
599 Gilbert, *Saints' Three Reasons*, 13–16; Pereda, *Imágenes*, 80–81 (*Images*, 39–40).
600 Peter K. Klein, "From the Heavenly to the Trivial: Vision and Visual Perception in Early and High Medieval Apocalypse Illustration," in *The Holy Face and the Paradox*, 247–78; Sansterre, "Deux témoignages," 273–85.
601 Gerhard Wolf, "From Mandylion to Veronica: Picturing the 'Disembodied' Face and Disseminating the True Image of Christ in the Latin West," in *The Holy Face and the Paradox*, 153–79.
602 Felipe Pereda Espejo, "Imagen y olvido: Imagen del lamento fúnebre entre la Antigüedad u la Reforma católica," *Codex Aqvilarensis* 34 (2018), 229–62.
603 Binski, "Rhetorical Occasions."
604 A fifteenth-century version of the manuscript in Einsiedeln (Stiftsbibliothek, MS 710(322), fol. 106^r) completes it as a painted Crucifixion triptych.
605 Hamburger, "Speculations," 360–68.
606 The type developed first in Franciscan circles during the course of the thirteenth century and was taken up especially by Dominicans; Bernard of Clairvaux, *Sermon Compendium* (Historisches Archiv der Stadt Köln, Ms. Best. 7010, nr. 255, fol. 117^v), which juxtaposes Longinus piercing Christ's chest with Mary swooning into John's arms, a sword penetrating her heart (*Krone und Schleier*, 460–61).

607 Paul Binski, "The Crucifixion and the Censorship of Art," in *The Medieval* World, ed. Peter Linehan and Janet Nelson (London: Routledge, 2001), 342–60; Beth Williamson, "How Magnificent was Medieval Art?," in *Magnificence and the Sublime*, 243–62; Meredith Raucher Sisson, "Beyond Blood: The *Crucifixus Dolorosus* and the Beauty of Christ," in *Art and Experience in Trecento Italy* (Proceedings of the Andrew Ladis Trecento Conference, New Orleans, November 10–12, 2016), ed. Holly Flora and Sarah S. Wilkins (Turnhout: Brepols, 2018), 79–93.

608 *La France romane au temps des premiers Capétiens (987–1152)* (cat. of an exhib., Paris), ed. Danielle Gaborit-Chopin (Paris: Musée du Louvre, 2005), 160; Nurith Kenaan-Kedar, "Pictorial and Sculptural Commemoration of Returning or Departing Crusaders," in *Crusades and Visual Culture*, 91–104; *Voyager*, 93 (*Viaggio*, 174).

609 Manuel Studer-Karlen, "The Depiction of the Dead in Early Christian Art (Third to Sixth Century)," in *The Faces of the Dead and the Early Christian World*, ed. Ivan Foletti (Rome: Viella, 2013), 149–60.

610 Jeffrey F. Hamburger, *St. John the Divine: The Deified Evangelist in Medieval Art and Theology* (Berkeley and Los Angeles: University of California Press, 2002), 72–73; Elina Gertsman and Barbara H. Rosenwein, *The Middles Ages in 50 Objects* (Cambridge: Cambridge University Press, 2018), 38–41.

611 Paul Binski, "The Angel Choir at Lincoln and the Poetics of the Gothic Smile," *Art History* 20 (1997), 350–74; *Seliges Lächeln und höllisches Gelächter: Das Lachen in Kunst und Kultur des Mittelalters* (cat. of an exhib., Mainz) (Regensburg: Schnell & Steiner, 2012); Sánchez Ameijeiras, *Rostros*, 152, 164.

612 Brown, *Holkham Picture Bible*, 31, 88. See Robert Mills, *Seeing Sodomy in the Middle Ages* (Chicago: University of Chicago Press, 2015), 279–97 et passim.

613 Kumler, *Translating Truth*, 2; Ganz, *Buch-Gewänder*, 11–12 et passim.

614 Zchomelidse, *Art, Ritual*, 36–41 et passim; Kessler, "Object as Subject"; Richard G. Newhauser and Arthur J. Russell, "Mapping Virtual Pilgrimage in an Early Fifteenth-Century *Arma Christi* Roll," in *Arma Christi*, 83–112; Don C. Skemer, *Binding Words: Textual Amulets in the Middle Ages* (University Park: Pennsylvania State Press, 2006); Hamburger, *Script*; Conrad Rudolph, "The Tour Guide in the Middle Ages: Guide Culture and the Mediation of Public Art," *Art Bulletin* 100, no. 1 (2018), 36–67.

615 Garrison, "Mimetic Bodies"; Robert A. Maxwell, "Sealing Signs and the Art of Transcribing in the Vierzon Cartulary," *Art Bulletin* 81, no. 4 (1999), 576–97; "Literate' Lay Donor," 264–68, and "La *memoria* du medium dans le monde juridique," in *Revue d'Auvergne* (forthcoming).

616 Newman, "Visionären Texte," 104.

617 The form reached Europe from North Africa: Shalev-Eyni, *Jews Among Christians*, 2–6.

618 Katrin Kogman-Appel, "Christianity, Idolatry, and the Question of Jewish Figural Painting in the Middle Ages," *Speculum* 84, no. 1 (2009), 73–107.

619 Henrike Manuwald, "How to Read the 'Andachtsbüchlein aus der Sammlung Bouhier (Montpellier, BU Médecine, H 396)'? On Cultural Techniques Related to a Fourteenth-century Devotional Manuscript," in *Reading Books and Prints as Cultural Objects*, ed. Evanghelia Stead (New York: Palgrave, 2018), 57–77.

620 Cannon, *Religious Poverty*, 119–37.

621 Frank O. Büttner, "Der illuminierte Psalter im Westen," in *The Illuminated Psalter: Studies in the Context, Purpose and Placement of its Images*, ed. Frank O. Büttner (Turnhout: Brepols, 2004), 1–106.

622 Chazelle, *Crucified God*, 242–43.

623 Diane J. Reilly, "Giant Bibles and their English Relatives: Blood Relatives or Adopted Children?," *Scriptorium* 56, no. 2 (2002), 294–311.

624 Dutton and Kessler, *Poetry and Paintings*, 65–66; Kessler, *Spiritual Seeing*, 175–87.

625 Wilhelm Koehler and Florentine Mütherich, *Die Karolingischen Miniaturen* 6, pt. 2 (Berlin: Deutscher Verlag für Kunstwissenschaft, 1999), 109–74; *La Bibbia carolingia dell'Abbazia di San Paolo fuori le Mura*, ed. Marco Cardinali (Rome: Edizioni Abbazia San Paolo, 2009).
626 Ulrich Kuder, "Die dem Hiobbuch vorausgestellten Bildseiten des 2. Bandes der Bible von Floreffe," in *Per assiduum stadium*, 109–36; Anne-Marie Bouché, "The Spirit in the Word: The Virtues of the Floreffe Bible Frontispiece: British Library, Add. MS 17738, ff. 3v-4r," in *Virtue & Vice: The Personifications in the Index of Christian Art*, ed. Colum Hourihane (Princeton: Department of Art and Archaeology of Princeton University, 2000), 42–65, and "'Vox imagines': Anomaly and Enigma in Romanesque Art," in *Mind's Eye*, 306–35; Hamburger, *St. John the Divine*, 83–91; Joyner, *Hortus deliciarum*, 127–29.
627 *Bibbie atlantiche*; Reilly, "Giant Bibles."
628 Nees, "Problems"; Christopher De Hamel, *The Book: A History of the Bible* (New York: Phaidon, 2001); Diane J. Reilly, *The Art of Reform in Eleventh-Century Flanders: Gerard of Cambrai, Richard of Saint-Vanne and the Saint-Vaast Bible* (Leiden: Brill, 2006), 45–104, and "Lectern Bibles and Liturgical Reform in the Central Middle Ages," in *Practice of the Bible*, 105–25; Larry Hurtado, *The Earliest Christian Artifacts: Manuscripts and Christian Origins* (Grand Rapids, MI: Eerdmans, 2006), 95–134.
629 Catherine E. Karkov, *Text and Picture in Anglo-Saxon England: Narrative Strategies in the Junius 11 Manuscript* (Cambridge: Cambridge University Press, 2001); Mary Coker Joslin and Carolyn Coker Joslin Watson, *The Egerton Genesis* (London: The British Library, 2001); *Anglo-Saxon Kingdoms*, 212–61.
630 Karkov, *Text and Picture*.
631 Benjamin C. Withers, "A 'secret and feverish genesis': the Prefaces of the Old English Hexateuch," *Art Bulletin* 81, no. 1 (1999), 53–71, and *The Illustrated Old English Hexateuch, Cotton Claudius B.iv: The Frontier of Seeing and Reading in Anglo-Saxon England* (London: The British Library, 2007); Herbert Broderick, *Moses the Egyptian in the Illustrated Old English Hexateuch* (London, British Library Cotton MS Claudius B.iv) (Notre Dame, IN: University of Notre Dame Press, 2017).
632 Flora, *Devout Belief*.
633 Eran Lupu, Sussan Babaie, and Vera Basch Moreen, "Übersetzungen," in *Die Kreuzritterbibel: Pierpont Morgan Library, New York, M 638*, ed. Daniel H. Weiss (Luzern: Faksimile Verlag, 1999), 91–174; William Noel, "The First Iconographer of the Morgan Picture Bible," in *Book of Kings*, 109–19.
634 Susanne Wittekind, "Bild-Text-Gesang: Überlegungen zum Prümer Tropar-Sequentiar (Paris, Bibliothèque National, MS. lat. 9448)," in *Bild und Text im Mittelalter* (Cologne: Böhlau Verlag, 2011), 99–124.
635 Hahn, *Portrayed on the Heart*, 18–28.
636 Arnulf, *Versus ad Picturas*, 265–302 et passim; *Pictor in Carmine*.
637 Hahn, *Portrayed on the Heart*, 21–28 et passim; Lowden, "Illuminated Manuscripts and the Liturgy," in *Objects, Images*, 17–53.
638 Hahn, *Portrayed on the Heart*, 232–48.
639 Diebold, *Word and Image*; Donatella Nebbiai et al., *Le discours des livres: Bibliothèques et manuscrits en Europe IXe–XVe siècle* (Rennes: Presses universitaires de Rennes, 2013); Kumler, *Translating Truth*; Jeffrey F. Hamburger et al., *Liturgical Life and Latin Learning at Paradies bei Soest, 1300–1425* (Münster: Aschendorff Verlag, 2016), 744–50.
640 Susanne Wittekind, "Die Makkabäer als Vorbild des geistlichen Kampfes: eine kunsthistorische Deutung des Leidener Makkabäer-Codex Perizoni 17," *Frühmittelalterliche Studien* 37 (2003), 47–71.
641 Gearhart, *Theophilus*, 17–18, 48–50.

642 Kathryn B. Gerry, "The Alexis Quire and the Cult of Saints at St. Albans," *Historical Research* 82 (2009), 593–612, and "Reading between the Lines: Alexis, Christ and the Construction of the Saintly Ideal in the St. Albans Psalter," *Arte medievale* ser. 4, 4 (2014), 81–94.

643 Jeffrey F. Hamburger, "Idol Curiosity," in *Curiositas: Welterfahrung und ästhetische Neugierde in Mittelalter und früher Neuzeit*, ed. Klaus Krüger (Göttingen: Wallstein Verlag, 2002), 19–58; Anton von Euw, *Die St. Galler Buchkunst vom 9. bis zum Ende des 11. Jahrhunderts* (St. Gall: Monastery, 2008), 1:502–03; David Ganz, "Der lineare Blick: Geometrie und Korperwelt in mittelalterlichen Bildern der Himmelsschau," in *Sehen und Sakralität in der Vormoderne*, ed. David Ganz et al. (Berlin: Reimer, 2011), 266–91; Francesco Stella, "Poesie computistiche e meraviglie astronomiche: sull'horologium nocturnum' di Pacifico," in *Mirabilia: gli effetti speciali nelle letterature del Medioevo; atti delle IV Giornate internazionali interdisciplinary di studio sul Medioevo* (Torino: 10–12 aprile 2013), ed. Francesco Mosetti Casaretto and Roberta Ciocca (Alessandria: Edizioni dell'Orso, 2014), 181–26.

644 Fabio Guidetti, "Texts and Illustrations in Venice, Biblioteca Nazionale Marciana, MS lat. VIII 22 (2760)," in *Certissima signa: A Venice Conference on Greek and Latin Astronomical Texts*, ed. Filippomaria Pontani (Venice: Edizioni Ca'Foscari, 2017), 97–125; Isabelle Draelants, "Le *Liber Nemroth de astronomia*: Mise au pointe et nouveaux indices," *Revue d'Histoire des textes*, n. s. 13 (2018), 245–329.

645 Dana Katz, "From Norman to Hohenstaufen Rule of Sicily: The Representation of Matthew of Ajello in the *Liber ad honorem Augusti* and the Church of La Magione in Palermo," *Convivium* 5, no. 1 (2018), 66–79.

646 Christel Meier, "Illustration und Textcorpus: Zu kommunikations- und ordnungsfunktionaler Aspekten der Bilder in den mittelalterlicher Enzyklopädiehandschriften," *Frühmittelalterlichen Studien* 31 (1997), 1–31; Brigitte Roux, *Mondes en miniatures: L'iconographie du* Livre du Trésor *de Brunetto Latini* (Geneva: Librairie Droz, 2009), 15–42.

647 Evelyn Edson, *Mapping Time and Space: How Medieval Mapmakers Viewed Their World* (London: The British Library, 1997), 36–51.

648 Giulia Orofino, *I codici decorati dell'Archivio di Montecassino* (Rome: Istituto Poligrafico e zecca dello stato, 2000), 50–86.

649 Joyner, *Hortus deliciarum*.

650 Lina Bolzoni, *La rete delle immagini: Predicazione in volgare dalle origini a Bernadino da Siena* (Turin: Einaudi, 2002), 61–71 (English trans., *The Web of Images: Vernacular Preaching from its Origins to St Bernardino da Siena*, trans. Carole Preston and Lisa Chien [Aldershot: Ashgate, 2004], 50–57).

651 Allegra Iafrate, "Of Stars and Men: Matthew Paris and the Illustrations of MS Ashmole 304," *Journal of the Warburg and Courtauld Institutes* 76 (2013), 139–77.

652 Newhauser and Russell, "Mapping."

653 *The Cambridge Illuminations: Ten Centuries of Book Production in the Medieval West* (cat. of an exhib., Cambridge), ed. Paul Binski and Stella Panayotova (London: Harvey Miller, 2005), 315–16; Paul Binski et al., *Western Illuminated Manuscripts: A Catalogue of the Collection in Cambridge University Library* (Cambridge: Cambridge University Press, 2011), 139–41; *The Medieval Craft of Memory: An Anthology of Texts and Pictures*, ed. Mary Carruthers and Jan M. Ziolkowski (Philadelphia: University of Pennsylvania Press, 2002), 120–23; Mary Carruthers, "Intention, sensation et mémoire dans l'esthétique médiévale tardive," in *Cinq sens*, 59–77; Thea Summerfield, "'Aprendre e enseigner': The Contents of Cambridge University Library, MS Gg.1.1," in *The Dynamics of the Medieval Manuscript: Text Collections from a European Perspective*, ed. Karen Pratt et al. (Göttingen: Vandenhoeck & Ruprecht, 2017), 327–36.

654 Éric Palazzo, *L'invention*, 252–66, and "La mise en action des images dans L'illustration du sacramentaire de Gellone: le canon de la messe et le ritual baptismal," *Codex Aqvilarensis* 29 (2013), 49–60; Cynthia Hahn, "The Performative Letter in the Carolingian Sacramentary of Gellone," in *Sign and Design*, 237–57.
655 Palazzo, *L'évêque*, 111–81; Le Goff et al., *Sacre royal*; Lowden, "Illuminated Manuscripts and the Liturgy."
656 Christine Jakobi-Mirwald, *Text-Buchstabe-Bild: Studien zur historisierten Initiale im 8. und 9. Jahrhundert* (Berlin: Reimer, 1998), 40–45 et passim; Laura Kendrick, *Animating the Letter: The Figurative Embodiment of Writing from Late Antiquity to the Renaissance* (Columbus: The Ohio State University, 1999), 80–81, 86–90 et passim.
657 Winterer, *Sakramentar*; Waldhoff, "Synagoga."
658 Pierre Alain Mariaux, *Warmond d'Ivrée et ses images: Politique de création iconographique autour de l'an mil* (Bern: Peter Lang, 2002).
659 *Bonifacio VIII*, 138; Alessandro Tomei, "Pittori per la miniatura tra Duecento e Trecento," in *Il libro miniato a Roma nel Duecento: Riflessioni e proposte*, ed. Silvia Maddalo (Rome: Istituto Storico Italiano per il Medio Evo, 2016), 353–74.
660 Nino Zchomelidse, "Descending Word and Resurrecting Christ: Moving Images in Illuminated Liturgical Scrolls of South Italy," in *Meaning in Motion: The Semantics of Movement in Medieval Art*, ed. Nino Zchomelidse and Giovanni Freni (Princeton: Department of Art and Archaeology, 2011), 3–34.
661 Hamburger, *Visual and the Visionary*, 149–90; *Women and The Book: Assessing the Visual Evidence*, ed. Jane Taylor and Lesley Smith (London: The British Library, 1997).
662 Shalev-Eyni, *Jews Among Christians* and "Tradition in Transition"; Kogman-Appel, "Hebrew Manuscript Painting"; Marc Michael Epstein, *The Medieval Haggadah: Art, Narrative & Religious Imagination* (New Haven: Yale University Press, 2011), and *Skies of Parchment*; Cohen, *Signs and Wonders*, 2–7.
663 Thomas Lentes, "'Textus Evangelii': Materialität und Inszenierung des 'textus' in der Liturgie," in *Textus im Mittelalter: Komponenten und Situationen des Wortgebrauchs im schriftsemantischen Feld*, ed. Ludolf Kuchenbuch and Ute Kleine (Göttingen: Vandenhoeck & Ruprecht, 2006), 133–48; John Lowden, "The Word Made Visible: The Exterior of the Early Christian Book as Visual Argument," in *The Early Christian Book*, ed. William E. Klingshirn and Linda Safran (Washington, DC: Catholic University of America Press, 2007), 13–47; Kathryn Rudy, "Words as Devotional Objects," *Simulacrum* (May 2007), 29–33; Bruno Reudenbach, "Der Codex als Verkörperung Christi: Mediengeschichtliche, theologische und ikonographische Aspekte einer Leitidee früher Evangelienbücher," in *Erscheinungsformen und Handhabungen heiliger Schriften*, ed. Johann Friedrich Quack and Daniela Christina Luft (Berlin: De Gruyter, 2014), 229–44.
664 *Expositio super Librum generationis*, ed. R.B.C. Huygens (CCCM 224) (Turnhout: Brepols, 2008), 66; Gertsman, "Phantoms of Emptiness," 806–08.
665 Orth, "Widmungsgedicht," 42–43.
666 Michele Ferrari, *Il "Liber sanctae crucis" di Rabano Mauro: testo-immagine-contesto* (Bern: Peter Lang, 1999); Chazelle, *Crucified God*, 99–131; Hamburger, *Hrabanus redivivus*; Beatrice Kitzinger, "Recasting Hrabanus: Romanesque Praise for the Holy Cross," in *Romanesque and the Past: Retrospection in the Art and Architecture of Romanesque Europe*, ed. by John McNeill and Richard Plant (Leeds: British Archaeology Association, 2013), 221–41.
667 Hamburger, *Script*, 6–10.
668 Kessler, "Medietas /Mediator."
669 Rudy, *Postcards*, 41–52.
670 Vincent Debiais, "Les inscriptions médiévales de la Péninsule ibérique et les recherches européennes en épigraphie," *Revista Diálogos Mediterrânicos* 2 (2012), 34–47, and "From Christ's Monogram to God's Presence: An Epigraphic Contribution to the Study of Chrismon in Romanesque Sculpture" in *Sign and Design*, 135–51, Hamburger, *Script*, 11–19.

671 Cynthia Hahn, "Letter and Spirit: The Power of the Letter, the Enlivenment of the Word in Medieval Art," in *Visible Writings: Cultures, Forms, Readings*, ed. Marija Dalbello and Mary Shaw (New Brunswick: Rutgers University Press, 2011), 55–76, and "Performative Letter."

672 Carol Farr, *The Book of Kells: Its Function and Audience* (London: The British Library, 1997); Jennifer O'Reilly, "Gospel Harmony and the Names of Christ in the Book of Kells," in *The Bible as Book: The Manuscript Tradition*, ed. John L. Sharpe III and Kimberly van Kampen (London: The British Library and Oak Knoll Press, 1998), 73–88; Małgorzata Krasnodębska-D'aughton, "Decoration of the *In principio* Initials in Early Insular Manuscripts: Christ as a Visible Image of the Invisible God," *Word & Image* 18, no. 2 (2002), 105–22; Heather Pulliam, *Word and Image in the Book of Kells* (Dublin: Four Courts Press, 2006); Catherine E. Karkov, *The Art of Anglo-Saxon England* (Woodbridge: Boydell & Brewer, 2011).

673 Jennifer O'Reilly, "Patristic and Insular Traditions of the Evangelists: Exegesis and Iconography," in *Le Isole Britanniche e Roma in Età Romanobarbarica*, ed. Anna Maria Luiselli and Éamonn Ó Carragáin (Rome: Herder, 1998), 49–94, and "St. John the Evangelist: Between Two Worlds," in *Insular and Anglo-Saxon Art and Thought in the Early Medieval Period*, ed. Colum Hourihane (University Park: Penn State Press, 2011), 189–218; Hamburger, *St. John the Divine*, 9; Karkov, *Anglo-Saxon*, 256–58 et passim.

674 Ganz, *Medien der Offenbarung*, 174–76; *Buch-Gewänder*, 208–10 et passim; Éric Palazzo, "Le 'livre-corps' à l'époque carolingienne et son rôle dans la liturgie de la messe et sa théologie," *Quaestiones Medii Aevi Novae* 15 (2010), 31–63; Kingsley, *Bernward Gospels*.

675 Horst Wenzel, "Die Schrift und das Heilige," in *Die Verschriftlichung der Welt: Bild, Text und Zahl in der Kultur des Mittelalters und der Frühen Neuzeit*, ed. Horst Wenzel, Wilfried Seipel, and Gotthart Wunberg (Milan: Skira, 2000), 14–57; Silke Tammen, "Blut ist ein ganz besonderer 'Grund': Bilder, Texte und die Farbe Rot in einem kartäusischen Andachtsbüchlein (British Library, Ms. Egerton 1821)," in *Bild und Text*, 229–51; Marlene Villalobos Hennessy, "The Social Life of a Manuscript Metaphor. Christ's Blood as Ink," in *The Social Life of Manuscript Illumination: Manuscripts, Images, and Communication in the Later Middle Ages* (Turnhout: Brepols, 2013), 17–52; Ganz, *Buch-Gewänder*, 45–48.

676 Kogman-Appel, *Jewish Book Art*, "Jewish Art and Cultural Exchange," and "Role of Hebrew Letters"; Epstein and Frojmovic, *Skies of Parchment*.

677 It recalls the Gradual of Johann von Valkenburg made in Cologne a few years later; see Hamburger, "Work of Art," 390.

678 Skemer, *Binding Words*; Ryan D. Giles, *Inscribed Power: Amulets and Magic in Spanish Literature* (Toronto: University of Toronto Press, 2017), 26–56.

679 Ganz, *Buch-Gewänder*. The Oviedo *arca* may, in fact, once have sheltered an evangelistary but eventually housed relics; García de Castro Valdes, "Arqueta."

680 Michele P. Brown, *The Lindisfarne Gospels: Society, Spirituality, and the Scribe* (Toronto: University of Toronto Press, 2003), 209–10; Barbet-Massin, *L'enluminure*, 413–15.

681 Palazzo, "'Livres-corps'"; van Asperen, "'Veronique.'"

682 Ursula Peters, *Das Ich im Bild: Die Figur des Autors in volkssprachigen Bilderhandschriften des 13. bis 16. Jahrhunderts* (Cologne: Böhlau, 2008).

683 Hamburger, *St. John the Divine*, 49–50; Crivello, "Handschrift."

684 Pulliam, *Kells*, 180–88.

685 O'Reilly, "St. John the Evangelist," 193–97.

686 In the Weingarten Gospels (Stuttgart, Württembergische Landesbibliothek, Cod. HB II 40), John, alone among the evangelists, is shown enthroned on an orb like Christ in Majesty to portray the accompanying words "flying like an eagle the word of John aspires

to the heavens"; Hamburger, *St. John the Divine* 50–52; Herbert L. Kessler, "Carolingian Art as Spiritual Seeing" and "'Hoc visibile imaginatum figurat illud invisibile verum': Imagining God in Pictures of Christ," in *Seeing the Invisible*, 293–328. Christ was the *persona* of God; Belting, *Echte Bild*, 47–52.

687 Reilly, "Lectern Bibles"; *Cistercian Reform*, 181–85; Alessia Trivellone, *L'hérétique imaginé: Hétérodoxie et iconographie dans l'occident médiéval, de l'époque carolingienne à l'inquisition* (Turnhout: Brepols, 2009), 174–88 et passim; "'Styles' pour enlumineurs dans le scriptorium de Cîteaux? Pour une relecture des premières miniatures cisterciennes," *Cahiers de Saint Michel-de-Cuxa* 43 (2012), 83–93, and "Images et exégèse monastique dans la Bible d'Étienne Harding," in *L'exégèse monastique au Moyen Âge (XIe–XIVe siècle)*, ed. Gilbert Dahan and Annie Noblesse-Rocher (Paris: Institut d'Études Augustiniennes, 2014), 85–131.

688 Sánchez Ameijeiras, *Rostros*, 199–213.

689 Kahsnitz, "Adagruppe," 34–40.

690 Herbert L. Kessler, "Jerome and Vergil in Carolingian Frontispieces and the Uses of Translation," in *Le Manuscrits carolingiens: Actes du colloque de Paris, Bibliothèque nationale de France, le 4 mai 2007*, ed. Jean-Pierre Caillet and Marie-Pierre Laffitte (Turnhout: Brepols, 2010), 121–40.

691 Alessia Trivellone, "Culte des saints et construction identitaire à Cîteaux: les images de Jérôme dans les manuscrits réalisés sous l'abbatiat d'Étienne Harding," in *Normes et hagiographie dans l'occident latin (VIe–XVIe)*, ed. Marie-Céline Isaïa and Thomas Granier (Turnhout: Brepols, 2014), 215–34; Reilly, *Cistercian Reform*, 62–80.

692 The Bible illuminated in 960, under the supervision of the "magister" Florentius (León, Real Colegiata de San Isidoro, Cod. 2), for instance, introduces nearly one hundred small pictures within the columns of the Old Testament; John Williams, "The Bible in Spain," in *Imaging the Early Medieval Bible*, 179–218. Generally: John Lowden, "The Beginnings of Biblical Illustration," in *Imaging the Early Medieval Bible*, 9–59; Henrike Manuwald, "'Eine blühende Nachkommenschaft und ein hürendehmender Steuerberater': Zur medialen Struktur und Funktion von Wortillustration," *Archiv für Kunstgeschichte* 92 (2010), 1–45; Catherine Brown, "Remember the Hand: Bodies and Bookmaking in Early Medieval Spain," *Word & Image* 27, no. 3 (2011), 262–78; Hamburger, "Word Illustration," in *Liturgical Life*, 750–51.

693 David Wright, *Der Vergilius Romanus und die Ursprünge mittelalterlichen Buches* (Stuttgart: Belser, 2001). The fifth-century Greek Genesis that served as the basic model of the San Marco atrium mosaics is a famous example; *Atrium von San Marco*.

694 Midori Tsuzumi, "The Utrecht Psalter and the Late Antique Paintings: Source of Its Composition," *Memoires of the Faculty of Education of Toyama University* 54 (2000), 63–77; William Noel, "Medieval Charades and the Visual Syntax of the Utrecht Psalter," in *Illustration of the Psalter*, 34–41.

695 Chazelle, "Ebo and Hincmar"; *Crucified God*, 242–43 et passim; Hamburger, *Script*, 33–37.

696 Peter K. Klein, "Stellung und Bedeutung des Bamberger Apokalypse-Zyklus," in *Das Buch mit 7 Siegeln: Die Bamberger Apokalypse*, ed. Gude Suckale-Redlefsen and Bernhard Schemmel (Luzern: Faksimile Verlag, 2000), 105–36.

697 Renana Bartal, *Gender, Piety, and Production in Fourteenth-Century Illustrated Apocalypse Manuscripts* (London: Routledge, 2016).

698 Flora, *Devout Belief*, 117–86.

699 Williams, *Beatus*; Klein, "Prototypes and Models."

700 Withers, *Hexateuch*, 86–120 et passim.

701 Kessler, "Real Absence," 116–19.

702 Wolfgang Hartl, *Text und Miniaturen der Handschrift "Dialogus de laudibus sanctae crucis"* (München, Bayerische Staatsbibliothek Clm 14159), and *Ein monastischer Dialog und*

sein Bilderzyklus (Hamburg: Verlag Dr. Kovač, 2007); Jeffrey Hamburger, *Diagramming Devotion: Berthold of Nuremberg's Transformation of Hrabanus Maurus's Poems in Praise of the Cross* (Chicago: University of Chicago Press, 2019), 136–39.

703 Conrad Rudolph, *Violence & Daily Life: Reading, Art, and Polemics in the Cîteaux Moralia in Job* (Princeton: Princeton University Press, 1997), 159–64 et passim.

704 Lowden, *Bibles Moralisées*, 2:199–209.

705 Alejandro García Avilés, "Imagenes 'viventes': Idolatria y herejia en las Cantígas de Alfonso X el Sabio," *Goya* 321 (2007), 324–42; Francisco Prado-Vilar, "Parchment," 490–93, and "Arte y diplomacia: el discurso del regalo en las relaciones con Oriente," in *Alfonso X el Sabio: Catálogo de la exposición celebrada en Murcia (2009–10)*, ed. Isidro Bango Torviso (Murcia: Caja de Ahorros del Mediterráneo, 2009), 186–89; Sánchez Ameirjeiras, *Rostros*, 213–50; Kennedy, "Seeing is Believing"; Giles, *Inscribed Power*, 26–30; Estefanía Piñol Álvarez, "Alfonso X y el Mediterráneo: algunas reflexiones acerca de la influencia de los manuscritos iluminados árabes en las *Cantigas de Santa María*," *Territorio, Sociedad y Poder*, 13 (2018), 71–99.

706 Kathrin Müller, *Visuelle Weltaneignung: Astronomische und kosmologische Diagramme in Handschriften des Mittelalters* (Göttingen: Vandenhoeck & Ruprecht, 2008), 54–56.

707 Martina Bagnoli, "Making Sense," in *A Feast for the Senses: Art and Experience in Medieval Europe*, ed. Martina Bagnoli (cat. of an exhib., Baltimore) (Baltimore: The Walters Art Museum, 2016), 22–23 (incorrectly labeled), 137–38; Tanja Klemm, "Life from Within: Physiology and Talismanic Efficacy in Marsilio Ficino's *De vita* (1498)," *Representations* 133 (2016), 110–29; Lakey, *Sculptural Seeing*, 28–29; A similar but distinct diagram of the brain in a fourteenth-century compendium, also in Cambridge (University Library, MS Gg.1.1), has been discussed extensively: Camille, "Before the Gaze"; Carruthers, *Craft of Memory*, 118–88, and "Mechanisms for the Transmission of Culture: The Role of 'Place' in the Arts of Memory," in *Translatio or the Transmission of Culture in the Middle Ages and the Renaissance: Modes and Messages*, ed. Laura H. Hollengreen (Turnhout: Brepols, 2009), 1–26; Tanja Klemm, *Bildphysiologie: Wahrnehmung und Körper in Mittelalter und Renaissance* (Berlin: Akademie Verlag, 2013), 12–13; Hartnell, *Bodies*, 34–36.

708 Lynn Ransom, "Innovation and Identity: A Franciscan Program of Illumination in the *Verger de soulas* (Paris, Bibliothèque Nationale de France, MS. fr. 9220)," in *Insights and Interpretations: Studies in Celebration of the Eighty-Fifth Anniversary of the Index of Christian Art*, ed. Colum Hourihane (Princeton: Department of Art and Archaeology, 2002), 85–105, and "Eyes Have It"; Hélène Bouget, "Le *Miroir de vie et de mort*: une enluminure du *Vrigiet de solas*," *Miroirs et jeux de miroirs dans la littérature médiévale*, ed. Fabienne Pomel (Rennes: Presses universitaires de Rennes, 2003), 109–24; Kumler, *Translating Truth*, 63–68.

709 Isidore of Seville, *Etymologiae*, VI, vxiii–xxiv; Ganz, *Buch-Gewänder*, 288.

710 Ganz, *Medien der Offenbarung*, 323.

711 Ganz, *Medien der Offenbarung*, 162–88; Jeffrey F. Hamburger, *Ouvertures: La double page dans les manuscrits enluminés du Moyen Âge* (Dijon: Presses du Réel, 2010); Tina Bawden, "The Relationship between Letter and Frame in Insular and Carolingian Manuscripts," in *Graphic Devices*, 143–62.

712 Texts and ornament also tie the paired dedication pages in the Bernward Gospels together. The verses bearing on the gift extend from the one to the other, and the church represented by three arches behind the bishop is understood as the earthly realization of the heavenly church rendered in the three arches behind the Virgin and Child, just as the paten and chalice on the altar are figures of Christ on Mary's lap; Kingsley, *Bernward Gospels*, 15–17 et passim.

713 Ganz, *Medien der Offenbarung*, 30–100.

714 Kumiko Maekawa, *Narrative and Experience* (Frankfurt am Main: Peter Lang, 2000); Harvey Stahl, *Picturing Kingship: History and Painting in the Psalter of Saint Louis* (University Park: Penn State University Press, 2007), 19–23 et passim.
715 Biernoff, *Sight and Embodiment*, 158–62; Lindquist, "Nudity," 14–15.
716 Lucy Freeman Sandler, "The Study of Marginal Imagery: Past, Present, and Future," *Studies in Iconography* 18 (1997), 1–49; Andreas Bräm, "L'Évolution de la mise en page et du décor marginal," in Jean Wirth, *Les marges à drôleries des manuscrits gothiques* (Geneva: Librairie Droz, 2008), 45–77; Zchomelidse, "Liminal Phenomena," 249–51; Bawden, "Relationship between Letter and Frame."
717 Norbert H. Ott, "Texte und Bilder: Beziehungen zwischen den Medien Kunst und Literatur in Mittelalter und früher Neuzeit," in *Verschriftlichung*, 104–43.
718 Palazzo, "Mise en action"; Pulliam, "Exaltation"; Hahn, "Performative Letter."
719 Anna Somfai, "The Nature of Daemons: A Theological Application of the Concept of Geometrical Proportion in Calcidius' *Commentary* to Plato's *Timaeus* (40d-41a)," in *Ancient Approaches to Plato's Timaeus*, ed. R.W. Sharples and Anne Sheppard (London: University of London, 2003), 129–42; "Calcidius' *Commentary* on Plato's *Timaeus* and Its Place in the Commentary Tradition: The Concept of *Analogia* in Text and Diagrams," *Bulletin of the Institute of Classical Studies* 47 (2004), 203–220; Bruce Eastwood and Gerd Graßhoff, "Planetary Diagrams for Roman Astronomy in Medieval Europe, ca. 800–1500," *Transactions of the American Philosophical Society* 94 (2004); Peter Dronke, *The Spell of Calcidius: Platonic Concepts and Images in the Medieval West* (Florence, 2008), xviii-xix; Kessler, "Dynamic Signs."
720 Müller, *Visuelle Weltaneignung*, 51–54; Hahn, "Performative Letter," 252.
721 As the Tours Sacramentary did to capture the essence of the Preface's Trinitarian argument; Kessler, "Dynamic Signs," 127–28.
722 Pulliam, "Exaltation," 99–112.
723 Provoked by the letter's sound, the initial *S* that begins Psalm 68 in Peter Lombard's Commentary on Psalms produced for Archbishop Hartwig of Bremen in 1166 (Bremen, Staats- und Universitätsbibliothek, MS a.244, fol. 113ᵛ) pictures the brazen serpent typology to contrast the Jews who lack faith with Mary and John; Walter Cahn, "Illuminated Psalter Commentaries," in *Psalms in Community: Jewish and Christian Textual, Liturgical, and Artistic Traditions*, ed. Harold. W. Attridge and Margot E. Fassler (Atlanta: Society of Biblical Literature, 2003), 241–63; Stahl, *Picturing Kingship*, 132–67.
724 Elizabeth Sears, "'Reading' Images" in *Reading Medieval Images*, 1–7.
725 Michele Brown, "The Visual Rhetoric of Insular Decorated Incipit Openings," in *Graphic Devices*, 127–42.
726 Reudenbach, *Godescalc-Evangelistar*, 51–67; Lafitte, *L'évangéliaire*, 30–31.
727 Klein, *Apocalypsis Carolingio*.
728 Kumler, *Translating Truth*, 87–90.
729 Aden Kumler, "Handling the Letter," in *St. Albans and the Markyate Psalter*, 69–100.
730 Rudolph, *Violence & Daily Life*; Reilly, *Cistercian Reform*, 154–64.
731 Kendrick, *Animating the Letter*; Jakobi-Mirwald, *Text-Buchstabe-Bild*; Charles S. Buchanan, "Late Eleventh-Century Illuminated Initials from Lucca: Partisan Political Imagery during the Investiture Struggle," *Arte medievale*, 2nd ser. 12/13 (1998/1999), 65–73.
732 Heck, *L'échelle*, 70–73; Constant Mews, *Listen, Daughter: The* Speculum Virginum *and the Formation of Religious Women in the Middle Ages* (New York: Palgrave, 2001).
733 Rudolph, *Mystic Ark*, 49–51 et passim.
734 Mary J. Carruthers, "Ars oblivionalis, ars inveniendi: The Cherub Figure and the Arts of Memory," *Gesta* 48, no. 2 (2009), 99–119.
735 Rudolph, *Violence & Daily Life*, 44–49.
736 Dutton and Kessler, *Poetry and Paintings*, 94–95.

737 Herbert L. Kessler, "'Facies bibliothecae revelata': Carolingian Art as Spiritual Seeing," in *Spiritual Seeing*, 149–89.
738 Wenzel, "Schrift"; Rudy, *Postcards*, 225–66. Carmela Franklin, "Words as Food: Signifying the Bible in the Early Middle Ages," in *Comunicare e significare nell'alto medioevo* (LII settimana di studio) (Spoleto: CISAM, 2005), 733–62; Reilly, *Cistercian Reform*, 141–59.
739 Recht, *Croire et voir*, 97–250 (*Believing and Seeing*, 69–174); *L'Église, lieu de performances*.
740 *Gerardi Cameracensis Acta synodi Atrebatensis*, ed. Steven Vanderputten and Diane J. Reilly (CCCM 270) (Turnhout: Brepols, 2014); Samuel W. Collins, *The Carolingian Debate over Sacred Space* (New York: Palgrave/MacMillan, 2012); Bynum, *Materiality*, 163–67.
741 Regnerus Steensma and Justin E.A. Kroesen, *The Interior of the Medieval Village Church*, rev. ed. (Leuven: Peeters, 2012).
742 Palazzo, *L'espace rituel*.
743 Thomas E.A. Dale, "Introduction," in *Shaping Sacred Space*, 1–32; María Luisa Martin Ansón, "El ajuar litúrgico de las Iglesias románicas: objetos para el culto," in *Mobiliario y ajuar litúrgio en las Iglesias romanicas* (Aguilar de Campoo: Fundación Santa María la Real, 2011), 205–48; *Romanesque Cathedrals in Mediterranean Europe: Architecture, Ritual and Urban Context*, ed. Gerardo Boto Varela and Justin E.A. Kroesen (Turnhout: Brepols, 2016).
744 For instance, despite intense research, whether the Salerno ivories originally decorated doors, an antependium, or a throne has yet to be determined; *Salerno Ivories*, 211–39; Borsook, "Solomonic Throne."
745 On the strong ties to Jerusalem, see Palazzo, *L'espace rituel*, 165–66; Alexander Nagel, *Medieval Modern: Art Out of Time* (London: Thames & Hudson, 2012), 100–14 et passim; as a provisional paradise, see Jérôme Baschet, Jean-Claude Bonne, and Pierre-Olivier Dittmar, *Le Monde roman par-delà le bien et le mal* (Paris: Arkhe editions, 2012), 43–97.
746 Eivor Andersen Oftestad, "Beyond the Veil: Roman Constructs of the New Temple in the Twelfth Century," in *Visual Constructs of Jerusalem*, ed. Bianca Kühnel et al. (Turnhout: Brepols, 2014), 171–78.
747 Hediger and Kurmann-Schwarz, "Reliquie und Skulptur."
748 Sicard von Cremona, *Mitralis der Gottesdienst der Kirche: Einleitung, Übersetzung und Anmerkungen*, ed. Lorenz Weinrich (Turnhout: Brepols, 2011); Timothy M. Thibodeau, *The Rationale Divinorum Officiorum of William Durand of Mende* (New York: Columbia University Press, 2007).
749 Jung, "Beyond the Barrier," and *Gothic Screen*, 17–25 et passim.
750 Bruno Phalip, "Les grilles de choeur liturgique dans le Massif Central (XIe–XIIIe siècles): D'infranchissables transparences," in *L'Église, lieu de performances*, 39–54.
751 Pablo Ordás Díaz, "El mundo por cosas trabaja: la doble fortuna de Aristóteles en la Edad Media," *Goya* 361 (2017), 271–85.
752 Iogna-Prat, *La Maison Dieu*; Baschet, Bonne, and Dittmar, *Monde roman*, 29–31.
753 Hansen, *Spolia Churches*. The term "triumphal arch" was first applied to the wall between the nave and transept in the ninth century.
754 Michael Jacoff, "Fashioning a Façade: The Construction of Venetian Identity on the Exterior of San Marco," in *San Marco, Byzantium*, 113–50.
755 Baschet, Bonne, and Dittmar, *Monde roman*, 28–38; Susannah Crowder, "Ivory and Parchment, Flesh and Stone: Performance and the Activation of Sacred Space," in *L'Église, lieu de performances*, 137–48.
756 Stéphanie Diane Daussy, "*Quanto cultu auroque templa fulgerent*: toitures et beauté de la vision comme expression des pouvoirs," *Hortus Artium Medievalium* 21 (2015), 273–83.
757 Grooves in the exterior fabric of some Italian churches united them with adjacent marketplaces; Emanuele Lugli, "Hidden in Plain Sight: The *Pietre di Paragone* and the

Preeminence of Medieval Measurements in Communal Italy," *Gesta* 49, no. 2 (2010), 77–95.
758 Rudolph, "Gothic Portal," 575–79; Vincent Debiais, "Writing on Medieval Doors: The Surveyor Angel on the Moissac Capital (ca. 1100)," in *Writing Matters: Presenting and Perceiving Monumental Inscriptions in Antiquity and the Middle Ages*, ed. Irene Berti et al. (Berlin: De Gruyter, 2017), 285–308.
759 Kuder, "Christus Scheibe," 77.
760 Henry Maguire, "The Political Content of the Atrium Mosaics," in *Atrium*, 271–79; Beat Brenk, "Zur Funktion des Atriums von San Marco in Venedig," in *Atrium*, 49–72.
761 Stefano Riccioni, "From Shadow to Light: Inscriptions in Liminal Spaces of Roman Sacred Architecture (11th–12th Centuries)," in *Sacred Scripture/Sacred Space*, 217–44.
762 Rituals of dedication included the opening and closing of a saint's tomb; Lakey, *Sculptural Seeing*, 39.
763 Binski, "Rhetorical Occasions," 11.
764 Michele Bacci, *Lo spazio dell'anima: Vita di una chiesa medievale* (Bari: Giuseppe Laterza e filli, 2005), 79–85.
765 Deshman, "Disappearing Christ," 528 (*Eye and Mind*, 253–54).
766 Low, "'You Who Once Were Far Off,'" 473–81.
767 Hermann Kern, *Through the Labyrinth*, trans Abigail H. Clay, ed. Robert Ferré and Jeff Saward (Munich: Prestel, 2000), 106; Angelika Schineller, "Die Fussbodenmosaiken von San Savino in Piacenza: Überlegungen zu Ikonographie, Ikonologie und Funktion im Kirchenraum," *Arte Medievale* 8 (2008), 47–68; Giancarlo Pavat, "The Labyrinth of St. Petronio in Bologna, Italy," *Caerdroia* 45 (2016), 9–31. See also the labyrinth at the start of the ninth century Gospels of Otrid von Weissenberg (Vienna, ÖNB, Cod. Vind. 2687, fol. 1r); Beatrice E. Kitzinger, *The Cross, the Gospels, and the Work of Art in the Carolingian Age* (Cambridge: Cambridge University Press, 2018), 106–14.
768 Paul Binski, "Reflections on the 'Wonderful Height and Size' of Gothic Great Churches and the Medieval Sublime," in *Magnificence and the Sublime*, 129–56; *Gothic Wonder*, 32–33.
769 Elaine M. Beretz, "Adjustments for the Innovative: Installing a Rose Window into the North Façade of Saint-Étienne, Beauvais," *AVISTA Forum Journal* 14 (2004), 17–24; Nigel Hiscock, *The Symbol at Your Door: Number and Geometry in Religious Architecture of the Greek and Latin Middle Ages* (Aldershot: Ashgate, 2007), 165–71.
770 Mathieu Beaud, "Images de l'Épiphanie: une cérémonie de l'offrande," *Revue d'Auvergne* (2013), 77–94.
771 Low, "'You Who Once Were Far Off,'" 470–76; Thunø, *Apse Mosaic*, 69–72 et passim; Rudolph, "Gothic Portal," 580–91.
772 Also, the portal of San Leonardo al Frigido (c. 1175) at the Cloisters (Metropolitan Museum in New York); Anita Moskowitz, *Italian Gothic Sculpture, c. 1250–c. 1400* (New York: Cambridge University Press, 2001), 13–14.
773 Heyman, "Fulcher's Bestiary," 105–34.
774 For example, in Pisa and on the remote early twelfth-century church of San Nicola in Sardinia; Karen Rose Mathews, "Other Peoples' Dishes: Islamic Bacini on Eleventh-Century Churches in Pisa," *Gesta* 53, no. 1 (2014), 5–23; Alberto Virdis, *San Nicola di Trullas gli affreschi: Intersezioni mediterranee nella Sardegna del XIII secolo* (Ariccia: Aracne, 2014), 91.
775 Substituting for John the Baptist, as seen in the refashioned version portrayed by Cimabue in the crossing of San Francesco at Assisi: Romano, *San Francesco ad Assisi*, 101–39; Chiara Frugoni, "L'Ytalia di Cimabue nella basilica superiore di Assisi: Uno sguardo dal transetto alla navata," in *Imago Urbis*, ed. Francesca Bocchi and Rosa Smurra (Rome: Viella, 2003), 33–63; Cooper and Robson, *Assisi*, 82–85; Peter Bokody, *Images-within-Images in Italian Painting (1250–1350): Reality and Reflexivity* (Farnham: Ashgate, 2015), 62–63; Erik

Thunø, "The Pantheon in the Middle Ages," in *The Pantheon: From Antiquity to the Present*, ed. Tod A. Marder and Mark Wilson Jones (Cambridge: Cambridge University Press, 2015), 231–54; Herbert L. Kessler, "Façade, Face, and Frontal Photo," *Codex Aqvilarensis* 31 (2016), 13–36.

776 Ilene Forsyth, "Narrative at Moissac: Schapiro's Legacy," *Gesta* 41, no. 2 (2002), 71–93; Meyer Schapiro, *Romanesque Architectural Sculpture*, ed. and intr. Linda Seidel (Chicago: University of Chicago Press, 2006), 45–48, 186–87, et passim; Marcello Angheben, "La théophanie du portail de *Moissac*: une vision de l'Église céleste célébrant la liturgie eucharistique," *Les cahiers de Saint-Michel de Cuxa* 44 (2014), 61–82.

777 Ilene H. Forsyth, "The Date of the Moissac Portal," in *Current Directions in Eleventh- and Twelfth-Century Sculpture Studies*, ed. Robert A. Maxwell and Kurt Ambrose (Turnhout: Brepols, 2010), 77–99; Palazzo, *L'invention*, 142–51.

778 Trinks, *Antike*, 10–13, 110–21 et passim; Francisco Prado-Vilar, "The Marble Tempest: Material Imagination, the Echoes of *Nostos* and the Transfiguration of Myth in Romanesque Sculpture," in *Icons of Sound: Voice, Architecture and Imagination*, ed. Bissera V. Pentcheva (New York: Fordham University Press, forthcoming).

779 Jérôme Baschet, *Le sein du père: Abraham et la paternité dans l'occident médiéval* (Paris: Gallimard, 2000); Ilene Forsyth, "Narrative at Moissac"; Jean Wirth, *La datation de la sculpture médiévale* (Geneva: Droz, 2004); Dany Sandron, *Amiens: La cathédrale* (Paris: Zodiaque, 2004); Thomas E.A. Dale, "The Nude at Moissac," in *Current Directions*, 61–76; Angheben, *D'un jugement à l'autre*, 570–95.

780 Rudolph, "Gothic Portal," 589.

781 *Conservation of the Last Judgment Mosaic St. Vitus Cathedral, Prague*, ed. Francesca Piqué and Dusan C. Tulik (Los Angeles: Getty Publications, 2004).

782 Ambrose, *Vézelay*, 14–15.

783 Jaromir Homolka, "The Pictorial Decoration of the Palace and Lesser Tower of Kalstein Castle," in *Magister Theodoricus*, 74–86; Hana Šedinová, "The Precious Stones of Heavenly Jerusalem in the Medieval Book Illustration and Their Comparison with the Wall Incrustation in St. Wenceslas Chapel," *Artibus et Historiae* 21 (2000), 31–47.

784 Rudolf Dellermann, "Die Vorhalle von San Marco vor den Genesismosaiken-Aspekte der Bau-, Ausstattungs- und Nutzungsgeschichte," in *Atrium*, 21–47; Brenk, "Funktion des Atriums."

785 Ambrose, *Vézelay*, 13–15.

786 Low, "'You Who Once Were Far Off,'" 484.

787 Debiais, "Writing on Medieval Doors," 285–86.

788 Bredekamp, *Bildakts* 77 (*Image Acts*), 50; Michael Brandt, *Bernwards Tür*; "Mentem et oculos pascere—Bernwards Kunst," *Niederdeutsche Beiträge zur Kunstgeschichte*, n. s. 2 (2016) 9–26; Weinryb, *Bronze Object*, 70–73.

789 Bredekamp, *Souverän*, 88–103.

790 Weinryb, "Avant-Garde," 747–58.

791 Cohen and Derbes, "Bernward and Eve"; Stahl, "Eve's Reach"; Brandt, *Bernwards Tür*; Marchesin, *L'arbre*, 97–99. The Marian allegory is explicit in the arches over the Virgin's head in the dedication of the miniature of Bernward's Gospel inscribed: "The door of Paradise closed through the first Eve, now is through Holy Mary thrown open to all"; Kingsley, *Bernward Gospels*, 20.

792 Krause, "Venedigs Sitz im Paradies"; Reed, "Blessing the Serpent," 41.

793 Caroline Roux, *La pierre et le seuil: Portails romans en Haute-Auvergne* (Clermont Ferrand: Presses universitaires Blaise-Pascal, 2004).

794 Basing his claim on Bede's *De templo* (Book I, chap. 6), *Mitralis*, Book I, chap. 4, *ed. cit.*, 13; Jérôme Baschet, *L'iconographie médiévale* (Paris: Gallimard, 2008), 77; Baschet, Bonne, and Dittmar, *Monde roman*, 28–38.

795 Fabio Barry, "Walking on Water: Cosmic Floors in Antiquity and the Middle Ages," *Art Bulletin* 89, no. 4 (2007), 627–56; Rebecca Molholt, "Roman Labyrinth Mosaics and the Experience of Motion," *Art Bulletin* 93, no. 3 (2011), 287–303.

796 Barral I Altet, *Décor*, 327–29; Arturo Carlo Quintavalle, "Testi e figure della memoria: pavimenti musivi e imagine del mondo," in *Medioevo: imagine e memoria* (acts of an international congress, Parma), ed. Arturo Carlo Quintavalle (Parma: Università di Parma, 2009), 13–39; Maddalena Vaccaro, "La scacchiera del mosaico di S. Savino: Due letture della virtù," in *Gli scacchi e il chiostro: Atti del convegno nazionale di studi (Atti del convegno nazionale di studi, Brescia, 2006)*, ed. Angelo Baronio (Brescia: Fondazione civiltà bresciana, 2007), 129–54; *"Pavia città ragguardevole": Mosaici pavimentale e cultura figurative nel XII secolo* (Mantua: SAP Società Archaeologica, 2016)," 231–41 et passim; Schineller, "Fussbodenmosaiken."

797 Grazio Gianfreda, *Il mosaico di Otranto: Biblioteca medioevale in immagini* (Lecce: Edizioni del Grifo, 2001); Barral i Altet, *Décor*.

798 Barral I Altet, *Décor*, 306–07.

799 In San Tommaso at Acquanera, the arrangement even made specific connections between the creatures in conflict and the inferno of judgment; Maddalena Vaccaro, "Il mosaico pavimentale: frammenti, connessioni, visioni," in *San Tommaso ad Acquanegra sul chiese: Storia, architettura e contesto figurative di una chiesa abbaziale romanica*, ed. Fabio Scirea (Mantua: SAP Società Archeologica, 2015), 251–74.

800 Baschet, Bonne, and Dittmar, *Monde roman*, 72–97.

801 Gerardo Boto Varela, "Caracterización icónica y delimitación visual de los lugares postiminares en las Iglesias románicas españolas," in *L'Église, lieu de performances*, 265–81.

802 Marcello Angheben, *Les chapiteaux romans de Bourgogne: Thèmes et programmes* (Turnhout: Brepols, 2003); Ambrose, *Vézelay*, 20–28.

803 Angheben, *Chapiteaux*, 219; Ambrose, *Vézelay*, 103; biblical exegesis maintained that the calf is the devil, but no knowledge of theology is needed to decipher the dramatic scene.

804 Robert Maxwell, "La sculpture romane et ses programmes: questions de méthode," in *Le programme: Une notion pertinente en histoire de l'art médiévale*, ed. Jean-Marie Guillouët and Claudia Rabel (Paris: Leopard d'or, 2011), 135–63; Kirk Ambrose, *The Marvellous and the Monstrous in the Sculpture of Twelfth-Century Europe* (Woodbridge: Boydell, 2013); Trinks, *Antike*, 110–21.

805 Marta Serrano and Ester Lozano, "The Cloistral Sculpture at La Seu d'Urgell and the Problem of the Visual Repertoire," in *Romanesque Cathedrals in Mediterranean Europe*, 275–89.

806 See p. 32. On Theophilus's fascination with Byzantium: Pentcheva, *Sensual Icon*, 223–24.

807 Uggé, "Rotolo," 22, 77–80.

808 *Die Bilderdecke der Hildesheimer Michaeliskirche. Erforschung eines Weltkulturebes*, ed. Rolf-Jürgen Grote and Vera Kellner (Munich: Deutscher Kunstverlag, 2002).

809 Wirth, *L'Image à l'époque romane*, 333–61 et passim; Serena Romano, "Il ciclo di San Pietro in Valle: strutture e stile," in *Affreschi*, 41–76.

810 Jeremy Johns, "Le pitture del soffito della Cappella Palatina" in *Cappella Palatina*, 387–407.

811 *Saint-Savin: L'Abbaye et ses peintures murales*, ed. Robert Favreau et al. (Poitiers: C.P.P.P.C., 1999); Marcello Angheben, "Saint-Savin-sur-Gartempe, nouvelles recherches: problématique et méthode," in *Couleurs et lumière à l'époque romane: Colloques d'Issoire 2005–2007* (Clermont-Ferrand: Revue d'Auvergne, 2011).

812 Binski, *Gothic Wonder*, 307.

813 Erik Inglis, "Gothic Architecture and a Scholastic: Jean de Jandun's 'Tractatus de laudibus Parisius' (1323)," *Gesta* 42, no. 1 (2003), 63–85; Cohen, "Indulgence."

814 Baschet, *L'iconographie*, 67–151; Steffen Bogen, "Itinerarprinzip und Ortsreferenz: Bilderzählung im sakralen Kontext (*Wiener Genesis* und Reichenau Oberzell)," in *Bild im Plural*, 135–60.
815 On animals, Baschet, Bonne, and Dittmar, *Monde roman*, 101–11.
816 Hahn, "Seeing and Believing"; Cécile Voyer, *Faire le ciel sur la terre: Les images hagiographiques et le décor peint de Saint-Eutrope aux Salles-Lavauguyon* (XIIe siècle) (Turnhout: Brepols, 2007), 217–37 et passim.
817 Geymonat, "Disegno," 55.
818 *Alfa e omega: Il giudizio universale tra oriente e occidente*, ed. Valentino Pace (Milan: Italica, 2006). At Reims, the wall of statues "suspended like a tapestry from the west triforium" connects the interior with the façade; Donna Sadler, *Reading the Reverse Façade of Reims Cathedral: Royalty and Ritual in Thirteenth-Century France* (Abingdon: Routledge-Ashgate, 2012).
819 Herbert L. Kessler, *Old St. Peter's and Church Decoration in Medieval Italy* (Spoleto: CISAM, 2002), 152–57 et passim; Müller, *Omnia in mensura*, 193–202.
820 *Universo di simboli*; Cappelletti, *Affreschi*; *Il Restauro della Cripta di Anagni*, ed. Alessandro Bianchi (Rome: Artemide, 2003); Francesca Romana Moretti, "La parabola delle dieci vergini nell'oratorio di S. Tommaso Becket ad Anagni: Rappresentazione pittorica di un drama medieval," in *Il Molise medievale: archeologia e arte* (Borgo S. Lorenzo: All'insegna del Giglio, 2010), 249–59; Claudia Quattrocchi, *Un martire inglese alla Curia di Roma: L'oratorio di San Thomas Becket di Canterbury nella cattedrale di Anagni* (Rome: Campisano Editore, 2017).
821 Herbert L. Kessler, "Sacred Light from Shadowy Things," *Codex Aqvilarensis* 32 (2017), 237–69.
822 Eva Frojmovic, "Giotto's Circumspection," *Art Bulletin* 89, no. 2 (2007), 195–210; Derbes and Sandona, *Usurer's Heart*, 150–52.
823 Jean-Claude Schmitt, "Les reliques et les images," in *Les reliques: Objets, cultes, symboles*, ed. Edina Bozóky and Anne-Marie Helvétius (Turnhout: Brepols, 1999), 145–59.
824 Filippini, "Functions."
825 Dale, *Relics, Prayer*, 66–76.
826 Osborne, "Dado Imagery"; Manuela Gianandrea, "Geschichtsschreibung und Erinnerung: Die Rolle von Papst Silvester in der Selbstdarstellung des römischen Papsttums (6.-12. Jahrhunderts)," in *Die Päpste und Rom zwischen Spätantike und Mittelalter: Formen päpstlicher Machtentfaltung*, ed. Norbert Zimmerman et al. (Regensburg: Schnell & Steiner, 2017), 55–76.
827 Romano, *San Francesco ad Assisi*, 101–39 et passim.
828 Hauknes, "Emblematic Narratives," 29–36.
829 Zsombor Jékely, "Narrative Structure of the Painted Cycle of a Hungarian Holy Ruler: The Legend of St. Ladislas," *Hortus Artium Medievalium* 21 (2015), 62–74.
830 Milagros Guardia and Carles Manco, "Pedret, Boí o dels origens de la Pintura mural romànica catalana," in *Les fonts de la pintura romànica*, ed. Milagros Guardia and Carles Mancho (Barcelona: Publicacions I Edicions de la Universitat de Barcelona, 2008); Milagros Guardia, "De lo supuestatmente profane y de lo sacro en las pinturas de Sant Joan de Boí," *Codex Aqvilarensis* 33 (2017), 85–105.
831 Milagros Guardia, "*Ioculatores et saltator*: Las pinturas con escenas de juglaría de Sant Joan de Boí," *Locus Amoenus* 5 (2000–2001), 11–32, and "De lo supuestamente profano," 103–05; Shalev-Eyni, *Jews Among Christians*, 59–60.
832 Kurmann-Schwarz, "Fenestre vitree," 67–68.
833 Herbert L. Kessler, "Shaded with Dust: Jewish Eyes on Christian Art," in *Judaism and Christian Art*, 74–114.
834 Gerald Guest, "The *Prodigal's Journey*: Ideologies of Self and City in the Gothic Cathedral," *Speculum* 81, no. 1 (2006), 35–75.

835 Caviness, "Stained Glass Windows," 135–48.
836 Zchomelidse, *Art, Ritual*, 15.
837 As also the later pulpits by Nicola Pisano in the Pisa and two by his son Giovanni in Pistoia and cathedral of Pisa: Anita Moskowitz, *Gothic Sculpture*, 74–90, and *Nicola and Giovanni Pisano: The Pulpits; Pious Devotion, Pious Diversion* (Turnhout: Brepols, 2006); Jules Lubbock, *Storytelling in Christian Art from Giotto to Donatello* (New Haven and London: Yale University Press, 2006); Seidel, *Nicola and Giovanni Pisano*.
838 Zchomelidse, *Art, Ritual*, 11–14 et passim.
839 Binski, *Gothic Wonder*, 101.
840 Foletti and Quadri, "Dialogo."
841 Tripps, "Man hole einen Schmied."
842 Claudia Bolgia, "Icons 'in the air': New Settings for the Sacred in Medieval Rome," in *Architecture and Pilgrimage*, 113–42.
843 Claudia Bolgia, "The Felici Icon Tabernacle (1372) at S. Maria in Aracoeli Reconstructed: Lay Patronage, Sculpture and Marian Devotion in Trecento Rome," *Journal of the Warburg and Courtauld Institutes* 68 (2005), 27–72.
844 Bolgia, "Icons," 124–25.
845 Peter Kovác, "Notes on the Description of the Sainte-Chapelle in Paris from 1378," in *Court Chapels of the High and Late Middle Ages and Their Artistic Decoration*, ed. Jiří Fajt (Prague: National Gallery, 2003), 413–18.
846 Achim Timmermann, *Real Presence: Sacrament Houses and the Body of Christ, ca. 1270–1600* (Turnhout: Brepols, 2009).
847 Rüdiger Becksmann, "Bildprogramme in der Glasmalerei des Mittelalters: Gesalt—Funktion—Bedeutung," in *Glasmalerei im Kontext*, 17–48.
848 Sandler, *Reims*, 237–39; Rowe, *Jew, Cathedral*, 203–16: Jung, "Moving Viewers," 33–34; Terrier Aliferis, *L'imitation*, 112–18.
849 Romano, *San Francesco ad Assisi*, 82–85.
850 T.A. Heslop, "*Contemplating Chimera in Medieval Imagination: St. Anselm's Crypt at Canterbury*," in *Raising the Eyebrow: John Onians and World Art Studies; An Album Amicorum in his Honour* (Oxford: Archaeopress, 2001), 153–68.
851 Yves Christe, "L'autel des innocents: Ap 6, 9–11 en regard de la liturgie de la toussaint et des saints innocents," in *Kunst und Liturgie*, 91–100.
852 *Universo di simboli*, 4–7; Cappelletti, *Affreschi*.
853 Lorenzo Proscio, *Il bestiario della Cattedrale di Anagni: Un viaggio all scoperta del simbolismo medievale* (Rome: Edizioni Efesto, 2015), 70–73.
854 Bonne, "Concordia discors temporum"; Russo, "Espace peint."
855 Brigitte D'Hainaut-Zveny, "De l'implication des paramètres spatio-temporels dans la constitution de ces *Locis competentibus*," in *L'Église, lieu de performances*, 209–23.
856 Peter Cornelius Claussen, *Die Kirchen der Stadt Rom im Mittelalter 1050–1300* (Stuttgart: Franz Steiner Verlag, 2002), 325–33.
857 Emanuelle Polack, *Les fresques de l'église Saint-Martin de Vic* (Paris: Lancosme, 2012).
858 Ehrenfried Kluckert, "Romanesque Painting," in *Romanesque: Architecture, Sculpture, Painting*, ed. Rolf Toman (Cologne: Könemann, 1997), 434–45; Jung, *Gothic Screen*, 91.
859 Jung, "Beyond the Barrier"; *Gothic Screen*, 17.
860 Pierre-Yves Le Pogam, "The Hagioscope in the Princely Chapels in France from the Thirteenth to the Fifteenth Century," in *Court Chapels*, 171–78; Rocio Sánchez Ameijeiras, "A través de la ventana: metáforas arquitectónicas y arte 1200 en Castilla y León," in *Contextos 1200 i 1400: art de Catalunya i art de l'Europa meridional en dos canvis de segle*, ed. Rosa Alcoy (Barcelona, 2012), 213–28.
861 Romano, *San Francesco ad Assisi*, 77–100.
862 Joanna Cannon, "Dominican Shrines and Urban Pilgrimage in Later Medieval Italy," in *Architecture and Pilgrimage*, 143–63; *Religious Poverty*, 29–45 et passim.

863 Willibald Sauerländer, "Die Naumburger Stifterfiguren: Rückblick und Fragen," in Willibald Sauerländer, *Cathedrals and Sculpture* (London: Pindar Press, 2000), 593–711; Jung, *Gothic Screen*, 81–88 et passim; Pinkus, *Simulacra*, 29–70.

864 Michael Viktor Schwarz, "Retelling the Passion at Naumburg: The West-Screen and its Audience," *Artibus et historiae* 26 (2005), 59–72.

865 Marcello Angheben, "Les théophanies composites des arcs absidaux et la liturgie eucharistique," *Cahiers de civilisation médiévale* 54, no. 214 (2011), 113–42.

866 Paul Binski, "The Ante-Reliquary Chapel Paintings in Norwich Cathedral: The Holy Blood, St. Richard and All Saints," in *Tributes to Nigel Morgan*, 241–61.

867 Maria Andaloro and Serena Romano, "L'immagine nell'abside," in *Arte e iconografia a Roma da Costantino a Cola di Rienzo*, ed. Maria Andaloro and Serena Romano (Milan: Jaca Book, 2000), 93–132.

868 Thunø, *Apse Mosaic*, 131–34.

869 Baschet, Bonne, and Dittmar, *Monde roman*, 39–42.

870 Binski, "Angel Choir"; *Seliges Lächeln*.

871 Jean-Claude Bonne, "Entre l'image et la matière: la choséité du sacré en Occident," *Bulletin de l'institut Belge de Rome* 21 (1999), 78–111; Endrödi Gábor, "De materialibus ad inmaterialia excitans: Commentary on the Stained Glass Windows by Suger, Abbot of Saint-Denis," in *Kép és kereszténység: Vizuális médiumok a középkorban / Image and Christianity: Visual Media in the Middle Ages*, ed. Péter Bokody (Pannonhalma: Pannonhalmi Főapátság: 2014), 112–33.

872 Bianca Kühnel, *The End of Time in the Order of Things: Science and Eschatology in Early Medieval Art* (Regensburg: Schnell & Steiner, 2003), 65–115; Hamburger, *Haec Figura demonstrat*, 11–43; Lautier, "Sacred Topography," 188–95.

873 One of the lancets below pictures Christ's infancy and another, devoted to Theophilus, introduces the theme of the glorification of the Maria-Ecclesia at the end of time; Claudine Lautier, "Les vitraux de la cathédrale de Chartres: Reliques et images," *Bulletin monumental* 161 (2003), 260; Michael Cothren, "Some Personal Reflections on American Modern and Postmodern Historiographies of Gothic Stained Glass," in *Minor to Major*, 268–70.

874 Paolo Piva, "'Los spazio liturgico': architettura, arredo, iconografia (secolo IV-XII)," in *L'arte medievale nel contesto 300–1300: Funzioni, iconografia, tecniche* (Milan: Jaca Book, 2006), 141–80; Hainaut-Zveny, "L'implication," 209–24; Phalip "Grilles," 41–46.

875 Donna L. Sadler, *Touching the Passion-Seeing Late Medieval Altarpieces through the Eyes of Faith* (Leiden: Brill, 2018), 15–43.

876 Krüger, "Aschaffenburger Tafelbild."

877 Éric Palazzo, "L'autel de Saint-Guilhem-le-Désert et l'iconographie des autels portatifs du haut Moyen Âge," in *Saint-Guilhem-le-Désert: Le contexte de la fondation, l'autel medieval de Saint-Guilhem* (Aniane: Amis de Saint-Guilhem-le-Désert, 2004), 115–23; Hedwig Rökelein, "Des 'saints cachés': les reliques dans les sépultures d'autel," in *Ad libros! Mélanges d'études médiévales offertes à Denise Angers et Joseph-Claude Poulin*, ed. Jean-François Cottier et al. (Montreal: Presses de l'Université de Montréal, 2010), 21–34; Didier Méhu, "L'évidement de l'image ou la figuration de l'invisible corps du Christ (IXe–XIe siècle)," *Images Re-vues* 11 (2013), 1–37.

878 Cynthia Hahn, "Narrative on the Golden Altar of Sant'Ambrogio in Milan: Presentation and Reception," *Dumbarton Oaks Papers* 53 (1999), 167–87; Steffen Bogen, *Träumen und Erzählen: Selbstreflexion der Bildkunst vor 1300* (Munich: Fink, 2001); Werner Telesko, "Bildgeschichte und Geschichtsbild: Untersuchungen zur Vorbildlichkeit christologischer Bildtypen von 'Teppich von Bayeux' bis zur 'Historia Troiana,'" in *Krieg und Sieg: Narrative Wanddarstellungen von Altägypten bis ins Mittelalter*, ed. Manfred Bietak and Mario Schwarz (Vienna: Eisenbrauns, 2002), 201–25; Erik Thunø, "The

Golden Altar of Sant'Ambrogio in Milan—Image and Materiality," in *Decorating the Lord's Table: On the Dynamics between Image and Altar in the Middle Ages*, ed. Søren Kaspersen and Erik Thunø (Copenhagen: Museum Tusculanum Press, 2006), 63–78; Ivan Foletti, "Le tombeau d'Ambroise: cinq siècles de construction identitaire," in *L'évêque*, 73–101, and "Le fléau des hérétiques: Ambroise de Milan, l'exclusion 'ethnique' et l'autel d'or de la basilique Ambrosiana," *Bulletin monumental* 175 (2017), 99–112.

879 Foletti, "L'autel," 105.
880 Resting his head on a stone, Jacob dreamt of angels ascending and descending; Heck, *L'échelle*; Palazzo, *L'espace rituel*.
881 Krüger, "'Hoc est corpus meum'"; Aavitsland, "Visual Splendour" and "Civitas."
882 Annika Elisabeth Fisher, "Cross Altar and Crucifix in Ottonian Cologne: Past Narrative, Present Ritual, Future Resurrection," in *Decorating the Lord's Table*, 43–62.
883 Georges Didi-Huberman, *L'image ouverte* (Paris: Éditions du Cerf, 2007), 184–85.
884 Justin E.A. Kroesen, "Ciborios y baldaquinos en Iglesias medievales: Un Panorama europeo/Ciboria and Baldachins in Medieval Churches: A European Panorama," *Codex Aqvilarensis* 29 (2013), 189–222. The use of stucco in Milan and Civate may have been intended to reinforce the transformation of humble hybrid material into an elevated substance; Foletti, *Oggetti*, 181–221.
885 Alessio Monciatti, "Il transetto meridionale della Basilica inferiore di San Francesco (entro il 1319?)," in *Pietro e Ambrogio Lorenzetti*, ed. Chiara Frugoni (Florence: Casa Editrice Le Lettere, 1998), 26–55.
886 *El cel pintat: El baldaquí de tost*, ed. Manuel Castiñeiras González (Vic: Museu Episcopal de Vic, 2008); Kroesen, "Ciborios," 199–200.
887 Anita Moskowitz, "Arnolfo, Non-Arnolfo: New (and Some Old) Observations on the Ciborium of San Paolo fuori le mura," *Gesta* 37, no. 1 (1998), 88–102.
888 Kessler, "*Realia* and *Spiritualia*," 127–28; Borsook, "Solomonic Throne."
889 Iafrate, "Artifex specialis."
890 Carola Jäggi, "Cathedra Petri und Colonna Santa in St. Peter zu Rom: Überlegungen zu 'Produktion' und Konjunktur von Reliquien im Mittelalter," in *Erzeugung und Zerstörung von Sakralität zwischen Antike und Mittelalter (Beiträge der internazionalen Tagung in München, 2015)*, ed. Armin Bergmeier, Katharina Palmberger, and Joseph E. Sanzo (*Distant World Journal: Special Issue* 1 2016), 109–31.
891 Westermann-Angerhausen, "Incense in the Space"; Blumer and Frontzek, "Recherchiert und kartiert"; Debaiš, "Mostrar, significar"; *Croisée*, 139–41.
892 Hanna Wimmer, "The Iconographic Programme of the Barbarossa Candelabrum in the Palatine Chapel at Aachen: A Re-interpretation," *Immediations* 1 (2005), 24–39; Debaiš, *Croisée*, 140–41. Also, Teuntje van de Wouw, *The Zutphen Chandelier in a New Light: A Search for the International Roots of a Local Masterpiece* (Utrecht: Utrecht University, 2016).
893 Zchomelidse, *Art, Ritual*, 234.
894 Beat Brenk, *The Apse, the Image and the Icon: An Historical Perspective of the Apse as a Space for Images* (Wiesbaden: Reichert Verlag, 2010).
895 Thunø, *Apse Mosaic*; Ivan Foletti and Irene Quadri, "L'immagine e la sua memoria: L'abside di Sant'Ambrogio a Milano e quella di San Pietro a Roma nel Medioevo," *Zeitschrift für Kunstgeschichte* 76 (2013), 475–92.
896 Riccioni, *Mosaico*, 37–47, 65–66 et passim.
897 Romano, *Apogeo*, 116–30.
898 Fassler, *Virgin*, 205–41.
899 Diana Norman, *Siena and the Virgin: Art and Politics in a Late Medieval City State* (New Haven and London: Yale University Press, 1999), 35–37; *Duccio: La vetrata del Duomo di*

Siena e il suo restauro, ed. Alessandro Bagnoli and Camillo Tarozzi (Cinisello Balsamo: Silvana editoriale, 2003).

900 Didier Mehú, "Les rapports dans l'image," in *Images dans l'occident*, 275–90; Silvia Schlegel, "Festive Vessels or Everyday Fonts? New Considerations on The Liturgical Functions of Medieval Baptismal Fonts in Germany," in *The Visual Culture of Baptism in the Middle Ages: Essays on Medieval Fonts, Settings and Beliefs*, ed. Harriet M. Sonne de Torrens and Miguel A. Torrens (Abingdon and New York: Ashgate, 2013), 129–47.

901 Franz Alto Bauer, "Überlegungen zur liturgischen Parzellierung des römischen Kirchenraums im frühen Mittelalter," in *Bildlichkeit und Bildorte von Liturgie: Schauplätze in Spätantike, Byzanz, und Mittelalter*, ed. Rainer Warland (Wiesbaden: Reichert, 2002), 75–103.

902 C.P.J. van der Ploeg, "How Liturgical is a Medieval Altarpiece?," in *Italian Panel Painting*, 102–12.

903 Palazzo, "Peintures murales," 60.

904 Heidrun Stein-Kecks, *Der Kapitelsaal in der mittelalterlichen Klosterbaukunst: Studien zu den Bildprogrammen* (Munich: Deutscher Kunstverlag, 2004); Cannon, *Religious Poverty*, 188–98.

905 Maria Cristina Pereira, "Les images-piliers du cloitre de Moissac," *Bulletin du centre d'études médiévales d'Auxerre*, special edition no. 2 (2008), 2–12.

906 Kessler and Zacharias, *Rome 1300*, 159–60.

907 Thomas E.A. Dale, "Monsters, Corporeal Deformities, and Phantasms in the Cloister of St-Michel-de-Cuxa," *Art Bulletin* 83, no. 3 (2001), 402–36; Peter K. Klein, "The Iconography of the Cloister of Gerona Cathedral and the Functionalist Interpretation of Romanesque Historiated Cloisters: Possibilities and Limitations," in Boto Varela and Kroesen, *Romanesque Cathedrals*, 259–74.

908 Rose Walker, "The Poetics of Defeat: Cistercians and Frontier Gothic at the Abbey of Las Huelgas," in *Spanish Medieval Art: Recent Studies*, ed. Colum Hourihane (Princeton: Department of Art and Archaeology, 2007), 187–213; Eduardo Carrero Santamaría, "The Creation and Use of Space in the Abbey of Santa María la Real de Las Huelgas, Burgos: Architecture, Liturgy, and Paraliturgy in a Female Cistercian Monastery," *Journal of Medieval Iberian Studies* 6, no. 2 (2014), 169–91; Gerardo Boto Varela, "Artífices en movimiento y transferencia de ideales artísticos en el reino de Alfonso VIII y Leonor: Arquitecturas y microarquitecturas para imaginar y presentar las utopías del Templo y la Ciudad de Dios," in *Alfonso VIII y Leonor de Inglaterra*, 271–314, and "Velum lapideo"; Vincent Debiais, *Le silence dans l'art* (Paris: Éditions du Cerf, 2019).

909 Hörsch, "Ausstattung," 261–68.

910 Thunø, *Apse Mosaic*, 52–55.

911 Draghi, *Affreschi*; Romano, *Duecento*, 136–76; Hauknes, "Painting of Knowledge"; Blume, "Aula Gotica."

912 As at St. Paul's in Rome: Romano, *Riforma*, 127–28; and Santa Croce in Florence: Diana Hiller, *Gendered Perceptions of Florentine Last Supper Frescoes, c. 1350–1490* (London: Routledge, 2013); Cannon, *Religious Poverty*, 198–99.

913 Reilly, *Cistercian Reform*, 167–81.

914 Kirstin B. Aavitsland, *Imagining the Human Condition in Medieval Rome: The Cistercian Fresco Cycle at Abbazia delle Tre Fontane* (Milton Park: Routledge, 2012); Romano, *Apogeo*, 94–100.

915 Sadler, "Reverse façade," 208–15.

916 Charity, it must be remembered, was a basis of medieval artistic ecology itself. John Henderson, *Piety and Charity in Late Medieval Florence* (Chicago and London: University of Chicago Press, 1997), 74–79; Philine Helas, "Die Repräsentation von Armut und

Armenfürsorge in italienischen Städten des 14. und 15. Jahrhunderts—ein 'republikanisches' Thema?," in *Armut und Armenfürsorge in der italienischen Stadtkulturzwischen 13. und 16. Jahrhundert: Bilder, Texte und soziale Praktiken*, ed. Philine Helas and Gerhard Wolf (Frankfurt: Peter Lang, 2006), 193–245; Rouchon Mouilleron, "Miracle et charité," 187–89; Michele Bacci, *"Pro remedio animae": Immagini sacre e pratiche devozionali in Italia centrale (secoli X III e X IV)* (Pisa: GISEM, 2000), 42–47; *Florence at the Dawn of the Renaissance*, 53.

917 Alejandro García Avilés, *El Tiempo y los Astros: Arte, Ciencia y Religión en la Alta Edad Media* (Murcia: Universidad Murcia, 2001); Paul E. Dutton, *Charlemagne's Mustache and Other Cultural Clusters of the Dark Age* (New York: Palgrave MacMillan, 2004), 93–127; Bruce Eastwood, *Ordering the Heavens: Roman Astronomy and Cosmology in the Carolingian Renaissance* (Leiden: Brill, 2007); Eric Ramirez-Weaver, *A Saving Science: Capturing the Heavens in Carolingian Manuscripts* (University Park: University of Pennsylvania Press, 2017); Marion Dolan, *Astronomical Knowledge Transmission through Illustrated Aratea Manuscripts* (Cham: Springer Verlag, 2017); Anderson, *Cosmos*, 138–42 et passim.

918 Cordez, "Échecs," 6–9.

919 Peter Rietbergen, "Sacralizing the Palace," in *Monuments & Memory*, 209–20.

920 *The Legend of Charlemagne in the Middle Ages: Power, Faith, and Crusade*, ed. Matthew Gabriele and Jace Stuckey (New York: Palgrave MacMillan, 2008); Joan Molina Figueras, *La memoria de Carlomagno: Culto, liturgia e imágenes en la catedral de Gerona* (Aguilar de Campoo: Santa Maria la Real, 2018).

921 *Westminster Retable*, 32–35.

922 Rushing, "Images at the Interface"; Oliver, "Between Flanders and Paris," 27.

923 Barral I Altet, *Décor*, 362.

924 Dale, *Relics, Prayer*, 71.

925 Christopher S. Wood, *Forgery Replica Fiction: Temporalities of German Renaissance Art* (Chicago: University of Chicago Press, 2008), 173–84; Assaf Pinkus, "The Giant of Bremen: Roland and the 'Colossus Imagination,'" *Speculum* 93, no. 2 (2018), 386–419.

926 As the portrayal of God creating the world with a compass in *Bibles moralisées* (constructed to educate rulers) asserted; Boespflug, "Créateur"; Martinez Ruipérez, "Compass."

927 Klemm, *Bildphysiologie*, 13–14; Summerfield, "Aprendre e enseigner," 339–42.

928 Richard G. Newhauser, "*Inter scientiam et populum*: Roger Bacon, Peter of Limoges, and the 'Tractatus moralis de oculo,'" in *Nach der Verurteilung von 1277: Philosophie und Theologie an der Universität von Paris im letzten Viertel des 13. Jahrhunderts; Studien und Texte/After the Condemnations of 1277: Philosophy and Theology at the University of Paris in the Last Quarter of the Thirteenth Century; Studies and Texts*, ed. Jan A. Aertsen et al. (Berlin: De Gruyter, 2001), 682–703; Jean Wirth, *L'image à la fin du Moyen Âge* (Paris: Éditions du Cerf, 2011), 19–46; Romano, *La O*, 117–21; Büttner, *Giotto*, 15–27.

929 Trans. Richard G. Newhauser (Toronto: PIMS, 2012); Jacques Berlioz, "Eyes in the Back of the Head: Exempla and Vision in the Moral Treatise on the Eye by Peter of Limoges," in *Optics, Ethics*, 65–83.

930 Carruthers, *Craft of Thought*, 213–20; Monika Otter, "Baudri of Bourgueil: 'To Countess Adela,'" *Journal of Medieval Latin* 11 (2001), 60–141; Vincent Debiais, "The Poem of Baudri for Countess Adéle: A Starting Point for Reading of Medieval Latin Ekphrasis," *Viator* 44 (2013), 95–106; Barral I Altet, *Souvenir*, 85–98 et passim.

931 Joanna Ochlawa, "Das neu erworbene Aquamanile in Hildesheim: Objekt- und Bedeutungsanalyse," in *Drachenlandung*, 17–40.

932 Draghi, *Affreschi*, 22–59; Romano, *Duecento*, 160; Hauknes, "Painting of Knowledge," 45–46; Blume, "Aula Gotica," 228–29.

933 Barral I Altet, *Souvenir*, 85–87.

934 Helmut Stampfer, *Schloß Rodenegg: Geschichte und Kunst* (Bozen: Pluristamp, 1998), 20–35; Michael Curschmann, "Aventiure bilde" and "Vom Wandel im bildlichen Umgang mit literarischen Gegenständen: Rodenegg, Wildenstein und das Flaarsche Haus in Stein am Rhein," in Curshmann, *Wort-Bild-Text*, 2:559–636; Helmut Stampfer and Thomas Steppan, *Affreschi romanici in Tirolo e Trentino* (Milan: Jaca Book, 2008), 248–50; Anne Dunlop, *Painted Palaces: The Rise of Secular Art in Early Renaissance Italy* (University Park: Pennsylvania State University Press, 2009), 138–39; James H. Brown, *Imagining the Text: Ekphasis and Envisioning Courtly Identity in Wirnt von Gravenberg's "Wigalois"* (Leiden and Boston: Brill, 2015), 208–09. Generally: Susanne Koch, *Wilde und verweigerte Bilder: Untersuchungen zur literarischen Medialität der Figur um 1200* (Göttingen: Universitätsverlag, 2014).

935 Bynum, *Materiality*, 200–05; Malcolm Jones, *The Secret Middle Ages: Discovering the Real Medieval World* (Westport, CT: Praeger, 2002), 254–56; Anne Marie Rasmussen, *Wandering Genitalia: Sexuality and the Body in German Culture between the Later Middle Ages and Early Modernity* (London: King's College London, 2009); Madeline H. Caviness, "A Son's Gaze on Noah: Case or Cause of Viriliphobia?," in *The Meanings of Nudity in Medieval Art*, ed. Sherry C.M. Lindquist (London and New York: Routledge, 2012), 103–48.

936 Bynum, *Materiality*, 177.

937 Guardia, "Supuestamente profane," 103–05; Shalev-Eyni, *Jews Among Christians*, 59–60. Also, Trinks, *Antike*, 246–52.

938 Valerie I.J. Flint, "The Hereford Map: Its Author(s), Two Scenes and a Border," *Transactions of the Royal Historical Society* 8 (1998), 19–44; Naomi Reed Kline, *Maps of Medieval Thought: The Hereford Paradigm* (Woodbridge: Boydell and Brewer, 2001); Patrick Gautier Dalché, "Décrire le monde et situer les lieux au XIIe siècle: L'Expositio mappe mundi et la généalogie de la mappemonde de Hereford," in *Mélanges de l'École française de Rome: Moyen Âge* 113, no. 1 (2001), 343–409; Scott Westrem, *The Hereford Map: A Transcription and Translation of the Legends with Commentary* (Turnhout: Brepols, 2001); Marcia Kupfer, "Medieval World Maps: Embedded Images, Interpretive Frames," *Word & Image* 10 (2004), 262–87, and *Art and Optics in the Hereford Map: An English Mappa Mundi c. 1300* (New Haven and London: Yale University Press, 2016); Dan Terkla, "The Original Placement of the Hereford Mappa Mundi," *Imago Mundi* 56 (2004), 131–51; *The Hereford World Map: Medieval World Maps and Their Context*, ed. P.D.A. Harvey (London: British Library, 2006); P.D.A. Harvey, *The Hereford World Map: Introduction* (London: The Folio Society, 2010); Thomas de Wesselow, "Locating the Hereford Mappa Mundi," *Imago Mundi* 65 (2013), 180–206; Diarmuid Scully, "Augustus, Rome, Britain, and Ireland on the Hereford mappa mundi: Imperium and Salvation," *Peregrinations* 4 (2013), 107–33; Jeffrey Jaynes, *Christianity beyond Christendom: The Global Christian Experience on Medieval Mappaemundi and Early Modern World Maps* (Wiesbaden: Harrassowitz, 2017); Debra Higgs Strickland, "Edward I, Exodus, and England on the Hereford World Map," *Speculum* 93, no. 2 (2018), 420–69.

939 Geymonat, "Disegno," 56.

940 Romano, *San Francesco ad Assisi*, 101–39; Frugoni, "L'Ytalia"; Cooper and Robson, *Assisi*, 82–85; Bokody, *Images-within-Images*, 62–63; Thunø, "Pantheon," 247–49.

941 Sarah M. Guérin, "Meaningful Spectacles: Gothic Ivories Staging the Divine," *The Art Bulletin* 95, no. 1 (2013), 71.

942 Sabine Utz, "Reprise et reinvention des manuscrits antiques à l'époque carolingienne: l'exemple du Prudence de Berne," in *Actualiser le passé: figures antiques au Moyen Âge et à la Renaissance*, ed. Jean-Claude Muhlethaler and Delphine Burghgraeve (Lausanne: Centre d'Études Médiévales et Post-Médiévales, 2012), 33–42.

943 Achim Arbeiter and Sabine Noack-Haley, *Christliche Denkmäler des frühen Mittelalters vom 8. bis 11 Jahrhundert* (Mainz: Philipp von Zabern, 1999), 152–53; Barbara Obrist, *La cosmologie médiévale: Textes et images* (Firenze: SISMEL-Edizioni del Galluzzo, 2004); Elly Dekker, *Illustrating the Phaenomena: Celestial Cartography in Antiquity and the Middle Ages* (Oxford: Oxford University Press, 2012); Horst Bredekamp and Stefan Trinks, "Continuatio statt Renaissance: Das Fortleben der Antike auf der Iberischen Halbinsel 500 bis 1300—ein Manifest," in *Transformatio et Continuatio: Forms of Change and Constancy of Antiquity in the Iberian Peninsula 500–1500*, ed. Horst Bredekamp and Stefan Trinks (Berlin: Walter de Gruyter, 2017), 1–61.

944 Vitali, "*Sicut explorator*," 18; Terrier Aliferis, *L'imitation*, 56–57.

945 Dolan, *Astronomical Knowledge*, 55–92; Anderson, *Cosmos*, 79–105.

946 Ramírez-Weaver, *Saving Science*, 71–83 et passim.

947 Binski, "Cosmati," 129–31.

948 M.A. D'Aronco, "Il ms. Londra, British Library, Cotton Vitellius C. III dell'erbario anglosassone e la tradizione medica di Montecassino," in *Incontri di popoli e culture tra V e IX secolo* (Atti delle V giornate di studio sull'età romanobarbarica), ed. Marcello Rotili (Naples: Arte tipografica, 1998), 117–27; Minta Collins, *Medieval Herbals: The Illustrative Tradition* (London: The British Library, 2000); Giulia Orofino, "Ad decus et utilitatem operis: caratteristiche e funzioni dell'illustrazione scientifica nel Medioevo," *Medicina nei secoli* 14 (2002), 439–60; Jean Givens, "Reading and Writing the Illustrated *Tractatus de herbis*, 1280–1526," in *Visualizing Medieval Medicine and Natural History, 1200–1550*, ed. Jean Givens et al. (Aldershot: Ashgate, 2006), 115–45; Walter Oberschelp, "Der Karlshof als Zentrum der Naturwissenschafte," in *Orte der Macht*, 306–15.

949 Alain Touwaide, "Latin Crusaders, Byzantine Herbals," in *Visualizing Medieval Medicine*, 25–50.

950 Transformed in the twelfth and thirteenth centuries into various editions of bestiaries; Strickland, "Jews."

951 Utz, "Reprise et reinvention"; Ramírez-Weaver, *Saving Science*, 169–76.

952 *Time in the Medieval World: Occupations of the Months and Signs of the Zodiac in the Index of Christian Art*, ed. Colum Hourihane (Princeton: Department of Art & Archeology, 2007); Winterer, *Sakramentar*, 438–44; *Das Kalenderhandbuch von 354—Der chronograph Des Filocalus*, ed. Johannes Divjak and Wolfgang Wischmeyer (Vienna: Holzhausen, 2014); Judith Oliver, "Christian Calendars and Secular Labors of the Months: A Reassessment," in *Tributes to Adelaide Bennett Hagens: Manuscripts, Iconography, and the Late Medieval Viewer*, ed. Pamela A. Patton and Judith K. Golden (Turnhout: Brepols/Harvey Miller, 2017), 111–32.

953 O'Reilly, "Patristic and Insular Traditions"; Kühnel, *End of Time*, 181–83; Lawrence Nees, "Reading Aldred's Colophon for the Lindisfarne Gospels," *Speculum* 78, no. 2 (2003), 333–77.

954 Massimo Bernabò, "Virgil Illustrated in Gaul: A Reassessment," *Bizantinistica Rivista di Studi Bizantini e Slavi*, 2nd ser., 16 (2014–15), 239–57.

955 Beatrice Radden Keefe, "The Manuscripts and Illustration of Plautus and Terence," in *The Cambridge Companion to Roman Comedy*, ed. Martin Dinter (Cambridge and New York: Cambridge University Press, forthcoming), and "Illustrating the Manuscripts of Terence," in *Terence between Late Antiquity and the Age of Printing: Illustration, Commentary, and Performance*, ed. Andrew Turner and Giulia Torello-Hill (Leiden: Brill, forthcoming).

956 Holger Grewe, "Die Pfalz zu Ingelheim am Rhein: Ausgewälte Bauerfunde und ihre Interpretation," in *Karl der Gross/Charlemagne*, 188–97; Giulia Orofino, "La storia nei

margini: I disegni dell'Orosio Va. lat. 3340 tra eredità tardoantica e creazione medieval," *Convivium* 3 (2016), 122–35.

957 Claudia Annette Meier, *Chronicon pictum: Von den Anfängen der Chronikenillustration zu den narrative Bilderzyklen in den Weltchroniken des Hohen Mittelalters* (Mainz: Chorus Verlag, 2005).

958 *Apollonius pictus: A Late Antique Illustrated Romance around 1000*, ed. Anna Boreczky and András Németh (Budapest: OSZK, 2011); Anna Boreczky, "The Illustrated Life of Apollonius and Tarsia: A 'Papyrus-style' Narrative in Ottonian Art," *Convivium* 3, no. 1 (2016), 76–91; András Németh, "Continuous Narration through Scenic Depictions," *Convivium* 3, no. 1 (2016), 106–22.

959 Ilaria Molteni, "Lo spazio del foglio: Sulla *mise en page* dei romanzi cavalereschi di origine italiana (XIII–XIV secolo)," *Convivium* 3, no. 1 (2016), 126–41.

960 Sánchez Ameijeiras, *Rostros*, 171–76. Diagrammatic interplay was embedded in objects themselves. The world of strife inherent in the Ballinderry fitchell board, for instance, took on ecclesiological and even liturgical significance through the circle in the square; Barbet-Massin, *L'enluminure*, 331–415.

961 Hamburger, "Haec Figura demonstrat" and *Hrabanus redivivus*.

962 Kühnel, *End of Time*; Bolzoni, *La rete*, 103–44 et passim (*The Web*, 83–114); Somfai, "Nature of Daemons," and "Calcidius' *Commentary* on Plato's *Timaeus*"; Steffen Bogen, "Verbundene Materie, geordnete Bilder: Reflexionen diagrammatischen Schauens in den Fenstern von Chartres," *Bildwelten des Wissens: Kunsthistorisches Jahrbuch für Bildkritik* 3 (2005), 72–84; Dieter Blume, "Körper und Kosmos im Mittelalter," in *Bild und Körper*, 225–41; Dronke, *Spell*, xviii–xix; Müller, *Visuelle Weltaneignung*; John Bender and Michael Marrinan, *The Culture of Diagram* (Stanford: Stanford University Press, 2010); Bruno Reudenbach, "Ein Weltbild im Diagramm—Ein Diagramm als Weltbild: Das Mikrokosmos-Makrokosmos-Schema des Isidor von Sevilla," in *Atlas der Weltbilder*, ed. Christoph Markschies et al. (Berlin: De Gruyter, 2011), 32–39; *Taxonometries of Knowledge: Information and Order in Medieval Manuscripts*, ed. Emily Steiner and Lynn Ransom (Philadelphia: University of Pennsylvania Libraries, 2015); Rebecca Zorach, *The Passionate Triangle* (Chicago and London: University of Chicago Press, 2011); *Sign and Design*.

963 Shimona Cohen, *Transformations of Time and Temporality in Medieval and Renaissance Art* (Leiden: Brill, 2014), 72–73.

964 Kumler, *Translating Truth*, 63–68.

965 Bolzoni, *La Rete*, 63 (*The Web*, 50–51); Kumler, *Translating Truth*, 80–82.

966 Müller, *Visuelle Weltaneignung*, 38–42.

967 Dieter Blume, Mechthild Haffner, and Wolfgang Metzger, *Sternbilder des Mittelalters: Der gemalte Himmel zwischen Wissenschaft und Phantasie*, part I 800–1200, and *Sternbilder des Mittelalters und der Renaissance: Der gemalte Himmel zwischen Wissenschaft und Phantasie*, part II 1200–1500 (Berlin: De Gruyter, 2012 and 2016); Dieter Blume, "Picturing the Stars. Scientific Iconography in the Middle Ages," in *The Routledge Companion to Medieval Iconography* (London: Routledge Ashgate, 2016), 310–21.

968 Ramirez-Weaver, *Saving Science*, 120–21, 165–66 et passim.

969 Bianca Kühnel, "Carolingian Diagrams, Images of the Invisible," in *Seeing the Invisible*, 359–89; Ramirez-Weaver, *Saving Science*, 223–24.

970 Oberschelp, "Karlshof," 313; Alejandro García Avilés, "El hombre y las estrellas: el imaginario astrológico en los siglos del románico," in *El románico y sus mundos imaginados* (Aguilar de Campoo: Santa María la Real, 2014), 85–107.

971 Herbert L. Kessler, "The Christianity of Carolingian Classicism," *Convivium* 3, no. 1 (2016), 22–39.

972 M.A. D'Aronco and M.L. Cameron, *The Old English Illustrated Pharmacopoeia: British Library Cotton Vitellius C III, Early English Manuscripts in Facsimile* (Copenhagen: Rosenkilde and Bagger, 1998) and M.A. D'Aronco, "Gardens on Vellum: Plants and Herbs in Anglo-Saxon Manuscript," in *Health and Healing from the Medieval Garden*, ed. Peter Dendle and Alain Touwaide (Woodbridge: Boydell, 2008), 101–27; *Anglo-Saxon Kingdoms*, 274–75.

973 Guidetti, "Texts and Illustrations"; Draelants, "Le *Liber Nemroth*."

974 Ramirez-Weaver, *Saving Science*, 103–04.

975 Kessler, "Memory and Models" and "Thirteenth-Century Venetian Revisions."

976 Prado-Vilar, "Parchment."

977 Herbert L. Kessler, "Jerome and Vergil," and "'Filled to the Brim': The Meaning of Perspective in Carolingian Art," in *Ars auro gemmisque prior: Mélanges en hommage à Jean-Pierre Caillet* (Zagreb: University of Zagreb, 2013) 181–87.

978 Heyman, "Fulcher's Bestiary," 138–43.

979 Müller, "Fragwürdige Bilder," 238–39.

980 Zchomelidse, *Art, Ritual*, 11–12.

981 Trinks, *Antike*, 151–52; Prado-Vilar, "*Superstes*," 175–79.

982 Ambrose, *Marvellous and the Monstrous*, 119–20.

983 Opicinus de Canistris, for instance, harnessed geometry to real experience; Whittington, *Body-Worlds*, 50–59.

984 Alexander Patschovsky, "Die Trinitätsdiagramme Joachims von Fiore: Ihre Herkunft und semantische Struktur im Roahmen der Trinitätsikonographie, von deren Anfängen bis ca. 1200," in *Die Bildwelt der Diagramme Joachims von Fiore: Zur Medialität religiös-politischer Programme im Mittelalter*, ed. Alexander Patschovsky (Ostfildern: Jan Thorbecke Verlag, 2003), 55–114; Müller, "Gott is (k)eine Sphäre."

985 Manuel Castiñeiras González, *Tapiz (Tapestry)* (Girona: Catedral de Girona, 2011).

986 Reynolds, "Vetera analecta," "Christ's Money," and "Eucharistic Adoration in the Carolingian Era? Exposition of Christ in the Host," *Peregrinations: Journal of Medieval Art & Architecture* 4 (2013) 70–153; Kessler, "Sign and Design" and "Medietas/Mediator"; Alfred Hiatt, "Worlds in Books," in *Taxonomies of Knowledge: Information and Order in Medieval Manuscripts*, ed. Emily Steiner and Lynn Ranson (Philadelphia: The Shoenberg Institute of Manuscript Studies, 2015), 37–55. The Arnstein window applies the coin metaphor to the seven gifts of the Holy Spirit showering Christ in the Tree of Jesse.

987 Hauknes, "Painting of Knowledge," 38.

988 Debiais, *Croisée*, 139–41.

989 Vincent Debiais, "Du monogramme du Christ à l'image de Dieu: Contribution épigraphique à la compréhension du chrisme monumental (France-Espagne, XIe–XIIIe siècle)," in *La lettre dans tous ses états* (acts of conferences, Poitiers) ed. Laurent Habot and Vincent Debiais (Poitiers, CESCM, 2012), 1–17; "Inscriptions médiévales," and "Christ's Monogram"; Peter Scott Brown, "The Chrismon and the Liturgy of Dedication in Romanesque Sculpture," *Gesta* 56, no. 2 (2017), 199–223.

990 Kline, *Maps*; Painton Cowen, *The Rose Window: Splendor and Symbol* (London: Thames and Hudson, 2005).

991 Brown, *Lindisfarne Gospels*, 209–10; Barbet-Massin, *L'enluminure*, 413–15.

992 O'Reilly, "Patristic and Insular Traditions"; Benjamin C. Tilghman, "The Shape of the Word: Extralinguistic Meaning in Insular Display Lettering," *Word & Image* 27, no. 3 (2011), 292–308.

993 Zorach, *Passionate Triangle*, 15.

994 Zorach, *Passionate Triangle*, 71.

995 Wamberg, *Landscape* 1:232–35; Andreina Contessa, "Between Art, Faith and Science: The Concept of Creation in the Ripoll and Roda Romanesque Bibles," *Iconographica* 6 (2007), 19–43. Although the geometry that God used to construct the world reflected his divinity, his viewpoint on the world was distinct from humankind's; Whittington, *Body-Worlds*, 44–45; Kupfer, *Art and Optics*, 53–73, 115–27 et passim.
996 Isabelle Marchesin, "Verbum Christi: Musical Iconography in the St Albans Psalter," in *Albani-Psalter*, 152–77.
997 Cohen, *Uta Codex*, 157–71.
998 David Rollason, *The Power of Place; Rulers and their Palaces, Landscapes, Cities, and the Holy* (Princeton: Princeton University Press, 2016), 91–96; Bucklow, *Riddle*, 161–64.
999 Didier Méhu, "*Historiae et imagines* de la consécration de l'église dans l'Occident medieval," in *Mises en scène et mémoires de la consécration de l'église dans l'Occident médiéval*, ed. Didier Méhu (Turnhout: Brepols, 2008), 293–98.
1000 Martina Bagnoli, "Le fonti e i documenti per l'indagine iconografica," in *Universo di simboli*, 71–86; Kathrin Müller, "Profane Knowledge, Sacred Insights: The Cosmological Diagrams in the Crypt of Anagni Cathedral," *Codex Aqvilarensis* 33 (2017), 55–71.
1001 Monica Green, "From 'Diseases of Women' to 'Secrets of Women,'" *Journal of Medieval and Early Modern Studies* 30, no. 1 (2000), 5–39; *Making Women's Medicine Masculine* (Oxford: Oxford University Press, 2008); Karl Whittington, "The Cruciform Womb: Process, Symbol and Salvation in Bodleian Library MS. Ashmole 399," *Different Visions: A Journal of New Perspectives on Medieval Art* 1 (2008), 1–24; Novacich, "Transparent Mary," 464–90; Faith Wallis, "Counting All the Bones: Measure, Number and Weight in Early Medieval Texts About the Body," in *Was Zählt: Ordnungsangebote, Gebrauchsformen und Erfahrungsmodalitäten des "numerus" in Mittelalter* (Cologne: Böhlau Verlag, 2012), 185–207.
1002 Bolzoni, *La Rete*, 162–66 (*The Web*, 132–35).
1003 Romano, *Riforma*, 28–31.
1004 MGH. *Poetae Latini aevi Carolini*, III, 297.
1005 Herbert L. Kessler, "From Vanitas to Veritas: The Profane as the Fifth Mode of Romanesque Art," *Codex Aqvilarensis* 33 (2017), 52–53; Strickland, "World Map," 427–32.
1006 On spiritual and bodily nourishment: Brian Patrick McGuire, "Sanctity: The Saint and the Senses; The Case of Bernard of Clairvaux," in *Saturated Sensorium*, 92–111.
1007 Kessler, "Vanitas," 42–44.
1008 Strickland, "Jews," 208–10; Nigel Morgan, "Pictured Sermons in Thirteenth Century England," in *Tributes to Jonathan J.G. Alexander*, 323–40; Kessler, "Vanitas," 42–43.
1009 Dale, "Nude at Moissac," 69–70.
1010 Dale, "Monsters," 418–20.
1011 Coker and Watson, *Egerton Genesis*, 176–77; Mills, *Seeing Sodomy*, 58–62; Binski, *Gothic Wonder*, 341.
1012 Skemer, *Binding Words*, 171–233.
1013 Benoît Grévin and Julien Véronèse, "Les 'caractéres' magiques au Moyen Âge (XIIe–XIVe siècle)," *Bibliothèque de l'École des Chartes* 162, no. 2 (2004), 305–79.
1014 Francisco Corti, "Cantiga 125: la nigromancia y las relaciones entre imágines y textos," *Alcanate: Rivista de estudios Alfonsíes* 5 (2006–07), 423–38; Veronica Menaldi, "Miracles and Magic," in *Magic and Magicians*, ed. Albrecht Classen (Berlin: De Gruyter, 2017), 423–38.
1015 Cordez, "Marbres," 18–19.
1016 Skemer, *Binding Words*, 199–212, 285–304.
1017 Skemer, *Binding Words*, 116–17.
1018 Skemer, *Binding Words*, 247–49; Tammen, "Blick und Wunde"; Caroline Bynum, "Violence Occluded: The Wound in Christ's Side in Late Medieval Devotion," in *Feud, Violence and Practice: Essays in Medieval Studies in Honor of Stephen D. White*, ed.

Belle S. Tuten and Tracy L. Billado (Burlington: Ashgate, 2010), 95–116; *Christian Materiality*, 197–200; Trinks, *Antike*, 348–59; Giles, *Inscribed Power*, 109–21 et passim.

1019 On vaginal imagery, Madeline Caviness, *Visualizing Women in the Middle Ages: Sight, Spectacle, and Scopic Economy* (Philadelphia: University of Pennsylvania Press, 2001), 158–62.

1020 George Ferzoco, "Il murale di Massa Marittima—The Massa Marittima Mural," *Toscana Studies* 1 (2004), 71–107; *Il murale di Massa Marittima* (Florence; 2005); Dunlop, *Painted Palaces*, 160; Matthew Ryan, "Reconsidering the 'Obscene': The Massa Marittima Mural," *Shift: Queen's Journal of Visual and Material Culture* (2009), 1–27; Whittington, *Body-Worlds*, 148–51; Elina Gertsman, "Sensual Delights: Fountains, Fiction, and Feeling," in Stephen N. Fliegel and Elina Gertsman, *Myth and Mystique: Cleveland's Gothic Table Fountain* (Cleveland: Cleveland Museum of Art, 2016), 59–90.

1021 Brian W. Spencer, *Pilgrim Souvenirs and Secular Badges: Medieval Finds from Excavations in London* (London: The Stationery Office, 1998); Jones, *Secret Middle Ages*, 258–73; A.M. Koldeweij, "'Shameless and Naked Images': Obscene Badges as Parodies of Popular Devotion," in *Art and Architecture of Late Medieval Pilgrimage in Northern Europe and the British Isles*, ed. Sarah Blick and Rita Tekippe (Leiden: Brill, 2004); Thomas A. Bredehoft, "Literacy without Letters: Pilgrim Badges and Late Medieval Literate Ideology," *Viator* 37 (2006), 433–445; Gerhard Wolf, "Phallus am Grillspiess und Vulva auf stelzen: Überlegungen zur kommunikativen Funktion erotischer und obszöner Tragezeichen aus den Niederlanden," in *Erotik aus dem Dreck gezogen*, ed. J.H. Winkelman and Gerhard Wolf (Leiden: Brill, 2004), 285–330; Tamen, "Blick und Wunde"; Bynum, *Materiality*, 201–05; H.J.E. van Beuningen et al., *Heilig en Profaan 3: 1300 laatmiddeleeuwse insignes uit openbare en particuliere collecties* (Langbroek: Medieval Badges Foundation, 2012); Hartmut Kühne et al., *Jungfrauen, Engel, Phallustieren: Die Sammlung Mittelalterlicher Französischer Pilgerzeichen des Kunstgewerbemuseums in Prag und des Nationalmuseums Prag* (Berlin: Lukas Verlag für Kunst- und Geistesgeschichte, 2012); Giles, *Inscribed Power*, 110–13; Ben Reiss, "Pious Phalluses and Holy Vulvas: The Religious Importance of Some Sexual Body-Part Badges in Late-Medieval Europe (1200–1550)," *Peregrinations: Journal of Medieval Art and Architecture* 6 (2017), 151–76.

1022 James Bugslag, "'Contrefais al vif': Nature, Ideas and Representation in the Lion Drawings of Villard de Honnecourt," *Word & Image* 17, no. 4 (2001), 360–78; Noa Turel, "Living Pictures: Rereading au vif 1350–1550," *Gesta* 50, no. 2 (2011), 163–82; Wirth, *Villard*, 57–60 et passim.

1023 Terrier Aliferis, *L'imitation*, 34–38.

1024 Wirth, *Villard*, 62–73 et passim; Pinkus, *Simulacra*, 77 et passim.

1025 Judith Collard, "Art and Science in the Manuscripts of Matthew Paris," *Medieval Chronicle* 9 (2015), 79–116.

1026 *El códice sobre medicamentos de Federico II* (Valencia: Patrimonio, 2003); Giulia Orofino, "Le tre vite di un erbario: Il Codex Vindobonensis 93," in *Le plaisir de l'art du Moyen Âge: Commande, production et réception de l'œuvre d'art; Mélanges en hommage à Xavier Barral i Altet* (Paris: Picard, 2012), 925–31, and "Gemelli diversi: Trasmissione e circolazione degli erbari in età sveva," in *Medioevo: Natura e Figura; La raffigurazione dell'uomo e della natura nell'arte medieval*, ed. Arturo Carlo Quintavalle (Milan: Skira, 2015), 505–16.

1027 Frederick II of Hohenstaufen, *De arte venandi cum avibus: L'arte di cacciare con gli uccelli*, ed. Anna Laura Trombetti Budriesi (Rome: Editori Laterza, 2000); Giulia Orofino, "Di padre in figlio: Federico II, Manfredi e l'illustrazione del De arte venandi cum avibus," in *Tempi e forme dell'arte: Miscellanea di Studi offerti a Pina Belli D'Elia*, ed. Luisa De Rosa and Clara Gelao (Foggia: C. Grenzi, 2011), 137–43.

1028 Rosen, "Republic at Work."

1029 Emanuele Lugli, "A Mathematical Land: Measurements in Twelfth- and Thirteenth-Century Modena and the Po Valley," in *Was Zählt*, 273–93.

1030 François-Xavier Fauvelle, *Le* rhinocéros *d'or* (Paris: Gallimard, 2014) (trans. *The Golden Rhinoceros: Histories of the African Middle Ages* [Princeton: Princeton University Press, 2018]), 191–98; Kathleen Bickford Berzock, "Caravans of Gold, Fragments in Time: An Introduction," in *Caravans of Gold*, 22–37.
1031 Romano, *La O*, 65–74.
1032 Kessler "Revisions," 87–89; Thomas E.A. Dale, "Pictorial Narratives of the Holy Land and the Myth of Venice in the Atrium of San Marco," in *Atrium*, 247–69.
1033 Stephen N. Fliegel, "The Art of War: Thirteenth-Century Arms and Armor," in *Book of Kings*, 82–97; M.C. Gaposchkin, "Louis IX, Crusade and the Promise of Joshua in the Holy Land," *Journal of Medieval History* 34, no. 3 (2008), 245–74.
1034 Epstein, *Medieval Haggadah*, 98–104. In general, Rubin, *Gentile Tales*; Merback, *Pilgrimage*, 113–15 et passim.
1035 Strickland, "Edward I," 431–42.
1036 Jékely, "Painted Cycle," 62–74.
1037 Sadler, *Touching the Passion*, 71–107.
1038 Cooper and Robson, *Assisi*, 63–72 Marcello Gaeta, *Giotto und die* croci dipinte *des Trecento* (Münster: Rhema-Verlag, 2013).
1039 Flora, *Devout Belief*, 145.
1040 Hamburger, "Seeing and Believing."
1041 Stephen Perkinson, *The Likeness of the King: A Prehistory of Portraiture in Late Medieval France* (Chicago: University of Chicago Press, 2009), 27–29.
1042 Wirth, "Peinture et perception visuelle"; Lakey, *Sculptural Seeing*, 92–109 et passim.
1043 Tamanti, "Il restauro," 13 and Figure 8; Serena Romano, "Il ciclo"; Herbert L. Kessler, "Optical Art before Assisi" in *L'image en questions pour Jean Wirth*, ed. Frédéric Elsig et al. (Geneva: Librairie Droz, 2013), 50–55. On the built-in geometry needed to transfer drawings and templates to monumental contexts, Leturque, "Scope," 316–20.
1044 Dominique Raynaud, "Geometric and Arithmetical Methods in Early Medieval Perspective," *Physis: rivista internazionale di storia della scienza* 45 (2008), 29–55; Herbert L. Kessler, "Topografias de la fe en el arte medieval," *Codex Aqvilarensis* 28 (2013), 11–28; Wirth, *Villard*, 175–76.
1045 Lakey, "'To See Clearly,'" 121–23.
1046 Pinkus, *Simulacra*, 29–50 et passim.
1047 On technique: Spencer, *Souvenirs*, 7–13.
1048 Kruse, *Wozu Menschen malen*, 318–28.
1049 Biernoff, *Sight and Embodiment*, 68–73 et passim.
1050 Klaus Bergdolt, *Das Auge und die Theologie* (Paderborn: Schöningh, 2007); Romano, *La O*, 51–52 et passim; *Duecento*, 331–38.
1051 Kessler, "Façade, Face"; Flora, *Cimabue*, 119–29.
1052 Marvin Trachtenberg, *Dominion of the Eye: Urbanism, Art, and Power in Early Modern Florence* (Cambridge: Cambridge University Press, 1997), 223–43 et passim; Raynaud, "Methods"; Büttner, *Giotto*, 86–99.
1053 Zorach, *Passionate Triangle*, 71–72; Kessler, "Topografias." Kupfer discovers a similar punning interaction in the Hereford Map: *Art and Optics*, 82–86, 157–67 et passim.
1054 Stephen N. Fliegel, "The Cleveland Table Fountain," in *Myth and Mystique*, 1–55; see it work: https://www.youtube.com/watch?v=jxAUCdoUTmY.
1055 Bagnoli and Gerry, *Medieval World*, 157.
1056 C. Jean Campbell, *The Game of Courting and the Art of the Commune of San Gimignano, 1290–1320* (Princeton: Princeton University Press, 1997).
1057 Garrison, "Mimetic Bodies," 223.

1058 Heidelberg, Universitätsbibliothek, Cpg 848 and Stuttgart, Württembergische Landesbibliothek, Cod. HB XIII 1; Ott, "Texte und Bilder," 106–07.
1059 Benedetta Chiesi, "Mobilité des artistes et des oeuvres," in *Voyager*, 124–26.
1060 Christopher Lucken, "Les Manuscrits du Bestiaire d'Amours de Richard de Fournival," in *Le Recueil au Moyen Âge: Le Moyen Âge central*, ed. Yasmina Foehr-Janssens and Olivier Collet (Turnhout: Brepols, 2010), 113–38; Christine Noacco, "La 'maison de Mémoire' et les sens dans le *Bestiaire d'Amour* de Richard de Founival," in *Penser les cinq sens au Moyen Âge: Poétique, esthétique, éthique*, ed. Florence Bouchet and Anne-Hélène Klinger-Dollé (Paris: Classiques Garnier, 2015), 183–202.
1061 Albrecht Hausmann, "Der älteste Tristan-Teppich im Kloster Wienhausen bei Celle," *Mitteilungen des Deutschen Germanistenverbandes* 64 (2017), 294–301.
1062 Dieter Blume, "Die imaginierte Natur des Papstes—Die Chambre du Cerf in Avignon," in *Nahsicht—Fernsicht, Kunst und die Erfahrung der Natur in Italien vom 14. bis zum 16. Jahrhundert*, ed. Hans Aurenhammer and Kathrin Müller (forthcoming).
1063 Dunlop, *Painted Palaces*, 120.
1064 The literature is vast: Suzanne Lewis, *The Rhetoric of Power in the Bayeux Tapestry* (Cambridge: Cambridge University Press, 1999); Werner Telesko, "'Quid est ergo 'tempus'?" Überlegungen zu den Verbindungslinien zwischen Zeitbegriff, Heilsgeschichte und Typologie in der christlichen Kunst des Hochmittelalters," *Mediaevistik* 13 (2000), 87–116; Peter K. Klein, "The Borders of the Bayeaux Tapestry: Visual Gloss or Marginal Images," in *Plaisir de l'art*, 626–42; Barral I Altet, *Souvenir*; Debiais, *Croisée*, 109–20; Elizabeth Carson Pastan, "Imagined Patronage: The Bayeux Embroidery & Its Interpretive History," *Patronage*, 54–75; Pastan and White, *Bayeux Tapestry*.
1065 Klein "Borders," 630–31; Debiais, *Croisée*, 111–16; Barral I Altet, *Souvenir*, 260–64.
1066 Bianca Kühnel, "The Perception of History in Thirteenth-Century Crusader Art," in *France and the Holy Land: Frankish Culture at the End of the Crusades*, ed. Daniel H. Weiss and Lisa Mahony (Baltimore and London: Johns Hopkins University Press, 2004), 161–86.
1067 Iafrate, "Artifex specialis."
1068 Katz, "Norman to Hohenstaufen," 69–72.
1069 Vinni Luccherini, "Il *Chronicon pictum* ungherese (1358): Racconto e immagini al servizio della costruzione dell'identità nazionale," *Rivista di storia della miniatura* 19 (2015), 58–72.
1070 Carrie E. Benes, *Urban Legends: Civic Identity and the Classical Past in Northern Italy, 1250–1350* (University Park: Pennsylvania University Press, 2011), 115–42; Weinryb, *Bronze Object*, 172–98.
1071 Elena Bianca Di Gioia and Claudio Parisi Presicce, *Carlo I d'Angiò, re di Sicilia e senatore di Roma: Il monumento onorario nel Campidoglio del Duecento* (Rome: Campisano Editore, 2009), 40–55.
1072 Pinkus, "Giant of Bremen."
1073 Kristin Marek, *Die Körper des Königs: Effigies, Bildpolitik, Heiligkeit* (Munich: Fink Verlag, 2009).
1074 Dale, "Individual"; Bedos-Rezak, *Ego*, 170–85 et passim; Shirin Fozi, "'Reinhildis Has Died': Ascension and Enlivenment on a Twelfth-Century Tomb," *Speculum* 90, no. 1 (2015), 158–94; Dutton, "The Identification of Persons."
1075 Ildar H. Garipzanov, *The Symbolic Language of Authority in the Carolingian World (c. 751–877)* (Leiden: Brill, 2008).
1076 Foletti, *Oggetti*, 161–80.
1077 Castiñeiras González, "Mateo," 45–51.
1078 Di Gioia and Presicce, *Carolo I d'Angiò*.

1079 Scott B. Montgomery, "The Saint and the King: Relics, Reliquaries and Late Medieval Coronation in Aachen and Székesfehérvár," in *Matter of Faith*, 32–39.
1080 Bedos-Rezak, *Ego*, 200.
1081 Perkinson, *Likeness*, 92–93 et passim; Wirth, *Villard*, 92–95.
1082 Hörsch, "Bildlichen Ausstatung," 292–93.
1083 Wirth, *L'Image à l'époque romane*, 304–14 et passim; Forsyth, "Narrative at Moissac"; Baschet, *Corps*.
1084 On restoring God's perfect order: Ramirez-Weaver, *Saving Science*, 209–13.
1085 Dale, "Individual."
1086 Fozi, "'Reinhildis,'" 160–63.
1087 Sánchez Ameijeiras, "*Monumenta* and *Memoria*," and *Rostros*, 108; Miguélez Cavero, "Embodied Emotions."
1088 On the representation of human souls, Baschet, *Corps*, 123–72; Fozi, "'Reinhildis.'"
1089 *Arnolfo di Cambio: Il monumento del Cardinale Guillaume de Bray dopo il restauro* (special issue of *Bollettino d'Arte*, [2009]), ed. Angiola Maria Romanini; Lakey, Sculptural Seeing, 157–59.
1090 Franz Kohlschein and Peter Wünche, *Heiliger Raum: Architecture, Kunst und Liturgie im mittelalterlichen Kathedralen und Stiftskirchen* (Maria Laach: Institut der Abtei, 1998); Éric Palazzo, *Liturgie et société au Moyen Âge* (Paris: Aubier, 2000); *Kunst und Liturgie im Mittelalter*; Bacci, "Pro remedio animae"; *Art Cérémonial et Liturgie*; Warland, *Bildlichkeit und Bildorte*; *Frömmigkeit im Mittelalter*; *La performance des images*, ed. Alain Dierkens, Gil Bartholeyns, and Thomas Golsenne (Brussels: Université de Bruxelles, 2010); *Art médiéval: Les voies de l'espace liturgique*, ed. Paolo Piva (Paris: Picard, 2010); Nicolas Reveyron, "Image performative et liturgie: Les sept chapiteaux de l'abside de la cathédrale de Lyon (XIIᵉ)," in *L'Église, lieu de performances*, 301–13.
1091 Donalee Fox, "Roman Theatre and Roman Rite: Twelfth-Century Transformations in Allegory, Ritual, and the Idea of Theatre," in *The Appearances of Medieval Rituals: The Play of Construction and Modification*, ed. Nils Holger Petersen et al. (Turnhout: Brepols, 2004), 33–48; Zchomelidse, *Art, Ritual*, 14–18, 104–07.
1092 Palazzo, "'Livres-Corps,'" 39.
1093 Cannon, *Religious Poverty*, 326–28.
1094 Klemm, "Corpus Animatum," 277.
1095 Bredekamp, *Souverän*, 94–100.
1096 Hahn, *Thing of Mine*, 123.
1097 Flood, "God's Wonder," 186.
1098 Divesting them would have signaled loss of sanctity; Miller, *Clothing*, 87–95.
1099 Peter Barnet, "Beasts of Every Land and Clime: An Introduction to Medieval Aquamanilia," in *Lions, Dragons, & Other Beasts: Aquamanilia of the Middle Ages, Vessels for Church and Table*, ed. Peter Barnet and Pete Dandridge (New Haven, CT: Yale University Press, 2006), 3–17; Ochlawa, "Aquamanile."
1100 Kinglsey, *Bernward Gospels*; Helga Lutz and Bernhard Siegert, "In der Mixed Zone: Klapp- und faltbare Bildobjekte als Operationen hybrider Realitäten," in *Klappeffekte*, 108–38; Harald Wolter von dem Knesebeck, "Faltbilder als Form der Ordnungs- und Sinnstiftung im Kostbaren Evangliar Bischof Bernwards von Hildesheim," in *Klappeffekte*, 161–83; Benjamin C. Tilghman, "Pattern, Process, and the Creation of Meaning in the Lindisfarne Gospels," *West 86th* 24 (2017), 3–28, and "Patterns of Meaning in Insular Manuscripts: Folio 183r in *The Book of Kells*," in *Graphic Devices*, 163–78.
1101 Cannon, *Religious Poverty*, 54–56 et passim; Palazzo, *Peindre*, 45–63.
1102 Dutton and Kessler, *Poetry and Paintings*, 95–96 et passim.
1103 Kumler, *Translating Truth*, 76–90.
1104 Kumler, *Translating Truth*, 63–68.

1105 Newhauser and Russell, "Mapping," 83–112.
1106 Daniel Connolly, "Imagined Pilgrimage in the Itinerary Maps of Matthew Paris," *Art Bulletin* 81 (1999), 598–622; Newhauser and Russell, "Mapping." The lintel of the Holy Sepulcher maps history onto actual pilgrimage, but see Rudy, *Postcards*, 175–76.
1107 Marius Rimmele, "Die Schreinmadonna: Körperlichkeit, Medienfragen und Bedeutungsschichten eines mittelalterlichen Bildes," in *Kanon Kunstgeschichte: Einführung in Werke, Methoden und Epochen*, vol. I: *Mittelalter*, ed. Kristin Marek and Martin Schultz (Munich: Wilhelm Fink, 2015), 192–213; Gertsman, "Performing Birth," 83–104, and *Worlds Within*; Pinkus, *Simulacra*, 148–78; Novacich, "Transparent Mary," 283.
1108 Gertsman, *Worlds Within*, 126–48.
1109 Allegra Iafrate, *The Wandering Throne of Solomon: Objects and Tales of Kingship in the Medieval Medditerranean* (Leiden: Brill, 2015).
1110 Fliegel, "Table Fountain," 4–22.
1111 Fliegel, "Table Fountain," 11–12; Pinkus, *Simulacra*, 9.
1112 Bynum, *Materiality*, 105–14; E.R. Truitt, *Medieval Robots: Mechanism, Magic, Nature, and Art* (Philadelphia: University of Pennsylvania Press, 2015), 119–21.
1113 Christopher Swift, "Technology and Wonder in Thirteenth-Century Iberia and Beyond" in *Performing Object and Theatrical Things*, ed. Maria Schweitzer and Joanne Zerdy (New York: Palgrave, 2014), 21–35.
1114 Robert Mills, *Suspended Animation: Pain, Pleasure and Punishment in Medieval Culture* (New York: Reaktion Books, 2005), 38–52; Koerner, "Icon as Iconoclash."
1115 Barbet-Massin, *L'enluminure*, 333–40.
1116 A bronze censer in Lille bears an inscription that likens the smoke to "true prayers intended for Christ"; Gearhart, "Word and Prayer"; Hiltrud Westermann-Angerhausen, "The Two Censers in the *Schedula diversarum atrium* of Theophilus and Their Place in the Liturgy," in *Cinq sens*, 189–211.
1117 Kessler, "Images Borne on a Breeze," 82–83.
1118 Debiais, *Croisée*, 298–300.
1119 Hahn, *Strange Beauty*, 134–41 et passim.
1120 Jacqueline Jung, "The Tactile and the Visionary: Notes on the Place of Sculpture in the Medieval Religious Imagination," *Looking Beyond: Visions, Dreams, and Insights in Medieval Art & History*, ed. Colum Hourihane (Princeton: Index of Christian Art, 2010), 236–39.
1121 Kumler, "Multiplication," 181–84.
1122 Ursula Nilgen, "Die römischen Apsisprogramme der karolingischen Epoche: Päpstliche Repräsentation und Liturgie," in *799, Kunst und Kultur*: 3: 542–49, and "Die Bilder über dem Altar: Triumph- und Apsisbogenprogramme in Rom und Mittelitalien und ihr Bezug zur Liturgie," in *Kunst und Liturgie*, 75–89; Thunø, *Apse Mosaic*, 119–42.
1123 Aavitsland, "Visual Splendour," 213–16; "Civitas."
1124 Klemm, "Corpus animatum," 276.
1125 Fisher, "Cross Altar and Crucifix," 43–62; Pierre-Alain Mariaux, "'Faire Dieu': Quelques réflexions sur les relations entre confection eucharistique et création d'image, IXe–XIIe siècles," in *Ästhetik des Unsichtbaren*, 94–111, and "Eucharistie et création d'image autour de l'an mil: le crucifix de Géron," in *Les pratiques de l'eucharistie dans les Églises d'Orient et d'Occident (Antiquité et Moyen Âge)*, ed. Nicole Bériou et al. (París: Institut catholique, 2009), 1043–56; Roger Wieck, *Illuminating Faith: The Eucharist in Medieval Life and Art* (New York: Scala Publishers, 2014).
1126 Reynolds, "Christ's Money," 43–49; Kessler, "Medietas/Mediator," 44–52.
1127 Hamburger, "*Haec Figura*" and *Hrabanus redivivus*; Sand, *Vision, Devotion*, 54–58 et passim; Rist, "Innocent III"; Jörg Bölling, "Face to Face with Christ in Late Medieval Rome:

The Veil of Veronica in Papal Liturgy and Ceremony," in *European Fortune*, 136–44; Uwe Michael Lang, "Origins of the Liturgical Veneration of the Roman Veronica," in *European Fortune*, 144–55.

1128 Zchomelidse, "Descending Word"; *Art, Ritual*, 34–71 et passim.

1129 Justin Kroesen, *The Sepulchrum Domini through the Ages: Its Form and Function* (Louvain: Peeters, 2000), 150–73; "Easter Sepulchres," in *Village Church*, 284–99; Amy Knight Powell, *Depositions: Scenes from the Late Medieval Church and the Modern Museum* (London: Zone Books, 2012), 81–101; Xavier Barral I Altet, "La escenografía de la tumba: Lugares de la muerte en la iglesia medieval: rios y atrevimientos," *Codex Aqvilarensis* 30 (2014), 13–35.

1130 Lutz, "Drop of Blood," 37–38.

1131 Hosts were occasionally stored in Shrine Madonnas, which were also fitted out with moveable figures of the Crucified that served the Holy Week rituals; Melissa Katz, "Marian Motion: Opening the Body of the *Vierge Ouvrante*," in *Meaning in Motion*, 63–91; Pinkus, *Simulacra*, 153–56; Gertsman, *Worlds Within*, 53–55 et passim.

1132 Marcello Angheben, "La crucifixion du chevet: Entre liturgie eucharistique et dévotion privée," in *La cathédrale Saint-Pierre de Poitiers: enquêtes croisées*, ed. Claude Andrault-Schmitt (Poitiers: La Geste, 2013), 350–63.

1133 Kamil Kopania, *Animated Sculptures of the Crucified Christ in the Religious Culture of the Latin Middle Ages* (Warsaw: Wydawnictwo Neriton, 2010).

1134 Lutz, "Drop of Blood," 39.

1135 *Sotto il Duomo di Siena: Scoperte archeologiche, architettoniche e figurative*, ed. Roberto Guerrini (Cinisello Balsamo: Silvano Editoriale, 2003); Herbert L. Kessler, "Joseph in Siena," in *Joseph of Nazareth*, 63–76.

1136 Johannes Tripps, "Scene di teatro sacro nelle miniature fiamminghe del Quattrocento: Reflessioni sull'opera dei fratelli Limbourg e dei loro contemporanei" in *Teatro delle statue*, 111–24.

1137 *Prozessionen und ihre Gesänge in der mittelalterlichen Stadt*, ed. Harald Buchinger et al. (Regensburg: Schnell & Steiner, 2017).

1138 Albert Dietl, "Per totum murorum ambitum: Papst Leos IV; Bau und Einweihungsprozession der civitas Leoniana," in *Prozessionen*, 119–59.

1139 Johannes Tripps, *Das handelnde Bildwerk in der Gotik: Forschungen zu den Bedeutungsschichten und der Funktion der Kirchengebäudes und sein Ausstattung in der Hoch- un Spätgotik* (Berlin: Gebr. Mann, 2000), 95–121.

1140 Lorenzo Carletti and Cristiano Giometti, "Medieval Wood Sculpture and Its Setting in Architecture: Studies in Some Churches in and around Pisa," *Architectural History* 46 (2003), 37–56.

1141 Cohen, "Indulgence," 874–75.

1142 Rollason, *Power of Place*, 268.

1143 Paul Crossley, "Bohemia Sacra: Liturgy and History in Prague Cathedral," in *Pierre, lumière, couleur*, 341–65; Williamson, "How Magnificent," 248–56.

1144 Sible de Blaauw, "Following the Crosses. The Processional Cross and the Typology of Processions in Medieval Rome," in *Christian Feast and Festival: The Dynamics of Western Liturgy and Culture*, ed. Paul Post et al. (Leuven: Peeters, 2001), 319–43; Joseph Dyer, "City Streets as Sacred Space: The Topography of Processions in Medieval Rome," in *Prozessionen*, 13–33; Chris Wickham, *Medieval Rome: Stability and Crisis of a City, 900–1150* (Oxford: Oxford University Press, 2014), 321–84. An enormous fourteenth-century gilt-silver processional cross still at the Lateran attests to the importance of this urban celebration; Herbert L. Kessler, *Old St. Peter's and Church Decoration in Medieval Italy* (Spoleto: CISAM, 2002), 55–59 et passim.

1145 On the complicated politics related to this mosaic made just before the papacy departed for Avignon, see Gardner, *Roman Crucible*, 275–80.
1146 Kessler and Zacharias, *Rome 1300*, 130.
1147 Debra J. Birch, *Pilgrimage to Rome in the Middle Ages* (Woodbridge: Boydell, 1998), 114–15; Serena Romano, "L'acheropita lateranense: storia e funzione," in *Volto di Cristo*, 39–41; Maria Andoloro, "L'acheropita in ombra del Laterano," in *Volto di Cristo*, 43–49; Enrico Parlato, "Le icone in processione," in *Arte e iconografia*, 69–92. It is still imitated in nearby Tivoli; Philene Helas and Gerhard Wolf, *Die Nacht der Bilder: Eine Beschreibung der Prozession zu Maria Himmelfahrt in Rom aus dem Jahr 1462* (Freiburg i. Breisgau: Rombach, 2011).
1148 By the thirteenth century, the procession was entrusted to members of the Confraternity of the Savior, a lay charitable organization: Barbara Wisch, "Key to Success: Propriety and Promotion of Miraculous Images by Roman Confraternities," in *Miraculous Image*, 161–84; Noreen, "Sacred Memory"; Rebekah Perry, "On the Road to Emmaus: Tivoli's 'Inchinata' Procession and the Evolving Allegorical Landscape in the Late Medieval City," in *Space, Place, and Motion: Locating Confraternities in the Late Medieval and Early Modern City*, ed. Diana Bullen Presciutti (Leiden: Brill, 2017), 127–53.
1149 Rist, "Innocent III"; by the fifteenth century, the *Veronica* was also part of the Christmas and Ascension Day liturgies; Bölling, "Face to Face," 140.
1150 Kessler and Zacharias, *Rome 1300*, 207; Gardner, *Roman Crucible*, 159–60.
1151 Rita Tekippe, "The Grand Procession at Tournai: The Community Writ Large," in *Push Me, Pull You*, 523–58.
1152 Werner Telesko, "Theologische Programm des Kölner Dreikönigenschreins," *Jahrbuch des Kölnischen Geschichtsvereins* 68 (1997), 25–50; Philippe Cordez, "La châsse des rois mages à Cologne et la christianisation des pierres magiques aux XIIe et XIIIe siècles," in *Trésor au Moyen Âge*, 315–32; Westermann-Angerhausen, "Spolia as Relic"; David Ganz and Stefan Neuner, "Peripatetisches Sehen in den Bildkulturen der Vormoderne Zur Einfürung," in *Mobile Eyes*, 38–39.
1153 Kessler and Zacharias, *Rome 1300*, 208; Rosamond McKitterick, John Osborne, Carol M. Richardson, and Joanna Story, "Introduction," in *Old Saint Peter's Rome*, 1–20.
1154 Frugoni, *L'affare migliore*, 145–46, 186–87; Tomei, "Dio Padre in Trono."
1155 Fricke, *Fallen Idols*, 180–83.
1156 Bacci, "Pro remedio animae," 82–83. Noble, *Images*, 243–44, and "Images, a Daydream and Heavenly Sounds in the Carolingian Era: Walahfrid Strabo and Maura of Troyes," in *Envisioning Experience in Late Antiquity and the Middle Ages: Dynamic Patterns in Texts and Images*, ed. Giselle de Nie and Thomas F.X. Noble (Farnham: Ashgate, 2012), 23–45; Christiane Veyrard-Cosme, "Polyphonie énonciative et variations stylistiques dans le *sermo de vita et morte gloriosae virginis Maurae* attribué à Prudence de Troyes," *Hagiographica* 20 (2013), 79–92; Palazzo, *Peindre*, 52–54; Maria Cristina Correia Leandro Pereira, "Exposition des ymages des figures qui sunt: discursos sobre imagens no Ocidente Medieval," *Antiteses* 9 (2016), 36–54.
1157 Elvio Lunghi, "Francis of Assisi in Prayer before the Crucifix in the Accounts of the First Biographers," in *Studies in the History of Art* 61 (2002), 340–53; Jean-Marie Sansterre, "Avant que le crucifix ne 'parle' à s. Francois: les mentions de crucifix parlants antérieurs à celui de San Damiano à Assise," *Analecta Bollandiana* 129 (2011), 71–79.
1158 Chiara Frugoni, *Quale Francesco? Il messagio nascosto negli affreschi della Basilica superiore ad Assisi* (Torino: Giulio Einaudi editore, 2015), 238–49.

1159 Thunø, *Apse Mosaic*, 133–34 et passim; Paul Davies, "The Lighting of Pilgrimage Shrines in Renaissance Italy," in *Miraculous Image*, 57–80.
1160 Russo, "Espace peint"; Juliette Rollier-Hanselmann, "Peintures et couleurs dans la mouvance clunisienne," in *Peintures murales médiévales, XIIe–XVIe siècles: Regards comparés*, ed. Daniel Russo (Dijon: Éditions universitaires de Dijon, 2005), 113–30; Lapina, "Mural Paintings"; Bergmeier, "*Traditio Legis*."
1161 Bogen, "Itinerarprinzip"; Jeannet Hommers, "Kaleidoskop der Bilder: Zur Mehransichtigkeit historisierter Kapitelle am Beispiel von Saint-Andoche in Saulieu," in *Bild im Plural*, 161–79; Tina Bawden, *Die Schwelle im Mittelalter: Bildmotiv und Bildort* (Cologne: Böhlau, 2014).
1162 Kessler, "*Realia* and *Spiritualia*," 130.
1163 Prado-Vilar, "*Superstes*," 140–41.
1164 Bynum, *Materiality*, 71–81; Suzanne Karr Schmidt, "Memento mori," in *Push Me, Pull You*, 261–94. Peter of Limoges saw a horrifying statue of Mary in a vision: Peter of Limoges, *Moral Treatise on the Eye*, trans. Newhauser, 181; Kessler, "Fenestra," 157–58.
1165 Ingo Herklotz, "*Miranda se non scribenda*: Il campus *Lateranensis* nel Medioevo," in *Eredi di Costantino/Il papato, il Laterano e la propaganda visive nel XII secolo* (Rome: Viella, 2000), 41–94.
1166 Moskowitz, *Gothic Sculpture*, 13–14.
1167 Fassler, *Virgin*, 205–41.
1168 Reed, "Blessing the Serpent," 41.
1169 Maguire, "Political Content," 100–01.
1170 Heyman, "Fulcher's Bestiary," 115 et passim.
1171 Leah Rutchick, "A Reliquary Capital at Moissac: Liturgy and Ceremonial Thinking in the Cloister," in *Decorations for the Holy Dead: Visual Embellishments on Tombs and Shrines of Saints*, ed. Stephen Lamia and Elizabeth Valdez del Álamo (Turnhout: Brepols, 2002), 129–50.
1172 Bacci, "Berardenga Antependium," 2.
1173 Jacqueline Jung, "Kinetics of Gothic Sculpture: Movement and Apprehension in the South Transept of Strasbourg Cathedral and the Chartreuse de Champmol in Dijon," in *Mobile Eyes*, 156; Guest, "Prodigal's Journey," 62–64.
1174 Gardner, *Roman Crucible*, 261–67; Thunø, *Apse Mosaic*, 37.
1175 Campbell, *Game of Courting*, 194–95 et passim.
1176 Alyce Jordan, "Stained Glass and the Liturgy: Performing Sacred Kingship in Capetian France," in *Objects, Images*, 274–97.
1177 Palazzo, *L'évêque*; Méhu, "Images, signes."
1178 Patrizia Caramassi, "Die hochmittelalterlichen Fresken der Unterkirche von San Clemente in Rom als programmatische Selbstdarstellung des Reformpapsttums: Neue Einsichten zur Bestimmung des Entstehungskontextes," *Quellen und Forschungen aus italienischen Archiven und Bibliotheken Deutsches Historisches Institut in Rom* 81 (2001), 1–66; Filippini, "La Chiesa e il suo santo"; De Blaauw, "Following the Crosses"; Dyer, "City Streets."
1179 Willibald Sauerländer, "Reliquien, Altäre und Portale," in *Kunst und Liturgie*, 121–34; Bruno Boerner, "L'iconographie des portails sculptés des cathédrales gothiques: Les parcours et les fonctions rituels," in *Art médiéval*, 221–61; "Les cinq sens et la sculpture gothique," in *Cinq sens*, 547–63. Also, Francisco Prado-Vilar, "Cuando brilla la luz del quinto día: El pórtico de la gloria y la visión de Mateo en el espejo de la historia," *Románico* 15 (2012), 8–19.
1180 Méhu, "Images, signes," 306–11.
1181 One of the acts of mercy, charity was a means to salvation that entered Last Judgment imagery and that underlies the marketplace miniature in the *Specchio umano*: Albert

Dietl, "Vom Wort zum Bild der Barmherzigkeit," in *Schwelle zum Paradies: Die Galluspforte des Basler Münsters*, ed. Hans-Rudolf Meier and Dorothea Schwinn Schürmann (Basel: Schwabe, 2011), 74–93; Federico Botana, *The Works of Mercy in Italian Medieval Art (c. 1050–c. 1400)* (Turnhout: Brepols, 2011); Rouchon Mouilleron, "Miracle et charité," 176.

1182 Klein, "Cloister of Gerona."
1183 Diane J. Reilly, "Picturing the Monastic Drama: Romanesque Bible Illustrations of the Song of Songs," *Word & Image* 17, no. 4 (2001), 389–400.
1184 Bolzoni, *La Rete*, 3–46 (*The Web*, 11–40); Niklaus Largier, *In Praise of the Whip: A Cultural History of Arousal* (New York: Zone Books, 2007), 101–74.
1185 Krüger, "Aschaffenburger Tafelbild"; van der Ploeg, "How Liturgical Is a Medieval Altarpiece?"
1186 Caviness, "Stained Glass Windows," 137–39.
1187 Bauer, "La frammentazione liturgica," 385–446, and "Überlegungen," 75–96; John Crook, *The Architectural Setting of the Cult of Saints in the Early Christian West c. 300–c. 1200* (Oxford: Oxford University Press, 2000); Jung, "Moving Viewers," 39–40.
1188 Nicolotti, *From the Mandylion of Edessa to the Shroud of Turin*.
1189 *Romei & Giubilei: Il pellegrinaggio medievale a San Pietro (350–1350)*, ed. Mario D'Onofrio (Milan: Electa, 1999); Gerhard Wolf, "'Or fu sí fatta la sembianza vostra?'"; *Schleier*, and "Vera Icon," in *Handbuch der Bildtheologie*, 419–66; Kruse, *Wozu Menschen malen*, 269–306; *L'immagine di Cristo dall'acheropita al mano d'artista dal tardo medioevo all'età barocca* (Studi e testi 432), ed. Christoph L. Frommel and Gerhard Wolf (Vatican, 2006), 143–65; *European Fortune*.
1190 *Bonifacio VIII*.
1191 Kessler and Zacharias, *Rome 1300*, 28–33; Gardner, *Roman Crucible*, 289–92; Romano, *Apogeo*, 208–12.
1192 Rudolph, "Tour Guide," 41–59.
1193 V.A. Kolve, *Telling Images: Chaucer and the Imagery of Narrative* (Stanford: Stanford University Press, 2009).
1194 Indeed, the entire sculptural ensemble can be understood as a guide through the church: Low, "'You Who Once Were Far Off,'" 484.
1195 Rocío Sánchez Ameijeiras, "Imagery and Interactivity: Ritual Transaction at the Saint's Tomb," in *Decorations for the Holy Dead*, 21–38.
1196 Joanna Cannon, "Popular Saints and Private Chantries: The Sienese Tomb-altar of Margherita of Cortona and Questions of Liturgical Use," in *Kunst und Liturgie*, 149–62, and *Religious Poverty*, 192–97.
1197 Spencer, *Souvenirs*; *Romei & Giubilei*, 338–65.
1198 The scene alone was isolated in a frame and provided with an altar when the church was transformed during the fifteenth century.
1199 Hauknes, "Painting of Knowledge," 30–38.
1200 Gerardo Boto Varela, "Caracterización icónica y delimitación visual de los lugares *postliminares* en las iglesias románicas españolas," in *L'Église, lieu de performances*, 265–81.
1201 D.K. Connolly, "At the Center of the World: The Labyrinth Pavement of Chartres Catheral," in *Late Medieval Pilgrimage*, 285–314; Asa S. Mittman, "Forking Paths? Matthew Paris, Jorge Luis Borges, and Maps of the Labyrinth," *Peregrinations: Journal of Medieval Art and Architecture* 4 (2013), art. 7; Kupfer, *Art and Optics*, 83.
1202 Debra Higgs Strickland, *Demons & Jews: Making Monsters in Medieval Art* (Princeton: Princeton University Press, 2003), 166; "Meanings of Muhammed in Later Medieval Art," in *The Image of the Prophet between Ideal and Ideology: A Scholarly Investigation*, ed. Christine Gruber and Avinoam Shalem (Berlin and Boston,

2014), 147–64; "Monstrosity and Race in the Late Middle Ages," in *Monsters and the Monstrous*, ed. Asa S. Mittman and P.J. Dendle (Abingdon: Ashgate, 2013), 65–86; "Edward I," 431. Also, Svetlana Luchitskaja, "The Image of Muhammad in Latin Chronography of the Twelfth and Thirteenth Centuries," *Journal of Medieval History* 26 (2000), 115–26.

1203 Craig M. Wright, *The Maze and the Warrior: Symbols in Architecture, Theology, and Music* (Cambridge, MA: Harvard University Press, 2001), 129–58; Constant J. Mews, "Liturgists and Dance in the Twelfth Century: The Witness of John Beleth and Sicard of Cremona," *Church History* 78 (2009), 512–48; Barral I Altet, *Décor*, 189–90. A chandelier in Zutphen pictures dancing; see van de Wouw, *Chandelier*.

1204 *Rationale divinorum officiorum*, chap. 120; Barral I Altet, *Décor*, 190.

1205 Largier, *Whip*, 145–46.

1206 Niklaus Largier, "The Art of Prayer: Conversions of Interiority and Exteriority in Medieval Contemplative Practice," *Rethinking Emotion: Interiority and Exteriority in Premodern, Modern, and Contemporary Thought*, ed. Rüdiger Campe and Julia Weber (Berlin: De Gruyter, 2014), 58–71; Carolyn Muessig, "Performance of the Passion: The Enactment of Devotion in the Later Middle Ages," in *Visualizing Medieval Performance*, 129–42.

1207 Büchsel, "Materialpracht," 166–67.

1208 Alejandro García Avilés, "*Transitus*," 34, and "Estatuas poseidas: idolos demoniacos en el arte de la Edad Media," *Codex Aqvilarensis* 28 (2012), 231–254.

1209 Schmidt, *Painted Piety*, 44–71; Kozlowski, "Trecento Diptych."

1210 Laura Katrine Skinnebach, "Devotion: Perception as Practice and Body as Devotion in Late Medieval Piety," in *Saturated Sensorium*, 152–79; Palazzo, *Peindre*, 65–132.

1211 Derbes and Sandona, *Usurer's Heart*, 146–48.

1212 It also portrays the lascivious priest conjuring up demons in a kind of anti-prayer posture, frontally but with one leg back and the other forward. Rocío Sánchez Ameijeiras, "'Ymagines sanctae': Fray Juan Gil de Zamora y la teoría de la imagen sagrada en las *Cantigas* de Santa María," in *Homenaje a José García Oro*, ed. Miguel Romani Martínez and Maria Ángeles Novoa Gómez (Santiago de Compostela: Universidade de Santiago de Compostela, 2002), 515–26; Jean-Marie Sansterre, "Miracles et images: Les relations entre l'image et le prototype celeste d'après quelque récits des Xe–XIIIe siècles," in *Performance des images*, 47–57; Avilés, "*Transitus*," 32–35.

1213 Kumler, *Translating Truth*, 228–29.

1214 Kamerick, *Popular Piety*, 37.

1215 Bolzoni, *La Rete*, 29–35 (*The Web*, 29–34); Nirit Ben-Aryeh Debby, "Italian Pulpits: Preaching, Art, and Spectacle," in *Charisma and Religious Authority: Jewish, Christian, and Muslim Preaching, 1200–1500*, ed. Katherine L. Jansen and Miri Rubin (Turnhout: Brepols, 2010), 125–46; Vibeke Olson, "Movement, Metaphor, Memory: Interactions between Pilgrims and Portal Programs," in *Push Me, Pull You*, 495–521; Carolyn Muessig, "'Can't Take My Eyes Off of You': Mutual Gazing Between the Divine and Humanity in Late Medieval Preaching," in *Optics, Ethics*, 17–27.

1216 Rudolph, *Mystic Ark*, 49–51 et passim.

1217 Hamburger, "Various Writings of Humanity."

1218 Hamburger, "Hand of God," 61.

1219 Rudolph, "Tour Guide."

1220 Rudolph, "Tour Guide," 51–52.

1221 Reveyron, "Image," 302; Adam of Eynsham, *Magna vita Sancti Hugonis*, Bk. V.9; Christopher Norton, "Henry of Blois, St Hugh and Henry II: The Winchester Bible Reconsidered," in *Romanesque Patrons and Processes*, 117–41.

1222 Norton, "Henry of Blois," 126.

1223 Norton, "Henry of Blois," 132.
1224 Rocío Sánchez Ameijeiras, "The Faces of the Words: Aesthetic Notions of Artistic Practice in the Thirteenth Century," in *Gothic Art & Thought in the Later Medieval Period: Essays in Honor of Willibald Sauerländer*, ed. Willibald Sauerländer and Colum Hourihane (Princeton: Index of Christian Art, 2011), 103–05, and *Rostros*, 65–80; Debby, "Italian Pulpits."
1225 Ambrose, *Vézelay*, 34–37 et passim.
1226 Stephen Murray, *A Gothic Sermon: Making a Contract with the Mother of God, Saint Mary of Amiens* (University of California Press, 2004); Jung, *Gothic Screen*, 191–93. Most sermons were ad hoc and ephemeral, but a mid-thirteenth-century compendium of pastoral texts (London, British Library, Harley MS 3244), including William Peraldus's *Summa de Vitiis*, suggests that some were collected, read, meditated, and even illustrated; Bolzoni, *La Rete*, 62–71 (*The Web*, 50–57); Kumler, *Translating Truth*, 80–81.
1227 Hamburger, *Diagramming Devotion*, 16.
1228 Opicino was best known for diagrams that provide a *tertium comparationis* between word and image: Stefan Bogen and Felix Thürlemann, "Jenseits der Opposition von Text und Bild: Überlegungen zu einer Theorie des Diagrammatischen," in *Bildwelt der Diagramme*, 1–22; Morse, "Seeing and Believing"; Whittington, *Body-Worlds*, 103–39 et passim.
1229 Giuseppe Ledda, "Filosofia e ottica nella predicazione medievale," in *Letteratura in forma di sermone: I rapporti tra predicazione e letteratura nei secoli XIII–XVI*, ed. Ginetta Auzzas, Giovanni Baffetti and Carlo Delcorno (Florence: Olschki, 2003), 53–78; Cannon, *Religious Poverty*, 52–53; Cooper, "Preaching," 39–44.
1230 Stephen Murray, "Pourquoi la polychromie? Réflexions sur le role de la sculpture polychrome de la cathédrale d'Amiens," in *La couleur et la pierre: Polychromie des portails gothiques (Actes du Colloque, Amiens 2000)* (Paris: Picard, 2002), 207–12.
1231 Jung, *Gothic Screen*, 191–92.
1232 Philine Helas, *Lebende Bilder in der italienischen Festkultur des 15. Jahrhunderts* (Berlin: Akademie Verlag, 1999); Palazzo, *Liturgie et société*, 162–63; Niklaus Largier, "Scripture, Vision, Performance: Visionary Texts and Medieval Religious Drama" in *Visual Culture*, 207–19; Michael Norton, *Liturgical Drama and the Reimagining of Medieval Theater* (Kalamazoo: Medieval Institute Publications, 2017).
1233 Moretti, "Parabola."
1234 Palazzo, "Peintures murales," 59–60.
1235 Sharon Mueller-Loewald, "Quatre figures féminines apocryphes dans certains mystères de La Passion en France," *Fifteenth-century Studies* 28 (2003), 173–183; Lipton, *Dark Mirror*, 221–23; Brown, *Holkham Picture Bible*, 76; Kessler, "Literary Warp and Artistic Weft," 11–29.
1236 Beatrice E. Kitzinger, "Judgment on Parchment: Illuminating Theater in Besançon MS 579," *Gesta* 55, no. 1 (2016), 49–78.
1237 Tripps, *Handelnde Bildwerk*; Helas, *Lebende Bilder*.
1238 Campbell, *Game of Courting*, 194–95 et passim.
1239 *Anglo-Saxon Kingdoms*, 238–39.
1240 Büchsel, "Materialpracht," 169; Dell'Acqua, "Gerlachus"; Parello, "Fünf Felder," 31–32. Hugh of Saint-Victor had referred to such exegetic readings as playful allegories.
1241 Ambrose, *Vézelay*, 68; Weinryb, *Bronze Object*, 65–73.
1242 Cordez, "Arrepentimiento," 136.
1243 Kessler, "Sanctifying Serpent," 161–62.
1244 Heslop, "Hugh's Choir," 72–74; Sánchez Ameijeiras, *Rostros*, 226.
1245 Ganz, "Blick," 271; Bynum, *Materiality*, 195–208.

1246 Nurith Kenaan-Kedar, "Interaction of Marginal and Official Iconography: The West Façade of St. Hilaire in Foussais—Its Oral, Visual and Literary Sources," in *The Metamorphosis of Marginal Images: From Antiquity to Present Time*, ed. Nurith Kenaan-Kedar and Asher Ovadiah (Tel Aviv: Tel Aviv University Press, 2002), 159–74; Binski, "Medieval Invention"; Kenaan-Kedar and Fishhof, "Patrons," 118–20.
1247 Barral I Altet, *Souvenir*, 275–92; Ordás "Mundo," 275–80.
1248 Trinks, *Antike*, 246–52; Shalev-Eyni, *Jews Among Christians*, 59–66.
1249 Brown, *Holkham Picture Bible*, 2.
1250 Connie L. Scarborough, "Laughter and the Comedic in a Religious Text: The Example of the 'Cantigas de Santa Maria,'" in *Laughter in the Middle Ages and Early Modern Times: Epistemology of a Fundamental Human Behavior, Its Meaning, and Consequences*, ed. Albrecht Classen (Berlin: De Gruyter, 2010), 281–94.
1251 Elizabeth Sears, "Ivory and Ivory Workers in Medieval Paris," in *Images in Ivory: Precious Objects of the Gothic Age*, ed. Peter Barnet (Princeton: Princeton University Press, 1997), 19–37.
1252 Elizabeth Sears, "Scribal Wit in a Manuscript from the Châtelet: Images in the Margins of Boileau's Livre des Métiers, BnF, MS fr. 24069," in *Tributes to Lucy Freeman Sandler: Studies in Illuminated Manuscripts*, ed. Kathryn A. Smith and Carol H. Krinsky (London: Harvey Miller, 2007), 157–72; Wirth, *Marges*, 181–364.
1253 Barral I Altet, *Décor*, 186–90; Kessler, "Vanitas," 42–48.
1254 Gertsman, *Worlds Within*, 147–48.
1255 Zorach, *Passionate Triangle*, 31–33.
1256 Dutton, *Carolingian Civilization*, 479; Ackermann, *Itinerarium*, 8, 127, 135.
1257 Eugene Vance, "Seeing God: Augustine, Sensation, and the Mind's Eye," in *Rethinking the Medieval Senses: Heritages/Fascinations/Frames*, ed. Stephen G. Nichols, Andreas Kablitz, and Alison Calhoun (Baltimore: Johns Hopkins University Press, 2008), 13–29; Mehú, "Augustin."
1258 Klemm, "Corpus Animatum," 268–73; the recent interest in neuro-aesthetics might be applied productively to this conception of cognition; Anjan Chatterjee, *The Aesthetic Brain: How We Evolved to Desire Beauty and Enjoy Art* (Oxford: Oxford University Press, 2014).
1259 Distinctly different from the arrangement in the better-known diagram in Cambridge, University Library, MS Gg. I. I, fol. 490ᵛ; Carruthers, *Craft of Memory*, 120–23; Klemm, *Bildphysiologie*, 12–14; "Life from Within," 118–22.
1260 Carruthers, *Craft of Thought*, 206–09.
1261 Wirth, *Villard*, 50–51; Carruthers, *Experience of Beauty*, 200–05.
1262 Dallas G. Denney II, *Seeing and Being Seen in the Later Medieval World: Optics, Theology and Religious Life* (Cambridge: Cambridge University Press, 2005), 91–96; Andrew Harrison, "What is Presence?," in *Presence*, 161–72.
1263 Rupert of Deutz (Herman-Judah's supposed interlocutor) had asserted, "Whoever makes and adores pagan idols, makes and adores lies. However, whoever makes and adores an image Jesus Christ who was crucified for the salvation of the world, makes truth and adores truth ... the image figures both God and man"; François Bœspflug, "La vision-en-reve de la Trinité de Rupert de Deutz (v.1100), Liturgie, spiritualité et histoire de l'art," *Revue des Sciences Religieuses* 71 (1997), 205–29; Kessler, *Spiritual Seeing*, 193–94 et passim.
1264 Kumler, "Manufacturing," 9–13.
1265 See p. 94; Kessler, *Neither God nor Man*, 29.
1266 Cannon, *Religious Poverty*, 52.
1267 Jane Bennett, *Vibrant Matter* (Durham: Duke University Press, 2009); Nagel, *Medieval Modern*.
1268 Some medieval sundial diagrams include crosses or crucifixions in the center; Barbara Oberist, "The Astronomical Sundial in Saint Willibrord's Calendar and its Early

Medieval Context," *Archives d'Histoire Doctrinale et Littéraire du Moyen Âge* 67 (2000), 71–118. Pacificus's *Horologium* still requires the viewer's imagination to find the nails in the sky Hamburger, "Idol Curiosity," 45; Guidetti, "Texts and Illustrations."
1269 Kumler, *Translating Truth*, 222–37 et passim.
1270 Jung, *Gothic Screen*, 191–97 et passim.
1271 Jansen, *Making*, 130–34; Binski, "Rhetorical Occasions," 24–25.
1272 Jung, *Gothic Screen*, 253; Rudolph, "Exegetical Stained-Glass Window," 406–18; Debiais, *Croisée*, 255–57; Bynum, *Materiality*, 129–31.
1273 *Sententiae*, Bk. 2, Chap. 12.
1274 Augustine had already identified the three theological virtues as the means to rise from the flesh, the world, and the devil; Méhu, "Augustine," 297–98; Cynthia Hahn, "Vision," in *Companion to Medieval Art*, 44–64.
1275 Biernhoff, *Sight and Embodiment*, 43; Büttner, *Giotto*, 15; Nirenberg, *Aesthetic Theology*, 23–34.
1276 Ledda, "Filosofia," 53.
1277 *Acta Synodi*, 52.
1278 Hamburger, "Idol Curiosity," 38–39.
1279 Kessler, *Spiritual Seeing*, 104–48; Krüger, "Medium and Imagination."
1280 Nirenberg, *Theology*, 15–78.
1281 Seeta Chaganti, "Figure and Ground: *Elene*'s Nails, Cynewulf's Runes, and Hrabanus Maurus's Painted Poems," in *Arma Christi*, 53–82; Kessler, "Arca arcarum," 104–06.
1282 Kumler, *Translating Truth*.
1283 Christian Trottmann and Arnaud Dumouch, *Benoît XII: La vision beatifique* (Paris: Éditions Docteur angélique, 2009).
1284 Winterer, *Sakramentar*, 431–32; Anderson, *Cosmos*, 73–77.
1285 Herbert L. Kessler, "Corporeal Texts, Spiritual Paintings, and the Mind's Eye," in *Reading Images and Texts*, 9–61; Müller, *Omnia*, 215–21.
1286 Peter Seiler, "Schönheit und Scham, sinnliches Temperament und moralische Temperantia: Überlegungen zu einigen Antikenadaptionen in der spätmittelalterlichen Bildhauerei Italiens," *Zeitschrift für Kunstgeschichte* 70, no. 4 (2007), 473–512; Ritchy, *Holy Matter*, 61; Büttner, *Giotto*, 15–17.
1287 Marchesin, *L'arbre*, 24–41.
1288 Stahl, "Eve's Reach"; Marchesin, *L'arbre*, 204–17.
1289 Maria Evangelatou, "Botanical Exegesis in God's Creation: The Polyvalent Meaning of Plants on the Salerno Ivories," in *Salerno Ivories*, 133–65.
1290 Kessler, "Topografías," 19–28.
1291 Winterer, *Sakramentar*, 414–18; "*Ewaldi-Decke*," in *Karolingische und ottonische Kunst*, ed. Bruno Reudenbach (Munich: Prestel, 2009), 306–07; Anderson, *Cosmos*, 73–77.
1292 Barbara Raw, *Trinity and Incarnation in Anglo-Saxon Art and Thought* (Cambridge: Cambridge University Press,1997), 90–91; Jakobi-Mirwald, *Text-Buchstabe-Bild*, 139–42; Peter Parshall, "The Art of Memory and the Passion," *Art Bulletin* 81, no. 3 (1999), 456–72.
1293 Hamburger, "Idol Curiosity," 40–41; Kumler, *Translating Truth*.
1294 Bonne, "Entre l'image et la matière," 78–96.
1295 Debiais, *Croisée*, 326–31 et passim.
1296 Büttner, *Giotto*, 160.
1297 Wolf, *Schleier und Spiegel*, 57–58.
1298 Grönwald, "Einzelfund," 300.
1299 In so doing, the confraternity assumed roles that clerics had previously served; Rudolph, "Tour Guide"; Holmes, *Miraculous Image*, 69–74, 172; Jane Garnett and Gervase Rosser, *Spectacular Miracles: Transforming Images in Italy from the Renaissance to the Present* (London: Reaktion Books, 2013), 115–20. The *Specchio umano* pictures the

lamps mentioned in texts but not the curtains; Orcagna's monumental tabernacle, however, renders them in stone.

1300 *Otia Imperialia: Recreation for an Emperor*, ed. S.E. Banks and J.W. Binns (Oxford: Clarendon, 2002), 606–07.

1301 *Vie de sainte Julienne de Cornillon*, ed. Jean-Pierre Delville (Louvain-la-Neuve: 1999), 80–81; Sansterre, "Deux témoignages."

1302 Bruno Reudenbach, "Der Altar als Bildort: Das Flügelretabel und die liturgische Inszenierung des Kirchenjahres," in *Goldgrund und Himmelslicht: Die Kunst des Mittelalters in Hamburg*, ed. Uwe Schneede (Hamburg: Dölling & Galitz, 1999), 26–33; Jens T. Wollesen, "Spoken Words and Images in Late Medieval Italian Painting," in *Oral History of the Middle Ages: The Spoken Word in Context*, ed. Gerhard Jaritz and Michael Richter (Krems: Medium Aevum Quotidianum, 2001), 257–76.

1303 David Wilkins, "Opening the Doors to Devotion: Trecento Triptychs and Suggestions Concerning Images and Domestic Practice in Florence," in *Italian Panel Painting*, 371–93.

1304 In general, the sensorium was understood misogynistically; Richard G. Newhauser, "Introduction," in *Sin in Medieval and Early Modern Culture: The Tradition of the Seven Deadly Sins*, ed. Richard G. Newhauser and Susan J. Ridyard (Woodbridge: Boydell & Brewer, 2012), 1–16.

1305 Matthew G. Shoaf, "Eyeing Envy in the Arena Chapel," *Studies in Iconography* 30 (2009), 126–67; Serena Romano, "Allégorie de la deviance: la *Folie* de Giotto dans la chapel d'Enrico Scrovegni à Padoue," in *L'image en questions*, 146–54.

1306 Fricke, *Fallen Idols*, 243–45; Fischer, "Facing Medusa," 26–30; Cordez, "Arrepentimiento," 136.

1307 Eva Frojmovic, "Giotto's Circumspection," *Art Bulletin* 89, no. 2 (2007), 195–210; Romano, *La O*, 220; Catherine Harding, "Speaking in Pictures: Reading, Memory and Interpretation in Francesco da Barberino's Advice to Women in his Reggimento e costumi di donna," *RACAR: revue d'art canadienne/Canadian Art Review* 36 (2011), 29–40; Dieter Blume, "Francesco da Barberino: The Experience of Exile and the Allegory of Love," in *Images and Words in Exile, Avignon and Italy during the First Half of the 14th Century*, ed. Elisa Brilli, Laura Fenelli, and Gerhard Wolf (Florence: SISMEL. Edizioni del Galluzzo, 2015), 171–92.

1308 Genevra Kornbluth, "Active Optics: Carolingian Rock Crystal on Medieval Reliquaries," *Different Visions: A Journal of New Perspectives on Medieval Art* 4 (2014), 1–36; Benjamin C. Tilghman, "Ornament and Incarnation in Insular Art," *Gesta* 55, no. 2 (2016), 157–77; Aden Kumler, "Seeing the Worldly with a Moral Eye: Illuminated Observation as Introspection," in *Optics, Ethics*, 47–63.

1309 Dunlop, *Painted Palaces*, 160–62; also, Beate Fricke and Tanja Klemm, "Conceptio und perceptio: Zum 'Weimarer Blatt' von Leonardo da Vinci," in *Modernisierung des Sehens*, ed. Matthias Bruhn and Kai-Uwe Hemken (Bielefeld: Transcript Verlag, 2008), 82–99.

1310 Hamburger, "Idol Curiosity," 43–46.

1311 Lentes, "Inneres Auge," 186–91.

1312 Anne Rudloff Stanton, "Turning the Pages: Marginal Narratives and Devotional Practice in Gothic Prayerbooks," in *Push Me, Pull You*, 76–115; Tilghman, "Shape of the Word."

1313 Kumler, *Translating Truth*, 64–66.

1314 Bedos-Rezak, *Ego*, 180–86.

1315 Anne Dunlop, "Black Humour: The Cappellone at Tolentino," in *Art and the Augustinian Order*, 79–98.

1316 Winterer, *Sakramentar*, 407–64.

1317 Kessler, "Speculum"; Kupfer, *Art and Optics*, 82–86 et passim; Hauknes, "Painting of Knowledge," 38–40. The Walters Art Museum mirror's spoof only underscores the mechanism's importance.

1318 Bynum, *Materiality*, 127.
1319 Akbari, *Veil*, 3–44; Pedone, "Vedere Bisanzio."
1320 Biernoff, *Sight and Embodiment*; Dale, "Nude at Moissac," 64–65; Lakey, *Sculptural Seeing*, 92–119 et passim.
1321 Tanja Michalsky, "Local Eye: Formal and Social Distinctions in Late Quattrocento Neapolitan Tombs," *Art History* 31, no. 4 (2008), 484–504.
1322 *Moral Treatise*, 143; Biernhoff, *Sight and Embodiment*, 123–28 et passim; Dennery, *Seeing*, 75–115; Noble, *Images*, 224–26 et passim; Rudolph, "Exegetical Stained-Glass Window," 406–07; Kessler and Newhauser, *Optics, Ethics*.
1323 Pedone, "Vedere Bisanzio."
1324 Gearhart, *Theophilus*, 129–39.
1325 Hans Belting, *Florence and Baghdad: Renaissance Art and Arab Science*, trans. Deborah Lucas Schneider (Cambridge, MA: Harvard University Press, 2011), 135–42.
1326 Klaus Krüger, "Mimesis als Bildlichkeit des Scheins—Zur Fiktionalität religiöser Bildkunst im Trecento," in *Eigensinnlichkeit der Bilder*, 54–73.
1327 Raynaud, "Methods."
1328 Whittington, *Body-Worlds*, 178–79.
1329 For a plan of the space, Richard Némic, "Kaple sv. Kateriny," *Pruzkumy Pamatek* 13 (2006), 145.
1330 Biernoff, *Sight and Embodiment*, 76–81; Kessler, "Fenestra," 149–53.
1331 For instance, the chess-like movements propelled by the capitals that converge eventually in the apse of Saint-Pierre at Mozat: Baschet, Bonne, and Dittmar, *Monde Roman*, Figure 66.
1332 David Ganz, "Touching Books, Touching Art: Tactile Dimensions of Sacred Books in the Medieval West," *Postscripts: The Journal of Sacred Texts and Contemporary Worlds* 8, no. 1–2 (2012): 81–84.
1333 Wittington, *Body-Worlds*, 112–24 et passim; Kupfer, *Art and Optics*, 120.
1334 Gardner, *Roman Crucible*, 32–34, 298–301; Serena Romano, "Giotto e la basilica di San Pietro: il politico Stefaneschi," in *Giotto, l'Italia*, 96–113; *Apogeo*, 281–86; Carlo Volken, "Stefaneschi in 3D," in *Ricerche sul polittico Stefaneschi*, ed. Antonio Paolucci, Ulderico Santamari, and Vittoria Cimino (Milan: Electa/Vatican, 2016), 176–98.
1335 Zchomelidse, "Bild im Busch," 185–89; Kessler, *Neither God nor Man*, 45–52.
1336 Katz, "Marian Motion," 77–78; Hartnell, *Bodies*, 230–31.
1337 Winterer, *Sakramentar*, 431–38; Ramirez-Weaver, *Saving Science*, 26.
1338 Whittington, *Body-Worlds*, 140.
1339 Kumler describes the depiction of the human condition on fol. 10^r as a "visual mise en abime"; *Translating Truth*, 63–68.
1340 Boto Varela, "Artífices en movimiento" and "Velum lapideo."
1341 Connolly, "Center of the World," 304.
1342 In Eldefonsus's tract, the wafer is marked as both the earthly Jerusalem where the human Son died and the cosmos where the majestic Lord reigns; Kessler, "Medietas/Mediator," 49–52; Bougard, "L'hostie, le monde."
1343 Kumler, "Multiplication," 186.
1344 The late–ninth-century Fuller brooch (London, British Museum) includes personifications of all five senses but pictures sight at the center, much larger than the others; see Bagnoli, *Feast for the Senses*, 138–39; *Anglo-Saxon Kingdoms*, 188–89.
1345 Klemm, "Corpus animatum," 264–65; Klaus Krüger, "Mute Mysteries of the Divine Logos: On the Pictorial Poetics of Incarnation," in *Image and Incarnation*, 76–108.
1346 Prado-Vilar, "Parchment," 485.
1347 Derbes and Sandona, *Usurer's Heart*, 146–48; Klemm, "Corpus animatum," 277–78.

1348 As Gerard of Cambrai detailed at the Council of Arras in 1025 (*Acta synodi*, 44); John H. Arnold and Caroline Goodson, "Resounding Community: The History and Meaning of Medieval Church Bells," *Viator* 43 (2012), 99–130; Weinryb, *Bronze Object*, 100–06 et passim. Trumpeting angels are often pictured at the entrances of churches, on the façade of Amiens, for instance, and within the portico of Santiago de Compostela.
1349 Weinryb, *Bronze Object*, 140–43.
1350 Rouchon-Mouilleron, "Miracle et charité," 161.
1351 Reilly, *Cistercian Reform*, 28–31, 40–44 et passim; Rudolph, *Mystic Ark*, 42–51 et passim.
1352 Vincent Debiais, "Au pied de la letter: Une lecture ouverte et liturgique des relations texte/image dans la peinture murale romane catalane," in *L'église, lieu de performances*, 71–84.
1353 Krüger, "Mute Mysteries"; Giovanni del Biondo's altarpiece in the Accademia in Florence realizes the Annunciation not only through light emerging from the shaded figure of God but also by Gabriel's animating words that move the curtain; Cannon, *Religious Poverty*, 326–27. Barbara Baert, *Pneuma and the Visual Medium in the Middle Ages and Early Modernity* (Leuven: Peeters, 2016), 53–80; Sarah Drummond, *Divine Conception: The Art of the Annunciation* (London: Unicorn, 2018), 53–61.
1354 Palazzo, *L'invention*, 346–48.
1355 Avinoam Shalem, "La voix du héros: Note sur la fabrication et l'utilisation des cors médiévaux comme instruments de musique," *Les Cahiers de Saint-Michel de Cuxa* 36 (2005), 117–26.
1356 Aline Kottmann, "Eine neue Interpretation der Burgfeldener Keramik: Vitruvs Echea und die mittelalterlichen Schalltöpfe," in *Michaelskirche Burgfelden* (Lindenberg im Allgäu: Beuroner Kunstverlag Josef Fink, 2004), 26–33; *Archéologie du son: Les dispositifs de pots acoustiques dans les édifices anciens*, ed. Bénédicte Palazzo-Bertholon et Jean-Christophe Valière (Supplément au bulletin monumental 5) (2012); Jean-Christophe Valière et al., "Acoustic Pots in Ancient and Medieval Buildings: Literary Analysis of Ancient Texts and Comparison with Recent Observations in French Churches," *Acta Acustica* 99 (2013), 70–81; Veyrard-Cosme, "Polyphonie"; *Resounding Images: Medieval Intersections of Art, Music, and Sound*, ed. Susan Boynton and Diane J. Reilly (Turnhout: Brepols, 2015); Palazzo-Bertholon, "Spatialisation."
1357 Palazzo-Bertholon, "Spatialisation," 410–11.
1358 Tracing the tubes to the destination in the room above is what led scholars to the discovery of the frescoes; Draghi, *Affreschi*, 69.
1359 Pereira, "Images-piliers"; Bauer, "Geological Imagination," 105–06; Prado-Vilar, *Portal*, 29–30; Debiais, *Silence*.
1360 Isabelle Marchesin, *L'image organum: La représentation de la musique dans les psautiers médiévaux 800–1200* (Turnhout: Brepols, 2000), 63–70 et passim.
1361 Olivier Manaud, "La note de resonance des édifices ou l'hospitalité sonore des abbayes médiévales," in *L'Église, lieu de performances*, 55–70.
1362 Rudolph, "Gothic Portal," 573–74; Mickey Abel, "Intellectual Projection, Liminal Penetration," in *Push Me, Pull You*, 421–65; Debiais, *Croisée*, 259–64.
1363 Draghi, *Affreschi*, 205–06; Frank Hentschel, "The Sensuous Music Aesthetics of the Middle Ages: The Cases of Augustine, Jacques de Liège and Guido of Arezzo," *Plainsong and Medieval Music* 20 (2011), 1–29.
1364 Marchesin, *L'image organum*, 65–75 et passim.
1365 Fassler, *Virgin*, 205–07.
1366 Sánchez Ameijeiras, *Rostros*, 111–20.
1367 Newman, "Trinity," 135–36.
1368 Alejandro García Avilés, "The Philosopher and the Magician: On Some Medieval Allegories of Magic," in *L'allégorie dans l'art*, 241–52.

1369 Marchesin, *L'image organum*, 96–98.
1370 Bland, *Artless Jew*, 117.
1371 Chiesi, "Mobilité," 124–25.
1372 Craig Wright, *The Maze and the Warrior: Symbols in Architecture, Theology, and Music* (Cambridge, MA: Harvard University Press, 2001); Mills, *Seeing Sodomy*, 58; Barral I Altet, *Décor*, 186–90; Connolly, "Center of the World"; Mittman, "Forking Paths?"; Gianluca Marovelli, "Il labirinto di San Martina a Lucca," in *In cammino ... Fino all'ultimo labirinto*, ed. Giancalo Pravat et al. (Tricase: Youcanprint, 2013).
1373 Kumler, "Handling."
1374 Jung, "Tactile and Visionary"; Akbari, *Veil*, 29.
1375 Biernoff, *Sight and Embodiment*, 90–92; Sadler, *Touching the Passion*, 2. The fingerlike growths Sight displays on the Fuller Brooch may illustrate the idea; *Anglo-Saxon Kingdoms*, 189.
1376 *Mitrale*, III, 6; Kessler, "Gregory," 153–54; Jennifer P. Kinglsey, "Le paysage sensorial de l'église et les images vers 1200: Le témoignage du *Mitralis* de Sicard de Crémone," in *Cinq sens*, 667–87.
1377 Francesca Dell'Acqua, "The Five Senses and the Knowledge of God: Mary Magdalene and Thomas in the Salerno ivories," *Cahiers de Civilisation Médiévale* 55 (2010), 571–98; *Cinq Sens*, 235–83.
1378 Lutz, "Drop of Blood," 43–44.
1379 Hamburger, *St. John the Divine*, 72; Jung, "Tactile and Visionary," 210–15; Gertsman and Rosenwein, *Middle Ages*, 38–41.
1380 Recht, *Croire et voir*, 252–69; Largier, *Whip*, 55–71 et passim.
1381 Bynum, *Materiality*, 24; Ganz, "Touching Books," 93–94; Kathryn M. Rudy, "Eating the Face of Christ: Philip the Good and his Physical Relationship with Veronicas," in *European Fortune*, 168–79.
1382 Lutz, "Drop of Blood," 40–41.
1383 Sara Lipton, "'The Sweet Lean of His Head': Writing about Looking at the Crucifix in the High Middle Ages," *Speculum* 80, no. 4 (2005), 1172–1208.
1384 Krüger, *Eigensinnlichkeit der Bilder*, 50.
1385 Guérin, "Meaningful Spectacles," 71.
1386 Paul Williamson and Glyn Davies, *Medieval Ivory Carvings, 1200–1550* (London: V&A Publishing, 2014), part 1, 352–57.
1387 Hahn, *Thing of Mine*, 233–34.
1388 Coker and Watson, *Egerton Genesis*, 176–77; Binski, *Gothic Wonder*, 338–41.
1389 A similar threat is evoked on the thirteenth-century knife in Milan (Castello Sforzesco): "I shall bring bad luck to those who wish to make me theirs. I shall bring happiness to the owner who keeps me. Let no one else desire me, therefore; let this be understood, small though I am"; Tasso, "Medioevo nella Milano." On such invocations: Bredekamp, *Bildakts*, 59–100 (*Image Acts*, 45–66).
1390 Martin Roch, "Conditions, modalités et significations des éxperiences olfactives de l'église dans le haut Moyen Âge," in *L'Église, lieu de performances*, 103–18.
1391 Westermann-Angerhausen, "Incense in the Space," 241.
1392 Romano, *Riforma*, 135–37.
1393 Fliegel and Gertsman, *Myth*, 42–46 et passim.
1394 The contrast underlies monastic refectory decoration; Reilly, *Cistercian Reform*, 176–81.
1395 Angheben, "*Moissac*," 79–80.
1396 Chazelle, *Crucified God*, 194; Lee Palmer Wandel, *The Eucharist in the Reformation: Incarnation and Liturgy* (Cambridge: Cambridge University Press, 2006), 14–45; Elizabeth Saxon, *The Eucharist in Romanesque France: Iconography and Theology* (Woodbridge: The Boydell Press, 2006).

1397 Lutz, "Drop of Blood," 38.
1398 Hamburger, *St John the Divine* 82.
1399 Lakey, *"Chiarito Tabernacle,"* 16; Saracino, *"Felix umbilicus."*
1400 Dutton and Kessler, *Poetry and Paintings*, 109.
1401 Isabelle Cochelin, "When the Monks Were the Book: The Bible and Monasticism (6th–11th centuries)," in *Practice of the Bible*, 61–83.
1402 Riccioni, *Mosaico*, 74–75.
1403 Dutton and Kessler, *Poetry and Paintings*, 105, 115; Pulliam, *Kells*, 105–09.
1404 Kessler, "Images Borne on a Breeze," 62–67.
1405 Ganz and Neuner, "Peripatetisches Sehen," 38.
1406 Catherine Vincent, "Images liturgiques de lumière et expression visionaire, à travers les témoignages de la *Vita* d'Alpais de Cudot (XIIe siècle et des *Revelationes* d'Ermine de Reims (XIVe siècle)," in *L'Église, lieu de performances*, 197–207.
1407 Zchomelidse, "Descending Word."
1408 Later Cistercians still referred to looking at art as ocular lust; Hamburger, "Idol Curiosity," 50–51.
1409 Éric Palazzo, "Art and the Senses. Art and the Liturgy in the Middle Ages," in *A Cultural History of the Senses in the Middle Ages* (London: Bloomsbury, 2014), 175–94.
1410 Francesca dell'Acqua, "Parvenus ecclettici e il canone estetico della varietas: reflessioni su alcuni dettagli di arredo architettonico nell'Italia meridionale normanna," *Römisches Jahrbuch der Bibliotheca Hertziana* 35 (2003/2004), 49–79; Sánchez Ameijeiras, *Rostros*, 219–42; Debiais, *Croisée*, 250–54; Carruthers, *Experience of Beauty*, 135–64; Lakey, *Sculptural Seeing*, 144–50.
1411 Hamburger, "Work of Art"; Carruthers, *Experience of Beauty*; Rudolph, "Exegetical Stained-Glass Window"; Hentschel, "Sensuous."
1412 Binski, "Medieval Invention."
1413 Kessler, "Vanitas," 50.
1414 Seiler, "Schönheit und Scham," 174–76.
1415 C. Stephen Jaeger, "Introduction," in *Magnificence and the Sublime*, 1–16.
1416 The appellation "Beau-Dieu" (beautiful God) was first applied only in the nineteenth century; Andreas Speer, "Beyond Art and Beauty: In Search of the Object of Philosophical Aesthetics," *International Journal of Philosophical Studies* 8 (2000), 73–78.
1417 Cannon, *Religious Poverty*, 26.
1418 The Tree of Jesse in the *Vrigiet de Solas* is also centered on the Virgin holding the Child and a rose, repeating the Edenic symbol of unblemished beauty (together with a lily).
1419 Trans. 182.
1420 Anthony Cutler, "Resemblance and Difference: Carving in Byzantium and Ottonian Germany in the Ivory Century," in *Spätantike und byzantinische Elfenbeinbildweke im Diskurs*, ed. Gudrun Bühl et al. (Wiesbaden: Reichert Verlag, 2008), 37–53; Michele Smargiassi, *Un'autentica bugia: La fotografia, il vero, il falso* (Rome: Contrasto, 2009); Michael Camille, *The Gargoyles of Notre Dame: Medievalism and the Monsters of Modernity* (Chicago: University of Chicago Press, 2009); Jas Elsner, "Art History as Ekphrasis," *Art History* 33 (2010), 10–27; *Photo Archives and the Photographic Memory of Art History*, ed. Costanza Caraffa (Munich and Berlin: Deutscher Kunstverlag, 2011); Ralph Lieberman, "The Art-Historical Photograph as Fiction: The Pretense of Objectivity," in *Fictions of Art History*, ed. Mark Ledbury (Williamstown: The Sterling and Francine Clark Art Institute, 2013), 118–38; Madeline H. Caviness, "Seeking Modernity through the Romanesque: G.G. King and E.H. Lowber behind a Camera in Spain c. 1910–25," *Journal of Art Historiography* 11 (2014), 1–26; Kessler, "Façade, Face"; Christopher Lakey, "Contingencies of Display: Benjamin, Photography, and Imagining the Medieval Past," *Postmedieval: A Journal of Medieval Cultural Studies* 7

(2016), 81–95, and *Sculptural Seeing*; Kathryn Brush, "Medieval Art through the Camera Lens: The Photography of Arthur Kingsley Porter and Lucy Wallace Porter," *Visual Resources* 33 (2017), 252–94.

1421 Ganz and Neuner, "Peripatetisches Sehen"; Jung, "Moving Viewers"; Lakey, *Sculptural Seeing*.

1422 Kessler, "Fenestra," 157–58.

1423 Sansterre and Henriet, "L'inanimis"; Jean Wirth, *L'image à l'époque gothique (1140–1280)* (Paris: Éditions du Cerf, 1999), 64–67; Avilés, "Transitus," 31.

1424 Stephen Murray, *Life of a Gothic Cathedral: Notre-Dame of Amiens* (2018), https://global centers.columbia.edu/events/life-gothic-cathedral-notre-dame-amiens.

1425 The issue is discussed in Kessler, "Façade, Face"; Marchesin, *L'arbre*; Lakey, *Sculptural Seeing*.

1426 As Pentcheva does for Byzantine Art in *Performative Icon*: Cothren, "Some Personal Reflections," 255–70.

1427 Michelle P. Brown, "The Modern Medieval Museum," in *Companion to Medieval Art*, 639–54.

1428 *L'abbaye de Saint-Maurice d'Agaune*.

1429 *Rothko/Giotto*, ed. Stefan Weppelmann and Gerhard Wolf (Munich: Hirmer, 2009).

1430 *Objects of Devotion and Desire: Medieval Relic to Contemporary Art*, ed. Cynthia Hahn (New York: Hunter College, 2011).

1431 *Heavenly Bodies: Fashion and the Catholic Imagination* (cat. of an exhib., New York), ed. Andrew Bolton et al. (New York: Metropolitan Museum of Art, 2018).

1432 Michel Pastoureau, *The Devil's Cloth: A History of Stripes and Striped Fabric*, trans. Jody Gladding (New York: Columbia University Press, 2001); Catherine Kovesi Killerby, *Sumptuary Law in Italy 1200–1500* (Oxford: Clarendon Press, 2002); Sarah-Grace Heller, "Limiting Yardage and Changes in Clothes: Sumptuary Legislation in Thirteenth-Century France, Languedoc, and Italy," in *Medieval Fabrications: Dress, Textiles, Clothwork, and Other Cultural Imaginings*, ed. E. Jane Burns (New York: Palgrave Macmillan 2004), 121–36; Miller, *Clothing*, 8–9; Kumler, "Seeing the Worldly."

1433 Smith, *Body of the Artisan*, 9–11; Cooper, "Projecting Presence"; Cannon, *Religious Poverty*, 172.

1434 William Niederkorn, "Artist Defends Depiction of Christ," *Boston Globe* (20 August 1989), 89.

1435 Carruthers, *The Experience of Beauty*, 1–3.

1436 Glenn Peers, "Utopia and Heterotopia: Byzantine Modernisms in America," in *Defining Neomedievalism(s)*, ed. Karl Fugelso (Cambridge: D.S. Brewer, 2010), 77–113; Nagel, *Medieval Modern*; Cynthia Hahn, *The Reliquary Effect: Enshrining the Sacred Object* (London: Reaktion Books, 2017), 232–71.

1437 George Tatge, *L'Italia metafisica* (Rome: Contrasto, 2015), 39.

1438 Cannon, for example, uses the word in connection with Cennino Cennini's reference to the authority of Greek models: *Religious Poverty*, 67.

1439 Madeline H. Caviness, "Revisiting Vaginal Iconography," *Quintana* 6 (2007), 30–37; *Rothko/Giotto*; Bredekamp, *Bildakts (Image Acts)*; Didi-Huberman, *L'Image ouverte*; Nagel, *Medieval Modern*; Powell, *Depositions*; Francisco Prado-Vilar, "*Silentium*: El silencio cósmico como imagen en la Edad Media y la Modernidad," *Revista de Poética Medieval* 27 (2013): 21–43.

1440 Alexander Nagel and Christopher S. Wood, *Anachronic Renaissance* (New York: Zone Books, 2010), 247–50.

1441 Anne Dunlop, *Andrea del Castagno and the Limits of Painting* (Turnhout: Harvey Miller, 2015), 103–22.

1442 Sadler, *Touching the Passion*.

1443 Ethan Matt Kavaler, *Renaissance Gothic: Architecture and the Arts in Northern Europe 1470–1540* (London and New Haven: Yale University Press, 2012).
1444 Merback, *Pilgrimage*.
1445 Felipe Pereda, *Crime and Illusion: The Art of Truth in the Spanish Golden Age* (Turnhout: Brepols, 2018).
1446 Manuel Castiñeiras González, "La iglesia del Paraíso el Portico de la Gloria como puerto del Cielo," in *Maestro Mateo*, 52–86.
1447 Hamburger, "Vision and the Veronica," 320–21; Nagel and Wood, *Anachronic Renaissance*, 123–30; also Gardner, *Giotto*, 7–8.

Photo Credits

Photographs are reproduced with permission from the following providers.

Pl. I Gerald Richter, © Art collections of the dioceses of Regensburg.
Pl. II George Tatge, Art Resource, NY.
Pl. III Real Colegiata de San Isidora, Leon—The Metropolitan Museum of Art, Art Resource, NY.
Pl. IV Pit Siebigs, Domkapitel Aachen.
Pl. V Jens Nober, © Domschatz Essen.
Pl. VI RMN-Grand Palais, Art Resource, NY.
Pl. VII RMN-Grand Palais, Art Resource, NY.
Pl. VIII Katholische Domgemeinde St. Peter in 34560 Fritzler, Deutschland.
Pl. IX © Dean and Chapter of Westminster.
Pl. X Opificio delle Pietre Dure, Florence.
Pl. XI Darmstadt, Hessische Landesbibliothek, Cod. 1640; fol. 20r.
Pl. XII Scrovegni (Arena) Chapel, Padua, ItalyCameraphoto Arte Venezia/Bridgeman Images.
Pl. XIII Branislav Stantchev.
Pl. XIV Polo Museale del Lazio—Archivio fotografico, under license from Italian Ministero per i Beni e le Attività Culturali.
Pl. XV Laon Cathedral, Laon, France, Bridgeman Images.
Pl. XVI Hereford Cathedral.

Fig. 1 National Museum of Ireland, Dublin, IrelandPhoto © Boltin Picture Library, Bridgeman Images.
Fig. 2 Private collection, The Hague.

PHOTO CREDITS

Fig. 3	P. Portuer, Historisches Museum Basel.
Fig. 4	Münsterschatz, Katholischer Pfarramt.
Fig. 5	Manuel Cohen, Art Resources, NY.
Fig. 6	© Foletti/Ventura Foto: Domenico Ventura.
Fig. 7	Walters Art Museum, Baltimore.
Fig. 8	Ecole des Beaux Arts, Paris.
Fig. 9	Florian Monheim, Dommuseum Hildesheim.
Fig. 10	Catarina Gomes Ferreira, @Calouste Gulbankian Foundation, Lisbon.
Fig. 11	Anja Runkel, @Stadtbibliothek, Stadtarchiv Trier.
Fig. 12	Author's archive.
Fig. 13	© Victoria and Albert Museum, London.
Fig. 14	Károly Szelényi, Magyar Képek, Budapest.
Fig. 15	Michele Bacci.
Fig. 16	Biblioteca Laurenziana, Florence, Art Resource, NY.
Fig. 17	© Museu Nacional d'Art de Catalunya, Barcelona.
Fig. 18	Schatzkammer, Munich.
Fig. 19	Rheinisches Museum, Cologne, plat. 13332.
Fig. 20	Wikimedia Commons.
Fig. 21	Foto Lensini, Siena.
Fig. 22	BNU de Strasbourg.
Fig. 23	Foto Marburg, Art Resource, NY.
Fig. 24	Thomas Dale.
Fig. 25	Manuel Cohen, Art Resource, NY.
Fig. 26	Matthias Rutkowski. Archiv. Vereingte Domstifter zu Merseburg und Naumburg und des Kollegiatstifts Zeitz.
Fig. 27	Antonio García Omedes.
Fig. 28	© The Metropolitan Museum of Art, New York, Art Resource.
Fig. 29	Kunsthistorisches Institut in Florenz, Max Planck-Institut.
Fig. 30	© CESCM/CIFM, Jean Michaud.
Fig. 31	Bayeux Museum.
Fig. 32	Académie de Mâcon.
Fig. 33	LWL-Museum für Kunst und Kultur (Westfälisches Landesmuseum), Hanna Neander.
Fig. 34	© The Israel Museum, Jerusalem, by Moishe Caine.
Fig. 35	Bibliothèque nationale de France.
Fig. 36	Marta Serrano Coll.
Fig. 37	Pierluigi Zolli.
Fig. 38	Universiteitsbibliotheek Utrecht.
Fig. 39	Pablo Ordás Diaz.
Fig. 40	Basilica of St. Godehard, Hildesheim.

PHOTO CREDITS

Fig. 41　Album, Art Resource, NY.
Fig. 42　Private Collection of Avital Heyman.
Fig. 43　RMN-Grand Palais, Art Resource, NY.
Fig. 44　St. Peter, Salzburg.
Fig. 45　Royal Danish Library, Copenhagen.
Fig. 46　De Agostini Picture Library, A. Dagli Orti, Bridgeman Images.
Fig. 47　© Bibliothèque municipale de Tours.
Fig. 48　Bibliothèque royale, Brussels.
Fig. 49　Archives de l'Assessorat du Tourism, des Sports, du Commerce, de l'Agriculture et des Biens culturels de la Région autonome Vallée d'Aoste—fonds du Catalogue biens culturels, Alessandro Zambianchi avec l'autorisation de la Région autonome Vallée.
Fig. 50　Jacqueline E. Jung.
Fig. 51　Erich Lessing, Art Resource, NY.
Fig. 52　British Library, London, UK © British Library Board, Bridgeman Images.
Fig. 53　By permission of the Ministry of Cultural Heritage and Activities, Marciana National Library.
Fig. 54　The Board of Trinity College, Dublin.
Fig. 55　The Master and Fellows of Trinity College, Cambridge.
Fig. 56　Bibliothèque nationale de France.
Fig. 57　De Agostini Picture Library, R. Carnovalini, Bridgeman Images.
Fig. 58　Author's archive.
Fig. 59　© Museu Nacional d'Art de Catalunya, Barcelona.
Fig. 60　Didier Méhu.
Fig. 61　Hubert Walder.
Fig. 62　© RMN-Grand Palaise, Art Resource, NY.
Fig. 63　Emanuele Lugli.
Fig. 64　The Cleveland Museum of Art.
Fig. 65　George Tatge.

Index

Page numbers in *italics* indicate illustrations. Authored works are located under the author's name. Works of art not having a specific name or title, as well as churches and buildings, will be found under the location.

Aachen
    artisans gathered at, 4, 31, 37, 39
    Barbarossa chandelier, 157
    diagram of heavens at, 169
    Dom
        ambo, 4, 31, 37, 39, 149–50, 162, 170, 207, 224, *Pl. IV*
        doors, 40, 144
abbots and abbesses, as art patrons, 75, 77
Abraham, 98, 101, 155, 197, 199, 212
Acheropita, Lateran, Rome, 20–21, *22*, 33, 70, 78, 95, 113, 149, 195, 198, 212, 220
Adam and Eve, 47, 60, 119, 143, 145–48, *147*, 155, 159, 166, 170, 172, 200, 206, 210, 211, 212, 222–24
Adam of Eynsham, 203
Adam the Premonstratensian, *De tripartito tabernaculo*, 137
Adela of Blois, 84, 163
Adémar de Chabannes, 52
Ælfgyfu (queen of England and Denmark), 78
Ælfric Hexateuch, 119, 131
Aesop's fables, 183
aesthetics, xv, 207–24
    anxiety over art and images, 91–94, 174, 224

    cognitive theory, xv, 168, 180, 207, 208, 214
    hearing and sound, 217–19
    lack of formal aesthetics, 223
    mise-en-abîme, 215–17
    multisensory perception, 217, 222–23
    seeing and vision theory, 162, 179–80, 204, 208, 209–15
    smell, 221–22
    subject and object, relationship between, 207–08, 214, 215
    taste, 222
    touch, 219–21
    varietas, 223–24
Æthelwold of Winchester, 56, 77
Aigeline of Burgundy, *115*, 116
alabaster, 52–53, 67
Alan of Lille, 94, 112
Alberti, *Ludi mathematici*, 229
Albertus Magnus, 42, 52, 53
Alcuin, 130
Alexander legends, 166, 168
Alexander of Halles, 94
Alexis (saint), 122
Alfonso X the Wise (king of Aragon and León), 42, 79, 83, 114, 132, 174, 183, 202, 217. See also *Cantigas de Santa Maria*

321

322 INDEX

Alhacen (Ibn al-Haytham), 162, 180
Alpais (saint), *Life* of, 223
Amata (of Sankt Gallen), 25
amber, 48–52, 68
Ambrosius Autpertus, 66
Amiens, cathédrale de Notre-Dame
  Chroma at, 226
  façade, 42, *44*, 101, 141, 143, 144, 176, 189,
    198, 203–04, 224, 226
amulets and amuletic powers, 1, 117, 127,
  174, 190, 213
Anagni
  crypt and Becket Chapel, 148, 151,
    172, 204
Andrew (saint), martyrdom of, 108, 200
Andrew III (king of Hungary), 20, 216
Angela of Folino, 202
Angilbert, portrait of,
  Milan, Sant'Ambrogio, *9*, 69
Annales regni Francorum, 111
Annunciation, 56, 69, 87, 101, 105, 111, 135,
  153, 173, 190–91, 193, 195, 214
Anselm of Canterbury, 77
  Why God Became a Man, 104
Aosta, Sant'Orso, Samson mosaic, 105, *106*,
  111, 145, 171, 174, 201
aquamanile, Hildesheim, 12, *13*, 47, 69, 110,
  163, 181, 189, 190
Aquileia Cathedral, 148–49, 162, 173
Aratea, 123, 167, 169
Aristotle, 52, 162, 175, 206
  De aspectibus, 180
  De memoria et reminiscentia, 95
Ark of the Covenant/Tabernacle, 14,
  48, 100–01, 137, 139, 140, 146, 166,
  195, 212
arma Christi, 17–18, *19*, 172, 191
Arnaud of Clermont, *Dialogue on Miracles*, 85
Arnolfo di Cambio, 61, 185, 187
Arnstein window, 62, *63*, 96, 98, 99, 100,
  105, 109, 112, 117, 153, 154, 196, 203,
  205, 217, 219
Arnsteiner Mariengebet, 112, 203, 217, 219
Arras, Bib. mun., MS 559 (Saint-Vaast
  Bible), 199
Arras, Synod of (1025), 139
art, medieval. *See* medieval art
Arthurian cycle, 183
artist/artisan, medieval concept of, 60–68,
  63, *65*, *66*
asbestos, 44
Ascension, 108, 113, 141, 194

Assisi
  church of San Francesco, 40, 67, 68, 72,
    77, 86, 149, 151, 152, 166, 180
  reliquary of Francis's stigmata (now in
    Louvre, Paris), 20, 31, 39, 60, 67,
    89, 108, 110, 191, Pl. VI
Assumption, 155, 194, 195, 198
astronomical/astrological and cosmological
  knowledge, xiv, 60, 111, 146, 162, 163,
  167, 169, 171, 172, 183
Audradus Modicus, 77
Augustine of Hippo, xv, 100, 113, 141, 214
Augustus (emperor), 166
aula gotica, Santi Quattro Coronati, Rome,
  72, 160, 163, 167, 170, 179, 183, 200,
  213, 218, Pl. XIV
Aulnay Cathedral, south transept portal, 218
Aurillac, golden effigy of Saint Gerald, 195
authentics, 20
Autun, sculpted lintel at, 62
Auxerre, Saint-Étienne, labyrinth, 201
Averroës (Ibn Rashd), 175
Avignon
  Palais des Papes, papal chambers, 183
  popes living in, 72, 87, 183, 199

Bacon, Roger, 174, 180, 208
Ballinderry fidchell board, 1–2, *2*, 54–55,
  181, 192, 206, 219
Baltimore, Walters Art Museum
  Catalan altar, 28
  Crown of Thorns reliquary, 39
  ivory mirror, *10*, 181, 205, 206
  Knight's Hall, 226
Bamberg, Staatsbibliothek
  Misc. Bibl. 22, 135
  Misc. Bibl. 140, 131
Banksy, 227
baptisteries and baptismal fonts, 157–59, *158*,
  172, 198
Barcelona, Museu nacional d'art de
  Catalunya
  Sant Joan de Boí frescoes, 149, *150*, 164,
    206, 221
  Vallbona altarpiece, 28, *29*, 31–32, 94,
    151, 155, 156, 178, 192, 193, 199,
    217, 222
Basel, Historisches Museum, reliquary, 4, *5*,
  39, 100, 206, 212–13, 224
Baudri of Bourgueil, 88–89, 94, 163
Bayeux embroidery, *54–55*, 55, 84, 163, 183,
  205, 206

INDEX 323

Beatus of Liebana, commentary on
 Apocalypse, 86, 131
Beauvais, Saint-Étienne, 142
Bede, 34, 100, 101–04, 169, 172
Benedetto da Maiano, 230
Berengaudus, 118
Berlin, Gemäldegalerie, Rothko/Giotto
 (exhibition, 2009), 226–27
Bern, Burgerbibliothek, Cod. 120.II (Peter
 of Eboli, *Liber ad honorem Augusti*), 123
Bernard of Angers, *Liber miraculorum sancte
 Fidis*, 91, 195, 200
Bernard of Clairvaux, 39, 75, 91, 149, 206
Bernard the Frank, 45, 207, 208, 215
Bernard Silvestris, 174, 175
Bernward of Hildesheim, 20, 40, 68, 72, 77,
 105, 126, 166
Berthold of Nuremberg, 77
Berthold von Sperberseck, 7, 55, 108
Berzé-la-Ville, Chapelle-des-Moines, apse,
 fresco, 56, 57, 75, 96, 101, 108, 110, 112,
 117, 151, 153, 157, 171, 173, 196, 197,
 204, 215
Besançon, Bib. mun., MS 579, 205
Beuys, Joseph, 227
Beverly Minster, ceiling paintings, 145
bibbie atlantiche, 71, 119
Bible. *See* scripture and tradition
bibles moralisées, xiii, 60, 81, 84, 86, 109, 132
biblical paraphrases, 119–22
bishops, 72, 77
Blanche of Anjou and Naples, 186
Blanche of Castille, 81, 83
Boethius, 167, 172
Boileau, Étienne de, *Livre des métiers*, 64, 85
Bonaiuto, Andrea, 159, 200
Bonaventure, 39, 54, 95, 207–08
 Legenda Maior, 60, 172, Pl. VI
Boniface VIII (pope), 72, 125, 199
"La Bonissima" (Modena town square),
 176, *177*
Bonizo of Sutri, 153
Book of Kells, 70, 126, 127–30, *128–29*, 133,
 135, 136, 171, 206, 213, 222
books, xiv, 117–38. *See also specific texts and
 manuscripts*
 Aachen ambo as, 149–50
 author portraits, 127–30, *128*
 codices, 117–18
 composite manuscripts, 122–25, *124*
 contents other than scripture, 122–25, *124*
 eating, 138, 222

 encyclopedias, 123
 geometry of, 171
 Incarnation, as recapitulation of, 126
 interpretive probes, illustrations as, 136–38
 liturgical manuscripts, 125
 monastic participation in book culture, 75
 parchment (vellum), 52, 56
 performativity of, 190–91
 scriptural manuscripts, 118–22, *120–21*
 scrolls, 117
 secular texts, 183–84
 shrines and covers for, 127
 visual glosses, illustrations as, 131–36,
 133, 134
 words and letters, illustrative power of,
 126–27, *128–29*, 135–36
Bourges, Sainte-Chapelle, 79, 160
brain map, pseudo-Augustine, *De spiritu et
 anima*, 132, *133*, 162, 168, 207, 214
Braunschweig, Dankwarderode Castle, 185
Brazen Serpent, 14, 70, 92, 101–02, 109,
 149, 210
Bremen, town square, 162
bronze, 40, 54, 68, 104
Bruno of Segni, 33, 100, 154, 207, 209
 Sententiae, 140, 156
Brussels, Bibliothèque royale, MS 10074
 (*Physiologus*), 101, *102–03*, 135, 210
Budapest
 Hungarian National Library (Országos
 Széchényi Konyvtár), Cod. Lat.
 4 (*History of Apollonius of Tyre*),
 168, 184
 Hungarian National Museum, coronation
 mantle, 20, *21*, 26, 33, 68, 79, 104,
 162, 190, 216
 Hungarian Parliament, "Holy Crown of
 Hungary," 10–11
Burgos
 Sant Maria la Real de las Huelgas, 159,
 191, 216
butterfly reliquary, Regensburg, 1, 16, 20,
 32, 72, 110, 190, 213, 216, Pl. I

Caesarius of Heisterbach, 126, 195–96
Calcidius, 136, 206
 Commentary on Plato's Timaeus, 60, 168
Calendar of 354, 167
Cambridge
 Corpus Christi College, MS 16 (Matthew
 Paris, *Chronica Maiora*), 70, 104, 175
 Saint John's College, MS B 18 (Psalter), 219

Trinity College Library
MS 0.7.16 (*De spiritu et anima*, pseudo-Augustine), 132, *133*, 162, 168, 207, 214
MS R. 16.2 (Apocalypse), 86
MS R. 17.1 (copy of Utrecht Psalter), 62, 86
University Library, MS Gg 1.1 (composite manuscript), 123–25
cameos, 4, 5, 39
Candide of Maubuisson, 216, 229
Canterbury
ampulla from, 200
Cathedral Library
MS Add. 23, 174
MS C 246, 203
tomb of Thomas Becket, 200
Cantigas de Santa Maria, 42, 56, 79, *80*, 83, 117, 132, 169–70, 174, 183, 202, 205, 217
cardinals, as art patrons, 72
carnality and eroticism, xiv, xv, 75, 91, 94, 100, 105, 143, 160, 163–164, *165*, 172–74, 181, 206, 211, 221, 222
Cassiodorus, 56
castle of love, 181, 205
Catalan Atlas, 176, 184
Celestine III (pope), 150
Celestine V (pope), 125
Cennino Cennini, 183
Ceri, Santa Maria Immaculata, murals, *71*, 86, 89, 98, 101, 104, 105, 108, 109, 147–49, 172, 173, 196–97, 200, 212, 215, 222, 223
chandeliers, in churches, 156–57
Chanson de Roland, 162, 185
Chantilly, Musée Condé, MS 65 (*Très riches heures*), 25, 112, 136, 151, 153, 200, 202, 221, 223, Pl. *VII*
Charlemagne, 40, 47, 78, 79, 118, 130, 160, *162*, *185*
Charles II the Bald (Holy Roman emperor)
antependium, Saint-Denis, 199
First Bible of, 25, 77, 84, 118–19, 138, 170, 190, 222
marriage of daughter Judith to king of Wessex, 83, 86
prayer book of, 33, *34*, 56, 110, 118, 126, 133–35, 181, 202, 206
throne of, 4, 10, 156, 195
Charles IV (Holy Roman emperor), 16, 23, 39, 87, 160, 181, 185, 194, 214
Charles V (king of France), 176, 206

Charles I of Anjou, 178, 185
Charles VI of Anjou, 78
Chartres
Bib. municipale, MS. 24 (*Liber comitis of Saint-Père of Chartres*), 77
Cathedral
La belle verrière, 7, *8*, 23, 31, 40, 60, 100–01, 112, 117–18, 140, 156, 157, 197, 203, 221
Charlemagne window, 162
Clara chorus sung at, 203, 219
corporate donors of stained glass in, 84
furriers' guild window, 109
Prodigal Son window, 149
sculptures, façade portals, 197
Chaucer, Geoffrey, *Canterbury Tales*, 200
Chicago, Art Institute, Weingarten Mass of Saint Gregory, 208
Chicago, Judy, 227
Chrétien de Troyes, 183
chrismon, 126, 174
Christ. *See also* Ascension; crosses; crucifixes; Crucifixion; Passion; Resurrection
arma Christi, 17–18, *19*, 172, 191
bleeding chest wound/Sacred Heart, 164
books as recapitulation of Incarnation of, 126
David as type of, 99–100, 119, 130
light, association with, 153, 196
as maker, 60
materials associated with, 39, 42, 47, 52, 56, 58
relics of, 16–18, 23, 45–47
rulers and popes as types of, 109
transformation of materials and, 53–54
two natures of, 33, 39, 51, 53, 55, 69, 94, 95, 96, 109, 110, 113, 136, 168, 171, 192, 225
Christian of Stavelot, 126
Christianity
art as instrument for teaching, 91, 108, 109
Ecclesia and *Synagoga*, 98, 100, 105, 193, 198
magic, necromancy, and superstition, 174
pagan legacy of, xiv, 40, 42, 47–48, 71, 96, 140, 151, 162, 166–70
secular world in dialogue with, 161–66, 174
Christianus II (archbishop of Mainz), 56
Christina of Markyate, 75
Chronicle of Dalimil, 14

INDEX

churches, xiv–xv, 139–61. *See also* stained glass; *specific buildings*
　Ark of the Covenant/Tabernacle, typology of, 139–40, 146
　baptisteries and baptismal fonts, 157–59, *158*
　barriers between nave and sanctuary area, 151–53, 199
　body symbolism of, 141
　cloisters, 68, *69*, 140, 159
　consecration of, 198
　crypts, 151
　façades, porticoes, and doors, 140–45, *142*, 190
　Jerusalem Temple, typology of, 139–40, 143, 152
　naves, aisles, and transepts, 145–51, *147*, *150*
　oratories, side chapels, and chapter houses, 159
　performativity of/in, 189–90, 197–99
　private chapels, 160
　pulpits, 149–50
　reception and dining areas attached to, xiv–xv, 139–61
　relics in, 79, 141, 148, 150–51, 152, 153, 154, 155, 198
　sanctuary area (choir, altar, apse), 151–57
　spolia, use of, 139–40, 143
Cimabue, *Ytalia*, 166, 180
circles, 170–71, 175
Civate, San Pietro al Monte, 148
Cividale del Friuli, Museo archeologico nazionale, Bib. cap., I–II (*bibbie atlantiche*), 119
classical heritage, 48, 59, 130, 141, 163, 166–70, 175, 192
Clement VI (pope), 23, 72, 183
Cleveland, Museum of Art
　paten of Bernward of Hildesheim, 20
　table fountain, 181, *182*, 191, 222
cloisters, 68, *69*, 140, 159
clothing and vestments, 181, 190
Clovis (Merovingian ruler), 162
Cnut (king of England and Denmark), 78
cognitive theory, xv, 168, 180, 207, 208, 214
Cologne
　Dom, Shrine of the Three Kings, 4, 27, 195
　Sankt Kunibert, embroidery, 210
　Sankt Severin, coronation of the Virgin, 218
color symbolism, 12, 39, 53, 56
Como, picture of Virgin and Child, 111
Conques, statues of Saints Gerard and Faith at, 91, 200

Conrad IV of Germany, 83
Conrad of Hirsau, 137
consecrations, 198
Constantine Africanus, 175
Constantine I the Great (emperor), 4, 14, 72, 78, 166, 229
Constantinople, Pharos Chapel, 24, 160
Contardo, Inghetto, 208
contemporary artists and medieval forms, 227–28
contemptus mundi, 160
Conti, Stefano (cardinal), 72, 183
Copenhagen
　Kongelige Bibliotek
　　MS. Hebrew 11 (Pentateuch), 92, *93*, 118, 127, 202, 213
　　MS Thott 190 2°, 167
　Nationalmuseet, Lisbjerg altar, 96, *97*, 155–56, 171, 193
Coronation Gospels, 78
coronation mantle, Hungary, 20, *21*, 26, 33, 68, 79, 104, 162, 190, 216
coronation rituals
　of Charles IV, 194
　De coronatione, 125
　ordo in Louis IX's time, 198
　Westminster pavement marking positions for, 198
cosmological and astronomical/astrological knowledge, xiv, 60, 111, 146, 162, 163, 167, 169, 171, 172, 183
courts and courtly life, 78–83, 181–85
Cremona, cathedral, pavement, 145
cross, sign of the, 155, 189
crosses, 7, 11, 16, 19, 20, 25, 47, 54, 55, 59, 79, 83, 96, 98, 105, 114, 126, 135–36, 143, 154–56, 167, 170–75, 179, 192, 193, 194, 196–98, 209, 210, 213, 214–16, 220, 228
crucifixes, 16, 28, 47, 56, 70, 78, 88, 92–93, 95, 105, 110, 114, 155, 178, 179, 190, 193–94, 196, 202, 204, 216, 217, 220, 221, 222, 227. *See also* Rosano Crucifix
Crucifixion, 1, 29, 47, 52, 70, 96, 98, 101, 106, 114–16, 122, 133, 149, 152, 154, 155, 187, 194, 208, 216, 219, 220. *See also* True Cross, relics of
Crusades, 7, 25, 87, 100, 139, 140, 143, 162, 178, 184, 191
curtains before images, 212
cypress wood, 48

Daddi, Bernardo, 78
Dagobert (Merovingian ruler), 20
Damasus (pope), 130
damnatio memoriae, 192
dance, liturgical/paraliturgical, 201
Dante, *Purgatory*, 52
Darmstadt, Hessische Landesbibliothek, MS 1640 (Hitda Codex), 25–26, 56, 111, 135, Pl. XI
David (biblical king)
    Arnstein window, Tree of Jesse, 105, 153
    as author of psalms, 130, 219
    Basel reliquary, 4, 5, 39, 100, 206, 212–13, 224
    rulership viewed as descending from, 162
    typology of, 99–100, 105, 119, 130, 136
De arithmetica, 167
De coronatione, 125
De modo orandi corporaliter sancti Dominici, 190
De sex alis cherubim, 137
Den Haag, private collection, pilgrim badge from Pantheon, Rome, 3, 3–4, 40, 70, 89, 164, 190, 212, 221
Desiderius of Montecassino, 40, 75
devotion, art and, 199–202
diagrams and diagramming, 28, 36, 100, 114, 123, 132, 136–37, 162, 167–72, 202, 207, 208, 214, 216–17
Dialogus de laudibus sanctae crucis, 132
Dijon, Bib. municipale
    MS 12–15 (Bible of Stephen Harding), 130
    MS 173 (Gregory I, *Moralia in Job*), 132, 137
Dioscurides, 167
Domingo Gundisalvo, *De divisione philosophiae*, 61
Dominic (saint) and Dominicans, 20, 77, 137, 159, 162
Dominic of Sora, *Life* of, 220
Donation of Constantine, 72
drama, liturgical, 172, 204–05
Drogo sacramentary, 125
Dublin
    National Museum
        fidchell board, Ballinderry, 1–2, 2, 54–55, 181, 192, 206, 219
        Soiscél Molaise (book shrine), 127, 171
    Trinity College Library
        MS 177 (Matthew Paris, *Passion of Alban and Amphibalus*), 184
        MS A. 1. [58] (Book of Kells), 70, 126, 127–30, *128–29*, 133, 135, 136, 171, 206, 213, 222

Duccio, 61
    Maestà, 157
Durand of Mende, 94, 95
    Rationale, 69

Ealdred (archbishop), 145
Ebo of Metz, 169
Ecclesia and *Synagoga*, 98, 100, 105, 193, 198
Écouis, church of Notre-Dame, Mary Magdalene, 81, *82*, 108–09, 116, 208
Eden, 16, 37, 40, 47, 101, 140, 144, 157, 163, 172, 186, 206, 210, 224, 228
Edward I (king of England), 178
Edward Plantagenet, signet ring of, 14
Edward the Confessor, 79, 160, 162
Egerton Genesis, 173, 221
Einhard (Bezazel), 78
Eldefonsus ("bishop of Spain"), 28
Eleanor of Aquitaine, 81
Eleanor of Castille, 81
Elias of Cortona, 178
Elisabeth of Hungary, 162
Eloy, cross attributed to, 20
emotion, art eliciting, 113–16, *115*
encyclopedias, 123
Enguerrand de Marigny, 81
Eriugena, *Periphyseon*, 168
eroticism. *See* carnality and eroticism
Escley (Herefordshire), Michael Church, "Sunday Christ" at, 18–19
Escorial, Real biblioteca del Monasterio, MS T.I.1 (*Cantigas de Santa Maria*), 42, 56, 79, *80*, 83, 117, 132, 169–70, 174, 202, 205, 217
Essen
    Domschatz, Theophanu Gospels, 12, 26, 48, 55, 64, 79, 83, 101, 106–08, 110, 117, 126, 127, 141, 212, 216, Pl. V
    Golden Madonna, 12, 83, 108, 212
    reliquary of Saint Blaise, 192
Eucharist
    blood libel, 178
    circle, significance of, 170
    eating, trope of, 138, 222
    Hosts, words and motifs embossed on, 96–98
    matter/materials/materiality and, 45
    as mise-en-abîme, 217
    objects associated with, 16–17, 27–29
    "ocular communion," 222
    as performance, 192–93
    seals and sealing associated with, 104

tabernacles for, 151
transubstantiation, 155, 168
visibility of, 199
Eve. *See* Adam and Eve
Exeter, Cathedral Library, MS 3501, 205
extramission, 180, 220
ex-votos, 25–27, 148
eyes. *See* seeing and vision theory

famine of 1329, 161
Ferentillo (Umbria), San Pietro in Valle, frescoes, 98, 146, 147–48, 179, 180, 210, 211, 223, 224
Ferrara, San Giorgio, tympanum, 179
fidchell board, Ballinderry, 1–2, *2*, 54–55, 181, 192, 206, 219
First Crusade, 7
flabellum of Tournus, 2, 48, 66–68, 192, 222–23, 229, Pl. II
flagellants, 199, 201
flagellation of Christ, *120–21*, 220
Floreffe Bible, 119
Florence
  Duomo, 159, 226, 230
  Kunsthistorisches Institut, *Cenobium* project, 226
  MS Plut. 73.16 (*Varia medica*), 175
  MS Tempi 3 (Domenico Lenzi, *Specchio umano*), 23, *24*, 59, 78, 122, 135, 141, 161–62, 173, 212, 217
  Museo del Bargello, flabellum of Tournus, 2, 48, 66–68, 192, 222–23, 229, Pl. II
  Osanmichele
    confraternity at, 59, 212
    cult image of Virgin and child, 23, *24*, 59, 78, 122, 135, 141, 161, 173, 212, 227
    tabernacle, 26, 152, 160, 185
  San Miniato, "Sunday Christ" painting, Mariotta di Cristofano, 18
  Santa Maria Maggiore, relief icon of Mary and Christ, 18–19
  Santa Maria Novella
    chapter house, 159
    Giovanni del Biondo altarpiece (now in Galleria dell'Accademia), 189
    Peter Martyr, grave of, 200
  Santissima Annunciata, 193
  secular art patronage in, 78
Fontevraud, abbey of, 226
Fourth Crusade, 25, 87, 140

Fourth Lateran Council (1215), 154, 193, 199
Francesco da Barberino, *Documenti d'Amore*, 213
Francis of Assisi
  Amiens cathedral, façade, 143
  Assisi, church of San Francesco, 40, 67, 68, 72, 77, 86, 149, 151, 152, 166, 180
  aula gotica, Santi Quattro Coronati, Rome, 163
  Bonaventure, *Legenda Maior*, 60, 172, Pl. VI
  elephant tusk presented to, 10, 12, 218
  on emotions stimulated by images, 213
  naturalism in art and, 178–79
  speaking crucifix and, 196
  stigmata reliquary of, 20, 31, 39, 60, 67, 89, 108, 110, 191, 196, 211, 213, Pl. VI
Franciscans, 40, 67, 77, 86, 162, 178–79, 180, 206, 213, 219
Frankfurt, Städel Museum, Jeffrey Koons installation, 227
Freckenhorst, Stiftskirche Sankt Bonifatius, baptismal font, 157–59, *158*, 172, 198
Frederick Barbarossa, 78
Frederick II the Great (Holy Roman emperor), 78, 175
  De arte venandi cum avibus, 83, 136, 175–76
Freiburg-im-Breisgau, Dom, north transept, 151
Fritzlar, Dom, Pietà, 32, 48, 56, 67, 104, 116, 164, 206, 214, 220, 222, Pl. VIII
Fulcoius of Beauvais, 89
Fulda sacramentary, 125
Fulk of Anjou, 12, 79

Gaddi, Taddeo, 214
Galen, 172, 180
gazzatum, 52
Gellone sacramentary, 125, 136
gems, 37–39, 55
Geneva, Bibl. Bodmeriana, Cod. 127, fol. 224, 77–78
Geoffrey of Vinslauf, *Poetria nova*, 61
geometry, 111, 168, 170–72, 175, 179, 218–19
Gerald of Wales, 70
Gerard of Arras, 139, 209
Gerbert of Aurillac (later Pope Sylvester II), *Isagoge geometriae*, 111, 171
Gerlach/Gerlachus (in Arnstein window), 62, *63*, 205, 216–17
Germigny-des-Prés, Theodulf oratory, apse mosaic, 72

Gerona cathedral, 170, 199
Gertrude of Hefta, 209
Gervase of Tilbury, 212
Géza (king of Hungary), 10
Ghiberti, Lorenzo, 229
gifts and gift-giving, 10–12, *11*, 25–27, 28, 119, 176, 184
Gilbertus Crispinus, 96
Gilliam, Sam, 227
Giordano of Pisa, 7, 204
Giotto, 61, 87, 185, 214, 227, 230
 Assisi, church of San Francesco, frescoes, 180
 Lateran, Loggia, fresco, 199
 Navicella, San Pietro, Rome, 72, 109
 Scrovegni Chapel frescoes, Padua, 110–11, 174, 180, 213
 Stefaneschi altarpiece, Vatican, Pinacoteca, 215
Giovannetti, Matteo, 87
Giovanni del Biondo, 189
Gisela (queen of Hungary), 20, 26, 79, 162
Gislebertus of Autun, 62
glass, 12, 39–40, 53. See also stained glass
Godescalc Evangeliary, 47, 126, 136–37
Godfrey of Viterbo, *Pantheon*, 168
gold, 33, 55, 56, 153
Golden Madonna of Essen, 12, 83, 108, 212
Gregory I the Great (pope), 91, 94, 96, 108, 109, 113, 130, 146, 210, 211
 Moralia in Job, 132, 137
 Registrum, 94
Gregory VII (pope) and Gregorian reform, 71, 79, 119
Gregory X (pope), 180
Groß-Comburg, Sankt Nicholas, wheel chandelier, 156, 170
Grosseteste, Robert, 180
Gubbio, Passion procession, 226
Guibert of Nogent, 32
Guido Aretinus, *Micrologus*, 218
Guido Guerra, 83
Guillaume De Bray, tomb of, 187
Guillaume de Seignelay, 218
Guillaume Martin, 62, 83
Gulbenkian Apocalypse, *15*, 21, 52, 95–96, 104, 118, 135, 139–40

Hadrian I (pope), 70–71, 181
Haimo of Auxerre, *Commentary on Ezekiel*, 131
Harding, Stephen, Bible of, 130
Hartmann von Aue, 183

hearing and sound, 217–19
Hebrew manuscripts
 "bird's head" Haggadah, 64, *65*, 92, 118, 125, 138, 176–78
 Copenhagen Pentateuch, 92, *93*, 118, 127, 202, 213
Helena (mother of Constantine), 16, 98, 210
Henry II (Holy Roman emperor), 4, 92–94
Henry II (king of England), 81
Henry III (king of England), 44, 45, 67, 78–9, 160, 175, 184
Henry of Blois, 26, 40, 111, 186
Henry of Ghent, 94
Henry the Lion, 185
Herbert of Bosham, *Liber Melorum*, 40
Hereford, Cathedral, *mappa mundi* (Hereford Map), 52, 164–66, 167, 172, 178, 201, 209, 213, 215, 216, *Pl. XVI*
Herman of Scheda, 208
Herrard of Hohenbourg, *Hortus deliciarum*, 27, 75, 123, 161, 224
Hildebert de Lavardin, 89, 159
Hildegard of Bingen, 40, 47, 53, 61
 Liber divinorum operum, 117
 Scivias, 33, *35*, 75, 85–86, 111, 112–13, 118, 170, 202, 225
Hildesheim
 Diözesannmuseum, aquamanile, 12, *13*, 47, 69, 110, 163, 181, 189, 190
 Dom, bronze doors, 40, *41*, 47, 72, 105, 144, 166, 210, 216
 Dombibliothek, MS Saint-Godehard 1 (Saint Albans Psalter), 75, *76*, 100, 111, 118, 122, 130, 136, 137, 171, 184, 219
 Dommuseum, MS 18 (Gospel Book of Bernward of Hildesheim), 72, 126
 Sankt Michael, painted ceiling, 146
Hilton, Walter, 202
Hincmar of Reims, 72
Hippocrates, 172
Hirst, Damien, 227
History of Apollonius of Tyre, 168
history texts, 183–184
Hitda Gospels, 25–26, 56, 111, 135, *Pl. XI*
Holkham Picture Bible, 63, 77, 116, 119–22, 120–21, 190, 205, 206, 209, 220
Honorius III (pope), 67
Honorius Augustodunensis, 61, 94, 96–98, 146, 224
 Clauis physicae, 168
 Expositio in Cantica Canticorum, 131

Sigillum sanctae Mariae, 89
Hoppertad (Norway), wood altar canopy, 156
Horace, 175
Hrabanus Maurus, 77
  De laudibus sanctae crucis, 86, 126
  De natura rerum, 123
Hrotsvit of Gandersheim, 172
Hugh of Fouilloy, 174
Hugh of Lincoln, 203
Hugh of Meaux, 179
Hugh of Poitiers, 19
Hugh of Saint-Victor, 60, 61, 77, 100, 113–14, 202, 213
  Ark of Noah, 77
  Mystic Ark, 137
Hugh of Vaudemont, *115*, 116, 175, 186

Ibn al-Haytham (Alhacen), 162, 180
Ibn Rashd (Averroës), 175
iconoclasm
  Byzantine, 71, 94
  Carolingian controversy over images, 32, 72, 91
  Jewish range of views regarding, 91–92
  medieval anxiety over art and images, 91–94, 174, 224
impressing, 89, 100
Incarnation, 48, 56, 94, 95, 98, 100, 104, 112, 126–30, 137, 140, 148, 157, 167, 179, 192, 210, 212, 218, 223, 227, 228
Innocent III (pope), 23, 27, 33, 61, 71, 72, 193, 195, 199, 220
inscriptions associated with images, 96–99
intromission, 180
Isidore of Seville, 114
  De natura rerum, 123
Islam and Islamic art, xiii, xiv, 7, 12, 67, 132, 143, 146, 162, 163, 175, 191
ivory, 48, 53, 55, 154, 220
Ivrea, Bib. Capit. Cod. LXXXVI (sacramentary of Warmond of Ivrea), 125
Iwain, chivalric tale of, 163, *164*, 189

Jaca, Museo Diocesano, capital from funerary chapel of Don Sanchez Ramirez, 42, *46*, 109–10, 170, 196
Jacobus da Voragine, 94
Jacques de Vitry, 202
James (saint), 12, 20, 79, 87, 101, 191, 200
James II of Aragon, 186
James le Palmer, *Omne bonum*, 123, 191

Jan of Oplava, Evangeliary of, 70
Jean, duc de Berry
  Bourges, Sainte-Chapelle, 79, 160
  Très riches heures, 25, 112, 136, 151, 153, 200, 202, 221, 223, Pl. *VII*
Jean II le Bon (king of France), 23, 72
Jehoshaphat, abbey of Mary in Valley of, 79
Jerome, 130, 170
  Commentary on Isaiah, 61
Jerusalem
  Armenian church of Saint James, 79
  Holy Sepulcher, 79, *81*, 87, 142–43, 170, 197
  Israel Museum, MS 180/57 ("bird's head" Haggadah), 64, *65*, 92, 118, 125, 138, 176–78
  Temple, 14, 69, 92, 100–01, 137, 139–40, 143, 152, 195, 214
  Tower of David, 100
  as world's umbilicus, 171
Jews and Judaism. *See also* Hebrew manuscripts
  aesthetic theory and, 208, 209, 210, 211, 218
  blood libel, 178
  books and, 118, 125, 126, 127, 176
  Ecclesia and *Synagoga*, 98, 100, 105, 193, 198
  expulsion from England, 178
  making and, 64, *65*, 85, 89
  objects and, 28–29, 173
  Old Testament typology in Christian art, 99–109, *102–03*, *106*, *107*
  spirituality and, 91–94, *93*, 96, 100, 104, 105, 173
Joan of Navarre, 81
Johanna von Pfirt, 83
John Lackland (king of England), 203
John the Apostle/Evangelist, 52, 86, 101, 108, 114, 116, 118, 119, 127–30, *129*, 138, 143, 155, 171, 178, 187, 220
John the Baptist, 20, 23, 25, 153–54, 194, 222
John Beleth, 136, 201
John of Jandun, 146
Joseph (saint), as carpenter, 69
Joseph Bekhor Shor of Orléans, 92
Judaism. *See* Jews and Judaism
Judith of Wessex, 83, 86
Julian of Vézelay, 203
Juliana of Cornillon, 212

Kaprow, Allan, 227
Karlstejn Castle, chapel, 16, *18*, 45–47, 79, 87, 144, 154, 185, 194, 214

Kassel, Landesbibliothek und Murhadsche Bibliothek, 2° ms phys. et hist. nat. 10 (*Pseudo-Apuleius*), 167, 169
Koons, Jeffrey, 227

La Tour, Georges de, 229
labyrinths, 141, *142*, 144, 145, 166, 201, 219
Ladislaus/Ladislav (saint), 149, 162, 178
Lambach, adoration of the magi at, 204–05
Lambeth Palace Apocalypse, 137, 190
lance of Longinus (Holy Lance), 16, 17, 135, 194
Lando di Pietro, 227
Laon
  cathédrale de Notre-Dame, rose window, 153–54, 172, 222, 224, pl XV
  Mandylion (*La sainte face*), 83
lapis lazuli (ultramarine), 44
Last Judgment, 83, 84, 98, 106, 116, 123, 137, 143–44, 147–48, 159, 166, 172, 187, 203, 210, 216, 217
Last Supper, 16, 23, 27, 116, 130, 157, 160, 192, 220
Lateran Council (1215), 154, 193, 199
lay orders and confraternities, 59, 77–78, 84, 108, 212
lay/secular patronage, 78–85
Le Mans, donor portrait in stained glass window, 27
lead, 40
Leiden, Universiteitsbibliotheek
  Cod. Perizoni, F.17 (Vegetius and Book of Maccabees), 122
  VLQ 7 (*Aratea*), 169
Lenzi, Domenico, *Specchio umano*, 23, *24*, 59, 78, 122, 135, 141, 161–62, 173, 212, 217
Leo III (pope), 25, 159–60
Leo IV (pope), 194
Leo IX (pope), 71
Léon
  catedral de Santa Maria
  cloister, Phyllis riding Aristotle, 206
  façade, 203, 219
  tomb of Rodriguez Alvarez, 72, *74*, 114, 186–87, 198
  San Isidoro, Urraca chalice, 4, 26, 28, 37, 45, 60, 110, 207, Pl. III
Liber Nemroth, 123
Liège, Archives de l'État, drawing of great reliquary of Saint Remaclus, 26
Life of Dominic of Sora, 220
light

Christ, association with, 153, 196
  churches and, 153, 189
  divinity communicated through, 111–13
  performative nature of, 189, 196
Lille, Palais des Beaux-Arts, bronze censer of Reiner, 27
Lincoln Cathedral, 116, 153, 203
Lindau Gospels, 127
Lisbjerg altar, 96, *97*, 155–56, 171, 193
Lisbon, Gulbenkian Collection, MS. L.A. 139 (Gulbenkian Apocalypse), *15*, 21, 52, 95–96, 104, 118, 135, 139–40
liturgy and paraliturgy
  drama, liturgical, 172, 204–05
  manuscripts, liturgical, 125
  performance, 189, 192–94, 197–99, 204–05
  processions, xv, 27, 174, 189, 194–95, 198, 200, 218, 226
  smell, role of, 221
  sounds of liturgical objects, 218
London
  British Library
    MS Add. 17737–38 (Floreffe Bible), 119
    MS Add. 42130 (Luttrell Psalter), 78, 219
    MS Add. 47682 (Holkham Picture Bible), 63, 77, 116, 119–22, *120–21*, 190, 205, 206, 209, 220
    MS Add. 49598 (Benedictional of Saint Aethelwold), 56, 77
    MS Arundel 83 (*De sex alis cherubim*), 137
    MS Arundel 157 (psalter), 114
    MS Cotton Claudius B.IV (Ælfric Hexateuch), 119, 131
    MS Cotton Vitellius C III (pharmacological texts), 169
    MS Egerton 1139 (psalter of Melisende), 12, 79
    MS Egerton 1821 (Egerton Genesis), 173, 221
    MS Harley 603 (copy of Utrecht Psalter), 86
    MS Harley 3244 (preacher's manual), 123
    MS Harley MS 3244 (Peraldus, *Summa de virtutibus et virtiis*), 168
    MS Royal 6.E.VI (James le Palmer, *Omne bonum*), 123
    MS Royal 14. C. VII (Matthew Paris, *Historia Anglorum*), 95
    MS Stowe 944 (*Liber Vitae*), 78

MS Yates Thompson, 11 (*La sainte abbaye* manuscript), 202
Lambeth Palace Library, MS 209 (Apocalypse), 137, 190
Palace of Westminster, painted chamber, 162, 184
Victoria and Albert Museum, *arma Christi* polyptych, 17, *19*, 36, 70, 104, 114, 139, 191, 210, 221
Westminster Abbey
  Cosmatesque floor, 44, 67, 79, 111, 153, 167, 171–72, 200, 207, Pl. IX
  as royal burial church, 160
  tomb of Edward the Confessor, 79
Longinus, 16, 17
Lorenzetti, Ambrogio, Massa Marittima altarpiece, 33, 34, *37*, 52, 58, 113, 171, 174, 179, 180, 193, 209, 213, 214, 223, 228
Loreto, house of Mary at, 18
Los Angeles, J. Paul Getty Museum, Chiarito triptych, Pacino di Buonaguida, 28, 113
Louis I the Pious (Holy Roman emperor), 105, 126, 169
Louis VIII (king of France), 84
Louis IX (king of France), 24, 79, 83, 109, 135, 139, 151, 160, 162, 175, 198, 200
Louis of Toulouse, 52
Lucas/Luke of Tuy, 72, 94, 225
Lucca
  San Martino, labyrinth, 141, *142*, 144, 216, 219
  "Volto Santo," impressions of, 89
Luke (saint), 20–23, *22*, 23, 69–70, 95, 113, 118
Lund, University Library, Medeltidshandskrift 1 (*De arithmetica*), 167
Luttrell Psalter, 78, 219
Lyon, Musée des Beaux-Arts, knob of bishop's crozier, 48, *51*, 98, 111, 118, 192

Madonna. *See specific entries at* Virgin
Madonna Advocata, Rome, 70
Madrid, Bib. nac., MS 3307 (computus textbook), 169
Maestro Mateo, 185, 229
magic, 174. *See also* amulets and amuletic power
Mainz Cathedral, 208
Majestas Domini, 28, 33, 42, 47, 56, 109, 154, 156, 169, 171, 190, 193, 195, 211, 217
making, xiv, 59–89

artist/artisan, medieval concept of, 60–68, *63*, *65*, *66*
  collaborative nature of, 65–67
  as family business, 85
  originality and standardization in, 85–89, *88*
  patrons, donors, sponsors, and conceivers, 60, 62, 68, 70–85, *71*, *73*, *74*, *76*, *80*, *81*, *82*
  regional specialties, 67–68
  saints, as makers, 69–70
  in scripture and tradition, 60, 68–70
  spirituality, role of, 61
  workshops, 62, 68, 88
Al-Malik al Kamil (sultan), 10
Manfred (son of Frederick II), 136, 176
manuscripts. *See* books; *specific texts and manuscripts*
Marcus Aurelius (emperor), 4, 166
Margaret of Cortona, tomb of, 200
Marguerite of Florence, 84
Mariotta di Cristofano, 18
Mark (saint), 20, 39, 118, 197
Mary. *See specific entries at* Virgin Mary
Mary Magdalene, 81, *82*, 108–09, 116, 125, 144, 185, 208
Massa Marittima, Museo di Arte Sacra Medievale, Ambrogio Lorenzetti altarpiece, 33, 34, *37*, 52, 58, 113, 171, 174, 179, 180, 193, 209, 213, 214, 223, 228
Master Honoré, 85
Matilda of Canosa, 79
matter/materials/materiality, xiv, 31–58
  alabaster, 52–53, 67
  amber, 48–52, 68
  bronze, 40, 54, 68, 104
  Christ, spirit and matter linked by dual nature of, 94, 95, 96, 110, 113
  color symbolism, 12, 39, 53, 56
  glass, 12, 39–40, 53
  ivory, 48, 53, 55, 154, 220
  lead, tin, pewter, and stucco, 40–42
  parchment (vellum), 52, 56
  precious metals and gems, 33–39, 55, 153
  purity, importance of, 33, 52
  relics and, 32
  in scripture and tradition, 32, 37, 39, 42, 47, 52, 56
  spirituality and, 32
  stone, 42–47
  textiles, 52, 55, 56–58, 68, 70, 154

transformations and combinations of materials, 53–58
water, 47, 157
wax, 52, 59, 89, 104
wood, 47–48
Matthew (saint), 23, 204
Matthew Paris, 45, 64, 96, 114, 123, 201
  Chronica maiora, 70, 104, 175, 184
  Historia Anglorum, 95
  Passion of Alban and Amphibalus, 184
Matthew of Vendome, 96
Mechtild of Hackeborn, 52
Mechtild of Magdeburg, 222
medieval art, xiii–xvi. *See also specific subheads below as expanded entries in the index*
  aesthetics, xv, 207–24
  anxiety over art and images, 91–94, 174, 224
  books, xiv, 117–38
  churches, xiv–xv, 139–61
  contemporary artists and, 227–28
  environments of display, 225–30, *228*
  historiography of, 229–30
  as instrument for teaching, 91, 108, 109
  making, xiv, 59–89
  matter/materials/materiality, xiv, 31–58
  objects, xiv, 1–29
  performance/performativity, xv, 189–206
  secular world and, xv, 161–87
  spirituality and, xiv, 89–116
Meditations on the Life of Christ, 77, 119, 131, 179, 212
Meir ben Baruch, 92
Melisende of Jerusalem, 12, 97
mendicant and lay orders, 77–78, 178
Merseburg, cathedral, slab effigy of Rudolph of Swabia, 186
Michael Scot, 175
Michael VII (Byzantine emperor), 10
Micon of Saint-Riquier, 172
Milan
  Castello Sforzesco, Eucharistic knife, 16–17, 48
  Sant'Ambrogio, interior, 7–10, *9*, 42, 44, 58, 69, 117, 140, 150, 154, 156, 185
mirrors, 12, 94, 132–33, 181, 185, 213, 224
  Holkham Bible, monkey gazing in mirror, 77, 206
  ivory mirror, Walters Art Museum, *10*, 181, 205, 206
  Massa Marittima altarpiece, 58, 113, 180, 213, 223, 228
  in *Vrigiet de solas* page, 191

mise-en-abîme, 215–17
Modena
  Cathedral, Porta della Pescheria, 162, 183
  "La Bonissima," 176, *177*, 184
Moissac, l'abbaye Saint-Pierre, façade and portal, 42, *43*, 116, 143, 173, 186, 197, 222
monastic culture and art, 75, 77–78
Monreale, cathedral, mosaic, 170
Montebourg Psalter, 162
Montecassino, Abbazia, Cod. 132 (Isidore of Seville, *De natura rerum*), 123
Montpellier, BU Médecine, H 396 (devotional book), 118
Moses
  Brazen Serpent, 14, 70, 92, 101–02, 109, 149, 210
  at Burning Bush, 14, 89, 98, 105–06, 203, 212, 215, 223
  Mount Sinai and golden calf, 68, 92, 106–07, 117, 145, 146, 149, 173–74, 201
  Pharaoh and, 176, 197
  rod of, 25, 162, 205
  San Marco, Venice, atrium, 197
  typology of, 42, 99, 101–02, 105–07, 119, 138
motion. *See* performance/performativity
Munich
  Bay. Staatsbibliothek
    Clm 210 (collection of astrological texts), 169
    Clm 4450 (Honorius Augustodunensis, *Expositio in Cantica Canticorum*), 131
    Clm 13601 (Uta Codex), 25, 75, 127, 171
    Clm 14159 (*Dialogus de laudibus sanctae crucis*), 132
    Cod. Germ. 193, III (Wolfram von Eschenbach, *Willeham*), 135, 205
  Residence, Schatzkammer, prayer book of Charles the Bald, 33, *34*, 56, 110, 118, 126, 133–35, 181, 202, 206
Münster
  Landesmuseum, Arnstein window, 62, *63*, 96, 98, 99, 100, 105, 109, 112, 117, 153, 154, 196, 203, 205, 217, 219
  Sankt Theobald, façade sculptures, 83

Nancy, Musée Lorrain, funeral monument of Hugh of Vaudemont and Aigeline of Burgundy, 115, 116, 175, 186
naturalism in art, 175–80
nature and natural world, 101, *102–03*, 131, 135, 162, 167, 169–70, 175–78, *177*

INDEX

Naumburg, Dom, choir screen, 42, 45, 58, 152, 178, 179, 186, 199, 204, 208, 220
Nazareth, Church of the Annunciation, 87
necromancy, 174
New Haven, Yale University, Beinecke Rare Book and Manuscript Library
   MS 404 (Rothschild Canticles), 111, 135, 219, 220
New York
   Hunter College, *Objects of Devotion and Desire* (exhibition, 2011), 227
   Metropolitan Museum of Art
      amber relief (at The Cloisters), 52
      environments of display (at The Cloisters), 226
      Heavenly Bodies exhibition, 227
      San Leonardo-al-Frigido lintel (at The Cloisters), 197
      shrine Madonna, 48, *49*, 89, 94, 191, 213–14, 216
   Pierpont Morgan Library
      Lindau Gospels, 127
      MS 240 (Toledo *bible moralisée*), 81, 83, 84, 109, 119, 176, 186
      MS 736 (*Life of Saint Edmund*), 122
Newman, Barnett, 227
Nicholas III (pope), 26
Nicholas IV (pope), 71–72
Nicholas Maniacutius, 113
Nicholas of Verdun, 167
Nicodemus, as sculptor of *Volto Santo*, 70
Nicomachi-Symmachi diptych, 167
Nikolaus von Ybbs, 72
Noah, 14, 48, 69, 70, 77, 145, 147, 153, 176
nobility, art patronage by, 83–84
Norwich Cathedral, 153

objects, xiv, 1–29
   burial goods, 2
   defined, 1
   Eucharist, objects associated with, 16–17, 27–29
   exoticism and strangeness, 12
   as gifts/ex-votos, 10–12, *11*, 25–27, 28
   interchangeability of, 28–29
   mechanically animated, 191
   natural objects, 12
   performativity of, 190–96
   pilgrim souvenirs, 2–4, *3*
   relics, 7, 14–25
   in scripture and tradition, 4, 12, 14

spolia and recycled objects, xiv, 4–10, *5*, *6*, *8*, *9*, 14, 25, 44, 52
   subject and, 207–08, 214, 215
Officium stellae, 205
Ofili, Chris, *Holy Virgin Mary*, 227
Old Testament, typology of, 99–109, *102–03*, *106*, *107*, 200–01, 215
Oliba (abbot), 75
Opicino di Canistris, 86, 204, 214, 216
opus anglicanum cope for bishop of Ascoli, 71–72
Opus Caroli regis contra synodum (*Libri Carolini*), 32
Orcagna (Andrea di Cione), 78
originality and invention, 85–89, *88*
Orosius, *Historia adversos paganos*, 166, 167–68
Orvieto
   Duomo, reliquary of the corporal, 155
   San Domenico, tomb of Guillaume De Bray, 187
Otranto, cathedral, 145
Otto II (Holy Roman emperor) and Theophanu, marriage charter of, 60, 79, 110, 117, 141, 183
Otto III (Holy Roman emperor), 78, 109
Otto IV of Braunschweig, 89
Ovid, 59
Oviedo
   Asturian palace doors, 166
   Cathedral
      agate box, 48, 140, 221
      Camera Santa, 15, 39
      red-stained linen handkerchief, as relic, 58
Oxford, Bodleian Library
   MS Ashmole 304 (composite manuscript illustrated by Matthew Paris), 123, 172
   MS Bod. 717 (Jerome's *Commentary on Isaiah*), 61
   MS Junius 11 (biblical paraphrase), 119

Pacificus of Verona, *Horologium nocturnum*, 122–23, *124*, 162, 169, 170, 208
Pacino di Buonaguida, Chiarita triptych, 28, 113
Paderborn, Erzbischöfliches Diözesanmuseum und Domschatzkammer, portable altar, 45
Padua
   basilica of San Antonio, sarcophagus, 152

Scrovegni Chapel, 58, 84, 101, 110, 146,
    148, 149, 152–53, 160, 174, 180,
    187, 189–90, 195, 202, 210, 213,
    214, 217, Pl. XII
pagan legacy, xiv, 40, 42, 47–48, 71, 96, 140,
    151, 162, 163, 166–70
Palencia, cathedral, 152
Palermo, Cappella Palatina, 47, 65, 67, 78,
    89, 146, 152–53, 160
Panofsky, Erwin, 228
Pantéléon, Jacques (later Pope Urban IV),
    83, 114
Pantheon Bible, 119
Panziero, Ugo, 179
Papeleu Master, 85
parchment (vellum), 52, 56
Paris
    Bibliothèque Mazarine, MS 406, 25
    Bib. nationale de France
        MS Esp. 30 (Catalan Atlas), 176, 184
        MS fr. 9220 (*Vrigiet de solas*), 132–33,
            134, 168, 191, 213, 216, 219
        MS fr. 13342 (Mass tract), 28
        MS fr. 19093 (Villard de Honnecourt's
            sketchbook), 64, *66*, 85, 87, 175,
            191, 206
        MS Ital. 115 (*Meditations on the Life of
            Christ*), 77, 119, 131, 179, 212
        MS lat. 1 (First Bible of Charles the
            Bald), 25, 77, 84, 118–19, 138,
            170, 190, 222
        MS lat. 1203 (Godescalc Evangeliary),
            47, 126, 136–37
        MS lat. 1246 (coronation ordo), 198
        MS lat. 6734 (Honorius Augustodunensis,
            Clauis physicae), 168
        MS lat. 8846 (Psalter), 86
        MS lat. 9428 (Drogo sacramentary),
            125
        MS lat. 10525 (Psalter of Louis IX),
            79, 135
        MS lat. 12048 (Gellone sacramentary),
            125, 136
        MS lat. 12302 (Haimo of Auxerre,
            Commentary on Ezekiel), 131
    École des Beaux-Arts, charter, Saint-Martin-
        du-Canigou, *11*, 11–12, 16, 27, 56,
        58, 98, 108, 117, 151, 154–56, 192–93,
        223, 225
    Musée Cluny
        environments of display at, 226
        erotic pilgrimage badge, 163–64, *165*, 206

Musée du Louvre
    Francis reliquary, 20, 31, 39, 60, 67,
        89, 108, 110, 191, 196, 211, 213,
        Pl. VI
    ivory box, 166
    signet ring of Edward Plantagenet, 14
Saint-Denis, abbey church, 20, 23, 40, 77,
    100, 153, 157, 173, 197, 199
Sainte-Chapelle, 24, 25, 53, 67, 72, 79, 81,
    109, 112, 146, 151, 152, 160, 162,
    194, 198, 200, 202, 223, Pl. VII
Paris, Council of (825), 32
Paschal I (pope), 25
Paschal II (pope), 71
Passion, 16, 17, 25, 54, 56, 108, *120–21*, 126,
    142, 152, 179, 204, 205, 209, 210, 220,
    223, 226
patrons, donors, and sponsors
    gifts, objects as, 10–12, *11*, 25–27, 28, 119
    making, role in, 60, 62, 68, 70–85, *71*, *73*,
        74, *76*, *80*, *81*, *82*
Paul (saint), 12, 23, 100, 101, 108, 119, 138,
    146, 152, 157, 170
Pecham, John, 180
Pedro IV of Aragon, 176
Peraldus, *Summa de virtutibus et virtiis*, 168
Pere III of Aragon, tomb of, Santes Creus, 44
Peregrinus, 204
performance/performativity, xv, 189–206
    in church buildings, 189–90, 197–99
    dance, 201
    devotion, art and generation/control of,
        199–202
    drama, liturgical, 172, 204–05
    liturgy and paraliturgy, 189, 192–94,
        197–99, 204–05
    objects in motion, 190–96
    people in motion, 196–99
    play and playfulness, 205–06
    prayer, 189–90, 191, 201–02
    processions, xv, 27, 174, 189, 194–95, 198,
        200, 218, 226
    speaking, 202–05
    troubadour and minstrel performance,
        181, 183
perspective, 179, 229
Perugia, Fontana Maggiore, 185
Peter (saint), 10, 20, 23, 65, 70, 75, 87, 101,
    108, 109, 112, 114, 142, 143, 146, 156,
    157, 159, 185, 195, 210
Peter Abelard, 89
Peter Berchorius, 127

INDEX

Peter of Celle, 207
Peter the Chanter, 201
Peter Damian, 47
Peter of Eboli, *Liber ad honorem Augusti*, 123, 184
Peter of Limoges, 47, 204
    The Moral Treatise of the Eye, 162, 180, 212, 214, 215, 224, 225
Peter Lombard, 201
Peter Martyr, grave of, 200
Peter the Venerable, 222
Peterborough Cathedral, 47, 146
Petrarch, 111
Philip IV the Fair (king of France), 81
Phyllis riding Aristotle, 206
Physiologus, 101, *102–03*, 131, 135, 167, 169
Piacenza, San Savino, labyrinth, 145
Pictor in Carmine, 89, 94–95, 174
Pierre de Roissy, 112
pilgrims and pilgrimage, 2–4, *3*, 32, 70, 89, 141, 163–64, *165*, 190, 199–200, 206, 213, 216
Pisa
    Campo Santo, *flagilanti* rituals, 199
    Duomo, bronze griffin, 7, 217
    Santa Caterina d'Alessandria, sarcophagus of Giordano of Pisa, 7
Pisano, Giunta, 178
Pisano, Nicola and Giovanni, 85
Plato and Platonism, 111, 168, 175
play and playfulness, 205–06
Poliziano, Angelo, 230
popes. *See also specific popes by name*
    in Avignon, 72, 87, 183, 199
    as promoters and sponsors of art, 70–72
porphyry, 44
portable altars, 42, 45, 139
portraiture, 185–87
Poussin, Nicholas, 229
Prague, Cathedral of St. Vitus
    mosaic, exterior of south transept, 143–44
    Wenceslaus Chapel, 42
Prato (Tuscany), cathedral, belt of Mary at, 18
prayer, performativity of, 189–90, *191*, 201–02
preaching, 203–04
Princeton, University Library, Ms. 138, 174
processions, xv, 27, 174, 189, 194–95, 198, 200, 218, 226
Profiat Duran, 92
Prudentius, *Psychomachia*, 167

Pseudo-Apuleius, 167, 169
pseudo-Augustine, *De spiritu et anima*, 132, *133*, 162, 168, 207, 214
Pseudo-Dionysius, 77
pulpits, 149–50. *See also* Aachen, Dom, ambo; Milan, Sant'Ambrogio
puns and punning, 205–06
Pythagoras and Pythagoreans, 169

Quadrans vetus, 179, 229
Quem quaeritis, 204

Radulphus Ardens, 108
Ramirez, Don Sanchez, 42, *46*
Rashi (Schlomo Yitzchaki), 53, 92
Ravello, Cathedral, Rufolo pulpit, 26
Raynard de Fonoyll, 68
rectangle and rhombus, 171
Regensburg
    Diözesannmuseum, butterfly reliquary, 1, 16, 20, 32, 72, 110, 190, 213, 216, Pl. I
    Sankt Emmeram, *Majestas Domini*, 42
Reichenau (Konstanz), Münster
    gilt disk, 33, *36*, 112, 118, 141, 217–18
    Schatzkammer, green glass slab, antependium, 12, 39, 118, 141, 217–18
Reims
    Cathedral, labyrinth, 201
    Saint-Remi, 149, 154–55
Reinhildes, gravestone of, 186
relics
    in churches, 79, 141, 148, 150–51, 152, 153, 154, 155, 198
    matter/materials/materiality and, 32, 45–47, 58
    as objects, 7, 14–25, 27
    performativity of, 194, 195, 198, 200
    smell of, 221
    Thiofrid of Echternach on, 16, *17*, 20, 32, 47, 58, 135, 221
    of True Cross, 16, 19, 20, 23, 194, 197, 215
reliquaries. *See also specific reliquaries*
    in churches, 141, 149
    as objects, xiv, 1, 4–7, 16, 18–20, 23–25, 26
    performativity of, 195, 198
    "portraits" on, 186
    Rosano Crucifix as, 83
    skills needed for making of, 64
    "speaking reliquaries" fashioned as arms, 192
    spirituality and, 95, 96

Remaclus (saint), great reliquary of, 26
Resurrection, 7, 12, 40, 42, 54, 83, 108, 113, 114, 125, 148, 157, 193, 211, 220, 225
Richard of Fournival, *Bestiaire d'amour*, 183
Richard of Saint-Victor, 61, 91, 211, 213
Riesenbeck, Sankt Callixtus, gravestone of Reinhildes, 186
Robert de Mozat, 85
Rodenegg, Castello, frescoes, 163, *164*, 183, 205
Rodriguez Alvarez, tomb of, 72, *74*, 114, 186–87, 198
Roger I of Sicily, 78
Roger II of Sicily, 160, 183
Roger of Helmarshausen. *See* Theophilus
Roland, depictions of, 162, 185
Roman de la Rose and Romance literature, 181
Rome. *See also* Vatican
   Arch of Titus, 14, 139–40, 195
   Capitoline, senatorial palace, 185
   in Cimabue's *Ytalia*, 166
   Clement (Saint), portrait of, 27
   Curia (Sant'Adriano), 40, 195
   Lateran
     Acheropita, 20–21, *22*, 33, 70, 78, 95, 113, 149, 195, 198, 212, 220–21
     Boaz and Jachim columns, 14
     Capitoline wolf (*lupa Romana*), 4, 10, 68, 86, 181, 185
     Loggia, Giotto fresco, 199
     reception and dining halls, 159–60
     San Giovanni in Laterano, 14, 166
     San Lorenzo chapel, 23, 160
     Sancta Sanctorum, *22*, 23–25, 27, 40, 44, 45, 48, 109, 140, 149, 152, 154, 207, 214
     spolia at, 196
     in stational liturgy, 194
     statue of Marcus Aurelius, 4, 166
   Madonna Advocata, 70
   Monastery of San Paolo fuori le mura, San Paolo Bible, 72, 119
   Pantheon (Santa Maria ad Martyres)
     bronze doors, 40
     in Cimabue's *Ytalia*, 166
     pilgrim badge from, *3*, 3–4, 40, 70, 89, 164, 190, 212, 221
     rose petals at, 22
     in stational liturgy, 194
     Virgin Hodegetria, 212
   processions in, 194–95
   San Clemente

     lower church, 26, 71, 148
     portico, 144
     translation of Clement's body to, 198, 221
     upper church, 96, 151–52, 157, 222
   San Lorenzo fuori le mura, 144
   San Paolo fuori le mura, 67, 71, 159
   San Pietro
     Charles the Bald, throne of (throne of St. Peter), 4, 10, 156, 195
     in Cimabue's *Ytalia*, 166
     crypt, brass lunette, 195
     dedication of new walls around, 194
     epitaph of Pope Hadrian, 181
     Giotto's *Navicella*, 72, 109
     nave paintings, 71, 86
     papal restoration of, 71
     portico, 144
     relics displayed in, 150
     veneration of *Veronica* in, 199
     Veronica tokens for pilgrims, 89
   Santa Maria Maggiore
     apse, 72, 157, 179, 198
     in Assumption procession, 195, 198
     rose petals released on worshippers, 194, 221
     Salus populi romani, 23
     tabernacles for icons and relics in, 151
   Santa Maria Nova, 195
   Santa Prassede, lintel from sarcophagus with scenes of Jonah, 7
   Santa Pudenziana, lintel, 141
   Santi Quattro Coronati
     aula gotica, 72, 160, 163, 167, 170, 179, 183, 200, 213, 218, Pl. XIV
     Saint Sylvester chapel, 72, 218
   Santo Spirito, hospital of, 195
   Temple of Romulus (Santi Cosma e Damiano), bronze doors, 40
Rosano, Abbazia di Santa Maria, Crucifix, 47, 67, 83, 89, 96, 108, 114, 155, 156, 193, 213, Pl. X
rosaries, 202, 221
rose petals, in Roman churches, 194, 221
roses as symbol of Mary, 194, 221–22, 227–28, *228*
Rothschild Canticles, 111, 135, 219, 220
Rudolph of Swabia, 186
Rufillus (white canon and illuminator), 77–78
Rule of Saint Benedict, 75
Rupert of Deutz, 32, 77, 220

INDEX   337

Saint Albans Psalter, 75, *76*, 100, 111, 118,
    122, 130, 136, 137, 171, 184, 219
Saint Clare, Order of, 77
Saint Martin de Vicq (church), 152
La sainte abbaye manuscript, 202
Saint-Guilhem-le-Désert, altar, 154
Saint-Martin-du-Canigou charter, *11,*
    11–12, 16, 27, 56, 58, 98, 108, 117, 151,
    154–56, 192–93, 223, 225
Saint-Maurice d'Agaune, treasury, 226
Saint-Michel-de-Cuxa, cloisters, 159, 173
Saint-Pierre-de-l'Isle, doorway, 144
saints. *See also* relics; reliquaries
    on church façades, 141
    church interiors depicting, 148–49, 151
    as makers, 69–70
    rituals at tombs of, 200
    vitae of, 122
Saint-Savin, 153
Saint-Vaast Bible, 199
Salerno, Museo Diocesano
    Exultet roll, 109
    ivory plaques, 48, *50,* 53, 65, 104–05, 156,
        175, 196, 211, 220
Salimbeni brothers, angel fresco, Urbino, 36
Salzburg, Stift Sankt Peter, drawing for a
    chapel, 87–88, *88,* 98, 111, 148, 159,
    164, 171
San Gimignano, Communal Palace, paintings,
    181, 205
San Paolo Bible, 72, 119
San Pietro in Valle. *See* Ferentillo
San Sepolcro, crucifix, 47
Sanchez Ramirez (Don), capital from
    funerary chapel of, 42, *46,* 109–10, 170,
    196
Sankt Gallen, Switzerland
    Cod. 18 (composite manuscript), 122–24
    Cod. Sang. 53 (*Evangelium longum* of
        Amata), 25
Sant Joan de Boí frescoes, 149, *150,* 164,
    206, 221
Santes Creus (Catalonia)
    cloister sculptures, 68, *69,* 159, 186, 219
    tomb of Pere III of Aragon, 44
Santiago de Compostela
    censer, 226
    main atrium portals, 144
    Porta de las Platerías, 87
    portico sculptures, 229
    portrait of Maestro Mateo, 185, 229
Santo Domingo de la Calzada, 20

sator arepo tenet opera rotas palindrome, *106,*
    171, 174
Schwarzrheindorf, double church of Saints
    Mary and Clement, 77, 152
science. *See* secular world
scripture and tradition
    light in, 111
    making in, 60, 68–70
    manuscripts of scripture, 118–22, *120–21*
    matter/materials/materiality in, 32, 37,
        39, 42, 47, 52, 56
    objects in, 4, 12, 14
    typology in Christian art and, 99–109,
        102–03, 106, 107, 200–01, 215
    Vulgate, 118, 170
Scrovegni, Enrico, and Scrovegni Chapel,
    Padua, 58, 84, 101, 110, 146, 148, 149,
    152–53, 160, 174, 180, 187, 189–90, 195,
    202, 210, 213, 214, 217, Pl. XII
seals and sealing, 89, 100, 104, 185–86
secular world, xv, 161–87
    art used in secular ceremonies, 205
    books, 183–84
    brain map, pseudo-Augustine, *De spiritu
        et anima,* 132, *133,* 162, 168, 207,
        214
    carnality and eroticism, xiv, xv, 75, 91,
        94, 100, 105, 143, 160, 163–64, *165,*
        172–74, 181, 206, 211
    Christianity, in dialogue with, 161–66, 174
    classical heritage, 48, 59, 130, 141, 163,
        166–70, 175, 192
    contemptus mundi, 160
    cosmological and astronomical/astrological
        knowledge, xiv, 60, 111, 146, 162,
        163, 167, 169, 171, 172, 183
    courts and courtly life, 78–83, 181–85
    everyday life, art in, *10,* 181, *182*
    geometry, 111, 168, 170–72, 175, 179,
        218–19
    magic, necromancy, and superstition, 174
    naturalism in art, 175–80, *177*
    nature and natural world, 101, *102–03,*
        131, 135, 162, 167, 169–70
    portraiture, 185–87
    vision theory, 162, 179–80
    Worms Cathedral, *Lady World,* 196
seeing and vision theory, 162, 179–80, 204,
    208, 209–15, 225
Seguer, Guillem, 28, *29,* 31–32, 94
senses. *See under* aesthetics
sensuality. *See* carnality and eroticism

338 INDEX

Serenus of Marseilles, 210
Sermo de vita et morte gloriosae Virginis Maurae,
 195
Serrano, Andres, *Piss Christ,* 227
Seville, *Virgin de los Reyes,* 191
sexuality. *See* carnality and eroticism
Shroud of Turin, 199
Sibylle, abbess of Montreuil-les-Dames, 83
Sicard of Cremona, 145, 202, 220
Siena
 Duomo, so-called crypt, fresco, 194
 Museo del Duomo, Duccio's *Maestà,* 157
 Pinacoteca nazionale, Berardegna antependium, 194
sight. *See* seeing and vision theory
silk, 52, 68
silver, 34–35
Sisebutus (Visigothic king), 123
smell, 221–22
Smithson, Robert, 227
Soiscél Molaise (book shrine), 127, 171
Soissons, slipper of Mary at, 18
Solomon, 14, 69, 70, 92, 101, 143, 151, 156, 161, 163, 171, 174, 214
sound and hearing, 217–19
speaking, 202–05
Speculum Virginum, 137
spirituality, xiv, 89–116
 assertion of spiritual potential of images, 94–96
 butterfly imagery, 1, 110, *Pl. I*
 Christ, spirit and matter linked by dual nature of, 94, 95, 96, 110, 113
 emotion, art eliciting, 113–16, *115*
 imbuing art with, 109–11
 of impressing, stamping, sealing, and stenciling, 89
 inscriptions associated with images, 96–99, *97, 99*
 light and, 111–13, 153
 making, role in, 61
 materiality and, 32
 medieval anxiety over art and images, 91–94
 typology, use of, 99–109, *102–03, 106, 107*
 water as medium of, 47
spolia
 in churches and other sacred spaces, 139–40, 143
 making art from, 60, 65
 materiality of, 52, 60
 as objects, xiv, 4–10, *5, 6, 8, 9,* 14, 25

patrons encouraging use of, 72
performativity of, 196
secular and religious worlds, dialogue between, 162
Sponsus, 204
Stagel, Elsbeth, 114, 202, 219
stained glass, 27, 31, 67, 75, 100, 109, 111–13, 149, 153, 157, 160, 202–03, 224. *See also* Arnstein window; Chartres, Cathedral
stamping, 89, 100
standardization, seriality, and copying, 85–89, *88*
Stefaneschi, Giacomo Gaetani (cardinal), 72, 125, 215
stenciling, 89
Stephen I (saint and king of Hungary), 20, 78, 162
stone, 42–47
Strasbourg
 Bibliothèque de la Ville, Herrard of Hohenbourg, *Hortus deliciarum* (destroyed), 27, 75, 123, 161, 224
 Bibliothèque nationale et universitaire, Cod. 2929 (Henry Suso, *Exemplar*), 36, *38,* 111, 114, 116, 133, 170, 202, 219–20, 221
 cathédrale de Notre-Dame, south transept exterior, figures of *Ecclesia* and *Synagoga,* 105, 198
 iconography of, 151
 interior, windows and column sculptures, 105, *107,* 111, 112, 151, 217
stucco, 40–42
Stuttgart, Württembergishe Landesbibliothek, HB XIII 1 (songbook), 64
subject and object, 207–08, 214, 215
Suger (abbot of Saint-Denis), 20, 40, 53, 67, 75, 77, 100, 140, 153, 157
Summaga, dado pictures at, 173
superstition, 174. *See also* amulets and amuletic power
Suso, Henry, *Exemplar,* 36, *38,* 111, 114, 116, 133, 170, 202, 219–20, 221
Sylvester I (pope), 149, 196–97
Sylvester II (pope). *See* Gerbert of Aurillac

Tabernacle/Ark of the Covenant, 14, 48, 100–01, 137, 139, 140, 146, 166, 195, 212
table fountain, Cleveland, Museum of Art, 181, *182,* 191, 222
Tarragona, cathedral, portal, 72
taste, 222

INDEX

Tatge, George, *Il miracolo e lo specchio*, 227–29, *228*
Tauler, Johannes, 202
Temple, Jerusalem, 14, 69, 92, 100–01, 137, 139–40, 143, 152, 195, 214
Temple curtain, 14, 52, 56, 69, 75, 96, 101, 114, 135, 140, 152, 212
Terence, 167
    Andria, 172
textiles, 52, 55, 56–58, 68, 70, 154. *See also* Bayeux embroidery; coronation mantle
Thangmar (biographer of Bernward of Hildesheim), 77
Theodulf of Orléans, 27, 72, 91, 98
    Opus karoli, 185
Theophanu
    Gospels of, 12, 26, 48, 55, 64, 79, 83, 101, 106–08, 110, 117, 126, 127, 141, 212, 216, *Pl. V*
    marriage charter of Otto II and, 60, 79, 110, 117, 141, 183
Theophilus/Roger of Helmarshausen, *De diversis artibus/Schedula diversarum atrium*, 32, 60–61, 122, 146
Thietmar (chronicler), 77
Thiofrid of Echternach, 16, *17*, 20, 32, 47, 58, 135, 221
Thomas (saint), 18, 39, 47, 220
Thomas Aquinas, 95
Thomas Becket
    Anagni, chapel at, 148, 151, 172
    tomb of, Canterbury, 200
Thomas of Perseigne, 53–54
Thomas von Zerclaere, *Der welsche Gast*, 109
Throne of Mercy, 94, 113, 211
Throne of Wisdom, 19, 156
thrones
    of Charles II the Bald (throne of St. Peter), 4, 10, 156, 195
    in churches, 156
    of Dagobert, 20
Titus (emperor), 14, 140
Tomaso da Modena, 87
Torriti, Jacopo, 72
touch, 219–21
Tournai, relics of Saint Eleutherius, 195
Tournus flabellum, 2, 48, 66–68, 192, 222–23, 229, *Pl. II*
Tours
    Bibliothèque municipale

MS 193 (sacramentary), 98, *99*, 100, 136, 138, 168, 193, 221
    MS 1018 (*Vita sancti Martini*), 122
Saint-Julien, frescoes, 148
Traditio legis, 75, 96, 109, 117, 156, 169
transubstantiation, 155, 168
Tree of Jesse, 32, 105, 146, 153, 203, 211, 216, 217
Tree of Life, 16, 47, 48, 105, 145, 157, 222
Très riches heures, 25, 112, 136, 151, 153, 200, 202, 221, 223, *Pl. VII*
triangles, 171
Trier
    Cathedral, bronze door, 59
    Domschatz, gilt bronze censer, 101
    Stadtbibliothek, MS. 1378 (Thiofrid of Echternach), 16, *17*, 20, 32, 47, 58, 135, 221
Trinity Apocalypse, 86
triplex ratio, 94
Tristan legend, 183
True Cross, relics of, 16, 19, 20, 23, 194, 197, 215
Tuotilo of Sankt Gallen, 62, 64, 67, 77
Türje, Hungary, Premonstratensian abbey church, 149
typology, 99–109, *102–03*, *106*, *107*, 119, 184, 200–01, 215

Ugo Panziera da Prato, *Trattato della Perfezione*, 95
Ugolino di Vieri, 155
University Bibles, 118
University of Pennsylvania, Rare Books Collection, MS LJS 194 (Gerbert of Aurillac, *Isagoge geometriae*), 111, 171
Urban II (pope), 71
Urban IV. *See* Pantéleon, Jacques
Urban V (pope), 23
Urraca chalice, 4, 26, 28, 37, 45, 60, 110, 207, *Pl. III*
Urraca of Léon-Castille, 4, 79
Uta Codex, 25, 75, 127, 171
Utrecht, Universiteitsbibliotheek, MS Bibl. Rhenotraiectinae I Nr 32 (Utrecht Psalter), 34, 62, 72, *73*, 86, 104, 118, 130, 131, 136, 169

Valencia, reliquary, 18, 23
Valenciennes, Bib. municipale, MS 99 (Apocalypse), 137

Vallbona altarpiece, 28, 29, 31–32, 94, 151,
    155, 156, 178, 192, 193, 199, 217, 222
Varia medica, 175
varietas, 223–24
Vasari, Giorgio, 229, 230
Vatican
    Bib. Apostolica
        Cod. Reg. lat. 1351 (Baudri of
            Borgeuil), 163
        Cod. Vat. lat. 12958 (Pantheon Bible), 119
        MS Pal. Lat. 1071 (Frederick II, *De
            arte venandi cum avibus*), 83, 136,
            175–76
        MS Vat. lat. 3225 (*Aeneid*), 130, 170
        MS Vat. lat. 3340 (Orosius, *Historia
            adversos paganos*), 168
        MS Vat. lat. 4933 (*De coronatione*), 125
    Pinacoteca
        Giotto, Stefaneschi altarpiece, 215
        Last Judgment panel, 83
        procession of *Veronica* from, 195
Vegetius, *Epitoma rei militaris*, 122
Vendôme, chapter house, 159, 204
Venice
    Biblioteca Marciana, MS lat. VIII 22
        (*Horologium nocturnum* and other
        texts), 122–23, *124*, 162, 169, 208
    San Marco
        asbestos relief of reliquaries, 44
        Byzantine spolia, 24, 40, 140
        campanile, as Tower of Babel, 176
        creation cupola, sunlight on, 113
        doges as patrons of, 79
        mosaics, atrium, 60, 79, 87, 99, 144,
            169, 197, *Pl. XIII*
        Porta da Mar, 144–45, 197
        Porta Sant'Alippo, 197
        portico, 141, 176
        sculptures on façade, 64, 176
Vercelli
    Archivio e Biblioteca Capitolare, scroll
        illustrating Book of Acts, 88
    San Eusebio, ceiling frescoes, 145
Veronica, 14, 21, 23, 52, 70, 71, 83, 89, 95, 104,
    113, 114, 137, 150, 195, 199, 201, 212
Vespasian (emperor), 14, 140
vestments and clothing, 181, 190
Vézelay, Sainte-Madeleine
    nave supports, 145
    tympanum, 144, 200
    wood statue of Virgin at, 19

Vic, Museu Episcopal, baldachin of Tost, 156
Victor III (pope), 71
Vienna
    Cathedral, reliquary of Saint Stephen, 78
    Öst. Nationalbibliothek
        Cod. 93 (*Varia medica*), 175
        Cod. 397 (collection of astrological
            texts), 169
        Cod. 1179 and 2554 (*bibles moralisées*), 84
        Cod. 1182 (Evangeliary of Jan of
            Oplava), 70
    Schatzkammer, Coronation Gospels, 78
Vienne, Saint-André-le-Bas, 62, 83
Villard de Honnecourt, sketchbook, 64, *66,
    85,* 87, 175, 191, 206
Vincent of Beauvais, 53
Virgil, 167, 175
    Aeneid, 130, 170
    Bucolica, 48, 192
    Eclogues, 169
Virgin and Child, 3, 4, 7, 21, 23, 25, 48, 70,
    78, 100, 111, 153, 155, 164, 192, 195, 199
Virgin Mary. *See also* Annunciation;
    Assumption; *specific representations*
    Arnsteiner Mariengebet, 112, 203, 217, 219
    black Madonnas, 23
    books equated with, 126
    as heaven's gateway, 191
    Saint Luke's portraits of, 20–23, *22,* 23,
        69–70
    as maker, 69
    as *mater dolorosa*, 114–16
    materials associated with, 39, 52, 56, 112
    medieval art, centrality to, 224
    relics of, 18–19, 21–23, 45, 140
    reliquaries, images of Virgin as, 18
    roses as symbol of, 194, 221–22, 227–28, *228*
    as *speculum sine macula* (unblemished
        mirror), 181
    as vessel of God, 140
Worms Cathedral, *Lady World*, as
    anti-Mary, 196
vision. *See* seeing and vision theory
*Vision of Edmund, Monk of Eynsham / Vision of
    Saint Edmund*, 193, 222
Vitelo, 180
Viterbo, Museo Civico, *Marmo Osiriano*, 229
Vitiis mystica (attrib. Bonaventure), 54
Vitruvius, 218
Volvinus, portrait of,
    Milan, Sant'Ambrogio, *9,* 69, 154

Vrigiet de solas, 132–33, *134*, 168, 191, 213, 216, 219
Vulgate, 118, 170

Walsingham, house of Mary at, 18
Warmond of Ivrea, 125
water, 47, 157
wax, 52, 59, 89, 104
Wibald (abbot), 26
Wienhausen, monastery, Tristan tapestry, 183
Wiesbaden, Nassauische Landesbibliothek, MS 1 (Hildegard of Bingen, *Scivias*; Rupertsberg codex), 33, *35*, 75, 85–86, 111, 112–13, 118, 170, 202, 225
William I the Conqueror (king of England), 84
William of Tyre, *Histoire d'Outremer*, 184
William of Volpiano, 194

William of Winchester, 81
Wolfenbüttel
  Herzog August Bibliothek, Cod. Guelf. 61.2 Aug. 8, 87
  Niedersächsisches Landesarchiv, 6 Urk 11, 60
Wolfram von Eschenbach, *Willeham*, 135, 205
women, as art patrons and art makers, 75, 77, 79, 81–3, 84
Worms Cathedral, *Lady World*, 196
Wycliffe, John, 94

Xanten, antependium, *Majestas Domini*, 33

Zillis, Sankt Martin, ceiling, 47, 145
Zwiefalten, Katholischer Pfarramt, reliquary, 4, *6*, 14, 20, 31, 37–39, 55, 59–60, 108, 215–16

rethinking the middle ages
SERIES EDITOR: PAUL EDWARD DUTTON

Rethinking the Middle Ages is a series committed to re-examining the Middle Ages—its themes, institutions, people, and events—with short studies that invite readers to think about that era in new and unusual ways.

Series Titles

Volume One • Experiencing Medieval Art
By Herbert L. Kessler

Volume Two • The Story of a Great Medieval Book: Peter Lombard's *Sentences*
By Philipp W. Rosemann

Volume Three • Rethinking the School of Chartres
By Édouard Jeauneau
Translated by Claude Paul Desmarais